RB Aged About 26

The Brownings' Correspondence

Edited by

PHILIP KELLEY & RONALD HUDSON

Volume 4

———

January 1838 – December 1840
Letters 602 – 783

Wedgestone Press

The editorial work on this volume was made possible in part by a grant from the National Endowment for the Humanities, an independent federal agency.

The plates for this volume were made possible by a subvention from the John Simon Guggenheim Memorial Foundation.

Copyright © Browning Letters, John Murray, 1986
Copyright © Editorial Matter, Wedgestone Press, 1986

All rights reserved. No part of this publication may be reproduced, stored in a retrieval system, or transmitted, in any form or by any means, electronic, mechanical, photocopying, recording or otherwise, without the copyright owners' prior permission.

Published and Distributed by
Wedgestone Press
P.O. Box 175
Winfield, KS 67156

Library of Congress Cataloging in Publication Data

Browning, Robert, 1812–1889.
    The Brownings' correspondence.
    Correspondence written by and to Robert and Elizabeth Barrett Browning.
    Includes bibliographical references and indexes.
    Contents: v. 1. September 1809–December 1826, letters 1–244 — v. 2. January 1827–December 1831, letters 245–434 — [etc.] — v. 4. January 1838–December 1840.
    1. Browning, Robert, 1812–1889—Correspondence.
2. Browning, Elizabeth Barrett, 1806–1861—Correspondence.
3. Poets, English—19th century—Biography.
I. Browning, Elizabeth Barrett, 1806–1861. II. Kelley, Philip.
III. Hudson, Ronald. IV. Title.
PR4231.A4   1984   821'.8B   84-5287
ISBN 0-911459-09-X (v. 1)

Manufactured in the United States of America by Inter-Collegiate Press, Shawnee Mission, Kansas.

A Request

The editors invite all users of this edition to convey any additions or corrections by writing to them through the publisher.

Illustrations

The Legend of the Browne Rosarie 193
Engraving, for which EBB wrote her poem.
Reproduced from *Findens' Tableaux* (London, 1840).

Alfred Domett 254
Engraving by Emery Walker from the water-colour by George Lance, 1836.
Reproduced from *Robert Browning and Alfred Domett* (London, 1906).

Walter Savage Landor 255
Oil by William Fisher, ca. 1840.
Courtesy of the National Portrait Gallery.

RB to William Charles Macready 294
Letter 770, [?27 July] [1840].
Courtesy of the Armstrong Browning Library.

Cue Titles, Abbreviations & Symbols

ABL	Armstrong Browning Library, Baylor University, Waco, Texas
Altham	Mary V. Altham, Babbacombe, England
BBIS-5	"Diary of Miss Evelyn Barclay, Letters to Walter Savage Landor, Three Letters of Browning," ed. A.J. Armstrong, *Baylor Browning Interests Series Five* (Waco, 1932)
Berg	The Henry W. & Albert A. Berg Collection, The New York Public Library, Astor, Lenox and Tilden Foundations
B-GB	*Letters of the Brownings to George Barrett*, ed. Paul Landis (Urbana, 1958)
BL	British Library, London
Brims	Eve Brims, London, England
Brown	Brown University, Providence, Rhode Island
Browning Collections	*The Browning Collections. Catalogue of Oil Paintings Drawings & Prints; Autograph Letters and Manuscripts, Books ... the Property of R.W. Barrett Browning, Esq.* (London, 1913). Reprinted in Munby, *Sale Catalogues*, VI (1972), 1–192
Checklist	*The Brownings' Correspondence: A Checklist*, comps. Philip Kelley and Ronald Hudson (New York and Winfield, Kansas, 1978)
Chorley	*Letters of Mary Russell Mitford*, second series, ed. Henry Chorley, 2 vols. (London, 1872)
DeVane	William C. DeVane, *A Browning Handbook*, 2nd ed. (New York, 1955)
Diary	*Diary by E.B.B.: The Unpublished Diary of Elizabeth Barrett Barrett, 1831–1832*, eds. Philip Kelley and Ronald Hudson (Athens, Ohio, 1969)
DNB	*Dictionary of National Biography*
Duke	Duke University, Durham, North Carolina
EBB	Elizabeth Barrett Barrett / Elizabeth Barrett Browning

Cue Titles

EBB-HSB	*Elizabeth Barrett to Mr. Boyd. Unpublished Letters of Elizabeth Barrett Browning to Hugh Stuart Boyd*, ed. Barbara P. McCarthy (New Haven, 1955)
EBB-MRM	*The Letters of Elizabeth Barrett Browning to Mary Russell Mitford, 1836–1854*, eds. Meredith B. Raymond and Mary Rose Sullivan, 3 vols. (Winfield, Kansas, 1983)
EBB-RHH	*Letters of Elizabeth Barrett Browning, Addressed to Richard Hengist Horne, with Preface and Memoir*, ed. S.R. Townshend Mayer, 2 vols. (London, 1877)
ERM-B	Edward R. Moulton-Barrett, Platt, England
Eton	Eton School Library, Eton College, Windsor, England
G & M	W.H. Griffin and H.C. Minchin, *The Life of Robert Browning* (New York, 1910)
Garnett	R. & E. Garnett, *Life of W.J. Fox* (London, 1910)
Hereford	County Council of Hereford and Worcester, Records Office, Hereford, England
Hunt	*The Correspondence of Leigh Hunt*, ed. J.H.L. Hunt (London, 1862)
HUP	*Elizabeth Barrett Browning. Hitherto Unpublished Poems and Stories*, ed. H. Buxton Forman, 2 vols. (Boston, 1914)
LEBB	*The Letters of Elizabeth Barrett Browning*, ed. F.G. Kenyon, 2 vols. (London, 1897)
L'Estrange (1)	*Friendships of Mary Russell Mitford*, ed. Alfred Guy Kingham L'Estrange, 2 vols. (London, 1882)
L'Estrange (2)	*Life of Mary Russell Mitford*, ed. Alfred Guy Kingham L'Estrange, 3 vols. (London, 1870).
Lilly	The Lilly Library, Bloomington, Indiana
LRB	*Letters of Robert Browning Collected by Thomas J. Wise*, ed. Thurman L. Hood (New Haven, 1933)
Macready	*The Diaries of William Charles Macready 1833–1851*, ed. William Toynbee, 2 vols. (London, 1912)
Maggs	Maggs Bros., Ltd., book dealers, London
Maynard	John Maynard, *Browning's Youth* (Cambridge, Mass. and London, 1977)
MM-B	Myrtle Moulton-Barrett, Ringwood, England
NL	*New Letters of Robert Browning*, ed. W.C. DeVane and K.L. Knickerbocker (New Haven and London, 1950)
North	Ernest Dressel North, book seller, New York (later, Summit, N.J.)
OED	*Oxford English Dictionary*
Orr	Mrs. Sutherland Orr, *Life and Letters of Robert Browning*, revised and in part rewritten by Frederic G. Kenyon (London, 1908)

Cue Titles

RAM-B	Ronald A. Moulton-Barrett, Aberdeenshire, Scotland
RB	Robert Browning
RB-AD	*Robert Browning and Alfred Domett*, ed. Frederic G. Kenyon (London, 1906)
RB-EBB	*The Letters of Robert Browning and Elizabeth Barrett Barrett, 1845–1846*, ed. Elvan Kintner, 2 vols. (Cambridge, Mass., 1969)
RB, Sr.	Robert Browning, Sr., RB's father
Reconstruction	*The Browning Collections: A Reconstruction*, comps. Philip Kelley and Betty A. Coley (London, New York, Waco, Texas and Winfield, Kansas, 1984)
SD	Supporting Document. For checklist of contemporary supporting documents see: Volume 1, Appendix II, SD1–SD577; Volume 2, Appendix II, SD578–SD749; Volume 3, Appendix II, SD750–SD844; Volume 4, Appendix II, SD845–SD1144
Sotheby's	Sotheby & Co., auctioneers, London
V & A	Victoria and Albert Museum, London
Weaver	"Twenty Unpublished Letters of Elizabeth Barrett to Hugh Stuart Boyd," ed. Bennett Weaver, *Publications of the Modern Language Association*, 65 (1950)
Wellesley	Wellesley College Library, The English Poetry Collection, Wellesley, Massachusetts
[ ]	Square brackets indicate material inserted by editors
⟨ ⟩	Angle brackets denote some irregularity in the manuscript. The absence of a note indicates that the information within the brackets is a conjectural reconstruction caused by seal tear, holes or physical deterioration of the manuscript
⟨…⟩	Angle brackets enclosing ellipsis show an actual omission caused by a defect or physical irregularity in the manuscript. Except in the case of text lost through seal tears, holes, etc., the nature of the irregularity is indicated by a note. This symbol appears on a line by itself if lost text exceeds half a line
⟨★★★⟩	Angle brackets enclosing triple stars indicate the lack of a beginning or end of a letter
| |	Vertical bars are used before and after a word which, though not physically obliterated, is a word of uncertain transcription
…	Ellipses indicate omissions from quoted material in notes and supporting documents, but in the actual texts of the Brownings' correspondence they merely reproduce the writers' style of punctuation

Chronology

1838: EBB's "A Romance of the Ganges" published in *Findens' Tableaux: a Series of Picturesque Scenes of National Character, Beauty, and Costume* (published October 1837).

    mid-April: EBB moves to 129 Crawford St. for a few days and then to 50 Wimpole St.

    April–July: RB's first Italian journey. RB recorded his itinerary in diary form, now at University of Toronto; it is here reproduced in full.

    April 13, Good Friday, left St Katharine's Docks 4 p.m. Anchored in Halfway Reach, 6. pm. Brig. "Norham Castle," Matt. Davidson—Courier, (John Graham, Mate) Snow.

        Apr. 14. Norfleet 10. am.
    Sund. 15. Gravesend. 5. p.m. 8. anchored in the Hope. Noon, in the Nob channel.
        16. (P.M.) 6. Anchored in the Downs. gales.
        17. Strong gales with snow.
        18. Strong gales, showers of sleet. 5. a.m weighed anchor and proceeded. observed a vessel on fire off Deal. noon, off Dungeness.
        19. Strong breezes with snow.
        20. P.M. St Katharine's point N.E. by N. Ditto weather. Midnight, Start light, distance 7 leagues, from which the ship "takes its departure," in lat. 50, 13 N. long. 3, 38 W.
        21. Squally with rain.
    Sund. 22. Strong gales, rain.
        23. Strong gales, squally, rain. Ship labouring and shipping much water.
        24. 10. a.m. Cape Finisterre, E.S.E distance, 10 miles.
        25. Steady breeze with showers.
        26. Rock of Lisbon, E.N.E, distance 40 miles. 8 a.m.
        27. Cape St. Vincent, N. by W. dist. 16 miles. noon. Spoke the "Mary & Isabella" bound to London.
        28. Fine.
    Sund. 29. Cape Spartelle, S.S.W dist. 5 miles. 8 p.m. Midnight, strong gales with rain; Ceuta fort, S.S.W. 4 miles. Thro' the Gut of Gibraltar.
        30. ½ p 1. p.m. passed Alboran Island. Fine, very hot.
    May 1. Light breezes, hot & sultry weather.
        2. Light variable winds. burning heat.

Chronology

         3. do.
         4. do; spoke a brig, name unknown.
         5. variable; calms. hot.
Sund. 6. † calms. † observed 5. a.m. let go, 4 p.m. (Lat 37, 33. Long. 3, 39 E.)
         7. Light variable winds.
         8. Do.
         9. Calm, cloudy.
        10. Fresh breezes, Cape Bugrone [sic] S.E by S. 30 miles.
        11. 5 p.m. Galita Island. S.S.W 5 miles. noon, Cape Bon, squall, 8 miles.
        12. Pantelleria Island, S.W by S, 12 miles—4 a.m.
Sund. 13. 1. a.m. Goza [sic]. 7. a.m. Valetta, S.W by W, 7 miles.
        14. 6 p.m. Cape Pesaro, Noon Syracuse, N, 7 miles.
        15. Variable light weather.
        16. Calms—sultry weather. Mt. Ætna, N.W by N. all day.
        17. Do–
        18. Noon, caught a bonito. light airs, showers.
        19. Steady breezes. Noon, Fano Island. N.E distant 12 miles (Corfu in sight.) Coast of Albania, one side and Cape St Mary's on the other.
Sund. 20. Light airs and calms. N. Cape St Mary's W. half N. Otranto.
        21. Calms, sultry weather; noon, do: Sassino Is. N.E. saw two sperm-whales close astern, of from 80 to 90 feet.
        22. Weather do. 6. pm. Sassino Is. E.N.E. Tacking ship occasionally.
        23. Fresh breezes and clear weather, winds N.N.W. Brindisi, W.N.W, dist. 10 mile, 8. Tacked ship.
        24. Light Airs & Calms. Three sail in company.
        25. Do. Sultry weather. 13 Sail in comp.
        26. Do. Do. Isl. of Cazza N.E.
Sund. 27. Fresh wind, Scirocco. N. Poma, W.S.W. (6. pm). Is. St. Andrea. S. by E.
        28. Light airs and calms. Lissa Is. E.S.E. (noon).
        29. Calms, cloudy weather. Rovigno E by S, Noon.
        30. Arrived at Trieste—anchored 4 p m.
        31. Left by Steam-boat for Venice, 10. ½ pm.
June 1. Arrived at Venice, 7. a.m.
         2. Lodgings. Casa Stefani, Calle Giacomuzzi, S. Moise, 1139.
Sund. 3.
         4.
         5.
         6.
         7.
         8.
         9.

Sund. 10.
   11.
   12.
   13.
   14.
   15.
   16.
Sund. 17. Mestre, Treviso, Castelvecchio [sic], Rossano.
   18. Bassano
   19. Asolo, Possagno, Asolo.
   20.
   21. St Zenon, Asolo.
   22.
   23. Bassano.
Sund. 24. Vicenza.
   25. Padua.
   26. Venice.

6 June: EBB's *The Seraphim, and Other Poems* published by Saunders and Otley, London.

28 June: Coronation of Queen Victoria.

25 August: Under medical advice, to recuperate from a lung hæmorrhage, EBB leaves London for "The Braddens," Torquay.

27 August: EBB arrives at Torquay.

1 October: EBB moves to 3 Beacon Terrace, Torquay.

1839: EBB's "The Romaunt of the Page" published in *Findens' Tableaux of the Affections: A Series of Picturesque Illustrations of the Womanly Virtues* (published October 1838).

EBB's "A Sabbath on the Sea" published in *The Amaranth: A Miscellany of Original Prose and Verse* (published October 1838).

26 January: EBB's "L.E.L.'s Last Question" published in *The Athenæum*.

18 May: Richard Barrett dies at Montego Bay, his dispute with the Moulton-Barretts unsettled. Some claims awarded to his principal heirs Samuel Goodin Barrett and George Goodin Barrett.

1 October: EBB removes to 1 Beacon Terrace, Torquay.

1840: EBB's "The Dream" and "The Legend of the Browne Rosarie" are published in *Findens' Tableaux: the Iris of Prose, Poetry, and Art for 1840* (published October 1839).

10 January: Penny postage begins.

10 February: Queen Victoria marries Prince Albert of Saxe-Coburg-Gotha.

15 February: EBB's "The Crowned and Wedded Queen" published in *The Athenæum*.

17 February: EBB's brother, Samuel Moulton-Barrett, dies at Cinnamon Hill, Jamaica, and is buried there.

29 February: The announced date of publication of RB's *Sordello*, which was actually published the following week by Edward Moxon, London.

April: EBB's "A Night Watch by the Sea" published in *The Monthly Chronicle*.

July: EBB's "A Lay of the Rose" published in *The Monthly Chronicle*.

4 July: EBB's "Napoleon's Return" published in *The Athenæum*.

11 July: Bro drowns in a sailing accident in Tor Bay. EBB suffers a near-fatal illness as a result.

late-December: RB's family removes from Camberwell to New Cross, Hatcham, in Surrey.

The Brownings' Correspondence

Volume 4
January 1838 – December 1840
Letters 602 – 783

602. EBB TO JOHN KENYON

[London]
[ca. 1838][1]

We gratefully accept dear M.ʳ Kenyon, the present you have sent us—and altho' we had not the happiness of knowing personally Her to whom it bears so mournful a reference, yet *do* believe that we cannot make this connection between the worth of the dead, and the confidence & kindness of the living, in these thanks to *you*, with unaffected feelings.[2]

My sisters desire me to express their thanks—& I linger over those of mine just to say, that I receive from you my dear friend this kindness, both as a proof of *your* friendship, and a token of what you kindly tell me,—that *She* would not have considered me quite unworthy of *Her's*——

Your obliged
E B Barrett.

Address, on integral page: John Kenyon, Esq.ʳ / 4 Harley Place.
Publication: None traced.
Manuscript: Michael Meredith.

1. Dating is approximate, based on handwriting and watermark (1837).
2. From the context, the gift was probably some memento of Kenyon's second wife, Caroline (*née* Curteis), who had died on 7 August 1835.

---

603. RB TO THOMAS NOON TALFOURD

Camberwell,
Wednesday M.ᵍ [ca. 1838][1]

My dear Talfourd,
I am heartily vexed to find myself engaged for next Sunday: pray excuse and believe me,

Yours ever faithfully,
Robert Browning.

Publication: None traced.
Manuscript: Berg Collection.

1. Dated by handwriting and form of signature.

604. RB TO RACHEL TALFOURD

Camberwell
Wednesday Eve^g [ca. 1838]¹

My dear Mrs Talfourd,
 I accept your kind invitation with nearly as much shame as pleasure: even the poor visit I was about to pay you last Monday Evening—came to nothing thro' a blunder--but I shall trust to your goodness for a hearing on Sunday. Pray believe me meanwhile,
My dear Mrs Talfourd,
Yours ever faithfully,
Robt Browning.

Publication: None traced.
Manuscript: Armstrong Browning Library.

 1. Dated by handwriting and form of signature.

---

605. EBB TO MARY RUSSELL MITFORD

London.
1st Jany—— [1838]¹

I wrote a letter to you dearest Miss Mitford last week which turned out, by force of the destinies, to be for the fire instead of the post. It was heavy with stupidity—& I had no fear of your being uneasy about Mr Kenyon—& I had no frank,—& without one, you w^d have paid triple postage for a letter of lead!–

 Yet I wished to write to you, after what you told me of your being unwell & of your wish that I should try to do something for you in the pension business. Glad & proud I should have been to do it!– Dearest Miss Mitford! if there ever appears to you the least possibility of my being able to do the least thing for you in any way, you will never if you love & care to please me, hesitate about saying '*do it*'– In the present case, I fear that I & my doves are equally powerless!——nobody in this house knowing a single member of the Committee. I fancied that Mr Tulk knew Mr Hume² & might have some influence,—but he says that he has none whatever—that if he had, he would with pleasure have used it, in the manner suggested. Then, there is Sir William Gosset the Serjeant at Arms & my franker. I dont know him personally—altho' he is my very obliging franker—having an unlimited power of franking & kindness in using it, & a son who married my first cousin & to whom I send my letters whenever I can find a carrier for them down to Westminster. This

No. 605 1 January [1838]

son, an amiable person, is at present in Ireland. On his return which must be at the opening of parliament (for he holds office under his father) I will immediately persuade him to persuade Sir William to persuade the Committee to make the "pig go over the style", which if it be a true pig & no donkey, it is sure to do of its own accord!– You see this is all indirectness, & feebleness!– May you my very dear friend, have friends with a directer influence, & no less affectionate thoughts than mine towards you!——[3]

I am so grieved to hear of your suffering– Are you not too sedentary?—and will you not lie down a little more & manage the writing in that way?—— Whenever you are so kind as to write again to me, do mention yourself particularly– May God bless you the whole year thro!—— I am writing on the first day of it!– Do receive for yourself & D^r. Mitford every kindest wish & thought which must always be *seasonable* from me to you!—— As for the season, I doubt whether it be Christmas, notwithstanding the mince pies & Sette's orisons that Papa may buy a twelfth cake[4] with *M^r. Pickwick at the top of it!*– And by the way I must tell you that Sette had made your suggestion of the Pickwick resemblance long before it occurred in your letter!–[5] Sette & Occy are great Pickwickians. "What are you thinking of Occy"?—Occy being in a deep grave reverie, with eyes fixed upon the fire– *"Of M^r. Pickwick".*

Three times this week has Papa seen dear M^r. Kenyon—seen him in his sitting room, & dressed & inclined to talk, & looking, tho' of course thinner & paler, very much better than Papa had any hope of. He is thinking of going, I believe soon, to Tunbridge Wells for the change of air of a day or two—& this seems to be a prudent plan. Papa told him of your anxious kindness respecting him—and the answer was "I mean to write myself to Miss Mitford very soon".

Papa met in his room your correspondent Capt. Jones, & was much pleased with him. I was wrong in imagining him to be no intimate friend of M^r. Kenyon's, for such he appears to be!–[6]

How grievous it is that M^r. Carey's name sh^d. be disassociated from the British Musæum![7] I am very sorry! When you once mentioned that name to me, the sound struck into the midst of a heap of old dusty thoughts of mine, & made an odd confusion, half humourous & half pathetic. You spoke of the *venerable* M^r. Carey!– And I never before had any M^r. Carey in my head except *"young Carey"* who with "young Lister" enacted the Pylades & Orestes of Miss Seward's Letters.[8] The translator of Dante & Pindar I knew & reverenced well; but as to his personality, I took all that I ever heard of it from Miss Seward; & if it had not been for you, "young Carey" he w^d. have been to me for ever & ever! Shall I tell you—shall I confess––wont you bid me wear sackcloth for it––that in my childish days & for some days afterwards I have read & re-read Miss Seward's Letters. They had a charm for me notwithstanding their vanity & elaborateness & bombast; and that charm was from the earnest love of poetic literature with which they are penetrated, & the generous thoughts & feelings which light them up. I can be animal-magnetized thro' a wall.[9]

        Dearest Miss Mitford's
         Ever affectionate
          E B Barrett.

Addressed and franked, on integral page: London Jany. four 1838 / Miss Mitford / Three Mile Cross / nr. Reading / [undecipherable signature].
Publication: EBB-MRM, I, 60–63.
Manuscript: Wellesley College.

 1. Year provided by the frank.
 2. Joseph Hume (1777–1855), a member of Parliament from 1812 until his death, except for two short breaks, and leader of the radical party for 30 years, "served on more committees of the House of Commons than any other member" (*DNB*).
 3. Miss Mitford was hoping to obtain an increase in her government pension, and was seeking through her friends a means of bringing the matter before the appropriate Parliamentary committee. Sir William Gosset's son Ralph had married EBB's cousin Arabella Butler in 1835.
 4. A cake made for Twelfth Night, 5 January. It contained a bean, and the person finding it in his piece of cake was named Bean King, to direct the festivities.
 5. John Kenyon, when wearing his glasses, was held to resemble Mr. Pickwick. For a sketch of Kenyon by EBB see *EBB-MRM*, II, facing p. 320.
 6. William Jones (?–1846) was a member of the party travelling in France the following summer, Kenyon, Southey and Henry Crabb Robinson being the other members. He was described as "an active, intelligent man, by birth a Welshman, who kept us in good-humor by his half serious, half-jocular zeal for the honor of his countrymen the Welsh" (*Diary, Reminiscences, and Correspondence of Henry Crabb Robinson*, ed. Thomas Sadler, 1870, II, 266).
 7. Henry Francis Cary (1772–1844), a friend of Miss Mitford, had been appointed Assistant Keeper of Printed Books at the British Museum in 1826. When the post of Keeper became vacant in 1837, Cary applied for it, but was passed over in favour of Antonio Panizzi (1797–1879). Cary then resigned his post, and devoted himself to literary endeavours. He had published some poetry of his own, together with a translation of Dante; he now undertook editions of various English poets and a series of critical observations on Italian poets.
 8. In 1788 Cary had met Thomas Lister, of Armitage Park, Lichfield, another young prodigy. Both were fifteen at the time, and formed a very close friendship, writing poetry together. As EBB indicates, the friendship was mentioned by Anna Seward (1747–1809) in her correspondence (*Letters of Anna Seward: Written Between the Years 1784 and 1807*, 1811, II, 96–97).
 Pylades and Orestes, nephew and son respectively of Agamemnon, are renowned in Homeric legend for their closeness, always linked as are Damon and Pythias, David and Jonathan.
 9. "Animal magnetism" (later known as mesmerism) claimed to effect a cure of certain ailments by manipulating the magnetic fluid supposedly contained in the body. EBB was later much intrigued by Harriet Martineau's assertion that she had overcome an incurable malady by these means.

606. EBB TO MARY RUSSELL MITFORD

74 Gloucester Place–
Tuesday. [January 1838][1]

Do write one line to me my dearest Miss Mitford, just to say how you are– I might have asked as much as this before—but felt unwilling to be in your way when so much else was there. One line—*I* must ask for now!—— It haunts me that you are suffering. May God grant that such a thought be one of my many vain ones!—& that the amendment you spoke of be not vain at all.

This is the first day of my release from prison—for during this terrible weather which held daggers for all weak chests, I was not permitted to get up before it was *deep* in the afternoon,—& so have scarcely had a pen in my hand for a fortnight past. I was glad to be able to breakfast as usual with Papa this morning—& feel an early-rising-vain-gloriousness almost as "thick upon me"[2] as Mr Boyd's is upon him—when (& he always does it) he gets up at four or five o clock in the morning & looks down upon the rest of the world. You cant think how much scorn I and my half past nine o clock breakfasts have met with from him. *You* would meet with no mercy. He has intimated to me again & again, that it was both a moral & religious sin not to get up before the second cock crowing– And that Peter's repentance, besides a good deal of sackcloth, sh^d wait upon the third–[3] I believe I inferred the last—being logical: but the "moral & religious sin" was just his own expression.

How high you bribe dearest Miss Mitford! To *stand alone by your side* in praising Hayley[4] & his contemporaries—or in doing anything else! That *is* a bribe,—& when I have read the essays on scu[l]pture Painting & epic poetry,—anything more than the Triumphs of Temper,—I will make a desperate effort towards admiration. I admire him now as a *man*—and as Cowper's friend! I admire Miss Seward, not as a letter writer or a poet or a critic,—but as a kindly, generous hearted woman who loved poetical literature "not wisely"[5] but very well,—who loved her friends still better than her vanities,—& who was not frozen to her pedestal! (she had one in her day!)—as many are apt to be in all days. When Sir Walter Scott edited her poems he cancelled such praise as he had given them in his own letters to her–[6] It was an ungenerous act! The poor poetess could no more have committed it than she c^d have written Waverley!——

My dear friend! as you have changed your mind about the season of application for increase of pension, I have not said a word to Mr Gosset.[7] If I am wrong, tell me immediately.

Finden is a triumph for you!– I am so glad of it. Dearest Miss Mitford, whenever I am able to do anything, or you fancy so & like me to try, by making me do it pray remember that you make me obliged–

The poor little dove, weak for the last three weeks, perished one cold night a fortnight since. I mean the poor little cockney dove. The others, I took up to my bedroom & kept very warm—& after some spiritless songless days, they revived & are perfectly well now. If I were to lose either of them, I should name it as a grief–

Goodbye—God bless you, dearest Miss Mitford. Do tell me that you are better. D! Chambers says that I shall lose my cough in the warm weather—April or May—& not before. So there is nothing for it but patience. And nothing makes one so patient, as knowing that patience is not needed for those one loves!——

Your ever affectionate
E B Barrett.

I have not yet seen M! Kenyon. He sent me M! Landor's last most exquisite book[8] of which I have no time to speak–

The kind regards of all the house—do accept them!——

Publication: EBB-MRM, I, 59–60 (as [19? December 1837]).
Manuscript: Wellesley College.

1. Dated by the further reference to Miss Mitford's pension, mentioned in the previous letter.
2. Cf. *Henry VIII*, III, 2, 354.
3. Cf. Mark, 14:72.
4. William Hayley (1745–1820). The following references are to *An Epistle on Painting* (1777), *Poetical Epistle on Epic Poetry* (1782), *An Essay on Sculpture* (1800) and *The Triumphs of Temper* (1781).
5. *Othello*, V, 2, 344.
6. At the request of Miss Seward (known as "the Swan of Lichfield"), Scott edited and published her poetical works in 1810, a year after her death. In a memoir of her included in the first volume, Scott was somewhat less enthusiastic about her poetry than he had professed to be in letters to her.
7. As EBB mentioned in the previous letter, her cousin's husband, Ralph Gosset, was obliged to return from Ireland prior to the opening of Parliament; this took place on 16 January, thus dating this letter to the first half of the month.
8. *The Pentameron and Pentalogia* (1837).

---

607. EBB TO JOHN KENYON

74, Gloucester Place
[ca. January 1838][1]

Offered for sale by Sotheby's, 14 July 1898, lot 475, and Maggs' Catalogue 166 (1899), item 811. A 2-page letter expressing her opinion of Walter Savage Landor. "I believe I ought to return more books than I do return, were it only to make you think that I have not been asleep over Landor's. It is easier to dream than to sleep over a volume of his, and perhaps very beautiful as these are in many parts, one of my dreams is that they express coldly, and with a hard stiff stoney outline, what the Greeks were—there were living Greeks, as well as Greek stories, were there not?[2] ... how ungrateful it appears that the acknowledgment of the beauty in Landor's Books should come in as an afterthought, and the complaint in full length. I am not so bad as my note."

1. This letter could have been written at any time during EBB's residence at Gloucester Place (Summer 1835–April 1838). However, EBB's having mentioned in the previous letter that Kenyon had lent her Landor's latest work suggests that this may be one of the books she is now returning.
2. EBB's comments about Landor's Greeks make it probable that one of the volumes in question was his *Pericles and Aspasia*, published in March 1836.

608. RB TO JOHN KENYON[1]

Camberwell
Jan 11. [1838]

My dear Sir,
    I shall be delighted to dine with you to-morrow week: had I guessed you were a house-keeper thus long, something more substantial than a card should have assured you how much I am,

Yours very faithfully,
R Browning.

My father sends his kindest regards—and will assuredly see you this season, I hope.

Publication: None traced.
Manuscript: Armstrong Browning Library.

1. Correspondent inferred from letter 569. As it was RB's habit to include his full address early in a correspondence, and thereafter to shorten it, the presumption is that RB, Sr. still had not met Kenyon, and that this letter was written later than no. 569.

609. EBB TO HUGH STUART BOYD

[London]
[mid-January 1838][1]

My dear friend,
    I shall be glad to see Mrs Smith[2] whenever she is kind enough to come—should I be up, & as well as usual. For the last fortnight I have not left my bed until the afternoon, in consequence of the severe weather,—but this being, to my great joy, at an end, I mean tomorrow morning

to get up as early as you know I always used to do, to your great admiration! Therefore pray say to Mrs Smith the message I have already written—together with two things more—my thanks for her caring to see me—& my hope that she wont come *far* out of her way to do so, lest I should happen to be put into prison again by a confluence of cough and frost. But Mr Murphy the prophet of the almanacks[3] who said that Saturday sh^d contain the *pith* of the frost, & Sunday the thaw, declareth that we shall have no more until friday or Saturday & Sunday.[4] Have you heard of him? He is considered the seer of seers, & *sees* all about the weather in the stars.

As to your good counsel dear Mr Boyd, I assure you that I *do* consider myself *better*. Dr Chambers told me openly that my indisposition would not go, for medicine. He told me that, in his *conviction*, my lungs were without desease—but so *weak*, that they struggle *against* the cold air—which occasions the cough. It is a sensible deduction that until the warm weather comes, I cannot be well. In the meantime, he gives me soothing medicines—to produce as much as possible of quiet & sleep. If it pleases God I shall be better in time—

If you see Mr Woodforde, do say how obliged I feel by his expression of kind interest, in calling three times here to enquire after me. ⟨★★★⟩

Publication: EBB-HSB, pp. 224–225.
Manuscript: Wellesley College.

1. Dated by the reference to Murphy's *Almanack*.
2. Mary Ann, the daughter of Boyd's late friend, Dr. Adam Clarke.
3. Patrick Murphy (1782–1847), author of *The Weather Almanack (on Scientific Principles ...)*.
4. Murphy's *Almanack* forecast the day-by-day weather for 1838. EBB's comment about "the *pith* of the frost" relates to his prediction that 20 January would bring the lowest temperature of the winter. By luck, coincidence or divination, that day brought a sunrise temperature of −4°F, whereupon the public clamoured for copies of the *Almanack*. It quickly ran through 45 editions and sold over 100,000 copies. Murphy also forecast frost for the 27th and 28th, after a few days of fair and changeable weather.

---

610. Lady Margaret Cocks to EBB

[Reigate]
[25 January 1838]

Cover sheet only.

Addressed and franked by Lord Somers: Reigate Jan^{ry} Twenty fifth / *1838* / Miss Barrett / Wimpole Street / London / [and presumably in hand of Lady Margaret Cocks, on reverse when folded:] Miss Barrett / Wimpole S^t / London.
Publication: None traced.
Manuscript: Myrtle Moulton-Barrett and Ronald A. Moulton-Barrett.

611. EBB TO LADY MARGARET COCKS

74 Gloucester Place
Monday. [?29] [January 1838][1]

Thank you my dear Lady Margaret for the kind interest you express towards me & in me. I am better than I have been—altho' this severe weather has been hard to bear, & enforced the precaution of keeping me more in bed than out of it, for a fortnight past. The illness arose entirely I believe from cold—one cold upon another falling upon the chest & producing cough—so that for four months past, I have not left the house. D[r] Chambers says that he is very confident of there being *no disease on the lungs*—"not the least bit" was his expression—but that the lungs & chest being in a weak & delicate state, I am not likely to lose the cough until the warm weather—April or May. In the meantime he gives me soothing medicines which I am sure do me good– Still I am suffering a good deal from lassitude & feebleness—(scarcely at all from *pain*—a great blessing) and do not sleep well at nights– May God teach me more & more that His providence & His love are one! a lesson often learnt in weeping, tho' the fulness of its knowledge be the fulness of all joy!——

Thank you for the good news about Finden. M[r] Tilt has been doubting as to continuing it thro' another year—notwithstanding its selling so much better than it did last year under M[rs] Hall's editorship.[2] And I do hope that he may go on with it—that being or involving a pecuniary object, to dear Miss Mitford.– Have you seen M[r] Chorley's annual of living authors?[3] which did not sell, & to no surprise of hers Miss Mitford says, as she always feared for the fate "of 13 ugly profiles & a long volume of short lives". Her own profile is among the "ugly" ones! & notwithstanding this liveliness & fear *I am* very much surprised that a book of a character so lastingly interesting, could not sell for one Christmas day.

Dear Lady Margaret, I rejoice in hearing of your enjoyment during the past one! and I rejoice too, more selfishly, at the news of your being about to go so soon to Reigate[4]—remembering as I do, among my shreds of geographical learning, that Reigate is nearer London than Worcester is!– I do indeed hope to see you this spring—tho' you give me no hope of it, by word or breath.

I have not coughed away my ambition yet—and your Ladyship wont think me very very bad when I tell you that I am still thinking gravely of publishing in the present spring. The booksellers tell horrible tales about poetry not selling—yet I am not frightened quite from the thoughts of trying mine. Thoughts however have been my only activity, hitherto—& if there is not soon some of another kind, the season will be too far advanced for even thoughts.

10 [?29] [January 1838]   *No. 611*

We are not in Wimpole Street. The workmen have been there for six weeks, and have not yet prepared the way for the furniture. It will be March I dare say before we leave Gloucester Place.

May God bless you dear Lady Margaret!

Ever believe me
Your affectionate & obliged
E B Barrett.

Publication: None traced.
Manuscript: Hon. Mrs. Elizabeth Hervey-Bathurst.

1. EBB's statement "We are not in Wimpole Street" suggests that this is a reply to letter 610, which was addressed to Wimpole St.

2. Anna Maria Hall (*née* Fielding, 1800–81), the wife of Samuel Carter Hall (1800–89), had edited the 1837 edition of *Findens' Tableaux*.

3. *The Authors of England* (1838). It dealt with fourteen eminent writers, including Scott, Byron, Southey, Coleridge, Shelley, Wordsworth, and, of course, Miss Mitford, accompanying the text with medallion portraits by Achille Collas (1795–1859); that of Miss Mitford is reproduced facing p. 40.

4. EBB's comment may appear to disprove the assumption in note 1, as letter 610 was postmarked Reigate; however, as it was common practice for a bundle of correspondence to be sent to Earl Somers for franking, his doing so at Reigate Priory was not of itself proof that Lady Margaret was herself there.

---

612. MARY RUSSELL MITFORD TO EBB

Three Mile Cross,
Feb. 1, 1838.

My dear Love,

I have got to think your obscurity of style, my love, merely the far-reaching and far-seeing of a spirit more elevated than ours, and look at the passages till I see light breaking through, as we see the sun shining upon some bright point (Oxford, for instance) in some noble landscape. I have just been reading Racine's "Letters," and Boileau's. How much one should like both, if it were not for their slavish, servile devotion to the king (and I think it was real), and to that odious woman Madame de Maintenon.[1] Also Racine was a bigot, but sincere. My liking for Madame de Sevigné, is, I suppose, owing to my very ignoble love of gossip, which, if it be but honest and natural, I always like, whether on paper or *de vive voix*.[2] And French, being the very language of chit-chat and prittle-prattle, is one reason why I like so much the *mémoires* and letters of that gossiping nation. Certainly Molière is their greatest man. Do you know Foote's farces?[3] They have more of Molière than any other English writer, to say nothing of a neatness of dialogue the most perfect imaginable—as perfect as the dialogue part of the "Critic,"[4] which I take to be the most finished bit of Sheridan. I think you will like Mr. Townsend's smaller pieces.[5] Lady Dacre you will love. Heaven bless you! Love to all.

Ever most faithfully yours,
M.R. Mitford.

Address: Miss Barrett, Gloucester Place.
Text: L'Estrange (2), III, 85–86.

1. Françoise D'Aubigné, Marquise de Maintenon (1635–1719), mistress and later second wife of Louis XIV, the "Sun King" (1638–1715).
2. "By word of mouth."
3. Samuel Foote (1720–77), actor and dramatist, whose works included *The Minor* (1760) and *All in the Wrong* (1761), a version of Molière's *Cocu Imaginaire*.
4. *The Critic* (1779) by Richard Brinsley Sheridan (1751–1816).
5. The further reference to Townsend's poems in letter 647 suggests that this was Miss Mitford's friend, Richard Edwin Austin Townsend.

613. EBB TO JOHN KENYON

[London]
[ca. February 1838][1]

My dear Mr Kenyon,

I am so sure that you are not laughing at me, that I am ready to act the "critic" for your *good-natured* amusement at any time,—& the more ready, as I feel very sure of greater pleasure being in store for me from the reading of your MSS,[2] than even that great human pleasure of finding fault. You will not have to find fault with *me* for being uncandid. I wish I were as free from every other deficiency & inadequacy.

Thank you for your indulgence to my *mysticism*. It was not indeed meant to be so much so!——but your servant is here again.

Believe me
Ever truly yours
EBB.

Address, on integral page: John Kenyon Esq.[r] / 4 Harley Place.
Publication: None traced.
Manuscript: Armstrong Browning Library.

1. Dated by the reference to Kenyon's manuscript.
2. When Kenyon's volume of *Poems: For the Most Part Occasional* was published, it contained a note dated 26 April 1838. As EBB is reading the poems in manuscript, this letter must antedate April by some weeks.

614. EBB TO JOHN KENYON

74 Gloucester Place
Thursday morning. [ca. February 1838][1]

Dear M.ʳ Kenyon,

I am inclined to use the words you would not translate from Constant's poem—"stringite lumina."[2] Certainly I *am* ashamed & fearful at the idea of your looking upon the papers accompanying this note, the length & breadth of which, supply such convicting measures of my presumption.

But I am quite sure you *meant what you said*, when you desired me to speak candidly: *much more* sure, than that it was altogether becoming in me to be so obedient.

The objections—to do them justice—refer, in by far the greater part—only to little roughnesses & apparently forced constructions—which—even if they are properly objected to—will not occasion you much trouble in their dismissal. If your opinion is, that any or EVERY OBJECTION is "vexatious opposition" (altho' you will *not* think it was meant so) do "dismiss the complaint"—& you will serve me rightly. This is said as candidly as all the rest.

And now, altho' you have tried so often, dear M.ʳ Kenyon, you shall not *quite* spoil me. Perhaps you have succeeded in producing presumption—or the image of it—but ingratitude you cannot produce. Therefore I *will* thank you for all the pleasure I have had in reading these poems—so full of strong thoughts & lovely stedfast feelings—& that *belief in beauty* which is at once the poet's enthusiasm & his inspiration. You shall not think that I admire nothing, but what, in the papers, I have noticed admiringly—*their* amiable object being the detection, or as you will suggest, the *imagination*, of all possible faults. 'Moonlight' is full of beauty. The 'Rhymed Plea' pray, for *me*, sit at its feet. But this you may call a simple prejudice,—& even speak the epithet advisedly. Of the 'occasional verses,' many of which are so graceful & so strong, I like least the "neglected wife" & like most, among others, the musical & feeling "music"—& "Bromfield Churchyard", & 'Reminiscence', & the 'Two harps' & the powerful 'Destiny' which is so to honor mine.[3] There are besides some touching poems, which I do not forget, & shall not, easily.

Thank you for all the pleasure—& in addition to it,—*forgive* ME.

Ever truly yours
E B Barrett.

With a great many thanks, I return the books you kindly lent me.

Publication: None traced.
Manuscript: Fitzwilliam Museum.

1. Dated by EBB's further criticisms of Kenyon's manuscript, the subject of the previous letter.
2. "Song of the Manes" (pp. 117–118 in the printed text) was translated from some modern Latin verses in Benjamin de Constant's *Traité de la Religion*, III, 391. The words "stringite lumina" ("let the torches be extinguished") appear in line 3 of the 6th verse of "Le chant des mânes" in de Constant's book. Kenyon's rendering was "Bid our wan torches gleam."
3. All these references are to poems included in Kenyon's book, except "Rhymed Plea," which is an earlier work of his, *Rhymed Plea for Tolerance* (1833). "Destiny" was preceded by a four-line quotation from EBB's *Prometheus Bound* (583–586). A very detailed, 10-page critique by EBB of some of these poems is extant (see *Reconstruction*, D1285).

615. EBB TO HUGH STUART BOYD

[London]
Monday morning. [*Postmark:* 26 February 1838]

My dear friend,

I saw the following advertisement in the Athenæum of Saturday, & believing that it may interest you, do not delay to send it.

To clergymen &c–
To be sold by order of the proprietor, a copy of Archbishop Cranmer's Bible, the very rare edition of 1539, folio, black letter, in very fine condition, wanting only the first title, which has been replaced by a facsimile from Lewis's Translation.
Apply to Smallfield & Son. 69 Newgate St.[1]

You may have perhaps heard that we have lost a beloved relation, poor Papa's only brother, & one who was once more than uncle to *me*.[2] But we have the only comfort for his absence from us, in the perfect security of his presence with our Lord. May God so comfort us all, in all our griefs–

My cough is quieter since the frost went away,—but I am very weak & far from being well.

M.[r] Curzon has been in London for a few days,—or rather at *Fulham*. But in spite of the distance he was so kind as to make his way to see us—& I had great pleasure in seeing him once more, & so little altered that these five long years seem to have passed for nothing with him. He left M.[rs] Curzon & his boy at Plymouth,[3] to which place he returns—but with no intention of joining the church there—rather of returning to London,—and even this plan appears to be at present a mere uncertainty. He enquired with great appearance of interest after you, & desired me to give you his very kind remembrances.

I never hear anything of you dear Mr Boyd! May you be quite well & happy.

                    Your affectionate friend
                    E B Barrett.

Do you know that Mr Valpy is giving up business?
Remember me—do—to Miss Holliday.
Daisy is quite well again, thank God.

Address, on integral page: H S Boyd Esqr / 4 Circus Road / St. John's Wood.
Publication: EBB-HSB, pp. 225–226.
Manuscript: Wellesley College.

   1. *The Athenæum,* 24 February 1838 (no. 539, p. 155).
   2. Samuel Moulton-Barrett had died in Jamaica on 23 December, but the news only reached England in the middle of February.
   3. Curzon had married Eliza Joynes in 1822. Their son, Henry George Roper-Curzon (1822–92), later became 17th Baron Teynham.

---

616. EBB TO JOHN KENYON

                    74 Gloucester Place
                    Wednesday. [ca. March 1838]¹

Indeed dear Mr. Kenyon, I have not *at all* liked leaving your two notes unanswered several days in this manner—wishing as I did even before I received them to write and assure you how gladly & thankfully I have heard of every step taken by you towards recovery. Some other people's friends may need a frightening such as yours have had, to teach them their value,—and tho' yours did never & can never need *such*, yet a fear followed by so much gladness can scarcely be called a useless thing– May God bless you in all ways & always!–

It was very good of you to indulge my "particular taste for cutting & slashing"—which, considering that expression, is, tho' particular, not peculiar-— And here, enclosed, are the fruits of the steel. And do observe that even if you were bound to believe in its striking always or generally or often or at all, wisely, you would have very little trouble in consequence—there being scarcely any except verbal findings-fault!—— It seems to me that you have dealt triumphantly with the potatoes—& may put to shame the poetical mob with roses lilies & violets by basketfulls!– What a mistake it is, to make a locality for Beauty! It is as well to make one for the Chief Spirit!——

Your description of evening is very lovely—beginning—[']'evening now

          Was slanting her long shadows &c"

The *pause* of the cloud—the *laboring* of the rook—& that line which undulates so expressively—

"*Swayed leisurely by to* food & needful rest"—

these are all *rests* for the memory. I must thank you for the pleasure this Amphitheatre has given me,[2] independently of the particular one of cutting & slashing.

As to your vow of not writing any more, I hope that those are among the perjuries at which Jove laughs! that it is a mere eastern idiomatic vow, & that M!˚ Landor made his at the same time & upon the same Zendavesta!——[3] His book is quite exquisite—with pages in it almost too beautiful to be turned over![4]

It is quite as well to say upon *another sheet*, that I did think of "trying the public" & not at all of printing a book without publishing it. I have wanted very much to ask your advice almost ever since you went into Devonshire, about the manner of doing this—for as to sending you any of the sheets, which I would do still more eagerly, I am afraid of provoking your kindness into putting you to inconvenience— I know that you have not as much leisure as kindness.

But I will tell you, if you will hear so far dear M!˚ Kenyon, just what I have thought of printing.

First, the *Seraphim*, the first part of which I once mentioned to you as being sent to & lost at M!˚ Colburn's. Partly from a very rough copy, & partly from memory, I recovered it,—& added to it a second part of about twice the length. The length of the whole is within twenty lines I think, of that of *my* (not Æschylus's) Prometheus—& the form, rather a dramatic lyric, than a lyrical drama, & the subject, the supposed impression made upon angelic beings by the incarnation & crucifixion—a very daring subject, which suggested itself to me whilst I was *doing* that translation from Æschylus .. which makes me shiver to think of, this cold day.

Then, would come the Poets' vow, & Margret, & several poems of a length almost equal to them, & some shorter ones at the end.— The whole book might be between two & three hundred pages thick—or more—or less.

Now do you not think that there wᵈ be no *harm* in submitting some of these mss, by the mediation of a note or my brother, to a publisher—just to see, whether he wᵈ take just so much of the risk as wᵈ secure his taking a little interest about the sale— I wᵈ rather not be asked again as M!˚ Valpy asked me, (after he had enquired whether I had been skaiting on the Regent's Park Canal—women who meddle with such being thought brave or bad enough for anything) if my books had sold at all—when no human being except himself, cᵈ know a word about them. I have "a lady's oath"[5] (not upon the Zendavesta) to put no more mss to be changed to print, in M.ʳ Valpy's hands–

Perhaps it is almost too late, & w.ᵈ at any rate be vain to put them into anybody's– And I dont very much mind if it is, & w.ᵈ be– For altho' ambition is a grand angelic sin, I fell a good way from the sphere of it, soon after I left the nursery. I have at any rate a long futurity of coughing abstract me from it by thinking of⁶––until April or May, D.ʳ Chambers says! But I am better—particularly as there is a hope of a little thawing. I do trust that this terrible weather has not affected you——and that besides, you dont think me the most tiresome person in the world—which I am sure you must do, if *you* are not the most patient. But indeed you have brought it upon yourself by your too great kindness to me.

Dear Miss Mitford wrote again & again to me during your illness, in the utmost anxiety: & now I fear that she is herself very unwell–

Sette & Occy are so much obliged to you for your intention with regard to the fossils—but you sh.ᵈ not rob yourself any more– The repairs are going on busily in the house—which reminds me (too late) that I ought not to begin our neighbourhood of twenty five years by tiring you thus!——

Believe me dear M.ʳ Kenyon,
Ever & most truly yours,
E B Barrett–

Thank you for Alford's poems.⁷ There is much beauty in some of them—but *there is a want of abiding power*. Do you not think so?– It might be a fault in my humour at the time I read them. The boys told me to enclose the book which you leant [*sic*] to them LAST YEAR—& they have gone out without giving it to me– It shall be sent.

With many thanks Occy & Sette return the long detained book–

Address, on integral page: John Kenyon Esq.ʳ / 4 Harley Place.
Publication: None traced.
Manuscript: Armstrong Browning Library.

1. Dated by the further references to Kenyon's manuscript poems, and the fact that EBB was still at Gloucester Place.
2. The lines quoted by EBB refer to "Dorchester Amphitheatre," which appeared on pp. 168–185 of the printed text (the lines quoted: p. 170).
3. The sacred writings of Zoroaster that formed the basis of the prevailing religion in Persia from the 6th century B.C. to the 7th A.D.
4. Presumably EBB refers to Landor's latest work, *The Pentameron and Pentalogia* (1837).
5. Cf. Fletcher, *The Chances*, II, 1, 118.
6. EBB originally wrote "a long futurity of coughing to think of––". When she altered that to the present reading, it seems probable that she intended the phrase to end with "thinking of me" but omitted to add the final word.
7. Henry Alford (1810–71), later (1857) Dean of Canterbury, had published *Poems and Poetical Fragments* (1833) and *School of the Heart, and Other Poems* (1835).

617. EBB TO MARY RUSSELL MITFORD

74, Gloucester Place,
Monday [March 1838][1]

I cannot hope, my dearest Miss Mitford, that it may have seemed to you half as long as it has seemed to me since I wrote last to you, and yet it is a month since your delightful letter brought the *first* pleasure to me at a season of deep sadness. We had heard from the West Indies of the death of poor Papa's only brother, of one in past times more than an uncle to me, and, notwithstanding all the comfort with which God in his mercy did soften this affliction, it could not but be felt, even as the affection which preceded it had been, and must ever be. Dearest Miss Mitford, the passing away of everything around us would break the hearts of many of us, if we did not know and feel that *we* are passing too. I long to hear of you, and should have said so before, and have thought day after day I will write to-morrow, and then again, not being very well, I have put it off to some less dull moment for your sake. The turning to spring is always trying, I believe, to affections such as mine, and my strength flags a good deal, and the cough very little; but Dr. Chambers speaks so encouragingly of the probable effect of the coming warm weather, that I take courage and his medicines at the same time, and, "to preserve the harmonies,"[2] and satisfy some curiosity, have been reading Garth's "Dispensary," a poem very worthy of its subject.[3] Yes, and, besides, I have been going through heaps of poets ("oh, the profaned name!")[4] laid up in Dr. Johnson's warehouses—Duke and Smith, and King and Sprat[5] (never christened in Hippocrene),[6] and Pomfret, with his choice, not mine, and his Pindaric odes, not Pindar's, in which he exclaims in a rapture—

> "Good Heaven would be extremely kind,
> Either to strike me dead, or strike me blind,"[7]

when striking him *dumb* would be more to *my mind*! By the way, I am not at all sure of that not being as good a line as either of his.

Thank you for your most interesting remarks upon the drama; Victor Hugo's plays I never read, but will do so. His poems seem to me not very striking, more bare of genius than such of his prose writings, as I have happened to see. And little have I seen of the new school of French literature, and must see and know more of it. De Lamartine's "Pilgrimage"[8] is the only traveller's book, except "Sinbad the Sailor," and "Robinson Crusoe," that ever pleased me much; and his poetry is holy and beautiful, though deficient, as it appears to me, in concentration of expression and grasp of thought. To speak generally, my abstract idea of a Frenchman is the antithesis of a poet, but pray do not, if the prayer does not come too late, think me quite a bigot. There is nothing, as you say, like the Greeks, *our* Greeks let them be for the future, and although I can scarcely consent to crowning Philoctetes over all,[9] it would still be more difficult to take a word away from your just praise. The defect of that play is that it is founded upon physical suffering, and its glory is that from the physical suffering is deduced so much moral pathos and purifying energy. The "Œdipus" is wonderful, the sublime truth which pierces through it to your soul like a lightening seems to me to be the humiliating effect of guilt, even when unconsciously incurred. The abasement, the self-abasement, of the proud, high-minded king before the mean, mediocre Creon, not because he is wretched, not because he is blind, but because he is criminal, appears to me a wonderful and most affecting conception.[10] And there is Euripides, with his abandon to the pathetic, and Æschylus who sheds tears like a strong man, and moves you to more because you know that his struggle is to restrain them.

But if the Greeks once begin to be talked of, they will be talked of too much. I should have told you when I wrote last that Mr. Kenyon lent me Mr. Harness's play, which abounds in gentle and tender touches, and not, I think, might I say so, in much concentration and dramatic *power*.[11] As to its being a domestic tragedy, I do not object to it on that account, and really believe that I don't share your preference for imperial tragedies. Do not passion and suffering pervade Nature? Tragedies are everywhere, are they not? Or, at least, their elements are, or is this the pathos of radicalism? My book is almost decided upon being, and thanks for your kind encouragement, dearest Miss Mitford, you, who are always kind. There is a principal poem, called the "Seraphim," which is rather a dramatic lyric than a lyrical drama, and as long, within twenty or thirty lines, as my translation, "The Prometheus of Æschylus," and in two parts. I can hardly hope that you will thoroughly like it, but know well that you will try to do so. Other poems, longer or shorter, will make up the volume, not a word of which is yet printed. Would not by E. B. B. stand very well for a name? I have been reading the "Exile," from Marion Campbell, with much interest and delight;[12] besides, she made me forget Dr. Chambers, and feel how near you were. A pleasant feeling to everybody, but how very pleasant to your affectionate and grateful

E. B. Barrett

P.S.—My kind regards to Dr. Mitford, and Papa's and my sister's to you. Our house in Wimpole Street is not yet finished, but we hope to see the beginning of April in it. You must not think I am very bad, only not very brisk, and really feeling more comfortable than I did a fortnight since.

Text: L'Estrange (1), II, 16–19 (as 1837).

1. Dated by the references to EBB's health, and the impending move to Wimpole Street.

2. Cf. Hazlitt, *Table Talk*, Essay 22.
3. *The Dispensary, a Poem* (1699), by Samuel Garth (1661–1719), physician and poet, ridiculed apothecaries and dealt with the first attempts to establish out-patient rooms.
4. Jonson, *Poëtaster; or, His Arraignment* (1616), IV, 6, 29.
5. Samuel Johnson's *Lives of the English Poets* (1779–81) included text on Richard Duke (1658–1711), Edmund Smith (1668?–1710), William King (1663–1712) and Thomas Sprat (1636–1713).
6. The fountain on Mt. Helicon that sprang up where the hoof of Pegasus struck the rock. It was sacred to the Muses, and thus signified poetical inspiration.
7. A slight misquotation of lines 10–11 of stanza VI of "Eleazar's Lamentation Over Jerusalem: Paraphrased Out of Josephus." This appeared in *The Choice: a Poem Written by a Person of Quality* (1700) by John Pomfret (1667–1702). Pomfret gave to some of his poems the sub-title "A Pindaric Ode" or "A Pindaric Essay."
8. *Le Dernier Chant du Pèlerinage d'Harold* (1825), by Alphonse Marie Louis de Lamartine de Prat (1790–1869), which EBB recorded reading in 1831 (*Diary*, p. 54). At the same time, she mentioned having read some of Hugo's poetry.
9. Sophocles' *Philoctetes* deals with the most famous archer of the Trojan War, to whom Hercules gave arrows.
10. At the conclusion of Sophocles' *Œdipus Tyrannos*.
11. *Welcome and Farewell: a Drama* had been published by Miss Mitford's friend William Harness in 1837, under the pseudonym George Taylor.
12. One of Miss Mitford's fugitive pieces.

---

618. EBB TO HUGH STUART BOYD

74 Gloucester Place
Friday– [9 March 1838][1]

I heard last night my dear friend of the grief sent to you by God.[2] I am sure that you will remember its being sent by Him, & receive it resignedly & calmly, &, read upon it the mark of His love—and yet I am so sure besides of the painfulness of that grief, that I must tell you how much & truly I feel with you & for you. Do my dear friend, accept this expression of sympathy from me. Such sympathy always goes to you from me,—& is the deeper in proportion to the depth of your gladness or your sorrow.

If there is anything which you wish to be done for you, Arabel will certainly be glad to do it. Would that there were anything for *me* to do! I am a helpless useless being just now—but your kindness will care to know that I feel better today than I was yesterday.

May God bless you—and then there will be no more need of human actions––or words.

Your affectionate friend
E B Barrett.

Address: H S Boyd Esq[r] / 3. Circus Road / St. John's Wood.
Publication: EBB-HSB, pp. 226–227 (as [10 March 1838]).
Manuscript: Wellesley College.

1. Letter is postmarked 10 March 1838, which fell on a Saturday.
2. The death of his only sister.

619. EBB to Lady Margaret Cocks

74 Gloucester Place.
Tuesday. [?13] [March 1838][1]

I must intrude a short letter upon you my dear Lady Margaret, just to ask how Lord & Lady Eastnor are, and indeed how your own self is, for I well know the affectionateness of your feelings & that the affliction lately sustained by your family cannot have passed you by without a pang—[2] Will you, when it is not disagreeable to you to do so, write me one line of reply to this enquiry. I had not heard of any illness—but I trust that the blow did not fall very suddenly, and that the dear little girl went to God without a great deal of suffering, to forget the short trouble of time in His blessed eternity. The youngest of us all is old enough to go to Him,—and the case being so, it is only the *foolishness* of grief (perhaps all grief is foolish except grief for sin) to lament immature years, & unfulfilled earthly expectations.

You will be kind enough to wish me to say how I am. A blister submitted to a few days since, seems to have relieved the chest a little,—& the warm weather being so near, D.ʳ Chambers & I *both* hope that I may be *much* the better for *that*- I am however in a very weak state of health, & incapable of any occupation which should not rather be called an imitation of idleness, & have not been out of the house since September. We have also been very unhappy; having lost our beloved relative in the West Indies—poor Papa's only brother,—who was once to *me* Uncle brother friend & nurse when I lay in the long weary sickness at Gloucester. I never can forget *that*—& the gratitude & the love were as one. Every comfort that the *so* bereaved can have, we have had. He died *in Christ*—in the alone hope of safety by Him—and selfish is the sadness which can live thro' such assurance. My brother Sam is coming to England for a few months,—which will be a great happiness to us, & an advantage to him both as to spirits & health. How the waves of pleasure & mournfulness chase each other over the sand of life! But it will dry at last. I have just selected as a motto for one of my poems (my volume is in the press & is promised to emerge from it in a month) a line from an old poet whose antiquity has buried his name--"All goeth, but Goddis' will."[3] Yes! and all *should* go but That!-

We hope to remove into our new house early in April—but frosts & floods have so delayed the arrival of the furniture that the time of removal is still doubtful. Do, my dearest Lady Margaret, forgive this scribble, which blushes black to appear before you. Finden's sale has been beyond expectation—I mean the Tableaux- I had such an affectionate letter from my dear friend Miss Mitford this morning. I do believe she dearly loves me, and I am sure I gratefully love her—altho we have seen each other only four times. There never was a heart more tender in its affections than Her's—or more skilfull to *draw out* love.

May God bless you, dear Lady Margaret! Shall I hear from you? *Do let me.* I send this note to Reigate, from want of knowing where else to send it.

Your sincerely affectionate
E B Barrett.

Address, on integral page: The Lady Margaret Cocks.
Publication: None traced.
Manuscript: Hon. Mrs. Elizabeth Hervey-Bathurst.

1. Dated by the death of Lord and Lady Eastnor's daughter.
2. Isabella Jemima Cocks, third daughter and fourth child of the Eastnors, had died on 8 March, aged 10.
3. EBB used this motto for "An Island," included in *The Seraphim, and Other Poems* (p. 185).

---

620. EBB to Hugh Stuart Boyd

[London]
Monday morning. [26 March 1838]¹

My dear friend,

I do hope that you may not be very angry,—but Papa thinks and indeed I think that as I have already *had* two proof sheets of forty eight pages, and the printers have gone on to the rest of the poem, it would not be very welcome to them if we were to ask them to retrace their steps. Besides I would rather—*I* for myself, *I*—that you had the whole poem at once and clearly-printed before you, to insure as many chances as possible of your liking it. I am *promised* to see the volume completed in three weeks from this time,—so that the dreadful moment of your reading it, I mean the Seraphim part of it, cannot be far off; and perhaps, the season being a good deal advanced even now, you might not on consideration wish me to retard the appearance of the book except for some very sufficient reason. I feel very nervous about it—far more than I did, when my Prometheus crept out the Greek, or I myself out of the shell, in the first Essay on Mind. Perhaps this is owing to D.ʳ Chambers's medicines! or perhaps to a consciousness that my present attempt *is* actually, & will be considered by others, more a trial of strength than either of my preceding ones.

Thank you for the books! and especially for the *editio rarissima*, which I should as soon have thought of your trusting to me, as of your admitting me to stand *with gloves on*, within a yard of Baxter.² This extraordinary confidence shall not be abused.

I thank you besides for your kind enquiries about my health. Dr Chambers did not think me worse yesterday, notwithstanding the last cold days which have occasioned some uncomfortable sensations—and he still thinks that I shall be better in the warmer season. In the meantime he has ordered me to take ice—out of sympathy with nature I suppose,—and not to speak a word,—out of contradiction to my particular, human, feminine nature!

Whereupon I revenge myself you see, by talking all this nonsense upon paper & making you the victim.

To propitiate you, let me tell you that your commands have been performed to the letter,—& that one Greek motto (from Orpheus) is given to the First Part of the Seraphim, and another from *Chrysostom* to the second.[3]

Henrietta desires me to say that she means to go to see you very soon. Give my very kind remembrance to Miss Holmes[4]—& believe me

Your affectionate friend
E B Barrett.

I saw Mr Kenyon yesterday. He has a book just coming out. I sh.^d like you to read it. If you would, you would thank me for saying so!–

Address: H S Boyd Esqr / 3 Circus Road / St John's Wood.
Publication: LEBB, I, 57–58 (as 27 March 1838).
Manuscript: Wellesley College.

1. Letter was postmarked 27 March 1838, which fell on a Tuesday.
2. Richard Baxter (1615–91), best known for *The Saints' Everlasting Rest* (1650), and his *Paraphrase of the New Testament* (1685), which resulted in his being tried and imprisoned on the charge of libelling the Church.
3. The two mottoes selected by EBB were, respectively, "Σῳ δε θρονῳ τυροεντι παρεστᾶσιν πολυμοχθοι Αγγελοι" ("Long-suffering angels stand by the fiery throne," Fragmenta, III, 9–10, in Hermann's 1805 edition of *Orphica*) and "Ετερως γαρ ουκ οιδα φιλεῖν, αλλ 'η μετα του και την ψυχῆν εκδιδοναι την εμαυτου" ("For otherwise I do not know how to love, except that I also surrender my life," from St. John Chrysostom).
4. As letter 551 indicates that Boyd knew Mrs. Mary Anne Holmes, this was probably her sister-in-law. Repeated references to her suggest that she was caring for Boyd in some way, perhaps as housekeeper, now that his daughter was no longer living with him.

---

621. EBB TO MARY RUSSELL MITFORD

74 Gloucester Place
Monday. [early April 1838][1]

My dear friend, I am going to put one question into as few words as possible,—being in great haste. Have you the least shadow of preference for my NOT comprizing the Ganges ballad, written for your Tableaux, in my little volume of poems? Do answer me quite plainly. I have not any wish about it, believe me; and even if I had, the stronger one would still be to attend to *your* wish.–

Some of the MSS have actually *gone* to press– So now, there is room for only "the *late* remorse of *fear*".² The Ganges is not wanted, even to fill up–

Are you quite well? Would that I could hear you say 'yes'—but I suppose there is no hope of that pleasant sound coming, actually & sensibly, to supersede my coughing. I am rather better I think, & do 'honor due' to a blister which I submitted to so reluctantly a few days ago–

Occy is a great *Murpheist*,³ notwithstanding all the proved frailty of the prophecies,—& when Sette & I laugh at him for it, the retort is that *we* both believe in animal magnetism—which is much worse!—— '*Alice or the mysteries*' is magnetizing me just now!⁴ I have read one volume.

Dearest Miss Mitford, I must say goodbye! You will readily forgive a short post[s]cript to my long letter of last week.

Your affectionate
EBB–

Publication: EBB-MRM, I, 66–67.
Manuscript: Wellesley College.

1. Dated by the reference to *The Seraphim* being in the press, and by EBB's still being at Gloucester Place.
2. A modification of Byron's "late remorse of love" (*Childe Harold's Pilgrimage, Canto the Fourth*, 1818, stanza 137, line 9).
3. A reference to Patrick Murphy, the weather prophet (see letter 609, notes 3 and 4).
4. Bulwer's novel, published in February 1838.

622. RB TO HARRIET MARTINEAU[1]

[London]
Monday. [?9 April 1838][2]

My dear Miss Martineau,

I am unluckily engaged on Wednesday; but will endeavour to see you, if only for a minute, in the course of the evening.

Yours faithfully
Rob.ᵗ Browning.

Pray remember me very kindly to Mrs Martineau.³

Publication: None traced.
Manuscript: Harvard University.

1. For details of RB's friendship with Miss Martineau, see pp. 325–327.
2. This letter has no watermark, and could have been written any time between 1836, when RB is thought to have first met Miss Martineau, and April 1839, when Miss Martineau left London. Lacking any more definite evidence, we have assigned this

conjectural date, as Miss Martineau recorded that RB visited her on Wednesday, 11 April 1838 (*Harriet Martineau's Autobiography*, ed. Maria W. Chapman, 1877, II, 337).

3. Elizabeth Martineau (*née* Rankin, 1773–1848).

623. RB TO JOHN ROBERTSON[1]

[London]
Good Friday, [13 April] 1838

Dear Sir,

I was not fortunate enough to find you the day before yesterday—and must tell you very hurriedly that I sail this morning for Venice—intending to finish my poem among the scenes it describes.[2] I shall have your good wishes I know.

Believe me, in return,
Dear sir,
Yours faithfully and obliged,
Robert Browning.

Text: Orr, p. 88.

1. According to Mrs. Orr, Robertson was connected with *The Westminster Review*, and had been introduced to RB by Miss Martineau. He had expressed admiration for *Paracelsus* and had promised careful attention to *Sordello*. However, he demanded an early reading of the poem; RB thought this would be unfair to other reviewers, and refused to comply, thus losing Robertson's goodwill (Orr, p. 88).

2. i.e., *Sordello*.

624. RB TO UNIDENTIFIED CORRESPONDENT

[London]
[13 April 1838][1]

⟨★★★⟩ information happens to be sufficiently precise—and he may assure himself I will look into the matter on my return: I sail in a few hours—not unluckily for him.

I put up Landor and Tennyson. Do not forget,
Yours ever most
truly and obliged,
R Browning.

Publication: None traced.
Manuscript: Armstrong Browning Library.

1. Dated by his sailing for Venice on his first journey to Italy.

625. Leigh Hunt to RB

Chelsea,
15.th April. [ca. 1838][1]

My dear Sir,—Your *Corelli* gratified me extremely. The only pleasure I had in the other was in looking at the beautiful name (Arcangelo Corelli),[2] and thinking how very unlike the face must have been. Yours, in the rich pulpy lips, mild eyes, and yet, somehow irritable expression, must come much nearer to the aspect of the sweet and sensitive musician, whose name, I think, was singularly happy, for no man seems to me to have written such air-drawn, trust-heaven-and-earth strains as he did. When you return from the country, I hope you will not forget the promise you made me of again coming to see me. It will be both a pleasure and an honour to, dear sir,

yours truly,
Leigh Hunt.

Text: Hunt, I, 316.[3]

1. This letter could have been written any time after RB first met Hunt (believed to be in the mid-1830's) and the summer of 1840, when Hunt moved from Chelsea.
2. Arcangelo Corelli (1653–1713), the influential Italian violinist and composer.
3. We have some doubts about RB's being the addressee, in view of the context of the letter, but, as the original has not come to light, we are accepting, with reservations, the ascription in the printed source.

---

626. EBB to Hugh Stuart Boyd

129 Crawford St.
Monday. [16 April 1838][1]

My dear friend,

I was thinking of writing to you when your kind enquiry came. In the Athenæum of saturday is a notice which is likely, or rather, sure, to interest you. It is to this effect.

"The examination of a m.s. entitled ["]*The Homilies of St Chrysostom,*" which was bequeathed to the Royal Library of Dresden, has discovered five homilies of St Chrysostom which have been hitherto unedited, & in fact unknown. A copy has been forwarded to Dr Becken, a distinguished theologian and Greek scholar at Leipsic, with orders for him to make a Latin translation of them."[2]

Thank you for your notices of *seraphical* passages in Gregory,—tho' I had examined them previously & found nothing reflecting any particular light on *my* subject. I have just sent away a proof sheet up to the 216.th page.

There can be no question as to your being *perfectly in the right*, with regard to Lady Olivia Sparrow,—so much so, that upon reconsideration it must appear [so] to whomsoever your view of the subject was displeasing. Do not be angry with me, my dear friend,—but I *would not let* Henrietta apply for an opinion elsewhere. You will at once know my reasons: and after abusing me for a quarter of an hour by the clock, are sure to forgive me in your abundant indulgence—particularly when I tell you that D! Chambers condemned me yesterday to two applications of leeches before Wednesday. And so for my sake, you must smooth your frowns away—I mean such as were meant for *others*, as well [as] for me!——

He found me yesterday in a very weak state—with what he calls a 'miserable pulse': & it could not be expected to be much better today, after 'Leeches the first' last night. I feel however better this morning in some respects. He says that he "hopes to overcome the complaint in time,["]—& considers it a favorable circumstance that all the warm weather sh^d be before me!——

I wish I had a prospect of seeing you! May God bless you dear M! Boyd!—— M! Kenyon's book is splendid—I mean as to type & paper,—& beautiful, as to composition.[3] You ought to read some of it at least? Will you? Would you, if I were to send it to Circus Road? Give my kind remembrances to Miss Holmes.

Affectionately yours
E B Barrett

Address, on integral page: H S Boyd Esq! / 3 Circus Road / St John's Wood.
Publication: EBB-HSB, pp. 227–228.
Manuscript: Wellesley College.

1. Dated by the reference to *The Athenæum*.
2. *The Athenæum*, 14 April 1838 (no. 546, p. 277).
3. *Poems: For the Most Part Occasional*, which EBB had criticized in manuscript (see letters 613, 614 and 616).

---

627. EBB TO MARY RUSSELL MITFORD

[London]
Monday– [16 April 1838][1]

My beloved friend,

If I *had* heard of your being in such anxiety & distress, you would have known before now of my hearing of it. But since last Sunday week I have not seen M! Kenyon, & from no other except yourself could I have heard it. Into all that you must have felt I deeply enter—& thank

God that this sympathy is so much too late. May you not need it for very very long again! Indeed it is not likely that from *me* you may ever need it! Not that I am going to die immediately you know—but that from what you tell me of the abstraction of blood & unslackened energy afterwards, I am led to muse upon differences of constitutional strength, & to count up my own years to be some fifty five *more* than those of D[r] Mitford. A few leeches, if applied oftener than once, reduce me almost to the last position suggested by the Sphinx's riddle[2]—& draw from D[r] Chambers (notwithstanding the advantage I receive from them otherwise) the oracular "We *cannot* continue them"–

But I was speaking & wished to speak, not of myself but of D[r] Mitford. May God long bless you both with the blessedness of tracing much earthly happiness to each other—for if we sorrow because we love, it is no less true than we rejoice because we love—& the purest human loves are those which came first from the spring!—— Do when you write dearest Miss Mitford, mention him particularly,—& moreover your own health & spirits–

And how are the flowers?– None the better I fear for this doubling upon us of the winter. I felt as sorry to hear of the perished ones, as if I could have seen them—nay, more so—for then I should have seen *you*. But THE BAY IS NOT DEAD!![3]

Now will you 'take notice'?– I began this letter the day after receiving yours, altho' I would not go on with it,—franks being so rare at Easter time. Do remember that it was begun the day after receiving yours. I would not have you think (oh surely you *could not* think so) that my sympathy did not respond quickly to every mention of—a grief of yours: & even if without it, my heart had not "leapt up"[4] to thank you for the tenderness to me myself of many of your words, my heart had been no heart but the 'large black stone' which wears in oriental phrase the 'small black beetle'![5] How kind of you to say that you w[d] have read my poor MS for me, had I sent it to you! And indeed my not sending it involved no doubt—of even such a kindness. But I love you too well to try to tempt your love for me (an infidel sh[d] I be, if I disbelieved it!) into misusing your time for my sake.

Thank you for the tableau[6] .. which I have kept determinedly out of my head ever since, because you did not acquaint me with the *nationality* which belongs to it. Will you tell me, when you write?—— I am sure that much might be made of it! If I were but as sure of the *maker!* ——

M[r] Kenyon's book is indeed beautiful—& in all ways. I will praise 'Pretence' up to your highest wish of praising it, if you will take delight with me afterwards (as you certainly will) in 'Moonlight'. For Moonlight is vivid with picture,—& the manner in which the moral glides in upon the graphical (towards the end),—sad, solemn, & chastened like one of its own rays—appears to me exceedingly beautiful. I have not seen the writer since he was so kind as to send me his work,—but I hear of his being very well & haunted with society. Through it all, I had to thank him for bestowing a thought on me, & lending me Mr Milnes's Poems just printed for private circulation.[7] They are of the Tennyson school, to which you know (after all the harm we grave critics are obliged to say of *schools*) only poets can belong,—& very much delighted me. Some of them & those not a few, appear to me most exquisite.

You knew so well what I sh^d like, when you sent me Mr Spring Rice's letter!!–[8] Indeed your whole packet had its share in lighting up my spirits for days afterwards.– But *your* "charmëd words"[9] which beguiled the stern statesmen of softer & purer thoughts than were "in their bond"[10]—what would I not give to see *those*?– I was obliged in my fulness of joy to let Papa into the 'confidence'—& you must forgive me for it—because he said "*This* does indeed give me pleasure"–

We are no longer in Gloucester Place—nor yet in Wimpole Street. At least I & my sisters are not. The house was so unfinished, that we were obliged & glad to accept the charities of a kind friend & go to Crawford Street until the ghost of paint had been sufficiently exorcised.[11] But direct to 50 Wimpole Street—both because our stay elsewhere is very uncertain, & because our letters are brought from thence instantly.

The scratches I have sent you lately are remorseful subjects with me– These (for the most part) are made in bed: not that I am worse, but have been obliged for some time, to rest until rather late in the day. I am better—but I fear, not VERY much so. God's will be done in all things. May I have wisdom & strength to rejoice that it *must*. Dr Chambers seems to regard the warm weather with hopefulness– In the meantime, he frowns most awfully at the snow– Nevertheless down it comes!——

Do give my kindest regards to Dr Mitford! The doves are with me here! I w^d not come without them!——

My very dear friend's most affectionate & grateful
E B Barrett

I hope Mr Chorley has recovered from indisposition– Mr Carey's information I was thankful for. Though a *fond* reader of some of the Greek Fathers, I know nothing of Origen except from report.——[12]

Tuesday. [24 April 1838]

Dearest Miss Mitford, I was disappointed in the frank yesterday: & now I am glad of it, because I forgot then to tell you a story about your last letter. While the postman was in the act of delivering it, out of it fell a little packet of seeds inscribed as far as my ignorance wotteth of, Mixed *Zinnias*. I am sure it must have slipped into your envelope without a consciousness on your part. I once received, just by a like process, a *prescription*—in the letter of an invalid friend residing at Geneva!— The wonder in the present case is, that the supernumerary packet should have kept in, just long enough to admit of its falling out at our door.

I thought at first of retaining it until I had your direction—as you MIGHT have meant to send it to some other correspondent in London. But I believe the safest way is, to return it to you at once. And so here it is!——

Addressed and franked by John Somerset Pakington on integral page: 1838 / London April twenty five / Miss Mitford / Three Mile Cross / Reading / J.S. Pakington. / [and in EBB's hand on two integral pages:] Miss Mitford / Three Mile Cross / near Reading.
Publication: EBB-MRM, I, 67–71.
Manuscript: Wellesley College.

1. Concluding date provided by the frank; date of commencement by the reference to Easter.
2. The Sphinx of Greek mythology plagued the inhabitants of Thebes by posing riddles, and then devouring those unable to solve them. The Thebans were told by an oracle that the Sphinx would kill herself if they could solve this riddle: "What goes on four feet, on two feet, and three / But the more feet it goes on, the weaker it be?" Œdipus gave the correct answer: "Man" (who goes on all fours as an infant, on two feet in his prime, and in old age requires the support of a cane).
3. Presumably a reference to the bay tree that flourished in Miss Mitford's garden.
4. Cf. Wordsworth's poem, "My heart leaps up when I behold" (1807).
5. A Moslem proverb tells that "On a black night on a black stone stands a black ant; but God sees him and does not forget."
6. The illustration (reproduced facing p. 192) to accompany EBB's contribution to the 1839 *Findens' Tableaux*. It showed a girl, dressed as a page, hiding behind a tree while a knight rode by, providing the theme of "The Romaunt of the Page."
7. Richard Monckton Milnes (1809–85), later (1863) 1st Baron Houghton, was a friend of Thackeray, Tennyson and Hallam. The volume of which EBB speaks was *Memorials of a Residence on the Continent, and Historical Poems*. He had earlier (1834) published *Memorials of a Tour in Some Parts of Greece, Chiefly Poetical*.
8. Thomas Spring-Rice (1790–1866), later (1839) 1st Baron Monteagle, was Chancellor of the Exchequer under Melbourne at this time, so it is probable that his letter to Miss Mitford related in some way to her government pension.
9. Cf. Shelley, *The Revolt of Islam*, IV, 28, 3.
10. Cf. *The Merchant of Venice*, IV, 1, 262.
11. Crawford Street was in the immediate neighbourhood of Gloucester Place and Wimpole Street. Street directories and rate books for 1838 show that no. 129, the Barretts' temporary home, was owned by a Mrs. Ann Smith. It seems probable that this was Boyd's friend, the youngest daughter of the late Dr. Adam Clarke.
12. Origen (ca. 185–ca. 254), one of the Fathers of the Church, wrotte the first textual criticism of the Bible, and many commentaries. Cary had commented to Miss Mitford that the subject of EBB's *The Seraphim* had "never been touched except by one of the Fathers (Origen), and an old divine of the Church of England—a Bishop Andrews of the age of Elizabeth" (Chorley, I, 272).

628. EBB TO JOHN KENYON

129 Crawford Street
Wednesday– [18 April 1838][1]

Hearing last night dear M.ʳ Kenyon, of your return, I do not delay to tell you, by Miss Mitford's desire, that her father is very much better—indeed so well as to be able to attend the Quarter Sessions & to relieve her from present anxiety. I had such a delightful affectionate letter from her a few days ago which is refreshing to me even now to think about!——

Besides, I wish to know—or rather Henrietta does—whether your parcel goes to Torquay today or tomorrow. Papa told us of your allowing us to send a letter in it;[2] but he was a little uncertain in respect to the *chronology*.

I like your book better & better, the more & more I am familiar with it. As to the type & paper, my brother George is of opinion that I have suffered *agonies of envy* ever since they met my eyes,—but whether this be true or not, the agonies have not distorted me yet from the pleasure of being obliged to you for a gift, the beauty of whose print does not put out the beauty of its poetry.[3]

I have been trying to beguile M.ʳ Boyd into reading it—but English poetry he scarcely ever will read,—& for modern typography & paper has the utmost contempt,—extending itself to my opinions on the same– He paid me the very questionable compliment of reading "nine tenths" according to his own calculation, of my 'Poet's vow',—& is under a vow himself of going thro' the Seraphim; and so, altho' there is not a chance of his admiring your printer he may give himself an opportunity of estimating *you*.

My last note was sent to you on Saturday; & it was only on Sunday that I knew of Papa's wishing to send me & my sisters here.

Ever most truly yours
E B Barrett–

Address, on integral page: John Kenyon Esq.ʳ / 4 Harley Place.
Publication: None traced.
Manuscript: Armstrong Browning Library.

1. Dated by EBB's removal from Gloucester Place earlier in the week.
2. i.e., to EBB's aunt, Jane Hedley, who was living at Torquay.
3. EBB's presentation copy of *Poems: For the Most Part Occasional* formed part of *Browning Collections* (see *Reconstruction*, A1361).

629. EBB TO HUGH STUART BOYD

[London]
[ca. May 1838][1]

Thank you my dear friend for your kind enquiry. I am better today than I felt yesterday,—& *then*, Dr Chambers perceived some improvement upon my state some days ago. He thinks that the warm weather, when it comes, will really do much for me: and it will, if God sees fit that this should be.

I want to tell you about the Seraphim. I do not know whether the sheets are completed. I rather believe that they are not. But at any rate, I have a fancy in my head that you should see the whole book instead of a part of it—that you should read the preface before the poem,—in which I mean to teach you exactly how much to admire it!! I have had an affectionate & very pleasing letter from Miss Bordman. She speaks feelingly of your late loss—as being to her the loss of one of her earliest & kindest friends–[2]

Do give my regards to Miss Holmes,
& believe me
Your affectionate friend
E B Barrett.

Address, on integral page: H S Boyd Esqr
Publication: EBB-HSB, p. 228.
Manuscript: Wellesley College.

1. Dated by the imminent publication of *The Seraphim*.
2. It was through Boyd's sister that Miss Bordman was introduced to the Boyds' circle, and hence to EBB.

---

630. EBB TO HUGH STUART BOYD

[London]
[May 1838][1]

My dear friend,

I am rather better than otherwise within the last few days—but fear that nothing will make me essentially so except the invisible sun– I am however a little better—& God's will is always done in mercy.

As to the poems—do forgive me dear Mr Boyd,—& refrain from executing your cruel threat of suffering "the desire of reading them to pass away".

I have not one sheet of them—and Papa, and to say the truth, I myself would so very much prefer your reading the preface first, that you must try to indulge us in our phantasy. The book, M.[r] Bentley half promises to finish the printing of, this week.[2] At any rate it is likely to be all done in the next: and you may depend upon having a copy *as soon* as I have power over ONE–

With kind regards to Miss Holmes, believe me

Your affect.[te] friend
EBB–

Address, on integral page: H S Boyd Esq.[r] / 3 Circus Road.
Publication: LEBB, I, 60–61.
Manuscript: Wellesley College.

1. Dated by the impending publication of *The Seraphim*.
2. Samuel Bentley (1785–1868), of Dorset Street, was the printer chosen for *The Seraphim*.

---

631. EBB TO MARY RUSSELL MITFORD

[London]
Monday. [May 1838][1]

My ever dearest friend,

I write one word to say that I am not ill—or worse—indifferent to *your* illness & dearest love to me, & all dear D.[r] Mitford's kindness in pulling the violets for me. How can they fade in the glass, & I not have thanked him? Thank him for me, will you? & as *you* only, can.

I have been breathless with *business* such as it is, these two days—but will write to you at length either tomorrow or Wednesday. Say Wednesday & forgive

your own EBB

Publication: EBB-MRM, I, 71.
Manuscript: Edward R. Moulton-Barrett.

1. Dated by EBB's preoccupation with seeing *The Seraphim* through the press.

---

632. EBB TO HUGH STUART BOYD

50 Wimpole Street
Wednesday. [late May 1838][1]

Thank you for your enquiry my dear friend. I had begun to fancy that between Saunders & Otley & the Seraphim I had fallen to the ground of

No. 633 [late May 1838] 33

your disfavor. But I do trust to be able to send you a copy before next Sunday.

I am thrown back a little just now by having caught a very bad cold, which has of course affected my cough. The worst seems however to be past, & D.* Chambers told me yesterday that he expected to see me in two days nearly as well as before this casualty. And I have been, thank God, pretty well lately—and altho' when the stethescope was applied three weeks ago it did not speak very satisfactorily of the state of the lungs, yet D.* Chambers seems to be hopeful still, & to talk of the wonders which the summer sunshine (when it does come) may be the means of doing for me. And people say that I look rather better than worse, even now.

Did you hear of an autograph of Shakespeare's being sold lately for a very large sum (I *think* it was above a hundred pounds) on the credit of its being the only genuine autograph extant?–[2] Is your's quite safe? And are *you* so, in your opinion of its veritableness?

I have just finished a very long barbarous ballad for Miss Mitford & Finden's tableaux of this year. The title is "The romaunt of the page", & the subject, not of my own choosing.

I believe that you will certainly have The Seraphim this week. Do Macadamize[3] the frown from your brow in order to receive them!——

Give my love to Miss Holmes——

Your affectionate friend
E B Barrett.

Address, on integral page: H S Boyd Esq.* / 3 Circus Road / St John's Wood.
Publication: LEBB, I, pp. 61–62.
Manuscript: Wellesley College.

1. Dated by the imminent publication of *The Seraphim*.
2. *The Times* of 16 May 1838 had reported that "Yesterday there was sold by Mr. Evans, Pall-mall, *Montaigne's Essays*, by Florio, First Edition. Shakspere's Copy, with his Autograph, in the original binding, 1603.... The authenticity of this autograph of Shakspere is unquestionable" having "already passed the ordeal of numerous competent examiners ... The lot was ... knocked down at 100*l*. to Mr. Pickering." Nothing is known of Boyd's supposed autograph of Shakespeare.
3. i.e., smooth; McAdam's process provided an even surface for roads.

---

633. EBB TO JOHN KENYON

50 Wimpole Street.
Monday. [late May 1838][1]

My dear M.* Kenyon,

The gift of the fossils is only too kind—and my brothers are both glad & grateful—and I am their *thanks bearer*, though "so late in the day".

I am very sorry to hear that you are suffering so much in this universal plague of colds. To prove my own strict veracity I must confess to having a cold too, which, as all my colds make a point of doing, has diverged to my chest & increased the cough today & yesterday. I am however more comfortable this evening & hope to be still more so tomorrow, & have not been bad enough at the worst of the badness, to trouble Dr Chambers about it.

You may be sure that I shall see my book & think of you JUST at the same time—particularly as Papa tried to frighten me yesterday by hypothesizing that you will not like it. If the gentle critics grow severe, what will be done (or suffered) with the ungentle?–

Ever truly yours
E B Barrett.

Address, on integral page: John Kenyon Esqr / 4. Harley Place.
Publication: None traced.
Manuscript: Pierpont Morgan Library.

1. Dated by the reference to EBB's cold and cough, mentioned in the previous letter.

---

634. EBB TO JOHN KENYON

[London]
[late May 1838]¹

My dear Mr Kenyon,

The books are just come. You know you are not obliged to read yours until you have leisure for doing so, even though you go into Normandy for such leisure.²

I have always forgotten to say that perhaps I have spoilt the last stanza of the sea mew. I waited to consult you about it long & long, & after all did not see you until I was obliged to send it to press. You suggested—did you not—

"And with it, grief, our destiny"—

but we neither of us observed that a repetition of '*grief*' was incurred by the suggestion. See the first line of the stanza–

And so when I came to be or to try to be, very exact indeed in order to printing, I was obliged to find another way of attending to your criticism.³

The "forward shade" in the first stanza, is right I believe—is what you wished me to write.

You must forgive the plagiarism as confessed in a note to 'Sounds.'⁴ It is the consequence of my early association with "*Fire-thieves!*"⁵

Pray send the ballad back, if it is troublesome.⁶

Most truly yours
EBB–

Address, on integral page: John Kenyon Esq!
Publication: None traced.
Manuscript: Columbia University.

1. Dated by receipt of copies of *The Seraphim*.
2. See letter 605, note 6.
3. The first line of the final stanza of "The Sea-Mew" reads "He lay down in his grief to die." In lieu of Kenyon's suggestion, involving the repetition of "grief," EBB made the last line read "And, with our touch, our agony."
4. Line 38 of "Sounds" reads "Like a singing in a dream." A note quotes four lines from Kenyon's poem "Reverie," the last one reading "Like music mingling in a dream," and acknowledges an unconscious debt to Kenyon.
5. A reference to EBB's reading and translating *Prometheus*. After Jupiter had taken fire away from the earth, Prometheus climbed to the heavens with the aid of Minerva and stole fire from the chariot of the sun. (*Prometheus Bound*, line 1124, refers to Prometheus as "The reverencer of men, the thief of fire.")
6. EBB had sent Kenyon the manuscript of her poem for the 1839 *Findens' Tableaux*. He returned it on 4 June, and EBB then sent it on to Miss Mitford (letter 636).

---

635. EBB TO JOHN KENYON

50 Wimpole Street
Saturday– [ca. June 1838]¹

My dear M! Kenyon,

The opening stanzas of your poem² would charm Criticism into silence, even if she had a little to say. They contain some beautiful & true description, & in flowing sound.–

In the 4.th, I do not quite like either of the concluding lines–— 'strengthen hearts *yet not* deform.' There is not *contrariety*—(is there?)— between strength & deformity? and then the 'sturdier powers' are the powers of the heart—are they not—and if so, the strengthening of the heart is involved in them, & you have fallen into a *pleonasm*– Then with regard to the last line, I dont much like the 'stern' & the 'storm' so near each other. The sound is deformed without being strengthened, by this nearness.

In the 6.th, you do not seem to me to carry out your idea with sufficient distinctness. "Hence Too" &c[.] The sense of the preceding stanza sh.d be continued. Now because Man's nature is strengthened by storm, you do not "stand & watch" the storm, "with straining eye"– Yes! I see now that you may so mean to express your interest in it– Still, I think that *kindling* eye (or some similar epithet) would say better what you wish to say. The last line of this stanza; I much admire–

As to the 8th, I would not on any account omit it. How could you *think* of *thinking* of doing so?– But—I do not—willingly agree to your proposed alteration of the last lines,—except in the word 'faithful' for 'constant'.– The next

> In love, that only *dies with breath*,
> And plucks new force from thoughts of death.

are false, if I may dare to say what appears true to me, as to their sentiment– For *if* love dies with breath, there would be no plucking of strength from thoughts of death– Were the poem mine, I certainly would try to prevail upon stanzas 8 and 9 to exchange their concluding distichs. I would connect the 'flickering light' with the 'faithful hand'—vainly faithful; and when I had proceeded as far as "the torch is dim" I should think it just the time for exclaiming

> "Cease raging Demons of the dark
> And spare the light—& spare the bark."

If it could be managed so, the 10th stanza would begin very naturally "If that brave bark"—and 'the guardian spirit' of the next line, would follow the 'Demons', according to a philosophical law of Association! vide Hume on contrarieties–

But I must not forget to say that "would rush to tread" &c is a great improvement upon the 2d line of stanza 9.

In stanza 10, I object to the Fates—particularly as the next refers to "how tis doomed *above*".

I am not inclined to recall from banishment the stanza about Ebydos[3]– It is certainly desirable to refer to the three figures—but you need not pay a price for it, and are surely right in suspecting the prolonged allusion, of "destroying the unity of impression". Besides, both 'the deeper' & 'the holier ties' may, as you observe, have 'temper' & 'logic' against them. Besides, I have either a confusion of memory, or Musæus or the more modern author of the poem called Hero & Leander, attests the celebration of their marriage.[4] Had not Turner's picture a Hymen in it, as well as a Cupid?– I think so!––.[5]

Thank you for the great pleasure I have had in reading this poem– Its concluding stanzas are animated & forcible, & leave an impression—& this is as it should be– I would rather *not* admit the proposed change on the last–

The leaves shall be inserted in the book– The explanation or apology, I like *very* much—I mean the gracefulness of the *manner of it*.

As to *Jephtha*[h][6]—what I can say of him must be "in a whisper" indeed—& a very low one—so low as to be inaudible even to you. But

No. 636 1–6 June [1838] 37

when I confess that I could not read the whole book through, you may guess what it is!——

Dear M.ʳ Kenyon,
Most truly yours
E B Barrett.

The enclosed note came to us from Torquay this morning.

Publication: None traced.
Manuscript: Huntington Library.

1. This letter falls between the publication of *Jephthah* in May 1838, and late August, when *Findens' Tableaux* went to press.
2. The subject of this letter is "The Greek Wife," the poem Kenyon was writing for inclusion in *Findens' Tableaux* (reprinted, with revisions, in his *A Day at Tivoli: With Other Verses*, 1849). A comparison of the printed text with EBB's quotations shows that he made extensive changes before submitting the poem to Miss Mitford.
3. *Sic*, for Abydos, the point on the shore of the Hellespont from which Leander swam over to meet Hero.
4. The "modern author" was Leigh Hunt, whose "Hero and Leander" was published in 1819. Neither he nor Musæus Grammaticus, the classical author of the legend, mentions any formalization through marriage of the relationship. Kenyon's poem, through not mentioning Hero and Leander, has parallels with the legend, in that the wife of the title holds aloft a torch to guide her husband's boat across the Hellespont in a storm; he, like Leander, fails to complete the crossing.
5. "The Parting of Hero and Leander," by J.M.W. Turner (1775–1851), was exhibited at the Royal Academy in 1837. A verse accompanying the painting included the lines "But Love yet lingers on the terraced steep, / Upheld young Hymen's torch and failing lamp."
6. *Jephthah, and Other Poems*, by George Pryme (1781–1868). Pryme, a barrister and political economist, was M.P. for Cambridge (1832–41). *The Athenæum*, reviewing the poem in the issue of 22 December 1838, apparently agreed with EBB, saying "the images are not so vivid, nor is the passion so deep, or the impulse so strong, as to manifest the afflatus of creative genius."

---

636. EBB TO MARY RUSSELL MITFORD

50 Wimpole Street–
June 1 [1838][1]

Perhaps it is lucky for me that my dearest Miss Mitford's last letter has no date, to be read in capitals now by my accusing conscience. Oh! but do not let her think that my conscience is accusing me of want of love for her—or of forgetfulness of her during one of these many days of silence! Or this speech at last, would be a double to the Statue scene in Don Giovanni,—& I should be doubly stone!——

We have been moving & settling—& I have been sometimes very unwell & sometimes better (never too unwell to write to YOU—no excuse is meant by *that!*) & the proof sheets abstracted me—who am light to abstract just now—from the ballad, & I did not like to write to you late in May without being able to tell you of having even begun it. And then the book—I waited for my book—& the printers & binders were waiting I suppose for something else; but here we all are at last, letter ballad & book, & you must welcome us gently for the love's sake that runs through us all!——

The ballad, I ought to blush—as ladyes always do in ballads—"scarlet-red", to send you—being quite aware that its length is sufficient to keep it separate from your tableaux, & fearing besides that this length is not its most pardonable fault.[2] Now my very dear friend, you will prove your affection for me,—JUST AS MUCH by sending back my ballad as by keeping it– Do remember *that*. It is a gift-*poney* not a gift-horse—& you may look it all over, & finish by overlooking it, just as much as you please, & the more to please *me* that *you* are pleased!– If you should prefer keeping it—upon the whole—it must be of course as my gift to you & not to Mr Tilt;[3] & if you send it back, why then I shall only have to beg your forgiveness for not giving you more time to engage another page. By the way, the pictured one pretty as she is, has a good deal exaggerated the ballad-receipt for making a ladye page– Do you remember?——

"And you must cut your gowne of green
An INCH above the knee"!——[4]

She comes within the fi fa fum of the prudes, in consequence–

My good intentions of making a ballad of less than half the length of mine, are all spent in 'pavement' for some critical 'Inferno'.[5] Indeed I do *try* to blush the 'scarlet-red'.

And here is a book to be blushed for besides. You will see that your opinion & Mr Kenyon's have had their due weight, & that the name is on the title-page.[6] Would that the book were as your kindness w.^d have wished it in other things. You will tell me your impression my beloved friend as openly as if you did not care for me—or rather as candidly as if you did!—for if we love truth, we must surely speak truly to such as we love. For the rest I fear I know too much of the truth in this case, to be disappointed in hearing the darkest of it—& I may assure you that you could only discourage me totally, by telling me of my incapacity *ever to write better*.

In speaking of my silence I should have told you that I had heard from Mr Kenyon of you & Dr Mitford—that you were both better. Otherwise a conspiracy of ballads & books would not have kept me silent.

Do you know that M.[r] Kenyon is going into Normandy—but not until July, & for no longer period than six weeks—with M.[r] Southey & M.[r] Robinson?[7] This will be very enjoyable. He is looking as well as possible—at least, *was* last week—for I have since been sorry to learn in a note from him that he has been state prisoner to a cold & swelled face. His account of D.[r] Mitford & yourself dearest Miss Mitford, was pleasant to hear; but still I do want to hear more details from you than I could hear so. Are you not advised to abstain from strong medecines—such as salts? Would not an attention to your diet prove as effectual as any? Do you ever take figs—or tamarinds?– I often feel uneasy in thinking of the system of night-watchings in union with the as bad system of submitting to strong medecines, which seems to be almost forced upon you. Do be careful of yourself, my dear friend– And be careful to tell me when you write, exactly how you are, & how D.[r] Mitford is. And offer to him my very kind regards, & the gladness with which I have heard of his recovery!—if indeed *that* do not belong exclusively to *you*!—— May God bless both of you!——

For my own part, I am going on very tolerably well– A cold this week threw me back a little—but it seems to be gone, & without doing as much harm as might have been feared. The lungs are said to be affected—they did not respond as satisfactorily as heretofore to the latest application of the stethescope,—but still there are good symptoms, & D.[r] Chambers insists upon my not having lost ground lately & is hopeful of my gaining some in a settled sunshine, such as I hope we *shall* have this summer. He is at once a kind & a skilful man—& my confidence in him is the greater that he has not tried to deceive me by calling things by cowardly names. Indeed he does me good, & if it pleases God, may do more still. In any case I have much to be thankful for, to God's mercy, & I wish that I could thank Him as I ought. Do not say much about my health when you write—for it is a great pleasure to Papa to read your letters (when I will LET him—when they are not '*private*') & I would not have him fancy me worse than I am– No, nor *you*, dearest Miss Mitford! And the *real truth* is (be sure) that I am better at this time, & going on to D.[r] Chambers' satisfaction.

M.[r] Milnes the poet, *is* M.[r] Milnes the member.[8] M.[r] Kenyon tells me of his having printed an additional volume of poems; but this I have not seen.[9] He was born a crowned poet!——

Do tell me of your Tableaux, whether I have anything to do with them or not.

Is M.[rs] Howitt a contributor?—& M.[r] Procter?[10]—and are your own contributions in an advanced state? Dont let me forget to say that in the case of my ballad's being found usable, I shall be obliged by your affixing to it EBB—or E B Barrett—or Elizabeth B Barrett—just as you prefer, & as will best suit the *manners* of your book. I leave a blank on purpose: Would that last year's were a blank too!—[11]

Here is the end of my paper; but one word notwithstanding in respect to book & ballad. Do not fancy that I shall care more for an unpleasant truth, because I happen to be not quite well. It is JUST THE CONTRARY– But indeed at anytime, my caring intensely for poetry does not mean that I care intensely for my own poems: & I am not wounded easily except through my affections. In *them* I never can be wounded by *you*—& so speak plainly!——& forgive all this egotism!——

Your grateful & affectionate
E B Barrett.

We like the house very much indeed! How I shall like it better still when I see you in it!——

The doves & my books & I have a little slip of sitting room to ourselves,—& dearest Papa in his abundant kindness surprised me in it with a whole vision of majestic heads from Brucciani's—busts of poets & philosophers[12]—such as he knew that I would care for- You may think how it startled & affected me to look round & know that he had found time in all his bustle & vexation of house furnishing, to remember so light a thing as my pleasure!——

Wednesday. June 6.

Dearest Miss Mitford,

You will *see* by the date of the enclosed, that I did not *mean* to make so many paces into June without sending my Page to your feet—or without sending there besides the volume wearing the same livery.

I have however dared to be so troublesome to dear Mr Kenyon as to ask him to pause in his multitudinous businesses & I hope pleasantnesses, just to read over my ballad for me—& in obedience to his useful criticisms I have been doing some good to it since, which could not have been done without him. But I did not receive the ms back from him until Monday evening—& yesterday, on accomplishing my first drive out for many months, I was too exhausted to do anything but lie on the sofa with your 'wedding slippers' in my *hands*. Thank you for all the good they did me—the delight they gave me. Your Elizabeth is so lovely & serene,— that the very *heart* rests, upon her!—& I enjoyed the walk thro' Belford Regis,[13] just as if nothing could tire me. Was I not walking there with *you*?

In great haste—(*at last!!* you will say)
Your ever affectionate
EBB——

Mary Russell Mitford

Dr. George Mitford

My sisters saw D.[r] Mitford's portrait, & were much pleased with it, at the Royal Academy yesterday![14] But dearest Miss Mitford! it vexes me so to think that the picture is there only NOW—too late for *me!!*

I trust to your *kindness* (let me repeat) to send back the ballad in the case of your book's being the better for its absence.

Publication: EBB-MRM, I, 71–76.
Manuscript: Wellesley College.

1. Year provided by the publication of *The Seraphim*.
2. EBB's "The Romaunt of the Page," despite her fears about its being too long, did appear in *Findens' Tableaux of the Affections: A Series of Picturesque Illustrations of Womanly Virtues* (pp. 1–5) when it was published in October 1838.
3. EBB means that Charles Tilt's £5 payment for each contribution should be retained by Miss Mitford.
4. A slight misquotation from "Child Waters" in Thomas Percy's *Reliques of Ancient English Poetry* (1765, III, 60, 41–42). The brevity of Ellen's tunic invites criticism from prudes.
5. A reference to Dr. Johnson's "Hell is paved with good intentions" (James Boswell's *The Life of Samuel Johnson, LL.D.*, 1791, I, 484).
6. *The Seraphim* was the first of her compositions to carry her name in full.
7. Robert Southey (1774–1843), the Poet Laureate, and Henry Crabb Robinson (1775–1867).
8. Richard Monckton Milnes had been elected to Parliament in 1837, as Member for Pontefract.
9. *Poems of Many Years*. See also letter 627, note 7.
10. Mary Howitt (*née* Botham, 1799–1888), a prolific writer, was best known for her children's stories and translations of Hans Christian Andersen. She had contributed "A Story of the Indian War" to the 1838 *Findens' Tableaux*, but did not write for the 1839 issue. Bryan Waller Procter (Barry Cornwall) had also contributed to the 1838 issue of *Findens' Tableaux* ("The Death of the Bull") but did not provide anything for the 1839 issue.
11. Owing to a misunderstanding, "A Romance of the Ganges" in the 1838 *Findens' Tableaux* had been printed over EBB's initials, against her father's wishes (see letter 591).
12. EBB's busts included those of Chaucer and Homer. Lewis Brucciani was a plaster-model maker, with premises at 5 Little Russell Street, Drury Lane.
13. Miss Mitford's story, "Wedding Slippers," had been printed in *Tait's Edinburgh Magazine* (1838, V, 366–371). It was set in Belford Regis, Miss Mitford's fictional village, loosely based on Reading.
14. The portrait of Dr. Mitford by John Lucas (reproduced on facing page) was no. 288 in the catalogue of the 1838 Royal Academy exhibition.

637. THOMAS NOON TALFOURD TO EBB

Temple
2 June 1838

M.[r] Serj.[t] Talfourd presents his compliments to Miss Barrett and begs to express to her how much he is gratified and honored by the gift of her charming volume of poems;[1]—at which he has already glanced with singular pleasure—and which he hopes to enjoy thoroughly in the first leisure he can obtain. He takes leave to request her acceptance—not in return but in acknowledgment—of a very hasty and imperfect drama,[2] written for a purpose which has been frustrated, and having claim only on the charitable allowance to which he commends it.

Address: Miss Barrett / (care of Mess.rs Saunders & Otley).
Publication: None traced.
Manuscript: University of Iowa.

1. Talfourd's copy of *The Seraphim* is now at the University of Texas (see *Reconstruction*, C174).
2. *The Athenian Captive* (1838).

638. EBB TO HUGH STUART BOYD

[London]
[6 June 1838][1]

My dear M.r Boyd,

Papa is scarcely inclined, nor am I for myself, to send my book or books to the East Indies. Let them alone poor things, until they can walk about a little!—and then it will be time enough for them to 'learn to *fly*[']!–

I was so sorry that Emily Harding saw Arabel & went away without this note which I have been meaning to write to you for several days, & have been so absorbed & drawn away (all except my thoughts) by other things necessary to be done, that I was forced to defer it. My ballad containing a Ladye dressed up like a page & gallopping off to Palestine in a manner which would scandalize you, went to Miss Mitford this morning. But I augur from its length, that she will not be able to receive it into Finden.

Arabel has told me what Miss Harding told her of your being in the act of going through my Seraphim for the second time. For the feeling of interest in me which brought this labour upon you, I thank you, my dear friend. What your opinion *is*, & *will be*, I am prepared to hear with a good deal of awe. You will *certainly* NOT *approve of the poem*.

There now! You see I am prepared. Therefore do not keep back one rough word, for friendship's sake—but be as honest as––you could not help being, without this request!–

If I should live, I shall write (*I believe*) better poems than the Seraphim: which belief will help me to survive the condemnation heavy upon your lips.

Affectionately yours
E B Barrett.

No. 639 [7 June 1838] 43

Address: H S Boyd Esq! / 3. Circus Road / St John's Wood.
Publication: LEBB, I, 62–63.
Manuscript: Wellesley College.

1. The reference to sending off the manuscript of "The Romaunt of the Page" dates this letter as 6 June 1838; it is postmarked 7 June 1838.

---

639. EBB TO JOHN KENYON

50 Wimpole Street.
Thursday morning. [7 June 1838][1]

I meant to have thanked you before dear M! Kenyon for the kindness which has been as useful to me as I fear it was troublesome to you with your engagements αναριθμοι![2]—but my first writing was obliged to be given to the ballad & Miss Mitford & to the thought that I had already stepped over the bound she had set for me in regard to Finden. And tuesday was a blank day,—for on it, I was subjected to the 'Spallanzani process'[3] of going out to drive, & could do nothing afterwards but feel tired– This morning however my parcel is on its road to judgment & Reading,—& my gratitude is ready to tell you, that the ballad seems to me *far* the better for my obedience to the greater number--almost all . . of your criticisms, & that I had the less remorse in receiving them, because the good they did, might be a little for Miss Mitford, as well as a great deal for me. *Might* be! *for her!* but I do not *think* the ballad will appear among her Tableaux after all. It is far too long for the purpose–

Now I am not going to tire you over again along the same road—but I just want to say—for fear you should think me obstinate—*why* I have not after all your recommendation, connected the Beati Mortui[4] &c with the story, by the expression 'Not prophecy' or any other. The adoption of that expression or its equivalent, w!d have, in the first place, told the poor page's fate too plainly to the reader, & prematurely: and then again, it is according to my conception,—that the convent music & mourning sh!d be kept *as distinct & separate as possible* from the story. It comes when the page is happiest, & so absorbed in happy thought that he is unconscious even of the sound. And the reference to HIM, to the destiny reserved for him (for none are blessed but the dead!) I would rather that the reader remembered at the close of the poem than felt at the time, according to the natural process of reading our omens by the light of our actual griefs. At the close of the poem, I have written some lines to make (at least I hope so) the whole clearer—& to show that the dirge begun for the Abbess was as suited for the page[5]—there being no lament begun underneath the sun which ere it end will suit but *one*.

I have left the Judge's hand 'little' instead of making it either 'gentle' or 'delicate'[6]—because you see, tho' you may not have thought of it at the time—she was speaking of her own—and as dear little Mary Hunter used to say "It is very wrong to self-praise oneself"- The 'energy' & 'passiveness' are both sent away—& very properly—but I left the 'dead' & 'death'—& the 'bodily' besides,[7]—as you said you liked them yourself, & only doubted whether others would.

And this is all that I can remember, to tire you with.

It pleased me very very much that you should, on the whole, like the ballad—& none the less so that I turned over the leaves of Mr Reade's poem[8] for some minutes before I opened your letter—for the fear of what it might say! Bro observed "What a want of curiosity"!—but I responded & explained--"What a want of *courage*"!

I hope that you say only in jest, & think in no way—I would not have anyone to think so—and still less *you* to whom I am grateful for so much more indulgence than I can meet with from others—that in being obscure I am 'proud & perverse' or at all doing what I choose to do. Indeed it is VERY different. I see plainly that this fault of obscurity, even if it were alone, would do the work of all other faults—& also that it is NOT the prevailing fault of true poets- And so if I sh^d live, & if you will sometimes help me, I must try to keep it farther off.

Your affectionate but very tiresome
friend & cousin
E B Barrett.

I sent for Tait for the name's sake of Miss Mitford's "Wedding Slippers"[9]—& it was a pleasant surprise to see besides them a review of your book.[10] You have probably seen it—but if not, you can have it from this house at any minute.

Address: John Kenyon Esqr / 4. Harley Place.
Publication: None traced.
Manuscript: Mills College.

1. Dated by the dispatch of EBB's manuscript to Miss Mitford (see previous letter).
2. "Without number."
3. Lazaro Spallanzani (1729–99), an Italian, was a natural scientist, writing on such subjects as respiration, digestion, etc. He demonstrated that it was the action of the gastric juices that accomplished digestion, rather than its being purely mechanical. What exactly EBB means by "the Spallanzani process" is not clear; it was presumably some prescribed regimen of diet and exercise.
4. Lines 71 and 86 of "The Romaunt of the Page" read "Beati, beati, mortui!" ("Blessed, blessed, be the dead!").
5. Lines 341 ff.
6. Line 211.
7. Stanza XII.

8. *Italy* (1838) by John Edmund Reade (1800–70), who was best known for *Cain, the Wanderer* (1829).
9. Miss Mitford's story, "Wedding Slippers," was printed in *Tait's Edinburgh Magazine* (1838, V, 366–371).
10. In the same issue of *Tait's* (pp. 395–397) was a review of Kenyon's *Poems, For the Most Part Occasional*, "a volume of graceful and classic poetry . . . 'fit audience, though few,' will be found for these polished and classic effusions, though they display few of the qualities which beget either an instantaneous, a wide, or a fervid and headlong popularity." Many of the poems are said to have a "pensive and tender cast . . . versified with equal elegance; so that . . . the delicate workmanship enhances the value, or gives a value of its own." The book was also reviewed at length in *Blackwood's Edinburgh Review* (December 1838, pp. 779–794).

640. EBB to Hugh Stuart Boyd

50 Wimpole Street.
Wednesday morning. [June 1838][1]

My dear friend,

Do not think me depraved in ingratitude for not sooner thanking you for the pleasure, made so much greater by the surprise, which your note of judgment gave me. The truth is that I have been very unwell, & delayed answering it immediately until the painful physical feeling went away to make room for the pleasurable moral one—and this I fancied it would do every hour, so that I might be able to tell you at ease all that was in my thoughts. The fancy was a vain one. The pain grew worse & worse, & Dr Chambers has been here for two successive days shaking his head as awfully as if it bore all Jupiter's ambrosial curls,—& is to be here again today, but with I trust a less grave countenance, inasmuch as the leeches last night did their duty & I feel much better– God be thanked for the relief. But I am not yet as well as before this attack, & am still confined to my bed—and so you must rather imagine than read what I thought & felt in reading your wonderful note. Of course it pleased me very much, very very much—and I dare say, would have made me vain by this time, if it had not been for the opportune pain & the sight of Dr Chambers's face!–

I sent a copy of my book to Nelly Bordman *before* I read your suggestion. I knew that her kind feeling for *me* would interest her in the sight of it.

Thank you once more, dear Mr Boyd! May all my critics be gentle after the pattern of your gentleness!

Believe me
affectionately yours
E B Barrett.

Arabel will try to go to visit you tomorrow—that is, if it shd be fine–

Address: H S Boyd Esqr / 3 Circus Road / St John's Wood.
Publication: LEBB, I, 68–69.
Manuscript: Wellesley College.

1. Dated by Boyd's "judgment" of *The Seraphim*.

641. EBB TO MARY RUSSELL MITFORD

[London]
Monday– [?June] [1838]¹

I do not know how to thank you ever dearest Miss Mitford for these lovely flowers, so full of sun & air & *you*, that whether their perfume travels fastest to my senses or my heart is almost a doubtful thing! Almost!—not quite! And indeed I am not sure of the 'almost'. And I never should have thought of such a word in looking at flowers from *you*, if a more than two years imprisonment in London² had not made me "high fantastical"³ in affection for everything from the country. And after all, our affections towards the natural & the human are more identical than some of us wot of. One thing I know, that I delight in these flowers both for being themselves & for coming from yourself.

They came as brightly as if they were unconscious of not growing still,—and we have filled four or five large vases with them—& now but for the thought of having stolen a *Pleiad*⁴ from your garden & darkened some of its brightness, what have we to do but to thank you—gladly? But my sisters have another gift from you—and they thank you for it gladly & gratefully . . the pretty little book which I, for one, value without having read, for the sake of one page in it, & two lines written on another⁵—notwithstanding a certain *formality* which, as Mr Kenyon very justly observes, *is not Greek*. I have not seen him, nevertheless, since I received the hamper, & sent the contents belonging to him, to Harley Place.⁶

I was going to tell you that Mr Crosse was with him still—but there is more thankfulness belonging to you, behind,—& I must not forget to say how your "Miss Barrett" & "Isobel" shame me & mine, & make me pleased, & grateful to you for an honor so much brighter than the bay. Beautiful blossoms they are,⁷—but the best of the beauty is that it is
⟨...⟩⁸

And so you thought that Papa was not grateful to you! I have half a mind to be angry! but I will offer you his acknowledgments & regards instead.

Publication: EBB-MRM, I, 78-79.
Manuscript: Wellesley College.

1. Dated by the reference to "two years imprisonment in London" and to "Isobel."
2. The Barretts had moved to London from Sidmouth during the first week of December 1835; this reference therefore provides the year.
3. *Twelfth Night*, I, 1, 15.
4. The Pleiades were the seven daughters of Atlas, who were transformed into a cluster of stars.
5. We cannot identify this book; it did not survive to form part of *Browning Collections*. No doubt it was a collection of Miss Mitford's stories.
6. Kenyon's residence, on the edge of Regent's Park, not far from Wimpole Street.
7. Flowers named by Miss Mitford for EBB and her poem "Isobel's Child." As letter 627 makes it clear that Miss Mitford had not seen EBB's manuscript prior to publication, the naming of "Isobel" suggests that the letter was written after Miss Mitford received a copy of *The Seraphim* at the beginning of June.
8. The remainder of the letter is missing. The final paragraph was cross-written at the top of the first page.

642. EBB TO THOMAS NOON TALFOURD

50 Wimpole Street–
June 13.th 1838——

Miss Barrett presents her compliments to M.r Serjeant Talfourd, and desires to express to him her thankfulness both for his very obliging note,[1] and also and in particular for the valued present accompanying it. She is glad to be able to associate with the true pleasure with which she lately read his beautiful play, the gratification of now receiving it from its author.

Publication: None traced.
Manuscript: Huntington Library.

1. Letter 637.

643. EBB TO JOHN KENYON

[London]
Friday. [15 June 1838][1]

I felt rather like a criminal in remembering how long I have kept two new books, even when I remember besides my own *intentional* innocence & the probability of your never having had a moments time to miss the books from your table. But I have had rather a bad attack & was too unwell for several days to do more than *imitate* reading, which tho' a process not altogether uncongenial perhaps with *one* of the books (I dont mean the unMiltonic Miltonic "Speech")[2] did not cause me to turn over its leaves very quickly.

You are quite right I think in your thoughts of this book,—the large one.[3] A little *humeur*[4] (for a wonder, a French word is more graceful than an English one) was in mine, as remembrances of the Childe swept across almost every page with their [']'Why do you mock me"?——The parallel passages as to ideas dispositions & cadence are seventy times seven! and I know C. Harold *so* well, & wonder *so*, how any human being could write upon Felino[5] in that measure, & print the writing afterwards! But there are powerful lines—yes, & passages—& altho' an imitative work of such a length & from a practised writer does to me argue a deficiency in inherent, what is called, *original* power, yet every one has a heart & mind apiece, & if this writer had drawn from his, we sh^d all have been satisfied.

The 'Speech' has talent, but it is not after Milton, I think, either in the character of style or thought—— Now you see what discontentedness comes of being shut up for a week! No! not quite for a week. This is Saturday, & I received last night the medical permission to go down stairs today, on the condition of *very* quiet behaviour–

A letter this morning from dear Miss Mitford. She is so anxious to see you, & altho' not daring (she says) to ask your "fit comrade" Mr Southey to accompany you, would feel happy & honored by his doing so! Do contrive it for her if you can! Do you know that Dash is dead?–

Your affec^{te} cousin
E B Barrett

Address, on integral page: John Kenyon Esqr
Publication: None traced.
Manuscript: Armstrong Browning Library.

1. Dated by the mention of the same events as in letter 644.
2. It is difficult to interpret this enigmatic remark. It is possible that EBB refers to the 1837 French prose translation of *Paradise Lost* by François René, Vicomte de Chateaubriand (1768–1848).
3. The following remarks make it clear that the book in question is John Edmund Reade's *Italy*, just published, which drew much criticism because of its astonishing parallels with Byron's *Childe Harold's Pilgrimage*. The review in *The Athenæum* (no. 557, 30 June 1838, p. 453) commences "We have rarely addressed ourselves to the ungracious task of criticism with greater reluctance than in the present instance" and later says that "in cast of thought, simile, allusion,—in the use of language and of imagery,—nay, in the very artifices of cadence and versification, do we find a strong unmistakeable leaven of Byron"; examples of similar passages in both works follow.
4. "Ill-humour."
5. *Sic*, for Velino, a river N.E. of Rome. Its cataract, 5 miles E. of Terni, in Umbria, had a total fall of about 650 ft. in three separate stages. Both Byron and Reade give a description of the falls, in passages starting "The roar of waters!—from the headlong height" (Byron, stanza LXIX) and "Velino rushes from his mountain home" (Reade, pt. II, stanza xxxiii).

644. EBB TO LADY MARGARET COCKS

50 Wimpole Street
Saturday. June 16. [1838][1]

My dear Lady Margaret,

You will forgive my writing to you in words rather than sentences, on account of my having been so unwell all the week as to be kept in bed for that time by Dr Chambers, & disciplined with leeches & two blisters in two days. But God has blessed these means to me—& the acute pain in the side from which I suffered is diminished to the ghost of a *sensation*,—& I am allowed to go down stairs today, on condition of behaving very well & *silently*. There is of course however a good deal of weakness—& I will not do more than thank you my dear Lady Margaret, for the interest with which I have gone thro' your 'gentle-hearted' (Wordsworth's own word you know)[2] poems, & felt the abiding sense of religion on every page. May God teach all those who sing, to *pray!*

A much less modest volume is the one which I send now[3] in company with your Ladyship's– Dear Lady Margaret, as you are good enough to be interested in its appearance, I must request your acceptance, as I *did*, your opinion, of it. You will at least believe *this* good of its author—that she remains

faithfully & affectionately
yours
E B Barrett.

Publication: None traced.
Manuscript: Hon. Mrs. Elizabeth Hervey-Bathurst.

1. During EBB's residence in Wimpole Street, 1838 was the only year in which 16 June fell on Saturday.
2. Cf. line 55 of his poem "Nutting": "In gentleness of heart."
3. A copy of *The Seraphim*, now in the Clark Memorial Library (see *Reconstruction*, C157).

---

645. EBB TO HUGH STUART BOYD

50 Wimpole Street
June 21.st Thursday. [1838][1]

My dear friend,

Notwithstanding this silence so ungrateful in appearance, I thank you at last & very sincerely for your kind letter. It made me laugh, & amused me—& gratified me besides. Certainly your "quality of mercy is not strained".[2]

My reason for not writing more immediately, is, that Arabel has meant day after day to go to you, & has had a separate disappointment for every day. She says now, "*Indeed* I hope to see Mr Boyd tomorrow." But *I* say that I will not keep this answer of mine to run the risk of another day's contingencies—& that *it* shall go, whether *she* does or not.

I am better a great deal than I was last week, & have been allowed by Dr Chambers to come down stairs again, & occupy my old place on the sofa. My health remains however in what I cannot help considering myself, & in what I *believe* Dr Chambers considers a very precarious state—& my weakness increases of course under the remedies which successive attacks render necessary. Dr Chambers deserves my confidence—& besides the skill with which he has met the different modifications of the complaint, I am grateful to him for a feeling & a sympathy which are certainly rare in such of his profession as have their attention diverted, as his must be, by an immense practice, to fifty objects in a day. But notwithstanding all, one breath of the east wind undoes whatever he labours to do. It is well to look up & remember that in the eternal reality, these second causes are no causes at all.

Dont leave this note about for Arabel to see. I am anxious not to alarm her, or any one of my family,—and it may please God to make me as well & strong again as ever– And indeed I am twice as well this week as I was, last.

Your affectionate friend,
dear Mr Boyd,
E B Barrett.

I have seen an extract from a private letter of Mr Chorley editor of the Athenæum, which speaks *huge* praises of my poems. If he were to say a tithe of them in print it w.^d be nine times above my expectation![3]

Address, on integral page: H S Boyd Esqr / 3. Circus Road / St John's Wood.
Publication: LEBB, I, 70–72.
Manuscript: Wellesley College.

1. Dated by the reference to EBB's health, and the fact that 21 June fell on a Thursday in 1838.
2. *The Merchant of Venice,* IV, 1, 184.
3. Chorley did, in fact, commit his praises to print in *The Athenæum* (7 July 1838), pp. 466–468). (For the text of his review, see pp. 375–378.)

---

646. EBB TO LADY DACRE

50 Wimpole Street.
June 21.st [1838][1]

Dear Lady Dacre,

As I am encouraged to say so! I am at least obliged to explain to your Ladyship why it is that I do not express my thankfulness for the kindness of your note and the honor of your visits by immediately waiting upon you in Chesterfield Street. I need not, *indeed*, invoke Miss Mitford, to dispense my formalities. Dear Miss Mitford is a great teacher of the art of feeling kindness—but then it is, her *own* kindness—and pray believe that to feel your Ladyship's, I have only need of Lady Dacre.

The "not at home" which, I am sorry to learn, was said of me last week, has not been true of me since last September, excepting once for ten minutes. Since September I have been in a very weak state of health, & was during the whole of the past week so increasedly unwell as to be confined to my bed. And altho' I am now better & down stairs again, yet there appears to my sanguinest hope, no prospect near enough to be spoken of, of my being able to pay any visit under the impulse of any desire—

Nor do I venture to say what your Ladyship must believe in my feeling—that I should very gladly see you here—because I am aware how doubly dull would be a visit to an invalid who is scarcely fit even for the sofa until late in the day, & whose voice is most audible in coughing. Indeed that same voice is not strong enough just now to "fight out" any question, unless it be the *right* side of the one suggested by the note before me—viz—whether Lady Dacre's book proves her to be "more than a good hardworking drudge"![2] I could "fight out" such a "right" even now, but without much glory! And where could I find an antagonist except in Lady Dacre and the Windmills?

With every sentiment of respect & still some hope of being honored hereafter with your Ladyship's acquaintance I remain your very obliged

E B Barrett.

Publication: None traced.
Manuscript: Armstrong Browning Library.

1. Dated by the reference to EBB's health.
2. Lady Dacre's most recent work, *Translations from the Italian* (1836) had been sent to EBB with letter 567.

---

647. EBB TO MARY RUSSELL MITFORD

50 Wimpole Street.
Thursday. [21 June 1838][1]

We thank you gratefully dearest Miss Mitford— Papa & I and all of us thank you for your more than kindnesses. The extracts were both gladdening & surprising—& the one the more for being the other also. Oh! it was so kind of you in the midst of your multitude of occupations, to make time (out of love) to send them to us![2]

As to the Ballad, dearest Miss Mitford, which you & M? Kenyon are indulgent enough to like, remember that he passed his criticism over it—before it went to *you*—& so if you did not find as many obscurities as he did in it, the reason is—HIS merit & not mine. But dont believe him—no!—dont believe even M? Kenyon—whenever he says that I am *perversely* obscure. *Unfortunately* obscure—not *perversely*—that is quite a wrong word. And the last time he used it to me (and then I assure you another word still worse was with it) I begged him to confine them for the future to his jesting moods. Because INDEED I am not in the very least degree perverse in this fault of mine which is my destiny rather than my choice, & comes upon me I think, just where I would eschew it most. So little has perversity to do with it's occurrence, that my fear of it makes me sometimes feel quite nervous and thought-tied in composition.

M? Townsend's poems have just reached me.[3] I have had no time to read them, except at a rail road speed, & that not continuously. They seem to have much thought & poetic beauty; and my pleasure (certain) in receiving them, & my pleasure (I may say certain too) in reading them, is made the more pleasurable by thanking you for it, my dear friend!

Is *Flash* or *Flock* the hero of your story—which interested us all, to say nothing of Sette & Occy. How like you was the impulse to a stockingless vengeance! How very very like!–[4]

I am writing in such haste to meet a franker at Westminster. But do give my thankful remembrance & regard to D? Mitford—and do believe how gratefully Papa has felt every word of your letter—& accept my expression of his feeling.

I have not seen M? Kenyon since I wrote last. All last week I was not permitted to get out of bed, & was haunted with leeches & blisters. And in the course of it, Lady Dacre was so kind as to call here—& to leave a note instead of the personal greeting which I was not able to receive. The honor she did me a year ago, in sending me her book, encouraged me to offer her my poems. I hesitated about doing so at first, lest it should appear as if my vanity were dreaming of a *return*—but M? Kenyon's opinion turned the balance. I was very sorry not to have seen Lady Dacre, & have written a reply to her note expressive of this regret. But after all, this inaudible voice (except in its cough) could have scarcely made her understand that I was obliged by her visit, had I been able to receive it.

D? Chambers has freed me again into the drawing room, & I am much better or he would not have done so. There is not however much strength or much health—or any near prospect of regaining either. It is well that in proportion to our feebleness, we may feel our dependence upon God.

I feel as if I had not said half—& they have come to ask me if I have not said *all!* My beloved friend, may you be happy in all ways!——

Do write whenever you wish to talk & have no one to talk too [*sic*], nearer you than I am! *Indeed* I did not forget D.r Mitford when I wrote those words—altho' they look like it!——

Your gratefully affectionate
E B Barrett

Publication: EBB-MRM, I, 76–77 (as [14 June 1838]).
Manuscript: Wellesley College.

1. Dated by the reference to EBB's note to Lady Dacre (646).
2. Apparently Miss Mitford had copied extracts from reviews of *The Seraphim*.
3. Miss Mitford's friend Richard Edwin Austin Townsend (1801?–58) had printed privately in 1838 *Visions of the Western Railways*.
4. The "hero of your story" was, of course, Flush, as is made clear in later letters; he was the father of EBB's own Flush. EBB's reference to "stockingless vengeance" is unclear; it may refer in some way to Miss Mitford's acquiring the dog after his leg was broken by a boy (see L'Estrange (2), II, 206).

648. EBB to Hugh Stuart Boyd

[London]
Monday. [25 June 1838][1]

My dear friend,

I send you the Examiner wherein is a review, which I cannot but consider a favorable & gratifying one, of my book.[2]

And I send to dear Miss Bordman my deep repentance for an omission on Saturday evening which has haunted my conscience ever since. I suffered her to go away without any of Miss Mitford's flowers!! And now, that their petals are frailer, I dare not put them into motion again. Beg her not to think me the most selfish & miserly, but only the most careless person of her acquaintance—for indeed I *did* MEAN to give them to her,—but you know my meanings are apt to be obscured—& for want of any other kind of obscuration, came forgetfulness, on the present occasion.

The *'betterness'* in which she found me has lasted until now,—& D.r Chambers called me yesterday a most astonishing person for *rallying!*—not for 'sneering', mind, whatever the Reviewer may think—& with regard to the Reviewer *I* think that if I had said D.r Johnson *was* Longinus, the saying would be less pardonable (even from "a woman") than the "sneer" itself.[3] It would be as great a mistake as my chronology about Adam[4]—I dont say, as "the stars roll on afar"[5] which indeed I cannot admit to be a mistake at all. The Virgin is sitting in the sunlight, & can therefore discern no stars visible or invisible. But she may infer the vainness of her adjuration, & the consequent calm on-rolling of the bodies she adjured, by the continued darkness, & the uncrownedness of the Infant's brow. Have I spoken clearly? *at last*?

My dear friend, I *cannot* let you have the extract you ask for. If ever I see you again I will explain the why; and you in the meanwhile must try to forgive me.

Is not this, blessed sunshine?—to thank God for?—— D.ʳ Chambers thinks that if I try the carriage again while it lasts & while there is a south wind, I shall be able to breathe *this time*.

⟨...⟩[6]

And I mean to try—but as to being able to go to *you*, there seems to be not a hope of it. Even if I went to your door, & were carried up stairs, there would be no power of talking for long afterwards. I say this, to prevent your reproaching me in a thought.

I thank you my dear friend, for all your kind expressions, & if I did not, should still *feel* them gratefully. M.ʳ Crosse is staying with M.ʳ Kenyon.

Affectionately yours
E B Barrett.

I *petition* for Miss Bordman to come & see me sometimes!——
Her parcel has not arrived *yet!*
Will you return the Examiner when you have quite done with it?–

Address: H S Boyd, Esq.ʳ / 3 Circus Road / St John's Wood.
Publication: EBB-HSB, pp. 229–230.
Manuscript: Wellesley College.

1. Dated by *The Examiner* review.
2. *The Seraphim* was reviewed in *The Examiner* of 24 June 1838 (no. 1586, pp. 387–388): "This book opens with a preface which is very remarkable for power and beauty of expression." After quoting "a few of its striking and brilliant bursts of fancy and of passion," the reviewer continued: "Who will deny to the writer of such verses as these ... the possession of many of the highest qualities of the divine art? ... Miss Barrett is indeed a genuine poetess, of no common order; yet is she in danger of being spoilt by over-ambition ... She has fancy, feeling, imagination, expression; but ... she aims at flights which have done no good to the strongest, and therefore falls infinitely short ... of what a proper exercise of her genius would infallibly reach.... The entire volume deserves more than ordinary attention." (For the full text, see pp. 373–375.)
3. In the course of the review, there is a reference to "the sneer ... in Miss Barrett's admirable preface, at the unlucky critic who was '*not* Longinus' (Doctor Johnson, we presume)."

EBB had said (p. xiv): "The generation of such as held the doctrine of that critic who was *not* Longinus, and believed in the inadmissibility of religion into poetry, may have seen the end of vanity." A note in the Porter-Clarke edition of EBB's works (1900) identifies the critic as Nicolas Boileau Despréaux.

4. "Adam dead four thousand years" (line 972 of *The Seraphim*).
5. Cf. the third stanza of "The Virgin Mary to the Child Jesus."
6. About one line obliterated, apparently by EBB.

649. EBB TO MARY RUSSELL MITFORD

[London]
[*Postmark:* 26 June 1838]

⟨★★★⟩ note, *ask* her to come again—[1] That would be so dull a visit for her—& my voice is now so weak that it could scarcely I fear, make my thankfulness audible to her. Perhaps I shall see her & Shakespeare's autograph together & with YOU, next year.

Ever your
EBB.

Envelope only, addressed and franked by Matt Bell: London June Twenty Six 1838 / Miss Mitford / Three Mile Cross / Reading / Matt Bell / [and in EBB's hand on back of envelope:] Miss Mitford / Three Mile Cross / near Reading.
Publication: EBB-MRM, I, 78.
Manuscript: Wellesley College.

1. The reference may be to Lady Dacre, who did call again at Wimpole Street, as mentioned in letter 650.

---

650. EBB TO HUGH STUART BOYD

[London]
[2 July 1838][1]

My dear friend,

I begged your servant to wait—how long ago I am afraid to think—but certainly I must not make this note very long. I did intend to write to you today in any case. Since Saturday I have had my thanks ready at the end of my fingers waiting to slide along to the nib of my pen. Thank you for all your kindness & criticism, which is kindness too—thank you at last. Would that I deserved the praises as well as I do most of the findings-fault—and there is no time now to say more of *them*. Yet I believe I have some thing to say, & will find a time to say it in.

D[r] Chambers has just been here, & does not think me quite as well as usual. The truth is that I was rather excited & tired yesterday by rather too much talking & hearing talking—& suffer for it today in my *pulse*. But I am better on the whole.

M[r] Crosse, the great lion, the insect-making lion,[2] came yesterday with M[r] Kenyon—and afterwards Lady Dacre. She is kind & gentle in her manner. She told me that she had "placed my book in the hands of M[r] Bobus Smith, the brother of Sidney Smith, & the best judge in England,[3] & that it was to be returned to her on Tuesday". If I *should* hear the "judgment," I will tell you, whether you care to hear it or not. There is no other review, as far as I am aware.

Give my love to Miss Bordman. When is she coming to see me? The thunder did not do me any harm.

Your affectionate friend—in great haste—altho' your servant is not likely to think so!——

EBB.

Address: H S Boyd Esq.ʳ / 3 Circus Road / St John's Wood.
Publication: LEBB, I, 72–73.
Manuscript: Wellesley College.

1. Dated by Lady Dacre's visit; as the following letter makes clear, this occurred on 1 July.
2. See letter 565, note 15.
3. Robert Percy ("Bobus") Smith (1770–1845) had been Advocate-General of Bengal from 1803 to 1810. He was a wit and scholar, Landor having said that his Latin hexameters would not have discredited Lucretius (*DNB*). His brother Sydney (1771–1845) was co-founder of *The Edinburgh Review* and Canon of St. Paul's.

651. EBB TO MARY RUSSELL MITFORD

Wimpole Street.
Tuesday. [3 July 1838][1]

Your note my very dear friend "burns the stick that whips the pig"[2]—impels the impulse towards writing to you, which I felt before it reached me. For I wanted to tell you how Lady Dacre came here on Sunday & how I was able to see her, & what a pleasure the seeing was. Unfortunately & most unusually our drawing room happened to be full when she called here .. some old friends from the country having drawn a whole congregation of my brother's together[3]—so that the hum of many voices made mine I fear more inaudible than it need have been, & a little hindered conversation. But I could hear Lady Dacre, & delighted in hearing her & felt the full pleasure & pride of making her acquaintance at last. It was very kind & quite unexpected that she should come again after my sombre & forbidding account of myself—but she said—she thought she would give me a little time to get better & then make another attempt. I was pleased unexpectedly too in another way. Notwithstanding all that you said & all that Mʳ Kenyon said, I had an idea suggested by what I had heard elsewhere & unconfessed to either of you that in seeing Lady Dacre I should see a *woman of the masculine gender*, with her genius very prominent in eccentricity of manner & sentiment—an idea the more admissible to my mind, as the only literary woman I ever knew—except ONE who IS ONE—was Lady Mary Shepherd whose kindness & *terribleness* I equally remember.[4] There is no terribleness in Lady Dacre, to confront her kindness—no keenness of eye or speech, or intent to dazzle by either—but as much gentleness & womanlyness as if she could be content with being loved. And that is what I like in a woman—yes, and in a man too, I like this *spirit* of it. I mean that I do *not* like in man or woman the constant carrying about of an intellect rampant, like a crest! as if thinking were a better thing than loving!——

Well—but without a dissertation—how could I help being pleased with Lady Dacre, or rather *won* by her, when she said so much about *you*—when she told me how she had brought together the cleverest people to meet you, & how you were the Queen of all—& how she delighted in your frankness—& how she was indignant that Lady Morgan's pension sh^d be larger than yours[5] (when mere amusement was the end & object of *her* writings)—& how the question as to the continuance of yours was carried by acclamation, & how at the reading of your note a tear was seen to trickle even from Mr Grote's eye![6] "This" she continued "was, indeed to draw iron tears down Pluto's cheek"[7]– And all this was, of course, to please *me* very much. But she paid an undeserved compliment to my fortunes in fancying you an old friend of mine. Yet I did not feel much abashed for them, in replying—"Not an old friend, but a *dear* friend"—dearness being better than oldness, which anyone may have for waiting for!–

I saw too on Sunday, Mr Crosse the insect-maker!—who can write fervent verses besides.[8] Nobody can be more ignorant, nor *you* more indifferent about science than I am—and yet I thanked Mr Kenyon (in my heart) for letting me see this Talked-about by all talkers, and I think I sh^d like him too, in defiance of acid & alkali. There is a curious contrast of quietness & energy in his deportment—perfect silence for ten minutes, & then a spasmodic outburst of speech & gesticulation, as if he could not hold any more thought.

I told Mr Kenyon some little time since that he was "bidden" to Three Mile Cross[9]—but he seemed to doubt whether he c^d go; & when I proposed his going with Mr Southey on his way to Normandy, begged to know whether I had ever been taught geography. (I was thinking of Southhampton, & he was'nt.)– And then on Sunday, he talked of transmigrating to Wales for a week—"On your way to Miss Mitford?—" "No"—again! But still I dont think that he will be finally able to resist looking in upon you this summer.

Oh yes! we were very very KIND, to be sure, in being pleased with your geraniums—& in being grateful besides to you & Dr Mitford for the promise about the dahlias. That sort of kindness is not hard to meet with– Is it, dearest Miss Mitford?

I was given into the safe keeping of Digitalis yesterday, for my *pulse* which keeps pace with the Wild Huntsman[10]—and it is tamer today; & Dr Chambers goes on to think me in a better state upon the whole. If it be God's will I may emerge into health yet—and if not, I would hope from His grace that no wish of mine or of those dearest to me may cross His *other* will. The only wrong—kindest wrong!—which the living have ever done me, is in attaching me too much to life by an affection & tenderness which were I to live very long I never c^d repay.

Do keep the Examiner, as you care for doing so—[11] And thank you for caring to do so!– It would seem quite like a dream that *you* sh^d care so much for *me*, if it were not an incontestable reality that I love you dearly—and love, you know, *will* witness for love. It grieves me that another indisposition of however transient a character should have been harrassing you,—& you, obliged to write notwithstanding it!– Do take care of yourself. But your health *is* improved—a blessing to more than *you*!—& you have the better blessing (to yourself) of seeing Dr Mitford tolerably well—may it be, better & better! And do say to him a little of what I feel thankfully & affectionately for his kind feeling towards *me*. It is so kind to care to please me, as you tell me he does. Why the very knowing that *your father* has such a care, is *made* to please me of itself!——

Here must be room for Papa's regards & those of all of us. How inconsiderate to crowd such a lengthy letter in among the rest & when you have just told me of their multitude! But we of the coronation are used to crowds, & inclined to count being squeezed to death among the luxuries of life. Everybody except myself & our housekeeper who cannot walk, went out of this house to see the sight—& Sette was on his feet, Queen-devoted, for thirteen hours.[12]

Ever dearest Miss Mitford's
affectionate EBB.

Did you see the notice for Miss Landon's marriage?[13] I have written to Mr Townsend. The more I read some of his poems, the more deeply I feel their beauty.[14] I *did* read the romance of Mr Osggood.[15]

Addressed and franked by Matt Bell on integral page: London July five 1838 / Miss Mitford / Three Mile Cross / Reading / Matt Bell / [and in EBB's hand on reverse when folded:] Miss Mitford / Three Mile Cross / near Reading.
Publication: EBB-MRM, I, 79–82.
Manuscript: Wellesley College.

1. Dated by the frank.
2. A slight misrendering of "The Old Woman and Her Pig," a folk-story describing a series of consequential actions, such as pouring "water that quenches the fire, that burns the stick, that whips the dog."
3. In a letter to Miss Mitford, 26 October 1841, EBB explained that "in addition to our ordinary household" there were "country neighbours of Irish extraction" (Mrs. and Miss Cliffe) and EBB's cousins, "the Mr. Clarkes of Kinnersley castle."
4. For further comments by EBB on Lady Mary, see letters 653 and 713.
5. A few weeks before Miss Mitford's pension of £100 per annum was granted, one of £300 p.a. had been awarded to Lady Morgan (Sydney Owenson), the Irish novelist.

6. George Grote (1794–1871), poet and historian. He sat in the House of Commons from 1832 to 1841, but did not then seek re-election, devoting himself instead to his monumental *History of Greece*, begun as early as 1822, published in stages from 1846 to 1856.

7. Cf. Milton, "Il Pensiero," line 107.

8. EBB must have seen Crosse's poems by courtesy of Kenyon, either in manuscript or some privately-printed volume, as there is no formal record of publication of his poetry prior to his widow's *Memorials, Scientific and Literary, of Andrew Crosse, the Electrician* (1857).

9. See letter 643.

10. The title of one of Scott's earliest poems (1796), an imitation of "Der wilde Jäger" (1786) by Gottfried Augustus Bürger (1748–94).

11. See letter 648, note 2.

12. Victoria's coronation took place on 28 June 1838.

13. *The Times*, 23 June 1838: "On the 7th inst., at St. Mary's, Bryanston-square, by the Rev. Whittington H. Landon, M.A., Letitia Elizabeth, only daughter of the late John Landon, Esq., to George Maclean, Esq., Governor of the Cape Coast, eldest son of the Rev. James Maclean of Urquhart, Elgin."

14. See letter 647, note 3.

15. "Mr." is either a slip of the pen or EBB is confusing "Frances" and "Francis," as the reference must be to Frances Sargent Osgood (*née* Locke, 1811–50), American poet and author of *A Wreath of Wild Flowers from New England* (1838); EBB's reference to "the romance" may have been to "Elfrida, A Dramatic Poem in Five Acts" contained in this volume. Mrs. Osgood was a contributor to the 1839 *Findens' Tableaux*.

---

652. EBB TO MESSRS. SAUNDERS & OTLEY

50 Wimpole Street
Wednesday evening. [ca. July 1838][1]

Miss Barrett would be much obliged to Mess.rs Saunders & Otley if they would send by the bearer a copy of the "*Seraphim*."

Address, on integral page: Mess.rs Saunders & Otley / Conduit Street.
Publication: None traced.
Manuscript: Yale University.

1. Based on the publication of *The Seraphim*, 6 June, and the handwriting.

---

653. EBB TO MARY RUSSELL MITFORD

50 Wimpole Street.
Saturday– [14 July 1838][1]

My ever dearest Miss Mitford's discernment was at fault when she decided that we must want the papers again. Perhaps the late arrival of the Atlas made her decide so—but we sent it late, only because we heard late of the review contained in it—& now I am provoked that this little mistake sh？ have driven you into the trouble—you, with so much to bear for yourself & to do for the whole world—of writing extracts about *me!* That it sh？ have done so has at once provoked & touched me! How kind you are! But pray for the future *keep* whatever we send to you. Papa had packed up a number of the Athenæum to the same destination, & was withheld from sending it only by the *fierce* evidence contained in your letter, of its being already in your possession.

And this fierce evidence is just one of my excuses (call it a reason by courtesy) for writing to you *quite* so soon again—for indeed while your kindness 'rejoices' in hearing from me, I am not easy in adding to those burdens which your most affectionate friends (& should *I* appear the least so?) would rather *not* add to, even by such a straw as this.

I am anxious to say that dear as your love is to me, & dear therefore as every proof of it must be, it w？ pain me the only way it ever could, if it led you to be displeased with any who see me & judge me & whose office it is, to see me & judge me, by a colder & less deceptive light. And I wish besides to impress it upon you my very dear & generous friend, that so far from being annoyed or even disappointed by the review in the Athenæum I was abundantly satisfied & gratified by it. There are more who will complain of its praising me too much than of its blaming me at all—and I have good reason to be obliged to the critic, to M？ Chorley, both for the actual praise he gives my poetry & for the *willingness* to praise, manifest I think in all parts of his criticism. As to the blame— certainly it is not pleasant to be called "affected" as in the Atlas (I confess to eschewing some things in that review) or even to be charged with *attitudinizing* as in the more gentle Athenæum.[2] But you know if things appear so to critics, it is quite right & *honest* for corresponding statements to be made. *Indeed* I am not *'perverse'* as dear M？ Kenyon calls it. I can understand what *he* means in his charge of unintelligibility, & often try tho' so often in vain, not to deserve it. But I do not understand how anyone who writes from the real natural impulse of feeling & thought,—& if I know myself, I[3] DO—can write affectedly, even in the manner of it. As to attitudes I never did study them. I never did take any thought as to forming a style—which formed itsel⟨f⟩ by force of writing, & which (without perverseness) it will be a hard thing to form anew. But this is "a groan" *aside*—& expressive of my misfortune & of nobody's fault. If I live I hope & believe I shall write better—not more from natural impulse—I cannot do that—I *deny that charge of affectation*—but better. But were I to do so, I would turn from the pleasure & the pride of hearing it confessed (were that also mine) to the dearer pride & pleasure of being so loved by *you*—I would indeed. You may believe it, for all this egotism.

Your note is so characteristic that it made me smile again & again. Lady Mary Shepherd *is* a kind & cordial woman—& I admire her talents

No. 653 [14 July 1838] 61

& conversational eloquence. But she is 'terrible' notwithstanding, without the *intent* of being so—& whenever I used to like to hear her talk, it was always under the proviso, that she did'nt talk to *me*. And I have know⟨n⟩ gentlemen shrink away from her, from a mor⟨e⟩ definite fear than mine— for fear of being examined in metaphysics!!– Yet, I admire & like her—& the strongest remembrance I have of the short & distant period of our acquaintance is a grateful one. She once gave me sympathy when I needed it.

Your note—the chapter on authoresses—how it amused me—& how characteristic, I mean in the manner of it, of the most earnest & womanly authoress in all England! I had asked (long ago) M.ͬ Kenyon, on the subject of Miss Landon—but he never met her anywhere, & could tell me nothing.

Your mentioning M.ͬˢ Opie has dovetailed an old dream. With all her feeblenesses, yes, & sillinesses sometimes, she is very moving in her best stories. Her 'Father & daughter' used to draw my childish tears—& so did 'Valentine's Eve'—& these constitute my chief impressions of her writings. The Illustrations of lying, which I read more lately, I made it a point of *conscience* (very congenially) to forget immediately. If she sh.ᵈ come here I shall be glad & with reason.[4]

M.ͬ Townsend had been so kind as to send me a supplement to his Rail Road—the Poems on the Liverpool Association[5]—& a very flattering & pleasing letter—some more of the reflection of your friendship.

But if I write any more you will believe what I do already, that it is nearly *impossible to write a short letter to* YOU. I assure you I began this one with the best intentions—& you see how they end– Give my thankful regards to D.ͬ Mitford. I do hope he continues tolerably well—& you yourself!— I am better for the sun–

My beloved friend's grateful
E B Barrett.

M.ͬ Kenyon we said goodbye to, on tuesday. He went on Wednesday to Cheltenham & Malvern & the Wye for ten days. On reading the Athenæum, I sent my brother out on a vain search for Edgar Quinet whom I never heard of before.[6] A foreign bookseller told him that he *had had* one or two copies from Paris—"*But*" (he added ominously) "the English wont buy poetry".

Publication: EBB-MRM, I, 82–85.
Manuscript: Wellesley College.

    1. Dated by Miss Mitford's returning the magazine reviews of *The Seraphim*.
    2. For details of *The Atlas* and *Athenæum* reviews, see letter 655, notes 2 and 3.
    3. Underscored twice.
    4. Amelia Opie (*née* Anderson, 1769–1853), poet and novelist, the widow of John Opie the painter, was a friend of Miss Mitford. EBB refers to *Father and Daughter*

(1801), *Valentine's Eve* (1816) and *Illustrations of Lying in All Its Branches* (1825). Mrs. Opie became a Quaker in 1825, at which time she abandoned the writing of novels.
  5. Presumably a privately-printed work, as there is no formal record of publication.
  6. The reviewer (Chorley) remarked on "a remarkable coincidence" in spirit, in EBB's preface, to some observations in the prelude to *Prométhée* (1838) by Quinet (1803–75), the French poet-philosopher, "in which the lofty-thoughted but wild genius also proposes to himself the completion of the Pagan fable." He then quoted Quinet at some length.

654. EBB TO JOHN KENYON

[London]
[ca. 15 July 1838][1]

In default of commissions to trouble you ⟨...⟩[2] to thank you my dear friend for a letter which wa⟨s...⟩ pleasantness. Do let me in the first place assure ⟨...⟩ did not doubt your having seen the note long ago, a thoug⟨ht...⟩ my mind to make me wonder why you did not say so. Certainly I wonder now—but it is that you should think it worth while to say so much. The note was meant only to be *once*-blessed—only to please myself; and if it is 'twice blessed' in the result & has pleased you besides, there is a reason for *my* thanking *it* but none for *your* thanking *me*. *I* too "know my place",—& did not presume to pretend to 'puff' *you* in saying what I thought of your book,—& no critic except you, would be malignant enough to dream of such a thing. But I felt it to be a natural pleasure to record, under circumstances when those who have been kind to us are most remembered by us, & close to my poetry in which & near which I could not write untruly, the name of one who truly has been & truly is a valued friend to me—albeit himself so very great an infidel as neither to "believe in thieves" nor in his own kindnesses. As to the last scepticism I might easily—as Johnson said of Berkeley's system—"confute it *thus*"[3]—by an appeal to my own experience & sense of those kindnesses– And indeed & without a jest, my dear friend, I have often felt them *silently*, just because I did not feel them lightly—& being you know so PERVERSE by nature, am not likely to be persuaded by you out of the pleasure of my gratitude. And all this time I am magnanimously forgetting to congratulate ⟨...⟩ed for my note instead of reproached for my ⟨...l⟩ost one limb of your infidelity—& learnt to "believe ⟨...⟩ very very much that the greater part of my book ⟨...⟩ in pleasing you—& altho' so much of your pleasure is of course owing to your kind intent of being pleased, yet that shall not & ought not to diminish my pleasure. The book is full of many sorts of faults—but if I should live I may write a better one—& in the meantime, will make such a glad use of the kindness of my friends, of your kindness & dearest Miss Mitford's which

I owe to yours, as to build a hope upon your praise that I have written in this book something better than I did formerly—& helped to confute (for my own private satisfaction) a dreadful theory of M.[r] Boyd's, that "women never improve". Notwithstanding it, by the way, & to my extreme surprise, he has praised my book most unduly & kindly—with some exceptions—Margret for instance, which is said to be "ridiculous stuff & nonsense"- M.[rs] Coleridge's opinion[4]—you once told it to me here— was upon this account i.e. the hope of making progress—a very gratifying one—but it closed with a great hyperbole,—for nothing "justifies what Miss Mitford says" except her own nature—according to which she wears her heart & her imagination in the same place. But speaking of M.[rs] Coleridge--I wont lose another opportunity of begging you to disclaim for me, whenever *you* have any, the *knowing more Greek than she does*. Indeed it is very improbable. M.[r] Boyd told me once that he admired! how I could possibly read so fluently & *be* so ignorant,—& it used to be a favorite triumph of his malice to close a long reading, by a catechism upon the grammar (his & Gascoigne's "Ladye Gram̃ar"[5] who was never a liege lady of mine) until I cried out for mercy & begged to be sent to school where *he* said I deserved to be sent—just to escape his "cruel smile". Not that M.[r] Boyd would tell you any of this scandal about me. Oh no!—he has far too sublime ideas upon friendship. Because I said to him once before Arabel, with regard to a literary habit of his, involving no opprobrium--"How can you M.[r] Boyd, do so?"—I had a long lecture on our next interview for referring to such a thing before my sister- He did not expect it of me- He really thought that any objection I had to make before a third person, ought at least to refer to hi⟨...⟩ character, & that I might spare his literary reputation—assure⟨...⟩ THAT *was the way in which he always acted by* ME!"— And this, ⟨...⟩ simplicity & gravity that I *dared* not laugh—& answered as ⟨...⟩ could,—that I was very much obliged to his ⟨...⟩ *my* literary reputation being of less ⟨...⟩ much for my moral!" ⟨...⟩ & unfortunately for me, ⟨...⟩ to you how in reading ⟨...⟩ this from the beginning to ⟨...⟩ skipping reader- I did ⟨...⟩ study it as I ought to hav⟨e...⟩ grammar-phobia—NO ⟨...⟩ study of language per se ⟨...⟩ Only certainly the Greek is ⟨...⟩ near philosophy than any othe⟨r...⟩ is rather, like *truth* in the ab⟨stract⟩ form, than philosophy, which is man's aspect towards the truth.

Ought you not to have been thanked before this moment, dear M.[r] Kenyon, for the vision you allowed us to have of him of the Quantock hills?[6] I was as interested in seeing him as any such ignoramus could be- Neither did I ever mention M.[r] Milnes' memorials—which I did not enjoy so much as his former volume,—not that they manifest less genius,—but that there is to me more interest in the *character* of the first manifestation. Others however, & perhaps most others, will think otherwise: but as to his being a true & original poet, all must agree.[7]

It is years since we were at Ross. I was there only once—but I remember the field—& the churchyard!—and Goodrich Castle,[8] & the beautiful Wye whose beauty we only traced as far as the ruin. Where you now are is of course more familiar to me—very familiar—at once gladly & sadly so, as everything near & dear to us, is or becomes. How strange it is—and yet not strange!--that every earthly joyfulness will in time, if it be remembered, grow into an occasion for sadness!——

I heard from Miss Mitford this morning. She says that M.r Chorley has been spending four days with her—a very good example, as it seems to me. If you call me good natured, dear M.r Kenyon (*why*, I dont quite understand) for wanting you to go to Three Mile Cross, what am *I* to call *you* for *not* going?--- *I* PAUSE FOR A REPLY!

Thank you,—I have felt & been better for some days—but with a betterness liable to change with the winds & the coming on of any occasions for exertion or excitement. D.r Chambers did however tell me, unasked, last week—(& I have a moral as well as professional confidence in him, on account of the honesty & sincerity I have observed in him)—that he has grounds for hoping that with care & in time ["]the lung will entirely recover itself"- And if it pleases God, it will be so-

Papa is not in the house—neither are my sisters—to send their kind regards to you. I take the liberty of sending them notwithstanding. We shall all be very glad to see you back again.

Your affectionate & obliged—however distant is the relationship—cousin.

E B Barrett.

Address, on integral page: ⟨... Malvern⟩ Wells.
Publication: None traced.
Manuscript: Manuscript Division, New York Public Library.

1. Dated by Kenyon's being at Malvern, as mentioned in the previous letter.
2. The manuscript of this letter is extensively damaged: the upper corner of the first leaf is torn off, and a large part of the central portion of the second leaf is missing.
3. "We stood talking for some time together of Bishop Berkeley's ingenious sophistry to prove the non-existence of matter ... Johnson answered, striking his foot with mighty force against a large stone ... 'I refute it *thus*'" (Boswell, *The Life of Samuel Johnson, LL.D.*, 1791, I, 257).
4. Sara Coleridge (1802–52), the daughter of Samuel Taylor Coleridge, had married her cousin Henry Nelson Coleridge (1798–1843) in 1829; she was the author of *Phantasmion*, a fairy-tale (1837).
5. Possibly a reference to "Certayne Notes of Instruction" at the end of *The Posies of George Gascoigne, Esquire* (1575).
6. i.e., Kenyon's friend Andrew Crosse, who had visited Wimpole Street with Kenyon on 1 July. He lived at Broomfield, Somersetshire, on the slopes of the Quantock Hills.
7. See letter 627, note 7.

8. Goodrich Castle, dismantled in the Civil War, stood on a precipice rising sheer above the River Wye, four miles below Ross-on-Wye.

655. EBB TO HUGH STUART BOYD

50 Wimpole Street—
June [sic, for July] 17. [1838][1]

My dear friend,

I send you a number of the Atlas which you may keep. It is a favorable criticism certainly—but I confess this of my vanity, that it has not altogether pleased me.[2] You see what it is to be spoilt!——

As to the Athenæum, although I am *not* conscious of the quaintness & mannerism laid to my charge, & am very sure that I have always written too naturally (that is, too much from the impulse of thought & feeling) to have studied '*attitudes*', yet the critic was quite right in stating his opinion, & so am I in being grateful to him for the liberal praise he has otherwise given me.[3] Upon the whole, I like his review better than even the Examiner's, notwithstanding my being perfectly satisfied with *that*.[4]

Thank you for the question about my health. I am very tolerably well—for *me!*—& am said to look better. At the same time I am aware of being always on the verge of an increase of illness—I mean, in a very excitable state—with a pulse that flies off at a word & is only to be caught by digitalis. But I am better—for the present—while the sun shines.

Thank you besides for your criticisms, which I shall hold in memory, & use whenever I am not particularly *obstinate*, in all *my succeeding editions!!*

You will smile at that, & so do *I!*

Arabel is walking in the Zoological Gardens with the Cliffes[5]—but I think you will see her before long.

Your affectionate friend
E B Barrett.

Dont let me forget to mention the Essays. You shall have yours—& Miss Bordman, hers—& the delay has not arisen from either forgetfulness or indifference on my part—altho' I never deny that I dont like giving the essay to anybody because I dont like it.[6] Now that sounds just like "a woman's reason", but it isn't, albeit so reasonable! I meant to say—— "because I dont like THE ESSAY".

Address, on integral page: H S Boyd Esq.r / 3 Circus Road / St John's Wood.
Publication: LEBB, I, 69–70.
Manuscript: Wellesley College.

1. The three magazines to which EBB refers were, respectively, the issues of 23 June 1838, 7 July 1838 and 24 June 1838, making it apparent that her dating of June was incorrect.

2. *The Atlas*, no. 632, 23 June 1838, p. 395, in a review of *The Seraphim*, commented that EBB "merely gives us a distant glimpse of the crucifixion, and throws a poetical obscurity over it which may probably impress her readers more solemnly than if she had ventured to delineate it with a bolder hand.... The form of the dialogue is irregular, and it constitutes, as the author justly describes it, a dramatic lyric, rather than a lyrical drama. In this conception there is not much power, nor does it admit of that breadth and force in the treatment of which the subject is susceptible, and, indeed, which it demands. But ... the suggestion is sufficiently striking to excite the imagination, and, although in some parts the poem is feeble and obscure, there are occasional passages of great beauty, and full of deep poetical feeling.... Miss Barrett is sometimes chargeable with affectation. She overworks the tints, and ... the tapestry has consequently a cumbrous appearance, here and there, from the excessive weight of colouring. But she possesses a fine poetical temperament, and has given the public, in this volume, a work of considerable merit." (For the full text, see pp. 372–373.)

3. *The Athenæum*, no. 558, 7 July 1838, pp. 466–468, called *The Seraphim* "an extraordinary volume ... Miss Barrett's genius is of a high order; active, vigorous, and versatile, but unaccompanied by discriminating taste. A thousand strange and beautiful visions flit across her mind but she cannot look on them with steady gaze;—her descriptions, therefore, are often shadowy and indistinct, and her language wanting in the simplicity of unaffected earnestness." Later in the article, the reviewer [Chorley] speaks of being "constantly drawn downwards from ecstatic visions ... to consider some peculiarity of attitude and utterance ... distracting our attention from the divine wisdom" issuing from the angel's lips. The review ends with the hope that "our words,—which ... have not been hastily conceived,—sink into her mind, and like 'bread cast upon the waters' be found again 'after many days,' in a strengthened resolution on her part to give her fancy, and her strength, and her learning, the only assistance they require to become widely as well as warmly recognized,—that is, a simpler and less mannered clothing than they at present wear." (For the full text, see pp. 375–378.)

4. For *The Examiner* review, see letter 648, note 2.

5. Mrs. Cliffe and her daughter Eliza, neighbours of the Barretts in the Hope End days, were guests of Boyd's daughter and son-in-law (see SD926).

6. Copies of *An Essay on Mind*, finally sent in August (see letter 659).

---

656. RB TO EUPHRASIA FANNY HAWORTH

[London]
Tuesday Evening. [24 July 1838][1]

Dear Miss Haworth,

Do look at a Fuchsia in full bloom & notice the clear little honey-drop depending from every flower .. I have but just found it out, to my no small satisfaction,—a bee's breakfast,—I only answer for the *long* blossomed sort, though,—indeed, for this plant in my room. Taste & be Titania,[2]—you can, that is.– All this while, I forget that you will perhaps never guess the good of the discovery: I have, you are to know, such a love for flowers and leaves—some leaves—that I every now & then,—in an impatience at being unable to possess myself of them thoroughly, to see them quite, satiate myself with their scent,—bite them to bits .. so there will be some sense in that. How I remember the flowers—even grapes—of places I have seen!—some one flower or weed, I should say, that gets some strange how connected with them. Snowdrops & Tilsit in Prussia go together; Cowslips & Windsor-park, for instance: flowering palm and some place or other in Holland. Now to answer what can be answered in the letter I was happy to receive last week. I am quite well– I did not expect you would write; for none of your written reasons, however. You will see Sordello in a trice, if the fagging-fit holds.[3] I did not write six lines while absent (except a scene in a play, jotted down as we sailed thro' the Straits of Gibraltar)—but I did hammer out some four, two of which are addressed to you, two to the Queen .. the whole to go in Book 3—perhaps. I called you, "Eyebright"—meaning a simple & sad sort of translation of "Euphrasia" into my own language: folks would know who Euphrasia, or Fanny was;[4] and *I* should not know Ianthe or Clemanthe.[5] Not that there is any thing in them to care for, good or bad. Shall I say "Eyebright".? I was disappointed in one thing, Canova.[6] What companions should I have? The story of the ship must have reached you "with a difference" as Ophelia says;[7] my sister told it to a Mr Dow, who delivered it, I suppose, to Forster, who furnished Macready with it, who made it over &c&c&c– As short as I can tell, this way it happened: the Captain woke me one bright Sunday Morning to say there was a ship floating keel uppermost half a mile off; they lowered a boat, made ropes fast to some floating canvass, & towed her towards our vessel. Both met half-way, and the little air that had risen an hour or two before, sank at once. Our men made the wreck fast, and went to breakfast in high glee at the notion of having "new trousers out of the sails," and quite sure she was a french boat, broken from her moorings at Algiers, close by. Ropes were next hove (hang this sea-talk) round her stancheons, and after a quarter of an hours pushing at the capstan, the vessel righted suddenly, one dead body floating out; five more were in the forecastle, and had probably been there a month under a blazing African sun .. don't imagine the wretched state of things. They were, these six, the "watch below"—(I give you the results of the day's observation)—the rest, some eight or ten, had been washed overboard at first. One or two were Algerines, the rest Spaniards. The vessel was a smuggler bound for Gibraltar; there were two stupidly-disproportionate guns, taking up the whole deck, which was convex and—nay, look you, these are the gun-rings, and the black square the place where the bodies lay. Well, the sailors

(All the "bulwarks," or sides at the top, carried away by the waves) covered up the hatchway, broke up the aft-deck, hauled up tobacco & cigars, good Lord such heaps of them, and then bale after bale of prints & chintz, don't you call it, till the Captain was half frightened—he would get at the ship's papers, he said; so these poor fellows were pulled up, piecemeal, and pitched into the sea, the very sailors calling to each other "to cover the faces": no papers of importance were found, however, but fifteen swords, powder & ball enough for a dozen such boats, and bundles of cotton &c that would have taken a day to get out, but the Captain vowed that after five-o clock she should be cut adrift: accordingly she was cast loose, not a third of her cargo having been touched; and you can hardly conceive the strange sight when the battered hulk turned round, actually, and looked at us, and then reeled off, like a mutilated creature from some scoundrel french surgeon's lecture-table, into the most gorgeous and lavish sunset in the world: there,—only, thank me for not taking you at your word and giving you the whole "story". "What I did"? I went to Trieste, then Venice—then thro' Treviso & Bassano to the mountains, delicious Asolo, all my places and castles, you will see. Then to Vicenza, Padua & Venice again. Then to Verona, Trent, Inspruck [*sic*] (the Tyrol) Munich, "Wurzburg in Franconia"![8] Frankfort & Mayence,— down the Rhine to Cologne, thence to Aix-la-Chapelle Liège, and Antwerp—then home. Forgive this blurring, and believe it was only a foolish quotation:[9]– Shall you come to town, any where near town, soon? I shall be off again as soon as my book is out whenever that will be. This sort of thing gets intolerable and I had better have done. I never read that book of Miss Martineau's so can't understand what you mean. Macready is looking well; I just saw him yesterday for a minute after the play: his Kitely was Kitely[10]—superb "from his flat cap down to his shining shoes"–[11] I saw very few Italians, "to know," that is. Those I did see I liked. Your friend Pepoli has been lecturing here, has he not?[12]

I shall be vexed if you don't write soon,—a long Elstree-letter:– What are *you* doing—drawing—writing?

Ever yours truly
R Browning.

Address, on integral page: Miss Haworth, / Barham Lodge, / Elstree. / RB.
Publication: LRB, pp. 1–3.
Manuscript: British Library.

1. Dated by RB's return from Italy and his seeing Macready in the role of Kitely.

2. Queen of the Fairies. From the context, it seems probable that RB was thinking rather of Ariel's song, "Where the bee sucks" (*A Midsummer Night's Dream*, V, 1, 88).
3. Despite this comment, it was not until May 1839 that the poem was finished, and March 1840 when it was published.
4. "My English Eyebright, if you are not glad" etc. (*Sordello*, III, 967ff.)
5. Ianthe, in Ovid's *Metamorphoses*, was a Cretan girl transformed into a young man. The name was much used in 19th century literature: Byron dedicated *Childe Harold* to Ianthe, meaning the 11-year-old Lady Charlotte Harley; Landor used the name for his early sweetheart, Sophia Jane Swift; Shelley gave the name to his eldest daughter, and also to a maiden in *Queen Mab*. Clemanthe, daughter of Medon, High Priest of the Temple of Apollo, was a character in Talfourd's *Ion*.
6. Antonio Canova (1757–1822), Italian sculptor, patronized by Napoleon. While in Italy, RB had visited Possagno, where Canova's studio had been made into a small museum, in which some of his work was exhibited. Katharine de Kay Bronson, in her article "Browning in Asolo" (*The Century Magazine*, no. 59, April 1900, pp. 920–931; reprinted in *More Than Friend*, ed. Michael Meredith, 1985, pp. 127–145), wrote of RB's visit: "Such was his interest in art in all its branches that he had the patience to examine the uninteresting collection of Canova's drawings in water-color, which present the appearance of very early attempts of a not very promising aspirant to fame."
7. *Hamlet*, IV, 5, 183.
8. The locus of the first part of *Paracelsus*.
9. RB has obliterated a passage of about three lines.
10. In *Every Man in His Humour* (1598) by Ben Jonson (1572–1637), performed on 23 July 1838 at the Theatre Royal, Haymarket.
11. *Every Man in His Humour*, II, 1, 103.
12. Count Carlo Pepoli (1796–1881), Italian author who wrote the libretto for Bellini's *I Puritani*, had established a course in Italian history and beaux-arts in Paris in 1837. *The Times* of 19 June 1838 referred to a course of lectures in the history of music being given by him during June and July (in French) at the Marylebone Institute in London. He held the Chair of Italian Literature at London University from 1839 to 1848.

---

657. EBB TO JOHN KENYON

[London]
Wednesday morn^g [?1] [August 1838][1]

Arabel forgot to tell me dear Mr Kenyon, until late in the evening, that you wished to have the Athenian Captive.[2] I take the opportunity of returning to you the Magazine, you were so kind as to send, but with which we had already provided ourselves.

I have felt all the pleasure & honor of being praised by Professor Wilson & associated with Mr Milnes[3]--& very much all the kindness of *your* being pleased in this pleasure of mine. Papa had looked thro' Blackwood, & came home to be surprised with your discovery!——

Your affec^{te} cousin
EBB

Publication: None traced.
Manuscript: Armstrong Browning Library.

1. Dated by the reference to the article in *Blackwood's*.
2. Talfourd's play, sent to EBB with letter 637.
3. *Blackwood's Edinburgh Magazine* for August 1838 contained a review of *The Seraphim* (XLIV, 279–284). John Wilson (1785–1854), the editor of *Blackwood's*, was the author, using his pseudonym "Christopher North." Earlier in the article, Wilson quotes from Monckton Milnes's *Poems of Many Years*. (For the full text of his comments on *The Seraphim*, see pp. 379–382.)

658. EBB TO LADY MARGARET COCKS

50 Wimpole Street.
Saturday. [4 August 1838][1]

My dear Lady Margaret,

I trust that it has seemed to you rather strange than unkind that I have not written to you before. Indeed it *was* my intention to do so—and then sometimes I waited to be better & sometimes to see the end of very uncertain plans, but never I fear for a sufficiently availing reason to justify this long silence before the kind interest you have expressed in me, & in which it gives me so much pleasure to believe.

I am better—with a *betterness* however very dependent, to speak humanly, upon the wind, & upon the degree of repose & freedom from emotion in the body & mind. The cough & expectoration of blood continue—though not with violence enough to demand the application of leeches, made so frequently some time ago: and I have had no return of the ACUTE pain in the side. Dr Chambers—the *sincerest* of physicians! has told me that there seems to be no *ulceration* of lungs, & that he has grounds for hoping for my ultimate complete recovery. But he has made an essential condition of my leaving this part of England for the winter– He w^d not, he said, be answerable as to any result if I attempted to stay here. And so, I am going—sad at heart, since I am going at the same time from my family—to Torquay for the winter & autumn months.

But to stay at the risk of my life w^d be wilfulness & foolishness at once: and indeed this necessity of going has assumed the gentlest form it could. I go direct to my uncle Hedley's house, there to remain until my aunt Bell, Miss Clarke, leaves Gloucestershire for Torquay on purpose to be with me. In the midst of so much kindness, lamenting w^d be out of place even if it did not imply unthankfulness. I shall be quite as happy as I can be under the circumstances. And I shall hold fast the hope of seeing my dearest Papa occasionally, & of having my sisters with me

No. 658 [4 August 1838] 71

alternately—& my brother will be my escort there. We go by sea. I am unable to bear the motion of a carriage,—& a sea voyage does not, Dr Chambers thinks, involve any risk. But indeed to a helpless being like me, whose migrations have for so many months been from the bed to the sofa, it looks in importance & hazard very much like an expedition to the North Pole. But I suppose it is not like it, after all!——

My book has been the means to me of a good deal of pleasure– It has pleased some whom I cared to please: and the half dozen reviews which I have seen, have all treated me graciously more or less. What gratified me particularly was Professor Wilson's graciousness in the last Blackwood—in the article called Christopher's cave. It pleased me very much to be taken into a cave in company with Mr Milnes who was born a crowned poet, by perhaps the first poetical critic of the day, to say nothing of being praised there besides. But it is not all praise—nor is the praise so emphatic as that of some other critics! But even blame, hard critical blame, in *that cave*, would have seemed praise to *me!!*——[2]

I know that the book is full of faults. Tell me the whole truth of your impression of it– you may, & without disappointing me. I have a kiss ready for every rod![3]

And do say dearest Lady Margaret, as much of your own self as I may hear! If you write *after* a week or ten days, I believe it must be to Torquay––Robert Hedley's Esqr Torquay. May God bless you! How all of us need blessing of God! *always!* but we feel the need sometimes more deeply than at other times! *I* feel it *now!*

Your affectionate
EBB.

My sisters beg to be very fondly remembered to your Ladyship. They are quite well.

Addressed and franked by Lord Somers: Tewkesbury Augst fifth / 1838 / The Lady Marg.^{t} Cocks / Neen Savage / Cleobury / Bewdley / Somers / [and on reverse of envelope in EBB's hand:] The Lady Margaret Cocks.
Publication: None traced.
Manuscript: Hon. Mrs. Elizabeth Hervey-Bathurst.

1. Dated by the frank.
2. The article in *Blackwood's* (see previous letter, note 3) was generally favourable ("pregnant with lofty thoughts"; "In 'The Seraphim' there is poetry and piety—genius and devotion"; "passages of deep pathos"), but Wilson said of the smaller poems "they are all disfigured by much imperfect and some bad writing—and the fair author is too often seen struggling in vain to give due expression to the feelings that beset her, and entangled in a web of words."
3. Cf. *Two Gentlemen of Verona*, I, 2, 59.

659. EBB TO HUGH STUART BOYD

[London]
Thursday. [?9] [August 1838][1]

My dear friend,

I was about to write to you just as I received your *last* note. For it, as well as for some kind & gratifying ones which preceded it, do receive my grateful thanks. My book *'if it had a voice'*,[2] would speak to you as eloquently as ever could the walls of Agamemnon's palace, & more gladly!

To many of your criticisms I bow very low. To others, I am inclined to be rebellious. Several are founded upon misprints—such as the word *'these'* to which you objected in Cowper's Grave, & which was written originally *those*.[3] I must mention besides the punctuation in a passage of Isobel's Child– It is true that there are no stops after the words "unweened" & "cry": but if you had been told of the *parenthesis* conspicuous in that place, you would not have complained of any obscurity induced by the omission.[4] At least, I think not. The Greek words in 'Night & the Merry Man' ARE in Greek characters already.[5]

Thank you for being delighted with Blackwood's Magazine. *I* was much delighted with it. I was pleased both with the words said, with the character of the Sayer, & the company in which they were said. It is something to be in a cave with M.̱ Milnes, who was born a crowned poet, & dear old Christopher, who is the first *professionally poetical* critic of the day, even if I were not praised there. Professor Wilson's praise I have always coveted . . yet scarcely dared to hope for.[6]

The essay goes to you at last.[7] The real truth is, that Papa forgot all about it. I am sure you must have wondered at the delay. Miss Bordman's copy I mean to send to her.

And this was the cause of my not writing to you before—this waiting for the essay—*this*, & not my ingratitude, whatever you may have thought of it!——

D.̱ Pye Smith is delightful—with a countenance whose radiancy I scarcely know whether to attribute to intelligence or benevolence. It may come of either—or both. If it pleases God that I should return in better health, I shall hope to see him often again & to *converse* with him– Conversation was out of the question last week—he being very deaf even with a ear trumpet,—& my voice, naturally so weak, having fallen into a *'swound'* through illness.

The day of my departure is not yet fixed. When it is, I will write to you again. This is not a farewell.

With the truest thankfulness for all the kindness you have shown me, believe me my dear friend

affectionately yours
E B Barrett.

Will not *Apolyptic* do,—tho' it does not mean Apocalyptic?[8] Find some excuse for it!– And pray do not mention to any person what Arabel told you on the subject of the intended length of the Athenæum-critique. Miss Mitford mentioned it to me in confidence: & you know that critics are very jealous of their mysteries!——

Publication: Weaver, pp. 416–418.
Manuscript: Huntington Library.

 1. Dated by the reference to *Blackwood's* and the continuing uncertainty regarding the date of EBB's departure for Torquay.
 2. Æschylus, *Agamemnon*, line 36.
 3. "Beneath these deep pathetic eyes" (line 40 of "Cowper's Grave," subsequently corrected to "those deep").
 4. Lines 383–387. This passage was modified slightly for the 1850 reprinting.
 5. Line 109: "And αι αι" ("woe, woe") "written upon none!"
 6. See letters 657, note 3, and 658, note 2.
 7. *An Essay on Mind*, promised in letter 655.
 8. Line 107 of "Sounds" read "As erst in Patmos apolyptic John." When the poem was included in the 1850 edition, the line was changed to read "As the seer-saint of Patmos, loving John."

---

660. EBB TO MARY RUSSELL MITFORD

[London]
Friday. [10 August 1838][1]

Ever dearest Miss Mitford,

With the parcel of reviews which your kindness makes you care to see, I venture to put up a little memorial[2] of the object of it—who although she w^d trust without any memorial to the pleasant likelihood of remaining unforgotten by you, yet feels that she cannot hold your memory of her (that being so precious!) by too many knotted threads!——

   "And *She* must be
   A *sterner* than thee,
  Who would break a thread of mine".[3]

I am going away dearest Miss Mitford, possibly in a very few days & certainly as soon as the weather will let me, to Devonshire—to Torquay—there to remain over the winter. The plan involves a sadness of heart to me—for we cannot all go; but it is one which is to be submitted to, D? Chambers having used very strong language as to its necessity. Indeed he told me plainly that my recovery *depended* upon its adoption. I am therefore going—with the *cold* hope of seeing Papa *sometimes*. My aunt & uncle Hedley who have resided at Torquay for the last two or three years under D? Chambers's jurisdiction, on account of my uncle's being affected in some similar way to myself—are kind enough to receive me very gladly & to wish to keep me with them; but after a while & in the case of the climate agreeing tolerably with me, I shall remove to another house & to the companionship of another aunt, Miss Clarke, a dear favorite relative, who has promised to leave Gloucestershire for Devonshire just for that purpose. Here you see, is plenty of kindness. I ought not to talk of "cold" hopes in the midst of it. But I cannot help the pang with which I think of those who must be left—altho' it would, I know all the time, be unkind to them & a wrong thing in itself, to risk my life by staying. As it is,—that is, if I go—D? Chambers seems to be hopeful.- He believes that there is not at present, any ulceration of the lungs—only a too great fulness of the bloodvessels upon them; & he told me a fortnight ago, that he had grounds for hoping in the affected lung's eventually recovering itself altogether. And it may please God, that I sh^d return next spring to rejoice in better health & a less helpless condition—& to rejoice in seeing *you* dearest Miss Mitford besides!

This is Saturday—& I began the letter I am writing, yesterday—& yesterday, too, I received yours. Thank you for letting me see M? Hughes's gratifying note[4] which I *shall* thank you for allowing me to keep in order to confront it with the proof. It shall be returned to you afterwards. But perhaps now that I am going to Torquay, I must not expect the proof? Must I not? Yet I hope I may. Do get it sent to me if you can. I have no corrected copy of the ballad by me.

There was some sort of reason for my alteration of the line in Margret[5]—though what it was, has quite escaped my memory. My impression however is, that I had detected the counterpart of the idea in some other person's writings—& took refuge from a possible charge of plagiarism, of which I always have a nervous dread,—in the flow of the universe. I do not say that this was so—but that this is my impression & that a very faint one it is.

Keep the reviews which are sent to you—at least do not return them to us. The Metropolitan, M? Kenyon says, I certainly wrote myself.[6] Blackwood pleased me very much. It is something to be in a cave with Professor Wilson & M? Milnes—without being praised there. But you see, opinion runs almost everywhere—even in the Metropolitan article which I wrote myself!—*against* the Seraphim, & in favor comparatively,

Joseph Arnould

Bryan Waller Procter

of the shorter poems– The extracts from M.[r] Milnes's poems in Blackwood, will deeply delight you. The lay of the humble—The Long Ago—Familiar Love—Youth .. they are surpassingly exquisite!——[7]

Your praise of my 'candour', my beloved friend, tells more of your own warm affections than of my praise! And let it be so!

But was M.[r] Henry Chorley really surprised that "Sister Seraphina-Angelica" did not fly into the tempest of a passion without any manner of reason for it?– Now it seems to *me*, that we of the Port Royal may very well keep our tempers––until we are provoked to lose them. Our saintship may prove itself so far!–[8]

What you tell me of him is very interesting, & makes me respond to your wish that I knew him personally. Does he write for the Tableaux this year? And does M.[r] Proctor?[9]

M.[r] Kenyon I saw yesterday. His continental plans are deferred as to the execution of them, until after the 15.th before which day M.[r] Southey cannot come to London.[10] In the meanwhile M.[r] Landor is coming.

You do not say whether you are both well. I trust you are. Offer my kindest wishes & regards to D.[r] Mitford—and accept such from Papa & all this house. *No* day is fixed for my departure—which is to be by sea, for lack of strength for a land journey. May God ever bless you! I shall hear from you—shall I not?—at Torquay—whenever you can write without adding wearily to your too many occupations? Never tire yourself for me! May God bless you! It is foolish to feel as if this were a farewell to *you*—but forty miles and a hundred & seventy are so different!

Dearest Miss Mitford's
EBB–

I am better. If M.[r] Townsend hath sent you or do send you some verses written by a female friend of his, requesting your opinion of them, will you tell *me* what it is?

You will think that there is at least as much disadvantage to me as honor, in the association with Mr Milnes—& you will think rightly—albeit I choose to dwell in my own thoughts upon the *honor*. If he be—as struck me at first—of Tennyson's school .. quære .. whether he does not sit in the seat of the Master?——

I am so glad that Mr Deffell said good to *you* about my sister.[11] One day I do trust that you will know & love both my sisters––who are already well prepared—to use the coldest word—to love *you*! Henrietta's predominant fondness is for music, & Arabel's for drawing––for which I think she has a good deal of talent. I do trust that you will love my sisters.

The wind is audible– It seems to me that I *cannot* be on the sea until late in the next week, if then. Perhaps I *hope* I cannot—& yet it might be as well if the business were over. Adieu once more.

M.[r] Deffell's family live in Harley Street close to us. His mother & sisters we have known by a very long acquaintanceship,—since our childhood—altho' I dont *feel* as if I know them very well!—which is possible, *you* know. Henrietta has far more intercourse with them than I.

A letter 'without an end'! in opposition to M.[rs] Austen!—— [12]

Publication: EBB-MRM, I, 85–88.
Manuscript: Wellesley College.

1. Dated by the still-tentative plans for EBB's departure for Torquay.
2. This may be the pencil-case mentioned in letter 662.
3. Cf. Southey, *Thalaba the Destroyer*, VIII, 26, 13–15.
4. John Hughes (1790–1857), author, linguist, draughtsman and wood-carver, was a friend of the Mitfords. He had published *An Itinerary of Provence and the Rhone Made During the Year 1819* (1822) and *The Boscobel Tracts* (1830); he later put in print some of his early poetry, *Lays of Past Days* (1850). His note referred to EBB's ballad for the new *Findens' Tableaux* (see letter 662).
5. When EBB reprinted "The Romaunt of Margret" in *The Seraphim*, she made several changes from the text originally submitted to *The New Monthly Magazine* in 1836.
6. The review of *The Seraphim* in *The Metropolitan Magazine* (August 1838, pp. 97–101) said: "At our first glance at this extraordinary little book, we were singularly struck with the originality, ideality, earnestness, and masterly power of expression and execution; and a more careful examination has deepened this first impression, and awakened in us a great respect for the fair author's uncommon learning. Whether she be qualified to split critical straws with a Parr or a Porson we know not, but she seems well read in the Greek poets, and perfectly imbued with their spirit.... The style and manner ... remind us more of Shelley than of any other recent English writer. But there is a devotional glow, an almost seraph-like enthusiasm in this lady, which the unfortunate Shelley never reached ... There is also here and there a happily reflected light from the great and good Wordsworth; and one or two of Miss Barrett's minor pieces might be mistaken for the productions of the greatest of our poets since Milton.... We cannot quite agree with this truly-gifted writer that the awful mysteries of the christian faith are suited to mortal verse—we remember that even a Milton could here make the sublime ridiculous, or something worse—but we admire with a heart-warm admiration her *intentions* in this way; and the all-absorbing enthusiasm with which she advocates the cause of devotional poetry." (For the full text, see pp. 383–385.)
7. See letter 657, note 3.
8. Chorley's unsigned review in *The Athenæum* included the comment (p. 466): "She addresses herself to sacred song with a devotional ecstasy suiting rather the Sister Celestines and Angelicas of Port-Royal, than the religious poets of our sober Protestant communities." Port Royal was a convent near Versailles censured by the Vatican for adherence to Jansenism. (For the full text of Chorley's review, see pp. 375–378.)
9. Chorley's "The Sister of Charity" was included in the 1839 *Findens' Tableaux*. Procter (Barry Cornwall) did not contribute.
10. See letter 605, note 6.
11. John Henry Deffell and his family lived at no. 38 Upper Harley Street. As EBB later indicates, the Deffells had been family friends for a number of years—the earliest reference to them occurring in 1825 (see SD512).
12. A reference to *The Story Without an End* (1834), a translation from the German by Sarah Austin (*née* Taylor, 1793–1867).

661. EBB TO HUGH STUART BOYD

[London]
[?11] [August 1838][1]

My dear friend,

You must let me *feel* my thanks to you, even when I do not *say* them. I have put up your various notes together—& perhaps they may do me as much good hereafter, as they have already, for the most part, given me pleasure.

The "burden pure *have* been"[2] certainly was a misprint. As certainly, "nor man nor nature satisfy" is ungrammatical.[3] But I am *not so* sure about the passage in Isobel

> I am not used to tears at nights
> Instead of slumber—nor to prayer–[4]

Now I think that the passage may imply a repetition of the words with which it begins, after "nor": thus—"nor *am I used* to prayer" &c. Either you or I may be right about it—and either 'or' or 'nor' may be grammatical. At lease, so I pray.

You did not answer one question. Do you consider that 'Apolyptic' stands without excuse?[5]

I never read Greek to any person except yourself, & M.r MacSwiney my brother's tutor. To him I read longer than a few weeks,—but then it was rather guessing & stammering and tottering through parts of Homer & extracts from Zenophon [*sic*], than reading– *You* would not have called it reading, if you had heard it!

I studied hard by myself afterwards—and the kindness with which afterwards still, you assisted me, if yourself remembers gladly *I* remember *gratefully* & gladly.

I have just been told that your servant was desired by you *not to wait a minute!!*

The wind is unfavorable for the sea. I do not think there is the least probability of my going before the very end of the week, if then. You shall hear.

Affectionately yours,
E B Barrett

I am tolerably well– I have been forced to take digitalis again, which makes me feel weak; but still I am better I think.

Address: H S Boyd Esq.r / 3 Circus Road / St John's Wood.
Publication: LEBB, I, 73–74.
Manuscript: Wellesley College.

1. Dated by the still-tentative plans for EBB's departure for Torquay, and the repetition of her question concerning "Apolyptic," posed in letter 659.

2. Line 114 of "The Virgin Mary to the Child Jesus." The misprint was corrected in *Poems* (1850).
3. Line 32 of "Cowper's Grave."
4. Lines 194–195 of "Isobel's Child." "Nor" was changed to "not" when the poem was reprinted in *Poems* (1850).
5. See letter 659, note 8.

---

662. EBB TO MARY RUSSELL MITFORD

50 Wimpole St.
Tuesday. August 14 [1838][1]

It is not yet sure on what day I go—and they are trying to persuade me that I *may* go tomorrow. I do not think that I may. Everything depends upon Papa's resolve & I do not think that he has resolved so. But even if I "*may* go tomorrow", I *must* not go then or any day without writing a few words to you my beloved friend. I will write them on the strength of that "may", though I do not believe in it—having waited to write them for some decision of wind & plan. Certainly I could not go without trying to thank you for all your great & most touching & tender kindness as expressed in the letters lying beside me. If I did, I should sink in the sea by the weight of my own heart! and as it must be a heavy one, any way, I may unload it of some of its feelings of gratefulness & affection, thus, & to you my kindest & dearest Miss Mitford.

And you would—were it not for one golden chain—may God keep every link of it strong![2]—go to Torquay, pass the winter there, & all for me! And you *will* as it is, write to me once a week, oftener if I please (if I please!!) & love me & pray for me always! I thank you for all this surpassing kindness! But you shall not write to me as often as I please. You shall not write to me *even* once a week—& never—except when you can do so without harrassing yourself & tiring yourself—you who have *so* many *too* many occupations. But you shall do what I know you will—write to me when you have snatches of time in which you might talk to me—did we happen to be near enough for talking—whenever you are least likely to be tired by writing!—and then I can be happy over your letters without remorse, & you can be acknowledged most worthily (in virtue of the good & cheerfulness done by those letters) a 'sœur de la charitè'[3] in opposition to us of the Port Royal.

If it be God's will to bring me here again, I shall very gladly make Mrs Anderdon's acquaintance, & her daughter's—both for the sake of what you say of them—and for a reason which might stand by itself . . that they are friends of yours.[4]

Not many more words shall be added to these; & I will keep these until the day of going is a fixed one. The '*may*' for tomorrow makes me feel uncomfortable—& I cannot just now ⟨w⟩rite about ballads or anything thereto pertaining. There shall be however as little delay as possible in returning the proof.[5] I wish that you *your own self* had given something *dramatic* to Finden!——

The 'favorite maid'! That struck a strained string. Think of our maid—my sisters' & mine—deciding just now—only two days ago,—that she would not go with me! We have been obliged to engage another, with great difficulty & haste,—& she came as a stranger last night![6] It is another shade upon the Torquay journey!— The reason given for the sudden decision was, the state of her health; and indeed she is not well, poor thing, nor does she look so! But still under the circumstances she might have decided either before or afterwards—not just at this moment—particularly as she had lived between two & three years with us, & had professed her willingness to go anywhere with me. I thanked her for saying so just three weeks ago! We have some reason for suspecting a fear of the sea-voyage to have had a little to do with the change—but I shall not mind this inconvenience much, or any other at all, if I MAY have with me one of my dear sisters. Another '*may*' to make me anxious! Nothing is decided.

May God ever bless you! You shall hear from Torquay! Does Dr Mitford, or do you, like *Devonshire cream*? Tell me whether either or both of you do?

Your attached
E B Barrett.

I am so obliged both to the carpenter for stealing the old pencil case and to you for not scorning the new one.

Monday *August 20th*

Dearest Miss Mitford, you must *dree*[7] this antique of a letter, because I cant afford to let you think it possible that I could live so long without at least *writing* a reply to some words of yours. After many uncertainties, my sister Henrietta, my eldest brother who boasts of having once been introduced to you, & my brother George are promised to go with me—& I am going possibly, I wont say certainly, on *Wednesday* to Plymouth where we may be detained a day or two before any other vessel will take us back to Torquay. Therefore dont imagine us to be among Mr Tennyson[']s Mermen & maids,[8] if you shd not hear of our arrival for a week to come or more— Oh! this going! It does cost me so much—more than I dare write about today. I had given up the whole attempt for three days last week! but it *is* to be made I suppose after all!— May God bless you—

The proof *has come*. How c^d you put me in the first place—not *my* place I am sure!—— I shall feel as ashamed as my short-petticoated heroine *ought* to feel!——[9]

By an anachronism (common you know to the poets) here is a double letter written, & no franker in all London, as far as I can find, to direct it!- I sent last night in vain to Mr Kenyon—& so now nothing is left to me but to make a parcel of my mistakes!——

Mr Hughes was right I think about *dree*. At least I have not succeeded in finding an instance of that word being used substantively. I have changed it.[10]

As to *ble*, I accept your permission & leave it.[11] A ⟨★★★⟩

Address: Miss Mitford / Three Mile Cross / Near Reading.
Docket, on reverse of envelope in Miss Mitford's hand: Zinnia.
Publication: EBB-MRM, I, 89–91.
Manuscript: Edward R. Moulton-Barrett and Wellesley College.

1. Year provided by EBB's impending departure for Torquay.
2. i.e., Miss Mitford's responsibility to her invalid father.
3. "Sister of charity." This was the title of Chorley's contribution to the 1839 *Findens' Tableaux*.
4. Mrs. Oliver Anderdon and her daughter, Lucy Olivia Hobart Anderdon.
5. The proof sheets of "The Romaunt of the Page," EBB's poem for the 1839 *Findens' Tableaux*.
6. Miss Crow, a native of Lancashire, remained with EBB until the spring of 1844, when it was discovered that she had married secretly another member of the household staff, William Treherne, the son of John Treherne, who was originally employed in the stables at Hope End and finally as butler. The Trehernes set up a bakery shop in Camden Town. "Favorite maid" probably refers to Miss Mitford's Martha.
7. "Suffer; bear" (*OED*).
8. "The Merman" and "The Mermaid" were included in Tennyson's *Poems, Chiefly Lyrical* (1830).
9. Ellen, the subject of EBB's poem. See letter 636, note 4.
10. "Dree" did not appear in the final text.
11. Lines 155–156 of "The Romaunt of the Page" read "For white of blee with waiting for me / Is the corse in the next chambère." "Blee" means colour, hue, and, by extension, complexion or form (*OED*).

---

663. EBB to Hugh Stuart Boyd

50 Wimpole Street
Friday. [24 August 1838][1]

My dear friend,

It seems to be at last definitively fixed that we go tomorrow. The wind is silent & I must be so too—though very very sad at heart.

My dearest Papa has kindly permitted one of my sisters to be my companion; and Henrietta is going with me for the first part of my absence, & then Arabel will take her place. Bro & George are going too.

And all this companionship is more than I hoped for, & I ought to be contented with it—& thankful for every brightness which has fallen, beyond my hope, upon my present circumstances. But still I cannot help being very sorrowful even while I write about the brightness!

May God bless you. It may please Him for me to return & visit you again. In the meantime I must once more thank you for the kind interest & trouble you have taken about my book & me! Two notes of yours lie unanswered to this moment—but while our uncertainties lasted, I did not like to write. Good bye dear M! Boyd! Do let me hear from you when the disinclination to letter-writing is least strong—& ever believe me your affectionate friend

E B Barrett.

We sail at eight in the morning to Plymouth, or rather Devonport, & shall not reach it until Monday night. Afterwards we avail ourselves of the earliest Torquay packet![2]

Once more, Good bye!—— Remember me to Emily [Harding].

Publication: Weaver, p. 418.
Manuscript: Huntington Library.

1. Dated by the impending departure for Torquay.
2. EBB and her companions sailed on *The Shannon* for Plymouth on 25 August, then on to Torquay, which they reached on 27 August (see SD943).

---

664. EBB TO MARY RUSSELL MITFORD

[Torquay]
Tuesday– [25 September 1838][1]

I sit down in the ashes my beloved friend to grieve that I sh.ᵈ have allowed you to be uneasy about me. Oh yes!—I have indeed received the three the four letters which your kindness sent, & also the separate delight from each which that kindness intended. And many many times on every day (the 'many' does not express *how* many!) I have thought of & thanked you in my heart, & felt that I truly loved you. But after all I did not write until now—and after all this silence can your affection for me make an effort & believe & understand how it was that I did not write yet did not forget you—yet did not remember you less often & affectionately than I always must? Do let it try at least!——

The physician attending me here was anxious for me to have as much air as possible before the cold came[2]—& would not allow me to keep up my late London habit (very useful in enabling an invalid to get thro' a good deal of writing without fatigue) of lying in bed until two. I was made, on coming here, to get up at ten & am always subject to a certain lassitude in the morning after little exertions—even the exertion of dressing. Then at one or two out I was sent in the chair, & seldom failed to come back quite exhausted & fit for nothing better than reading nonsense. In this way--by these little things--I have been--not *prevented* from writing to you--but tempted on from hour to hour & day to day into procrastination. You shall not hear of them again. To write to you is one of my best pleasures—*do* believe *that*—and to read even a little note from you is better than writing. Tell me if M.ʳ Serg.ᵗ Talfourd is at all likely to think me a bold person in doing what you suggest. My position with regard to him, not being that of an ordinary stranger (as we *have* had a very little intercourse by one or two notes)—nor of a personal acquaintance, makes me more scrupulous & fearful of intruding upon him than I could otherwise be. But if you really think that he would have nobody in his remembrance except YOURSELF, in receiving & forwarding my letters to you, I would gladly avail myself of your suggestion.[3]

Indeed my dearest Miss Mitford, I do believe that I am better in some respects. The stethoscope was tried on Sunday for the second time since my arrival, & the report is more favorable. D.ʳ Barry seems to be quite sure that the respiration is clearer on the affected side—& the spitting of blood is very little,—almost less than it has been at all since the first appearance of that unpleasant symptom. At the same time the last ten days have been dreary, uncomfortable ones to me, haunted throughout by weakness, an oppressive *sense* of weakness, & a lowness of spirits from which I am generally free. Such lowness of spirits, that I could have cried all day if there were no *exertion* in crying!—and feel the consciousness of there being no cause for gloom, just as a new mortification instead of as a comfort, the whole time!—— This was the result of taking digitalis for three weeks instead of one! & now I am reviving, & rising again to the 'high estate'[4] of common sense & cheerfulness.

D.ʳ Barry takes D.ʳ Chambers's view of the case exactly—which is satisfactory to me who trust so very much in D.ʳ Chambers. The opinion given to Lady Sidmouth[5] is quite mine—as far as I am able to judge of 'the physicians of the world'. But what I value in him more than even his ability, is the combination which exists in him, of frankness & feeling. Abernethy had one without the other.[6] D.ʳ Chambers never attempts to deceive you as to your state, and yet never by a word appears to forget .. I will not say your *feelings*, but even your preferences & prejudices. Did you hear the cause of his dismissal from Holland House? He TOLD[7] Lady Holland that she had a desease of the heart.[8] That was the crime. I have no Tyburn for it:– Have *you*?–

I am considered likely to recover; at least such recovery is not considered by any means either impossible or improbable. The locality of the complaint is very small—& the *right* lung perfectly unaffected. I tell you these things because I know you will care to hear them. There is a favorite psalm of mine—[']'The Lord is my Shepherd, *therefore* I shall not want". THEREFORE I would not FEAR to want! The lovely succeeding images of 'green pastures' and 'silent waters' are surely meant to make very green the hopes & very calm the depths of the soul!–⁹

You are not, or have not been well my dearest Miss Mitford—and have lost one friend by death, & are about to lose her whom you name another, by marriage.¹⁰ Do believe how I sympathize in the last two griefs—the first is *my own!* Take it away from me as soon as you can by writing to tell me that you are really better. Punish me in any way except by *not* writing to me––or by not loving me––or by not believing that I love you.

As to Martha, I shall be very glad to hear of her happiness, and yet I do hope that the beginning of it will be put off until you have quite made up your heart to lose her. You certainly *will*. And for all that you say about tragedies I wont believe that anybody's happiness can be at last in the least degree tragical to *you*—I wont indeed! The thought of a successor will not be a pleasant thought—notwithstanding which, pray think about it in time– Otherwise you will be vexed & disturbed more than you need be. It is quite right that your Martha sh.ᵈ marry a gardener. I like *that* very much. There is *symmetry* in it!––

M.ʳ Townsend too is married.¹¹ My particular sofa in Wimpole St most properly derives its genealogy from the tripod. *Dont tell him so*—*now mind you dont*—but *really* a vision of his Ladye love when I knew nothing of the existence of one, did pass between my eyes and the verses of his lady-poet!¹² Have you seen her?—and what are your thoughts? A spirit, pleasant to meet with, moved thro' those verses, besides the poetic *feeling* assuredly contained in them—but they failed in proving to my mind the being of the poetic faculty—and this I confessed to M.ʳ Townsend, nothing daunted by the vision! I was going to praise him for not being angry—but I wont. Perhaps he was—and at any rate a Tempter of his order deserves no praise. Just the same ploughshare had I walked over twice before. First in the case of a cousin of mine who asked me what I thought of a gentleman whom we both knew. I said—"Very amiable & of no common ability—but of a fidgetiness both in conversation & manner which spoils everything with the idea of *littleness*". A like question—something like— came to me from a friend whom I esteemed . . 'What do you think of M.ʳ Newnam's [*sic*] preaching'—and my answer was to the effect that if I were HE I w.ᵈ not preach at all. In both these instances was my innocence abused!—the fidget & the preacher being betrothed at the time of the questions to the questioners.[13] Was'nt it too bad dearest Miss Mitford?— yes, and just as bad in your M! Townsend as in the rest!——

Will you tell me what I have been doing? Indeed I mean what I say. M! T. K. Hervey of whom I know nothing except that he sometimes writes very sweet & rather effeminate verses, wrote to me a little time ago in very great haste & equal courtesy, to request a contribution from me to some imperial quarto, splendidly illustrated, which he further described as of an annual character & yet no annual, & graced with a noble train of contributors– All this he said—without naming its name. I sent him a little poem 'A Sabbath on the sea', too grave for an annual– Nevertheless a proof sheet of it arrived in company with his thanks. And now I only want to know what I have done. Can you tell me the title of this mysterious imperial volume?[14] If it is worth anything you are probably a contributor. I do trust you are—just for *my* sake!

Dont laugh at me for not knowing what I have done. Do *you* always know what *you* do?– Is there anybody in the world likely to say 'no' when you offer them flowers from your garden? What with the flowers & what with the associations, there is no escape for you—and to illustrate all this, M!ˢ Hedley is quite delighted & ready to be grateful for any seed or cutting which your kindness grants to her. And as for me I shall delight in seeing them in her garden—& do thank you again & again for this exercise of your art of giving pleasure, She is very kind & affectionate to me, and has a countenance & a character like one another in being full of sweetness. Her little daughter *Ibbit* Jane as she calls herself, is the Elizabeth Jane H—of some verses in my book—and the very dream of a lovely child—with golden hair drooping in long ringlets below her waist, & cheeks reddened with their own smiles.[15] Yesterday she was four years old—and when many more years were wished to her, she said with great animation "You are *very* welcome!" Such an imaginative little talker I never listened to—& she cant move her lips to say a word, without two or three smiles at least! And yet when the other day she brought me a miniature of her brother[16] at school, asking if I did not think it like *her*, & when I (of course) thought it "far too pretty for *that*", she did stand grave for a moment, & incredulous besides– "Why Ibbit! *do* you think you are as pretty as Robin is?" "Yes! *I* think *me* is the prettiest"— "But how can you judge? you cant see your own face"— She looked in mine with a very droll expression .. "Tant I look in the glass, Ba"—and then turning away with a smile half sly & half penitent, her *aside* was "Vain Wady"!!——

We are going from the kindness of this house next week—to 3 Beacon Terrace which is considered the warmest situation I could

No. 664 [25 September 1838]

occupy—& there my aunt from Frocester will come to pass the winter with my sister & myself.

Dearest Miss Mitford, I send—I venture to send—a little Devonshire cream, although you wont tell me whether you & Dr Mitford like it at all. If either of you do I shall be so glad.

If ignorant people are allowed to think, *I* think that Wisdom Barrett was the son of Papa's uncle.[17] I *think* he was.

My God bless you my beloved friend. I must not write any more, though with a hundred reasons for wishing to do so. You shall not be uneasy again on account of a silence of mine!– And *you*—whenever writing to me is not an unkindness to yourself do remember that there is no other way so good of being kind to your

EBB–

I "remind you" to tell me all about Miss Landon's husband. I have a full conviction that he is the author of *Duty & Inclination*, of which I could only read the first volume. The reason of my conviction is, that it is unaccountable otherwise how Miss Landon could consent to edit & *praise* such--trash.[18] I tried in vain to think of some softer word which was also true. And besides there is a trace of Scotland in it. Is Dr Mitford quite well?– Forgive *my* trash--that is, wherever you can read it. Have you heard anything of dear Mr Kenyon & his fellow tourists? I quite quite agree with you about him—& with my full & grateful & admiring knowledge not only of his intellect but of his heart, I often look at him in a sad wonder, that he sh.^{d} use & wear both as if they were common clay!—— I do not say--"how can he choose it?"—but "how can he endure it?"

I sh.^{d} indeed like very much to see Miss Anderdon's sketch of your garden. Dearest Miss Mitford, why dont you understand that it is for your sake that your friends wish kindly about me. But I should not be, & I am not, *less* grateful to them on that account.

Here are *four* letters in *one*!——

Address, on integral page: Miss Mitford / Three Mile Cross / Near Reading.
Publication: EBB-MRM, I, 92–97.
Manuscript: Wellesley College.

1. Dated by EBB's reference to the proof sheet of "A Sabbath on the Sea," mentioned in SD945.
2. The physician attending EBB in Torquay was Dr. Robert Fitzwilliam De Barry Barry (d. 1839).
3. From the context it is apparent that Miss Mitford had suggested that EBB approach Talfourd and ask him to frank her letters to Miss Mitford. He was M.P. for Reading.
4. Dryden, "Alexander's Feast" (1697), line 78.
5. Mary Anne, Viscountess Sidmouth (1783–1842), the daughter of Lord Stowell, was the second wife of Henry Addington, 1st Viscount Sidmouth (1757–1844). She was a friend of Miss Mitford.

6. John Abernethy (1765–1831) was an eminent surgeon and medical author. Despite a "vigorous and attractive personality," he was notorious for his "rudeness and even brutality of manner" (*DNB*).

7. Underscored four times.

8. Elizabeth, Lady Holland (*née* Vassall, 1770–1845) had formed an adulterous relationship with Henry Richard Fox, 3rd Baron Holland, which led to her divorce from Sir Godfrey Webster; she and Lord Holland were then married. Holland House, a centre for literary and political figures of the day, had a wide reputation for brilliant conversation and sumptuous entertainment.

9. EBB has taken "therefore" from the version of the 23rd Psalm contained in *The Book of Common Prayer* ("therefore can I lack nothing") and added it to the biblical text ("I shall not want"). However, neither version uses the adjective "silent"; *The Book of Common Prayer* has "the waters of comfort" and the Bible "the still waters."

10. We cannot identify the first of these friends; the second was Martha, her maid, who was about to marry Miss Mitford's gardener, John Lediard.

11. "Mr. Townsend, too is going to be married—a second marriage—he being a widower of seven and thirty—and to a poetess—a Miss Shepherd, of the neighbourhood of Frome" (Chorley, I, 157).

12. Miss Shepherd had published *Illustrations of the Scripture, the Hebrew Converts, and Other Poems* (1837).

13. Francis William Newman (1805–97), the youngest brother of John Henry, Cardinal Newman (1801–90). His religious beliefs were not in sympathy with those of his more famous brother: after first embracing Calvinism, he later abandoned that in favour of Theism. He was the author of several religious and philological works. His betrothed was Maria Kennaway, whom he married in 1834. The cousin of whom EBB speaks was probably Arabella Butler, who had married Allen Ralph Gosset in 1835.

14. Thomas Kibble Hervey (1799–1859), poet and editor, had contributed to magazines and annuals. EBB's "A Sabbath on the Sea" appeared in *The Amaranth: A Miscellany of Original Prose and Verse*, which he edited. Although dated 1839, the volume was published on 12 October 1838.

15. Elizabeth Jane ("Ibbit") Hedley (b. 1834). EBB had addressed "A Song Against Singing" to "My Dear Little Cousin Elizabeth Jane H———" (*The Seraphim*, pp. 318–320).

16. Robert ("Robin") Hedley (d. 1912).

17. Wisdom Barrett (1729–98) was EBB's father's great-uncle; his son was Samuel Wisdom Barrett, to whom EBB probably is referring.

18. *Duty and Inclination* (1838) was advertised as "A New Novel Edited By Miss Landon," but the author was Mme. de Grandrion, not Miss Landon's husband George Maclean.

---

665. GEORGE BARRETT HUNTER TO EBB

Ax[mins]t[e]r
Sept. 26.th/38

Dearest & ever dearer Friend—. If I thought you would be grieved by telling you that I am, I would not tell you so. In every other case than this, I believe I know that your kindness & sympathy would make you sorry with me in my sorrows— Yet in this case let me presume that you will not be grieved, because I am so, for having GRIEVED YOU. To give you any pain at any time, is a thought exceedingly distressing—how much more exceedingly so, must the thought be of in the least degree grieving you NOW![1] Be most assured my dearest Friend that I was most utterly unconscious of having written in my last anything unkind— And I am at this moment quite unable to remember or imagine to what you refer by "hard thoughts" and "silence" called "ingratitude". Dearest Friend there *must* be some mistake here. Have I left out, in hurried writing, some word or words, and by such an omission, entirely altered the intended expression or did I write so unintelligibly that you have mistaken some word, for it's very opposite? I beseech you to tell me from *what* you derived the impression that I had "hard thoughts"—and was "angry"—and deemed your silence "ingratitude"! for my most laborious recollections do not furnish me with the slightest surmize. All was the contrary! As to *silence* there was *none*—and if there had been, I should have ascribed it to your fatigue & feebleness—and to your kind effort to comply with a repeated request of mine, *not* to write, when doing so would in the least degree fatigue you—— And for such a silence (out of its cause) I should have been *grateful*—as one wh. spared you from an injurious exercise. O, my ever kindest & dearest Friend! how COULD I ever associate "ingratitude" and YOU? It is in *many* ways *utterly* IMPOSSIBLE—and I am altogether bewildered & astonished. Had I ever made such an association—my very consciousness would become a shuddering self disgust—and I should wear away in the wretchedness of having impaired—yea, of having deservedly & for ever forfeited a regard wh. is dearer to me than that of all the world besides— Did you think me angry when I was but joking about the D[r] or at least very nearly joking? The only expressions wh. I can remember as giving occasion perhaps to the view you took of my temper in my last letter, are those about "*Aristocracy.*" Could my dearest Friend, imagine that they referred, even in the remotest manner, to *Her*?! Does She remember having once jocosely but truly applied the term to the moral or mental temperament of a certain friend of Her's? He took the application, as he felt it, to be a true one—and regard[d] it as one proof that She knew him— And the knowledge wh. it intimated, from some cause or other, *pleased* him. He does not know that he ever referred to the matter, before he did so in a late letter, in wh. he said something wh. some foolish sensitive imagination suggested, but wh. could not in any possibility refer to *Her*.— But after all, I do, on several accounts, most sincerely & painfully regret that I ever used those expressions—and I do most anxiously & affectionately ask your forgiveness. I assure you—that I had no feeling while writing them that suggested they would grieve you—if I had had, would they have been there! O. no! Will you pardon them for the MOTIVE'S sake? *I wanted to see you.*

I fully understood, just as I do now, the suggestion about delaying a certain journey—I fully understood it in all its gentleness & kindness—and it was as *wise* as it was kind & gentle—but if it were so, that I foolishly imagined an obstacle (altogether apart from your own wishes) and wrote nonsense, Aristocracy—forgive it, my dearest Friend—for *I wanted to see you*.— But I am sure you will wish me to leave this subject—and I will do so.—— I need not inform you that I received your parcel this morning. I cannot tell you—therefore imagine, how I thank you—and prize the unwearied kindness wh. sent it. I am almost reluctant to touch on its contents now I have so little room left. That "*Sabbath on the Sea*" is most beautiful & dear—and *it* too is MINE. I cannot, may not tell you how & what I intensely feel of your kindness—while I call that and others—*Mine*—and the feeling is so intense as it is because *you* taught me to call them *so*— "The Romaunt"—if there could be brighter & warmer and purer tears than Miss Mitford's—or admiration more worthy than that of Walter Scott's most intimate friends—it is worthy of them—and would give more honor than it would receive .. (Do expressly and affectionately thank dear Henrietta, for me, for having written out the former) *The Reviews*— It was like Bulwer to perceive "sublimity," "natural grace" and "etherial beauty"—and to tell of "pure & lustrous gems" and "perfect models."[2]— "Christopher's Cave" was a little too gloomy when he wrote of "OUR ELIZABETH"!!![3]— Critics of Her Seraphim should be judges in Eyre[4] (ie in one, perhaps the least correct etymology of the term) (I appeal to the Templar). To write of Seraphim in a *Cave!* I am vexed to find that Christopher uses some expressions like—nay the very same as those of the Atlas. Yet he has written some things truly & beautifully. His predictions *have now* their beauty— may the future give them *truth*. You know *what* predictions I mean— One of them is of "*conspicuous splendour.*"[5] Besides he writes with a certain devoutness wh the rest of your critics want.— (By the way—the spirit of *our* poor "Sea-mew" will be jealous of "The Doves."-)[6]————— This is Wed^{dy} evening and it is probable that I shall see your Brother. Yet I fear the probability is not much for there will be no coach from Exeter till 1/2 past eleven. I shall meet it however. How glad I shall be to meet *him*. I heard from Mary to day. You shall *see* her letter. She says "*Papa* is going to Newcastle" &c and talks about the house being "turned onto its chimneys" before he comes back again. She tells me of "a BEAUTIFUL *Polar Bear*" in the Z. Gardens—and asks permission to *ride on the Elephant* the next time she goes.— She says of Miss Trepsack that she likes her (Miss T.) very much indeed—and that she is "a kind *lovely* old lady."— She has a very poetical passage about the Harrow cemetary—part of it runs thus. "I wish Carissima-Ba could see it. I am sure she would write such eloquent Poetry—as well as YOURSELF."[7] I commend the compliment & the Grammar to your especial admiration.— "The dear little Doves have had a young one—and all are doing well." She speculates about coming back in *May!!* Her epistle contains Latin, French & Italian—so you see what Carissimabella[8] is making of her.

I thank you for transcribing so much of dearest Bella's account of Mary—but have I written thus far without a word about your *health*—my dearest Friend?— I fear the best news only amounts to—much as usual. I have constantly hoped & prayed that the change of climate might prove decidedly beneficial before this— I yet hope & pray—and feel the consolation of commending you to the tenderest care—and the recovering mercy of Him who so mercifully cares for you. Dont dont I beseech you give way to anxieties & regrets about leaving your beloved ones in London. Their beautiful & precious love! I thank you for the view you have given me of it .. O! how could it be but what it is! Do let the cheerfulness & gratitude wh. such love demands prevail over the painfulness of being removed for a while from the scene in wh. its fulness gathered round you .. May you my most beloved Friend soon be restored to all its endearments—in health—happiness and all the blessedness of *His love* who "giveth His beloved sleep."[9]— As you love *them*, try to make us cheerful by your cheerfulness. Forgive me if I have written to you in some cases too cheerfully—but *our* darling Bella charged me to be very cheerful with you. How could I—how *could* I be *angry* and have "*hard thoughts.*"— *Tell* me that it is *not*—that it *never can be so.*— I wrote yesterday to your Brother—for I was very anxious to hear of you. I am almost fearful lest I should have said any thing to grieve you. Give to him & Mr Geo. and to dear Henrietta my kindest regards. Dr Smith[10] said nothing whatever to me in his letter that could unfold the secret—but of course I know or conjecture *now* what it is. By the way how surely *Woman can* keep a secret!— How glad I shall be to hear that you have entered on your own cottage. Regard it as a temporary & merciful *home*— May it abound with mercies in the fulness of wh you shall return to your own dearer home.

Your ever most affecte friend,
G B H.

1/2 past 12. I have been to meet the Coach, but I found no one in it who had seen you a few hours ago. It would have been a great pleasure to have seen them—but it is a greater to think they are with you. I prophesy that your beloved Bro will be appointed your guardian at Torquay. It *should be so*. It is more than midnight and my thoughts remind me that you have never told me whether you sleep well at night.—

Thursday Morn^g 27.th

I have a few minutes this morning to add a few lines. Neither my waking nor dreaming thoughts during the night have dissolved yesterday's mystery and yet I rose with a surmise that my dearest Friend must have absolutely mistaken my *jocoseness* for ANGER (about the *hard thoughts*, I can win no hint either from light or darkness.) Is it possible that my abruptness in some sayings about the D^r was mistaken for snappishness and anger—when positively it was my object to make you laugh at them— By the way I do think that there were some criticisms of a similar character in my last letter to Bro—criticisms on a critic of yours—and I fear that you will become still surer than you were before about my having turned to a sad ill natured mood since my Guardian Angel left me;[11] well I will give up this trying to make you laugh– I am the *beautiful White Polar Bear* trying to dance & sing for your amusement—and you take it for a growling passion– Ah my Friend I assure you that mine is no mood of merriment—a far other mood is mine. Well forgive it all. Mary tells me that you go onto the sea every day almost– And she says too (wh I pray you observe) that you have not yet granted her request to be made Lady of your study chamber. After writing a letter fuller if possible than this—she hopes in the *last line* that I will excuse her for not writing any *more* as she was going to write to you. There is *such* a passage about Mr Boyd! She says that great Greek scholars can talk a great deal of nonsense (pray observe that) and that as for Mr Boyd he does not know where Madagascar is. Good bye again.

Address, on integral page: Miss Barrett / (———Hedley's Esqr.) Braddon's Hill / Torquay.
Publication: B-GB, pp. 350–354.
Manuscript: Pierpont Morgan Library.

1. Underscored three times.
2. His review of *The Seraphim* in *The Monthly Chronicle* (August 1838, p. 195) included this passage: "The combination of sublimity—suggested, but not developed—of natural grace and ethereal beauty in this production, may be at once admitted as a favourable evidence of the poetical temperament of the writer. There are some passages in this sketch of unusual delicacy, and, on the other hand, many feeble and affected lines. In the same volume there are several minor pieces, which, though less ambitious in design, are more perfect in execution. The more simple of these are indeed gems equally pure and lustrous; and in them every lover of poetry must find delight, and every student of poetry a model." (For the full text, see p. 385.)
3. *Blackwood's Edinburgh Magazine* (August 1838, pp. 279–284) devoted the major part of an article, "Christopher in his Cave" (by John Wilson, the editor, but unsigned), to a review of *The Seraphim*. The passage EBB refers to occurs after Wilson has made reference to other authoresses: "And our Elizabeth—she too is happy—though in her happiness she loveth to veil with a melancholy haze the brightness of her childhood—and of her maidenhood—but the clouds we raise we can ourselves dispel—and far away yet beyond the horizon are those that may gather round the decline of her life." (For the full text, see pp. 379–382.)
4. The Judges in Eyre were itinerant judges, travelling on circuit to hear cases. They were made redundant in the 14th century by the introduction of Justices of Assize.

5. In his review, Wilson predicted that EBB would "some day shine forth with conspicuous splendour."
6. "My Doves," one of the minor poems in *The Seraphim*, was quoted in full by Wilson.
7. Underscored three times.
8. i.e., Arabella Moulton-Barrett, with whom Hunter's daughter Mary was staying.
9. Psalms, 127:2.
10. John Pye Smith (1774–1851), who had recently visited EBB (see letter 659).
11. i.e., his daughter Mary, now in London.

---

666. EBB TO ARABELLA MOULTON-BARRETT & MARY HUNTER

[Torquay]
Thursday. [27 September 1838][1]

My beloved Arabel *do pray* write, & dont wait for me to do it. I have not paid "five shillings for letters" one day since I went away from you, and all last week you kept your words to throw to Resolute[2] I suppose without any compassion for other poor dogs at a greater distance. Henry's Austrian officer never waited so impatiently under the German lady's window as I do for a letter from home[3] .. and if you could but imagine to yourself how it is with me here, with the disconsolate kind of feeling which the consciousness of distance from you all *fastens* upon me, you w^d not let three days pass without writing. And now dearest Brozie & dearest Georgie are going away—& tomorrow—I scarcely dare to think of it! These partings are *dyings*. But I sh^d not be ungrateful for the longer than hoped for pleasure they *have* kept near us here—and *you* will feel glad in having them back with you again, & *I* do indeed too dearly love you, not to be glad in any possible gladness of yours!——

They will if they speak the truth give you a very hopeful account of my health—notwithstanding the leeches & blister I have been visited by within the last few days, & other threatenings of the same kind. Dr Barry said to me yesterday unasked—"I think that your chest is certainly better"—and the expectoration (tho' I could not rely too much on anything which has proved itself to be so fluctuating) continues diminished down to *very little indeed*. The pulse is much lower—I am not stronger. And as I am still taking digitalis (it was a mistake to say in my letter to Papa that I had left it off) the only wonder is that I am not very very much weaker than is actually the case. As far as I can judge, Dr Chambers's medecines have been continued with but little variation—only the digitalis is given more continuously—& the blister &c applied without any particular call for it. Now mind!—you are not to fancy that I am in the least worse if you hear any more of blisters. D! Barry made up his mind from the first I believe that he w.^{d} give me plenty of them—& the better I declare myself, the firmer becomes his resolve. He provokes me sometimes into a fever notwithstanding his digitalis. And yet it may be ungrateful & foolish of me—for really he does take most incessant pains, & everybody says with a corresponding ability, to do me good—and doing good does not always mean in this world, giving pleasure. You see I had made up a hope of my own, encouraged by D! C's permission, to manage here without medical visits, & to trust simply to God's sun & air as the means of accomplishing whatever mercy He intended for me. So that I had the less ready patience for certain persecutions—& for not being allowed to write or read or eat or drink or go out or stay in, or put on my stockings, without a certificate from D! Barry. And really it has come to this.

Now fancy—on the occasion of my writing case being accidentally visible—"Have you been writing today Miss Barrett". "No"- "Did you write yesterday?" "Yes". "You will be so good as not to do so any more".!!—— And again— "You have observed my directions & been idle lately Miss Barrett?" "Yes". "And within these last three weeks you have never written any poetry?" The remembrance of M! T K Hervey kept me silent.[4] "Well then! I may as well take my leave! I have told you the consequence. You must do as you please; but if you please to do this, neither I nor anyone else can do anything for you". And then there are flannel waistcoats up to the throat—& next the skin—& most of the most disagreeable things you can think of besides .. provided that you happen to be particularly imaginative *while* you think!——

Thank you my own dearest Arabel for writing that Papa might consent to Bro's staying. He *did* consent—but plainly against his own wish—and as dear Bro's individual opinion was that he would do better in returning to London, I had not the bravery to urge him to stay—indeed I should have had no happiness in keeping him when he evidently would please dearest Papa better by going. And so much, so very much has been granted to me that I felt myself wrong in writing for another sacrifice to my bare convenience, & Papa felt it too even while ready to oblige me. At the same time it is a worse pain to part with Brozie now, from there being a *possibility* of keeping him. I almost wish there had been a downright no!—but this is ungrateful of me!——

They will tell you that Henrietta, Crowe & I go next week to Beacon Terrace.[5] I wish you w.^{d} write every morning, so that you may seem to be there too before YOUR TURN COMES. From Bummy I heard this morning—and she will not be able to join us before the second or third week in October—so that we & D! Barry of course!!! will be there many days by ourselves. Now do remember every one of you. There is room!!

No. 666 [27–28 September 1838] 93

Dear Jane means to keep us here until Thursday; but we certainly shall not wait longer before leaving this hospitable house—on account of the nearness of winter. I had a fourth letter from Miss Mitford two days ago, begging for a word of answer which has gone at last! and one day ago Mr Hunter wrote to Bro praying for the same. So you will understand how abominably I have behaved lately even to those whom I most care for—& will give up your very foolish scheme of expecting letter for letter. The truth is, that for the most part—the halves of my days have been wearying ones thro' getting up—& the other halves, with going out—and then lately this dreary digitalis makes one far more inclined to cry than to write. Yesterday I began to inhale something--*what*, Dr Barry WONT[6] tell me for I asked him twice & was answered each time by an evasion. Nothing to strengthen me!–

Tell us everything about everybody—*us* meaning Henrietta & me. I never *show* your letters & so you may open your heart! My beloved Arabel, mine rejoices whenever I think of our darling Mary's being with you, because I am sure you must be cheerful in her cheerfulness of which I am sure besides! Tell me more about her– Tell me whether you make her practice, as to music—and whether the drawing goes on—& whether you have taken her to the coliseum .. *That* reminds me of Westminster Abbey & Mr Boyd. Thank you for interposing your shadow between him & the Sunbeams! I would not have had such a letter written for the whole world![7]—and although abundantly grateful for being shone upon so benignantly, the more silent the gratitude, the better! Miss Mitford says "not merely the truest review but the ablest"—which is *not* true. She is very much out of spirits, because *Martha* is going to be married!—to a gardener—& about to remove from her neighbourhood. Nevertheless she has time to think of little kindnesses & to propose sending some seeds cuttings &c to Jane's garden that I might see the planting!– I shall not see it—but Jane is too pleased at the idea of having them, for me not to respond thankfully & acceptingly to the kind proposal.

Dearest Arabel, I am very glad that you know better & like the Bazelgettes[8]– Dont forget to take Mary to see Mr Stratten's children when they return. *Are* the Strattens returned? Tell me. And if they are give my kind regards to M^r & Mrs Stratten when you next speak to either. It is a pleasant placed hope to me that I shall get out beside you in the chapel at Paddington & hear with you what we used to hear so delightedly—with the same words of prayer & gladness upon our lips: It is a pleasant hope—but an earthly one after all. And on such hopes we should lean lightly. The reed will pierce if it flower or not—for if the dew of heaven fall on it or not, its root being in the earth, it is a reed for *piercing!*——

How blessed it is to look up & know that as God's sky is over the city & the fields, so is God's love!- Pray for me my own dear Arabel!- I know you do & will--that I may feel more continually & distinctly the omnipresence of His love—& let us both remember that while you are praying for me, & I for you, we must still pray *together!*——

Thursday night.

Thank you my own ever dear Arabel for your letter. So I am *forced* to keep Bro! But Georgie wont be kept--*will* go tomorrow morning--& indeed I am half angry with him & *whole* disappointed! it is so very very kind of my beloved Papa to let Brozie stay—& *his* face is as bright to hear of it (almost) as mine—& that is as bright as can be. His presence is not *necessary* in the strict sense of that word; perhaps no happiness IS; but besides the sorrow it will save me from,—between you & me the "officiating chairman" was only *less* disagreeable that [*sic*] the officiating Dr Barry w^d have been, who *did* actually lament his being prevented by an engagement from taking Bro's place on the day of his absence at Sidmouth!! There was a great fuss about the boat that day. I yielded to Jane's *entreaty* to go—but it was *so* disagreeable,—tho' less so than it might have been—that Bro's going away looked more horrible than ever. And they WOULDNT let me walk!-

Tell my dearest Minny & your dearest self not to be uneasy about digitalis or anything else--*now Bro is going to stay!*—without a joke do believe me to be better in essential things. As to your fancy about the pulse & pain in my side I do assure you that the perseverance has *not* been caused by an increase in either—but by a resolution to prevent that certain excitability which has you know from the first hung about the system. Therefore is it determined that I sh^d take digitalis & not write poetry. I might have deceived you if I had pleased by being silent—& in return for all this openness, you are BOUND[9] to believe my assurance that neither for digitalis (except occasionally) nor for leeches nor for blister has there been a necessity—but an advisability in D^r B's opinion, in order to subdue the *complaint*--not any new or worse development of it. He has fixed upon the very spot upon the left side of the chest which Dr Chambers did, as the locality of the complaint—which appears as if he knew something. Everybody says he knows everything. Tell dear Minny that as to missing my medicine he w^d as soon *miss a day in coming here* as let me do it. I have no chance. He not only asks "Have you taken your medicines today?" . . & "How often have you taken your medicine today?"—but he counts the bottles to see that they are regularly emptied. So that I sh^d be forced into a double iniquity—into upsetting *them* . . & telling *him* a story. Tell dear Minny the truth—that I did mean & do wish to write to her! but it is so late & I have told you everything & she will forgive me this time!

Oh my darling Mary how I delight to hear of you & from you! Write yourself & make Bella write! Her observation about postages & purses, I do not reply to—not having a pistol by me. It is an insult. Of course the little dove which came on purpose for you, is yours!—— Always let me hear of the doves—& do take care of my 'untidy' room! Dont love Bella more than a mile more than me!—— Your father wrote a very angry kind letter to Bro to enquire if we were all alive—& I have written to him—& Georgie will see him tomorrow—& we are likely to see him very soon– At least I *imagine* that we are likely to do so!—— God bless you darling Mary!—— Make Bella laugh hard all day!——

            Your ever affectionate
            Ba.

Will Georgie really go today (Friday morn^g) I am sitting up in bed wondering & wishing perhaps vainly about it.

Send two chickens & the smallest tin case to Trippy—& one chicken to poor old Mrs Nuttall.[10] The other three & larger case of Devonshire cream is for you. I believe some of you like it (does not Stormie?) with apple tart—& I dont insist upon its commixture with your coffee!——

We shall not go, I think, to Beacon Terrace (called Beacon from Beacon Hill--the wooded one above it) until Thursday. I have heard at last from Bummy who cant come until the second or third week in Oc^{ber} & wont, in my opinion, until the very end of the month.

My own dearest Bella, I never forget *your* turn!—& you need not wait for Mr Kenyon you know, with escorts all round you. Do you think (because I some times dream it) that Papa will bring you himself? But then he is coming very soon—I dare say immediately on his return from the north. Almost his last words to me were a promise (unasked for) that he w^d see me sooner than I expected—& in his letters since he has mentioned this journey to the north as something that must necessarily precede his coming here.

Do give Mr Boyd my love—& tell him that I will write soon to him.

        Your own ever *ever* attached Ba.

⟨Is it not *very wrong* of Daisy? I am so ...⟩[11]

Tell me of Mr Patch. Sette & Joc[12] why dont you write to me? And then there is dearest Stormie & Henry--why dont you write to me?– I think of you every one--one by one--all y^r faces & kindnesses. I love you more than ever & pray God to bless you!——

The poor Russells——

Say how you are my dearest Arabel—& all of you. How are Minny's legs?——

The blister was kept on 12 hours– It was covered with silver paper— & is not *very* sore, tho' quite sufficiently so.

Pray beg Henry not to go to Boulogne or Botany bay while Papa is absent. Open the parcel containing the Amaranth.[13] It is for Papa.

Address, on integral page: Miss Arabel Barrett. / 50 Wimpole Street / London.
Publication: None traced.
Manuscript: Berg Collection.

1. Dated by the impending move to Beacon Terrace.
2. One of the dogs belonging to EBB's brothers Henry and Charles John; EBB later described him as "an Alpine mastiff."
3. We cannot explain this reference, beyond suggesting that it must deal with an incident that occurred during Henry Moulton-Barrett's tour of Germany and Switzerland.
4. See letter 664.
5. No. 3 Beacon Terrace had been leased from 1 October at £180 per annum (see SD943).
6. Underscored three times.
7. An extensive discussion of EBB's works to date (*An Essay on Mind, Prometheus Bound,* and *The Seraphim*) appeared in five numbers of *The Sunbeam* (1 September 1838, p. 243; 8 September, pp. 254–255; 22 September, pp. 269–270; 6 October, p. 287; and 13 October, pp. 293–295; for the full text, see pp. 387–400). According to Mrs. Orme, the reviewer was a Mr. Frank, "a person of no celebrity" (see SD945). From the context, it seems that Boyd was ruffled by something in Frank's remarks, and had contemplated writing to the magazine, but was dissuaded by Arabella.
8. The family of Louis Bazalgette, living at 1 Pembroke Terrace, St. John's Wood.
9. Underscored three times.
10. The mother of George Ricketts Nuttall, the doctor who had attended EBB in London prior to Dr. Chambers. She had been very friendly with EBB's paternal grandmother, the Nuttalls also having a Jamaican background.
11. Slightly more than one line scored over in an unidentified hand.
12. Octavius Moulton-Barrett. Mr. Patch is identified in SD993 as a tutor to Septimus and Octavius.
13. See letter 664, note 14.

---

667. MARY RUSSELL MITFORD TO EBB

Three Mile Cross,
Sept. 20 [*sic,* for ?29], 1838.[1]

Ten thousand thanks, my dear young friend, for the clouted cream, that pastoral luxury, which is so welcome to me, because my father is so fond of it. I am not myself suffered to partake of the delicacy, but what my father enjoys is more than enjoyment to me, and it is mere selfishness that makes it so. I love to feed Flush even, and to see my tame pigeons feed at the window, and the saucy hen tap the glass, if the casement be shut. She likes to come in and to sit on the innermost ledge of the window-sill, and listen and turn her pretty top-knotted head to this side and that while I talk to her. This pleasure I owe to you, having taken to the homely pigeons as a rustic imitation of your doves, and they blend well with my flowery garden.

No. 667 [?29] September 1838

In spite of his physical debility, Mr. Thatcher is in no common degree *manly*;[2] and when I say this, and add that he is also mild and gentle, I say more for him than can be said for most of the "pen and ink" people, who are by very far the most effeminate class in existence. If it take nine tailors to make a man,[3] according to my calculation it would take nine authors to make a tailor.

I hope favourably for Miss Landon's marriage.[4] Dr. Buckland had seen (he told me) her husband, a little boyish-looking fair-haired Scotchman, but really thirty-six. He spoke well of him; and a story, which I will tell you, looks liberal and gentlemanly: Mr. Maclean was showing some rings of negro workmanship at a party, where he accidentally met Dr. Buckland,[5] and offered him a large and heavy one. "Not that," said Dr. Buckland, unwilling to accept so valuable a present; "give me one of the small and slight ones, for my wife or daughter." Upon which Mr. Maclean forced three rings upon him, the original and two of the slighter fabric. This looked well. The rings I saw, and they were beautiful. The things that go under Lady Stepney's *title* were all written over by Miss Landon, or the grammar and spelling would have disgraced a lady's maid.[6] This is a want of self-respect which one can not pardon; and, coupled with other facts of a similar nature, they explain my distaste toward her as a sister authoress.

Did I tell you that I have had accounts of Joanna Baillie, who was seventy-six on the 11th of this month?[7] She is losing her memory, and conscious of her loss. Heaven bless you, my ever dearest! Let me hear soon, soon.

Ever yours,
M. R. Mitford.

Address: Miss Barrett, Torquay.
Text: L'Estrange (2), III, 93-94.

1. As Miss Mitford is acknowledging the clotted cream sent by EBB with letter 664, this letter must be dated after 25 September; L'Estrange probably misread Miss Mitford's handwriting.

2. We have not been able to identify Mr. Thatcher.

3. A common expression derogating the physical abilities of tailors, but it has been suggested that "tailor" is a corruption of "teller," referring to the ancient custom of tolling the funeral bell three times for a child, six for a woman, and nine for a man.

4. See letter 651, note 13.

5. William Buckland (1784-1856), geologist and theologian, was a friend of Miss Mitford. He had written one of the Bridgewater Treatises (*The Power, Wisdom, and Goodness of God as Manifested in the Creation*) in 1836. He was a Fellow of the Royal Society and President of the Geological Society; he later (1845) became Dean of Westminster.

6. Catherine, Lady Stepney (d. 1845) had published two novels, *The Heir Presumptive* (1835) and *The Courtier's Daughter* (1838).

7. Joanna Baillie, playwright and poetess, had published *Miscellaneous Plays* in three volumes in 1836. She continued to write poetry until she was nearly 80, and died in 1851, aged 88.

668. EBB TO MARY RUSSELL MITFORD

3. Beacon Terrace
Wednesday. [10 October 1838][1]

Ever dearest Miss Mitford,
I wanted to write to you very very soon in reply to your last welcome note. I wanted to say to you very soon some words which it suggested. But I have been exceedingly unwell—confined to my bed nearly a week by a sudden return of bad symptoms & so weak since as scarcely to bear without fainting even the passive fatigue of being carried from this bed to the sofa down stairs, by all the gentleness of my brother's love for me. The prevalency of the east wind & sudden coldness of weather connected with it, are considered the causes of the attack- I was not suffered to write—& have only by mainforce written two post[s]cripts to two of Henrietta's many letters to London,—which I insisted upon doing because I knew that my writing & my *living* were ideas very closely associated in Wimpole Street. But *you*—I hope my beloved friend that another silence simply made you a *little cross* with me—& not uneasy. It is a disagreeable kind of hope—& I *indulge* in it (on the principle of a rustic friend of Papa's who always used to respond to his enquiry by--("Why Sir, I *enjoys* very bad health indeed") because almost anything is better than making you anxious, at a time too when you may be anxious enough without *me*. Henrietta proposed writing to you- I would not let her do it just to sadden you—& the physician here being very sure of my being better again, I dared making you think "she is not worth a thought" rather than the worse risk. The pulse is quiet now, & I can *sleep*—indeed the attack itself has quite passed away- And as to the weakness it is passing. From two days to two days I can perceive an increase of strength—and if it pleases God,—He has been *so* merciful!— in two or three weeks more I may be as strong as I was previous to the last pulling down.

My sister & brother & I removed to our present residence just in time—the very day before this illness. Since it, I could not have removed—and the difference between the Braddons & Beacon Terrace is all the difference between the coldest situation in Torquay & the warmest[2]—& my *body* was so ungrateful as to require another sun besides that of kind looks & words.

Here, we are immediately *upon* the lovely bay—a few paces dividing our door from its waves—& nothing but the "sweet south"[3] & congenial west wind can reach us—and *they* must first soften their footsteps upon the waters. Behind us—so close as to darken the back windows—rises an abrupt rock crowned with the slant woods of Beacon hill! and thus though the North & East wind blow their fiercest, we are in an awful silence & only guess at their doings.

The wind has changed now—and the gulf between autumn & winter or at least between the summer-part & winter-part of autumn is surely passed, & therefore no longer to be feared.

One thing I fear– Indeed I do—and so I will speak to you at once about it. In the first place my very dearest Miss Mitford, names that are worth gold & names that are worth nought cant be weighed in the same balance. Therefore the exclusive dedication of your name to the Tableaux could be no example to the nameless unless they were also modesty-less!– And then again there is a distinction between the office of an Editor & a contributor. I understand these two differences far too well to fancy even, that you meant a *word* in reference to *me* of what you said respecting your own resolve. But still when I had finished your note, I did fancy that you would—for some reason & perhaps for the simple one that you loved me—have preferred my having *not* written for M.̱ Hervey's annual.[4] Now this might just have been a fancy of mine--I am given to be tormented by such. But it has helped to make me restless, more restless than usual, in wishing to write to you.

I need not tell you my beloved & kindest friend that if the very shadow of a like fancy had crossed my mind before, my *no* sh.ᵈ have been said civilly to M.̱ Hervey. He wrote two letters—which in consequence of the difficulty he had had in finding my address reached me the same day,—to ask me, (not given you know to write for annuals) to send something to him for his. His request was made so very courteously & the making it seemed to have given him so much trouble, that I wrote down for him some stanzas, before floating about in my head, & sent them just for goodnature's sake--thinking no more of it, than if I had sent such to magazine or journal. Now if by a straw's breadth you had *rather* that I had not sent them, I shall most assuredly wish all the annuals—always excepting the great one—with M.̱ Hervey's ancestors! Not that I regard *them*—the ancestors--with *much* malice!

Do let me hear from you when you can write--*whenever* you can. I have *so* few pleasures!—and a few words from you bring many!– A true one to me was, that D.̱ Mitford liked the cream. He shall have some more. How is he? How are you? *Do* go on caring for me!——

Did Papa send you the last Sunbeam?[5] I hope so. They are "friendly beams" indeed,—& everybody who happens to see them, will be sure to think that we made them up among us in Wimpole Street. The editor wrote to me before I left London, begging to have the Prometheus & Seraphim sent to him for reviewing purposes– He had seen extracts from the latter & intended *an 'important essay upon my genius'*.[6] We had a good deal of laughing about it—and little did I anticipate being made such a "Sun's Darling" of!——[7]

Nothing yet of dear M.[r] Kenyon. I know nobody here--but the people seem very kind– M.[r] & M.[rs] Bezzi[8] have ceased to live here, & are I believe on the continent.

May God bless you! Do you write now—& what?—or are you resting from the Tableaux? Was M.[r] Chorley well or tolerably well, when you heard from him?——

Your always affectionate & grateful
E B Barrett.

Is anything *decided* about Martha?[9]

Publication: EBB-MRM, I, 100–103 (as [7 November 1838]).
Manuscript: Wellesley College.

1. Dated by the onset of EBB's relapse immediately after the move to Beacon Terrace on 1 October.
2. "The Braddons," the Hedleys' house, was on a hill overlooking Torquay, and thus was much more exposed than EBB's new quarters on the shore.
3. *Twelfth Night*, I, 1, 5. The usual reading is "sweet sound," although there had been much controversy over "sound" versus "south." Pope used the latter, and EBB follows his reading.
4. See letter 664, in which EBB asked Miss Mitford about Hervey.
5. EBB presumably refers to the most recent issue, that of 6 October.
6. The "important essay" appeared in five numbers of *The Sunbeam* (see letter 666, note 7).
7. *The Sun's Darling* was the title of a play, published in 1656, by John Ford and Thomas Dekker.
8. Giovanni Aubrey Bezzi, an Italian, had fled to England because of his association with the Silvio Pellico plot and the Carbonari, a secret political organization. He was a friend of Kenyon, and was to be instrumental in the rediscovery in 1846 of a portrait of Dante, hidden for 200 years beneath whitewash in the Bargello in Florence (see L'Estrange (2), III, 126). EBB referred to him as being "very musical" and so popular that "he draws everybody after him like Orpheus" (letter to Miss Mitford of 23 September 1841).
9. i.e., about her marrying and leaving Miss Mitford's service.

---

669. EBB TO MARY RUSSELL MITFORD

[Torquay]
Oc.[t] 30.th [1838][1]

Oh my beloved friend, *who* less than yourself gives pain where she would give pleasure? What a wrong do you do to your "destiny"!

Was it not an inspired one who said "Miss Mitford diffuses happiness everywhere"—?[2] And is it not an experienced one (experienced believe me in gratitude as well as in kindness) who sets her seal to the verity of that inspiration?

It was very wrong of me to teaze you with my fancifulness & tremors. This is the only excuse I can find for the existence, much less the obtrusion of either upon you— Had there been no love, there could have been no such sins. I always feel so deeply & equally your affectionateness & my own unworthiness as contrasted with its brightness, that the very idea of offending or seeming to offend against the first in ever such a trifle—is as bad as an east wind to me— The "sweet south"[3] of your letter set me at ease.

I did not receive Finden immediately.[4] I had desired Papa to unpack & take possession of it—because I fancied (you will think 'What an immense deal of vanity there is in all her fancies'!) it might be a pleasure to him. From this arrangement I have scarcely finished my own vision of the beautiful volume, while you may well be wondering at the apparent unthankfulness of my silence. And indeed if silence means any harm I confess to having suffered a *coup de silence* from one of the first pages[5]— only the kind of *harm* cant be unthankfulness, for I was indeed my dearest kindest Miss Mitford, at once surprised & pleased & touched by the manner in which you named my ballad—there! I do not presume to tell you that it was too much for you to say—but I must feel that it w^d have been enough for *me*, if *either* my ambition or affections had been gratified— —without this gratification of both at once!——

Well! Let me apply my theory about "spoiling children" to your practise of spoiling *me*—& go on to maintain that nobody is injured by too much love!——

The volume is a very splendid one! As to your stories they are delightful.[6] You cut away the 'pound of flesh'[7] in vain—they *would not die*. Nor is it likely that they would for all your cruelty--being works of yours!— I dare say I helped with my fellow-poets & sinners to whet the knife—and yet it does console me to observe in the very passion of my remorse that *my* poem is NOT *the longest!*

Those poems which are, bear within them the atonement for much sin. Mr Townsend's he kindly sent me in the proofs[8]—& I was touched by its purity of beauty—& recognized in it a great increase of clearness & even of unity. I do however still think & ventured to say so to him, that his lovely thoughts are too fragmentary—that his parts do not suggest his whole. Thank you for the justice you did me in believing that I should admire Mr Hughes's ballad[9]—which dares to be natural & to stand free from conventionalisms. My own feelings & faults lean towards the *mystical* whether in poetry or philosophy—but I am not so far gone as to be unable to appreciate the practical—*particularly when* lit up partially with the moonshine of the ideal so as to alternate the 'ivory' with the 'ebony'–

They are coming to take away my pen. Mr John Chorley & Mr Henry Chorley--I liked both of them in prose & verse.[10]

Your tales should be spoken of when I write next. The Buccaneer & the Cartel mentioned in the Athenæum,[11] I pass over, not with an indifferent love, but because I care more for the Baron's daughter. Is it right or wrong to *do* so?– It *is* right to be very sure of the loss which all who care for beauty, sustained, by the cutting away you spoke of—and yet you are as surely wrong in imagining any substitution of "baldness for beauty" in consequence of anything!—you *are* surely. When I read your account it sounded bad & sad. It sounded as if your stories must be spoilt in such a process—& I never felt so cross with poets before—"A poet! oh! base".[12] And then too, the crossness was not improved by a consciousness of utter powerlessness as to critics—by a certainty of not being able to *"explain"* a word of the matter to any critic much greater than Sette. I dont know one of them—not one. Nor do I know a person who knows one—except your own self & M:r Kenyon the wanderer—& as to my "friend of the sunbeam", altho' he *has* been friendly to a wonderful degree, & altho' he *has* a name I suppose, I cannot guess what it is.[13] Well! but reading the stories put out of my head all the bad & sad thoughts. They have enough in them to propitiate the critics, without explanations—& for my own part I prefer them to those of last year. Do you observe that M:r Fo[r]ster who found fault with you then for not keeping among the lanes, cant help being pleased now in meeting you anywhere?[14] Indeed the whole volume seemed to take a higher place than the former one. The literal *Tableaux* are very very beautiful—I congratulate you my beloved friend.

I have had such a pleasing note from – – –you cant guess from whom– –M:r Townsend's *betrothed*[15]—but I cant tell you about it.

I am indeed grateful to the Athenæum. Will you say to M:r Chorley how it pleased me with its honor *un*due.[16]

There remains so much to say. I *cant* say it. May D:r Mitford like the cream—& may you be able to give me a good account of him. I am better—& what is better than being so, *Papa is with me*. Your letter was enclosed to me from London by those who knew that tho' I could wait for books & seeds, I could not for *that*. Thank you dearest Miss Mitford for the seeds– So kind it is in you!——

Ever your attached
EBB——

Publication: EBB-MRM, I, 97–100.
Manuscript: Wellesley College.

1. Year provided by the reference to *Findens' Tableaux*.
2. Landor's remark; see letter 582.
3. See letter 668, note 3.

4. *Findens' Tableaux of the Affections: a Series of Picturesque Illustrations of the Womanly Virtues*, in which EBB's poem "The Romaunt of the Page" was given first place, came out in late October 1838.
5. "Stunned silence." Its cause was Miss Mitford's description, in the preface to *Findens'*, of EBB's contribution as "best and dearest."
6. Miss Mitford contributed "The Buccaneer," "The Baron's Daughter," "The Cartel" and "A Story of the Woods."
7. *The Merchant of Venice*, IV, 1, 99. Miss Mitford had been forced to prune her own stories to keep within the prescribed number of pages for the volume. In a letter to Lucy Anderdon, 5 November 1838, she speaks of cutting the proofs "within an inch of their lives," adding that she preferred that course to risking "the damage I should have done to my contributors by cutting away their poetry" (Chorley, I, 159).
8. Townsend's contribution was "The Coronation."
9. "The Minstrel of Provence."
10. They contributed "The Treason of Gomez Arias" (poetry) and "The Sister of Charity" (prose) respectively. John Rutter Chorley (1807?–67), the brother of H.F. Chorley, was for some years secretary of the Liverpool-Birmingham Grand Junction Railway. He had devoted himself to the formation of a superb collection of Spanish dramas, many restored by himself; the collection was given to the British Library.
11. The review of 20 October 1838 (pp. 757–758) includes the comment: "There are few capable of writing such stories as 'The Buccaneer,' and 'The Cartel,' who would have been content to exhibit so self-denying a good taste."
12. Cf. Dryden, "The Fourth Satire of Persius" (1692, line 127).
13. See letter 666, note 7.
14. The reviewer (Forster) in *The Examiner* (28 October 1838, p. 677) refers to "poems of higher tone and aim than are usually found in embellished publications" and says of EBB's contribution that it is "a poem with the spirit of the elder and better day of poetry in every line of it—in truth, a very sweet and noble composition." (For the full text, see p. 405.) For his comments on the previous *Findens'*, see letter 596, note 6.
15. Miss Shepherd (see letter 664, note 11).
16. For the full text of Chorley's review, see pp. 375–378.

---

670. EBB TO MARY RUSSELL MITFORD

Torquay,
Friday, November 13 [*sic*, for 23], 1838.[1]

Whenever I forget to notice any kindness of yours, do believe, my beloved friend, that I have, notwithstanding, marked the date of it with a white stone,[2] and also with a heart *not* of stone...

You said "distribute the seeds as you please," so, mindful of "those of my own household,"[3] I gave Sept and Occy leave to extract a few very carefully for their garden, composed of divers flower-pots and green boxes a-gasping for sun and air from the leads behind our house, and giving the gardeners fair excuse for an occasional coveted colloquy with a great chief gardener in the Regent's Park. Yes, and out of a certain precious packet inscribed (as Arabel described it to me) *from Mr. Wordsworth*, I desired her to reserve some for my very own self, because, you see, if it should please God to permit my return to London, I mean ("pway don't waugh," as Ibbit says, when she has been saying something irresistibly ridiculous)—I mean to have a garden too—a whole flower-pot to myself—in the window of my particular sitting-room; and then it will be hard indeed if, while the flowers grow from those seeds, thoughts of you and the great poet may not grow from them besides.

Dearest, dearest Miss Mitford, pray never, *never* do tear up any old letter of yours for the sake of sending me a new one. Send old and new together. Postages upon *your* letters never can be thought of, and besides, my correspondents are not like yours, millions in the way of *number*. They in Wimpole Street knew my doxy upon such subjects too well to keep your letters back with the seeds. They did not *dare* to wait even a day for Papa's coming, but sent it at once to me, double as it was, and *in* a letter of Arabel's own, making a triple; and those "discerners of spirits"[4] at the post-office marked it (for all the thick paper) a *single letter*[5]—immortal essence not weighing anything.

I can tell you a very little of dear Mr. Kenyon. I have heard indirectly from my sister, who had only *heard* of his return to London. His poem in "Finden" has both power and sweetness,[6] and I have heard it preferred, though without an assent on my own part to such a preference, to his last more elaborate contribution.[7] It is, however, very *stirring* in some parts, and liking it in MS.—in which state he hardly allowed me to see it,—I like it still better now. Is not your "Baron's Daughter" much admired? It *ought* to be. There is a half-playfulness and half-sentiment which touch my fancy just where it lies nearest to my heart, besides the practical *good sense* (perhaps my sin may be to care something less for that) which Mr. Kenyon says "is always to be found in Miss Mitford's writings, in the very midst of their gracefulness." Yes, I have seen some kind opinions of my "Romaunt" in the *Chronicle*[8] and elsewhere. *You* set the kind fashion by overpraising it; and indeed the stiff-necked critics must have caught fresh cold not to be able to bow their necks to receive a tunic from your hands.

May the "Pilgrim's Rest" as constructed be worthy of the "Pilgrim's Rest" as composed. There must be a "meeting of the waters" in their brightness for the accomplishment of that wish.[9]

My beloved father has gone away; he was obliged to go two days ago, and took away with him, I fear, almost as saddened spirits as he left with me. The degree of amendment does not, of course, keep up with the haste of his anxieties. It is not that I am not better, but that he loves me too well; *there* was the cause of his grief in going; and it is not that

I do not think myself better, but that I feel how dearly he loves me; *there* was the cause of my grief in seeing him go. One misses so the presence of such as dearly love us. His tears fell almost as fast as mine did when we parted, but he is coming back soon—perhaps in a fortnight, so I will not think any more of *them*, but of *that*. I never told him of it, of course, but, when I was last so ill, I used to start out of fragments of dreams, broken from all parts of the universe, with the cry from my own lips, "Oh, Papa, Papa!" I could not trace it back to the dream behind, yet there it always was very curiously, and touchingly too, to my own heart, seeming scarcely *of* me, though it came *from* me, at once waking me with, and welcoming me to, the old straight humanities. Well! but I do trust I shall not be ill again in his absence, and that it may not last longer than a fortnight.

Have you seen the "Book of Beauty?"[10] There is in it a little poem very sweet and touching, the production of Miss Garrow, a young lady residing in this place.[11] I do not yet know her personally, but she is a friend of Mr. Landor and Mr. Kenyon, and I have heard from the latter high estimation of her genius—it was the word used,—and accomplishments both literary and musical. She has been very kind in sending me flowers and vegetables, but up to this day I have scarcely been fit for a stranger's visit. May God bless you,

Ever dearest Miss Mitford's
EBB.

Text: L'Estrange (1), II, 34–37.

1. In 1838, 13 November fell on a Tuesday, but the 23rd was a Friday. It seems probable that L'Estrange misread EBB's writing.
2. Cf. Cervantes, *The Ingenious Gentleman Don Quixote of La Mancha*, part II, chapter 10.
3. Cf. Proverbs, 31:27.
4. Cf. I Corinthians, 12:10.
5. Postage was paid on the basis of the number of sheets, as well as weight. As there were enclosures in EBB's letter from Wimpole Street, additional postage should have been assessed.
6. Kenyon's contribution was "The Greek Wife." He had just returned to England from his tour in France.
7. His contribution to the 1838 *Findens' Tableaux* was "The Shrine of the Virgin."
8. Reviewing *Findens' Tableaux*, *The Monthly Chronicle* (November 1838, p. 465) said "Two poems, one by Miss Barrett, and the other by Mr. Hughes, are works distinguished by poetical qualities of the highest order. They are both dipped in the hues of ballad minstrelsy. The 'Romaunt of the Page,' by Miss Barrett, is full of the early spirit of English poetry—quaint, simple, and pathetic." (For the full text of the review, see pp. 405–406.)
9. EBB's allusion is unclear; it may refer to a musical setting of Thomas Moore's ballad "The Pilgrim," the first line of the last verse of which reads "Where rests the Pilgrim now?" "The Meeting of the Waters," included in Moore's *Irish Melodies and Songs* (1807), referred to the confluence of the rivers Avon and Avoca, in Co. Wicklow.
10. The annual edited by Lady Blessington.
11. Theodosia Garrow (1825–65) had contributed two poems, "The Gazelles" and "On Presenting a Young Invalid With a Bunch of Early Violets," to Lady Blessington's

annual. EBB's comment makes it probable that she was referring to the latter poem. Miss Garrow later (1848) married Thomas Adolphus Trollope (1810–92) and they lived in Florence while EBB and RB were there.

671. EBB TO THEODOSIA GARROW

[Torquay]
[late November 1838][1]

I cannot return the *Book of Beauty* to Miss Garrow without thanking her for allowing me to read in it sooner than I should otherwise have done, those contributions of her own which help to justify its title, and which are indeed sweet and touching verses.[2]

It is among the vexations brought upon me by my illness, that I still remain personally unacquainted with Miss Garrow, though seeming to myself to know her through those who actually do so. And I should venture to hope that it might be a vexation the first to leave me, if a visit to an invalid condemned to the *peine forte et dure*[3] of being very silent, notwithstanding her womanhood, were a less gloomy thing. At any rate I am encouraged to thank Miss Fisher[4] and Miss Garrow for their visits of repeated inquiry, and their other very kind attentions, by these written words, rather than by a message. For I am sure that wherever kindness *can* come thankfulness *may*, and that whatever intrusion my note can be guilty of, it is excusable by the fact of my being Miss Garrow's

Sincerely obliged,
E. Barrett.

Text: What I Remember, T.A. Trollope, 1887, pp. 402–403.

1. Dated by Miss Garrow's gifts, mentioned in the previous letter.
2. See letter 670, note 11.
3. "Intense and severe punishment." A torture, not abolished until 1772, in which the accused was subjected to increasing pressure while placed between two boards.
4. Harriet Fisher (d. 1850) was Miss Garrow's half-sister, being the daughter of Mrs. Garrow's first marriage.

672. EBB TO GEORGE GOODIN MOULTON-BARRETT

[Torquay]
[late November 1838][1]

Ever dearest Georgie,

My gratitude has been *rankling sore* within me for very very long! And I am sure that your anxiety for my morals demonstrated by the advice accompanying your present,[2] must have been rankling within *you*—& that my silence has been suggesting to you the probability of this want of thankfulness being a symptom of a more general corruption of the moral sense. Acquit yourselves dearest Georgie & Beaumont & Fletcher. You are yet innocent of corrupting me—& I am innocent of being ungrateful to any one of you!– And though upon the appearance of the great poets I did feel properly indignant with the great lawyer for his breach of all consistency (except the consistency of his own dear always remembered kindness to me) yet the "blushing apparitions"[3] of my wrath owed most of their colour to a very glowing affection & gratitude which have not left me at this present writing. But really Georgie, I did think that you considered it very improper to give anything away! *I* at least, if I had done such a thing, sh^d never have heard the last of it.

You are obeyed to the letter. I jump over all the puddles—& when I stand upon the dry ground & look round, the scenery is exquisite! Whatever light falls upon my poetry from Fletcher's—& some *must*—I shall remember that it came thro' *you*—*you* are the conveyancer—& my thankfulness holds the fee!——

Dearest Georgie, do you know it is very impertinent of you to write anything in Arabel's letters to me, not addressed to me. I really cant allow such a thing any more. Why wont you write yourself to me? You promised & vowed to me that you would. Do you think nothing of perjury?–

The manner of your introduction to Mr Wyghtman[4] *made* me pleased in spite of all prejudices poetical. And after all, there *is* a nobleness in the act of concentrating the mind, whatever the object upon which it is concentrated, may be. The law is a low object (suffer a poet to assume so much) but mind contemplating Law is sublime in itself, & in that energy of contemplation. At any rate (I wont puzzle about the reason) I am proud of your energy & stedfastness of purpose Georgie—& if I live to witness your success in your profession I shall be very proud. The most consistent of us—even YOU[5]—& far less *I!!* grow inconsistent sometimes.

May God bless you my dearest Georgie!——

Your attached Ba.

Address, on integral page: George Goodin Barrett, Esqr
Publication: B-GB, pp. 37–38.
Manuscript: Pierpont Morgan Library.

1. The dating is approximate. George was in Torquay with EBB at the end of September 1838; the letter (watermark 1838) was probably written subsequent to that visit, but before letter 679, in which EBB taxes George with extravagance for sending her another gift.
2. The three-volume edition of the *Dramatic Works* of Beaumont and Fletcher, ed. George Colman (1811); see *Reconstruction*, A178.

3. *Much Ado About Nothing*, IV, 1, 159.
4. William Wightman (1784–1863), an eminent lawyer who was highly regarded by his peers for his accuracy and learning. He served on two Royal Commissions deliberating on legal matters, was appointed a judge of the Queen's Bench in 1841 and was knighted. In a letter to Miss Mitford of 21 February 1842, EBB confirmed that George "*was* Mr. Wightman's pupil" (i.e., articled clerk). There is also a reference in SD1059 to George's being in Mr. Wightman's chambers.
    (In this note, and some others relating to the series of letters to George Moulton-Barrett, we have drawn on material researched by Professor Paul Landis for his *Letters of the Brownings to George Barrett*. We here record our debt to his scholarship.)
5. Underscored four times.

673. EBB TO MARY RUSSELL MITFORD

[Torquay]
Monday, December 3, 1838.

Ever[1] dearest Miss Mitford,

To-day was the day fixed in my mind for writing to you, even if I had not heard from you yesterday. I thought I would wait one day more, and then write, and in the meantime went on building my Bastille in the air[2] about your unusual silence. And do you know, dearest Miss Mitford, the truth came to me among my fancies. I fancied that some illness, and of one dearest to you, kept you silent. It was such a relief to read the first page of your letter, and such a sad confirmation to turn to the second. Well, the evil has passed now. May the shadow of it be kept from your path for very long. While it is, other shadows will fall lightly, and may be trodden upon by a light and, some of them, by a very scorning foot.

My scorn, really indignation is too good a word for such a subject, unites itself to yours as closely as all my sympathies do to *you* in regard to every detail of your most interesting letter. I am most astonished. Can "high-toned" instruments be strung with such cracked wires?[3] That *you* should pay, and *he* "*seem* to pay." Yes! and seem to be a poet besides!! Upon which there comes into my head a saying of Plato. I had thought before that it ought to come nowhere, albeit Plato's, "*Poets speak nobly, but understand not what they speak.*"[4] I feel sorry. It is disappointing to be thrust aside from our estimation of any person. I have been accustomed to associate certain noblenesses with certain intellectualities. And although I never dared quite to use the words of your prophecy, "He will be a great poet," on account of the present want of what you call vividness, and I the power of conception, both of us referring to the same deficiency, the one to the effect, and the other to the cause, yet I did see in him a poet, and expect from him more than *this*.

And you think others capable of *this* besides! Don't let us say so till the experience comes. At any rate, dear Miss Mitford, I am unwilling to base the suspicion upon the ground of literary pursuits, small or great. Human nature is surely a better ground than poetical nature, and may it not be very true that the low opinion you have been led to form of a certain class of minds may have arisen from the circumstance, the accidental circumstance of your seeing those minds in a closer relation to their vanities and interests than other minds, and also by naturally expecting something better from such minds, and also by necessarily, however unconsciously, comparing what you yourself think and do in similar situations, and that is always generously and nobly. I am afraid that human nature is corrupt everywhere. I hope it is not most so where corruption is most "without excuse."

But I am thinking, as I ought and must, more of you, my beloved friend, than of any of those people. I cling to the hope that although Mr. Tilt may be irritated into incivilities towards you, and abominable it is that he should, he is too wise a man to sacrifice his interests to his ill-humour, and lose your editorship of his annual just for the sake of annoying you. But, however it may be, as you think it worth while to put the question (and, while you put it, I do trust you were quite certain what the answer will be) *you may make whatever use of me you please, as long as I am alive, and able to write at all.* I hope, if he, Mr. Tilt, ventured to dismiss *you*,[5] he would pay me the compliment of forgetting my existence altogether, but, whichever way it is, "foul me fall" as a minstrel, if I serve liege ladye in "Findens' Tableaux" except your own self, therefore do not wrong my fealty....

Of dear Mr. Kenyon I have heard more from you than from anyone since his return. My sister had seen him, and Papa was going to see him. I had heard nothing of his doings and enjoyments abroad from either. And so he won't have anything to say to our narrative poetry in Finden? But he is a heretic, therefore we won't mind. After all, I am *afraid* (since it displeases you) that what I myself delight in most, in narrative poetry, is NOT the *narrative*. Beaumont and Fletcher, strip them to their plots, [make] them your own Beaumont and Fletcher, and you take away their glory. Alfieri is more markedly a poet of *action* than any other poet I can think of, and how he makes you shiver! Mr. Wordsworth told me that he could read him only once.

Is there much "heresy" in all this? Forgive it, if there be.

Little thinks the bishop, whose right reverend autograph conveys my letter to you,[6] that he is aiding and abetting the intercourse of such very fierce radicals. Indeed the last time I thought of politics, I believe I was a republican, to say nothing of some perilous stuff of "sectarianism," which would freeze his ecclesiastical blood to hear of. My uncle and aunt know him very well, and that way came my frank. Were omens busy around him, that he made such great haste and brevity about the name of *your village*?⁷ Do observe the direction. ⟨★★★⟩

Text: L'Estrange (1), II, 43–46.

    1. L'Estrange gives "You," an obvious misreading.
    2. A reversal of "castle in the air," to give the meaning of a dark fantasy rather than a bright one.
    3. Apparently this and the following remarks refer to Miss Mitford's friend Townsend and his poem "The Coronation" in the 1839 *Findens' Tableaux*. Miss Mitford had praised it as "pure and high-toned" in her preface to the volume. It is not known what particular action of his prompted these remarks.
    4. *Dialogues*, 534B.
    5. Charles Tilt, the publisher of *Findens' Tableaux*, had apparently expressed dissatisfaction with some aspect of Miss Mitford's editorship, and had threatened to replace her for the 1840 edition. It may have had to do with the pruning necessary to limit the number of pages in the 1839 edition (see letter 669, note 7).
    6. The Bishop of Exeter, Henry Phillpotts (1778–1869), who was known to the Hedleys. As one of the Lords Spiritual, he had the franking privilege.
    7. This suggests an abbreviation of "Three Mile Cross" to "3 Mile †."

---

674. EBB TO THEODOSIA GARROW

Beacon Terrace [Torquay]
Saturday [?8] [December 1838]¹

My dear Miss Garrow,

    I have just received a parcel from our friend Mʳ Kenyon & he requests me to send you the accompanying volume–

    Very many thanks—while I am writing—for the beautiful flowers which I owe to your & Miss Fisher's kindness some days ago—the very day I think, that you were in this house without my seeing you– I did not *like it at all*—but the hour being so late & the penalties so high, there was no choice left to me– In a few days I indeed hope to see you & your sister—to whom do offer my regards.

                                    Very truly yours
                                      Elizabeth B Barrett–

Publication: None traced.
Manuscript: Gordon N. Ray.

    1. The form of salutation clearly places this after letter 671. The reference to Kenyon suggests that it follows letter 673, as EBB had not then heard from him.

675. WILLIAM CHARLES MACREADY TO RB

13. Cumberland Terrace.
Dec. 10. [1838][1]

My dear Browning

On Sunday next I am going to test the effect of a play, as far as I can, by reading it to a select auditory:[2]—it has high pretensions, but particular circumstances interfere to perplex us in arriving at a clear judgement, and therefore I wish to pass it though another ordeal.– Will you come to us at three o'clock, and undergo it—and afterwards at half past six, give us the pleasure of your company at dinner:—of course you will make your whole day with us, if you are good enough to come.– Write per C.G.T.[3]

Always and ever sincerely
yours'
W. C. Macready.

R. Browning Esq.[r]

Docket, at top of first page, in RB's hand: Bulwer's "Richelieu".
Publication: None traced.
Manuscript: Southwark Central Reference Library.

1. Year provided by the entry in Macready's diary.
2. Macready's diary entry for 10 December 1838 reads: "Wrote notes of invitation to Browning, Fox, Rintoul, Wallace, H. Smith, Blanchard, asking them to dine and hear Bulwer's play on Sunday." The entry of 16 December recorded that "Henry Smith and Serle called first, then Browning, Fox, Blanchard, and Lane to hear the reading of the play." (*Macready*, I, 481, 482.) As RB's docket indicates, it was *Richelieu*, and Macready's diary entry goes on to say that the opinions of all were favourable, and that he wrote an account of the results to Bulwer.
3. Covent Garden Theatre.

---

676. EBB TO MARY RUSSELL MITFORD

Torquay.
Wednesday. [?19] [December 1838][1]

I do from my heart congratulate you my very dearest Miss Mitford!—yes, & my own self too—I having received two notes of a gladder character than with all my habitual hopefulness I had dared to hope– May the day which gave you to your beloved father prove indeed the one of his restoration to you! & oh! may the blessing of the Giver rest upon either gift!——

Will M.[r] May[2] frown over the *cream*! If he *do*, it *need* do no harm! If he do not, it may serve to tempt the dear invalid to take some additional sustenance—tho' "for *your* sake" be so far the stronger charm. Tell me whether he is permitted to take any of this cream—because you know I shall feel *exultant* to be permitted on my part, to send him more—& it is but fair that I as well as those happier friends who can be near you, sh^d be able to accomplish some little service.

The silence had begun to make me *so* afraid! And I was repentant too for not having thought in time of asking you to depute Mary Anne[3] to write a word to me in the event of your being unequal to do so! I must beseech you not to wear yourself out with watching. I fear you are doing it. *Pray* do not! Give your place to another sometimes—I beseech *that* of you dearest Miss Mitford—not for your own sake—knowing the vanity of such an adjuration to *you*—but for the very sake of your dear invalid! Consider dearest Miss Mitford! The strength of love is not the strength of body actually—tho' it serves so often & so well in its stead—& when the excitement of this time is over, you are likely, nay, certain, without some precaution, to be utterly exhausted, & from such exhaustion unfit & unable to support & cheer him in the progress of convalescence! While he is taking food for your sake, you must take rest for his! Do consider this dearest Miss Mitford!

I am better than I have been—for I have not been very well—& only emerged from an imprisonment of ten days in my bedroom, this day! But *all* the imprisonment was not *necessary*—only precautionary on account of the east wind! I hear from Wimpole Street that Mr Kenyon is confined to the house with rheumatism!——

I do trust to have better & better accounts. I seem to prophecy in my heart that I shall—& yet I am fearful sometimes lest you sh^d be too sanguine & make pain for yourself. God's will is best—& *we* are best when we feel so!—and we *shall* feel so some day if we do not on this!——

Your ever affectionate
Elizabeth B Barrett

Publication: EBB-MRM, I, 108–109.
Manuscript: Armstrong Browning Library.

1. The first paragraph appears to refer to Miss Mitford's birthday, 16 December; the following Wednesday was the 19th.
2. George May (1799–1884) was the medical attendant to both Miss Mitford and her father up to the time of their respective deaths. He took up residence in Reading in 1822 and shortly thereafter was appointed surgeon to the Reading Dispensary. In 1835, he was elected to the Borough Corporation. When the Royal Berkshire Hospital was established in 1839, he was appointed to the medical staff, and he remained associated with the hospital until his death. His obituary in *The Berkshire Bell and Counties' Review* (1884, p. 99) said that he arrived in Reading with less than half-a-crown, and attained his subsequent prominence "solely by reason of his skill and integrity."
3. Miss Mitford's new maid, replacing Martha, who left Miss Mitford's service when she married.

677. RB TO JOHN PAYNE COLLIER[1]

[London]
[ca. 1839][2]

Offered for sale by Sotheby's, 22 March 1905, lot 327. 1 p., 4to. RB apologizes for troubling Collier without an introduction. He is going out of town, hence he writes: "Mr Browning is desirous of obtaining Mr Collier's permission to look over the MS Ballad 'The Atheist's Tragedy,' of which mention is made in the 'Further Particulars, &c',[3] as it would be of essential service to him in a work he is about to begin. ... He will call anytime convenient ... "

1. John Payne Collier (1789–1883), reporter, author and Shakespearean critic.
2. Dated by the reference to Collier's book.
3. *Farther Particulars Regarding Shakespeare and His Works* (1839), derived mainly from material in the Earl of Bridgewater's library.

678. RB TO EDWARD MOXON

[London]
Monday, 4. p.m. [?January 1839][1]

My dear Moxon,

Here is Shelley—I wish there were time to go thro' the book carefully. You will see at a glance which are the real corrections of errors, and which mere attempts to clear the text by tracing the construction,—as in the lines on the "Medusa", "Song for Tasso" &c Don't be in any haste to get done with the book which I am in no want of—

Ever yours
R Browning.

Publication: NL, pp. 14–15.
Manuscript: Huntington Library.

1. In the spring of 1839, Moxon published the *Poetical Works of Shelley*, edited by Mary Wollstonecraft Shelley. In view of RB's known interest in Shelley, it is possible that Moxon consulted him during the pre-publication phase. This provides our conjectural dating. This hypothesis is strengthened by the fact that Moxon presented RB with an inscribed set of the *Poetical Works*, which formed lot 1081 in *Browning Collections* (see *Reconstruction*, A2111). For details of RB's association with Moxon, see pp. 328–330.

679. EBB to George Goodin Moulton-Barrett

[Torquay]
[ca. January 1839][1]

My ever dearest Georgie,

I entreat your forgiveness for the inscrutable & mystical wrong I have done you, together with your acceptance of some expression of my gratitude for Ben Jonson[2] whom I accepted before as your gift upon Sette's affidavit. Considering everything you certainly are excusable in being so ashamed of sending such a gift, as to disavow the doing so. A pretty person you are to preach against extravagances—& then to behave so!—— Nay, to behave so again & again & again!! If you had been Socrates you w^d have sacrificed a pair of doves to Venus, (doves!) as well as the cock to Æsculapius![3]—you are inconsistent enough, qualified enough for two sides of every question, to be fit already for the heights of your profession. Seriously Georgie, were you Attorney General, I sh^d say 'I am obliged to you,'—were you on the Woolsack,[4] I sh^d say "Thank you"—but in the present state of things, you are one of the very most incorrigible abominable people I ever knew.

So I *wont* thank you. I read Ben Jonson, & think of you dearest Georgie instead.

In a letter from Miss Mitford, dated not very long ago, she says—"I hate the law & *all its* PROFESSORS. Dont *you*?"—Why of course I do–

You are none of you to abuse me for writing—I have done it day by day. I dare'nt write to Stormie, unless my courage revives.

Your attached Ba–

Address, on integral page: George G Barrett Esqr
Publication: B-GB, pp. 39–40.
Manuscript: Pierpont Morgan Library.

1. Dated by EBB's reference in letter 700 to George's having "sent me in the winter Barry Cornwall's Ben Jonson."
2. *The Works of Ben. Jonson, With a Memoir of his Life and Writings*, ed. B.W. Procter, 1838 (see *Reconstruction*, A1324).
3. i.e., to give thanks for recovery from an illness, as described in Jonson's Epigram XIII: "When men a dangerous disease did 'scape, / Of old, they gave a cock to Æsculape: / Let me give two, that doubly am got free; / From my disease's danger, and from thee" (II, 666 in Procter's edition).
4. The seat in the House of Lords of the Lord Chancellor while presiding over the proceedings of the House. It is stuffed with wool as a symbol of England's one-time staple trading commodity.

680. EBB TO MARY RUSSELL MITFORD

Torquay,
January 5, 1839.

Ever[1] dearest Miss Mitford,

I do thank you, my beloved friend, for your kindness in making me a partaker of your gladness. I wish all happiness to both of you—to you and dear Dr. Mitford—gratefully responding to your wishes to me on the occasion of this putting on of Dan Time's new doublet.[2] They have come true already, for *Papa has come*. May mine for you come true as truly—may God keep you both from January to January, and grant that you may have and feel no less occasion to look gladly on each other than we all have to look thankfully up to him! I *may* send my love and earnest wishes to Dr. Mitford—now may I not?

Papa says that Mr. Kenyon is out, and looking very well, but a letter from my sister tells me that, when she saw him last in Wimpole Street, his spirits did not appear to be as animated as usual, and I don't like hearing Mr. Harness's report of him. It must be that the life he leads will tell at last, and at least, on his *spirits*. Only the unexcitable by nature can be supposed to endure continual external occasions of excitement. As if there were not enough—too much that is exciting *from within*. For my own part, I can't understand the craving for excitement. Mine is for *repose*. My conversion into *quietism*[3] might be attained without much preaching, and, indeed, all my favorite passages in the Holy Scriptures are those which express and promise peace, such as, "The Lord of peace Himself give you peace always and by all means," "My peace I give you, not as the world giveth give I," and "He giveth his beloved sleep"[4]—all such passages. They strike upon the disquieted earth with such a *foreignness* of heavenly music—surely the "variety," the *change* is to be unexcited, to find a silence and a calm in the midst of thoughts and feelings given to be too turbulent.

My beloved friend, how very glad must be your gladness to watch, as I trust you are doing, the return of health to your dear invalid—the dearer for the thought of what "might have been"—day after day, and to feel in the respect and attachment demonstrated so affectingly around you that there is a sympathy for your gladness as well as your fearing grief. But still I am anxious for you; I am anxious lest your past and present fatigues should prove presently too great for you, and that, when the exultation of joy has subsided, this proving may begin. Do be careful, and do not, at any time you have thirty-six letters to write, write a thirty-seventh to *me*. I am very thankful for the frequent accounts you have sent me, yet if they helped to tire you—oh, don't let me tire you ever, dearest Miss Mitford, pray do not.

And this suggests a termination to my letter.

I must, however, say how sorry and glad Papa has been with you through the late changes. The patience and the silence *for your sake*, the love stronger than pain, they are beautiful to hear of, and very touching they must have been to *you*.

Poor L. E. L.! You will have been, as I was, startled and saddened to hear the sudden news. I had a *prophet in my thoughts* about her ever since she went away. It is a fatal climate, and the longest years do not seem to go to the lives of poetesses. Did you know her personally at all?[5]

Good-bye, dearest Miss Mitford. The cream shall be with Dr. Mitford's coffee as soon as possible.

Your ever attached,
Elizabeth Barrett.

P.S.—I am tolerably well just now, and all the better for the sight of Papa. He arrived the day before yesterday, and I must remember him to you, although he is out walking, and cannot authorize me to intrude upon you in that way.

Text: L'Estrange (1), II, 46–49.

    1. L'Estrange gives "You," an obvious misreading.
    2. i.e., the New Year. "Dan" is a poetic form of "Master, Lord."
    3. "A form of religious mysticism (originated by Molinos, a Spanish priest), consisting in passive devotional contemplation, with extinction of the will and withdrawal from all things of the senses; ... a state of calmness and passivity of mind or body" (*OED*).
    4. The quotations are, respectively, II Thessalonians, 3:16; John, 14:27 and Psalms, 127:2.
    5. Letitia Elizabeth Landon, after her marriage on 7 June 1838 to George Maclean, had gone to Africa, where her husband was Governor of the Cape Coast. She died there on 15 October 1838, but the news was slow to reach London. The first printed announcement of her death appeared in *The Watchman*, 31 December 1838, but EBB would probably have read the news in *The Athenæum* of 5 January 1839, which carried an obituary notice. Miss Mitford later said she had met L.E.L. only once (Chorley, I, 280).

681. EBB TO CHARLES WENTWORTH DILKE

Torquay
Tuesday. [?15] [January 1839][1]

Miss Barrett presents her compliments to the Editor of the Athenæum, & submits to him, for insertion in that periodical, the preceding stanzas.

Publication: Goodspeed's Catalogue, date unknown.
Manuscript: Boston Public Library.

    1. This note is appended to a fair copy of "L.E.L.'s Last Question," first published in *The Athenæum*, 26 January 1839 (no. 587, p. 69).

682. EBB TO MARY MINTO[1]

[Torquay]
[*Postmark:* 17 January 1839]

My dearest Mary, As you are so kind as not to forget me but still to care to hear about me & from me, the whole Pharmacopœia's fi fa fum shall not keep me from writing the few lines you ask for. The first letter I received from you sh^d have been replied to long ago (I mean the first letter you sent to Torquay)—but at that time, October, I was so very unwell as to be disabled from any outward expression of the gladness with which its affectionateness came to me. For some time I have been much better—but still, weaker, than I used to be in London—the necessary & perhaps the transitory effect of a colder season. Our house here is *in* the sea– At least to my imagination it is—which is the same you know as its being so actually. From this sofa, I cannot see a yard of vulgar earth—except where the undulating hills on the opposite side of this lovely bay bound the clearness of its waters—and whenever the steam packet leaves it or enters it, my bed is shaken with the vibration. Torquay is a beautiful place—but as to its *human* aspect, it is much more like a hospital than anything else, & so, none of the gayest– Respirators & stethoscopes "go about the streets"–[2] I have not made one acquaintance since I came, except my physician's—a privation for which you wont pity me– So you are coming to England, dear Mary! I am so glad—I *shall* be so glad if it pleases God that I shall again see you! I shall certainly expect to see you *here* in "March", according to your word. And when the Spring advances a little, I for my part, if I am alive & able to move, shall be back again in London. I do long so to be at home again!– It almost broke my heart to leave it—& if by the great mercy of God, I am permitted to cross that dear threshold again, the joy will be past any words I can say, here or else where. Dearest Mary! I am very glad (& so is Papa) that your Englishisms are not expelled by your Gallicesms [*sic*]! I am glad that France is not to you what England must be!——

Your cousin's marriage[3]—of which I wish you joy—will introduce a Frenchman to you in all cousinly capacity– Dont let him try another.

Give my love to Mrs Minto!– I hear very often from Miss Mitford—who has been much distressed lately by the illness of her father– He is recovering almost miraculously. Ask for me whether there is an edition (in one work) of the Platonic philosophers—mind, *not* of *Plato*, but the *Platonists* in Greek—& what the expense w^d be– If your answer be very satisfactory, I may ask you to bring it over to me– My dearest Papa is with me just now. It is such a happiness! no room for a word more!

Ever your affectionate
EBB——

118 [17 January 1839] *No. 682*

Address, on integral page in Henrietta Moulton-Barrett's hand: à Mademoiselle / Mademoiselle Minto / 9. Avenue d'Antin / Champs Elysèes / Paris.
Publication: None traced.
Manuscript: British Library.

1. For details of EBB's friendship with Mary Minto, see pp. 327–328.
2. Ecclesiastes, 12:5.
3. EBB's letter is written at the end of one from Henrietta (SD979), in which Mary's cousin is identified as a Miss Scarlett.

---

683. EBB TO MARY RUSSELL MITFORD

[Torquay]
March 7 [1839][1]

Ever dearest Miss Mitford,

I must say so at the first word, though it may seem so contradictory to the long silence & neglect of which you have or surely *may* have (making every allowance for your tried kindness) judged somewhat severely– To explain it all, my beloved friend, I have been very ill—& your two last delightful letters were received by me when I was *quite* confined to my bed, & in such a state of debility as rendered writing a thing impossible– Even at this time, altho' more than a month has passed since this *laying up* began, the extent of my strength is to bear being lifted to the sofa for three hours a day—& I have not left my bedroom for six weeks. The cold weather at the end of January irritated the chest a good deal—& then most unaccountably—I never suffered from such a thing my whole life before—I had for ten days a kind of *bilious fever* which necessitated the use of stronger medecines than my state c^d very well bear—& then came on a terrible state of debility—the stomach out of sheer weakness, rejecting all sustenance except wine & water—& the chest, seeming to grudge the exercise of respiration. I felt oftener than once inclined to believe that the whole machine was giving way everywhere! But God has not willed it so! I am much better, & stronger— & growing with my strength has been the wish of assuring you--that indeed indeed I have *not* forgotten you, I am *not* ungrateful to you– As to the fish—oh what must you have thought!. But before your last letter brought me the permission of sending it, I was able to direct some to be sent to you—& the provoking fishermen or market people would not let us have any "fresh enough" according to the doxy of our cook. Torquay thinks more of pleasure boats than fishing boats. Indeed all the fish we have, or almost all, is the produce of Brixom[2]—& then the East winds set their faces against fishing anywhere– But I shall hope for better facilities henceforward—& in the meantime, if you will take the trouble of directing the empty basket back to me with *'returned basket'* written on the card, it will be ready to go to you again—& will reach me free of carriage. Thank you dearest Miss Mitford for believing that it *does* give me pleasure to do this little service. Would it were greater!-

And thank you for the memorial of poor LEL. How kind of you to spare those seeds to me!-[3]

I must not write any more—& have written far too much of myself— only I wanted to place my innocense of *not loving you*, beyond suspicion. Henrietta sh^d have written. I thought of asking her to do so—& then I thought again--"Why sh^d I not wait until I am better—if I *am* to be better? & spare her some gloomy fancies about me"—

I *do* feel so much for dear Lady Dacre.[4] If you sh^d be writing to her, & sh^d besides feel sure that the sound of a name so little familiar to her as mine, w^d not be or appear an impertinent intrusion, will you say how I have felt & do feel for her. When kindness has been shown to us—& hers was shown to *me*—we are apt to be intrusive in return. But without this, & indeed apart from it altogether—poor Mrs Sulivan was herself interesting to me as a writer. Her tale of the wife with two husbands affected me very much—& appeared most striking to me from its pathos & purity of tone.[5]

God bless you dearest Miss Mitford!-

Kindest regards to Dr Mitford—go on to send me good news about him. I am tired with writing as you will see-

Papa & *Sette* are here again! a good reason for my *betterness-*

Your ever attached
EBB——

I have not answered y^r letters I know- Say if there is any particular kind of fish which you & Dr Mitford prefer.

Thank you for letting me read Mrs Westmacott's letter[6]——& *for* LIKING *the* STANZAS.[7]

Tuesday morning.

The last sheet was written days ago—& to my great disappointment in vain. And now they have come up to me to hurry my letter to an end— First delay, & then hurry—both things for grumbling.

Retsch is very interesting in Mrs Westmacott's letter, & wild & grand & *Faustic* in his own productions. I have seen his illustrations of the Fridolin—accompanied by an English versification of the ballad—not a bad one but perfectly *uninspired*.[8] Your Buccaneer is certainly(—of course it struck me at the time to be—) an animated English version of that story out of the German Furnace-[9] By the way do you hear anything, have you heard anything from Mr Tilt & of his intentions?[10] Do you meditate the vivifying of any kind of annual this summer—or are they all to be annuals in the strict sense of your mignionette?—only without the perfume?——

I am sure you were polishing your dagger just when you asked me to agree with you in giving Goëthe's laurel to Schiller. You might as well ask our young Queen to prefer Shakespeare to Mr Van Amburgh.[11] My doxy is that there is (now you know what my doxy must be) that there is more essential genius in Goethe's mysterious Faustic growlings than in Schiller's most eloquent eloquence. He is of the schools. He lights his lamp like any common man—& I am quite sure not only that he wrote with a pen, but that it might very possibly have been a steel one. Now Goëthe's poetry comes like the wind--we cannot tell whence it cometh[12]—& what is more, never think of asking—and if *you* asked *me* I sh^d be obliged to shake my head & put on quite as mystic a face as his own.

Now you must forgive all this foolish criticism. Foolishness & criticism are so apt, do so naturally go together! and I am, for a critic, even unnaturally consistent, for I like Schiller's Robbers[13] better than any other play of his I have read.

I had in my hands (not of course for my reading) for a part of an evening years ago & at a party Lord Francis Gowers translation of the Faust. It was the only time I ever saw any translation of that untranslateable wonder--I never even saw the one you refer to.[14] On the other hand, the time I have given to German literature has been but little—none at all until the summer before last—and so you must find some good excuse for me if I have written anything *very*, more than critically, foolish.

Do mention poor Lady Dacre.

Thank you for all your encouraging kindnesses (how they multiply) about my poetry. But dearest Miss Mitford, if it were really the fashion to like it, w^{d}nt it be a little so to buy it! And Messrs Saunders & Otley gave bad accounts in the early part of the winter.[15] Do you think there sh^d be more advertisements?

I have not seen the Deluge—[16] Tell me your thought of it. And oh! do, when you can, write—& be sure that I am better—the pulse has been better for several days now——

Your hurried but most
affectionate EBB.

Mr Kenyon is quite well—but very seldom seen in Wimpole Street.

Address, on integral page: Miss Mitford.
Publication: EBB-MRM, I, 111–114.
Manuscript: Wellesley College.

1. Year provided by the reference to the death of Lady Dacre's daughter. Inclusive dating provided by EBB's "Tuesday morning."

2. *Sic*, for Brixham, on the southern arm of Tor Bay, opposite Torquay.

3. As later letters make clear, Miss Mitford had received from Africa some seeds sent by Letitia Landon (Mrs. Maclean) before her death, and EBB had been given two of them.

4. Arabella Jane Sullivan (*née* Wilmot), Lady Dacre's daughter by her first husband, Valentine Henry Wilmot, had died on 27 January 1839.

5. Mrs. Sullivan was the author of *Recollections of a Chaperon* (1831) and *Tales of the Peerage and Peasantry* (1835), both edited by Lady Dacre. EBB's reference appears to be to "An Old Tale, and Often Told," included in the former title.

6. The wife of the Rev. Horatio Westmacott, Rector of Chastleton, Oxfordshire.

7. Presumably EBB's reference is to "L.E.L.'s Last Question," published in *The Athenæum* of 26 January 1839 (no. 587, p. 69).

8. Maritz Retzsch (1779–1857), painter and engraver, furnished illustrations for the works of Schiller, Goethe and others, *Fridolin* (1798) being by Schiller. The English translation mentioned by EBB was *Fridolin, or the Road to the Iron Foundry* (1824), translated by John Payne Collier (1789–1883).

9. "The Buccaneer" was one of Miss Mitford's contributions to the 1839 *Findens' Tableaux*.

10. i.e., to ask Miss Mitford to edit another *Findens' Tableaux*.

11. Isaac Van Amburgh (1811–65), an American lion-tamer, was having a successful season in London; Queen Victoria went to see his performance six times.

12. John, 3:8.

13. *Die Räuber* was published in 1781; EBB presumably read an English translation, perhaps that of Benjamin Thompson (1776?–1816), published in 1801.

14. Francis Leveson-Gower (1800–57), later (1846) 1st Earl of Ellesmere, had published his translation of *Faust* in 1823. The English version mentioned by Miss Mitford cannot be identified positively, as there were at least seven translations, in addition to Gower's, published between 1833 and 1839. In view of the earlier comment about Retzsch, her reference might be to the translation by Jonathan Birch (1783–1847), with illustrations by Retzsch, the first part of which was published in 1839.

15. i.e., of sales of *The Seraphim*.

16. *The Deluge* (1839) was another of John Edmund Reade's derivative poems, owing much to Byron's *Heaven and Earth*. Landor told Lady Blessington that Reade "is now about to publish a drama of the Deluge, on which he tells me he has been employed for twenty years. You cannot be surprised that he is grievously and hopelessly afflicted, having had water on the brain so long" (*Richard Chenevix Trench, Letters and Memorials*, 1888, I, 195).

---

684. EBB TO MARY RUSSELL MITFORD

[Torquay]
[late March 1839][1]

My dearest Miss Mitford,

The fishermen in these waters certainly have not genius enough to pull up a Genius—& even after the promises of yesterday, I am advised by my maid "to write only what I might write any day" without any personalities touching the fish tribes. We are obliged to be particular as to the freshness on account of the distance. I am so glad that you & dear D[r] Mitford liked what I last sent, & so anxious that you sh[d] not have to wait another day. Were you visitors or residents at Lyme—Lyme Regis in this county? Then—in the latter case—you must have seen the Pinny Cliffs—& then (a still surer *then*) you never can have forgotten them. They seem to me the counterpart of Dreamland, on the earth. We made an excursion to Lyme, for the sake of the vision, when we resided at Sidmouth[2]—& I was obliged to lie in bed almost all the next day from the exercise, to which I was quite unequal but which that most surpassing scenery beguiled me into taking. Hills rocks & seas got *into my head*—& if I ever made oath in the Temperance Society, my conscience w^d consider itself bound never to let me look at them again– By the way I hope you are not *a member*!—& by the way again, I could not help smiling whilst I was writing *that*. Not that the whole system in question is not far too foolish, yes, & too anti-scriptural besides, for me to feel inclined to smile at it in general.

How very very kind of you my dearest Miss Mitford to send *more* seeds to my gardeners in Wimpole Street—how *too* kind! And then Arabel tells me of a kind note addressed to her which appears to have quite delighted her both for the kindness' sake & the autograph's.[3] They are all very busy she says, struggling for a garden!——& with your name for a charm, I sh^d think the flowers might grow without roots–

It is a great gladness to me to hear your good news of Dr Mitford—& altho' you say nothing of your own health, I try to believe in its being something to be glad about, too– I am better & stronger now—but since I wrote to you there has been—there was for some days—an exhausting increase of hemorrhage which however yielded to styptics—& Dr Barry is of opinion that if I can be kept from becoming worse thro' this trying early part of the spring, I am likely to be satisfactorily better as the weather settles. God's mercies have been very great to me—& it w^d be a no less ingratitude than a folly, to doubt His will to act out His own love whether by life or death. "*If* therefore there is any consolation in Christ Jesus———"— —![4] how beautiful that passage is—how pathetic that appeal––& how without an hypothesis that *if!*––

Beloved Papa & Sette were obliged to go away two days ago—& I miss them so as not yet to have left off hearing their footsteps on the stairs at the usual hours of their coming to sit with me. Sette's gossipings & secret-tellings were such delightful *old newnesses*. I used to think in quite the old times when he read Cæsar to me—his eyes (after the ubiquitous manner of Cæsar himself) holding communion with Punch out of the window,[5]—that I was unfortunate to have no more power in the way of enforcing discipline. It is better as it is– It is better to be loved than feared––or worse word of all!—*respected*. And if Sette had read

No. 685 28 March 1839 123

Cæsar to me without a look at Punch, I sh^d hear now none of the gossip or the secrets. You see how we great pedagogues console ourselves! ⟨★★★⟩

Publication: EBB-MRM, I, 114-116 (as [early April 1839]).
Manuscript: Wellesley College.

  1. Dated by the reference to EBB's father and brother leaving Torquay. Edward Moulton-Barrett was still in Torquay on 9 March (see SD990), but letter 686 makes it clear that he was back in London by the end of March.
  2. Miss Mitford had lived briefly at Lyme Regis as a child (see letter 685). EBB's outing to the Pinhay Cliffs is described in letter 508.
  3. See SD992.
  4. Philippians, 2:1.
  5. The reference to "old times" indicates that EBB is speaking of Hope End days, so Punch would have been a pet, probably a dog, rather than the Punch and Judy character.

---

685. MARY RUSSELL MITFORD TO EBB

Three Mile Cross,
Mar[ch] 28, 1839.[1]

My dear Friend,

  I should always doubt any preference of mine when opposed to yours, always, even if my ignorance of languages did not make my writing about foreign poetry a very great presumption. French I read just like English, and always shall, and I have a tendency towards the comedies and memoirs, that makes me open a French book with real gusto. And little as I know of Italian, I like the gem-like bits of Ariosto. But after all to be English, with our boundless vistas in verse and in prose, is a privilege and a glory; and *you* are born among those who make it such, be sure of that. I do not believe, my sweetest, that the very highest poetry does sell at once. Look at Wordsworth! The hour will arrive, and all the sooner if to poetry, unmatched in truth and beauty and feeling, you condescend to add story and a happy ending, that being among the conditions of recurrence to every book with the mass even of cultivated readers—I do not mean the few.
  I once remember puzzling an epicure by adding to an apple tart, in the making, the remains of a pot of preserved pine, syrup and all, a most unexpected luxury in our cottage; such would a bit of your writing be in a book of mine—flavour, sweetness, perfume, and unexpectedness.... Yes, for one year, from eight and a half to nine and a half—I lived—*we* lived, at Lyme Regis. Our abode was a fine old house in the middle of the chief street; a porch and great gables with spread-eagles distinguish it. It was built round a quadrangle, and the back looked into a garden,

which descended by terraces to a small stream, a descent so abrupt that a grotto with its basin and spring formed a natural shelter under the hilly bank, planted with strawberries. Arbutus, passion-flowers, myrtles, and moss-roses abounded in that lovely garden and covered the front of the house; and the drawing-room chimney-piece was a copy of the monument to Shakespeare in Westminster Abbey. How I loved that house! There is an account of a visit to Lyme in Miss Austen's exquisite "Persuasion."[2] Some of the scenery in the back of the Isle of Wight resembles Pinny, but it is inferior.

I shall tell dear Lady Dacre of your sympathy. Heaven bless you, my own sweet love.

Ever yours,
M. R. Mitford.

Address: Miss Barrett, Torquay.
Text: L'Estrange (2), III, 96–97 (as 28 May 1839).

1. L'Estrange dates this letter 28 May 1839. However, Miss Mitford's reference to adding pineapple to apple tart is mentioned by EBB in her letter of 10 April, so it appears probable that L'Estrange misread "Mar[ch]" as "May." Also, the reference to Lady Dacre makes it apparent that this is a reply to letter 683.
2. In chapter XI.

---

686. EBB to Arabella Moulton-Barrett

[Torquay]
Saturday. [30 March 1839][1]

My ever ever dearest Arabel,

Your letter came last night just as I had given it up in despair. The postman's raps died away, or seemed to do so, in the distance—& all hope of mine with them. It was well for you that you did write—& did not catch hold of dear Sam's letter as an excuse, or rather that dear Sam would not let you do so—your own inward corrupt inclinations being manifest enough—— Thank you, though, again & again for the letter! It came, & that was enough. Ask Sette what my reason is for NOT asking you to write everyday.

Well my dearest Arabel, I was down stairs yesterday!—the first time in ten weeks!- We have had no prevalence of cold wind since our beloved Papa & Sette went away, & I was half surprised not to have been ejected from "my lady's chamber",[2]—albeit not quite as summarily as the long legged hero of the long lived ballad,—long ago. I was glad on some accounts to be sent down—very very glad to be able to send you what you would all be sure to think good news. Being tired was a necessary consequence of such a transmigration– I was very very tired—& the more so from my extreme stupidity in not having *practiced dressing* all this time. It had seemed a rather rational excuse for laziness about doing so, that my strength was better spent in remaining up on the sofa longer than I might otherwise be able to do, & that the dressing process would have necessarily taken some to its own uses. So I have been satisfied all this time with donning Trippy's bright-hued flannel over my nightgown, & then nestling into a heap of shawls & cloaks. But you see such a costume would not quite do for an avatar into the world below. And not being used to sublunary petticoats I was tired before the removal took place at all. But it was managed, all of it, tolerably well;—and I stayed down stairs two hours—& when Dr Barry came at six, he said that I had done quite as well as he expected & did not suffer from fatigue more than he was quite sure I would do after such an exertion. And then (oh tuneful Barrytone accents!) he desired me to keep up stairs today & rest! Think of his humanity!– And dont scold me for being glad at this especial exercise of it—for indeed I was tired,—& came to a conclusion which made Henrietta laugh when I told it to her afterwards, that *that* drawing room was a detestable room. There seemed to me to be in it, such an immense superfluity of air & light, the weight was something past bearing—to say nothing of the straight sofa, which Crow had vainly tried to persuade me into letting her soften & breadthen (is there such a word?) by carrying down before me the featherbed to lay on it. Fancy a featherbed as one's avant courier[3] up & down stairs! Besides, a pillow does almost as well as any other thing after its kind. Dont suppose either Dr Barry or me to be daunted. I am to go down stairs again tomorrow.

And oh Arabel! in spite of your impertinence my cap is beautiful: & well it may be, for it cost very nearly two shillings. When I put it on for the first time a few days ago, Dr Barry exclaimed "Indeed, Miss Barrett, you do seem to me to be looking better today—or else .. IT IS YOUR CAP!"—

As you are investigating the subject, I will keep back no information. Be it known to you that having worn a nightcap for eight weeks my intention was to leave it off. I appeared accordingly cap-less—& was forthwith extinguished by the first person who came into the room, with a checked silk cravat & a white cambric pocket handkerchief—to which dearest Papa who came next, seemed inclined to *add* instead of substituting, the ancient nightcap. So I was forced to subside back again into that original element—revolving in my altered sole [sic][4] how I sh^d ever be able to alter the appearance of my head. If there were a risk in uncapping in this room, what w^d it be to do so suddenly upon my descent into the drawing room?– And very beautiful as all my nightcaps continue to be

(I hope Sette satisfied you on the subject) Oh w^d it not be rather FORT[5] to adjourn there in one of them—even if I preserved an unquestionable symmetry, by the adoption of Crow's project respecting the loco-motive feather bed?——

From such causes arose my day cap!– The velvet was superadded more accidentally, upon more Epicurean principles.[6] It happened to be already in my possession! Do you understand? Do you embrace the subject comprehensively?– Or, as you tell me you *"dont improve"*, is your intellect still too narrow for its vasty deepness?——

What nonsense you have provoked me into writing. You, & the pleasure of writing to you, & the inspiration of the asses milk this morning, altogether, are too much for me– But altogether I am afraid you wont think *I*[7] have "improved"!–

A letter from dearest Miss Mitford today—she says "Your dear sister's note delighted me.[8] She seemed to adopt me as a friend in right of my love for you—& indeed I love all belonging to you—those dear boys especially. How I hope the flowers may grow . . . And oh! how ardently I hope that the day may come when I shall see you all together my dear & most kind friends . . . you &c &c—being returned to them quite well! I pray for this next to my prayer for my father"—— And her father is going on as well as possible. Indeed he may be said to be perfectly restored.

Sunday.

O my beloved Arabel how many sabbaths have gone by since I conversed last with you. Here I am in bed for the night—it is seven—and I am quite helpless to resist the "sweet superstition"[9] of talking to you a little, before what may be called the *day*, is ended. I have your letter my dearest Bella. And if it were not for the unsightly void of one corner, & the extreme audacity (exactly the right word) of the other, my gratitude for it sh^d be laid undividedly at your feet. Make Sam write a copy & show it to you, before he attempts to insinuate anything into my letters, addressed to anybody else. You ought to have seen my face just as I caught the words "Dearest Bell" & . . . "uncle John's estates".[10] The lightening of my eyes singed both sides of my cap border––my beautiful cap! & even the black velvet fizzed. Who told him that I was an angel, & could bear it?——

There was a pleasant most welcome letter from dear Mr Hunter this morning—& *he is not coming here*. Thank you again & again for your wish that he should—knowing as you do, & knowing rightly how full of gladness such a visit would be to me– But if I could talk it all over with you you would be contented (as I am) in my disappointment. Henrietta wrote nearly three sides of a letter to him last week—& I covered the paper she left. Her letter took for granted that he was coming according to the old arrangement, but my codicil disinterestedly recommended a journey to London instead. He does not seem inclined to mind either of us. His decision against coming here is on account of my weakness— He knows he says that I sh^d exert myself in different ways, & determines that he *wont* come at present—that it w^d be quite wrong—& in short, *he wont*. And now I will tell you a little why I am satisfied to let it be so— The journey does involve both trouble & expence, & altho' he does not think of that (he is too kind) yet I ought to do so—& may do so with the less effort, as I see plainly that my being able to ENJOY his society & conversation down stairs is out of the question—-the sense of weakness upon removal made itself too convincingly felt last friday, & it w^d be unreasonable to expect to grow up into any great improvement of strength after only two more days. And then whether Dr Barry was not quite satisfied with what he called this morning the friday '*experiment*' I cant tell, but he wont let me go down any more until the weather is settled & sunny. He said "You must not go down today"—upon which I observed—- "It does not break my heart Dr Barry".— "I am glad of that—for really I *cant* dare let you go down stairs while the weather is so gloomy". It is very warm, but the south wind leaned rather to the east yesterday, & it rains today. I sometimes think that he did not like the pulse *much* on friday night, & Crowe says now that she suspected at the time from his manner I was not likely to repeat the experiment very immediately. Not that I am the least bit the worse for it. Only it may be considered prudent to wait a few days longer for more sunshine & more of the strength which by God's blessing, comes with it. Under such circumstances it would be foolish & inconsiderate to urge Mr Hunter's coming here—-when with every contrivance to see him I c^d scarcely compass it for more than an hour or two in the day at most. And then you see he w^d, notwithstanding Bro & Henrietta, be thrown a good deal upon Bummy for amusement—-for society I mean—at least she might fancy so—-and altho' she likes & admires him very much, yet I *am satisfied as it is*. There are some delicacies as we are situated—-she & we—and we have observed that notwithstanding her perfect acquaintance with the Easter plan & not unfrequent conversation about it, not a word on the subject has escaped her lately. I am glad to say that her cold is nearly quite well. I wish Henrietta's were—and it w^d be if her persuadibility had been equal to my wise counsellings. As it is, she walks about the house in a boa, & Dr Barry sent her some rose gargle yesterday, & I administer most disinterestedly all the gruel & arrowroot which I wont take myself. It was nonsense to tell you of *my* cold. It passed in a hurricane of pocket handkerchiefs in an hour or two!—— Here is April—summer at the doors! and oh Arabel! what a summer you make before it comes, with your vision of our sitting together in the happy happy chapel—kneeling together *there!* Should I ever get up again from that thankful prayer?——

You have prayed for me today, I know– How I love & pray for you always, you, all of you! You are so very very dear. I wish we could realize God's love to us as we do our own love for each other! I for one fail & with less excuse than any, fail continually in doing so. Strange that we sh^d fail! His blood upon the conscience, yet the near heart so cold. There is a wonderfulness in man's ingratitude & insensibility only surpassed by the long suffering of Him who is essentially the Wonderful.

Monday.

It is April. Tell that dearest April fool Sette (I know he is an April fool by this time, tho' Occy *may* have escaped) to carry the enclosed precious seed, one of two which came from poor LEL, from Cape Coast & were sent to me by Miss Mitford, to some most accomplished gardener, & to get as much information about it as he can, & in the case of its being considered likely to grow, to have it planted in some hotest of hothouses.

Tell yourself whenever the butterflies seem coming out (as perhaps they may this week)—& whenever you think Mary's[11] bonnet too warm for her,—to go to Miss Smith's (I forget the new name) & order for her either a silk or Tuscan straw Leghorn bonnet, whichever you & she prefer, to *my account*. I will settle for it when I go home.

When I go home! How happy those words look! How could I help writing them over again!

I wont have Dr Barry abused. I have taken him under my protection. Such a story as I heard two days ago of his kindness amongst the poor!—of his going twice a day two miles & a half out of Torquay to attend a poor woman who was severely ill, & not only refusing the slightest remuneration, but actually paying for the medecines he prescribed. And he is said to do this continually. And it was testified to in most emphatic gratitude by our charwoman at this house last week. For my own part I must be grateful too—& it is only commonly so to say that no one could be more kind & feeling than he was to me in my last illness.[12] All the professionalisms were cast away from the manner—while, in regard to professional services, I have every reason to subscribe to his ability. I was in what Sette w^d call a conglomeration of evils, at one time, quite enough to distract both physician & patient, & exigent of great judiciousness. Then as to the elixir you condescend to praise——I think it might immortalize him in your admiration. I am inclined to consider it (I may be wrong) that long sought elixir of life which used to run in couples with the philosopher's stone.[13] It re-vivifies you—refreshes you—if you sleep or not—& renders you sublimely indifferent to the nocturnal watchings of old women. The Bendemeer nightingales[14] sing all the night long just outside my curtains—and I feel myself smiling with complacency every now & then, & only too inclined to pull my check string & beg Henrietta to unders⟨tand⟩ how very particularly happy I am. It is sure to make me younger & younger—so that by the time I go home, I shall be wearing baby caps instead of *"these presents"*. All the *girl*-babies wear their cockades on the left side of the head—dont they? Let me know.

I meant to have written to my own beloved Papa,—but altho' beginning days ago this series of replies to letters sent to me so long since, I am tired today, & Henrietta, scolding like a virago!- Tell him how he is missed every night, & all day too—but *most* at night! & tell him he shall have a long letter from me very soon in reply to your blank corner- Dearest dearest Papa!. I hate sending so many MSS & none for him.

M! Stratten's silence has a promise in it. D! Payne D! Smith have been written to—& others of the influential- Dear M! Hunter seems sanguine, & not unreasonably so. In the meantime it has been proposed to him to supply at Albany Chapel. I am going to write to him. He OUGHT[15] to go to London. But as he has for once made some actual exertion, there is no use in being very violent!-

Dearest Henrietta's throat is better—D! Barry has just been here—& was so hardhearted as not to enquire about it. He says that I am not to go down stairs again until the weather is another thing,—& indeed that weather seems to be his only reason for keeping me where I am—the wind leaning eastwards—a *moist* east wind tho', which does not affect me so much as the dry—& the thermometer at 63 in my room this morning before any fire was lighted- Three letters next week for this!——

Your own Ba.

My love to M!ˢ Orme.

Best love to dearest Stormie. Ask him to send me O Connell's verses—& whether he sings them to an Irish harp.[16] I meant to write to Stormie—but really I *cant* now. The letters I *have* written are *just debts* & long owing. I read his Chaucer most fluently & admiringly—& am thinking of erecting it on a scaffold in my room covered with velvet. Speak of the doves—à propos of the velvet-

Send D! Elliotson[17] as quickly as you can, & Nelly Bordman's note.

I am so sorry about the Russells give my love to them-

Send two chickens & the smaller quantity of cream to Trippy—one chicken for M!ˢ Nuttall with my love. I meant to have written too to dearest Sam. *Tell him so.*

Address, on integral page: Miss Arabel Barrett.
Publication: None traced.
Manuscript: Berg Collection.

1. Dated by EBB's internal reference to Monday, April Fool's Day.
2. "Goosey, goosey, gander, whither shall I wander / Upstairs, downstairs and in my lady's chamber, / There I found an old man who wouldn't say his prayers, / So I took him by the left leg and threw him down the stairs" (old nursery rhyme).
3. "Forerunner."
4. Dryden, "Alexander's Feast" (1697), line 85.
5. "Outrageous; shocking."
6. Epicurus (ca. 340–ca. 270 B.C.) advocated reliance on the senses; for him, pleasure (i.e., freedom from pain) was the highest good.
7. Underscored twice.
8. i.e., in reply to SD992.
9. We have not located the source of this quotation.
10. Apparently Sam had used a portion of his sister's letter to address a message to his aunt, Arabella Graham-Clarke, who was with EBB in Torquay. A letter from her (SD996) thanks him for his "kind few lines."
11. Mary Hunter, who was with the Moulton-Barretts in London.
12. As late as September 1839, he had not submitted any bill for his frequent attendance on EBB, and she finally asked him for his account (see SD1042).
13. The "powder of projection," made from the philosophers' stone hypothesized by alchemists, could transmute any baser metal into gold.
14. Thomas Moore, "The Veiled Prophet of Khorassan" (*Lalla Rookh, an Oriental Romance*, 1817, p. 63): "There's a bower of roses by Bendemeer's stream, / And the nightingales sing round it all the day long." A note identifies Bendemeer as "A river which flows near the ruins of Chilminar," in Persia.
15. Underscored three times.
16. We have been unable to trace any published poems by O'Connell.
17. Dr. John Elliotson (1791–1868), professor of medicine at the University of London and founder of the Phrenological Society, was a student of Mesmerism. His experiments with it led to his resigning his Chair at the university. He was the author of *Principles and Practice of Medicine* (1839), the book EBB was asking for.

---

687. EBB TO MARY RUSSELL MITFORD

[Torquay]
April 10th [1839]^1

My beloved friend,

The east wind is here instead of the fish—& it seems that we must wait longer for the latter than one of us can, to reply to the dear interesting letter you sent me. I like the tour plan so much—so very much!^{2} and I am so very anxious to know your decision as soon as it is made, with regard to the book which is to play a more graceful part than the monument at Calais^3 & mark the footsteps of *la desireè*. You see I talk of a book—because you talked of two volumes. I conclude however from your reference to Wordsworth's work,^{4} that you mean the publication to take place every month & in numbers—& that the "two volumes" are the

No. 687 10 April [1839] 131

prophetic summing up of all. What "my public" is likely to be graciously pleased to be pleased with, is very often beyond prophecy—but if Casandra told me that it would be pleased with you & your undertaking, verily I should believe her–[5] As to Finden, supposing you & M.[r] Tait[6] keep to your coalition, why should not your friend's drawings[7] take the place of the tableaux, & the *memorabilia* of your journey wind Wye like amongst them. It would give a novel character to the whole—& the room for tradition & descriptions & antiquarian references of all sorts would be almost ample enough.

With reference to my own self my dearest Miss Mitford, you know very well that I am a slave to the genius of your lamp[8]—if the title be not too high for me always. In the present case I am afraid it is most surely so—although I thank you for the proud pleasure suggested to me by the very *idea* of being associated with you in your undertaking. There never was a more empty-headed body than I am, as to antiquities or local traditions—a more *wonderfully* empty-headed body, considering my delight from childhood until now in unbelievable irrational things--in all such wild stories as are most apt to stride down to us by tradition. But as to localizing or caring for the localities of any, just there is my deficiency—& here is a proof--that, living for years & years a three miles distance from Ledbury, I never had an opportunity of believing in St Catherine until Wordsworth gave me one.[9] Would that I were at least so far fit for localizing as to be *loco-motive*—& do something for you in the way of local tradition-hunting in books! Dear Sir Uvedale Price used to say that I was a very good ferret—& so I am--an indoor ferret. But what can I do bound hand & foot in this wilderness, in the way of book-ferreting? with a physician who groans in the spirit[10] whenever he sees within my reach any book larger & graver looking than "the last new octavo neatly bound"? Luckily my Plato looks as good as a novel on the outside—but you tempted me with Bishop Andrews, & the Bishop is in folio, & I was in an obstinate fit—& I *did* read--& *was* scolded[11]—& "all for the love of you"[12]—& for M.[r] Cary's[13] praise of the Bishop. By the way, the scolding went for nothing with me. He is not so high in compositional *art* (it seems to me) as Hooker, much less Barrow—nor in genius as Taylor[14]—but his heart is holy & beautiful & runs away into eloquence. But I must'nt run away from your antiquities. If you come into Devonshire, you wont forget Browne & his Pastorals[15]—and if you go near Malvern you are sure to think of Langlande & Piers Plowman[16]—and wherever you go, there is the Polyolbion to go with you[17]– I wish *I*[18] could go with you!– Notwithstanding my ignorances, if I can pick up sticks for you,[19] do let me try to do it! You shall have as many rhimes as you please, & as you want, for Finden or anything besides, if the subjects are within my reach. Only I want you to know my want of knowledge—& that I cant do what I cant do!——& that my head is more like Bottom's,[20] than an Antiquarian's!—— Remember—writing for you *will do me no harm*. Believe me it will not. And I consider myself bound with promises nine times round me,[21] & inducements of a softer kind besides, to do your bidding whenever I can—as slave of the genius of your lamp, not as "preserved pineapple" in your "apple tart"!!–[22] What a simile dearest Miss Mitford! And what faces your gentle readers would make when the pine apple turned out a crab-apple!

Why is the poor novel the last resource?[23] I do hope, ONLY because you cant do all things at once! But indeed I observe that you never assign to it any place of honor, & I cant help suspecting you of willing it away into the corner––for *our* penance I suppose! M.[r] Kenyon's report made me feel sure of its crowning you in the Capitol[24]—but you would rather go down the Wye than up the Capitol stairs—and indeed it will be much the same thing in the end.

Did you *see* Miss Roberts' Memoir of L E L– It is surely badly & injudiciously written—altho' its affectionate warmth sh.[d] be allowed to stand between it & criticism. But really there is no individualizing in the character—& as to the defence or explanation of that afflicting catastrophe how very strange to suggest as she does, that if it issued from a voluntary act, the act was more probably induced by impatience of bodily than of mental pain!–[25] 'Save me from my friends!'–[26] I do wish something satisfactory even in a measure, were known. Do you know whether the *maid* has appeared yet?–

How is M.[rs] Joanna Baillie?—& Lady Dacre?——

Is Alfred Tennyson among your personal acquaintances? I heard of him the other day as having an unduly large head, handsome features, & a fathoming eye—& that they had all settled into a cottage in Devonshire where he smoked & composed poems all day,[27] suffering many of the latter to escape him for lack of industry to write them down—& separating from his family *because they distracted him*– This was told to my brother by a friend of Mr Tennyson's, but may be very gossip after all.

I see that Deerbrook is highly spoken of in the Athenæum.[28] I confess my own disappointment. It seems to me all on a level, as some people say the earth was, before the flood—& I long for a flood to break it into pieces, because in that case beautiful & noble bits of landscape might be extracted for high admirations. As it is, I cant help fancying that the illustrations of Political economy suggested the existence of more vivid powers, more imaginat[i]vely vivid, than any visible here. Besides if I had been the hero I sh.[d] have managed to emerge from the last embarassment in half his time, tho' with but the thousandth part of his philosophy.[29] Tell me what you think.

No. 687 10 April [1839] 133

They carried me down stairs into the drawing room for two weary hours about ten days ago—but the weather has since kept me upstairs. I have had no new attack from this east wind—but feel very oppressed & uncomfortable— Dr Barry considers that upon a change of temperature I shall certainly come to the surface again—& it is satisfactory to be sure that I have gained strength surprisingly during the last two months, or rather six weeks. For weeks before I was reduced to all but the harmlessness of babyhood—lifting a spoon to my own lips being the only point on which I c^d claim precedence. Even now I am sure I c^d not stand a moment alone—but here is summer, *coming* tho' not in sight—& she sends a sort of mental sunshine *before*. It is wonderful that I should have rallied at all from the last attacks—& I cant help feeling very often that I *am* to rally from everything & fulfil some of those affectionate prayers of yours for which, in reference to all results I do most tenderly thank you. Of one thing I am very sure--the God of hope is the fulfiller of hope—of the hope of all such who look to his face thro' the agony of His Son! But we err in straightening hope to low & narrow objects, when we sh^d expand it to the embracing of *Good* in the abstract, & leave the meaning of *good* to the Supreme Mind. The God of hope will give the hopeful, *Good*--whether by life or death. May He forbid that I limit my conception of GOOD to only *life*—!——

Oh!—they were *so* delighted (in Wimpole St) with the seeds[30]—& Arabel's pleasure in hearing from you[31] (such kind words she said they were!) was worth a garland full-blown. You w^d laugh to see the primroses in this room—& the branch of yellow heath which I like better than all the rest, because it seems to me a token more directly from Nature's own heart! And yet it is a shame to bring them into the dark, to die,—& I could, if I tried, get up a very pretty tragedy of remorse about it.

Give my kind & grateful regards to dear Dr Mitford! How kind of him to drink my health,—& to think of me at anytime. He shall have more fish when they *will* be caught. Did you send the *basket*? We have not heard of it!—[32]

Pray pray do not fancy that I am suffering under any expectation of POPULARITY, sooner or later. I w^d just as soon cry for the Pope's tiara--& as vainly!——

Mr. Reade has power—a power of *elancement*[33] both of thought & language; but I do not think his Italy w^d have been "equal to Childe Harold if the latter had not been written first"[34]—simply because I *do* think that under such an hypothesis Italy w^d not have been written *at all*. It is the only poem of Mr Reade's I ever read; & without impugning any faculty of its author's, I may confess to *you* that it *provoked* me. He *can* walk alone & he OUGHT to walk alone. There is an individuality in all minds, which requires only an internal energy & a power of outward expression, to become an originality. M! Reade who has both, stands without excuse in that very singular *watch beside a* SHRINE selected by the idiosyncracy of his ambition. Oh!—how impertinent all this is!— Do forgive it & me. Your kindness tempts me & *spoils* me into impertinence. M! Naylor's book I never saw—[35]

Here must be the end, dearest Miss Mitford.

> I am ever & ever
> Your gratefully attached
> E B Barrett.

L? Methuen has the gout in his franking hand—& L? Sinclair[36] lives a mile off. But I shall struggle for a frank— Do remember,—this letter was written APRIL 10.th.

Publication: EBB-MRM, I, 116–122.
Manuscript: Wellesley College.

1. Year provided by internal references.
2. Miss Mitford was contemplating a tour of Herefordshire and serial publication of her impressions; EBB's knowledge of the area would have been helpful to her. However, nothing came of this plan.
3. EBB's reference is not clear; she may have had in mind the column erected outside Calais to mark the spot where Jean Pierre Blanchard (1753–1809) descended after the first cross-Channel balloon flight in 1785.
4. Wordsworth had undertaken a walking tour in Scotland in 1831, and this formed the basis for a series of poems published in *The Literary Souvenir* in 1833, later incorporated in his *Yarrow Revisited and Other Poems* (1835).
5. Cassandra's misfortune, of course, was that none of her prophecies was believed.
6. From the context, it would appear that EBB meant Mr. Tilt, the proprietor of *Findens' Tableaux*, rather than William Tait, the publisher of *Tait's Edinburgh Magazine*.
7. The friend in question was Lucy Anderdon.
8. A punning reference to the genie who materialized to do Aladdin's bidding whenever the magic lamp was rubbed ("Aladdin or the Wonderful Lamp" in *The Arabian Nights' Entertainments*).
9. "St. Catherine of Ledbury," dealing with St. Catherine Audley (ca. 1400), was included in Wordsworth's *Yarrow Revisited*.
10. Cf. John, 11:33.
11. Lancelot Andrewes (1555–1626), successively Bishop of Chichester, Ely, and Winchester, Dean of the Chapel Royal, was one of the eminent churchmen appointed by King James to make new translations of the Bible for an "authorized version." He was master of 15 languages and the author of many works. EBB's reference may be to his sermons, 96 of which were published in a folio edition in 1628.
12. Cf. the last line of verses 2 and 3 of Tennyson's "The Mermaid."
13. Henry Francis Cary (1772–1844), a friend of Miss Mitford, had published translations of Dante in 1805 and 1812; he had also translated Aristophanes and Pindar.
14. Richard Hooker (1554?–1600) was "the ablest living advocate of the church of England" (*DNB*), known for *Of the Lawes of Ecclesiasticall Politie* (1594–97). He was the subject of EBB's verse "On laying Hooker under my pillow at night" (see *Reconstruction*, D643). Isaac Barrow (1630–77), Master of Trinity College, Cambridge, classical scholar and mathematician, was the author of *Exposition of the Creed, Decalogue, and Sacraments* (1669). Jeremy Taylor (1613–67), Bishop of Down and Connor, delivered the "Gunpowder Treason" sermon in Oxford on 5 November 1638 and was the author

of many works, including *The Rule and Exercises of Holy Living*, the 1813 edition of which was sold in *Browning Collections* (see *Reconstruction*, A2259).
15. *Britannia's Pastorals* (1613–16) by William Browne (1591–1643?). EBB used some lines from this work as the motto for "A Vision of Poets" in *Poems* (1844).
16. William Langland or Langley (1330?–1400?), the putative author of *The Vision of William Concerning Piers Plowman*, in which the poet falls asleep in the Malvern Hills and dreams.
17. This work, published 1613–22, by Michael Drayton (1563–1631), was relevant to Miss Mitford's proposed tour, its full title being *Poly-olbion. Or a Chorographicall Description of Tracts, Rivers, Mountaines, Forests, and other Parts of this renowned Isle of Great Britaine, With intermixture of the most Remarquable Stories, Antiquities, Rarityes, Pleasures, and Commodities of the same.*
18. Underscored twice.
19. Cf. the old nursery rhyme, "One, two, buckle my shoe; three, four, shut the door; five, six, pick up sticks."
20. i.e., an ass's head, in reference to act III of *A Midsummer Night's Dream*.
21. Cf. Pope, *Ode for Musick. On St. Cecilia's Day* (1713), line 91.
22. See letter 685.
23. A reference to Miss Mitford's *Atherton*, in progress but not published until 1854.
24. It was in the Capitol, where Julius Cæsar was to receive the crown, that he was assassinated, 44 B.C.
25. Emma Roberts (1794–1840) contributed a memoir of Miss Landon (Mrs. Maclean) to *The Zenana, and Other Poems, By L.E.L.* (1839). On p. 14, she said of L.E.L.: "Though enduring illness with fortitude, the fine susceptibility of her nervous system rendered her very impatient under pain; she seemed to suffer more than others from spasms or cramps ... judging from my own acquaintance with her, I should say, that she was exactly the person who would fly to the most desperate remedy for relief from pain, but unless in some moment of actual delirium ... she never wilfully would have destroyed herself." EBB's copy of the book formed lot 812 of *Browning Collections* (see *Reconstruction*, A1385); it was the gift of Henrietta (see SD986).
26. The derivation of this saying is dealt with by William Carew Hazlitt (1834–1913) in his *English Proverbs* (1869, p. 328).
27. Tennyson spent the autumn of 1838 in Torquay, where he wrote "Audley Court" (*Alfred Lord Tennyson: A Memoir By His Son*, 1898–99, I, 165).
28. Harriet Martineau's novel, *Deerbrook*, was reviewed in *The Athenæum* of 6 April 1839 (no. 597, pp. 254–256). After speaking of "close observation of character, and a strong poetical feeling for nature" in her *Illustrations of Political Economy*, the reviewer spoke of expecting "in this her more mature effort, a work of fiction whose vitality and freshness should put to shame the feverish and conventional things, which are thrust upon us by the hundred, as pictures of human life. Such a work, though not in every point equalling our expectations, is the novel before us."
29. In Book II of *Deerbrook* (ch. XX ff.), the hero breaks off his engagement in the belief (based on falsehoods spread by his sister) that his betrothed loves another. All ends well—eventually.
30. Miss Mitford had sent EBB two of the seeds received from Miss Landon (Mrs. Maclean) in Africa (see letter 683).
31. See SD992.
32. EBB had given Miss Mitford instructions for the return, without expense to Miss Mitford, of the basket used for sending fish to Dr. Mitford (see letter 683).
33. "Force; ardour."
34. For comment on the close parallels between Reade's *Italy* and Byron's *Childe Harold's Pilgrimage*, see letter 643, note 3.
35. The book in question was *Ceracchi, a Drama and Other Poems* (1839) by Samuel Naylor (1809–65). EBB subsequently received from him a presentation copy, which sold in *Browning Collections* (see *Reconstruction*, A1722); she comments on the work in letters 702 and 703.

36. Paul Methuen (1779–1849) had been created 1st Baron Methuen following Victoria's coronation. From the context, he and Charles St. Clair, 13th Baron Sinclair (1768–1863) were both in Torquay at this time; both had franking privileges as peers.

688. EBB TO SAMUEL MOULTON-BARRETT (BROTHER)

[Torquay]
[*Postmark:* 19 April 1839]

My ever dearest Sam, not the chancellor's great seal could cover what I want to write to you—much less, Henrietta's little one.[1] I am afraid she is turning into a miser—but she need'nt & shant make me *misera*[2] by denying me the sweep of my plume[3] this morning,—you were so kind as to send me a very welcome & a very kind little note some time ago—& I do entreat you my dearest Sam to believe that I value your affection & respond to every breath of it whether *my* breath comes & goes silently or not!– It is something to feel that you are in England[4]—something but not all. And I cannot help sometimes being near to a murmur that your visit sh^d have hitherto been almost & so far a thing [']'to hear of & not to see"[5]—& what is to me still painfuller, that I sh^d be the means of interfering between you & the happiness you naturally expected in dearest Henrietta's society, & Bro's—& between them & your happiness– Oh! may we see you very soon, to put all this out of our heads–

You are not, any of you, to think a second time, of the blister[6]—which has maimed me so little, you see, this morning. The *impulse* given to the circulation by the last two or three days cold winds, wdnt come to an end at the first change to sunshine & west winds—altho' I fancied it w^d.– I felt so much better three days ago for one day– But the pulsation & a little feverishness have been disquieting me yesterday & the day before— & saline draughts w^d not do *all* the good, tho' apparently well inclined to do their share. So Dr Barry went last night to the root of the matter & ordered a blister, & I am the better for it this morning, & the action of the heart fallen to an ordinary and respectable jog trot. There was some slight pain in the chest—but nothing either to mind, or to make a fuss about.

Tell Arabel I cant wait any longer for Miss Bordman's note, or Dr Elliotson's pamphlet.[7] She must have quite forgotten me to have such an idea of my patience. Tell her she had far better put everything into a small bandbox & with them, a packet of letters & my *satin bonnet*. Dr Barry told me two or three days ago that he hoped to get me into the air in a month's time!! & I cant go out without a bonnet. That's certain! & I have not any here except a black one. So tell Arabel to pack up the bandbox, & send it—not in a month but NOW! I have been dreaming of walking with Papa. Such a walk we had!– He led me over gates & stiles & palings of all sorts, till I was quite out of breath. But it was a pleasant walk after all—& in the course of it, we met a child of Wordsworth's, & it held out its arms to kiss me! And then came a most tremendous rain in which Papa vanished away—and appeared a dreadful vision of Dr Barry in wrath– Did I mean to commit felo de &c.?[8] So I was transferred to a burning hot fire side, to dry my soaked shoes—and I could not find them when they were dried, to put on again! I cd find nothing but one immense shoe with Harriet Martineau written inside, & large enough for me to live inside of! So, like my illustrious predecessor who lived in a shoe,[9] I did'nt know what to do–

Unfortunate Ba to be forced to tell her dreams for lack of more amusing matter—& more unfortunate Sam to have to hear them——

Give my most tender love to my beloved Papa, & all the Beloveds. Tell Mary [Hunter] that her father has never written a word to me, & that I am inexorably angry. Love to dearest Trippy, to whom I am going to write a scold– Mention dear Minny's *eyes*—& say how Mrs Nuttall is!–

> My dearest Sam's
> sincerely attached
> Ba

The expectoration *very little*.

Address, on integral page: S M Barrett Esqr / 50. Wimpole Street. / London.
Publication: None traced.
Manuscript: Edward R. Moulton-Barrett.

1. This letter follows one written by Henrietta (SD998) and was sealed with a very small, green wax seal. Henrietta left EBB only one flap of the cover sheet upon which to write; uncharacteristically, EBB's letter is partly cross-written over Henrietta's.
2. "Unhappy."
3. A punning reference to "ma plume" (my pen).
4. Sam had returned to England from Jamaica in the previous November.
5. Cf. Matthew, 13:13.
6. See letter 599, note 2.
7. See the conclusion of letter 686.
8. Felo-de-se: suicide.
9. i.e., the Old Woman in the nursery rhyme, who had so many children that she didn't know what to do.

---

689. RB TO EUPHRASIA FANNY HAWORTH

[London]
Thursday Night. [?25] [April 1839][1]

Dear Miss Haworth,

You once said "letters were vile things"—they will be admirable things with me ere long, for the virtue and knack have gone out of me;

I talk better, rather, than I used,—certainly better; and as one swings over briar and puddle best with one pole only, so do "Come over into Macedonia and help us"[2]—besloughed in a comparison–

It must be this warm-chilly April weather, sweet-sour like violet punch, that undoes me. Soberly—eh? Oh! Those rhymes are rare: every body knows *I*[3] beat the world that way—can tie and untie English as a Roman girl a tame serpent's tail—but rare are those rhymes all the same. Do you know I was, and am, an Improovisatore of the HEAD—not of the *hort* (vide Cheveley)[4]—not you! (Know anything about me)[5]

You read Balzac's "Scènes" etc—he is publishing one, "Béatrix", in the feuilleton of the "Siécle", day by day–[6] I receive it from Paris two days old and usually post it off to a friend of mine, as soon as skimmed. But the four or five first chapters were so delightful that I hate myself for not having sent them to Barham[7]—and console myself only by knowing that you are spared a sad disappointment as well—for the going on of it all is naught—a story of Guérande in Bretagne–[8] He makes it out a sort of Venice. I told somebody, on the point of going to Bordeaux, to get there if he loved me (he does, I think). "Why" quoth he "I pass within five or six miles of it"—ie, overland, by Nantes;—yet all my wisest charming went to the deaf adder[9]—I don't believe the man will take the trouble to leave his route–

Did Mrs Macready tell you of the outrageous rascality of the Covent G. Renters, or their representatives?[10]

Don't let me leave out the praises of your nonsense.

My eye is caught by an old proof of an article by Fox, my Chiron in a small way:[11] I wonder whether this is not the style you like? Tell me—it is a good sample of his ware.

Do you know Milnes' Poems? or himself peradventure?

I shall put in a funny thing disinterred along with Fox's lucubration—very funny I thought it at the time: the print too!

Write very soon, pray.

RB

No. 690   29 April [1839]   139

What the children were singing last year in Venice, arm over neck.[12]

Publication: NL, pp. 15–18.
Manuscript: Huntington Library.

    1. Dated by the reference to *Le Siècle*.
    2. Acts, 16:9.
    3. Underscored twice.
    4. See letter 691, note 13.
    5. RB added this parenthetical phrase as an afterthought.
    6. *Béatrix ou les Amours Forcés* was serialized in *Le Siècle*, commencing on 13 April 1839. RB's reference to "the four or five first chapters" provides the conjectural dating.
    7. Barham Lodge, Miss Haworth's home in Elstree.
    8. Balzac devotes more than 100 pages of *Béatrix* to a description of Guérande and its people.
    9. Cf. Psalms, 58:4.
    10. Macready had held his position as actor-manager at Covent Garden for two years based only on a verbal agreement. The proprietors subsequently saw fit to disregard this pledge (see diary entries for 10–13 April 1839, *Macready*, I, 508–510).
    11. An acknowledgement of Fox's influence on RB. Chiron was a centaur who taught Achilles, Hercules and other heroes music, medicine and hunting.
    12. Attempts to identify this tune are dealt with by Jacob Korg in his *Browning and Italy* (1983), p. 230, note 19.

---

690. EBB TO ARABELLA MOULTON-BARRETT

[Torquay]
Monday– April 29. [1839][1]

My ever dearest Arabel,

You will be surprised to hear of me in such an out of the way manner—& must not be cross if only very few words are laid at their FULL[2] length upon this paper—seeing that they seem to go to you in a parenthesis of opportunities. I meant to have sent Mary's mantilla by the Hedleys & your drawing book by the same; but they don't go to London as soon as they intended I am very glad to find—and here is an opportunity——I "*say to all the world, 'this is a Mann'*"[3]—not a man of Ross[4] but of Torquay,—'an honest man' I do not doubt, & a very obliging one I am sure——Mr Mann linen draper,—successor to Mr Hall of the like profession——who offers to take anything to London for us on the coming evening. I therefore send mantilla & drawing book by the aforesaid. You used not to have a block drawing book—& you must not call me a block head for sending you such a book. In the first place I have coveted one for you ever since I saw Brozie's—and then it seems so likely that you may sit a good deal on the top of the monument[5] for air this hot weather, & so possible that you who recognize my handwriting on a letter in the postman's hand at the other side of the street (oh Arabel!!!) sh.^d be able to take a birds eye view of Hampstead & its adjacent pastoralities from any window in Wimpole Street, that I feel bound to provide you immediately with materials for sketching. Tell darling Mary with my love to unfold the mantilla very carefully, as there is a particular scolding wrapt up in it, and I should be sorry if she didn't receive it whole. Her father told me in his last letter that he had not heard from her since he last received mine. His was only poetical justice,—but there is neither justice nor poetry in her never writing to ME. But mind Arabel! Give my most affectionate love to dearest Sam, & say how glad I shall be when he can write to me! But mind, Arabel! I EXACT two letters from YOU every week, whether I have other letters or not. So pray keep to your own business,—& dont be curious about my other correspondents. I have noted a meddling disposition about you, good my Lady, for some time past—whereupon goes to you this gentlewomanly hint to reform it altogether.

You *do* improve after all. Yes! I knew of your farsightedness, but of your second-sightedness I never even heard. When you read my letter across the street, did you make out QUITE clearly what was under the seal?–

As to my degeneracies as contrasted with your improvements, I must I suppose try to defend myself. You think me something both to encounter the "delightful drawing room" & attribute the whole to a backsliding from my old sea-love. Now Arabel listen to me. Of your faithfulness to nature it is impossible to doubt, seeing that it has never been tried– Therefore do let me imagine you transported somewhere near the meetings of the waters––of the four Edenic rivers,—to sward, smooth as velvet (as men-milliner-poets say) to air, light & warm as mous[s]eline de laine,[6] among trees nodding like ostrich feathers. And suppose that somebody whom you highly respected (Adam for instance) was pleased upon your prostration before him, to stand upon your chest in clodhopper shoes (forgive the anachronism) while Dame Eve amused herself by whipping your ankles very earnestly with a branch of primæval birch. What w^d you do?—what w^d you say? W^d you cry out pastorally & passionately, [']' Oh dear me, how pleasant! what a delightful situation this is"—or w^d you be degenerate like me, & wish yourself at Jericho?– 'I pause for a reply.'——

The fact is, notwithstanding the sofa close to the window & the window close to the sea, I did most emphatically abominate & nauseate the going down stairs yesterday. The change from a four-month-long imprisonment to this room, where from habitude I had grown to like the air & the silence, was quite sure to be felt unpleasantly—& pretending to covet the change except at a distance, was out of the question. But dont fancy me a murmurer. I never ever said to Dr. Barry 'I dont like going down stairs'—& indeed was quite aware in my inward soul that going down was a very necessary step to take. So I went, & managed better than on the last trial– There was no fainting. I was just uncomfortable & oppressed, & a little irritated as to coughing—but I stayed down stairs two hours & a half & did I believe, my full duty. Dr Barry cant say so. Oh the treachery of doctor-kind! He gave me an imitation nightdraught, thinking I suppose (indeed he intimated as much) that the fatigue w^d make me sleep without an opiate. I knew it w^d*nt*: & it didnt. Fatigue never does me such a service. So I had the pleasure of lying all night as wide awake as I am at this moment when I hope you dont fancy me half asleep—though you MAY. The weather is not warm—but *hot*—& we are fire-less. I had meditated leaving off my merino today, but Henrietta's counsel defers it till tomorrow. Just done dinner, & just going again down stairs. Undaunted you see!– Dr Barry says, & common sense said it before him, that a few days will reconcile me & the second floor. So dont sympathize with me too painfully for yourself. Give me till Thursday, & I shall be ready with an 'Ode out of a balcony'– Only pray remember that the sea is visible even from the bed of this room, though from the windows being higher, there is some restraint upon the vision. As to London I dont & wont deny the extent of my affection for it—whether due most to the smoke or you, you may settle between you!—— Certainly (*that* may be a guide) I long for the most to see YOU![7]——

You say nothing about Mr Moody?[8] How do my dearest Sette & Joc like him? The name is ominous.

Think of an old gentleman in ringlets coming to call upon me the other day? "Is Miss Barrett at home"?—& upon an affirmative he was just walking in. "Oh Sir," said Patten—"she is ill, & never sees company." "Ill! I am very sorry to hear it"—& off he went without leaving his name. Of course I was in a phrenzy of curiosity—particularly as Crow told me that he forthwith walked down towards the London steamer. However he came again the next morning (just as I had persuaded myself that he must have been a deputation from Wimpole Street—SO likely you know) & left his card, the Rev^d ___ Cave, & a case about some Baptist chapel. And so perished the mystery of the old gentleman in ringlets.

Arabel! he is nothing to *you!* How can you be so tantalizing! First of all you are "engaged"––in what way being swallowed by an hiatus. Then you are going to ask me something––what, there is no room to particularize– Only it is something very "incomprehensible". How can you be so provoking! If you do it again, I will get a medical certificate from Dr Barry, to prove that it does'nt agree with me. It never did. You must remember that I was always of an Eveish constitution.

Not a word of poor D.̣ Chambers! Surely you have not been so unkind as never to have sent to ask how he was!——

I meant to have written to Treppy today—but she shall hear from me by Jane [Hedley]. Give her in the meantime my affectionate love & congratulation upon being well again.

The two blank corners. I looked very blankly at them in opening your dear letter—but that dearest dearest Papa sh.ḍ have even MEANT to write in them was something.

They make me go down stairs at once. And so goodbye, beloved Arabel. On thursday I shall hear: & mind you tell me every, the very least thing!——

May the Father of our Lord Jesus Christ surround you with the love which that filial name renders so tender!——

There is plenty of nonsense in what I have written—but I cant look over it to ascertain *how* much. Henrietta's letter will reach you on *thursday* instead of *wednesday*: so dont expect one before. I am going on very well!—& you are not to think of me any more except in the way of pure love. Poor dear Bummy is better today—but the rheumatism has not quite left her face & head, & it affects her spirits a good deal. Herein I send L E L's seed[9]—and you are not to wear out any more knees in looking for it on the carpet.

Your very ever attached Ba.

I shall write next to my beloved Papa—& in the meanwhile shall dream of hearing from him.

Love to Minny.

This is Jane's birthday—& Arabella came here to breakfast—& she & Arlette & Cissy[10] are gone out holidayizing upon donkeys. The two latter confided the other day to Henrietta, that they like Torquay so *very* much better than Frocester!!

M.ṛ Hamilton[11] will have worn out Henrietta's poplin before he arrives here, which he is to do in a '*fortnight*'! I hope I shall not catch cold by going out the first time without a hat!!!!!

I am so sorry to hear of M.ṛ Kenyon's illness. My kind regards to him, whenever there is an opportunity of giving them.

How critical you are about handwriting. Be merciful (& I am sure you SH.Ḍ) to this. I have put away the seeds somewhere & in so very safe a place that I cant find them. Therefore YOU need'nt look for them.

Iron out the mantilla, if squeezed to death.

Address: Miss Arabel Barrett.
Publication: None traced.
Manuscript: Berg Collection.

1. During the period of EBB's stay in Torquay, 1839 was the only year in which 29 April fell on Monday.
2. EBB originally wrote "fool," which was changed to "full" and underscored twice. Above the line she explained: "(written *fool* by instinct)."
3. Cf. *Julius Caesar*, V, 5, 75.
4. Pope, *Epistle to Several Persons* (1744), III, 250.
5. The Monument, a 202 ft. Doric column near the north end of London Bridge, marks the spot where the Great Fire of 1666 started.
6. Literally "muslin of wool." A dress material originally composed wholly of wool, but afterwards of wool and cotton (*OED*).
7. Underscored three times.
8. SD1067 includes the comment: "Tell George that the Governor thinks he will scarcely be rich enow to pay Mr. Moody his account," thus establishing Moody as a tradesman. However, it is not possible to identify him further; *Robson's London Directory for 1839* lists 24 tradesmen of that name.
9. One of the two sent to EBB from those received by Miss Mitford from Africa (see letter 686).
10. EBB's cousins, the daughters of her late aunt, Charlotte Butler.
11. SD965 describes Mr. Hamilton as a friend of EBB's brother Sam, and speaks of his going boating for four hours with Bro. SD1024 mentions his receiving a commission in the 62nd Regiment: "I suspect he had rather entered the holy state of wedlock than the bloody profession of war."

691. EBB TO MARY RUSSELL MITFORD

Torquay.
Tuesday. [30 April 1839][1]

Ever dearest Miss Mitford,

I have been a little anxious about your muteness as well as about the 'mute fishes'[2]—wondering whether I had any right to imagine you & D.' Mitford tolerably well. Do, when it does not too much cross your convenience, let me hear! It seems so long since I heard last, & there are so many disagreeable & painful things in the world notwithstanding all these spring flowers, & I have such a knack of imagining them, that I w.^d gladly be sure of none of them having touched you. Dont fancy me forgetful of the fishbasket. But our servant seems to be a nervous person as to the qualifications of travelling fish—and I told you before that fish in this market, when worth anything, is not very often fish directly from the sea.

Did you look into Blackwood this month—& (à propos to fish) perceive how Christopher's [']'Oystereater" congenially with Tait's Opium Eater, apostrophizes the "charming & adorable Mary Russell Mitford"—?—[3] You see no sort of diet will expel the admirations due to you—& the imaginative with their opium, & the literal with their oysters come to the same point at last. Nay—the very oysters are infected, if it be true that *"the* WORLD['] S *mine oyster.".*[4]

I am sorry, very sorry to hear of poor M.ʳ Kenyon's being laid up again with rheumatism—quite unable to move—& do trust that these attacks are not precursive of any such painful life as is led by his brother. That rheumatism is so fond of repeating itself!——

How right you are not to give away your time to languages. So is everybody who can do anything better-

"And Hebrew roots grow best on barren ground".[5]

The grammar & dictionary drudgery are past bearing, as soon as we have learnt to think- Faust's incantations threw me upon German a year or two ago, but could not keep me in a very exemplary humour notwithstanding. Yet there is a use for all things—for thistles & Babel too: and at painful times, when composition is impossible & reading not *enough*, grammars & dictionaries are excellent for *distraction.* Just at such a time .. when we were leaving Herefordshire .. I pinned myself down to Hebrew, took Parkhurst & Professor Lee for my familiars, & went through the Hebrew Bible from Genesis to Malachi, Syriac & all, as if I were studying for a professorship,[6]—& never once halting for breath. But I do hope & trust to learn no more new languages. There is no mental exertion, per se so little beneficial to the mind-

I covet your familiarity with all sorts of French literature .. a little: but not painfully. French poetry, so called by courtesy, always comes to me cold as prose—& this indisposition of mine has conveyed itself to the prose perhaps scarcely consciously. I believe Pascal stirs me more than any other French writer—at least strikes me as less French--& as endued with a sort of intellect that reaches deeper down to the feelings .. as deep intellectuality will always do .. than that of the national multitude. I am very backward as to the *Memoirs*—& a hundred miles behind everybody as to French literature of the present day—knowing scarcely anything except of Lamartine & Victor Hugo—& Edgar Quinet, by grace of the Athenæum,[7]—& the Athenæum's own Rhapsodist in criticism (Jules Janin) who in his proper particular practice you know, adopted the Siamese twins idealized, as heroines of romance- Peace to the souls of the heroines! They had two pairs of eyes .. black & blue .. had'nt they?—& only one heart—which was scarcely fair, & turned out to be very unfortunate.[8]

Do you know George Sand—& Paul De Kock?-[9] I am curious respecting the former-

What exquisite weather. They have carried me down to the drawing room—twice in the light of it—and I am very tolerably comfortable & well—longing to get back to London, longing to be with them all once more, in Wimpole Street. But moving is out of the question for me just now .. & must be, before quite the end of May or the first days of June—& even then, there is no plan fixed for me. I MUST[10] be with them this summer—I MUST *indeed*. I keep saying *that* day after day.

God bless you my beloved friend! Give my very kind regards—will you? to D! Mitford—& do tell me as much as I may hear of your plans loco-motive & literary. When do you go upon the *tour*?—[11] My love to the flowers! How beautiful they must look from your summer room! Have you ventured yet to begin its occupation?—

I hear good news of your seeds which are giving green promise in Wimpole Street.[12] But how disappointed the poor flowers will be when they come & see nothing but bricks!——& nothing of *you!*—

Is M! Chorley in better health?—Tell me.

Again disappointed about the fish! But there is hope for tomorrow.

Once more God bless you.
Most affectionately your
Elizabeth B B.

Cheveley or the man of honor—
Lady Cheveley or the woman of honor.

Have you observed the latter advertisement?[13] I have seen neither book, but am arrived at two conclusions— The first is, that however infamous Sir Lytton's conduct as a husband may have been—heaping it with every imaginable infamy—Lady Lytton deserves the whole of it— The second—that when a husband lives in London & his wife at Bath, there is no excuse for either, upon any disturbance of their *domestic harmony*. A hundred miles between, really ought to secure some degree of connubial felicity as the world wags—but unfortunately it *wages*— Seriously, how could a woman if ever so unwomanly achieve such an unwomanlyness?— The flippancy too of some of the extracts which is irreconcilable with the only excuse for her .. a good earnest downright fury of a passion .. is inexpressibly disgusting to me.

Publication: EBB-MRM, I, 122–125.
Manuscript: Wellesley College.

1. Dated by reference to the advertisement in *The Athenæum*.
2. William Congreve (1670–1729), *The Way of the World* (1700), IV, 9, 4.
3. *Blackwood's Edinburgh Magazine*, in an article entitled "Some Account of Himself. By the Irish Oyster Eater" (April 1839, pp. 463–475), included this passage: "'And where is your home, my dear little maid?' enquired I. 'Not far,' replied the little girl—'not very far—at *our village*.' Our village!—I thought of the charming—the adorable Mary Russel [*sic*] Mitford. Our village!—there was nature, kindliness, and simple-hearted tenderness in the very sound."

Tait's Edinburgh Magazine, under the heading "Lake Reminiscences, from 1807 to 1830. By the English Opium-Eater" (April 1839, pp. 246–254), spoke of Dorothy Wordsworth as being "thoroughly deficient (some would say painfully deficient—I say charmingly deficient) in ordinary female accomplishments, as '*Cousin* Mary' in Miss

Mitford's delightful sketch." Later in the article, the writer [Thomas De Quincey] says "We all know with how womanly and serene a temper literature has been pursued by Joanna Baillie, by Miss Mitford, and other women of admirable genius—with how absolutely no sacrifice or loss of feminine dignity they have cultivated the profession of authorship" and surmises that "the little cares of correcting proofs ... must inevitably have done much to solace the troubles, which, as human beings, they cannot but have experienced; and even to scatter flowers upon their path."

4. *The Merry Wives of Windsor*, II, 2, 3. The second word is underscored three times.

5. Cf. Butler's *Hudibras*, I, 1, 59–60.

6. EBB's copy of *An Hebrew and English Lexicon* (2nd edition, 1778), by John Parkhurst (1728–97), formed lot 967 of *Browning Collections* (see *Reconstruction*, A1813). Samuel Lee (1783–1852), Professor of Arabic at Cambridge and later Regius Professor of Hebrew, was said to have been master of 18 languages. He was the editor of scholarly editions of various parts of the Bible in Syriac, Malay, Arabic, Coptic, Persian and Hindustani. In 1827, he published *A Grammar of the Hebrew Language*, which reached a sixth edition in 1844. EBB's annotated Hebrew Bible is now at Union Theological Seminary (see letter 468, note 5).

7. See letter 653, note 6.

8. Jules Janin (1804–74) was a French journalist and critic, particularly of drama, who contributed reviews to *The Athenæum*. EBB's reference may have been to his *Une Femme à Deux Têtes* (1829), or to *Un Cœur Pour Deux Amours* (1833), which was based on the earlier work.

9. Charles Paul de Kock (1793–1871) wrote novels depicting middle- and lower-class life, including *André le Savoyard* (1825) and *Le Barbier de Paris* (1826).

10. Underscored four times.

11. See letter 687.

12. The two seeds sent to EBB (see letter 683) from those received by Miss Mitford from Africa.

13. Rosina, Lady Bulwer-Lytton (*née* Wheeler, 1802–82) had been separated from her husband, the well-known novelist and M.P., since 1836. Angered by what she believed to be his lack of generosity in the financial provisions he made for her, she attempted to obtain redress by legal and other means. She had recently published a novel, *Cheveley, or the Man of Honour*, in which the villain was a thinly-disguised depiction of her husband. *The Athenæum* of 27 April 1839, in its "List of New Books" (p. 314), included an anonymous rhyming brochure, *Lady Cheveley, or the Woman of Honour*. Lady Bulwer believed it to be her husband's work, but this he denied.

---

692. EBB TO MARY RUSSELL MITFORD

Torquay.
Thursday. [16 May 1839][1]

I knew it was so—I felt it was—& in the course of my long waking last night I had resolved to write to you today, if only six words just to beg for as many from you my beloved friend. I knew that dear Dr Mitford was not well, or that you were not well—& your letter this morning so eagerly seized & opened proves it true of both of you, & yet, I thank God, is far below my fears. Henrietta tried to persuade me that you had begun your tour,—of course all in vain! You w^d not have gone away without telling me what had become of you—I knew *that*. The weather is very trying & accounts for every indisposition—but I do trust & pray that you may have no more anxieties for him the dearest to you—nor any to give away to others, for yourself. Think of your stooping in the sun until you make yourself ill, & all for a garden!– Indeed it is almost unkind to us & *quite wrong* to do such a thing; & I beg & beseech you to try to find out some other John than the one who married Martha,[2] with some sort of horticultural acquirement, who would spare you from the effect of carrying on this apprenticeship system under the sun—just for a time you know. Surely any Belford Regis[3] gardener w^d be proud to be allowed to help you. At any rate, I shall think high treason against the geraniums—& if you dont let them die rather than injure you they shall be as nettles in my sight for ever & ever.

The winds have done me no more harm than to make me feel uncomfortable, & shut me up again in my bedroom where I have been for several days. But what makes me write to you so very soon as this morning, is to beg you not to take the slightest trouble about the baskets which are worth none, & also to beg for Mr Naylor's book[4] which as he was so kind as to permit me to see, I sh^d like to see whenever you have time to pack it up in brown paper & direct it to me, per coach or mail. If there SH^D be a note from you inside, the happier for *me* you know!—— Dont send it *in the basket*, because that w^d be to the overthrowing of the return-basket principle. I mentioned the returning of the baskets only because I had fancied that you w^d have no more trouble in accomplishing it than was involved in writing my name on the other side of the direction-card—(by the way, the *first* came back safely)—but I do assure you that the race of basket-makers is not extinct here, barbarous as we are, & that Dr Mitford may & *shall* have his fish sometimes without any *return*-basket to put it in. In the meantime, try to *forgive me*. I am sure it must need an effort—for if it had not been for this fussy & most unpoetical thrift of mine, you might not have known a word of the neighbourhood of the omnibus—not for another year at least!

Thank you my very dear friend, on the part of "*our* boys", for your meditated kindness to them—and as to Papa why I sh^d certainly *disinherit* him if he were not three-quarters as delighted as they will be. And then the nosegay for Arabel!—— You are *so* kind--& with that peculiar sort of kindness which comes close to us & makes us love you!—— It is not thus of all kindnesses--oh no!——

I am glad you have looked at Cheveley.[5] *Now* I can confess with one blush less that I have just read it through. People obliged to be dumb like me, & under a medical disciplinarian like Dr Barry have as good an excuse as any can have for reading it—but after all, my *curiosity* & "not my will consented".[6] I do believe, if it had not been for you, I sh^d have looked about for some large Harpocratic cabbage rose—very large—large enough & red enough to cover my offence immediately after its perpetration.[7] The book, if not the reader, is without excuse. It is wonderful in unwomanliness—one thing being easy & clear to see—that GRIEF NEVER MADE IT. My dearest Miss Mitford, if her children had all been rolled to Mount Taygetus[8] in wheelbarrows, grief would never have brought to pass such a book as Cheveley. Wounded vanity might—never, wounded affections! The book is a hard cold coarse book—a bold impudent book—& she who wrote it may have COUNTED many strifes but has *felt* none—*not one*—not even the worst & keenest which hardens after it has agonized.

And so I can scarcely agree with you that any possible circumstances c^d have made—a *woman* of her! I cannot, cannot think it. There is indelicacy of intellect & heart, from the root upward. Her very learning has a flippancy in it, & a coarse-coloured blueism in the display of it—nothing of the scholar's polish & reserve & depth & "signs of meditation"—& everything of the assumption & superficialness of third-form acquirement. Your words "clever & shrewd" are just the right words–Dearest Miss Mitford, Mrs Gore is not a woman of *genius*[9]––at least I think not—but she is a *woman*—& is this Lady Bulwer either?–

Forgive me for being so cross—or laugh, which will be better. I believe I feel a little angry for Bulwer's sake as well as for our womanhood's—& you *know* that *you* are angry simply for the latter cause. He may have acted "without excuse" *as she* has written—but not (I very much suspect) without provocation. That *he can feel*, I am as sure, as that *she cannot*. And it is as fixed in my creed as it is repudiated from hers, that no human being can write with passion & pathos to whom those *things* are mere *words*. *That* (the supposition of such possibility) is the cant of the world & of the Lady Byrons & the Lady Bulwers in it—& whenever I hear that cant,—I shrink from the canter as from one *unsound at heart*. Suppose *me* to write a treatise upon the Corn laws![10] or a disquisition on Jereny [sic] Bentham's panopticon![11] A fine business I sh^d make of it! And is the heart's ignorance less impotent than the head's—?– Oh, DO agree with me–

You made me laugh with your report (upon Mr Chorley's authority) of the process of Mr Tennyson's inspiration.[12] If I were a Miss Tennyson I sh^d be *so* inclined to retort––"Let the brother be taken away & the writing desk"[13]—only I conclude that writing desks are far too sublunary for the inspired. I never sh^d have expected the affectations of a "gentleman-parcel-poet"[14] from HIM, & do trust that he may smoke them into 'thin air'[15] as soon as may be. It w^d be the best use of tobacco, since Phillips's![16]

I was speaking of Mr May to Dr Barry—& he said "I think I have heard of him." Dr Barry is a very intelligent physician—devoted to his profession.

No plan fixed about my removal to London! I LONG to be at home—but am none the nearer for *that*. God's mercies are very very undeservedly great to me,—& for *me* to be *patient* under any little trial, sh.^d be called rather *gratitude* than patience—but I DO HOPE to be at home this summer.

Is Mr Townsend married?[17] Have you any communication with him now?

Tell me all you can about *yourself*. Mr Tilt's silence, if it continue silence, becomes ominous. Mr Kenyon is quite well again (so Arabel says) & Mr Wordsworth either is or has been staying with him, & Mr Southey has been *asked, in vain*—being about, you know, to marry a wife.[18] Think of Mr Rogers doing the like?—I mean as to marrying the wife[19]—"Deities, are you all agreed?"[20] You will forgive the Queen *now* for going to see the Lions![21] She deserves it of you!—and you deserve of me, that I sh.^d not weary you to death! Goodbye dearest dearest Miss Mitford. Love to Dr Mitford—he shall have more fish—& how c.^d you fancy that it was a trouble or anything except a pleasure, for me to send it!-

Thank you again & again, though so late, for your valued letter. May the next speak more blythely of you both!—that it may, *so* do the part of all your writings, letters & all--"bring delight & *hurt not*"-[22]

Most affec^{tly}
Your EBB.

I hear that Ld Methuen has had a letter from Sir John C Hobhouse in wh. he says that the Queen is in the utmost indignation—declaring that as long as she sits on the throne of England Sir R Peel shall never be reinvited to pass her palace gates.[23] Hic jacet Toryism-[24]

I am so glad Taite & Blackwood pleased Dr Mitford—& I will not forget to please him again when the opportunity arises.

How & where is Mrs Dupuy? And is Mr H. Chorley's health better?-Do you ever think of going to London?-

Addressed and franked by Lord Methuen: Torquay May Twenty 1839 / Miss Mitford / Three Mile's Cross / Reading / Methuen / [and in EBB's hand on reverse of envelope] Miss Mitford / Three Mile Cross / Near Reading.
Publication: EBB-MRM, I, 125-129.
Manuscript: Edward R. Moulton-Barrett and Wellesley College.

1. Dated by the frank.
2. i.e., a gardener to replace John Lediard, who had left Miss Mitford's employment after his marriage to Miss Mitford's maid.
3. i.e., local, Miss Mitford's fictional Belford Regis having been modelled on Reading.
4. See letter 687, note 35.
5. See letter 691, note 13.
6. Cf. *Romeo and Juliet*, V, 1, 75.
7. Harpocrates, the Greek version of the Egyptian sun-god Horus, was represented as a naked boy sucking his finger, and was venerated by the Greeks as the god of silence and secrecy. The association of Harpocrates with the large flowers of the cabbage rose suggests that EBB means she would have buried her face in the flower, in an embarrassed silence.

8. The Spartans killed deformed or unwanted children by throwing them from Mt. Taygetus, in the southern part of the Peloponnesus.

9. Catherine Grace Frances Gore (*née* Moody, 1799–1861), a prolific novelist, playwright and composer.

10. See letter 540, note 3.

11. Bentham, author of *Rationale of Punishments and Rewards* (1825), expended much time and effort advocating the use of the pantopticon, a design for a prison which was to be "circular, with cells on every story of the circumference. In the centre there was a lodge for the inspector, who would be able to see all the prisoners without being himself seen, and who could give directions without being obliged to quit his post" (*DNB*).

12. Doubtless a reference to Tennyson's being a heavy smoker.

13. In letter 700, also speaking of Tennyson, EBB says "let the sisters be brought & the harps." This phrase appears to be a humorous variation.

14. Jonson, *The Poëtaster; or, His Arraignment* (1616), IV, 6, 28.

15. *The Tempest*, IV, 1, 150.

16. John Philips (1676–1709) praised the properties of tobacco in most of his writings.

17. There is some doubt as to the date of Townsend's marriage. See letter 664, note 11.

18. His marriage to Caroline Anne Bowles took place on 5 June 1839.

19. Samuel Rogers (1763–1855) never married, but there was a rumour that he was to marry Miss Clarke, Lady Morgan's niece (L'Estrange (2), III, 98).

20. Jonson, *The Poëtaster*, IV, 5, 42.

21. Queen Victoria went six times to see the American lion-tamer, Isaac Van Amburgh (1811–65), at Drury Lane Theatre.

22. Cf. *The Tempest*, III, 2, 136.

23. When Melbourne's ministry resigned on 6 May, the Duke of Wellington was invited to form an administration, but he advised the Queen to entrust Peel with the formation of a new ministry. Peel was prepared to do so, but stipulated that the Mistress of the Robes and the Ladies of the Bedchamber (all appointed on the advice of Melbourne) be removed. The Queen wrote to Peel on 10 May, saying that she "cannot consent to adopt a course which she conceives to be contrary to usage, and which is repugnant to her feelings" and refusing to be parted from the "companions of her childhood, the friends of her youth." Peel then declined to take office, and Melbourne was recalled. Much discussion ensued regarding Peel's assertion that the appointments were more political than ceremonial and were, therefore, subject to change by any incoming ministry. See *The Times*, 13 May 1839.

24. "Here lies Toryism."

693. EBB to Hugh Stuart Boyd

Torquay.
May 21st 1839.

My ever dear friend,

I am very very sorry to understand from Arabel that you are not pleased with me for not having noticed even by a message the "*three or four*" letters which you have written to me. When did you write to me three or four letters? I am conscious of having in my possession only one unanswered letter which I was about to reply to at the end of January when the bad attack came on and prevented my writing at all for a very long time. *That* was the last writing project in my head!—& if I did not carry it into effect quite as soon as I was able, & as I did write to others, it was because I DO KNOW that you are not apt to be made uncomfortable by epistolary silences, & that the pleasure of our correspondence is rather more on *my* side than yours, notwithstanding your kindest feelings towards me. Lately I have been waiting for your return from Hampstead—& the cause of my sending no message is to be found in my intention of delivering it myself. You think this explanation dull enough. So be it—but pray dont think *me* ungrateful towards you or forgetful of you,—because, while I am alive, I can never deserve such a reproach; & there is a degree of painfulness in being *supposed* to deserve it, corresponding to that degree in which I value your regard.

Thank you my dear friend for the very kind opinions you sent me of the stanzas on LEL[1]—& on the care you took to give me pleasure by letting me know Leigh Hunt's of my poetry generally. Did it strike you that his criticism had two faces—one of them far from being as gracious-looking as the other? "Miss B– sits as a queen" &c &c "*but* her poetry is too elaborate" &c.[2] Now if "and" were substituted for "but" (and it sounds so much more natural in the place, that I can't help fancying its not being so an "error in the report") the first apparently complimentary clause becomes a mere illustration of the objecting second clause. Is Major Campbell, the *Calder* Campbell who is a poet?[3] Arabel did not say.

I have a confusion of poems running about in my head—a chaos of beginnings & endings & little pieces of middles, which are not likely to end in an Iliad, & so help Atheism to an argument. I sh^d be glad to be allowed to get them (not in the character of an Iliad) into some little nutshell of my own—but Dr Barry insists upon my not writing, and as you taught me passive obedience a long time ago I have been practising it like a St Aylmer[4]—not that I mean to do so all this summer, if it pleases God to spare me through it. I ought to say with a deep felt thanksgiving, how much better I am—*wonderfully* better to everybody who saw, & most of all to myself who felt, the manner in which I seemed to hang by a thread between life & death, & for two months at a time, the latter half of the past winter. The weakness was excessive—& indeed I have not even *tried* to stand up, since January—but everything is "in good time" Dr Barry says,—& it is planned for me to go upon the sea before the present week closes, which would be a "vision of delight"[5] for me if it were not for the fatigue. It was a true kindness in you my dear friend, to warn me of not suffering my natural affection (so naturally strengthened by the tenderness of some most dearly beloved) to bind me down too closely to the earth. The exercise of love, even of human love, is a suggester of God—& may God forbid, that what He permits as a suggestion sh^d be monstrously transfigured into an intervention, by the heart of His creature. Not that my heart has not often so transfigured it! I know that it has! Pray for me that it may not again! It is a foul sin, to sin *by* love, *against* Love!—even as if we used the mystic faces of the cherubim which enshadowed the Jewish altar,--the lion's the bull's & the eagle's faces--to bow down before the beast, & blaspheme the altar's God.

Do try to remember that you have not written three or four unanswered letter to me YET—& write *one* as soon as you can. I was glad to hear of your excursion to Hampstead,[6]—& hope that it made you fancy yourself two years old again—although as to the question of your settling there, it seems pleasanter for us in Wimpole Street that you should not entertain it. You see while *you* are fancying yourself two years old, *my* fancy is suggesting to *me* a renewal of our old intercourse,—and how many cups of coffee & pages of Gregory you & I are still likely to discuss. But "all goeth but Goddis' will" according to the ancient verse[7]—and the fulfilment of God's will is better, yes, & happier, than all that goes.

Arabel often mentions you in the long letters her long affection makes me so grateful for. It has been very very trying & disappointing to me never to have seen her all these months—and dreary ones they have been to me. But now, being in the summer & the sunshine, I would rather think of pleasures to come than of sadnesses past—and I am willing to believe that no obstacle in the common course of things can keep us apart much longer. My dearest Papa has visited me again & again—but I want Arabel—& I long to be tied fast to him & her & all of them--so that the words "*we*" & "us" may be used in their dear home sense. If I had my own way I sh^d be in London by this time,—before this time. I have not my own way—& everybody fancies that I could not yet bear the removal—and so there is no use in kicking against the goad.

Upon consideration I begin to be of opinion that a gynocracy[8] is the next best thing to a republic—and I do not despair of you, a thinking man, being *at one* with me in this opinion,—notwithstanding your favorite project for the future of which Arabel has told me--the combination-government,--consisting of the Pope's head & M^r O'Connell's tail. By the way, until I was assisted to it by your ready memory, I never for a moment suspected Dryden of loitering in M^r O'Connell's verses.[9] Certainly they had been "agitated" enough, to shake Dryden out of them—to say nothing of the "emancipation" from metres & meaning!—— Do let me ask one more question, notwithstanding this long letter. When Popery becomes the state-religion of England, is it to *stand*?[10]—or may we look forwards to a little Mohammadism and Heathenism?- Answer this—and believe that I balance my misfortune of being "*a female and a whig*," by the abundance of truth with which I remain

Your affectionate friend,
E B Barrett.

Poor M! Barker! I felt so very sorry and *memory-struck* in hearing of his death.¹¹ Have you heard any details?

Not knowing who is with you at present, I can send my remembrances to nobody.

Address, on integral page: H S Boyd Esq! / 3. Circus Road / St John's Wood / London.
Publication: EBB-HSB, pp. 231–233.
Manuscript: Wellesley College.

1. "L.E.L.'s Last Question," printed in *The Athenæum*, 26 January 1839 (no. 587, p. 69).
2. We have been unable to locate the source of these comments.
3. They were one and the same. Major Robert Calder Campbell (1798–1857), who was in the service of the East India Company from 1817 to 1836, was the author of *The Palmer's Last Lesson, and Other Poems* (1838). *The Athenæum* described him as a graceful writer of minor prose and poetry.
4. Presumably a reference to John Aylmer (1521–94), Bishop of London, the tutor of Lady Jane Grey and an opponent of the doctrine of transubstantiation. He was of an "arbitrary and unconciliatory disposition" (*DNB*), and his uncompromising zeal in enforcing the laws and orders of the church made him unpopular with both Papists and Puritans. His enemies made trouble for him at the court of Elizabeth I, and he attempted to secure translation to the see of Winchester or Ely. He was unsuccessful in this, and had to endure continued attacks.
5. Blake, *The Four Zoas: Night the Seventh* (1797), line 276.
6. Probably to see his old friend and mentor, Mr. Spowers.
7. EBB used this quote as the motto for "An Island" in *The Seraphim*. In letter 619 she said it was from "an old poet whose antiquity has buried his name."
8. i.e., petticoat government (*OED*).
9. We have been unable to trace any published verses by O'Connell.
10. See letter 484, note 2.
11. Barker, Boyd's friend and EBB's one-time correspondent, had died on 21 March. He had engaged in litigation to establish his claim to the family estates; this ruined him, and he died in poverty. A lengthy obituary notice appeared in *The Gentleman's Magazine* (May 1839, pp. 543–547).

---

694. EBB TO MARY RUSSELL MITFORD

Torquay.
Thursday. [23 May 1839]¹

I write in the utmost haste dearest Miss Mitford—that the fish may not go to you in their native silence. May you both be quite well when this reaches you! Give my regards to D! Mitford.

I heard the other day a story which amused me. M! Garrow² in writing to M! Landor said (of course in jest) that from the numerous Latin quotations in Cheveley he was generally supposed to have assisted in the composition. To which M.[r] Landor replied in great indignation & a very seriously crossed letter, that the report was quite untrue & he was much astonished at its having gone abroad—not that he cared so much about the book & its tendencies—but he was excessively annoyed at being considered a dealer in quotations—he, all the time, hating quotations, & feeling perfectly able to *walk without crutches!* How characteristic this is in all ways!—& very true—for my brother heard Mr Garrow talk of it only a few days since.

I am heartily glad to see in the Athenæum Sir Lytton Bulwer's denial of the brochure attributed to him.[3] In the meanwhile the "wife of Bath"[4] so far from wearing sackcloth, is heard of (since the infamous publication) at the Bath masquerade in a *Pompadour costume!* ——

Ever your most affectionate,
hurried Elizabeth B B ——

I am going on well—& Dr. Barry talks of having me out on the sea in a few days—sh.[d] the sunshine last & the winds turn to south winds. But ever since I have been ill, I think, north & east winds have been in fashion. I dont remember hearing of them before!——

Publication: EBB-MRM, I, 130.
Manuscript: Wellesley College.

1. Dated by the notice in *The Athenæum*.
2. Joseph Garrow (1789–1857) was the father of Theodosia Garrow, whose acquaintance EBB had made in November 1838.
3. *The Athenæum* of 18 May 1839 (no. 603, pp. 379–380) said "It was not our intention to notice a small rhyming brochure, lately published, called, 'Lady Cheveley, or the Woman of Honour.' ... it has no such distinctive character, merit or demerit, as to require from us a formal recognition. But, strange as it may appear, the work has been publicly attributed to Sir E.L. Bulwer; and we are therefore requested to state, not only that it was not written by him ... but that, so soon as the announcement appeared, the following letter was addressed to the publisher, in the hope that it might induce him or the author to stop the publication." A letter dated 24 April 1839 follows.
4. Chaucer's title refers, of course, to Lady Bulwer, who was living in Bath.

695. EBB TO ARABELLA MOULTON-BARRETT

[Torquay]
[*Postmark:* 4 June 1839]

Ever dearest Arabel,

This is your own due sheet—and yet I have been on the very point of transferring it to Papa. His letter called aloud for an answer—indeed I thought it *would* be answered, & even began, upon impulse, a letter in answer to it. But that w^d have been right down cheating—I know it would[.] I have your sheet upon sheet of letters, & you will be sure to expect one from me by Wednesday's post—and therefore to you this shall go—& my beloved Papa must believe how thankfully & tenderly all his kindnesses were read & that I mean to write to him very soon indeed.

Bummy has just interrupted me by bringing in a "water colour drawing, left as a gift by Mr Weale to me"[1] But no, no Bummy! you can t take me in quite so adroitly. It is a copy of a drawing of Mr Weale's, & very well executed by Brozie—excellently well considering that he never tried water-colours before, & I shall praise him for it up to the tops of the hills. In the meantime I am to tell you all about our late visitors. You may remember that I had the privilege of M^rs W's acquaintance only once before & for a very few minutes—& having forgotten the little I saw of her, I cant agree or disagree with Bro's opinion that she looks much older, or with Henrietta's that she *is* much quieter. I saw her last week only upon two days & but for a short time on either day,—& my impressions at either time (but for the *bygones*) w^d have been light enough to rub out with India rubber. She really seemed to me quite a commonplace very neatly dressed—talking quietly, & properly & amiably about the pretty hills & warm weather & pleasant walks. I sh^d never have thought that she c^d do anything worse than forget to mend her husband's stockings from looking too long out of the window. She embraced Henrietta—but I escaped with what Ibbit calls a *"shake hands"*, by virtue of my very solemn determination that it sh^d not be otherwise. We talked however together most amicably—& when Bro threw himself down at the company side of my bed in the evening, to confide to me in a torrent of a logical & liberal philosophy that nobody with a disagreeable voice c^d have any good in them, that M^rs W had the most disagreeable voice he ever heard, saying that there could be no good in *her*--I was able to find justice enough to take the part of the lady's voice against the gentleman's prejudices[.] Mr Boyd couldn't have been more outrageous now could he? And as to the voice, though it might as Bro declares it did, have spoken in fainter tones before me, by favour of my invalidness, I declare that I never heard one of the harsh shrill tones in it deprecated by Bro's ears--tuned to their peculiar nicety by the "most sweet voices"[2] of the Torquay dames. By the way, Agnes Walrond went away weeping like a Naiad[3]—& Henrietta has heard from Monti Garden (who is very uneasy I am sorry to say, about *me!* & begs Henrietta to write to her instantly) that she & Henrietta Garden her cousin,[4] sobbed themselves to sleep at Honiton at the thought of having left Torquay behind them. "Hydraulic exercises" Monti calls them—& very difficult to abstain from, when the Gardens dont come back before October! Well! but "come weal, come woe"[5] I must not diverge from the Weales to another subject, whatever may be its pathos, until I have done with them. And really M[r] Weale is worth talking of—& much & deeply as I always long for you my dear dear, Arabel, I did so in an especial manner while he was here in looking over the beautiful drawings which he brought & executed in the course of his visit. So rapidly executed too! And such character, & imagination, & painter's fire in them all! Not merely clever drawings! but beautiful & suggestive. I was delighted with them—& even was moved to wonder before the artist why he did not embrace the art as a profession instead of giving half a heart to medecine. He seemed to shrink from the uncertainty of success. But a *divided heart* never *will* do in anything; and M[r] Weale's faculty in art is too like *genius* to admit of the possibility of his not using it– And then his medical prospects are anything but bright I sh[d] think. He has the practice only in a naval hospital, & indeed, is not permitted by the rules, to extend it. And he is eccentric & wild, "half mad" Bro declares, & I sh[d] rather trust to his high imaginations in painting, than to his sober judgments in physic. Yet I must not despise his medical judgment upon me, nor fail to tell you of it. I saw him twice, for an hour & an hour & a half at a time. When I went from the room the first day, he said to Bummy & Henrietta as they told me afterwards, that my cough was like a spinal cough—& on the next day when he & I were alone together, he told me that it was like a nervous cough, & asked what other symptoms I had. I mentioned one or two—& besides, that I feared there was no room for doubt, as to the nature of the complaint which was said to be perfectly clear & simple—& that in fact, the chest had been examined & found wanting—"with the stethoscope?" he asked "because no examination is worth anything without *that*." "Yes"—I answered— "with the stethoscope". "Well" he said, "Miss Barrett—dont *you* despond! What I mean to say is this—there may be desease upon the lungs, but it is *not* beyond the reach of remedies, or you could scarcely have that countenance which buoys me up with hope everytime I look at you." I told him that I believed the physician who then attended me, thought hopefully of me, besides. Upon which he exclaimed very ecstatically, waving his painter's brush--"I knew it--I was sure of it--I am *very* glad of it"– Indeed, you never saw so ecstatic a person. He is likely to bleed a patient to death in a furor,—& shouldn't be trusted, with such an idiosyncrasy, in juxta-position with mortal drugs & mortal men. As to talking, oh how he did make me talk! Not on medical subjects—but on poetical![6] I could'nt help talking--he made me! and I do most earnestly believe that if I had stayed down stairs longer at a time, & if he had stayed here a very few days more, there w[d] have been a course of blistering successive to the course of talking. And unfortunately (or fortunately—for I really like & admire much in him) he took a great fancy to me & told M̲ͬ̄ˢ Weale that as long as I was in the drawing room he certainly w̲ᵈ not think of going out of the house—and as long as he was in the house, I, being in the drawing room, was silent scarcely a moment. And it might have been worse, for he said besides—to some of them--"I am a sensitive person—& while I was conversing with Miss Barrett, it was only by the strongest effort I c̲ᵈ keep myself from bursting into tears." Now in such a case,—it would have been only proper for me to have done the same--& if I had not happened to remember, just then, any particular reason for crying—how very unsymmetrical & embarrassing!! He is to send me a painting of Spenser's residence in Ireland, & an illustration of something in the Seraphim which Bummy gave to him—& some drawings for Bro—whom he considers "a young man of fine abilities"—confiding to him in their out-of-door sketch-time moments of privacy, his tendencies (before he married) to be constantly falling in & out of love, and an addiction to commit suicide which was still apt to recur. "In fact" he said very gravely "I do *hate* sometimes, to be alive"— Dont repeat all this, except among yourselves or even to Bummy—it being between Bro & me—& it might make her uneasy- In spite of the wildnesses, I do consider M̲ͬ̄ˢ Weale to have very full cause of thanking God for her lot in life. He seems to be a thoroughly amiable person, & not to be without some high excellences of disposition, both moral & mental. He is going to commence a series of graphic illustrations of English poetry—& I am to let him have some references to passages susceptible of such illustration.[7] There was a scene between M̲ͬ̄ˢ Weale & Bummy—& I was glad to hear of the former shedding many tears & being "very sure that she was insane" in times past. Bummy told her she was less insane than under the influence of Satan—but she has been very kind to her, is delighted with M̲ͬ̄ Weale, & is satisfied & in excellent spirits at their having both been here. There now! You are more than obeyed. I have told you everything. Oh! but I sh̲ᵈⁿᵗ forget a parting party on Friday night. D̲ͬ̄ & M̲ͬ̄ˢ Barry & the Fortescues & Miss Mackenzie[8] came—& if I may judge from the laughing & singing, made themselves as agreeable as c̲ᵈ be. D̲ͬ̄ Barry M̲ͬ̄ Weale & Bro sang trio after trio most divinely—only Bro & D̲ͬ̄ Barry stopped once or twice to beg M̲ͬ̄ Weale to moderate his ardour a little, as really nobody c̲ᵈ hear *them* for *him!* Certainly he does "roar like a nightingale".[9] But I kept my gravity admirably up stairs--having got over the first shock. Really that first night there did seem no prospect for me but to laugh on till dawn! And Crow's imperative "Now indeed Ma'am, you MUST[10] read your Psalms", did'nt do much good,—as you may suppose!——

    I have forgotten the bulletin all this time—which is a proof that you need not be anxious about having one. Pray dont take fancies into your head, Arabel, that I ever am worse than you hear of. I have not for the last ten days felt regularly every day quite as comfortable as the ten days before— Now & then I have had a bad day & stayed up stairs— But I do assure you that the chief symptoms, the only ones worth caring for—the expectoration the pulsation, intermission of the heart & perspiration at night are all in a very subdued state—& this fact *attests* that I am better. *I believe myself to be so.* When we were at dear Treppy's last spring, they were every one worse, much worse, than they are now—although I certainly have lost in strength a good deal, & a little in the tone of the stomach—but then after such a long continuance of illness, to say nothing of the terrible winter I have had, what else c^d be expected? I asked Crow (in my usual spirit of curiosity) what Minny had said in her note. Among other things, Crow told me that she was afraid I was "*only a little better*". I observed "She says so, because she did not see me in the Winter",—& Crow ... "Yes! everyone who saw you at one time in the winter, & sees you now, must think it wonderful! Nobody c^d believe the difference without seeing it. I am sure *I*[11] could not." —— —— You will never believe me when I talk about going out, I have talked so much in vain of it. I am sure to go this week if I am pretty well. It is "a pleasing dread"[12] to look forward to going—& sometimes I wonder how I shall bear the necessary *chair*-part of it. But I shall trust the arrangement to Dr Barry. He knows me thoroughly now, & is not likely to tax my strength beyond itself—indeed he is often far more cautious than I think it necessary to be. Jane [Hedley] need'nt laugh! When I complained last autumn of Dr B. it was not that I doubted his ability or knowledge of my case—but what I DID doubt, & still believe that I had reason for doubting, was his knowledge of *me* & of my constitution & degree of strength. —— He has been lending me his friend & patient's Dr Cummings book, to read—"Wanderings in search of Health"– There is some account of it in the Athenæum.[13] Dr Cumming leaves the famous chest surgeon Mr Andral of Paris,[14] with instructions to go to the Pyrennees for the summer & to Italy for the winter—but goes instead, to Italy for the summer & to Ægypt to the winter. His adventures in wandering down the Nile in search of health inclined me to laugh as much as his confession that he was "a physician in search of it" vide the Ægyptian Pasha– He thinks Ægypt the place for chest-patients to winter in! & that if you dont die of the plague or the cholera prematurely you are sure to be much better in your general health—& he has a delightful plan of building a wooden hospital at Thebes for the reception of European travellers. For the meantime there seems to be every facility of passing from heat to cold, from rain to drought—& you have the opportunity of a good deal of agreeable exercise in giving the necessary castigation to the Arabian boatmen who otherwise w^d be too happy to leave you to the crocodiles! I observed to Dr Barry

No. 695 [4 June 1839] 159

that unless I were ambitious of being buried in a Pyramid, I sh.^d be in no degree anxious to follow the steps of the Wanderer. Mr Andral must be flattered by Dr Cumming's attention to his advice, which he gives at full length, in the original French, in the preface to his book!!———[15]

The shoes fit admirably. As to the belt, Henrietta quite provoked me by sending for it—just because I happened to say that it would be a comfortable sort of cestus.[16] The sunday's letter *did* delight me so– How kind of my own dearest Papa to write such a long crossed one! I was by myself—& smiled at finding myself exclaiming out loud—"Oh how very delightful"! A long letter (more legible than this) shall go to him before many days.——

What do you mean Arabel, by not drawing or painting? Scold her well, Mary [Hunter]! Indeed, I shall be seriously displeased (so you need'nt laugh) if I hear any more of such degeneracy!—— It is enough to be angry with other people! I have no convenience for being angry with you. I am VERY angry with some people just at this moment. Fanny [Butler] says that "the sweet smile & curtsey of the Queen, went to her heart"—and a little afterwards "Jane [Hedley] is looking quite well, but as usual is always complaining. She has a habit of it, & it is not likely to be broken". Did you ever hear a more unprovoked unkindness—& at the same time a more manifest untruth? It is unfortunate when sisterly affection cannot go to the heart as a Queen's curtsey!——

I am sure to be too late, Crowe says!—& there is so much more to say– May God in Christ Jesus bless you all! I am with you in thought & prayer!—& oh how much, in love!

Your own Ba.

Love to dear Trippy——
Tell Mary I am ashamed to hear of her laziness!——
God bless you dearest dearest Bella!—do write!——
Love to Minny.

Address, on integral page: Miss Arabel Barrett / 50. Wimpole Street / London.
Publication: None traced.
Manuscript: Berg Collection.

1. As EBB indicates later in this letter, Weale was a naval doctor, and had to confine himself to amateur art. Henrietta, in a letter to her brother Sam (SD1006), said "Bro & Mr. Weale went out with their sketch books immediately after breakfast– The latter is indefatigable, he went yesterday to Ansteys Cove & made two most beautiful drawings in watercolors of it—& as soon as ever he comes home, he set to work again & did a sepia drawing in the even[in]g of the boats in the bay– I imagine his object is to distinguish himself as an artist before he dies– ... he has a great taste for the sister arts poetry & music but he speaks such broad Irish, you could not mistake him for a Paddy–" Mr. Weale and his wife were visiting Torquay from Plymouth, to which they had returned on 1 June.
2. *Coriolanus*, II, 3, 172.

3. In Greek mythology, the Naiades were the nymphs who presided over rivers, springs and fountains.
4. In SD1001, Henrietta speaks of Mr. and Mrs. Walrond as "our neighbours" and of Miss Walrond as being "Seppy's *friend*." The same letter talks of "an expedition to Dartmouth" with the Walronds and the Gardens.
5. "O'er the Water to Charlie" (*The Jacobite Relics of Scotland*, 1819–20), by James Hogg (1770–1835).
6. Weale gave EBB Coleridge's *Poetical Works* (see *Reconstruction*, A678).
7. See letter 698.
8. Nothing is known about Miss Mackenzie, other than that she belonged to a local family living at 8 Beacon Terrace. SD1059 speaks of EBB's aunt inviting Miss Mackenzie to tea, and SD998 mentions Bro going fishing with Mr. Mackenzie.
9. Cf. *A Midsummer Night's Dream*, I, 2, 83.
10. Underscored three times.
11. Underscored twice.
12. Cf. *The Campaign* (1704), V, 1, 10, by Joseph Addison (1672–1719).
13. *The Athenæum* of 25 May 1839 (no. 604, p. 393) reviewed *Notes of a Wanderer in Search of Health, Through Italy, Egypt, Greece, Turkey; Up the Danube and Down the Rhine*, by William Fullerton Cumming, M.D. (2 vols.). The review included this passage: "The tour, it seems, was undertaken to escape from the probable consequences of symptoms of consumption—and the Notes close with a page of cheerful resignation, which ... ought to charm the critics into silence."
14. Gabriel Andral (1797–1876), "whose reputation for a superior knowledge of thoracic diseases is well known throughout Europe" (*Notes of a Wanderer*, pp. viii–ix).
15. On pp. ix–x.
16. "Girdle."

---

696. EBB TO MARY RUSSELL MITFORD

Torquay.
Saturday. [?8] [June 1839].[1]

My dearest Miss Mitford,

I am beginning to write in a great hurry, & must soon end in a greater, or the post will be gone.

In the first place as you really do wish to have me & if you really dont change your mind as to that very questionable wisdom,—I am ready for any business or ballad.

I confess it has been a matter of regret to me, in regard to both your sets of Tableaux, that your poets did not for the most part bear *popular names*—& in the case of your having only four of them,[2] this regret will be stronger. I cannot help believing that the book would sell better if there were a *substratum of popularity* to rest the poetical part of it upon—the prose being safe. Where is Mrs *Howitt*? Above all, would Joanna Baillie send nothing to YOU[3]--no fragment no half scene--if you asked her? What a name *that* w^d be! *Do* write to Landor your very own self—he is at Bath—and I know by his countenance when you went away (that night at Mr Kenyon's) he could not say [']'*no*" if you asked him. And then Mr Talfourd--

Now dont be severe upon me dearest Miss Mitford, about "bubbles" & "popularities". The public is the public! Yes! and I know by my very own self who am no public, that in reading advertisements of literary collections, the interest fastens instantly to *names!*

This is all abundantly impertinent—but you asked for my mind, & I tell it to you the more frankly because remarks from others at different times upon *the subject in question* have strengthened my doxy. Of course the theory is against *my* own admission between your green covers, but I remain at your pleasure—— Will me between them or away from them according to it——

Let me hear from you when you resolve finally. If you wish me to ask Miss Garrow for a contribution I shall very gladly do it.[4]

Like the woods!—of course I do!— I cant say now how much!— But thank you for the delightful walk in them I have just taken with you!— "My public" might well envy me my letter!——

Your most affectionate
E B Barrett.

I am so glad, so very glad, to have this convincing proof of D![r] Mitford's being well. May God bless both of you.

Barry Cornwall— He may be moved—may he not?[5]

Publication: EBB-MRM, I, 131–132.
Manuscript: Wellesley College.

1. In letter 699, dated 12 June, EBB says she is "about ... to contribute again to Finden's Tableaux"; that provides an approximate date for this letter.
2. As EBB makes clear in letter 699, there were to be only four poetical contributors; the remainder of the text would be prose stories by Miss Mitford. The other writers suggested later in this paragraph did not contribute.
3. Underscored four times.
4. It is not known whether Miss Mitford did ask EBB to approach Theodosia Garrow, but she did not contribute.
5. He was; he furnished "Venice" for the 1840 *Findens' Tableaux.*

697. EBB to John Kenyon

[Torquay]
10 June 1839

Offered for sale by Sotheby's, 5 July 1900, lot 131. 3 pp., 8vo. EBB reports: "But Goddis will[1]—which is His mercy—and your kindness will induce you to hear gladly that with a full knowledge of the peculiar uncertainties of my complaint, I do consider myself—hopefully better..."

1. EBB used "'All goeth but Goddis will'—*Old Poet*" as the heading for her poem "An Island" in *The Seraphim.*

698. EBB TO MR. WEALE

[Torquay]
11 June 1839

Offered for sale by Maggs, Catalogue 333, Spring 1915, item 44. 4pp., 12mo. EBB discusses a work done by her correspondent: "The water colour drawing is extremely beautiful and suggestive. The moonlight in it cannot be said to have 'no business there'—for it comes like a spirit upon the ruin—the place for spirits—and reconciles us to desolation. You have done what is said to be impossible 'painted a thought.' And I am satisfied to hear in the silence of your picture, Spenser's very own voice:—'O Mulla mine, I whilome taught to weep'[1]—looking, with that moonlight on it, as if it wept still! Thank you again and again! I have written out some suggestions for paintings—as you asked me to do. Should you like any of them and wish for more, I shall be very glad to *purvey* for you again. These passages are all from the *old* poets—and you will not I think on that account, care less for them. . . . Browne, the writer of Britannia's Pastorals, is very graphic—more definitely so than most poets are. He is a poet too, to be read in Devon." With the letter EBB encloses 12 pp. (258 lines) of suggestions on subjects for further paintings. These include 34 extracts from poems by Chaucer, Prior, Spenser, Browne, and Fletcher, with occasional remarks by EBB. The catalogue carries some samples of the extracts, not reproduced here.

1. *Faerie Queene*, IV, xi, 41, 9, slightly misquoted. The picture for which EBB is thanking Weale is presumably the one of Spenser's residence in Ireland, which she mentions in letter 695 as having been promised her. She also says in that letter that Weale intends "to commence a series of graphic illustrations of English poetry"; her 12 pages of extracts obviously relate to this project.

---

699. EBB TO LADY MARGARET COCKS

3 Beacon Terrace, Torquay.
June 12th 1839.

My dear Lady Margaret,

I have mislaid your letter, & cannot remember the address which I think you gave me in it. Therefore I shall enclose what I am going to write in a cover to Lord Somers—and gladly do I begin to write, to renew the intercourse so long broken between us, & to thank you for keeping your interest in me so kindly unbroken.

That I am better is very true; & very wonderful in my own eyes it is, that I am as well as I find myself at this time. The winter has been very trying to me--and repeated attacks have brought & kept me so low that since October I have never walked without support, & since January *never in any way*. Indeed at that time & afterwards the state of debility, induced not merely by the complaint on the chest but by an incidental & unaccountable attack of jaundice, was excessive. No baby could be more helpless—only,—my voice having quite sunk away to a whisper,—I had not the baby's privilege of screaming. My own impression was that I should never rally—and indeed my physician, D.r Barry, a very able & kind helper to me, told a relation of mine that until March with its cold were past, he could not give any opinion as to consequences. But here is summer again!—and I am on the drawing room sofa & very much better—and from the last stethoscope examination, my chest is reported to be in a decidedly improved state—so that my prospects now are of going upon the sea almost immediately to gather a little strength from the external air & sunshine—and I am quite willing to be sanguine while God's providences will let me.

The joy of the summer comes however less (oh far less) from the sunshine than from the hope which I hold as fast as a child does its flowers, of being again with my beloved Papa & Arabel & all those who have hitherto found it impossible to be here with *me*. I want very much to go to London—I must do it, if it is not otherwise arranged, so that I may still be with THEM. Nothing is settled—& people look grave when I talk of London. Well! I do not mind about London—but I am self-willed upon one point--I must be with THEM.

Dearest Papa has been here, by a month at a time, & not unfrequently—and my sister Henrietta & my eldest brother have never left me. Miss Clarke too is here. There is kindness on all sides—but most kindness ABOVE--because *there* is the infinite Capacity of Love!- How coldly we stand beneath that Sunshine! Oh!—is it not true that we should look up & stretch out our hands, crying unto God, not for more gifts but for more gratitude—? The gifts are many--we cannot count them. The gratitude is very scant.

My dear Lady Margaret, that the one hour a year upon which I may talk to you & hear you talk should have gone by in silence for *me*, this year, makes me regretful indeed. I had heard of your visit to Wimpole Street before your letter reached me.

Do write again when writing is not a great trouble—& say dear Lady Margaret as much about yourself as I may hear. While I live I must care for you & yours & for whatever is of interest to you- Are you writing anything? or reading books that please you?

I have been dumb with my pen almost all the winter—& even now am under an awful medical ban in regard to any sort of composition.

Books too have been ordered away—but they, being faithful friends, *would'nt go*—so that now Dr Barry restricts his disapprobation to a shaking of the head when he happens to see one larger than usual.– I am about too, in spite of the ban, to contribute again to Finden's Tableaux—a vow having been vowed to that effect months ago, to my dear friend Miss Mitford, in the case of her retaining the editorship. There will be three other poets——I mean besides *me*—(all poets you know, in virtue of office)—and Miss Mitford will write the whole of the prose. What my subject is, I have no imagination of yet—& am only today beginning to expect the suggestive sketch. You will hope that whatever heroine may fall to my share, may have longer petticoats than she had last year.[1] So do I, most earnestly & decorously–

We have a house in the warmest situation of Torquay, which *just now* is scarcely an advantage. But the windows quite seem to hang over the beautiful bay, and our ears are as familiar as its rocks are, with the sound of its waters. And when I go to bed—where I always am at half past six, there is a crimson or golden sunset waiting for me, ready to be seen from my pillow, & pressing so heavily upon the opposite hills that they seem forced (for ease) to throw upon the intervening waves, some of the glory. This is nearly all I know of Torquay. Henrietta has mixed with the society, & liked a good deal of it; but Dr Barry's face is the only one I have seen thro' the winter. For four months I never left my bedroom at all—and the sight of a stranger having been from first to last forbidden to me,—I have had no chance of pleasure from the locality, except by means of the soft & mild temperature, which certainly does appear to agree with my shattered hapless chest.

Poor LEL. How soon she sang her last song!– Miss Mitford has heard dreadful intimations of the cause of her death![2] There was a dark woman with children in the castle, & the supposition is that the poisoning was intentional. Any supposition is better than the common one pointing to suicide! but however it was, the newly-made wife's heart was ready to break before it ceased to beat. *That* is said to be rendered clear by letters kept from publication.

My paper is at an end. I could write much more, but will not today. May God bless you my dear Lady Margaret!

Your affectionate
Elizabeth B Barrett.

I quite remember Mr. Martin—Mr. Joseph Martin[3]––& something of the general subject of our conversation. Was'nt it about Jove & fate? Or was it of Homer's recipe for making ghosts?[4] I see double after all.– Miss Clarke & Henrietta beg, both of them, their very kind remembrances.

My dear Mrs Martin (of Colwall) wrote to my sister not long ago. I *always* love her—

Addressed and franked by Lord Somers: London June Seventeenth / 1839 / The Lady Marg.^{t} Cocks / Neen Savage / Cleobury / Bewdley / Somers.[5]
Publication: None traced.
Manuscript: Hon. Mrs. Elizabeth Hervey-Bathurst.

1. A reference to the brevity of Ellen's tunic in "The Romaunt of the Page" (see letter 636, note 4).
2. Rumours abounded regarding the cause of Mrs. Maclean's death, so soon after her marriage. The obituary notice in *The Athenæum* (5 January 1839, p. 14) attributed death to "medicine taken improperly, or in too large a quantity," but gossip hinted at suicide or murder, rather than accidental death. The rumours were fuelled by there having been no post-mortem examination and the knowledge that her husband had destroyed two letters written just prior to her death. (See *L.E.L.: A Mystery of the Thirties*, by D.E. Enfield, 1928.)
3. Joseph Martin (1776–1867), a barrister, was the elder brother of James Martin, EBB's neighbour in the Hope End days.
4. References to ghosts abound in both *The Iliad* and *The Odyssey*, making it difficult to explain EBB's remark. The "recipe" may have been vengeance: Achilles slew twelve Trojan prisoners and cast them on the funeral pyre of his dead comrade Patroclus (*Iliad*, XXIII, 175–183).
5. On the front of the envelope, EBB wrote "The Lady Margaret Cocks .." This inscription was crossed out, apparently by Lord Somers at the time of franking.

700. EBB TO MARY RUSSELL MITFORD

[Torquay]
Monday. June 17.th [1839][1]

My beloved & kindest friend,

I have received your parcel & recovered my temper at its being withheld from me until *today* by those most impertinent dear people in Wimpole Street. Papa was half frightened lest your Messrs Finden sh.^{d} slay me with their speculative Beauties male & female—but he has quite got over *that*, and only prescribes that I content myself with looking at the engraving till the poetry comes of itself.[2] So pray for me to some gracious Muse, or "let the sisters be brought & the harps"[3] if Mr Tennyson can spare them,—for without inspiration, dearest Papa's plan for making a poem will scarcely be found practicable. But dont be afraid for the ballad, nor for me, nor for Papa. We shall agree together very well. He is not afraid now, but likes me to do it for *you*,—and as to me, if any other cause except the good of the book (*your* good as editress) had prevented my being with you this year, I sh.^{d} quite have taken it to heart. I sh.^{d} indeed. I am shut out from many things and persons dear to me,—&

please myself by being near you in the Tableaux still. The ballad shall be done as well as I can–

You interest me (how well you know the art of interesting!) by all you say of Miss Anderdon. Will you express to her from me how she has obliged me by her kind & flattering present—that is to be .. and by admitting me to a knowledge of her secret.[4] Some day I hope to have a friend's right to it. In the meantime I am very sorry that there was no room for *her* flowers among *yours*.

Is not her mother the Mrs Anderdon of Belford Regis?[5] And was I not promised a visit from both of them when my miserable removal from home became necessary?

What am I to do about Mr Naylor? Sh.^{d} I write my thanks to *him*?[6] And if so, where? Could a note pass thro' your hands?

Do let me hear about the Scarlatina. It makes me quite uneasy that you sh.^{d} be exposed to such an evil—and Dr Mitford. Do let me hear before *very* long.

Did your spirit walk Wimpole Street in magnetic separation from the body, a few days since? Arabel declares to me that you *called there, & asked for a book*. There c.^{d} have been no *clairvoyance* on *her* side, at any rate.

I hear of Mr Kenyon's having given an immense party the other evening—a desert full of lions & lionesses, among whom Mr Charles Dickens stood rampant. My brother was "there to see".[7]

By the way—talking of brothers—I mean to make an extract of your legal admirations[8] and send them to my brother George who begins his circuits next year as a BARRISTER!! I shall be curious to observe how his enthusiasm for his profession, which actually set him down to read Coke[9] among this exquisite scenery, when he came down with me last year, & his very high esteem for *your* opinions will bear up under the infliction. Oh yes! I *must*. I have a malignity about the law, & a particular pleasure in teazing him about it. I am always teazing him about it, & telling him that in time he will be worth an old bit of parchment, *ready* to be made a will but not made yet. And he, dear fellow, laughs very goodhumourdly, & goes on sitting up night after night, & sitting in chambers day after day--just as if he liked it—& I *cant* believe that anybody really *can*. He is too good for the woolsack[10] & you sh.^{d} give him a seat in your summerhouse. Well! I wont abuse his tastes any more today– He cares for mine, & sent me in the winter Barry Cornwall's Ben Jonson.[11] By the way, Ben says somewhere that there is no difference between law & poetry,--"it is all reading & writing".

I meant to have written six words. It is always so.

May success attend your applications my dearest Miss Mitford to the Landors Procters & Talfourds,[12] but I shall suffer for it—they will extinguish my "brief candle."[13] I tremble for my ballad & *me*. You will however be kind to us as usual—much too kind—there is the only danger!–

It wont be encouraging to you if I say what is in my head: it will prove how one kind act leads me to exact—no, not to exact—but to expect—(*that* isnt it either)—to *wish* for another. But I cant help saying it notwithstanding. Was Miss Anderdon the sketcher of your house at Three Mile Cross? You mentioned a sketch of it, being extant. Or does she ever sketch from nature? And would she, *if you asked her*, do a little slight sketch of it for *me*? Would she do it FOR YOUR SAKE, for *me*? Or ought'nt I to ask such a thing? If I ought'nt, say nothing about it, & try to forget my intention of being impertinent. But otherwise, I should thank her so very very much, & you too; & have such delight in looking at it—particularly if there were a sight in it of your window. But really I do feel ashamed (to do myself justice) of having written all this. I believe you must forget it & say nothing about it after all.

I am an ungrateful person. I began this note which is a letter, just to acknowledge the engraving, & to thank you again & again for your present to Wimpole Street—and not a word of thanking said yet!! Arabel begged me to tell you how much she was sensible of your kindness—and as to the boys, they are in ecstasies. I thank you for them & for myself. Dearest ever dearest Miss Mitford your kindness to *them* most nearly touches *me*. Let me hear of the scarlatina.

Your attached
E B Barrett.

I never saw Dr Parr, but Mr Barker his Boswell—no! a far more admirable man than Boswell—was a correspondent of mine at one time, & I have heaps of his valuable letters written in red & black ink within & without. I did not know *him* personally. I mean the author of the Parriana, & a most multifarious editor, & one of the most learned men, particularly in Latin matters, in England. You may have seen the notice of his death in the Athenæum.[14] I was *very* sorry,—& grieved at the allusion to some unhappiness as to his circumstances. Another time I will tell you more about him.

With regard to Dr Parr, his greatest point of originality lay in his wig. But there was powerful ponderous, *un*inspired eloquence about his latinity.

I am going on well in this lovely weather. May God preserve YOU! The Wimpole St plans are unarranged up to this moment– Is the life of Mrs Hemans done well?[15] I have not seen it yet.

Publication: EBB-MRM, I, 132–135.
Manuscript: Wellesley College.

1. Year provided by the reference to Barker's death.
2. i.e., the illustration (reproduced facing p. 193) that was to be the basis of "The Legend of the Browne Rosarie."
3. EBB is apparently modifying a quotation; the reference in some way relates to Tennyson's method of composition.
4. The "secret" was Lucy Anderdon's anonymous authorship of *Costanza of Mistra*, a copy of which she was sending to EBB (see letter 706).
5. A note at the end of "Mark Bridgman" in *Belford Regis* says "Mrs. Anderdon, whom I have the honour and pleasure of counting amongst my friends, will chide me for putting her name in a book.... she must forgive me, for the temptation was too great to be withstood. If she does not like to be talked about, she should not paint so well."
6. For the inscribed copy he had sent EBB of his just-published poem, *Ceracchi, a Drama* (see *Reconstruction*, A1722). EBB mentions writing her thanks to him in letter 703.
7. The dinner party was given on 11 June, and the American statesman, Daniel Webster, was one of the guests. In a letter to Charles E. Thomas he reported meeting Dickens: "Boz looks as if he were twenty-five or twenty-six years old, is somewhat older, rather small, light complexion, and a good deal of hair, shows none of his peculiar humor in conversation, and is rather shy and retiring" (*Life of Daniel Webster*, II, 8, by George Ticknor Curtis). For Sam's account of the dinner party, see SD1009.
8. EBB had quoted Miss Mitford on the subject of the law in letter 679.
9. Sir Edward Coke (1552–1634), judge and eminent legal author, had conducted the prosecution of Essex, Southampton, and Raleigh. His *Reports* had great influence on the legal profession.
10. See letter 679, note 4.
11. See letter 679, note 2.
12. i.e., to solicit contributions to *Findens' Tableaux*.
13. *Macbeth*, V, 5, 23.
14. The issue of 30 March 1839 (no. 596, pp. 243–244) said "Mr. Barker, of Thetford ... is also dead.... His death occurred after a short illness, which was unknown to his friends, and was not unattended, it is feared, by privations.... it was a principle of his life, frequently expressed, never to quarrel with any one." He had died on 21 March. See also letter 693, note 11. Samuel Parr (1747–1825), pedagogue and classical scholar, was the subject of Barker's book, *Parriana; or, Notices of the Rev. Samuel Parr* (2 vols., 1828–29; see *Reconstruction*, A1816).
15. *The Works of Mrs. Hemans, With a Memoir by her Sister* [Mrs. Harriet Hughes, née Browne] (1839).

---

701. EBB TO HUGH STUART BOYD

Torquay.
Monday. [*Postmark:* 24 June 1839]

My dear friend,

I take the liberty, which I know you will not be angry about, of enclosing to you a letter of *private gossip* for my dear Arabel. Will you be so very kind as to enclose it to *her* as soon as you conveniently can. Perhaps you would allow a servant to take it to her in the course of the day.

You wrote me a kind & welcome letter to which I mean to reply very soon—more at length than I can this morning, being quite tired with writing. Finden's Tableaux are to be edited again this year by Miss Mitford, and she has sent to me for a ballad,—& I have begun already a wild and wicked ballad.[1] There are so many monks & nuns in the engraving forwarded for me to fit my poetry to it, (think of the very annuals turning papistical!) that I am thinking of introducing you as a St John's Wood Bard versus Gray's "Welsh judges,"[2] taking a grand prophetic view of the Pope's dynasty which is to be in our O'Connellized country.

My dear Mr Boyd, believe me
truly & ever affectionately yours
E B Barrett.

I am better.

Address, on integral page: H S Boyd Esqr / 3 Circus Road / St John's Wood / London.
Publication: EBB-HSB, p. 234.
Manuscript: Wellesley College.

1. "The Legend of the Browne Rosarie."
2. A reference to *The Bard* (1757), in which Gray tells of Welsh bards put to death by Edward I.

---

702. EBB TO MARY RUSSELL MITFORD

Torquay –
Thursday. [11 July 1839]¹

Ever dearest Miss Mitford,

As you cant see me blush thro' all England, you can have nothing but my word for it, that I am ashamed of the proportions of this Patagonian[2] ballad– I *am* ashamed– Do take my word for it. Yes! and if I were not sure enough of your love to be able to trust to your candour, I sh^d hang back as to letting you see these sheets at all,—instead of begging you as I earnestly do, not to mind returning them & desiring me to accomplish the matter in half the space.

Is it not Montaigne who says that a horse shows blood by his power of stopping readily & with grace?[3] I am afraid, if it is, that he would "mean *me* by an *ass*".[4] I regularly run away with myself in poems & letters—waiting till my own breath & everybody's patience are exhausted before I stop, to wish I had stopped before.

But no horse is a type of my ballad. It is an ichthyosaurus of a ballad. Dr Buckland w^d refer it to the earliest stratum of "base ballads", and I may very possibly have to go back for readers, to the antedeluvians, correspondingly.[5]

So dearest dearest Miss Mitford, I do adjure you by your kindness for me not to let it lie in the way of your readers. It would not be longer than last year's Romaunt, nor perhaps so long, were it not for the dreadful long lines, the dreadful "wounded snakes"[6] of lines, which I fear will never coil up into columns. Could you put them out of the way into very small type? The types are not uniform, I think, in the preceding volumes. At any rate I adjure you by your kindness for me, (that Styx nine times round me)[7] not to put out a word of a line of a *page* of your beautiful stories for *me*. I couldn't bear the remorse of it.

All this time I am modestly appearing to confine your probable objections, to the quality of length! *Appearing!* I know too well that you are not likely to approve of me in any way as much or nearly as much as you did last year. Indeed I have my own private fears as to being approved of at all. Deal truly by me. I have lived upon ass's milk since January, & it is likely to *tell*. And whether you approve of me or not, I know you love me, & while you do so, I can afford to lose your sunshine for a ballad. Only dont pray dont, let me do harm even by a ballad, to anything of yours. I *trust to you* for safety from this danger, my beloved friend!—and you may trust to me that all the writing has done me no harm. Indeed I have been better lately, & was *out in the boat* four times last week. So concluded, for a time at least, my nine months imprisonment in this house—but the exertion was felt very much of course, marked by faintings, & an exhaustion which delayed me a little longer in sending this packet to you. When the sea is calm again, I am to repeat my visits to it– What tires me is the process of going down to it, not the dear sea itself, that being too sublime not to be gentle & harmless to the weak– And the intervening distance is not of many yards—not fifty, I sh^d think—only the chairs have earthquakes in them.

I forgot to answer a question put in a late letter of yours. I do not know whether Miss Garrow does or does not write ballads—but anybody who writes anything would climb at a ballad nor "fear to fall".[8] I have seen no writing of her's except what was published in Lady Blessington's annual last year, & some stanzas in MS. upon LEL's death, which appeared to me rather inferior to the rest. Her verses are, in my mind, to judge from these specimens, graceful & feeling, without much indication of either mounting or sinking into other characteristics—but it is scarcely possible or at least just to make a judgment of faculties, upon such scanty data. I have seen her only once– And of her accomplishments in Italian German & music, have heard much.

Oh my dearest Miss Mitford, I am in such a '*fuss*,' (to use an expressive word, which means here however something sadder than itself) about "my people" in Wimpole Street—about their coming here to spend

No. 702 [11 July 1839] 171

the summer with me. George at any rate is coming next week—& my dearest Papa will I know, do what he can about packing up the others—but nobody deals in positives & universals, & says "*we are* coming". The end of it is, naturally, that I am in a *fuss*. Do you think that I can really stay here until next spring—here, comparatively alone? That is proposed to me. I am told that I cant go back to London this winter without performing a suicide! If they w^d but come, I might think temperately of these things—but indeed it is necessary to gather strength of heart from the sight of everybody, to be able to look forwards to another year of exile.

In the meantime my dear relatives the Hedleys have taken a pretty place (under my particular ban, so if you ever heard any good of it, dont praise it to *me*) Merry Oak two miles from Southampton—leaving me as an inheritance, the flowers growing from your seeds in their Torquay garden, to make up into nosegays & sad morals. The worst grief of all (a very heavy grief at first—until I learnt to be wise & submissive about it) has been the departure for the West Indies of two of my dear brothers, who went from London without a last word or look from me.[9] It was all *kindly* done--and I am reconciled--but I cant write of it now-

May God bless you & yours my own dear friend! I venture to send some cream to Dr Mitford, notwithstanding his prohibition & the hot weather. The fruit season may make it welcome, if it can but be kept in good order from the sun. Tell me if it is spoilt or not.

Did Mr Landor vow on a BROWN *rosary* to Lady Blessington? I am quite out of humour about it.

Oh yes! I DID like Mr Chorley!– Have you applied to him?—& did you, at all to Mr Kenyon?

Is the Legend of the Brown rosary a good name! or w^d you like Lenora, the Ballad of Lenora, better?[10] But I quite expect to have it back to me—& in the meantime you may be perfectly sure that if I have done you no good, I have done myself no harm!——

Do you like Mr Horne's poetry?[11] It has to my judgment, great power & genius—and I was fancying some time ago that if you had wished to make him useful to you, access might be had to him through a friend of mine, a former governess of mine & my sisters, who used to talk to me about him when I was in dear Wimpole Street. But everything must be settled about the Tableaux for this year, by this time! and I am sure magnificently, were it not for my rags draggling on to the broaches!——

Poor *poor* Lady Flora Hastings!– *Was* it the Queen's doing? Do you think she really *has* no feeling?[12]

May God ever bless you!——

Your attached
Elizabeth B Barrett.

By the way I have written that name at the last year's *place of assurance*. Sh^d you *keep* the papers, you will put it for me wherever it ought to be– Is not Mr Naylor too like & too unlike Tennyson?——[13]

The cream would'nt come in time & has detained the packet– Arabel in her last letter particularly begged me to tell you that your flowers were growing beautifully—*"Not one has died."*

I c^d not put George out of admiration with you, if I tried.[14] Am I likely to try?——

Publication: EBB-MRM, I, 135–139.
Manuscript: Boston Public Library and Wellesley College.

1. Dated by the following letter, which mentions the despatch of EBB's ballad.
2. i.e., huge. EBB's poem occupied seven pages when printed in *Findens' Tableaux*.
3. "And there is nothing whereby the cleane strength of a horse is more knowne, than to make a readie and cleane stop" (*Essayes . . . by Michael, Lord of Montaigne, Done Into English by John Florio*, 1613, bk. I, ch. 9, p. 42).
4. Cf. *Much Ado About Nothing*, IV, 2, 76.
5. William Buckland, Miss Mitford's friend, was President of the Geological Society, and was the author of several works on geology and palæontology.
6. Pope, *Essay on Criticism* (1711), line 357: "That like a wounded Snake, drags its slow length along." In the second section of the poem, EBB used a 14-syllable line extensively.
7. Cf. Pope, *Ode for Musick. On St. Cecilia's Day* (1713), line 91.
8. Sir Walter Raleigh (1552?–1618), "Fain would I climb, / Yet fear I to fall" (written on a window-pane; quoted in Thomas Fuller's *The History of the Worthies of England*, 1662, p. 261).
9. Sam and Charles John sailed from London on 26 June. The former died in Jamaica on 17 February 1840, from a tropical fever; the latter returned to England in December 1840.
10. When the poem was reprinted in *Poems* (1844), EBB changed the title to "The Lay of the Brown Rosary" and the heroine's name to Onora.
11. Richard Hengist Horne (1802–84), who later became one of EBB's major correspondents, contributed "The Fetches" to the 1840 *Findens' Tableaux*. As EBB indicates later in the paragraph, he was known to Mrs. Orme, her former governess at Hope End.
12. Lady Flora Elizabeth Hastings (1806–39), the eldest child of the Marquis of Hastings, resided at Buckingham Palace as Lady of the Bedchamber to Queen Victoria's mother, the Duchess of Kent. In January, she had consulted Sir James Clark, the Queen's physician, and subsequently the rumour arose that she was pregnant, and this suspicion was communicated to the Queen and to the Prime Minister, Lord Melbourne. Lady Flora was subsequently required to undergo a further examination at Clark's hands, which resulted in a written statement from Clark, also signed by Lady Flora's personal physician, refuting the rumours. Her illness (later found to be due to enlargement of the liver) was aggravated by the mental suffering inflicted on her, and she died on 5 July. The Queen was much criticized for not taking a more supportive attitude.
13. Naylor's themes and imagery were similar to Tennyson's, but he employed a different metre. See EBB's additional comments in the following letter.
14. In letter 679, EBB had told George that Miss Mitford had said "I hate the law & *all its* PROFESSORS."

703. EBB TO ARABELLA MOULTON-BARRETT

[Torquay]
[13 July 1839][1]

My ever very dearest Arabel,
    But I am sure you dont believe it quite—you CANT, after the abominable manner in which I have behaved to you about your birthday! My very very dearest Arabel! *Can* you forgive me after all? Or have you & Minny (I am sure Minny has, at any rate) put me away in spirits & a corked bottle, as a moral monster of ingratitude? Your birthday is the FOURTH *of July*. Dont imagine that I forgot that. I thought of it in April & May & June. This morning I was sending away my packet to Miss Mitford, & in the process asked Crow the day of the month– "The 13th of July." "The thirteenth of JULY![2] so impossible!". She thought I was mad—& if remorse ever made anybody mad, I ought to have been so *in all conscience!* Do, do forgive me! and dont fancy, because I am away from you, that I forgot you, & because you had no letter from me on the right day, that I do not love you! I remember & love you *more* than if you were always before my eyes—a great deal more—and I am so very very sorry (for my own sake) that this has happened. I pray for you always, but I sh^d like to have done it upon that day *in reference to it.* But God remembered you upon it—& I scarcely needed this to prove to me how much better we are in the arms of His all rememb[e]ring & embracing Love, that is the tenderest care we can put out one towards another. According to *His* love, not to mine, may He bless you in earthly & spiritual things. Indeed I am *humbled*.
    If it had not been for this, my thoughts had tended towards my own beloved Papa– I had half meant to write to him today. Do tell him how deeply I felt the kindness of his solicitude in begging me off, from the overwork.[3] Neither that nor any other proof of his love c^d come to me as less than a pleasantness—altho' the fear of some anxiety on his part having preceded the proof-giving, must cause me to regret my own part in producing it. Indeed I am sure Bummy & others imagine me to have groaned sundry superfluities in Henrietta's letter—& I suspect myself that I wrote by no means like a hero. So you must not believe me for the future, should I happen ever again under such or similar circumstances, to be too demonstrative. One hero in a family is as much as can be expected—& we have Henry!!—and besides I am *not* the first poet who left his shield upon the battlefield.[4]—& besides I *am* apt, in writing to you, to leave the ohs & ahs sprinkled about, rather in the course of nature than of oratory! Do be sure of one thing, beloved Papa & all, that I am TAKEN CARE OF, in the extreme sense of the words,—"this side upper

most" being as strictly adhered to, as if I were made of Venetian glass. As to *fatigue*, you know that I c^d not but be expected—& when I *am* fatigued the effect in regard to sleeping, is always the same. My difficulty in regard to sleeping ordinarily, is from a want of calmness in the nervous system & circulation—therefore it stands to reason that whatever is of a disturbing character to body or mind, must increase the difficulty a little– But *use* will remove the obstacle––(i.e. the irritation from moving––) and in the process of doing this, my dearest Papa's wishes shall be attended to. There has been a week's rest in consequence of the weather, for me,—so that I ought to be fit for sailing round the world by today; and I expect Dr Barry every moment to come & say so. He does not *coersce* [*sic*], as it used to be his gracious pleasure to do once—and indeed Crow observed to me yesterday, "I am sure Ma'am you are a much greater favorite of Dr Barry's, than you used to be". "How do you mean, Crow?" [']'Why, I observe now that he does not seem to like to press you to do anything disagreeable to you. He gives up in a minute when he sees that you dont like what he proposes,—he seems so much more goodnatured altogether." He is very kind, & I have nothing to complain of––& certainly if he does (as he does) treat me like a child, it is now like a very good child indeed—("it *shall* have its sugar plum! *that* it shall!["]) and not like a naughty perverse child that looks best with its face in the corner. Oh no! Mr Squeers is put off—the Squeers discipline is at an end!–^{5} And yet I *was* a little frightened two days ago when the ballad came to light—and it *was*, I think, a struggle with Dr Barry as to whether he w^d be sublime or beautiful upon the occasion. He came into my room & found me dressed lying on the bed & thinking of the whole creation rather than of him. "I was ware"^{6} of the tableau near me, besides a writing case a half written letter & a pen guilty of ink. "In the very act, Miss Barrett! In the very act! Now what CAN you say for yourself?" "Only writing a letter Dr Barry––!" which was true, but I felt remorseful notwithstanding– I did not want to make a mystery of the business longer than was absolutely necessary & was not sorry when Henrietta placed the tableau in his hands, with the explanation that Miss Mitford had sent it for me to illustrate. "Put it into the fire! Take it away & burn it. Oh no, I cant indeed suffer such a thing."– She observed with an accent quite stone-melting, that the mischief was done. And then he looked vacillating between wrath & benignancy; & after a minutes mute horror on my part, I made out that I might as well throw away my medecines, for that nothing in the pharmacopœa c^d reach a case of such unmitigatable perversity—and a great deal besides that sounded very awful about ["]inexhaustible fuel & internal fires!" I appealed to him whether it was not much better to disobey *him* than to be perjured—and by degrees, between sundry quakes & shakes of the head, the smiles came back again—and we even grew calm enough to discuss the subject of the drawing. Dr Barry would have it to mean the dedication of a garland to the sepulchre of the lady's lover, upon which I quite made him laugh by assuring him that he was much too romantic for *me*, & that such a thing had never occurred to me before—so that it all ended very well. I made him understand too that the perpetration had taken place during his absence—at least for the most part—which sounded less like authority defied, altho' he took advantage of that communication to declare that he was *not* quite satisfied how it happened that I was not so well (as to expectoration) when he returned as when he left me! The ballad has *not* done me the very least degree of harm. I maintain that on the point of my sword. But medical opinions must be consistently maintained too, I suppose; & I am content in the cost to me being so little! And now there is nothing to be afraid of.

The ballad went away this morning. Brozie encourages me about it very much—but my impression still is that Miss Mitford wont like it nearly as well as the last—without reference to the length, which is past all reason. Above three hundred & fifty lines, for the most part of fourteen syllables! A ballad in four parts. I have told her that as she cant *see* me blush through England she must take my word for it! When you once begin a story you cant bring it to an end all in a moment—and what with nuns & devils & angels & marriages & deaths & little boys, I could'nt get out of the mud without a great deal of splashing, which Brozie likes extremely but which may cause less gentle critics to take up their doublets. The title is "The Legend of the Brown Rosary", & the heroine's name is *Lenora*.[7]

> ["]'Lenora, Lenora!' her mother is calling!-
> She sits at the lattice & hears the dew falling-"

There are the first two lines—& the only ones you shall see until I show them to you myself either HERE or in LONDON.[8] I have vowed upon my rosary that you shall not!——

Not a bit of my ["]poesisy"[9] was written to Mr Naylor—but a sufficiently civil note. I liked two sonnets & one rather longer poem & told him so, & told him besides that the gift of his book was the more gratifying to me as coming from a friend of Miss Mitford.[10] Praising the poetry of it generally, was quite out of the question. It is an excellent *mimicry from le comique* of Tennyson—Tennyson's mannerism & peculiarities *without his genius*. I felt myself quite laughing while I was reading some things in it. Nor could'nt have done it better!—— As to writing "hypocritical letters" in exchange for books, pray beware how you attribute such a thing to me again– That being the only point upon which I am superior to Sir Walter Scott, I pique myself proportionally upon it.——¹¹

Brozie brought me such pretty blue *two* vases this morning .. made of blue glass, very high & slim, so slim as not to be able to contain more than two or three flowers each—& you cant think how pretty they look upon the chimney piece opposite the bed, & on either side of a blue flowerpot wherein *groweth* a most splendid geranium so scarlet & luminous as quite to flare through the room. Sette will tell you about the flowerpot: & in regard to the others was it not kind of Brozie? So very kind. I keep them upstairs, because I dont like to be deserted by all the flowers, & am half the day or more in my bedroom. Being always up at eleven in the morning, Dr Barry allows me to remain in peace until one or a little after––this on days when I dont go out;—but upon those days, I go straight to the boat & straight back again without touching at the drawing room at all. This room is twice as pleasant as the drawing room, where the balcony cuts the sea into little stars, besides the restraint upon visitors & sundry noises, which my presence takes with it. The sea view is beautiful & uninterrupted from these windows—indeed if I sh^d be at *Torquay at all* at regatta time (the beginning of August) my intention is to let out sittings up stairs. It w^d answer quite as well as the house-buying. Dont you think so?–

Thank you my own dear Bella for your account of the sermon.¹² You are angry about something & with somebody. About what or with whom I do not know, but be sure of my sympathy of rage. I envied you all except the thunderstorm which if it lasted the whole of chapel time, (did it? I cant quite understand) must have distracted you a little. We had no storm that night—& I & my thoughts amused ourselves with drawing out the text to the best length we could reach, covetting every now & then our neighbours pew. We fancied rather that the first clause "Yet it pleased the Lord to bruise him,—to put him to grief"¹³ would be the one selected for consideration—but in this it seems that we went astray. It is a *full* verse—no one can go astray in it from the great *meaning* of God which informs it—and oh may that meaning overflow into our hearts & before our footsteps with its excelling sweetness– "Ay so! Let the roses & the lilies go!"–¹⁴ Do you intend me to understand that Mr Hunter was to go to Clapton last *friday*? & not to return to Wimpole Street?– How is this to be? I expect to hear a great deal about movements of all sorts by today's post (I am finishing these corners on Sunday morning) and woe to you Arabel, if you pass me by with any of your very sublime silences. So Georgie wont come by sea! and my drama of waving pocket handkerchiefs at five in the morning is got up for nothing!—– Mr Orange the new minister at the chapel[15] left a luminous *card* upon me the day before yesterday. I was not down stairs—and he told Crow that he had not been quite aware how unwell I was until then, & that it w^d give him great pleasure to come & see me whenever I was inclined to see him, & w^d let him know. Was it not very kind? I think so, & feel quite pleased about it—my only difficulty being as to the time. I would prefer seeing him alone—and this it is difficult to do in the drawing room— I think I shall fix upon their dinner hour, some day when I cant go out, & write a note to him— Crow has heard him preach, & was very much pleased indeed, and assures me that his manner, particularly in prayer, reminded her of Mr Hunter. She says too that he looks just like a missionary—and when I prayed for an explanation, she insisted upon his complexion being brown & his hair white, as distinctive signs— His family are arrived, & two little boys in straw hats have added to our population. It will be a great privilege to me to have some intercourse with him—if I can but manage it without brushing against the shirts of uncle Richard Dr Barry & other dramatis personæ–

There was a repetition yesterday of the going out—and it was managed pretty well. I should be so glad to have the Bella Donna (my yatch) brought to the side of the bed—or even (for I would not be extravagant in my expectations) to the house door! Henrietta & Crow have their share of the amusement agreeably interspersed with sensations of sickness so that altogether we have delightful parties. Oh! how I do wish you were part & parcel of the same!–

My best love to dearest Trippy. She is a very naughty person to think of sending me or Henrietta either these mantillas. Why wont she pack up herself to our direction, in a fit of generosity which we c^d appreciate?——

There has been a letter from Jane announcing uncle Hedley's safe arrival, & her own satisfaction with everything around her except with her own consciousness of having left *us*.[16] I do hope & trust they may be happy at Merry Oak—but my *prophecy* is that they wont stay there. In the meantime they are paying seven hundred a year upon a doubtful experiment. Walters, Jane's maid, told us that the house was very pretty— but that she was already sensible of its being a cold one– How indeed can it be otherwise, without the shelter of a hill on any one side?——

Miss Garrow & Miss Fisher paid me an hour's visit on friday—& thought me looking "*much better*" than when they saw me last, a month ago. I really think & believe I sh^d like Miss Garrow– Bro insists upon her exceeding affectation—to which I can only say that it is to me exceedingly innoxious. I perceive nothing of the sort—and I do perceive that she is in *earnest* in her love of poetry—which is always a pleasant & rare perception—at least in my experience–

You will pray for me today, my beloved Arabel—as I shall for you! May He in whom we are *one*,[17] in Jesus, bless us both!—bless all of *you*, my dearest dearest Papa & all of you!——

Your most attached Ba–

Henrietta desires me to wish you many happy returns of the day from *her!*—I am ashamed to write it either from her or myself.

My love to dear Minny– ⟨...⟩[18]

I cant read this over again– So forgive the *errata*[.]

Think of Mrs Brydges Williams[19] sending me the first fruits of her grapery– Most splendid grapes—& a basket of Eden flowers besides! The people here are very kind. Delightful weather for the beloved upon the sea!——

Address, on integral page: Miss Arabel Barrett / 50 Wimpole Street / London–
Publication: None traced.
Manuscript: Berg Collection.

1. The year is provided by a partial postmark; internal references supply the day and month.
2. Underscored three times.
3. This is probably a reference to a passage in SD1018, in which Henrietta tells Sam that their father had written to Torquay asking that EBB be spared the exertion of going out daily, despite Dr. Barry's wish for her not to miss benefitting from the fine weather.
4. Cf. *The Æneid*, bk. XII.
5. Wackford Squeers was the tyrannical master of Dotheboys Hall in Dickens's *Nicholas Nickleby*.
6. *Romeo and Juliet*, II, 2, 103.
7. Changed to Onora when the poem was reprinted as "The Lay of the Brown Rosary" in *Poems* (1844).
8. In view of this, it is interesting to note that George made a copy of the poem and sent it to Wimpole Street without EBB's knowledge. Mr. Moulton-Barrett called this "a breach of morality" and refused to read it until EBB gave her permission—but Arabella, "not being quite so strict," had no such scruples (see SD1023).
9. An obsolete word for poetry, from the Greek and Latin *poesis* (*OED*).
10. Naylor presented EBB with a copy of his *Ceracchi, a Drama and other Poems* (see *Reconstruction*, A1722).
11. See letter 606, note 6.
12. By G.B. Hunter. SD1018 tells how "Arabel walked through a violent thunderstorm to hear him, her admiration of his preaching could not have been evidenced in a stronger way than this."
13. Isaiah, 53:10.
14. We have not traced the source of this quotation.
15. Mr. Orange had just become the incumbent at the Independent Chapel in Union Street; he and his family were living at Penton Villa, Victoria Place. EBB gave him a copy of *The Seraphim*, inscribed "to the Revd. J. Orange, with the author's grateful remembrances, Torquay, October 1839" (see *Reconstruction*, C170).
16. As mentioned in the previous letter, the Hedleys had moved from Torquay to Southampton.
17. Cf. Galatians, 3:28.
18. Almost half a line obliterated, presumably by EBB.
19. Sarah Brydges Willyams (*née* da Costa) was the widow of Col. James Brydges Willyams, who had died in 1820. She lived at Mount Braddon, Torquay, and later became known for her close friendship with Disraeli. When she died in 1863 he was her residual legatee and inherited some £30,000 from her. She was buried at Disraeli's estate at Hughenden.

704. MARY RUSSELL MITFORD TO EBB

Three Mile Cross
[late] July, [1839][1]

My beloved Friend,

I am in great anxiety again. My dearest father has had in the past week two several attacks of English cholera. They have reduced him exceedingly, more than you can fancy, and I am now sitting on the ground outside his door, with my paper on my knee, watching to hear whether he sleeps. Oh! my dearest love, at how high a price do we buy the joy of one great undivided affection, such as binds us heart to heart! For the last two years I have not had a week without anxiety and alarm, so that fear seems now to be a part of my very self; and I love him so much the more tenderly for this clinging fear, and for his entire reliance upon me! You, with so many to love, and so many to love you, can hardly imagine what it is to be so totally the whole world to each other as we are. And oh! when sickness comes, when one attack of a different kind follows another, so that the insecurity of our treasure is pressed upon our attention every hour—oh! how tremblingly, throbbingly, sensible do we become to the consciousness of that insecurity! I hardly now dare leave him for half an hour. I have not left him for a drive, or to drink tea with a friend, for years. But I must not worry you with my depression. Heaven bless you!

Ever yours,
M. R. M.

Address: Miss Barrett, Torquay.
Text: L'Estrange (2), III, 79–80 (as July, 1837).

1. This letter, addressed to Torquay, was dated 1837 by L'Estrange; as EBB did not go to Torquay until August 1838, 1839 is a more probable date. If this inference is correct, the letter must have been written very late in July, as EBB would surely have referred to Dr. Mitford's health in her letter of 3 August, had she already known of his illness. She does mention Miss Mitford's anxiety about him in her next letter, dated 11 August.

---

705. EBB TO MARY RUSSELL MITFORD

Torquay–
August 3^d 1839

Ever dearest Miss Mitford,

Have you been thinking very hardly of me, "cudgelling me with your hard thoughts"[1] dearest Miss Mitford, for this dead silent way of receiving your letter? I fear it the more, on account of having heard from London that you must *suppose* me to be in possession of a parcel containing I dare say Miss Anderdon's book,² sent to Wimpole Street through M! Kenyon, and which has not reached me up to this moment. Dont be angry with anybody in Wimpole Street. They did not even wait for an opportunity!—they forwarded it to me immediately, inclosing your parcel in one of theirs, & sending the whole by the steamer—or rather, intending to do so. For the poor steamer broke its boiler in the river & exploded:³ without further injury to anybody I am glad to say than to the patiences of different people situated as I am, who must wait for the cargo by a sailing vessel & try to look placid everyday when they hear of the wind being right for Petersburgh.⁴ Day after day I have waited for this poor parcel—and besides, for M! Horne's reply to the enquiry I directed his way, via Mrs Orme, as to whether he w^{d} write a scene or poem of some sort, quickly & instantly for Miss Mitford's annual. I wrote to her by the post *next* to the one by which your letter reached me. It appears that M! Horne has been out of town—as far as I could understand what she wrote to me two days ago,—& this very day, I have received a most obliging letter directly from himself, from which here are extracts.- "I beg of you not to imagine that I am affecting to be, or really being, impertinent, when I say I never yet wrote a word in an annual,—and as I never could afford to buy one, nor ever lived in a house with one, so I never read one. It would give me great pleasure if I thought I c^{d} do anything that would be agreeable to Miss Mitford and yourself, in the work in question— but I really dont know what is wished. Anything I can do, pray command me, & to save time, allow me to tell you what I cannot. I know very well that the *majority* of the annuals entertain certain views of Art, to the bettering of Nature beyond all measure. The hands & feet of all the females excite pity,—their figures frighten one,—& perplex no less with scepticism as to how they are to *continue*. Nor are these hourglasses redeemed from the disbelief they excite as to all organic humanity, by the features & expressions of the faces—for 'each seems either'!⁵ I c^{d} not write of such without being guilty of offence to their arbitrary perfection." ---- "If you please, let me have some landscape with the least possible refinement or elegance in it, & the most old ruins. Amidst these, something might be built in descriptive or dramatic poetry,—but I can do nothing at all with the ladies & gentlemen-- You will perceive, no doubt, from all this, that I have derived my impressions from probably the worst annuals—to w^{h} Finden's Tableaux may be quite an exception. If this be the case and I can look at several of the subjects, I may be induced or compelled to alter my opinion—".

There are the extracts! I am personally quite unacquainted with M! Horne—but you will see through all this playfulness & oddity of satire upon the annuals, that he is at your disposal, & a willing victim besides!——— It will be right for me to send my own expression of thanks to him for his letter to me—& this I shall do on Monday, & I hope I shall not be wrong in telling him that you will write *directly* your instructions to himself. His address is 75 *Gloucester Place, Portman Square*. Of course he w?. like to select a subject, sh?. you have more than one drawing unappropriated[6]—but otherwise a few words from you w?. win him into contentment, even without the old ruins. Have you not *heard* of his Cosmo de' Medici?[7] He is a man of indubitable genius. I feel THAT quite distinctly, although I have read only a little of his poetry—and then his heart turns to the old poets as well as to the old ruins—& *that* I like, very much!——

After all, Barry Cornwall's heart may have turned to *you!*[8] I am an impetuous sort of person—my Italian master used to say that I was to be characterized by one English word which he dared not pronounce, but which, put into literal Italian, was "*testa lunga*".[9] Do you perceive the English word—& admit its application to me?—for I read your letter only once, & wrote just in time for the post, my few words of enquiry to M?.^{rs} Orme. Had I waited to read it twice, I believe I sh?. have paused for more precise directions from you.

But if your table is not filled, I do think you will like M?. Horne–And you will in any case, write to him—wont you?——

Ever dearest Miss Mitford, I feared that you might interpret my silence into a distaste to y?. criticism! You were wrong—very wrong—if you did!—— And altho' you recall your first impression, yet I am afraid more weight is due to it than to your merciful re-consideration. I had imagined that the penitence was implied, even were it not directly expressed by the words "Take pity on me––Let the sin be removëd"[10]—and to tell you the real truth, I have been taught to "walk softly"[11] upon all subjects connected with theologisms by the repeated intimations of my obstinate proclivity towards them. Let it *be* an obstinate proclivity!- I do hold, & do not slacken in holding, that all high thoughts look towards God, & that the deepest mysteries, not of fanaticism but of Christianity, yes, *doctrinal* mysteries, are,—as approachable by lofty human thoughts & melted human affections,—poetical in their nature. It w?. be a great mistake if I were to defend my own poetry from any imputation of intruding religious subjects, & of calling "vasty spirits"[12] whether they will come or not. I do not defend it. I only maintain that all such appearances of intrusion, arise from my own incompatibility, from some want of skill in *me*, & NOT from any unfitness of the subject—the subject meaning religion generally, & not such questionable selections as the subject of the *Seraphim*.-[13]

Do you remember anything of my stanzas upon LEL. Well! I heard of M?. Kenyon's speaking very kindly of them—& saying besides that it was a pity the *last* stanza was not cut away—that I *w?.* bring in religion upon all possible opportunities.¹⁴ And such things have made me, not afraid of my own opinions, but nervous sometimes about introducing wrongly or dwelling too much—and, in the ballad in question, I was satisfied with making as I thought one meaning clear & tried not to be too *verbally* theological—doing this very particularly in writing for an annual—not for *you* my beloved friend who never sent me any "advices" of the sort, but for your readers of whom you say such unflattering truths. Your "slightest of all readers" make an admirable pendant to M！ Horne's ideal of the engraved "ladies & gentlemen"!– In regard to yourself—[(]y！ own opinions)—I am sure they will agree with mine, against every experience of non-success or mal-success on the part of so many "religious poets", that the fault is more likely to lie in their not being poets than in their being religious—& that one truth is self evident—*wherever there is room for* HUMAN FEELING *to act, there is room for* POETICAL FEELING *to act*. We cant separate our humanity from our poetry—nor, when they are together, can we say or at least prove, that humanity looking downward has a fairer aspect than humanity looking towards God. I am afraid that the matter with some of us, may be resolved into our not considering religion a subject of *feeling*, of real warm emotion & feeling—but of creed & form & necessity. If we feel, it is wrong to show that we feel!—& this, only in religion!– Because you are kind to me, I must love you—& nobody will call me wrong for doing that. It is only grateful & natural that I sh！ love you—& there is no want of decorum & picturesqueness in loving you. Because Christ died for me, I must love HIM—but it is very wrong of me to say it,—& very improper—& above all things very unpoetical! Oh! the pitiful inconsistencies of this mortal world! And the inconsistency would be nothing, if it were not for the cold—if it were not for the cold & the baseness!—

Well! but it is easy to make the penitence more evident, dearest Miss Mitford—& respecting the short lines, which of them are the worst? I will try, & do what I can–

The address is,
R. H. Horne Esq！
75 Gloucester Place
Portman Square
London.

I have heard that he piques himself upon being very like the pictures & busts of Shakespeare!– People feel differently on every sort of subject. If I were like Shakespeare I sh！ be quite distressed, & take to wearing a wig, & green spectacles immediately. I sh！ be ashamed of being like Shakespeare, & afraid of profaning the shrine—I really should!——

Love to dear Dr Mitford. I must send more cream, as he liked the last.
                                  Your ever attached
                                      EBB.

I am going on very comfortable—my brother George is with me—& my dear Arabel is coming—& Papa is coming—& all this makes me very glad & happy—— But I am likely to remain here until next year– I am afraid there is no escape from it!—— Do you ever talk or dream of coming this way? I wish I had the loadstone which lies under y.^r threshold——

I had a very kind note from dear Mr Kenyon just before he went to Three Mile Cross. "Miss Mitford's lovely village" by the way, is praised in last month's Blackwood, in the *"Picture Gallery"*–[15]

Address, on integral page: Miss Mitford / Three Mile Cross / Near Reading.
Docket, near address, in Mary Russell Mitford's hand: Miss Barrett / Mr Kenyon.
Publication: EBB-MRM, I, 139–143.
Manuscript: Wellesley College.

1. Cf. *As You Like It*, I, 2, 183–184.
2. The reference in the following letter indicates that this was *Costanza of Mistra: a Tale of Modern Greece* (1839), although Miss Anderdon's authorship was not acknowledged on the title page.
3. *The Eclipse* was stated in *The Morning Chronicle* of 29 July to be departing on 4 August for Torquay and Dartmouth, but on 1 August the paper noted the cancellation of the sailing, owing to the need for repairs.
4. i.e., a wind favouring a vessel sailing for St. Petersburg would have been a contrary wind for a ship wanting to sail westward down the Channel.
5. *Paradise Lost*, II, 670.
6. Horne's contribution, "The Fetches," accompanied an engraving entitled "The Warning," showing a betrothed couple. In his poem, their fetches (fetch: an apparition or double of a living person, *OED*) appeared before them on their wedding eve.
7. Horne's tragedy, *Cosmo de' Medici*, had been published in 1837.
8. He contributed a poem, "Venice," to *Findens' Tableaux*.
9. "Head long." Her tutor would have had difficulty with the aspirate in English, as Italian does not have an equivalent.
10. A paraphrase of Psalms, 51:1–2. When reprinted in *Poems* (1844), EBB changed the line to "Now, O God, take pity — take pity on me!" (line 348).
11. Cf. Isaiah, 38:15.
12. Cf. *I Henry IV*, II, 1, 52–54.
13. In *The Seraphim*, Ador and Zerah have difficulty in comprehending the Divine Plan.
14. "L.E.L.'s Last Question" appeared in *The Athenæum* (26 January 1839, p. 69). The last stanza reads:
>But, while on mortal lips I shape anew
>A sigh to mortal issues, verily
>Above th' unshaken stars that see us die,
>A vocal pathos rolls—and HE who drew
>All life from dust, and *for* all, tasted death,
>By death, and life, and love appealing, saith,
>DO YOU THINK OF ME AS I THINK OF YOU?

15. *Blackwood's Edinburgh Magazine* (July 1839, p. 47), in an article lauding the scenic charms of England, said: "Landscapes superior to this are not, I am persuaded, to be found in any part of Europe ... What, for instance, can be lovelier of its kind, than Miss Mitford's village of Three-mile-cross, with its wild common, which should never be without a gipsy encampment, its clear gravelly springs, its one rustic mill ... and its broad daisied meadows, through which winds the sleepy Loddon."

706. EBB TO MARY RUSSELL MITFORD

Torquay.
August 11.th 1839.

I am so grieved my beloved friend, that the anxiety about dear D.r Mitford sh.d have returned under any form & alleviation--even as the light shadow of what once it was. When you are least beset with occupation, do let me learn by a word whether he is better—and in the meantime it has come into my head that he might like a little fish with the cream,—no!— not exactly *with* it!——"tho' by your smiling you seem to say so".[1] God grant that ere this your fear may be in blackletter.[2] To fluctuations all convalescents are exposed—particularly during the present summer's variable weather,—& I do hope & trust my dearest Miss Mitford that it is a mere fluctuation.

Thank you again & again for your delightful letter about M.r Webster,[3]—so nobly toned from your own heart!– I do like to read such letters—but I cannot say more, in my haste today, of yours, than that if I were to confess my ignorance until very lately, about him of the American senate, you w.d be sure to despise me very much. The first orator in the world, I think you call him—"except another Daniel." *Do* you mean M.r O'Connell? Oh! surely if he is a great orator, he must be the height of the sky above M.r O'Connell. Do you seriously consider M.r O Connell to be a great orator? Try to forgive a little astonishment. I disarm you by confessing my ignorance. I never heard him speak & seldom read his speeches—& when I do, my doxy is that M.r Shiel is a greater orator than M.r O Connell,[4] & that strictly speaking nothing oratorically great belongs to either of them.

I have read M.r Chorley's Lion[5]—and if we of the multitude, we of the literary laity, dared to remark upon persons set in authority over us, I sh.d wish the election a hundred books off, & more unity,—or rather more of that composure which arises from the *sense of unity*,—throughout the work. But it is a work highly indicative of ability—of an ability to come, as well as present—brilliant with allusion, yet not too dazzling to think by. A great part of the first volume & the greater part of the third struck & interested me much—only the Robin of the opening is too good

Miss Mitford's Cottage

Tor Bay with Beacon Terrace

for the Robin of the close—surely he is.[6] Why at this rate, Edwin, Beattie's Edwin might have turned into a Lion—"and yet poor Edwin was no vulgar boy"[7]—and *that* I never will believe. Put him into a menagerie & feed him as you will, the poor little giraffe & he w^d die together!——

The coteries must be very close offensive menageries,—& I am glad that I have none of their dust to shake from my feet.[8] But oh, dearest Miss Mitford if you were to shrive me & find out what a strong heart I have for making pilgrimages to certain shrines, & what impulses to lionizing hang about me, you w^d be ashamed of me—you w^d indeed. When I was between child & woman I prayed & teazed a dear old friend of ours into taking a long hot disagreeable walk in London (I happened to be there for a short time) just to look at Campbell's house——& I did just see the red curtains in the dining room, & with full contentment of heart——while my companion half amused & half annoyed declared over & over again that I was "*such* a child"——as if that was all to be said for me. And really I am just "such a child" at this moment— Mr Kenyon would not believe that I cared about the autographs he brought me[9]—he was sure that I was taking him in, & wanted them for a blaze. But the religion of genius, or you will say the *superstition*, is over me still. My organ of veneration is as large as a Welsh mountain.[10] I c^d kiss the footsteps of a great man—or woman either—& feel higher for the stooping. Now make allowances for me. I was never in literary society, & have not learnt the difference between books & the men who made them—or the distinctive signs by which you know a genius from an angel——I suppose there are some–

Mr Chorley's Sea port town was brought to me a little while ago—but not as Mr Chorley's.[11] Henrietta brought it from the circulating library– The *librarian had recommended it!*—& I am so forced to be dumb & to abstain from continuous attention to grave subjects, that amusing books of the class to which it belongs are necessary to me sometimes. Well! I did not like the name of the book—& was turning listlessly to the title page with the words "I cant read this",—when *there*, was Mr Chorley's name! Of course I c^d read it immediately,—& was much struck by the power it indicated, & the constructiveness of the stories—a rare characteristic, even in these story telling days.

All this time, not a word of Costanza! Will you tell the authoress whom I do seem to know, that the "*Ecclipse*" steampacket broke its boiler on purpose not to mar her volume by the evil omen of its name, & that the book came here by the "*James*"!—a sailing vessel.[12]

How true is what you say of it!—I mean of the book. Gentle & pure—& then you *feel her youthfulness* all through it![13] I have sent a little note which you will kindly let her have when she next comes to see you—& do impress upon her my sense of the kindness of the gift of her poem, & my hope of knowing her personally & her beautiful drawings too—*one* day.

What a singular imitative impulse is upon Mr Reade. Ld Byron's Cain Childe Harold & Heaven & Earth!—& now, is this Ben Jonson's *Catiline*? I have not seen the play. Have *you*? But it is singular that with rare Ben before his eyes any man sh.^d DARE to write a play & call it *Catiline*!–[14] "Can such things be?"–[15]

You did not *mind* writing to Mr Horne my beloved friend? And I do hope that everything by this time is settled with him & Mr Procter too.

And now I want to say one word– You told me of having made arrangements for the reception of *four* poems. Therefore, in the case of Mr Procter's doing what I earnestly trust he may do for you,[16] I very much wish that you would put my ballad away. You have received it with far too great kindness—& that kindness is guerdon enough for the writing, if it went into the fire instead of the press. Now consider my beloved friend—& dont injure the book or annoy anybody in connection with it "for love of me".[17] Rather prove the love by dealing with me as if I belonged to you, & waiving all ceremony of hesitation. The Messrs Tilt may expect to see only *four* poems—& as I have written for the tableaux two successive years already, you will be the better for the loss of me—for variety's sake ... we will put it *so* if you please, out of tenderness to my vanity.

God bless & keep you my ever dearest & kindest Miss Mitford!—& all dearest to *you*!

Your attached & grateful
Elizabeth B Barrett.

Between my physician & my maid I did what is called *walking* (by courtesy) a few days ago—about three yards of it—& I am better. Arabel is not come–

Publication: EBB-MRM, I, 144–147.
Manuscript: Wellesley College.

1. *Hamlet*, II, 2, 309–310.
2. i.e., superseded, as Gothic (blackletter) type in early printing gave way to Roman type face.
3. Daniel Webster (1782–1852), American statesman and member of Congress, had visited Miss Mitford on 18 July, in the company of John Kenyon. (See *Life of Daniel Webster*, II, 24, 26–27, by George Ticknor Curtis.)
4. As previously noted, EBB did not share Miss Mitford's admiration of Daniel O'Connell. Richard Lalor Sheil (1791–1851), dramatist and politician, had disagreed with his countryman, O'Connell, over the timing of Catholic emancipation.
5. *The Lion, a Tale of the Coteries* had just been published.
6. In the early part of *The Lion*, Robin Brandon is lauded as a successful poet; at its conclusion he becomes ill, after being humiliated when his play is laughed off the stage at its first performance.

7. Bk. I, xvi, 1 of *The Minstrel* (1771) by James Beattie (1735–1803). In the poem, Edwin is the child of a simple shepherd and his wife.
8. Cf. Matthew, 10:14.
9. EBB collected autographs, enlarging her collection by exchanging duplicates with friends. Letter 249 mentions an offer to exchange Campbell's autograph.
10. A reference to the Welsh penchant for exaggeration.
11. His *Sketches of a Sea Port Town* was published in 1834.
12. See letter 705, note 3.
13. The *Athenæum* of 10 August (no. 615, p. 594) said "'*Costanza of Mistra*' is a poem of some pretension, coming before us in all the dignity of five cantos, and Spenser's measure ... if the author will be advised by us, he will repose upon his laurels. We scarcely think him likely to add to his fame by any future attempt."
14. Reade was much criticized for his imitative style, Byron being his principal model. His *Cain, the Wanderer* (1829), *Italy* (1838) and *The Deluge* (1839) paralleled *Cain: A Mystery*; *Childe Harold's Pilgrimage*; and *Heaven and Earth*. His latest work, *Catiline; or, The Roman Conspiracy* (1839), was inspired by Jonson's play, *Catiline His Conspiracy* (1611). "Rare Ben" is a reference to the epitaph, "O rare Ben Jonson," carved above his tomb in Westminster Abbey.
15. *Macbeth*, III, 4, 109.
16. Procter (Barry Cornwall) did contribute a poem, "Venice," to *Findens' Tableaux*.
17. Tennyson's "The Mermaid" (last line of verses two and three).

---

707. EBB TO LADY MARGARET COCKS

[Torquay]
[mid-August 1839][1]

My dear Lady Margaret,

I am so much obliged to you for your kind letter that I cannot delay answering it. And you always seem nearer to me at Eastnor, & the law of attractions is the more imperative (is it not?) in proportion to the nearness– I believe this is so in physics– I am sure it is in morals—at any rate, & surest of all, I find myself wishing to write to your Ladyship & writing.

To your question as to my health, I will not wrong your kindness by putting off my answer to the last page. Dr Barry considers that I am better & that I *shall* be still better—and from his report to Dr Chambers whom he saw in London a month ago, much satisfaction was expressed by the metropolitan authority, & the assurance given that it "exceeded his expectation". The worst of it all is that I am constrained by advices from every quarter, & by the medical sentence that my going home this winter w^d involve an "act of absolute suicide", to look forwards to a prolonged exile, notwithstanding the earnest wishings & leanings of my heart. I *must* stay I suppose, here until next spring again—and indeed it is grievous to think of such an absence—grievous not merely on my own account but on my poor dearest Papa's whose comforts it breaks up in many ways. His tender affection for me has expressed itself so touchingly

& disinterestedly that I am deeply moved in adverting to it—and now he has made *presents* to me of my brother George who is here for his law vacation (he is to be called to the bar in November) & my sister Arabel who is coming to me immediately by some element or other,—which, I cannot guess at. And Papa too is coming—and I am as happy as I can be under the circumstance of feeling that they must one after another before the winter, go away again & leave me to the consciousness of exile & east winds. But it is ingratitude to God's mercy—(is it not, dear Lady Margaret?) to be sad *now* . . to begin to shiver before the time comes for lighting fires?

If you sh^d see dear Mrs Martin before she leaves England, do ask her to write to *me*—not to Henrietta,—but to *me*. I never forget her, & sh^d like both to hear from her & to write to her–

I was glad very glad of your good news about the Commelines. Mention them sometimes. Charlotte Peyton told Arabel & Arabel told me that Mr Commeline did not despise my book,[2] although he complained,—as you say & as I know most reasonable people do,—of its obscurity– But I felt pleased at his not despising it altogether—having desired his good opinion. Do you know I was "astonied"[3] the other day by hearing from the publisher that to his astonishment as well as mine, & in the teeth of the railroads, it was SELLING?!! I had expected most of the copies to be sent to me for waste paper by this time—& had put off all my notable sewing, as well as curling my hair, from last year, that I might peradventure come into an inheritance of thread papers & curling papers– You know Milton's idea of fame is, "to think to burst out into sudden blaze".[4] But in this utilitarian age, (& I w^d not be behind my age for the world!) I c^d not think of putting my books into the fire!– No! not for a 'sudden blaze' in our east wind!——

No poetry now? Have you seen Mr Milnes's? If you have not—*do!* He shall prove to you that there IS poetry, now. Believe *me* about it, dear Lady Margaret, rather than the Quarterly Review—which makes out that Mr Milnes is only best of the bad.[5] Mr Moiles's 'State Trials' too have power & poetry—and yet I w^d rather say power & *eloquence*. He is not such a poet as Mr Milnes– I hesitate to call him a *born poet*—but he has singular vehemence & eloquence of language[6]—& a versification parta-
⟨★★★⟩

Publication: None traced.
Manuscript: Hon. Mrs. Elizabeth Hervey-Bathurst.

    1. Dated by the reference to Arabella Moulton-Barrett's impending arrival; SD1024 speaks of her leaving London for Torquay on 19 August.
    2. i.e., *The Seraphim*, published the previous year.
    3. An archaic form of "astonished," used by Chaucer and others.

4. "Lycidas," line 74.

5. *The Quarterly Review*, in its June issue (pp. 59–64), spoke of the "unprecedented number of literary aspirants among the classes of society most favoured by fortune" and went on to say of Milnes' *Memorials of a Residence on the Continent* and *Poems* that his verses "contain abundant evidence that he possesses great cultural abilties ... but we think, upon the whole, he has shaken the tree a great deal too soon ... [but] in spite of all their weaknesses and affectations, they contain better English verses than have as yet been produced to the public by any living writer not on the wrong side of the *Mezzo Cammin*."

6. *State Trials—Specimen of a New Edition*, by Nicholas Thirning Moile (pseudonym of Henry Bliss, 1797–1873), was a poetic treatment of three famous trials: Anne Ayliffe's for heresy; Sir William Stanley's for treason; and that of Mary Queen of Scots. *The Athenæum* of 20 July (no. 612, pp. 538–539), in its review of the work, said "By turns impassioned, tender, and sarcastic, he touches every chord of human feeling ... so easy and unfettered is our author's style, that it rather resembles a brilliant improvisation than a studied and elaborate work."

---

708. EBB TO THEODOSIA GARROW

Beacon Terrace
Wednesday– [mid-August 1839][1]

My dear Miss Garrow,

I was too tired upon my return from the *voyage* yesterday,[2] to do more than feel very much pleased & honored too, by Mr Landor's gift.[3] Thank you for conveying it to me—& forgive me for not answering your note until now– The Admiral's daughter is the second of the "*Two old men's tales*".[4] I read it upon its publication several years ago, & was much struck with its passion & intensity, & "shed tears as fast" as Landor could, though mine wanted the embalming qualities of his— .. the "medicæan gums"–[5] Miss Boyle is to [be] envied. By the way I never heard [of] the book attributed to her,—or to a female writer at all– Surely she is not the State Prisoner Miss Boyle, Mr James's friend.[6] Not that I know anything of the Prisoner except from a review.[7]

If it sh^d be fine tomorrow

"There yawns the sack & yonder rolls the sea"[8]

& I am afraid I shall not escape being a victim. But in the case of the wind being a little rough, or a cloud being broad enough for an excuse, I shall be delighted to see you & your sister dear Miss Garrow—then—or any other day.[9]

And believe me on all days
Most truly yours
Elizabeth B Barrett.

I shall venture to write to M.ʳ Landor to Bath trusting to his name for including the advantage we need, of his address.

Docket, at top of page 1, in an unidentified hand: 1840. Miss Barrett.
Publication: None traced.
Manuscript: Armstrong Browning Library.

1. Despite the 1840 docket (probably written some time after receipt, perhaps by Miss Garrow's husband-to-be, T.A. Trollope), we think it impossible for the letter to have been written then—the prostration suffered by EBB following the successive deaths of Sam and Bro precluded any boating excursions in 1840. EBB was making such outings in August 1839.
2. A letter of 16 August 1839 (SD1024) says that EBB "bears her excursions upon the water (which are as frequent as the weather will permit,) with less fatigue to herself."
3. If our dating assumptions are correct, this would have been Landor's *Andrea of Hungary and Giovanna of Naples* (1839), mentioned in letter 710; the book formed lot 847 of *Browning Collections* (see *Reconstruction*, A1388).
4. *Two Old Men's Tales: The Deformed, and The Admiral's Daughter* (anon., 2 vols., 1834).
5. Cf. *Othello*, V, 2, 351.
6. Mary Louisa Boyle (1810–90) was the author of *The State Prisoner; a Tale of the French Regency* (2 vols., 1837). George Payne Rainsford James (1799–1860), novelist and historian, the author of *Henry Masterson* (1832), *The Gypsy* (1835) and *Attila* (1837), was described as Miss Boyle's "literary godfather" (see *Mary Boyle: Her Book*, ed. Courtenay Boyle, 1902). The book EBB had not heard of was perhaps Miss Boyle's just-published novel, *The Forester: A Tale of 1688* (3 vols., 1839).
7. *The Athenæum* of 25 March 1837 (no. 491, p. 214) had described *The State Prisoner* as "an agreeable and well-written novel."
8. Byron, *The Corsair* (1814), line 1509.
9. In letter 738, EBB tells Kenyon that she saw Miss Garrow "three times during the summer."

---

709. EBB TO MARY RUSSELL MITFORD

[Torquay]
August 29.ᵗʰ 1839.

Ever dearest Miss Mitford,

You could not please me better than by making me useful to you—& if anything crossed my pleasure in doing this spiriting it was thinking of your being too harrassed & unwell to do it yourself. Unwell again!—and what *was* the "*blow*"? Do say how you are. It w.ᵈ have been an assumption & presumption in me to try to "*set to rights*" verses of yours, & I am glad you preferred my sending verses of my own.¹ But WILL you, when you see them, prefer the same? Have I caught the idea in any measure? Am I out of all measure as to length? *Pray* dont use them unless you like them, but put somebody else into office. I have no right to expect you to like them—you have pleased me enough by treating me as one belonging to you––which I AM² you know!!- Do treat me so always, & never hesitate about making me do anything, even to mending y.' stockings .. particularly if you wish to have them spoilt. But tais toi Jean Jaques³—I am betraying myself, exposing myself, dishonoring myself .. in relation too to the great test of female excellence!

Wrong about the genii! My fancy about them a Dulcinea del Toboso— & you c.ᵈ prove it in a face to face talking of half an hour!! Well! To hear ⟨y⟩ou talk half an hour I w.ᵈ submit to be Dulcinea del Toboso myself. Appreciate the compliment--& consider her near connection with that detestable execrable Don Quixotte (the *book*, I mean) full of blasphemies against the ballads!! & that I w.ᵈ rather be a windmill in a hurricane than Dulcinea!-⁴

After shutting up my last letter I remembered having forgotten to speak to you of the State Trials.⁵ Certainly they have extraordinary power, & are eloquent supremely—with a versification partaking of Crabbe .. & Byron in his Lara & Corsair,—& the sense of *vehemence* which does occasionally quite take away your breath. At the same time they are not poetry in the *high meaning*. I hold that M.ʳ Milnes's poetry IS. Do *you?*- But then I know you delight in the pseudo-Moyle for the dear "action & passion's"⁶ sake, for which M.ʳ Milnes, in this early stage of his career is not t[h]ankworthy- I am so glad you estimate M.ʳ Horne. That is *genius* .. in the full acceptation of a great word.

In my niggardness of labor in the way of copying, I sent you the only fair copy I had of the ballad—& scarcely remember how many of the lines went to you. There is, I think a line ending—"but I must turn away."⁷ Now if the next were to begin "For though the ashes strew my sin, no soul of Adam's race", would ⟨the⟩ first part of that line express the *penitence* in any sufficient degree? Then there is a false quantity in the word "sacristan" as it stands in two places. Would you change the 4.ᵗʰ line in the 3ᵈ part to .. "And the saćristans slyly are jesting aside[".]⁸ And somewhere, midway in the same, the short line sh.ᵈ be changed to "As the sacristans told it"—unless "As the legends unfold it" w.ᵈ be better .. & I myself almost think it w.ᵈ.⁹ Tell me if you object in particular to anything I can alter.

You do not say how dear ⟨D.ʳ Mitford is. . . . May God⟩ bless both of you. I have been a little WILD for ⟨the⟩ last week—with joy at the sight of my dear dear Arabel—& perhaps this letter may not seem to you very particularly tame.

Ever my beloved friend
your EBB-

Address, on integral page: Miss Mitford / Three Mile Cross / Near Reading.
Publication: EBB-MRM, I, 147-149.
Manuscript: Wellesley College.

1. Miss Mitford had asked EBB for a second contribution to *Findens' Tableaux*. EBB responded by sending "The Dream," the manuscript of which is no longer with this letter.
2. Underscored three times.
3. "Be silent, Jean Jacques." A favourite expression of EBB, referring to a childhood incident recounted by Rousseau. As a result of a prank by his young cousin, the tips of two of Rousseau's fingers were trapped and crushed in the rollers of his uncle's mill. Rousseau cried out; his cousin, fearing to be punished, begged him to be silent. Rousseau did so, telling his aunt and uncle that a large stone had fallen on his hand ("Quatrième Promenade," *Les Confessions de Jean-Jacques Rousseau*, 1782).
4. Dulcinea del Toboso was the name given by Don Quixote to Aldonza Lorenzo, the country girl whom he took to be a great lady. EBB, who enjoyed using the ballad form of poetry, apparently resents Cervantes' criticism of that form.
5. See letter 707, note 6.
6. "Reason and Belief, no less than Action and Passion" were described by Carlyle as essential components of knowledge in his "Thoughts on History" (*Fraser's Magazine*, November 1830, pp. 413-418).
7. As printed in *Findens' Tableaux*, this line (in the 4th part of "The Legend of the Brown Rosarie") ended "but *I* must look away." EBB's suggested change to the next line was not made; the printed text reads "For never sinner, sin-convinced, can dare or bear to gaze". When reprinted in *Poems* (1844), EBB altered "look away" to "turn away," and the next line to "Because no sinner under sun can dare or bear to gaze" (lines 375 and 376).
8. This line was printed as "And the grave young sacristans jest slyly aside". EBB's suggested change was incorporated in the 1844 text (line 223).
9. The printed version reads "The sacristans have told it." The 1844 text was changed to "As the choristers told it" (line 319).

---

710. EBB TO MARY RUSSELL MITFORD

[Torquay]
Saturday. [?14] [September 1839][1]

My beloved friend,

I am afraid you have been cruelly buffeted by the Finden party when you were least able to bear it.[2] Tiresome people! If their book is the worse for it, just will be the retribution. Could you not have assumed some dignity of office & insisted upon artists being artists & yourself being editor? But after all, dignity is a troublesome thing either to set up or to keep up,—& far better is it, than that you sh^d be troubled when you are not well, for the bodies fond of "looking at pictures" to shut their eyes upon this volume of Tableaux (I mean literally the *tableaux*––the *prose* letter-press being safe) or content themselves with the vision of the golden mute lady upon the back, for the space of one twelvemonth.

As to my poems, depend upon it the prefatory little boy[3] will be found wandering somewhere to the end of all things, with a brown rosary tied round his neck. If he escapes hanging by it, it will be by miracle, & certainly not by virtue of the clearness of my manuscript.

The Picture for which EBB wrote "A Romance of the Ganges"

The Picture for which EBB wrote "The Romaunt of the Page"

The Picture for which EBB wrote "The Legend of the Browne Rosarie"

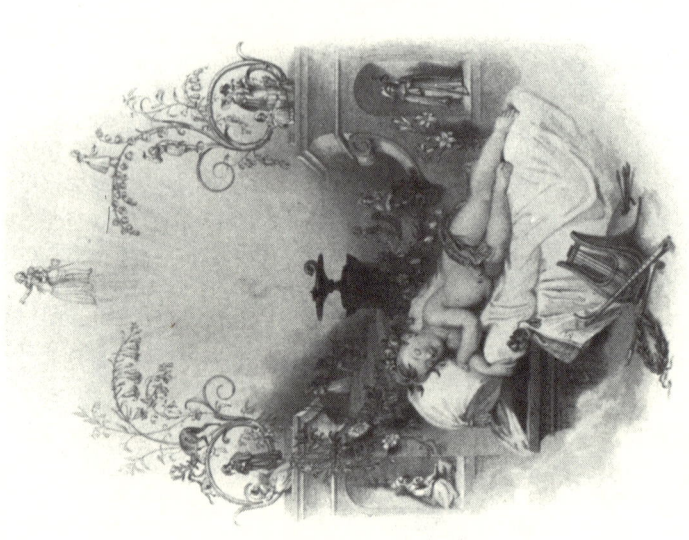

The Picture for which EBB wrote "The Dream"

Are you laughing at me, dearest Miss Mitford? or did you glorify my manuscript in a vision?

"Magnified from sight to dream."[4]

(may they print aright that one line at least, in the way of illustration!) for I remember moralizing over heaps of blots, & thinking--"Well, I am too tired to write all this over again,—& I can make everything straight in the proof"—little knowing what futurity was about to overwhelm me. And be it known to you that if you smile superior it is not only in your capacity of a "veteran author". All veteran authors do not attain to such high philosophy. There is Mr Boyd for instance whose whole existence is absorbed for the nonce in a question of errata, & who under my circumstances w^d hang himself in a brown rosary without pause, .. or put an end to himself by some more classical death without waiting to consider how Plato reasoned, before hand. Dont translate this into grave earnest dearest Miss Mitford! It is true only of Mr Boyd. But you & I may both wish Messrs Finden joy of my poems if they are printed as some proofs were, of my "*beautiful clear manuscripts*" of the Seraphim!![5] In that case too, I shall be less understandible than usual—which will be wonderful.

All which nonsense I am very little in a mood to write so gaily, though you may fancy so. Poor Dr Barry my able & most kind physician who for above a year has attended me almost every day—and at my best estate never left me longer than a day,—is seriously ill with rheumatic & nervous fever, has been confined to his bed for ten days & was yesterday in much danger. The crisis & danger are now said to be past—but I still feel anxious & saddened—& not the less so of course, from hearing of the continued solicitude he is expressing about me,—begging me to call in another physician .. which I cant & wont do. May God grant that the improvement in his state may be lasting! He has one dear little girl scarcely past her babyhood,—and his wife is about to become a mother again: and from his talents & rising reputation, & undeviating attention & kindness towards his patients, his loss w^d be greatly felt in this place, in a professional point of view as in many others. May God spare him to his family & friends! I am very anxious.

Has Mr Talfourd written for you?[6] I hope so. Mr Shepherd did not send me his poem, nor have I read it[7]—but I shall try to do so, since your opinion of it is so high. My acquaintance is confined to Lady Mary & her daughter—& even in this case seems to have come to an end—and Mr Shepherd I never saw in my life. It was when they were staying at Malvern & we were residing at Hope End, that I had my only intercourse with Lady Mary,—but two years afterwards Miss Shepherd visited the former place with the Chief Baron of Scotland,[8] & then she came over &

spent a week with me—& we parted as friends. I never was so near loving anybody very much whom I did *not* love very much! She might be .. or at least *have been* .. anything! Rapid intelligence & fancy—strong natural sensibility .. rendered peculiar .. at once interesting & repulsive to me .. by the very NAIVETÈ *of worldliness*. To explain what I mean, I need only tell you that she used words of this sort in talking to me--"I cannot be distinguished by either great beauty, great genius, or high rank. Nothing is left to me but to be faultless in high breeding—an *elegante par excellence*."[9] Words to that effect--I am not accurate as to syllables. And in order to compass an object so inglorious, i.e. this distinction *par Almacks*—she spoke openly of the necessity she was under of sacrificing friendships to surtouts,—& how friends in vulgar waistcoats & questionable situations never c^d be visible objects to her eyes, however dear to her heart. It is *all* vulgar—vulgar—vulgar!—more vulgar than any waistcoat or locality—the vulgarity on all sides of us every day in one form or another! But her openness in telling it, & the kind of principle upon which she based the profession struck & amused me,—& contrasted so blackly & whitely with much besides which I observed & estimated & admired in her, that I c^d have wept real tears & loved her through them all, to hear those shackles rattle "abhorred music"[10] as she cast them off. Her conversational powers were very nearly *brilliant*—but brilliant FOR *society*. "I can do two things well", she said once to me—"dance & speak French"! and 'well' meant "to perfection'['] in that sentence. And yet she was *not* a young lady's lady—by no means frivolous—by no means superficial. *There* was the peculiarity. She was a philosopher in triviality. Capable too of intense feeling—. I have seen her cheeks grow pale & her lips tremble with the strength of it.

Well! she was very affectionate to me: at least very kind & cordial: but our faults were not of the same kind, & some unfitness was felt I dare say on each side. When my Prometheus came out, I directed the publisher to send a copy to Lady Mary as from the author—which remains unacknowledged: and when we went to London & had ascertained that she knew of our being there, I did not like to be the first to break the silence & renew the acquaintance. I dont know much about etiquettes– Perhaps I sh^d have sent a card. But under the silence & the circumstances, & the remembrance of dear Miss Shepherd's old theories, I did not like to do it. Suppose I had been convicted of a vulgar waistcoat? What w^d have become of me? And certainly I felt by no means strong in Almacks & the Marchioness of Londonderry!——[11]

Was not Pedro (the first part) reviewed in the Athenæum?[12] Is it in the dramatic form?

I have *not* heard from Miss Anderdon. Will you call her attention to a notice of her poem on the last page of the last number of the New Monthly Magazine?[13]

Do let your next account of yourself be a better one. I am anxious about you my beloved friend. For my own part I have not been very well for some days—suffering from oppression on the chest & old symptoms consequent upon the changeable moist heavy state of the atmosphere. The fearful winter is at hand again!—— On the first of October we remove, or intend doing so now, to a new house, *1 Beacon Terrace*,— which is promised to be a warmer residence than our present one.

Whether Mr Horne is married or single I cannot, cannot tell you.[14] Dont make me responsible in a note. But dearest Miss Mitford, I quite agree with you that the 'Death of Marlowe'[15] over again, w^d not, with all its genius & power, do for your annual. I am sorry you did not make a point of seeing his contribution. He wrote to me to tell me that he had completed it,—& to ask besides I believe whether its title "*A German trilogy*" sounded in my ears very affected, or was likely to do so in the ears of your readers[16]—in which same letter, came a request that I w^d send him by return of post a short poem for insertion in the last Monthly Chronicle he having agreed to edit it for a month. I was very unwell when I received this letter,—confined to my bed & incapable of writing a short poem for the nonce, as I sh^d have liked to do. The shortest ready made ones I had access to were anything but short—yet rather than appear insensible to his much courtesy by my much crossness, I sent him two, together with applause (as far as I knew how) of the sound of the "German trilogy." I have not heard from him since; nor did the Monthly Chronicle contain either of my poems. By the way, one of them, called "The Madrigal of flowers" & occasioned by a dead flower being sent to me from Wimpole St, has a stanza in its middle consecrated to you & *yours*--flowers, I mean—not Dr Mitford.[17]

Give my love to him my dearest Miss Mitford—& my sisters' to yourself. Believe how very

truly you are loved by your
Elizabeth B Barrett.

Mr Landor has most kindly sent me his two last dramas. They are *Landor's*—& c^d be none other's– But they are not an achievement for Landor.[18]

My sister—Henrietta has made the acquaintance of the Miss Goldings, neighbours of yours,[19] & *nightingales*, I understand. They have left Torquay! Are they your acquaintances or your friends? I w^d rather have heard them talk of you—than sing!

Publication: EBB-MRM, I, 149–153 (as [September 1839]).
Manuscript: Wellesley College.

1. Dated by SD1042, which deals with some of the same subjects.
2. Apparently a reference to some arguments over editorial policy, involving the Finden brothers, responsible for the engravings, Charles Tilt, the publisher, and Miss Mitford, the editor.
3. The subject of EBB's second contribution, "The Dream."
4. Verse 3, line 4 of "The Dream."
5. A wry allusion to misprints occasioned by EBB's rather small handwriting.
6. Talfourd did not contribute to this issue of *Findens' Tableaux*.
7. Henry J. Shepherd, the husband of EBB's acquaintance of Hope End days, Lady Mary Shepherd, had published in 1838 *Pedro of Castile*.
8. Sir Samuel Shepherd (1760–1840), Member of Parliament 1813–19; Attorney-General 1817; Lord Chief Baron of the Court of Exchequer in Scotland 1819–30, was Henry Shepherd's father.
9. "Pre-eminent lady of style."
10. We have not located the source of this quotation.
11. Almack's Assembly Rooms, in King Street, St. James's, had been opened in 1765 by William Almack, a Scotsman, and soon became the Mecca of London society. The Rooms were ruled by the Patronesses, who alone distributed tickets of admission; as denial of entry was a fate almost worse than death, this power made them undisputed arbiters of fashion and manners. Lady Jersey was the most notable of the Patronesses, but Frances Anne Emily, Lady Londonderry (*née* Vane-Tempest, 1800–65), wife of the 3rd Marquis of Londonderry, had considerable influence also.
12. A review in *The Athenæum* (no. 536, 3 February 1838, pp. 88–89) conceded the poem some merit, but felt that the subject "required a sustaining power beyond that possessed by Mr. Shepherd."
13. The September issue (p. 144) said of *Costanza of Mistra* "This 'Tale of Modern Greece,' is pleasingly written, and with a feeling and fancy that evince the gratification its author must have derived from the composition ... its story being one of strict truth, connected with the Greek struggle for independence, and one which will amply repay perusal, without reference to the poetical merits of which it is made the medium."
14. Horne was single at this time; he did not marry until 1847.
15. Horne's *The Death of Marlowe* had appeared in *The Monthly Repository*, August 1837. It was published in book form that same year.
16. When printed in *Findens' Tableaux*, Horne's poem was entitled "The Fetches."
17. The poem was not published until its inclusion in *Poems* (1844), when it bore the title "A Flower in a Letter." Verse XI reads:
> By Loddon's stream the flowers are fair
> That meet one gifted lady's care
> With prodigal rewarding:
> (For Beauty is too used to run
> To Mitford's bower—to want the sun
> To light her through the garden.)

For the second poem sent to Horne, see letter 717. See also *Reconstruction*, D288 and D172.

18. *Andrea of Hungary and Giovanna of Naples* (1839). The book, inscribed by Landor, formed lot 847 of *Browning Collections* (see *Reconstruction*, A1388).
19. Possibly the family of Edward Golding, of Sonning, some 4 miles N.E. of Reading.

711. RB to Euphrasia Fanny Haworth

[London]
[16 September 1839][1]

Dear Miss Haworth,

The translation—with thanks. I am in haste, but mean to do something towards an answer to your letter (kind letter!) in a few days; meantime, I can't for my life remember what I meant, much less said or wrote, *that time*, whenever it was;—forgive it, with much beside.

Do not make a set at poor Harness—Miss Martineau intends to ask him all about the review— I see him every now and then.

Yours ever truly,
RB

Are you not sorry for L.E.L.? whom I never saw[2]—"Is she dead? Why—so shall I be!" quoth Barry Cornwall somewhere.[3] Wish "Paracelsus" luck, by the way, at the Great St Leger—for he, a horse, starts, I see by this morning's "Times", with a batch of the rarest—as does "Avicenna"—both gloried in by Mr C. Atwood![4]

Publication: None traced.
Manuscript: Dunedin Public Library.

1. Dated by RB's reference to *The Times*.
2. Letitia Elizabeth Landon (Mrs. Maclean) had died in Africa on 15 October 1838 (see letter 680, note 5).
3. "Ludovic Sforza" (*Dramatic Scenes and Other Poems*, 1819) contains the words "And is she dead?" but nothing approximating to the second phrase quoted by RB. "Juan," also in *Dramatic Scenes*, includes the words "I shall be dead." It seems probable that, at some distance of time, RB's memory produced a fusion of the two poems.
4. *The Times*, 16 September 1839, gave details of the week's programme of races at Doncaster, including Mr. Attwood's two horses, mentioned by RB. However, neither was listed for the St. Leger, to be run on 17 September. "Avicenna" was a possible starter for the Champagne Stakes, to be run on the 16th, and "Paracelsus" was down for the Two-Year-Old Stakes for the 19th. According to the results given later in the week, neither horse actually started.

---

712. EBB to Mary Russell Mitford

Torquay
Sunday. [?22] [September 1839][1]

Ever dearest Miss Mitford,

I am so grieved to hear this bad news .. I mean of your having been so unwell. But I should wait until tomorrow's post to say so, when I might say more besides than a great hurry & departing post will admit of now. My single reason for writing now is to apprize you that I have been troubled by NEITHER proof nor revise! Is it right or a mistake? If a mistake, will it be one likely to involve others .. in the printing?——

May God bless you both!——

I am in such a hurry.

But ever your
Elizabeth B Barrett.

Publication: EBB-MRM, I, 158 (as [29? September 1839]).
Manuscript: Wellesley College.

1. Dated by the reference to proofs of EBB's poems for *Findens' Tableaux*; EBB's comment about Miss Mitford's "improved health" in her letter of 27 September obviously follows the concern expressed here.

713. EBB TO MARY RUSSELL MITFORD

Torquay–
Septr 27.th 1839.

Thank you again & again my beloved friend for your kindest solicitude. Since I wrote to you last I have been much grieved & very anxious. Poor Dr Barry's illness c^d not have been simple rheumatic fever. At any rate, a few hours after Mrs Barry had written to beg that I w^d write to him most particularly about myself as he was much better & very anxious on my account, a relapse came, & for a night & a day his medical attendants had little or no hope of him. He lay for hours between life & death. I knew nothing of this until he was better—indeed until the crisis was quite over; and when I heard of it, even as a *past*, I was of course much moved by the thought of what might have been & of what still remained so precarious—especially with the thoughts of his late anxious kindness about myself warm beside *that* thought! I do thank God—everything is going right now, & there is no room for fear. I do thank God. Had the worst happened, I sh^d have scarcely borne to stay here! and I c^d not ever have shaken from my mind, in any case, that I must have been the involuntary cause of some of the evil,—poor Dr Barry having risen from his bed two days before he was quite confined to it, for the purpose of coming thro' an atmosphere saturated with rain, to see me between nine & ten at night.[1] I said at the time "Oh how ill you do look! How c^d you come out in such weather!" little thinking what was impending. Well—I thank God that all is bright or brighter now. And as to my sending for a substitute my dearest Miss Mitford, if you knew how I shrink from a *stranger* in the shape of a physician, you w^d not ask it. I dare say I shall see Dr Barry next week: and in the meantime I am better—the bad symptoms having receded, & the worst discomfort remaining, in an oppression upon the chest which impedes my voice very disagreeably— the effect probably of all this atmospheric changeableness & moisture. What weather it is .. even here where we are safe from the frosts of which you speak. How very very happy I am dearest dearest Miss Mitford to read your accounts .. or rather your expectations .. of improved health. God grant a realization to them all. It will be felt by me as a happiness. Mr May must be an admirable person—& I have a high respect for him all these miles off!——

Your view of things in relation to Miss Shepherd is right & bright together, I do not doubt. Sir Samuel Shepherd loved her dearly, when she was with him at Malvern––(that was when he was chief Baron of Scotland)––and if tender dispositions were suffered to evolve naturally from feelings naturally intense, she must have become year after year a more loveable person. Lady Mary IS a singular woman. I think gratefully of her from some passages of kindness which passed from her to me, when I wanted kindness most, & the saddest of domestic losses was nearer than I thought or *would* think.[2] I believe her to be a *kind woman*—a better if not a higher name than a great metaphysician. Have you seen her books upon the External Universe & Cause & effect?[3] She has high talents—but has not perhaps been *operative* enough to have done much undone before, altho' quite enough to raise her own name above the multitude. Metaphysicians, & I suspect, *poets* sh.^{d} live in a cave,—or at least live so, as to form habits of concentration & abstraction. Lady Mary (so her daughter told me) used to waltz until she was tired, & then sit down to write about algebra. Her daughter at once admired & *feared* her—feared her very much—& nobody else in the world. She seemed to love—in the clear meaning of love .. her father—with no fear in *that* love. There was love too in abundance, I am sure, between the metaphysician & the dramatist—& Lady Mary used to say jestingly—"We are *very* much in love with each other". Notwithstanding which, he used by her own account to take up his hat & walk out whenever she began to dissert (she *does* dissert you know) upon primary & secondary qualities in matter—and she on the other hand was the *authority* in all domestic matters & would'nt suffer any interference- "What can *he* know about children? Why he was only a boy *when I married him*".[4] Just those words! I am certain this time about the syllables. They are unforgettable.

Now you see what a gossip you have made of me. Dont tell it all again to Sir Samuel.

She used to keep Miss Shepherd up to three or four in the morning after a conclave of waltzers, to hear (she being "sole auditor") vocal dissertations upon spirit & matter & such high arguments,—then suddenly check herself with--"My dear!—how CAN you stand with your left foot before your *right*"! The most eloquent woman I ever heard speak, certainly—and the vainest in speaking of herself. But she is boldly vain. She justifies (almost) her vanity by her simplicity. She does not lay nets for praises.

When Miss Shepherd (to go back to the daughter) told me that she herself had not genius, I doubted her words. I used to think that she might be almost anything. She often wrote to me while she was at Malvern—years ago; & yet I have kept to this moment every line she sent me[5]—a sure sign—since they were not consecrated to me by any strong attachment—of how I thought concerning their writer—of how entirely she interested me. I remember her seal now,—*Per sempre*,[6]—& how in some of my musings about her, I used to lay the motto in contrast with others of her fancies, as things most contrastible.—— Tell me, when you hear anything about her.

The china asters are beautiful—rayed brightly as any stars of earth can be. Your flowers have grown in the desolate garden of that empty house[7] as beautifully as if my darling Ibbit Jane's blue eyes were looking out of the window upon them—or as if they had never left *you*. Nosegays upon nosegays of them have been gathered for me, & bloomed & blossomed with & been *survived by* thoughts of you, in my room. Thank you for all!–

Poor poor Lady Flora Hastings! Sir James Clark has *hallucinated* considerably from the high sphere in which you place his profession. The *ignorance* was the least of the injury. It appears to have been combined with coldness & coarseness of feeling. I w^d give much to rescue the young queen from any such imputation. *Can it be done?* I heard gladly of the tears she shed when tears were vain—but still the circumstances can scarcely be effaced by tears—& perhaps the most ineffaceable of all, was her cold long silence to the poor victim whose innocense was proved,— *in consequence of her uncle's publication of facts*.[8] That the queen could have been provoked by any publication, by any insult which that publication was *not*, by any injury which that publication was *not*, to give *more* pain to a heart so pained by herself, is an atrocity I w^d fain hear explained away.

> So much for human ties in royal breasts!
> Why spare men's feelings when their own are jests?[9]

But surely surely the young Queen with her fair happy-looking face, & her warm ready childish tears for the departure from office of her political friends, cannot be a mere Queen Stone, co-regnant with King Log.[10] I w^d fain hear differently. Have you heard anything?

In regard to poor Lady Flora, she was to my apprehension PERFECTLY WRONG in sacrificing her personal delicacy to any court slander upon lips noble or royal. She might have called in other medical men & insured their close attendance, & testimony together with Sir James Clark's.[11] And if such limited measures did not suffice to save her reputation if I had been she, I w^d have lost it. Let it go. I do not see why women sh^d not take as high ground in respect to one virtue as in respect to the rest. If anyone were to accuse me of secreting stolen goods, I w^d scarcely condescend to empty my drawers into the street, & so clear my character. Oh! this world! How we shake & crawl & die before it, if it do but bluster!–

And then surely the whole conduct of her family in regard to the publication of the letters is most blame-worthy. Tell me if you do not think so. *I* do, for many reasons: and everybody will consider one admissible if it go to prove that the publication is calculated to diminish rather than to heighten the interest & compassion. It has done so with me in this manner– I did not *quite like* poor Lady Flora's letter to her uncle. It did not seem to me the letter of a woman of deep sensibility, wrung to the cruellest. An amiable excellent woman I do not doubt her being,—& cruelly wronged she *was*—but after reading that letter, my mind is easy as to the wrong bringing her a step nearer to death. There is something in it, which if she were not in the grave, having put off, only with her living garments the aspersions of slander .. I sh^d be inclined to call, almos⟨t⟩ a *flippancy*. At any rate it was not, it c^d not have been, written in any degree of mental agony.

You have made me uneasy by your allusion to the Findens—& with the volume, too, in this unpromising state. But *your prose is in it*.[12] I always think THAT when I want to be comforted. Do give my love to Dr Mitford. We go to number one on this Terrace, on Monday or tuesday—& there wont be much risk for me in the removal for so short a distance. My brother means to fold me up in a cloak & carry me.

May God ever bless you!– Pray don't throw away more anxious thoughts upon me. If I had any really *bad* symptoms, I w^d call in another physician. As it is do let me enjoy the luxury of being obstinate—perverse as Mr Kenyon calls it–

Your obstinately affectionate
EBB.

Publication: EBB-MRM, I, 153–157.
Manuscript: Wellesley College.

1. It is interesting to note that, for all Dr. Barry's devoted attendance, he had "not received as yet a farthing" and that EBB had had to write to him to enquire the extent of her indebtedness (see SD1042).
2. i.e., the death of EBB's mother in October 1828.
3. In 1828, Lady Mary had presented EBB with copies of her books, *Essays on the Perception of an External Universe* (1827) and *An Essay Upon the Relation of Cause*

and Effect Controverting the Doctrine of Mr. Hume (1824), (see *Reconstruction*, A2124 and A2123.1).

4. Henry J. Shepherd, born in 1783, married Lady Mary in 1808, so was hardly "only a boy"!

5. As far as is known, these letters are no longer extant.

6. "For ever."

7. i.e., the one vacated by the Hedleys in July, when they moved to Southampton.

8. *The Times* published, in its issue of 12 August, two letters: one dated 8 March 1839 from Lady Flora to her uncle, Hamilton Fitzgerald, in which she expressed the belief that she was the victim of a conspiracy; the other, from Fitzgerald, dated 30 May 1839, explaining that his purpose in making public her letter was to counter suggestions that she was "guilty as charged." For details of the scandal, see letter 702, note 12.

9. Byron, *The Age of Bronze* (1823), 763–764.

10. When the frogs asked for a king, Jupiter threw down a log; when they complained, he then gave them a stork, which devoured them. "King Log" therefore symbolizes an ineffective, spiritless ruler. Suggesting that Victoria was "a mere Queen Stone" reflects a general feeling that she had been insensitive and ungenerous in her attitude towards Lady Flora.

11. The statement issued after Lady Flora's medical examination was, in fact, co-signed by her personal doctor, Sir Charles Mansfield Clarke (1782–1857), physician to Queen Adelaide.

12. Six of Miss Mitford's prose pieces were included in the 1840 *Findens' Tableaux*.

---

714. EBB TO SEPTIMUS MOULTON-BARRETT

[Torquay]
[*Postmark:* 18 October 1839]

My dearest Sette's repeated letters which always make me jump a little way into the air to meet them, have not, nevertheless, had one expression of gratitude from me all to himself. So that my conscience ought to begin the pricking system, as well as his. I told Arabel to leave me the corners which she has done—but without leaving the necessary accompaniment of time to write in them[1]—it being past nine o clock on friday morning at this moment of this being consigned to my hands. We try to console ourselves for losing Georgie,[2] by thinking & saying over & over again, that you will be glad to have him. After all it is scarcely sufficiently consolatory--if I may answer for the most selfish of us. You do not say what you think of his personal improvement--& whether my belief of his cheeks looking more rural, is or is not a fond illusion on my part. I was sure you w^d approve of Brozie's water color drawings. I did not see those which he sent to London; but his general progress is certainly very encouraging—& he does not falter or slacken yet in application, which is the great means. Arabel went with Bummy to Upton yesterday, & brought home a sketch of the stony valley—intended for an oil painting. She & Bummy & a donkey went all together.—— She has, I hope, given an improved account of me. Dr Scully³ said yesterday that the "storm was almost past"—& for the first time, wished me to remain half an hour on the sofa—intimating that the time sh.^d be gradually extended, & that, if the weather were good, I might be in the drawing room some time in the course of next week. This was a good deal for him to say—considering the timidity he has shown hitherto about my moving—even advising me to confine the bed making to three times a week! & it proves how very much calmer the action of the heart must be. I was beginning to think that my adjacency to the drawing room w.^d prove of little advantage for a long time.– The house appears to be very warm.– Whenever you write, do tell us everything you all do—bad or good. Even walking up stairs is an interesting circumstance. May He who is near to the far, bless you with the *chief* blessings in Christ Jesus. I love you all too much instead of too little—so I need not say I love you. Was it explained to dear Trippy, how the second goose failed Crow? I hope so. Tell her she is to write her own letters. Love to my beloved Papa & everybody—never forgetting dear Minny.

Your most affectionate Ba.

Address, on integral page: Mr Septimus Barrett / 50. Wimpole Street / London.
Publication: None traced.
Manuscript: Myrtle Moulton-Barrett and Ronald A. Moulton-Barrett.

1. This letter accompanies messages by Arabella Graham-Clarke and Arabella Moulton-Barrett. It is written on the final page of a four-page letter (SD1059), in spaces not occupied by the address (which is in EBB's hand).
2. He had left Torquay on 11 October, after a protracted stay with EBB.
3. Dr. Barry had died on 2 October; the shock of his death had an adverse effect on EBB's fragile health. To replace him, a senior local doctor, William Scully (d. 1842), was called in (see SD1058).

---

715. EBB TO MARY RUSSELL MITFORD

[Torquay]
[?25] October [1839]¹

I am afraid ever dearest Miss Mitford, to think what you may think of me with all these days nay, weeks between your last interesting letter & my acknowledgement of it. But I have been much grieved—& too unwell to *stir* to seek for your sympathy. Dear kind Dr Barry is no more. A second relapse followed fast upon the first, & you c.^d scarcely have read what I wrote in hope & gladness before all lay reversed, & by a startling decree of God, the physician was taken & the patient *left*—& left of course deeply affected & shaken. He was a young man—full of energy—

with a countenance seeming to look *towards life*—devoted to his profession & rising rapidly into professional eminence—a young man with a young wife & child, & baby unborn .. & in such circumstances there sh^d not be room for *me* to feel my own loss in his unslackening kindness & interest—yet I made room for my selfishness & have deeply felt it. To the very last his kindness did not slacken--but I need not bear down upon you with all this sadness. God's will be done .. be the close of all!——

You did your part in waging war against my obstinacy, beloved friend—but you see I *would* until dear Dr Barry was *gone* .. struggle on without medical advice—& the effect was a great deal of irritation superinduced into the system—so that upon my removal to this house[2] & the agitation of mind instantly succeeding, I was ill, & had my old attack of fever & imperviousness to sleep, & have not indeed left my bed for a longer period than three quarters of an hour, these three weeks or more. They called in the senior physician of the place, Dr Scully,—who is considered clever & safe—& his verdict upon the pulse this morning appears much more favorable. But you will understand that I have not been neglecting you through too much prosperity—& forgive a silence so sadly & heavily passed by me. And if you *do*, prove the clemency by the writing. I want to hear of you so very much, & besides of dear Dr Mitford!–

Oct. 29.th

The above was written some days ago. Would that it had been finished & sent then, because in such a case, I might be watching for a letter from you during this *now*. However, the delay allows me to tell you of my being better,—& able to get to the sofa for an hour every day, notwithstanding the terrible east wind .. Papa being here to counteract it with the 'sweet south'[3] of his presence– And he looks so well that everybody who loves him as I do, must begin to look well too.

I had the first glimpse of the new Tableaux on 'earthly ground' in the last Athenæum[4]—and to judge by such faintness of light & sight, we seem to have fallen upon our feet after all my dearest Miss Mitford. Not that I ever felt uneasy about YOU—but what you told me had brought around me some indefinite terrors about somebody or thing in or about the lonely ladye in gold & green. So you drew a song from dear Mr Kenyon after all!– I am very glad.[5]

Miss Anderdon has written. And do when you see her, express my thanks for the kindness which she did write, inclusive of her wish to begin our acquaintanceship to come, next summer. I am sure I cannot know her too soon—but our meeting them *at Torquay* depends on two great uncertainties, & one of them, the last, is most unpleasant for me to think of—viz—the continuance of my life .. & of my residence at this place. I *long* to go away. How we drag our weary wills after God's will .. reluctantly sadly heavily .. as if we did not recognize in *it* the chief wisdom! '*We*' is written & it sh.^{d} be "*I*"^{6}——"I" being the most inconsistent of all disquieted waters. God teach me & make me better & meeker & lower beneath His feet!——

Dearest dearest Miss Mitford, I liked the Athenæum note about your garden & the King of Prussia's policy!–^{7} I wish I c.^{d} see it & you—& love both of you at a distance.

Your attached
EBB——

The new house is warm & in all ways or *most*, superior to the last.

Address, on integral page: Miss Mitford / Three Mile Cross / Near Reading.
Publication: EBB-MRM, I, 158–160.
Manuscript: Wellesley College.

1. Inclusive dating provided by EBB; the year by reference to Dr. Barry's death.
2. The family had moved to 1 Beacon Terrace on 1 October.
3. See letter 668, note 3.
4. *The Athenæum,* 26 October 1839 (no. 626, pp. 809–810), under the heading "The Annuals for 1840," found the latest *Findens' Tableaux* "fully equal to the former volumes ... Miss Mitford, the editor, is also the principal contributor: and where shall we find a pleasanter narrator of a short, healthy, racy, story, just such a one as is sure to be the gem of an Annual!" The review quoted a lengthy extract from "a wild legend entitled 'The Brown Rosarie,' by Miss Barrett." (For the full text of the review, see pp. 409–411.)
5. Miss Mitford's story "The Roundhead's Daughter" incorporated a poem, "To an Æolian Harp," with a generous acknowledgement to its author, John Kenyon.
6. Underscored twice.
7. The same issue of *The Athenæum,* in an article dated "Leipsic, October 1839" (pp. 810–811), describes the Pfauen-Insel as "the worst piece of bad taste ... as if the *Schloss* were not already sufficiently incongruous ... in the midst of an English garden." A footnote at this point includes the comment that "There is a greater variety of plants in one patch the size of a table, in Miss Mitford's flower garden, than in the whole open-air 'policy' of the King of Prussia."

---

716. EBB to Mary Russell Mitford

[Torquay]
18.th Nov [1839]^1

My beloved friend,

Your note has distressed me & made me uneasy until I can have another. May God bless & restore the health so precious to many—& grant that even while I write, the cause of the painfulness with which I do so, may be passing away. Where is Mr May? You are obedient to him—are you not, my beloved friend? Does he not tell you to lie down or to walk—never to sit, when you can *choose* a posture.? Tell me what he says. Is a warm bath—a *hip* bath—considered good for you? a question to which, ignorant as I am, I almost fancy a 'yes'– Above all it must be injurious to you, if your mind continues haunted by uneasy thoughts of possible, surely not of probable disappointments & consequent difficulties—& I beat myself against the wires of my cage in wonderings & wishings about how I can ask you not to be uneasy under such circumstances, without saying a mockery. But surely dearest dearest Miss Mitford, these Mess.rs Finden who deserve to be drawn & quartered like their own 'tableaux' and your stories, cant meditate any pecuniary treason towards you.[2] They have done their worst, now—surely—and you have only to vow against forming any similar engagement without being secured against similar annoyances & disrespect. What your agreement is with them, of what nature & after what manner, I can know nothing—but I must hope them (*at* least) into being honest men, albeit for the nonce no gentlemen. The cutting down of your beautiful stories is lese majestè[3]— & unpardonable—& then cries for vengeance the omission of the dedication—indeed the whole series of their discourtesies towards you!– But— after all, dearest Miss Mitford, a fatality & *you* are in it, & the book will sell,—& then you see, these magnificent 'proprietors' however wilfully they may annoy you, will take care .. "stepping east & stepping west"[4] .. *as far as America* .. in their magnificent calculations, will take care not to offend & lose you irrepareably. Your popularity in America must raise your value as an editor: and for the rest I understand from a bookseller here that 'Finden's Tableaux' sells better than any of the annuals—that the '*trade*' winds set in, in such a sort. Thank you for the copy in Wimpole Street–[5] It is quite right in being there instead of here, inasmuch as it belongs to Papa—who, before your letter came, had bought & given one to my aunt Bell, Miss Clarke—so that I had both seen & read it. It is a beautiful book—& I hope the Mess.rs Finden may behave pretty well, were it only to give me the pleasure of admiring *comfortably* the engravings, vignettes & all. For I have quite (at heart) forgiven the vignettes— they are so graceful & have such an aerial significance. Your stories are full of beauty—cant be mutilated out of beauty. I am pleased with all; but with the 'king's page' most of all .. which last, I shall wonder about, if it do not find its way into the theatre. It has an inimitable spirit & delicacy—& is likely to be siezed upon for a '*petite piece*'––is it not?— only the lovely BLUSH wherein is involved the denoument, w.d vanish away before the footlamps.

Thank you for all this pleasure! Did you see a favorable notice in the Metropolitan which said in my ears some pleasant justice of you?[6] Indeed it spoke very graciously of more than you—of everybody I think or almost so, connected with the *late* green ladye.

No. 716   18 November [1839]

I am so glad in your satisfaction with Mr Horne's tragedy, & glad besides in the tragedy itself. The love scene by moonlight has to my apprehension a *Jessica feel* in it[7]—& that music of broken cadences is quite Shakesperian, which is to be recognized there also. Mr Horne has not denied himself in this composition, notwithstanding some obvious marks & results, of haste & confusion. Mr Chorley's ballad is too near the Ancient Mariner, not to be the Mariner himself.[8] Otherwise I sh^d admire it much. But 'Hence avaunt this holy ground'.[9] The Mariner must have his ship to himself.

Dearest dearest Miss Mitford, how I rejoice in your story of revived friendship, or rather of reunited friends.[10] It is a favorite doxy of mine——a favorite dream—do not speak loudly & wake me from it——that friendship—that love,—cannot by a law of its nature pass away, die away, as is the manner of mortal things, however we may look sometimes upon something dark & low, & call it ashes, & say "this is all that is left". Those who have once loved must love on in their hearts, if not in their words & faces &——alas, *lives!* And if this were otherwise, I c^d not yet willingly receive as a possibility, that Mr Sergeant Talfourd sh^d dishonor Ion by forgetting & denying *you*, & without recall & forgetfulness! "C^d such things, be?"[11] Your story of how it all came to pass touched & charmed me. That Ion did his part warmly & nobly I do not doubt,—your own nobleness & generosity being witness!—your own nobleness & generosity as seen in that relation!——

You have *dated* your letter, & I shall remember (if it please God for me to live) Dr Mitford's birthday on the 15.th of next Nov^r.[12] May God bless him & you—both of you in each other!—my love to him always!-

How *will* you read what I write on the 18.th of this Nov?—what I scratch rather than write?- I have not been out of bed except for an hour at a time & once a day, & never to *dress*, since the first of October—& Dr Scully seems afraid to permit me to do it or even to permit himself to think of my doing it. He called the pulse better this morning than it had been for a week—but indeed I am a useless & helpless person,—scarcely worth taking such care of, & not at all, except for love's sake. Do write to me for love's sake, & say how you are—that is, if you can without much inconvenience. Just a word will do. God make it a happy one for *me*—that is, a better one, of *you!-* Mr Talfourd kindly called me your "*dear* friend"- With or without such praise,—in any *case*,

                                        Your most affectionate
                                             Elizabeth B Barrett.

Thank you for your kindness (how *ever* kind you are) in charming a copy of Pedro from its author for me.[13]

I know I have faintly said everything I wished to say today—I have written so in the dark & so brokenly in all ways—not excepting my pleasure from the stories the beautiful stories in Finden. Believe how I love them & *you*!——

Publication: EBB-MRM, I, 160–163.
Manuscript: Wellesley College.

1. Year provided by the references to *Findens' Tableaux.*
2. The Finden brothers were apparently contemplating re-issuing the earlier *Tableaux* without Miss Mitford's sanction, even though it was her understanding that copyright had been assigned to her. The later legal wrangles over this matter are dealt with in letters to Miss Mitford between May and August 1842.
3. "Treason." Miss Mitford's stories had been somewhat arbitrarily edited to conform to the predetermined number of pages allocated to the book.
4. Cf. "I've wandered east, I've wandered west" (line 1 of "Jeanie Morrison" in *Poems Narrative and Lyrical*, 1832, by William Motherwell, 1797–1835).
5. Miss Mitford wrote a note (see SD1073) sending copies of the *Tableaux* to Wimpole Street.
6. *The Metropolitan Magazine*, November 1839, said "The literature of the volume is far superior in quality to any that we have lately seen in Annuals, and does infinite credit to Miss Mitford's taste.... 'The Dream,' by E.B. Barret [*sic*]; 'Venice,' by Barry Cornwall; and 'The King's Forrester,' by J. Hughes, are beautiful little poems. The 'Legend of the Brown Rosarie,' also by Miss Barret, seems to have been inspired by a part of the genius which suggested Goethe's Faust." (For the full text of the review, see p. 412.)
7. i.e., is reminiscent of the scene between Jessica and Lorenzo in act V, sc. 1 of *The Merchant of Venice*. See letter 717, note 3.
8. Several elements in John Chorley's contribution, "The Maid's Trial," parallel Coleridge's *The Rime of the Ancient Mariner*.
9. Cf. line 1 of Gray's poem, "The Installation Ode" (1769).
10. There had been an estrangement between Miss Mitford and Talfourd following the first performance of his *Ion* (see "'This Happy Evening': The Story of *Ion*" in *The Twentieth Century*, July 1953, pp. 53–61). On 29 October, Miss Mitford wrote to William Harness, saying she had received from Talfourd an "affectionate and cordial note" (see L'Estrange (2), III, 104).
11. Cf. *Macbeth*, III, 4, 109.
12. Dr. Mitford had just celebrated his 79th birthday.
13. *Pedro of Castile*, which EBB said, in letter 710, she had not read.

---

717. EBB TO RICHARD HENGIST HORNE[1]

Beacon Terrace, Torquay.
Nov.r 20.th 1839.

My dear Sir,

In passing to the immediate occasion of my troubling you with these lines, allow me to thank you .. to join mine to the thanks of many—for the *pleasure of admiration* (surely not the least of the pleasures of this world) with which I have read your trilogy.[2] It is so full of fine conception that its brevity grows into a fault– One would so willingly see it brought out into detail & consummation. But even as it is, believe in *my* contentment .. speaking for myself. The moonlight scene is exquisite—& there is (particularly distinguishable in *that*) a music of broken cadences which

I have seldom observed out of Shakespeare.³ It is the Fetch of a great tragedy—for all the briefness!–

I sh^d not have ventured to trouble you with opinions you might so easily take for granted, if it were not for another circumstance. Two months or more ago, you will remember asking me to send you a short poem by return of post for a particular purpose. I was ill able to write at the time, but still worse able to endure the appearance of discourtesy towards you in such a trifle,—& therefore I sent two MSS which I had by me, the shortest I had, but evidently too long to suit you. I did it, just & only that you might not think me ill natured.—and the event having proved their uselessness to you otherwise, perhaps you w^d be kind enough to enclose them back to me—that is, if you can readily put your hand upon them. 'The Madrigal of flowers' is one title, & [']The Cry of the human' the other.–⁴ I am afraid of involving you in some trouble of search for which you may well reproach me. So pray if you cannot readily put your hand upon them, put the subject out of your head.

         Very sincerely yours
         Elizabeth B Barrett.

Address: R H Horne Esqr / 75. Gloucester Place.
Publication: EBB-RHH, I, 10–12.
Manuscript: R.H. Taylor Collection.

 1. For details of EBB's friendship with Horne, see pp. 317–320.
 2. i.e., "The Fetches," his contribution to the 1840 *Findens' Tableaux*.
 3. In this scene the mad Theresa stands on the edge of a precipice, at the foot of which lies the body of the dead hero, and laments:

Ye birds of night!	For I would be chill
Lift all your spiritual voices sweet,	As a dead man's will
To lull the sleeping light!	With my blood lock'd up in a winter rill
Let it not touch my naked feet	All tender thoughts to drown.
With eastern ardours fleet	Good night! farewell!
On this rocky-hanging height,	Theresa sings a funeral knell
Only the moon	And nightingales carol from the dell!
So coldly smile a-down	Farewell, sweet bird, farewell!

 4. "The Madrigal of Flowers" was not published until 1844, when it was included in *Poems*, with the title "A Flower in a Letter." "The Cry of the Human" was printed in *The Boston Miscellany of Literature and Fashion*, November 1842 (pp. 197–199); it was reprinted in *Poems* (1844). (See *Reconstruction*, D288 and D172.)

---

718. EBB TO JULIA MARTIN

         Beacon Terrace, Torquay.
         Nov 24.th [1839]¹

My dearest Mrs Martin,
 Henrietta *shall not* write today, whatever she may wish to do. I felt in reading your unreproaching letter to her, as self-reproachful as anybody

could with a great deal of innocense (in the way of the world) to fall back upon. I felt sorry very sorry not to have written to you something sooner, which was a possible thing—although, since the day of my receiving your welcome letter, I have written scarcely at all nor that little, without much exertion. Had it been with me as usual, be sure that you sh^d not have had any silence to complain of. Henrietta knew I wished to write, & felt I suppose unwilling to take my place when my filling it myself before long, appeared possible. A long story—& not as entertaining as Mother Hubbard. But I w^d rather tire you than leave you under any wrong impression, where my regard & thankfulness to you dearest Mrs Martin are concerned.

To reply to your kind anxiety about me, I may call myself decidedly better than I have been. Since the 1st of October I have not been out of bed—except just for an hour a day, when I am lifted to the sofa, with the bare permission of my physician—who tells me that it is so much easier to make me worse than better, that he dares not permit anything like exposure or further exertion. I like him (Dr Scully) very much—& although he evidently thinks my case in the highest degree precarious, yet knowing how much I bore last winter & understanding from him that the worst *tubercular* symptoms have not actually appeared, I am willing to think it may be God's will to keep me here still longer. I w^d willingly stay, if it were only for the sake of that tender affection of my beloved family which it so deeply affects me to consider. Dearest Papa is with us now—to my great comfort & joy! & looking very well!—& astonishing everybody with his eternal youthfulness! Bro & Henrietta & Arabel besides, I can count as companions—& then there is dear Bummy!——— We are fixed at Torquay for the winter—that is, until the end of May: and after that, if I have any will or power & am alive to exercise either, I do trust & hope to go away. The death of my kind friend Dr Barry was, as you supposed a great grief & shock to me. How c^d it be otherwise, after his daily kindness to me for a year? And then his young wife & child—& the rapidity (a three weeks illness) with which he was hurried away from the energies & toils & honors of professional life to the stilness of *that* death!——— '*God's will*' is the only answer to the mystery of the world's afflictions.

And this reminds me of the poor Ricardos! & the terrible grief which has fallen upon them.[2] If you hear how Mrs Ricardo—indeed how they both bear up against it—do not forget to tell us in your letters.

I like so much to hear everything about you, & of the walks which you cant take as well as of those which you can. Our weather has kept pace as to wet, with yours.– Did you see Georgie gazetted "barrister at law" of the Inner Temple? My imagination has all gone to imaging him in a wig, for the last week.

Dont fancy me worse than I am—or that this bed-keeping is the result of a gradual sinking. It is not so. A feverish attack prostrated me on the second of October—& such will leave their effects—and D:̲ Scully is so afraid of leading me into danger by saying, "You may get up & dress as usual"—you sh:̲d not be surprised if (in virtue of being the senior Torquay physician & correspondingly prudent) he left me in this durance vile for a great part of the winter. I am decidedly better than I was a month ago, really & truly.

May God bless you dearest M:̲rs Martin. My best & kindest regards to M:̲r Martin. Henrietta desires me to promise for her, a letter to Colwall soon, but I think that one *from* Colwall sh:̲d come first. May God bless you! Bro's fancy just now is painting in water colours & he performs many sketches. Do you ever in y:̲r dreams of universal benevolence dream of travelling into Devonshire?

Love your
affectionate *Ba*.

found guilty of egotism & stupidity "by this sign"[3] & at once!

Publication: LEBB, I, 75–77 (in part).
Manuscript: Wellesley College.

1. Year determined by reference to the death of Dr. Barry.
2. Osman Ricardo and his wife were neighbours of the Martins, known to the Moulton-Barretts from their Hope End days. Mrs. Martin had presumably informed EBB of the death of their niece Mary in the spring of 1839.
3. According to legend, Constantine the Great had a vision in which a cross appeared to him in the sky; it bore the words "in hoc signo vinces" ("by this sign shalt thou conquer").

---

719. EBB TO HUGH STUART BOYD

1 Beacon Terrace Torquay
Wednesday. Nov:̲r 27– 1839

If you can forgive me my ever dear friend for a silence which has not been intended, there will be another reason for being thankful to you, in addition to the many. To do myself justice, one of my earliest impulses on seeing my beloved Arabel & recurring to the kindness with which you desired that happiness for me long before I possessed it, was to write and tell you how happy I felt. But she had promised, she said, to write herself—& moreover she & only she was to send you the *ballad*—in expectation of your dread judgment upon which, I delayed my own writing. It came in the first letter we received in our new house, on the first of last October. An hour after reading it, I was upon my bed,—was attacked by fever in the night, & from that bed, have never even been lifted since .. to these last days of November .. except for one hour a day to the sofa at two yards distance. I am very much better now, & have been so for some time,—but my physician is so persuaded, he says, that it is easier to do me harm than good, that he will neither permit any present attempt at further exertion, nor hint at the time when it may be advisable for him to permit it. Under these circumstances, it has of course been more difficult than usual for me to write. Pray believe my dear & kind friend in the face of all circumstances & appearances that I never forget you, nor am reluctant (oh—how could that be?) to write to you,—& that you shall often have to pay "a penny for my thoughts"[1] under the new Postage Act[2]--if it be in God's wisdom & mercy to spare me through the winter. Under the new act, *I* shall not mind writing ten words & then stopping. As it is, they w^d scarcely be worth eleven pennies.

Thank you again & again for your praise of the ballad,—which both delighted, & *surprised* me .. as I had scarcely hoped that you might like it at all. Think of Mr Tilt's never sending me a proof sheet. The consequences are rather deplorable, & if they had occurred to you might have suggested a deep melancholy for life. In my case, *I*, who am, you know, hardened to sins of carelessness, .. simply look *aghast*, at the misprints & mis-punctuations coming in as a flood, & sweeping away meanings & melodies together– The Annual itself is more splendid than usual—and its vignettes have illustrated my story, angels devils & all, most beautifully. Miss Mitford's tales (in prose) have suffered besides by reason of Mr Tilt—but are attractive & graphic notwithstanding—and Mr Horne has supplied a dramatic poem of great power & beauty.

How I rejoice with you in the glorious revelation (about to be) of Gregorys' 2^d volume– The 'De virginitate['] poem will, in its new purple & fine linen, be more dazzling than ever.[3]

Do you know that George is barrister at law of the Inner Temple—IS[4]!? I have seen him gazetted.

My dearest Papa is with me now, making me very happy of course. I have much reason to be happy—more to be grateful—yet am more obedient to the former than to the latter impulse. May the Giver of good, give gratitude with as full a hand! May He bless *you!*—& bring us together again, if no more in the flesh yet in the spirit!——

Your ever affectionate friend
E B Barrett.

Do write—when you are able & *least* disinclined.
Do you approve of Prince Albert or not?—[5]

Address, on integral page: H S Boyd Esqr / 3 Circus Road / St John's Wood / London.
 Redirected: 11 Mile Walk / Hampstead.
Publication: LEBB, I, 77–79.
Manuscript: Wellesley College.

1. John Heywood (1497?–1580?) included this phrase in his *Proverbs* (1546).
2. The Postal Duties Act of 17 August 1839 instituted reform of the postal system. As a temporary measure, postage in the London district was to be reduced to one penny, and general inland postage to fourpence, with effect from 5 December 1839, to be followed by the introduction of a uniform, prepaid, penny rate throughout the kingdom on 10 January 1840. Franking was abolished. For some details of postal charges prior to this Act, see vol. 1, p. xxxvii, note 6.
3. Apparently nothing came of this project; the British Library catalogue lists nothing by Boyd later than 1835.
4. Underscored three times.
5. Prince Albert and his brother, Prince Ernest, had returned home on 14 November, after a five-week visit to England. The following day, the Queen informed members of the Royal Family privately of her engagement to Albert, followed by her official declaration to the Privy Council on 23 November.

720. EBB TO MARY RUSSELL MITFORD

Torquay.
Friday. [13 December 1839][1]

Ever dearest Miss Mitford,

I do trust & pray that the better accounts may be followed by more & more betterness of which to take account. I was very uneasy about you—& am still so in a measure,—although reluctant to turn that trouble of mine into unnecessary trouble to you by intruding it & its interrogatives upon you oftener than I should. In the meantime your editorship is prospering. "Finden" says Sette in his letter yesterday "must be selling I think—for I see it in all the shops". And if I may stand next to Sette as an authority, why .. Finden must be selling, *I*[2] think too .. for I see it praised by all the critics: nemine contradicente[3] except M.ʳ Jerdan of the Literary Gazette who is so out of breath with lauding Miss Eliza Cook's poems that he cant do it for anything else. But even he was humane enough to pick up "two or three" of your stories & all the engravings, from the general wreck.[4]

I sent you the Atlas & Morning Chronicle[5]—the former most benignant,—& the latter scarcely less so, "hormis les coups" to me & M.ʳ Horne.[6] For my part, I felt incline⟨d⟩ to cry out, like children when they are whipt .. "Indeed I didnt mean it—indeed I didnt! It was all the fault of the geranium frame".[7] At any rate the moral is obvious .. that the poet of Rienzi sh.ᵈ never henceforward desert herself—& that the next tableaux must gather light around them from some of her dramatic scenes.

Well!—then, there is the united service Gazette which I have *not* seen—& the New Monthly which I have—& Tait who is as gracious as usual & ever,[8]—& who altho' he does not like my ballad as well as last year's, makes full amends (overflowing!) by speaking of me in reference to my '*friend* the editor'! Dearest dearest Miss Mitford, I must be sensible to the pride & pleasure of calling you my friend & of hearing you called mine, while any sensibility is left to me for the world's use.

Altogether I do trust you are pleased & satisfied—& that your own consciousness of having successfully accomplished your task, is seconded by something like gratitude from the Findens.

Mr. Hughes' poem I really believe never to have mentioned to you .. It is excellently done for a doing of that sort[9]—strong, & with a scent of 'morning air'[10] about it; but to you who know my frailties, I need not confess some indifference to the SORT.

Your Roundhead's daughter makes an impression & very justly. The tale opens with exquisite descriptive writing .. Miss Mitford's own .. & if I did not myself single out the whole for a chief niche, it was only from the story appearing afterwards rather broken & fragmentary—the obvious consequence of the Finden or Tilt sledge hammer[11]—Freemasons indeed! Niche after niche may well be made for your stories,—and the word "beautiful" be lip service for each!-

See what Tait says of MY! mistake of a 'manifest boy god' for a sleeping child in lady fashion ..

> But that little god upon roses reclining
> We'll make if you please Sir, a Friendship of him ..

or something as innocent as Friendship. But the mistake (if such) was Miss Mitford's not mine.[12] 'If you please Sir' not mine by any means! Oh that geranium frame! It was more fatal to me than to you—if not more fatal to the Findens than to either!——

Papa has gone away—but is coming again. So he promised, in the last good-bye two days since!- Coming again, very very soon. For my own part, my health's part I mean, I am going on tolerably well—still kept in bed, except for the one hour a day, & not very likely to emerge as long as the winter & Dr. Scully do after their will.

I have lately held within my hands Miss Eliza Cook's poems, as consecrated by Mr. Jerdan.[13] Have *you*? And, if you have, in which half of the world do you find yourself? She divides (in her introduction) the whole round literary world into two, in relation to her poetry; & being convinced of her own merits, equally by "the fierce malignity of the few, & the praises of the *impartial many!*", has "equal pleasure & confidence" in bringing herself before the public. Are you a 'fierce malignant' or an impartial applauder? I am inclined a little to fierceness. The modesty of the introduction, illustrated by the frontispiece .. a full length of the lady in mourning à la mode & hair à la Brute & a determination of countenance "to be poetical" whatever nature might say to it—are my provocatives!—

to say nothing of the facsimile of her handwriting obligingly appended, to show how great geniuses dot their i[']s like vulgar clay.[14]

There is malignancy for you!—but more mirth, I do hope. The sight of the book & its whole tone amused me very much. For the rest I c^d read nothing in it worth reading again. No, Mr Jerdan, it wont do: that is .. Miss Eliza Cook wont do to reign in the stead of LEL! though she has *courage* enough to match with Zenobia's regality!—— [15]

I have heard no word of Mr Kenyon, who however, on leaving England, thought it so possible that he might go onward to Italy that I cannot think his return this winter probable.

Have you heard lately of Lady Dacre? Will you tell me how she is?

God bless you & yours my beloved friend! Give my love & kindest wishes to Dr Mitford & ever believe me your own
affectionately attached EBB–

I will read Geraldine the very first opportunity. I believe it has made *converts*– [16] Do say particularly how you are.

Publication: EBB-MRM, I, 163–167.
Manuscript: Wellesley College.

1. Dated by the reference to EBB's father's date of departure, 11 December, which is also referred to by Henrietta in SD1090.
2. Underscored twice.
3. "No one opposing."
4. *The Literary Gazette* (no. 1188, 26 October 1839, p. 684), reviewing the forthcoming *Illustrations of Poems by Eliza Cook*, speaks of her "poetical genius." Page 676 in the same issue reviews *Findens' Tableaux*, and says EBB's "The Dream" "is a beautiful specimen of the whole plan." Miss Mitford's "The Bride" and "The Woodcutter" are considered to be "the only essays to be noticed with praise." (For the full text of the review, see pp. 411–412.) William Jerdan (1782–1869) had written poetry himself before turning to journalism. He wrote for, *inter alia, The Morning Post, The Sun,* and *The Literary Gazette.*
5. *Findens' Tableaux* was reviewed in *The Atlas* (26 October 1839, pp. 684–685) and *The Morning Chronicle* of 26 November 1839. (For the full text of the former, see p. 411.)
6. "Except for the blows." EBB's comment is perplexing; Horne is not mentioned in the *Chronicle*'s review, and EBB is not directly named, although the reviewer does say he would rather read Miss Mitford's poetry "than that of any of her contributors."
7. From the context, apparently some private joke relating to avoidance of blame.
8. Reviews of the *Tableaux* appeared in *The United Service Gazette,* 2 November 1839, p. 6; *The New Monthly Magazine,* December 1839, p. 559; and *Tait's Edinburgh Magazine,* December 1839, pp. 813–814. (For the full text of these reviews, see pp. 412–413.)
9. John Hughes (1790–1843) had contributed "The King's Forester" to the *Tableaux.*
10. *Hamlet,* I, 5, 58.
11. "The Roundhead's Daughter," one of Miss Mitford's six stories, had been somewhat arbitrarily edited by the publisher to keep the book to the prescribed size.
12. *Tait's* said of "The Dream" that "Miss Barrett, as many ladies have, wittingly or unwittingly, done before her, chooses to mistake a Sleeping Cupid—a very palpable boy-god—for a dreaming child." While the illustration accompanying EBB's poem does show Cupid (see the reproduction facing p. 193), her comment suggests that Miss Mitford did not make this clear in her original instructions to EBB.
13. *Melaia, and Other Poems* (1840).

14. In her preface, Miss Cook spoke of "the fierce malignity of the envious few, and the warm applause of the impartial many," claimed that the rapid sales "afford indisputable proof of the good opinion I have gained" and announced that "it is with equal pleasure and confidence I now issue my productions in a superior form."

The frontispiece shows Miss Cook in a severe black dress, relieved only by lighter cuffs and collar, with her hair arranged in side ringlets. Underneath, reproduced in her handwriting, are two lines from "The Old Arm Chair," her best-known poem, written in memory of her mother: "I love it, I love it and cannot tear / My soul from a mother's old armchair" followed by her signature.

Eliza Cook (1818–89) had written verses from the age of 14, the first being published when she was 17.

15. Zenobia Septimia, Princess of Palmyra, assumed the title Queen of the East and ruled as regent for her children. When Aurelianus became Emperor of Rome in A.D. 270, he led an expedition to punish Zenobia for her ambition. She herself led her army of 700,000 against him and fought with great courage, though eventually defeated.

16. *Geraldine; a Tale of Conscience*, by E.C.A. [Emily C. Agnew] had been reviewed in *The Athenæum* of 1 June 1839 (no. 605, p. 410): "The success of the two former volumes of 'Geraldine' has led their authoress to a bolder exposition of the doctrines of Catholicism, in this third volume, which, like its predecessors, is carefully and (better still) charitably written."

---

721. EBB TO JULIA MARTIN

Torquay–
Thursday [ca. 1840][1]

My dearest Mrs Martin,

I cannot delay offering to you & dear Mr Martin our true & affectionate sympathy upon the loss you have sustained, & which I am but too sure must grievously have affected you. May the God of all consolation who comforts by teaching us the *meaning* of affliction, have consoled & *be* consoling you & more & more day by day. The blessed consciousness of having been enabled to surround an object so beloved with every token of love, & comfort desirable from love, to the last hours of life will be strong with you & very reviving. When you can write without jarring any painful feeling, do let me hear from you,—& say particularly how dear Mr Martin is.[2]

I had heard of the sad illness—but only when it was hopeless & within a few days of the end. There w^d have been a selfish want of consideration for you in writing to you then—altho' I have longed ever since to lay my sympathy beside you.

There was something too about Miss Hanford's illness. How is she? Tell me when you *do* write. It has come into my head at moments that she & you might all come together *here* for a little time. The climate might reestablish her strength—& the change w^d do you and Mr Martin good—& the sight of you w.^{d} do good to *me*—for I must find room for that little bit of selfishness.

And I do so the more willingly because it goes to prove what I w.^{d} have you believe at all times but now more than usual, how very truly I regard you.

This is no answer to your kind letter long ago,—except in the spirit of it. I am tolerably well—not worse, nor essentially better. Bummy & both my sisters desire to be united in love to you—& ever believe me dearest Mrs Martin

Your affectionate
Elizabeth B Barrett

Publication: None traced.
Manuscript: Wellesley College.

1. This letter must have been written some time between the end of November 1839 (i.e., after letter 718) and June 1840, when Bummy left Torquay.
2. We cannot clarify the loss EBB speaks of; the reference to Mr. Martin suggests that it might have been the death of one of his three sisters.

---

722. RB TO ANNA BROWNELL JAMESON[1]

Camb.^{ll}
Friday. [ca. 1840][2]

Dear Mrs Jameson,

I must throw my poor self on your goodness: I set out last evening as in duty bound, but,—(that willingness of spirit should avail so little against weakness of flesh!)—was quite unable to proceed farther than a house where an engagement of importance obliged me to call in my way; (I ought to have said that I have been unwell this long while)—I am better today.

—You will forgive this, I trust, and suffer me to take the chance of seeing you for a minute in some morning or evening ere a week pass?

Ever my dear Mrs Jameson,
Most faithfully yours,
R Browning.

Publication: None traced.
Manuscript: Armstrong Browning Library.

1. For details of the Brownings' friendship with Mrs. Jameson, see pp. 320–323.
2. The Brownings moved from Camberwell to New Cross late in 1840. This letter must have been written prior to that.

723. RB TO CATHERINE FRANCES MACREADY

[London]
Friday Morning. [ca. 1840][1]

My dear Mrs Macready,
   Such a note would spirit me to Constantinople for the fellow to the barbaric attempt at a bottle you mention so kindly--yet I have barely to seek Cumberland Terrace! "My friend is cut, 'tis done at your request."[2] Pray believe me, with sincerest regards to all,
                              My dear Mrs Macready,
                                  Yours ever faithfully,
                                      Rob.[t] Browning.

Publication: None traced.
Manuscript: Armstrong Browning Library.

   1. The handwriting and form of signature place the letter in this approximate period.
   2. Cf. *Othello*, III, 3, 474.

---

724. RB TO RACHEL TALFOURD

[London]
Wednesday M.[g] [ca. 1840][1]

My dear Mrs Talfourd,
   To my extreme mortification I am prevented from availing myself of your kindness next Saturday; an engagement of a peculiar nature, & over which I have no control, will, I trust—(nay, am sure—) excuse me when I shall be able, in a few days, to procure a long intended pleasure by calling at Russell Square— Pray believe me, with truest regards to the Sergeant, My dear Mrs Talfourd,
                              Yours ever faithfully
                                  Robert Browning.

Publication: None traced.
Manuscript: Michael Meredith.

   1. Although this letter has an 1839 watermark, RB's habits in using stationery suggest that he would not have started using the 1839 paper before 1840.

725. EBB to Unidentified Correspondent

[Torquay]
[January 1840]¹

⟨★★★⟩ He was however at church on Christmas day--& upon M.ʳ Elliott's² being mercifully inclined to omit the Athanasian creed,³ prompted him most episcopally from the pew with a *"Whereas:"* & further on in the creed, when the benign reader substituted the word "condemnation["] for the terrible one ... "Damnation" exclaimed the Bishop!!⁴ The effect must have been rather singular.

⟨...⟩⁵

only by sympathy, ⟨...⟩ faultless in all ways. In regard ⟨...⟩ & shelter no house can be better adapted to me. The difficulty, even on cold days, has been to keep the thermometer low enough; notwithstanding which, we cant complain & of closeness. We have had some cold weather at Torquay even this year, & thermometers in the upper part of the town & out of doors did, I understand, stoop to two ⟨...⟩ the freezing point upon two several ⟨...⟩ the cold a mile off you know ⟨★★★⟩

Publication: None traced.
Source: Transcript in editors' file.

1. Dated by letter 727, which describes the same incidents.
2. The curate, described by EBB in letter 727 as "soft-hearted."
3. The creed embodying the opinions of Athanasius (ca. 298–373), Bishop of Alexandria, concerning the nature of the Trinity.
4. Henry Phillpotts (1778–1869), elected Bishop of Exeter in 1830, was a high churchman *par excellence*, being strenuously opposed to the current pressures in favour of Catholic emancipation, and having voted consistently against Parliamentary reform. He was known to the Hedleys, through whose intercession EBB had obtained his frank for letter 673.
5. Both the upper and lower parts of the sheet have been cut off.

---

726. EBB to George Goodin Moulton-Barrett

[Torquay]
Jany 4.ᵗʰ 1840–

My dearest dearest Georgie,

Arabel says you w.ᵈ much rather not hear from me & I dont contradict her—only you having just proved to me how pleasant it is to be pleased, I must be pleased again this morning by writing to you. The serpent tempted me & I did eat,¹ & now I take another apple. I do thank you for all the pleasure you have given me. It was so very very particularly kind of you to write, with your thoughts occupied as they must have been with novel & grave matters. It was more than I expected although you know I did pretend to expect it, & should have been rather furious if you had not done it— All *that* is excellent logic—& the end of it is my gratitude to you!— Thank you dear dear George!—

As to the rest I am astounded at the majesty of your first steps.[2] Papa will be more so still—for he told me that he did not think it at all likely you w^d have anything to do very soon— How pleased he will be! How I sh^d like to be first to tell him!!—

Was'nt it a breach of discipline to go by the *mail* to Ludlow?— How did you shake the straw at the bottom from the feet of your nascent chancellorship, & preserve your noli me tangere[3] from the attornies?— There are many questions I would ask. And Bro wants to know whether the prisoners whom you turned loose upon a grateful world, notwithstanding their crime & their character, were guilty of murder?— Certainly it w^d be as well to learn something of the particulars, before we raise your philanthropy to the rank of your legality. Of your consummate impudence there cant be a question. Oh Georgie!—how c^d you do so .. even under cover of the wig helmet!— Unprepared & at a moments' notice!! That was the very sublime of impudence, & makes my head turn round to think of it!!—

Just as I had finished y^r letter—in came Dr Scully—& I began to tell him what was the truth, that I had felt a little languor in the course of the morning. He felt the pulse & said .. "Well, Miss Barrett—I sh^d not have detected the languor in the pulse." "Oh no! because I have just had a letter from my brother Georgie, & it has answered the exact purpose of a cordial"— Upon which he began to laugh & to congratulate me—& then we diverged into law subjects (not into any particulars about you— dont be frightened!) & he told me how if his own brother had lived he w^d have been at this moment most assuredly the master of the rolls in Ireland .. & a great deal besides, not admissible into so small a sheet as this. Arabel says I must not have another, but I must & shall .. quod ita probatum est.[4] When you go to London you will hear the particulars of Dr Scully's having afflicted me with the presence of Dr Millar from Exeter[5] & a consultation. You may suppose how much oratory went to accomplish that— Yourself did not do more when you persuaded your gentlemen of the jury to honorably acquit your assassins— I have not been *worse* at all— Dont fancy *that!*— But a great deal was insisted upon the advantage of dyocephalus monsters, & upon the opportunity of D^r M's being in the town. *My* verdict (I mean their verdict upon me) was, tolerably satisfactory upon the whole. They agreed exactly as to the case—& thought that with care I sh^d bustle thro' the winter, & be better afterwards— But the way pointed out of "bustling through" is to keep on lying in bed—out of harm's way & air's way. I only hope & trust to be able &

quietly allowed to get back to London early in the summer—otherwise there will be a rebellion, & the chartists'[6] nothing to it!–

God's pleasure sh^d be mine, without any "hopes & trustings" except in *Him*. Surely I have had reason for knowing that His pleasure is His tender mercy—but how far I am from being reasonable!——

Dear Mr Hunter & Mary have left Axminster finally—& I had a joint letter from the two this morning from Exeter which place they past thro' yesterday on their way to Kingsbridge. He has an engagement at Kingsbridge for a few months—& after that comes a blank. He speaks of having written to his friend the independent minister at Gloucester to bestir himself & procure for you whatsoever business is going on amongst the dissenters there. It was kindly done–

Going on as usual at Torquay. Occasional quarrellings to clear the air & to keep up our respective characters. Bro was at Capt & Mrs Foleys yesterday . . last night. Great favorites of his—members of the Herefordshire Foley family[7] . . & come to live at the Knoll. Bummy & Henrietta went off in another direction to Mrs Inglise's—& Arabel & I talked wonderful sense tête à tête.

You are to restrain your wrath towards Arabel & Henrietta, & expand it upon your return to Wimpole St. Not a word did they remember to tell us about your last orders.

God bless & keep you dearest Georgie!–

I need not tell you how high & deep you are in my esteem & love—& now that you have not forgotten me on the reception of y^r first briefs, I rejoice in feeling sure that you wont cut me when you are chancellor.

Your truly affec^{te}
Ba.

Publication: B-GB, pp. 40–44.
Manuscript: Pierpont Morgan Library.

1. Cf. Genesis, 3:13.
2. George, having been called to the bar as recently as November, already had his first briefs and was on circuit in the west of England.
3. "Touch me not" (Vulgate: John, 20:17).
4. "Which is proved thus."
5. There were two doctors named Miller in Exeter at this time, both with practices among the monied classes; unfortunately, there is nothing in the correspondence to indicate which one was called in by Dr. Scully. The more likely of the two was Patrick Miller (1782–1871), M.D., F.R.S., Member of the Medico-Chirurgical Society of London and Extra Licentiate of the Royal College of Physicians; he was on the staff of the Royal Devon and Exeter Hospital. The other Dr. Miller, M.D., F.R.C.P., was the author of *Mortality of Exeter* and *The History of Cholera in Exeter in 1832.*
6. Proponents of a six-point "People's Charter," drawn up in 1838; its demands included equal Parliamentary constituencies, abolition of the property-ownership qualification for members of Parliament, and payment of M.P.s.
7. When the Moulton-Barretts were living at Hope End, one of their neighbours and social contacts was E.T. Foley, whose seat was Stoke Edith.

727. EBB TO MARY RUSSELL MITFORD

[Torquay]
Jany 15.th 1840.

Dearest dearest Miss Mitford,

Shame on me to have let you write again, without any words of mine, in grief & sympathy for your illness, coming in between! It seemed to me when I received your letter just now that I deserved much less than usual all your affectionateness & dear Dr Mitford's too!– And yet if loving you very much & thinking very much of you make the silence excusable, I am safe– You said you were a good deal better again,—& I on my own part was wrestling with the east wind or rather prostrated by it, & waiting for its going away, to get up again & write to you!—the getting up being altogether metaphorical, inasmuch as there appears no hope of leaving my bed until the warm months begin–

How very very ill you must have been—& suffering severe pain, I dare say, which is not the necessary consequence of illness– For the betterness I do thank God! May He grant it to grow better & better. I cannot bear to hear of your being ill––you are too dear, perhaps to the many, certainly to the few—& certainly, in a sense, to the many also!– What is Mr May doing? *Pray* if he sh.^{d} not quite & finally succeed, take an opinion when you go to London. Do you walk enough, & lie down the rest, almost all the rest of the time? Have you not learnt to write in a horizontal posture as I do? Remember how we love you––I cannot count how many do, but I feel well how some do, without algebra– Did not dear Dr Mitford forget Don Pedro[1] & me & everybody else when you were ill—& do we not feel honored by the forgetfulness? Yes—but we wont, at least one of us wont, be forgotten by him on other occasions—& pray give him my affectionate & thankful remembrances to that effect!——

I am very sorry to hear your bad tiding of poor Mr Brown, but Consumptive affections are so various in character, & so chronic sometimes that I w.^{d} hope something better for him than one is apt to take for granted from the first sound of Mrs Howitt's information.[2] You see how I have gone on,—& that the complaint is upon the lungs nobody can doubt—although what they call tubercular desease is supposed to have not yet taken place in me. The spitting of blood has never intermitted from last March twelvemonth, & my voice has never been able to lift itself above a whisper since October. There has been by Dr Scully's desire, a consultation lately with a physician high in authority in Exeter[3] whom I was ensnared into seeing,—& they agreed that after all I was likely with care to get through the winter safely, & to be better in the warmer season. I made an enquiry whether it was considered medically possible for me to be *ever* quite well,—and the answer modified my 'quite well' into a tolerably well--such a degree of health as w^d admit of my creeping about again with some comfort & independence; & this is considered both possible & probable. I heard it thankfully. As to strength, I must do without it, & bless God for what is left. The chest never does, I suppose, completely rally, after having undergone certain affections. I suffer no pain to signify—& the principal inconvenience, to my sensation, is debility & palpitation, & intermission of the heart's beating. Even the cough is not troublesome at all.

Think of your remembering Ibbit Jane.[4] Talking of my maladies reminds me of her philosophy such as I heard it a short time ago. "Mama" said she, lifting up her little foot in both her little hands in the triumph of vanity (& of all the Aphrodites[5] you ever saw Ibbit is the vainest) "have'nt I dot a pretty little foot." "You have a nice little foot enough Ibbit, to suit your little body". She stopped for a moment, & then said, rather disappointed I do not doubt but with a very reflective face, "Yes, it must be a nice little foot, *because* it is *glueded* on to my leg." Did you ever hear a better illustration of the doctrine of optimism?[6] She was learned in the "relations of things", of old, & amused me once last spring by an account of meeting an old gentleman on her way to Beacon Terrace, who begged her to give her one of her ringlets to fasten upon his own head– "I told him" she said with dramatic gesture, "I told him that my hair would'nt loot well at all, mixed with his! Only sink Ba!— bwown & white!!–"

How is your godchild?[7] Do tell me.

The Bishop of Exeter's dealing damnation round the church on Christmas day, is no romance. The curate was I suppose a soft-hearted man & tried to escape the Athanasian creed, when "Wher⟨eas⟩," prompted the episcopal voice from the episcopal pew, & "whereas" said the curate by constraint. And then again at the sacrament, he, in his benignity substituted the word "condemnation", . . "damnation" cried the Bishop,[8] holding up the book of Common prayer as if it were a miss*ile!*–[9] And then once again—for [']'thrice the brindled cat has mewed"[10]—he cried out "That bread is not consecrated!"—which really, taking one demonstration with another, was enough to tempt any person into responding "That bishop is not consecrated". He is the very parody of what a minister of peace sh^d be—& this is the consequence of crowning pamphleteers with mitres. Is'nt it enough to provoke many thinking & feeling people into dissent—or at least to beguile all thinking & feeling people into forgiving that offence?

I know you of old in your theory of names my dearest Miss Mitford (which parenthesis began itself by breaking through a reverie upon *Philpots*) but I thought then & think now that you stand upon terrible vantage ground in holding it. Mary Russell Mitford is simple & noble at once—but what are we of the commonalty to do—& others of the more decided mobocracy & cacology? What are they to do? Would you for instance sweep away all the multitudinous Smiths in the predestination of this new nominalism[11]—all the Thomsons & Simpsons & Browns without the e? As to my first name, you have made me like it—but

> "One name is Elizabeth
> Th' others let them sleep in death."[12]

Elizabeth Barrett Barrett .. so that I never never could by the shining of any connubial star, have put away both Barretts .. & have nothing as it is, for consolation except etymology .. Barrett Barrett meaning in the Saxon tongue helmet upon helmet,—& even *that* is indicative of some unheroic liking for a superfluity of defence. No, you can say nothing for the Barretts—therefore you could'nt expect me to embrace any theory of the sort! & have I not heard, not merely of 'savans in us' but of excellent & accomplished families in *Bottom*--& out of Titania's court?[13] And was I not told high praises only yesterday of an admirable M.[r] Sheepshanks who illuminated all Torquay[14] & its vicinity a few years ago? And as to Christian names, was there not a stern unbending "Rosalinda Theodora Mary" (yes, Mary!) who officiated as nurse when I lived in a nursery—? and did I not know a Clementina lovely in face & heart & mind,[15] yet simple & natural as any Lucy under Sun?[16]

Still there is something in your doctrine—some occult truth– And that reminds me of dear little Mary Hunter's question to me years ago. She was brought up a dissenter among dissenters, & amused herself one day when she & I were together in a bookseller's shop, with looking over for a novelty the church catechism—"*What is your name? M or N!*"[17] How very odd! Is that a *doctrine* of the Church of England"? If it had happened now of course I sh.[d] have answered—"No—not of the church of England but of Miss Mitford"!– Dear Child!– I think I see her grave considering little face!–

But now here is a problem. When two contradictory names come together, what happens?– Is one soluble in the other? Does one negative the other? What do you make out of a Sophonisba Anne? I *know* an Eliza Wilhelmina–[18]

I used to marvel sometimes at the two most popular poetesses of the day being each named after happiness; & each by a Latin derivative— Felicia Hemans .. Lætitia Landon. And, alas, an old latin adage was exemplified in each!—.[19]

They have not yet sent me the parcel, & will not, I know, for a more eloquent tongue than mine, until certain shoes are made in London, which they mean to put up with it. Be very sure that Mr Merry shall have a candid letter from me.[20] A want of truthfulness in such cases is not one of my sins & *I* always feel that the very obligation under which such undeserved attention as his must place me, extracts & necessitates my openness & gratitude together—

My beloved friend, good night. I am so tired. *Can* you make out this intolerable writing? May God bless & keep you & dear D.[r] Mitford.
Your ever attached
Elizabeth Barrett Barrett.

Yes—Eliza Cook suits the theory exactly. You have seen nothing if you have not seen her book—book, binding, frontispiece, autograph, preface & all!— You might make her out by the Brutus if you know anything of comparative anatomy—but the all is prodigious.[21]

I had heard some of the Jerdan murmurs, & had hoped them into slanders.[22] I never saw him in my life, nor any live critic.

Do thank M.[r] Townsend for so kindly sending me his hymns!—[23] Or ought I to do so myself? & if I ought, will you send me his address which I dont know— Once more goodbye— I long to hear again of your continuing better.

Publication: EBB-MRM, I, 167–171.
Manuscript: Wellesley College.

1. Henry J. Shepherd's *Pedro of Castile*.
2. In a letter of 8 January 1840, Mary Howitt congratulated Miss Mitford on the latest *Findens' Tableaux*, and said "We are so delighted with poor Mr. Brown's designs. ... Poor man! he is doomed, we fear, to die of consumption" (L'Estrange (1), II, 59–60). The 1840 volume was illustrated with engravings by W. and E. Finden from paintings by J. Browne. Browne also illustrated works by Dickens and Charles James Lever; in a letter of November 1841 Miss Mitford spoke of "their extraordinary individuality and variety" (Chorley, I, 190).
3. i.e., Dr. Miller (see letter 726).
4. EBB's cousin, Elizabeth Jane Hedley.
5. The Greek name for Venus, the goddess of beauty.
6. "The doctrine propounded by Leibnitz, that the actual world is the 'best of all possible worlds', being chosen by the Creator as that in which most good could be obtained at the cost of least evil" (*OED*). The German philosopher Gottfried Wilhelm Leibnitz (1646–1716) is also known for his formulation of calculus, independently of Isaac Newton.
7. Agnes Niven, the daughter of Miss Mitford's friend and frequent visitor, Mrs. Niven.
8. See letter 725, notes 3 and 4.
9. Punning "missile" and "missal," EBB wrote the letters "al" above "ile."
10. *Macbeth*, IV, 1, 1.
11. Nominalism is "the view which regards universals or abstract concepts as mere names without any corresponding realities" (*OED*). Miss Mitford's "new nominalism" propounded a correlation between name and personality.
12. Jonson, "Epitaph on Elizabeth, L.H." (*Epigrams*, 1616, CXXIV, 9–10), slightly misquoted.
13. In *A Midsummer Night's Dream*.

14. The Rev. J. Sheepshanks was licensed in 1823 as Perpetual Curate of the Torquay Chapel-of-Ease (later called St. John's Chapel). It is assumed that his having "illuminated all Torquay" refers in some way to his manner of preaching, or perhaps to some unorthodox opinions.

15. Mary Clementina Moulton-Barrett, the late wife of EBB's uncle Sam.

16. Lucy "grew in the sun and shower" in Wordsworth's "Stanzas Composed in the Hartz Forest" (1799).

17. In *The Book of Common Prayer*, the form of catechism prior to confirmation starts with the question "What is your name?" and answer "N. or M." The candidate for confirmation gives his name or names (M being a contraction of NN).

18. Her friend and neighbour of Hope End days, Eliza Wilhelmina Cliffe, with whom EBB still corresponded occasionally.

19. The names derive from the Latin *felicitas* (good fortune, happiness) and *lætitia* (gladness, delight). It is not possible to be sure which Latin adage EBB thought appropriate; as both ladies died young (41 and 36 respectively), it obviously had something to do with the transitoriness of life: perhaps Cicero's observation "Nature gives us a short life, but the memory of one well-spent is eternal" (*Philippicæ*, XIV, cap. 12).

20. Miss Mitford had obtained for EBB a copy of Shepherd's *Pedro of Castile* and Merry's *The Philosophy of a Happy Futurity*; she had sent them to Wimpole Street, and EBB was waiting for them to be forwarded to her.

21. See letter 720, note 14.

22. There had been gossip about the nature of Miss Landon's relationship with William Jerdan (1782–1869), editor of *The Literary Gazette* and Miss Landon's mentor.

23. In a letter dated 1 January 1840 to Lucy Anderdon, Miss Mitford had mentioned receipt "last week" of a sheet of Christmas carols from her friend Richard Townsend (Chorley, I, 167). It seems probable that EBB had received a copy also.

728. EBB TO HUGH STUART BOYD

Torquay.
Jany 29. 1840–

My ever dear friend,

It was very pleasant to me to see your seal upon a letter once more,—and although the letter itself left me with a mournful impression of your having passed some time so much less happily than I could wish & pray for you, yet there remains the pleasant thought to me still, that you have not altogether forgotten me. Do receive the expression of my most affectionate sympathy under this & every circumstance: & I fear that the shock to your nerves & spirits could not be a light one,—however impressed you might be & must be with the surety & verity of God's love working in all His will. Poor poor Patience!– Coming to be so happy with you, with that joyous smile I thought so pretty!– Do you not remember my telling you so?– Well—it is well & better for her,—happier for her, if God in Christ Jesus have received her, than her hopes were of the holiday time with you– The holiday is *for ever* now ..

"Gone from work, & taen her wages"–[1]

I am thinking of Kate—poor Kate!– How old is she?– Quite a child—is she not?[2]—yet not too young, having felt the "much affliction"[3] to rejoice in the "joy of the Holy Ghost"–[4] Do tell me when you write, dear M.[r] Boyd, how she is & how her spirits are, and whether you mean to let her return to school. If I were you I would not permit it– Do not, unless you cannot help it, or object to her remaining with you on other grounds than any I am aware of—for indeed that return w.[d] be very desolate & distressing to her—that return *alone!*–

I heard from Nelly Bordman only a few days before receiving your letter, & so far from preparing me for all this sadness & gloom she pleased me with her account of you whom she had lately seen—dwelling upon your retrograde passage into youth & the delight you were taking in the presence & society of some still more youthful, fair, & gay *monstrum amandum*,[5] some prodigy of intellectual accomplishment, some little Circe who never turned anybodies into pigs.[6] I learnt too from her for the first time that you were settled at Hampstead! Whereabout at Hampstead, & for how long? She did'nt tell me THAT, thinking of course that I knew something more about you than I do– Yes indeed! You DO treat me very shabbily– I agree with you in thinking so. To think that so many hills & woods sh.[d] interpose between us—that I sh.[d] be lying here, fast bound by a spell, a sleeping Beauty in a forest, & that *you* who used to be such a doughty knight sh.[d] not take the trouble of cutting through even a hazel tree with your good sword, to find out what had become of me!!– Now do tell me, the hazel tree being down at last, whether you mean to live at Hampstead, whether you have taken a house there & have carried your books there, & wear Hampstead grasshoppers in your bonnet (as they did at Athens)[7] to prove yourself of the soil!——

All this nonsense will make you think I am better—and indeed I am pretty well just now– Quite, however, confined to the bed—except when lifted from it to the sofa baby-wise while they make it,—& even then apt to faint. Bad symptoms too do not leave me,—& I am obliged to be blistered every few days—but I am free from any attack just now, & am a good deal less feverish than I am occasionally. There has been a consultation between an Exeter physician & my own[8]—& they agree exactly—both hoping that with care I shall pass the winter, & rally in the spring—both hoping that I may be able to go about again with some comfort & independence, although I never can be fit again for anything like exertion.

D.[r] Scully, the physician who attends me now & has done so since poor Dr Barry's death, (of which you may have heard as affecting me most painfully last October) is a highly intelligent man besides being one of the very kindest in the world. The world calls him a Roman Catholic,— & he calls himself a whig of the [illegible word] *æra*—rather a curious contradiction.[9] The explanatory truth is that he is no more a Roman Catholic than I am– He holds the right of private judgment as firmly with clenched hands as Luther did. I am not able to talk much—indeed my voice has wasted to a whisper,—but he & I talk a *little* every day on the occasion of his daily visit—and he brought me a book last week, a catalogue raisonnè of Dr Parr's library in which, among the *Patres ecclesiastici*[10] "my heart leaped up to see"[11] the mention of your select passages—by S Boyd, *1810*.[12] No observation upon it.

Do you know, did you ever hear anything of Mr Horne who wrote Cosmo de Medici & the Death of Marlowe, & is now desecrating his powers (I beg your pardon) by writing the life of Napoleon?–[13] By the way, he is the author of a dramatic sketch in the last Finden.

He is in my mind one of the very first poets of the day,—& has written to me so kindly (offering although I never saw him in my life, to cater for me in literature & send me down anything likely to interest me in the periodicals) that I cannot but think his amiability & genius do honor to one another.

Do you remember M[r] Caldicott who used to preach in the infant schoolroom at Sidmouth– He died here the death of a saint, as he had lived a saintly life—about three weeks ago–[14] It affected me a good deal. But he was always so associated in my thoughts more with heaven than earth, that scarcely a transition seems to have passed upon his locality. "Present with the Lord"[15] is true of him now,—even as "having his conversation in Heaven"[16] was formerly. There is little difference.

May it be so with us all—with you & with me, my ever & very dear friend!– In the meantime do not forget me. I never can forget YOU–

Your affectionate & grateful
Elizabeth B Barrett

Arabel desires her love to be offered to you–

Address: H S Boyd Esq[r] / 26 Downshire Hill / Hampstead / near London.
Publication: EBB-HSB, pp. 234–237 (as 29 May 1840).
Manuscript: Wellesley College.

1. *Cymbeline*, IV, 2, 261.
2. There is nothing in the secondary correspondence to help identification. The references to "holiday time" and "return to school" suggest that Patience and Kate were sisters visiting Boyd, perhaps related to his late wife.
3. II Corinthians, 2:4.
4. Romans, 14:17.
5. "Lovable monster," doubtless a play on the "monstrum horrendum" ("dreadful monster") of Vergil's *Æneid*, which EBB quotes elsewhere.
6. In *The Odyssey* (bk. X, 229ff.).

7. Thucydides (bk. I, cap. 6) tells of the older Athenian men "fastening up their hair in a knot held by a golden grasshopper as a brooch."
8. See letter 726.
9. The "curious contradiction" being that it was the Whigs who established the Protestant succession to the throne.
10. "Fathers of the church."
11. Cf. Wordsworth's lines "My Heart Leaps Up When I Behold" (1802).
12. A second edition, corrected and enlarged, of Boyd's *Select Passages of the Writings of St. Chrysostom, St. Gregory Nazianzen, and St. Basil* was published in 1810. The Catalogue mentioned by EBB was published by John Bohn and Joseph Mawman in 1827 (see *Reconstruction*, A1815).
13. Horne's *History of Napoleon* (1840); Mary Gillies was his collaborator.
14. Believed to be the Rev. William Marriott Caldecott (b. 1801?), who had died on 9 January.
15. II Corinthians, 5:8.
16. Cf. Philippians, 3:20.

---

729. EBB TO MARY RUSSELL MITFORD

[Torquay]
Friday– [late January 1840][1]

Ever dearest Miss Mitford

Our letters passing on the road without speaking, I must write a little more, too soon I fear to be at all in reason, in reply to your question as to whether Mr Shepherd's poem has reached me—which it has *not* done. I am very thankful to him & to the author of the Happy futurity for their kind intentions[2]—& certainly not less so to your own dear self who are at the bottom of so many of my pleasures of this sort. *You know you are*.

But I wish I could owe a better one to you, and hear that you are quite as well as my thoughts & prayers would make you. That rheumatic haunting pain in the face must be so worrying & incapacitating—& then the "*only* two" fits of sickness in a fortnight, sound anything but satisfactory to me. On the other hand I would not be unthankful to the mercy which has arrested the worse pain of mental anxiety. Dear Dr Mitford is pretty well—& you are easy about the Findens.

Is Mr Kenyon at Rome?[3] I do not quite make it out from what you say—& am willing to hope that he is not, .. that he will be in London, on the contrary, to praise Otto's cothurni[4] & see how you look in a new crown. Do tell me all & everything– I am *very* anxious to know. In the midst of the anxiety, I stop short to sigh, & think that whoever may be in London, *I*[5] shall not & you will. *I*[5] shall not see you in the new crown, or in any other—in truth the old one was regal & redolent enough for me!– Well!– I must be content with the smell of the new bays at a distance, & persuade some one shower out of a hundred to go away from this rainy cloud-land of Devon, & take my love with it & water them & keep them green.

Very green sort of writing is written up there—but when one is shut up in the dark, curtained all round, & under blister-torture, as I am "at these presents", one is glad to wander away from one's self & one's dreariness by favor of any sort of metaphor green or yellow,—without classical leave. D.[r] Scully has condemned me to a dynasty of blisters—each to be applied to the chest every three days for two or three hours at a time[6]—which just answers the purpose of a minor kind of flaying– Not that I am worse. But the spitting of blood which never has quite ceased, always increases with the fall of the thermometer—& it is found absolutely necessary to divert as far as possible (which is not very far) the morbid course of the circulation.

Have you seen M.[rs] Gore & M.[rs] Trollope in their late avatars?[7] "Preferment", with an undeniable cleverness, is dull & heavy—besides the *hardness*, as inseparable from that world-illustrating species of composition as from an old walnut shell. As to "One fault", with neither dulness nor heaviness, the book seems to *me* far less clever than M.[rs] Trollope's books generally or always are—and I am at a loss about the title, the applicability of the title, seeing that it is suitable neither to the work which is far from having *only* one fault, nor to the hero who really does in my eyes concentrate in his magnificent person most of the faults[8] & the worst ones, I can remember without "farther notice"—while the poor persecuted & perfect heroine has no fault at all .., if it be not that she might "have DONE IT" more gracefully, in making her proposals to that second husband with whom the third volume *leaves her*– But then again she was wet & in a hurry—there are excuses for her.[9] It w.[d] have been different if she had waited to change her stockings—& by the way, Eureka,!—in that one omission lies the *one* FAULT!⸺

Talking of Geraldine & converts,[10]—did you ever meet with an account partly translated partly composed by Miss Schimmelpenninck, of the Port Royal? It is long since I read, & will be longer before I forget that most interesting account of the most interesting establishment which ever owed its conventual name & form to the Church of Rome, & its purity & nobility to God's blessing & informing Spirit–[11]

They have come to warn me about the post. My beloved friend, do write whenever you can without crowding your employments unpleasantly, & *never* at another time.

My sisters say they w.[d] intrude their kindest regards—& mine *are* with dear D.[r] Mitford by permission––& intrusion too—fancying & wishing all sorts of seasonable good to both of you!-

Your most affectionate
E B Barrett–

Publication: EBB-MRM, I, 172–174.
Manuscript: Wellesley College.

1. Dated by the further reference to the books EBB was awaiting from Wimpole Street. EBB's references to Miss Mitford's health place this letter after no. 727.
2. See letter 727, note 20.
3. Kenyon was travelling in Italy (see letter 734).
4. The thick-soled boots worn by tragic actors. There was at this time a revival of interest in Miss Mitford's ill-fated *Otto of Wittelsbach*; she speaks of "present expectations" of the play's being staged in April (Chorley, I, 171). Nothing came of these hopes.
5. Underscored twice.
6. See letter 599, note 2.
7. *Preferment: or, My Uncle the Earl* (3 vols., 1840) by Catherine Grace Frances Gore (*née* Moody, 1799–1861), and *One Fault. A Novel* (3 vols., 1840) by Frances Trollope (*née* Milton, 1780–1863).
8. The "one fault" ascribed by Mrs. Trollope to her hero was his shortness of temper towards his wife.
9. After her husband was killed in a duel, the young widow was able to ensnare a former lover at the sea-shore during a storm.
10. See letter 720, note 16.
11. Port Royal, founded in 1204, was a Cistercian abbey a few miles S.W. of Paris, authorized by the Pope in 1223 to offer a retreat to women anxious to withdraw from the world without taking vows of poverty, obedience, etc. It later supported the Jansenists, who emphasized the personal relationship of each soul to God. The Jansenist doctrines were condemned in 1653 by Innocent X, and the abbey was forbidden to receive new members. After a brief rapprochement under Clement IX, Clement XI again condemned the Jansenists' teachings; in 1709 the nuns were forcibly removed from Port Royal, and in 1710 the abbey was razed.
    Mary Ann Schimmelpenninck (*née* Galton, 1778–1856) published *Select Memoirs of Port Royal* (3 vols., 1829).

---

730. Mary Russell Mitford to EBB

Three Mile Cross,
Jan. 3[0], 1840.[1]

My beloved Friend,

My father and I sat to-night looking at the fire in silence and in sadness, the wind rising and sighing with its most mournful rather than its more threatening sound through the branches, from which the snow was falling silently—contradicting by sight and feeling (for the cold was intense) the evidence of another sense, as the double Roman narcissus and the white and purple hyacinths shed their delicious fragrance from the window—my father and myself sat pensively over the wood fire, until he said suddenly, "You are thinking of dear Miss Barrett; so was I. God bless her! How long is it since you have heard from her?" Every night at that time I had thought of you, my sweetest, sitting over the glowing embers, and at last I determined to write to you before I slept. I have told you of my little girl, Agnes Niven, just twelve years old. Her mother and I sometimes call her our pet lamb. She sent me this week a pair of delicate mittens, knit of the finest wool and silk, with the following stanza:

> "A tuft of flax to a Grecian bride
> Was ancient Hymen's offer;
> A tuft of wool is England's pride:
> What more can a pet-lamb offer?"

Are not these lines, with their combination of point and gracefulness, their Mr. Kenyon-like terseness and turn, very remarkable in a girl of that age?

I have been reading "Jack Sheppard,"[2] and have been struck by the great danger, in these times, of representing authority so constantly and fearfully in the wrong, so tyrannous, so devilish, as the author has been pleased to portray it in "Jack Sheppard;" for he does not seem so much a man, or even an incarnate fiend, as a representation of power—government or law, call it as you may—the ruling power. Of course Mr. Ainsworth had no such design, but such is the effect; and as the millions who see it represented at the minor theatres will not distinguish between now and a hundred years back, all the Chartists[3] in the land are less dangerous than this nightmare of a book, and I, Radical as I am, lament any additional temptations to outbreak, with all its train of horrors.[4] Seriously, what things these are—the Jack Sheppards, and Squeers's, and Oliver Twists, and Michael Armstrongs[5]—all the worse for the power which, except the last, the others contain! Grievously the worse!

My friend Mr. Hughes[6] speaks well of Mr. Ainsworth. His father was a collector of these old robber stories, and used to repeat the local ballads upon Turpin,[7] &c., to his son as he sat upon his knee; and this has perhaps been at the bottom of the matter. A good antiquarian I believe him to be, but what a use to make of the picturesque old knowledge! Well, one comfort is that it will wear itself out; and then it will be cast aside like an old fashion.

Ever most faithfully yours,
M. R. M.

Address: Miss Barrett, Torquay.
Text: L'Estrange (2), III, 105–106 (as 3 January 1840).

1. The editors of *EBB-MRM* suggest that the date was misread by L'Estrange and should be Jan. 30 1840. This suggestion has merit; if L'Estrange's dating were correct, EBB would surely have commented on Agnes Niven's stanza in letter 727 or 729, rather than delaying comment until letter 732.
2. *Jack Sheppard: A Romance* (3 vols., 1839) by William Harrison Ainsworth (1805–82), novelist and historian, who had achieved popularity in 1834 with *Rookwood*.
3. See letter 726, note 6.
4. *The Athenæum* of 26 October 1839 (no. 626, pp. 803–805) described *Jack Sheppard*

as "a bad book, and what is worse, it is of a class of bad books, got up for a bad public." In view of this, and Miss Mitford's opinion of the book, it is interesting to note that *The Examiner* (no. 1659, 17 November 1839, p. 732) gave an account of the trial of an 18-year-old boy for burglary, in emulation of Jack Sheppard.

5. Wackford Squeers was the penny-pinching schoolmaster in Dickens's *Nicholas Nickleby*; Oliver Twist the foundling in Dickens's novel of the same name; Michael Armstrong's story was told in *The Life and Adventures of Michael Armstrong, the Factory Boy* (1840) by Frances Trollope.

6. See letter 660, note 4.

7. Dick Turpin (1706-39), a thief and highwayman, owes much of his lasting notoriety to Ainsworth, in whose *Rockwood* Turpin figured prominently. He was hanged on 7 April 1839.

731. EBB TO SEPTIMUS MOULTON-BARRETT

[Torquay]
Thursday. [6 February 1840][1]

My dearest Sette,

My conscience has fallen into a fit all at once, after various chronic symptoms, & is so unreasonable as to refuse to be revived unless I begin to write to you immediately. Indeed I do thank you for the dozens of 'penny a lines'[2] which you have sent me—none of them very long, but each proving that you think of me at odd times—which makes all even. Do believe that my not saying 'thank you' to each, is no proof of thankless thoughts—& do go on writing as often as you can. Any sort of nonsense does, you know—and really we ought to encourage the postage bill, were it only for patriotism's sake.

Thank dearest Papa for me for his enclosure & the lines in the envelope—but I believe I did it my own self. Tell him too what I forgot to tell, that I have finished Shelley's volumes[3] which, if it were not for the here & there defilement of his atrocious opinions[4] ⟨...⟩[5] would have very deeply delighted me. As it is there are traces of my pencil "*in a passion*" as dear Georgie w^d say. I have fallen out too with Shelley about his translations from Plato.[6] The general impression was, & my particular impression certainly was that he "ate Greek drank Greek"[7]—whereas it almost appears to me now that he starved upon it. At any rate he knew little or nothing of Plato—& the translations so extolled in the preface, are only wonderful from their extreme incorrectness.[8] I am wondering if any of the Critics par excellence will take notice of this. Tell me if you see it noticed anywhere–

Dr Scully came here this morning on his way to "looking in" he said "upon a meeting" at the hotel, "to consider the propriety of doing honor to Mrs Albert on monday".[9] He means to try to persuade the people to be satisfied with a subscription dinner for the poor—instead of disturbing the invalids of the place with threatened illuminations—& I do hope he may succeed– It w^d be a cruel mockery to permit such a public manifestation, in the midst of the dying—&—what many persons w^d think more of, tho' it inverts the climax,—"very bad taste"– He found my pulse in a "dead calm" (for me) this morning—at 84!! altho' 92 yesterday,—which he called a "pretty good pulse" (for *me*) also. It has been decidedly quieter now for ten days, & for the most part of that time, I have slept better. But when, in order to take advantage of this calm, & give some of the *strength*, which my dearest Papa wants me to have, he attempted to resume the iron, back came the palpitations & forced him to let it go again .. And now he says that there is no use,—that I can *not* bear *tonics* under present circumstances. The sun is the best tonic—the sunshine with God's blessing upon it,—the sunshine which promises to come the month after next!——

Today Mr Orange is coming to see me; and yesterday Mr Tagle,[10] in the course of his visit to Bummy, very kindly proposed of his own will, to do the same thing– He said that he knew "Miss Barrett was a dissenter", .. "so, indeed is her father, who knows the truth thoroughly" .. but that he c^d not consider such a circumstance any objection to his being admitted to talk & read & pray with me .. that he c^d not clash with Mr Orange who seemed to be a very good quiet man, not given to make disturbances in any dissenting manner whatever. "*That* is the worst of the dissenters!" Then he told Bummy to write my 'yes' to him, if I said it—which of course I did, immediately & very gratefully.

We have not heard from Jamaica, which is a shame. Bro went out to the Hopeful,[11] through such a foaming sea, that I sh^d have been terrified if I had known anything about it before his safe return. Dr Scully told me he tried to persuade him not to go—all in vain. We have had tremendous seas & winds,—& a chimney on the other side of the house, "nodding to its fall".[12] But nothing makes me fail to perceive the great advantages in point of shelter & warmth of this number one. My room particularly is quite a nest of a room—there being nothing at all like it, according to Dr Scully, in the whole of Torquay. During our short attack of frost, he used to stand before the fire every morning wrapt in admiration, while Crow reported the state of the thermometer.

The rock walk is falling to pieces. Indeed great rocky fragments have been hurled, in the manner of avalanches, so near some of the houses facing the quay that their inhabitants have fled—although one or two of the landlords came forwards with a generous offer of taking the responsibility .. "THEY w^d answer for the consequences." Tenants were unreasonable enough to run as fast as ever. Papa's artist, Mr Mills,[13] escaped crushing, just by six inches & a half.

Did anybody tell you of *my* artist M.ʳ Wyatt, being raised to the rank of chymist to Her Majesty[14]—& through no solicitation on his part? He shows an official letter, from Windsor I believe, & is a very great man indeed.

Do write & tell us all that you are all doing,—& in detail. Tell dearest Minny she is very very kind to send me so many letters, & that I do mean to write to her. My thoughts & affections are looking in upon you thro' all the windows, by daytime & night time.

The colour has come into the cheeks of my conscience, now Sette. She is pretty well, thank you!–

May God bless you always,
Your most affectionate Ba.

Best love to my dear Trippy. I cannot hear of M.ʳˢ Pierce[15] thro' D.ʳ Scully, my only source of news.

Poor Arlette & Cissy are rather better. They have had very very bad coughs for a fortnight past—in my private suspicion,—*the hooping cough*– But Bummy does not think so–

Publication: None traced.
Manuscript: Myrtle Moulton-Barrett and Ronald A. Moulton-Barrett.

1. Dated by reference to the forthcoming wedding of Queen Victoria.
2. Freelance contributors to newspapers used to be paid a penny a line.
3. EBB's father had sent her, in January, Shelley's *Essays, Letters from Abroad, Translations and Fragments*, ed. Mrs. Shelley (2 vols., 1840).
4. EBB took exception to Shelley's ideas on religion. In her copy of the book (now at Princeton; see *Reconstruction*, A2102) she has scored through some of his passages and has written her own opinions in the margin.
5. The words "by which they are defiled" have been deleted, apparently by EBB.
6. EBB considered Shelley's translations to be highly inaccurate; she noted 37 errors, and also complained of his failure to render the sense of a Greek pun. The tenor of her comments shows her real feeling for, and grasp of, the Greek language. A detailed listing of her notations can be found in "Elizabeth Barrett's Commentary on Shelley: Some Marginalia," by James Thorpe (*Modern Language Notes*, LXVI, 1951, 455–458).
7. We have been unable to locate the source of this quotation.
8. Mrs. Shelley's preface claims that "Shelley commands language splendid and melodious as Plato, and renders faithfully the elegance and gaiety which make the Symposium as amusing as it is sublime. The whole mechanism of the drama ... [is] given with grace and animation."
9. Queen Victoria's wedding to Prince Albert was to take place the following Monday, 10 February.
10. EBB's writing is clear, but we have not traced anybody of this name. Given her habitual carelessness with names, particularly any she was not familiar with, we believe this to be a reference to the Rev. John Eagles, Curate of Kinnersley and tutor to Bummy's nephew, John Altham Graham-Clarke. As his daughter, Emma Jane, was to marry Bummy's nephew later in the year, he would obviously call on her while in Torquay.
11. Presumably the name of the packet bringing mail from the West Indies.
12. Pope, *Essay on Man*, Epistle IV, 129.
13. Mills had made a chalk drawing of EBB's father that she had in Torquay, and later in Italy. In a letter of 19 November 1842, EBB mentions his being commissioned to do a fresco at Gravesend. He is thought to have been John Mills, who exhibited at the Royal Academy and the British Institute between 1801 and 1837.

14. EBB's reference is to the painter who accompanied the Moulton-Barretts to France in 1815 (see letter 26). We have been unable to elucidate his having been appointed "chymist to Her Majesty"; nobody of that name is listed in any capacity in any department of the Queen's Household, or in the listing of Queen's Tradesmen, in *The Royal Kalendar: and Court and City Register* for the years 1839 and 1840.

15. We have not identified Mrs. Pierce.

---

732. EBB TO MARY RUSSELL MITFORD

[Torquay]
[mid-February 1840][1]

Ever dearest Miss Mitford,

This little sheet must follow the step of my larger letter— I am not content with the latter's competency to say what I w^d say— I am constrained to more penitence before you for that unkindness of silence!— And yet how hard to repent, when the offence brought me such a vision of you & dear kind Dr Mitford sitting over the embers & thinking of *me*[2] .. all the snow being *without* .. as it always must, when you are *within!!*– Thank you,—both of you!— Do my beloved friend give my earnest & thankful love to Dr Mitford!— To think of *me!*—& to let me *see* you sitting over the fire & thinking of me!–! Never penitent smiled so before in sackcloth, as I did over that pleasant vision in that pleasant letter which, if my morals were properly balanced, w^d have brought me nothing but remorses. I caught myself smiling .. in the sackcloth & in the remorse .. "for a' that & for a' that"[3] .. with a kind of heir-in-mourning melancholy-mirth!

If Agnes were not *your* Agnes, & if you yourself were not the tale-bearer, I never c^d believe in the epigrammist being only twelve years old. I believe *now*, because it is impossible.[4] All you say about the terseness & Mr Kenyonness of the performance is as true as the other truth (viz about the age of the writer) is wonderful[5]—for the wonder of such characteristics & such childhood being synchronous has much more rare wonderfulness than any howsoever early development of imagination .. or genius, strictly so called. I sh^d be afraid of wearing the mittens for fear of being bewitched. It is very much like a snowdrop growing with the root in the air.

Can anything grow anywhere or any way with this terrible wind? The temperature of my bedroom is kept up day & night to 65 & I am not suffered to be moved from the bed even for its making—& yet the noxious character of the air makes me very uncomfortable & sleepless. I took two draughts of opium last night—but even the second failed to bring sleep. "It *is* a blessed thing!"[6] that sleep!—one of my worst sufferings being the want of it. Opium—opium—night after night!—& some nights, during east winds, even opium wont do, you see!——

Thank God that you dearest dearest Miss Mitford are able to hope about yourself. Oh may we soon rejoice about you .. without even the degree of fear which enters into the nature of hope— God grant it to be pure joy about you—not hope!— I am an insatiable person—

I have always forgotten to ask you— Did you ever hear how poor Mr Reade has compromised himself with Fraser .. in the magazine?— I always forgot to ask! I mean, how Fraser reviewed his poetry savagely last December or January, & published at full length still more savagely divers applications & supplications which the poet had addressed to his private tender mercies[7] through the post office .. said in observing that said poet's said supplicatory habits accounted for the degree of notice vouchsafed to said poems by more tender critic's than said untender Mr Fraser!![8] Did you hear this before. It made my blood run cold with sympathy for the poor poet when I read it first. Say compassion, rather than sympathy—for one cant feel altogether WITH anyone capable of canvassing his critics & assuring them *sous la rose*[9] of high esteem & devoted attachment. Fame is not woo[e]d so by "clear spirits"—[10] How c.^d Mr Reade do it, or think it, or imagine it .. or bear it all, as it turned out?—— Fraser is a monster—but that being undeniable, how c.^d Mr Reade *do it*?—

If you dont see the Athenæum I will send you my verses on the wedding—tho' they are not worth reading.[11]

Do you remember amusing me by enquiring whether a new contributor of yours to the Tableaux was married or single?[12] Well—do you know, I have not found out even yet. But I have, that he *deserves* to be married & well-married .. & to be like Shakespeare besides. A very very kind person—with an idiosyncrasy worth looking at, to say nothing of his genius as externally developped. He sent me by the post before last, Leigh Hunt's Feast of the violets[13] .. after my brothers had looked for it in London quite vainly— Have you seen it? I run the risk of that, & transcribe the verses respecting your dearest self & Apollo speaking to you ..

> "And Mitford, all hail!—with a head that for green,
> From your glad village crowners can hardly be seen!"
> And with that He shone on it & set us all blinking—
> And yet at her kind heart sate Tragedy, thinking!—

> God bless you beloved friend!—
> Your most affectionate EBB—

What do you mean by the week? [']'Do I remember the week"? what week?— I am always forgetting chronologies—times seasons .. & ages .. even Sette's. Do tell me—

Tell me of Flush--& pray dont insult me by doubting again whether I have natural affections– Poor little Flush! Perhaps if I lived in your neighbourhood I sh?. prefer him to "the Duke."[14] Which (mind!) is no want of respect to the Duke! only *the heart has its caprices*[15]—as they say in romances!

Publication: EBB-MRM, I, 178–180 (as [February 1840]).
Manuscript: Wellesley College.

1. Dated by the reference to EBB's "The Crowned and Wedded Queen."
2. See letter 730.
3. Burns, "For A' That and A' That" (1790).
4. Tertullian, *De Carne Christi*, 5; see letter 288.
5. EBB refers to the stanza quoted by Miss Mitford in letter 730.
6. Cf. Coleridge, "Oh sleep! it is a gentle thing" (*The Rime of the Ancient Mariner*, 292).
7. Cf. Luke, 1:78.
8. EBB refers to *Fraser's Magazine*, December 1839, pp. 758–762. Writing of Reade's *Italy* and *The Deluge*, the reviewer said of the latter "We are not sure that we ever attempted to read such a flood of foolery" and that the former "does not contain so much as one sentence that has a meaning." He continues "Who *is* Mr. John Edmund Reade? Is there really such a biped in existence?" but finds Reade's "*boná fide* presence among living men" proved by two letters uncovered from him, expressing hopes for the editor's "good report." The reviewer speculates that "Numbers of persons . . . have, if known at all, been pestered with presents of these silly books; for no other reason than that the author's vanity might be tickled by the note of thanks which common good breeding would, of course, extract from each of them. Now, really, we must enter our protest against such quackery." After giving some samples of Reade's verse, the reviewer protests that "Theodore Hook simply deserves to be hanged" for giving *The Deluge* a favourable notice in *The New Monthly Magazine*, but says that "a kinder-hearted fellow never lived" and that Hook "could not bring himself to resist the entreaties of Mr. Reade for a notice."
9. "Under the rose," i.e., secretly, the rose having been regarded by the ancients as emblematic of secrecy.
10. Cf. Milton, "Lycidas" (1638), 70.
11. *The Athenæum* of 15 February 1840 (no. 642, p. 131) printed EBB's verses celebrating Victoria's wedding, "The Crowned and Wedded Queen."
12. i.e., Horne. See letter 710.
13. Printed in *The Monthly Repository*, July 1837, pp. 33–57. See letter 538, note 20 and SD825.1.
14. Taken to be a reference to the Duke of Wellington, whose seat, Stratfield Saye, was about five miles from Three Mile Cross.
15. Cf. "La cœur a ses raisons" (Pascal, *Pensées*, pt. II, 17, 5).

---

733. EBB TO MARY RUSSELL MITFORD

Torquay.
Thursday. [20 February 1840][1]

My ever dearest Miss Mitford–

Two welcome letters from you, & one of them more than usually delightful—& no gratitude in the shape of an answer!! It *does* seem very abominable of me—& if I am black & blue with the "cudgelling" of "your hard thoughts",[2] I cannot say but that I deserve it to all appearances. Yet dearest dearest Miss Mitford, do forgive this mask of neglect, behind which I have loved, & thought of you much!– Do.

Your letters found me saddened by the death here of a friend with whom I had had little personal intercourse indeed, but who did not interest me the less on that account,—after a long illness of the same character as my own.[3] So that the end was affecting to me in many ways! But he is with God—passing tranquilly as one moves in a dream, from this earth to that Heaven .. almost, without the sign of transition. He walked to Beacon Terrace & up stairs very kindly last spring to see me upon my sofa. It was an exertion to him—but I c^d not stand: and I remember thinking within myself that if I were as well as he I sh^d be more sanguine about recovery than he seemed to be. How little we can count upon what will be!– He rallied in the summer as usual .. was looking almost *well*, Papa says .. in London: & returned here to die– But it was best & happiest for him—& even so his poor widow has strength to say with the smile upon her face!——

Well then!– I never received Mr Merry's book until a very few days since.[4] Was'nt it too bad of my dear people in Wimpole Street? I told you of their genius for "waiting for opportunities"—& in accordance with it, they opened the parcel, enclosed your letter to me, & kept the book until boots, & shoes enough for a colony c^d be made—allowing for that corresponding genius of procrastination common to shoemakers. I really was ashamed to write to you until I had the book—& when I had it & read it off my conscience & wrote to Mr Merry .. then came Dr Scully with the martyrdom of a perpetual blister in his right hand!-

Now do my dearest Miss Mitford, write & tell me all about yourself & dear Dr Mitford! It w^d revive me like an inward spring, to hear a great deal of good about you. Is it to be heard? God grant *that*. I have asked all I have access to about the maid, & cannot hear of a place for her,—& I do hope that by this time your success has been greater. My own maid & my sisters' is faultless in kindness & attention to me—or—had there been a vacancy near myself,—I sh^d have very much liked to fill it with anybody *consecrated by association with you!*–– Papa has not come yet!! so that I am not as silly as Dr Scully fancied, when he found me with tears running down my cheeks because of "a fortnight's absence",—& sate down in a kind of despair at my bedside, with his "Well Miss Barrett—there is no *reasoning* on such subjects!"– But I knew very well how these "fortnights" are apt to grow. *That* was a fortnight before Christmas!– Dearest Papa has so much occupation, & so many to care about & discipline in London, that it is very difficult for him to go two hundred miles away from it!—though Styx be 'nine times round him'[5] with promises!

I am tolerably well—but there is an east wind, & I feel it—& I feel too, by way of accessory *in* the way of inconvenience, this perpetual blister .. which is to do me good perhaps, & which in the meantime keeps me very quiet & *un*comfortable!——

Thank you for all your amusing *Mitfordiana*. I will tell you as a secret, that a Mr Henry Mitford (in the navy, I think he is) behaved nearly as ill to Mr Boyd's daughter as his uncle did to the Greeks.[6] (Forgive me—but I am sure you dont admire that *his*tory (pro *my*stery) of iniquity!–)[7] She is married now .. but she did at one time feel the cruelty very deeply—at least *as* deeply as a woman of rather quick than profound feelings c^d be supposed to do. They met at Malvern—she, a singularly pretty girl & very young: & a guitar between them & a great deal of flirtation .. causing them to separate under a tacit sort of engagement & with exchanged locks of hair, she received back a few days afterwards her ringlet wrapt up in an old newspaper, & without a word!– So I say "CRUELTY"– They met again after years & years; & he told a long tale about a plot against them both .. how he was persuaded that she had married, .. & was married himself in a kind of trance .. an absolute state of unconsciousness, he maintained it was!– Altogether the explanation sounded to me rather worse than the thing supposed to be explained—but SHE *believed it*, poor thing, *of course*– That a woman sh^d fancy herself beloved, & be mistaken, .. w^d always seem to *her* a stranger thing, than that a man sh^d. be married in a trance,—or any other miracle!–

Your "Annie" of yore & my Ibbit Jane must have a great deal in common. There never was a more absolute flirt than Ibbit. Indeed her love for "jeloms" as opposed to "wadys"[8] is honestly devulged upon every fitting opportunity—& her indignation too, wherever she c^d say of mortal man "he never speaked one word to me"! Nay! the very trick she has of catching the light with that lovely golden hair of hers, which hangs like a net of curls from brow to waist, is instinct with flirtation!– I wish you c^d see Ibbit!——

Mr Merry's little book pleased me much, for the most part. I have written to him just my thoughts: & if they get me into a scrape & he says to you "What a forward wrongheaded wrongmannered person she is" you are bound my dearest Miss Mitford to take my part & answer "Dont be angry—I spoilt her". Of course I made no reference to his letter to y^{r}self—which is here returned to you .. so that altogether I am blameless before YOU, & you must take my part. Did'nt you encourage me into this particular mischief, besides the general spoiling—now did'nt you?——

Mʳ Horne since I named him last to you, has sent me his *Marlowe*[9]— & moreover written in the very kindest way to propose amusing me to the end of the cold weather by sending anything amus*able* that might pass thro' his hands & thoughts—a proposition arising from his having heard something of the closeness of my imprisonment, through a mutual friend.[10] The whole manner of it was most abundantly kind .. most singularly so considering that we are strangers to each other. I am in a fit of gratitude—& believe more than ever in my edition of the Tales of the genii.[11] Your ordinary ladies & gentlemen wᵈ never think of doing such things– In the first place they coul'dnt make their way so close to a stranger as to make their kind feelings audible—they coul'dnt for conventionalisms—for the rustling of their petticoats & the creaking of their shoes.–

Mʳ Horne has told me too of what I never dreamt .. that I am named in Leigh Hunt's Feast of the Violets .. published two years ago!![12]—& very kindly named. Some lines he extracted .. but *not* those in relation to *you*, altho' he refers to *them* besides. Did you ever see the poem,—A pendant to the Feast of the Poets?[13] And have you seen the new tragedy .. this *Legend of Florence*? To judge from very scanty extracts it seems to have deep pathos & poetry—but rather, I shᵈ fancy, an ultra laxity of versification.[14] Where is Otto?[15] Are you arranging anything? Do tell me all—& with my love to dear Dʳ Mitford,

       believe me ever & ever gratefully
        yours, in true affection
         EBB–

Do mention your health *very* particularly!——

Publication: EBB-MRM, I, 174–177.
Manuscript: Wellesley College.

1. Dated by the reference to *A Legend of Florence*.
2. Cf. *As You Like It*, I, 2, 183–184.
3. See letter 728.
4. *The Philosophy of a Happy Futurity est. on the Sure Evidence of the Bible* (1839), by William Merry, who lived at "The Highlands," near Reading and was a friend of Miss Mitford.
5. Pope, *Ode for Musick. On St. Cecilia's Day* (1713), 90–92.
6. For EBB's earlier comments on William Mitford's *History of Greece*, see letter 568, note 5. Nothing is known of his nephew's alleged ill-treatment of Boyd's daughter.
7. II Thessalonians, 2:7.
8. i.e., "gentlemans" and "ladies."
9. *The Death of Marlowe* first appeared in *The Monthly Repository*, August 1837, pp. 128–140. It was published in book form that same year. EBB's copy formed part of lot 764 of *Browning Collections* (see *Reconstruction*, A1247).
10. i.e., Mrs. Orme, the one-time governess at Hope End.
11. James Ridley (1736–65), using the pseudonym Sir Charles Morell, had published in 1764 *The Tales of the Genii, or the delightful Lessons of Horan, the son of Asmar*, purporting to be translations from a Persian manuscript but being, in reality, Ridley's

own inventions, inspired by *The Arabian Nights*. EBB is equating the element of magic and improbability with the generosity of Horne.

12. See letter 538, note 20, and SD825.1.

13. *The Feast of the Poets . . . By the Editor of the Examiner* [Leigh Hunt] had been published in 1814.

14. Leigh Hunt's play, *A Legend of Florence*, was produced at Covent Garden on 7 February 1840. EBB's reference to reading "scanty extracts" suggests that her knowledge of the play came from *The Athenæum*, which reviewed the play, with extracts, in the issue of 15 February (no. 642, pp. 138–139).

15. There was a possiblity that Miss Mitford's play would be presented in April. See letter 729, note 4.

734. EBB TO MARY RUSSELL MITFORD

[Torquay]
Thursday. [27 February 1840][1]

Ever dearest Miss Mitford,

I send the Feast of the violets[2]—because I do fancy you will like to see them your own self. And now that you cant walk out to pick them, it is but fair that I sh^d bring them to you. There is occasional coarseness— which Leigh Hunt cant help or does'nt help—& the poem is less finished perhaps than the 'Feast of the poets'– But still it is clever & will make you laugh. Will you—when you have quite done with it—let me have it back?– It was published in 1837. How he came to put me into the violet beds (so long ago too) is a mystery for which I am very much obliged to him. Perhaps it is in illustration or coincidence with the parable of the tares!——[3]

But dont set it down to pure gratitude, if I admire Leigh Hunt as a poet, more than you seem to do. I think I admire him more. The story of Rimini[4] stands very near Chaucer's knight's Tale to my apprehension— & if Dr Scully ever caught me reading it, he w^d certainly say "Well! there is no reasoning on such subjects". And I do not cry for nothing, even over poetry I assure you. Oh! he is surely a true poet!– His affectations (I mean *verbal* affectations) have a certain poetesqueness about them—suited to the tastes of such as "in trim gardens take their pleasure".[5] The Legend has just lain down upon my bed. I have not read a word of it.

Here too is a letter from dear Mr Kenyon! dated Novr 20th & brought from Florence by private hand!![6] I am to write to him at Rome & to tell him "how dear Miss Mitford is" & all about the Tableaux which dont penetrate into Italy. His "life is a very quiet one" .. that is, I suppose considering that it is Mr Kenyon's. He seems to have made four or five friends worth calling so at Florence, & talks of how the Americans are winning honors on all sides of him, & how he was to dine the day he wrote, with two American sculptors.

And here is his "way of living" "done into English verse" .. very Kenyonianly—

Italy.

Fair blows the breeze! Depart—depart—
And tread with me the Italian shore;
And feed thy soul with glorious art,
And drink again of classic lore!—

Nor sometimes wilt thou deem it wrong
When not in mood too gravely wise,
At idle length to lie along
And quaff a bliss from bluest skies!—

Or—pleased more pensive joy to woo—
At falling eve, by ruin grey,
Muse oe'r the generations, who
Have passed, as we must pass, away.

Or mark oer olive tree & vine
Steep towers uphung; to win from them
Some thought of southern Palestine
Some dream of old Jerusalem.

JK.

Your story of dear Dr Mitford going back from Reading to Three Mile Cross with my letter quite moved me. May God bless you both. My beloved friend how I thank you for y^r letter!— The days of the 'Malvern flirtation['] were years ago—seven eight or nine!—& the poor heroine *very* young. But her feelings are rather quick than deep.[7]

You will like to hear of dear Mr Kenyon. I am so glad! He details no plan—but desires me to write to him at Rome & speaks cursorily of his going there previous to a return home— May God bless you. Love to dear Dr Mitford—

Your own
EBB—

Publication: EBB-MRM, I, 180–182.
Manuscript: Wellesley College.

1. Dated by the further reference to Leigh Hunt's poem, and receipt of Kenyon's letter, which EBB says in no. 738 arrived at "the close of February."
2. See letters 732 and 733.
3. Matthew, 13:36ff.
4. Leigh Hunt's *The Story of Rimini, a Poem* was published in 1816.
5. Cf. Milton, "Il Penseroso" (1673), line 50.
6. Letter 738 identifies the bearer as Mr. Fisher.
7. The brief Henry Mitford/Annie Boyd relationship mentioned in the previous letter.

735. EBB TO MARY RUSSELL MITFORD

Torquay.
Feb.y 31 [*sic*, for ?3 March], [1840][1]

Tell me my dearest Miss Mitford what I am to say for you to M.r Kenyon—that is unless you will write to him yourself. He desires me to write to him at Rome—& I forgot to ask you for at least a message, & I must have it before I write, and if I dont write soon my letter may miss him. So tell me. But he w.d rather, I know by instinct, have your own words in your own ink—only you may not be in a generous mood, having heaps of businesses in your right hand instead of a cornucopia–

By the way, I suspect you of some great scheme .. some gunpowder plot[2] for blowing people up into ecstasies. I long to hear all about it. I did hear a secret last night by the post—a *very highly connected* literary secret too .. but I mean to keep inviolate my integrity & not tell even you. M.r Horne told me. He had two to tell & promised them to me upon my making affidavit of secrecy[3] .. & then said in his humourous way that he w.d communicate one at a time "to see whether I sh.d *just mention it* in the course of a week". So I mean to do despite to his suspicions & my own femineity, by not telling even *you*.

Thank you again & again, my dearest kindest Miss Mitford, my beloved friend, for all your affectionateness—all your kindnesses of word & thought & deed. My heart leaps up[4] always to meet your letters! No—to be sure—if the people had not been talking, you w.d not have miscalled me so!– There was a strangeness in the 'Miss Barrett', which, as people were not talking round *me*, struck me at once. Oh no!– I belong to you my beloved friend by either of my names, Elizabeth .. or the other one sagaciously hinting at my immaturity in several respects .. 'BA' .. *by*—but the courtesy of the prefix & the "chivalry" of the *Barrett* are put aside between *us* .. are they not?—for ever?——[5]

Dear D.r Mitford! To know my writing!—& without spectacles!– Thank you for telling me everything!– And thank you—thank you both— for liking my poem, which I really did not hope you w.d like half so well. I wondered whether *you* might like it—but not at all about the Queen's liking it or seeing it– You are probably quite right in your devination that neither gods nor goddesses made her poetical– Otherwise she w.d care more for Shakespeare. Still there is much in her that interests me.

As to naming the poem to Miss Cocks, even if I were in habits of intercourse with her, I w.d as soon do such a thing as go to court myself with the Athenæum twisted into a foolscap!– Lady Margaret is my friend. I have not seen Miss Cocks, since she grew up–

But do just as you please, in regard to Miss Skennet.[6] I will not say that I sh.d not be pleased to hear of the Queen's having seen it—because

I *shd*, altho' you first suggested the thought. Only believe me to be as honest in assuring you besides that no Queen's look or Queen's smile c^d be worth either to my heart or mind, your approving words!——

Good bye– Terrible east wind—making my hands hot & pulse fast. But I bear up, thank God upon the whole! I thank Him that you are better! & remain with best love to dear Dr Mitford,

yours in truest affection,
EBB–

Publication: EBB-MRM, I, 182–184.
Manuscript: Wellesley College.

1. Year provided by the reference to EBB's verses on the Queen's wedding.
2. The Catholic plot to blow up James I, together with Lords and Commons, at the opening of Parliament on 5 November 1605. Barrels of gunpowder had been hidden under the House of Lords; because of this, a ceremonial search of the vaults is carried out before each opening of Parliament by the Sovereign.

Miss Mitford's "great scheme" involved publication of some of her letters.

3. Despite the "affidavit of secrecy," letter 746 appears to divulge the two secrets, namely, that Horne had asked EBB to write for *The Monthly Chronicle*, and that Horne was writing a new tragedy, not for the stage—this was *Gregory VII*, published in April 1840.
4. Cf. Wordsworth's lines "My Heart Leaps Up When I Behold" (1802).
5. In the following letter, Miss Mitford speaks of writing "in the midst of a quantity of people"; apparently while distracted, she had addressed EBB formally, instead of in her usual, more intimate style. EBB's comment about "chivalry" doubtless refers to the passage in letter 727 in which she said that "Barrett" meant "helmet."
6. EBB has misread Miss Mitford's handwriting. As SD1115.1 makes clear, Miss Mitford intended to send a copy of *The Athenæum* of 15 February, containing EBB's "The Crowned and Wedded Queen," to her friend, Marianne Skerrett, the Queen's Dresser, in the hope of its reaching the Queen. Before she did so, however, she wanted to be sure that EBB had not already taken steps in that direction through the offices of Lady Margaret Cocks, whose niece, Caroline Margaret Cocks, was one of the Queen's Maids of Honour.

736. MARY RUSSELL MITFORD TO EBB

Three Mile Cross,
March 3, 1840.

I had a kind message from Captain Marryat once,[1] when somebody whom he knew was coming here, but have never seen him. Without being one of his indiscriminate admirers, I like parts of his books (some of which I have read to my father), and have been told that they have done good in the profession—suggestions thrown out in them having been taken up and acted upon by the Lords of the Admiralty; and, although a Tory, he takes part with the common sailors. Did I tell you that, the day I wrote in the midst of a quantity of people, a niece of the late Mr. Trollope[2] called, and a nephew of Mrs. Trollope's[3]—both twins, she having a twin sister and he a twin brother. Odd, is it not?

Did you know Dr. Parry?[4] I did; and it is really sad how every lion, who behaves as if he thought himself a lion, shrinks into a very tame menagerie wild beast when one comes before him face to face. I suspect that Sir Walter[5] was about the only one that thoroughly stood the test, and poor Mrs. Hemans, because both were honest lovers of society, with no exclusive veneration for their own books, and therefore came within the exceptive clause in my first sentence.

Heaven bless you, my dearest! I am better, but have had two or three returns of sickness. These winds!

Yours ever,
M. R. M.

Address: Miss Barrett, Torquay.
Text: L'Estrange (2), III, 107–108.

1. Capt. Frederick Marryat, R.N. (1792–1848), novelist, had commanded one of the naval vessels patrolling off St. Helena during Napoleon's exile there. He drew on his experiences in the Navy when writing his novels, and this realism contributed to their success. Among his many works were *The Naval Officer* (1829), *The King's Own* (1830), *Peter Simple* (1834) and *Mr. Midshipman Easy* (1836).
2. Probably Frances Trollope's brother-in-law, the Rev. Henry Trollope, who had died in 1839.
3. Her brother, Henry Milton, had twin sons.
4. Parry being a common name, the reference is insufficient to identify this gentleman, even though the title "Dr." narrows the field.
5. Assumed to be Sir Walter Scott, as Miss Mitford names him and Mrs. Hemans again, in a similar context, in her letter of 20 June 1841.

---

737. EBB TO MARY RUSSELL MITFORD

Torquay.
6th March 1840–

My beloved friend,

I was hesitating whether or not to write when your letter came telling me to do so. I *wanted* to write very much—to assure you of my gladness about 'the PLAN':[1] and then again what you said in regard to the pressure upon your time seemed to say 'Tais toi Jean Jaques'[2] to *me*. All your affectionateness c^d not prevent my letters taking up time in reading as well as answering. Pray my ever dearest Miss Mitford, dont let them teaze you. Now dont write to me again for .. how many weeks? No– The time shant be measured or it will look too sadly long—but dont write until you have time to throw away by handfuls– It will be kind to *me* if you dont.

And I am the more remorseful for my in-the-way-ingness (I recommend that word to your authorship) because I do feel about to be useless in your new undertaking. People have different manners of reading, & I know that very many from the Laureate[3] downwards, are in the habit of filling voluminous commonplace books. I put ashes upon my head in the confession that I am not one of them. 'Every *woman* to her humour!'[4] That commonplacing always seemed to me wearying work, & scarcely calculated, in my own particular experience, to make amends for the expenditure of time which it exacts. I have a legal sort of memory, & when my associations imply the existence of a passage, I know tolerably well where to find it out. Poor Sir Uvedale Price used to call me "a good ferret." Books of mere reasoning & philosophy, I have often fixed in my memory by an analysis—and pages of such analyzing are somewhere nailed up in old boxes of papers, in Wimpole Street—but such, even if I c.d reach them, w.d be of no manner of use to you or anybody in the world— Extracts from books I have scarcely any even there. I never did care to make them—except in the case of books which I was not likely to have access to again. Yes!—and a little MS book beside me now, has extracts from the Greek Fathers &c arranged so as to show their views of certain doctrinal points. And here is a long arch-angelical passage from Swedenborg[5] whom I intended to part from eternally at the time I clipped that lock of hair!– Oh how can I be of use to you?–– You know Fuller, old Fuller, I dare say–[6] Otherwise, two pages of dislocated oddities from him, sh.d go to you, in my handwriting, & might prove usable as quotations applicable or inapplicable. Shall I send *them*?

How can I be of use to you? I am a ferret in a cage here—lying in bed as weak as a baby, & out of reach of books such as might profit you most–

The plan is delightful—I mean for *us*, the readers, the world,—your letters being always very attractive parts of you, & your *early* letters essentially & relatively interesting, of necessity. Do they refer to any particular subject—I mean, are they what are called 'literary letters' or *scenic* letters—or do they gossip "at their own sweet will"[7] (think of Miss Roberts attributing those words to Miss Landon!)[8] on all sorts of subjects? There!—I meant to ask no questions. But it will do as well,—if you dont answer any!–

Surely it is a book for selling—& living besides—whatever name you put to it. And it seems to me that nothing can be better than M.r S.jt Talfourd's suggestion, which I w.d modify by your own in some such manner as this

Letters before Authorship
by an Author.

Surely that arrangement cannot be objectionable on the ground of length,—while it is perfectly applicable & expressive, & catches the ear. I shall be so very glad to hear of triumphant success & profit & praise together. And I shall be sure to hear of it,—if I live out a few months longer. May your undertaking prosper my beloved friend—*may* it!-

In the meantime I am very sorry that you sh.^d be so hummed about by the great swarms of your admirers .. altho' I really could'nt help laughing at the diffident request of the lady unknown, praying for the transcription of her three volumes. Such shadow falls from such laurels!—but people are pardonable for fancying that the Miss Mitford of our village sits in a perpetual sunshine of her own which all their Alexandering⁹ cant disturb,—& that moreover she has an omnipresent smile, to smile the whole world round at once!- Oh I can well believe that *you* are more pestered than others even of equal notoriety—& the reason of it is a crown above the crown!—& not because you are taken for "a good-natured fool". What a reason to suggest!—— *That* made me laugh too!-

As for me, you *have* spoilt me to be sure—but the new pinnacle you forsee for me "above the notoriety," made me laugh again. [']'Thrice the brindled cat hath mewed".¹⁰ No—no—dearest Miss Mitford! I shall always be safe, *below* the danger of notoriety,—were I to live more years than I am likely to do months.

And yet I do believe that I can match your modest lady with another—an absolute stranger to me & mine, who wrote to me several years ago to beg me to lend her a thousand pounds!¹¹ She wanted the money, she said, to enable two young men to go to the university: and understanding that I was an only child & an heiress & very eager about literature besides, she thought me just the person to apply to!- After my first astonishment, I really did rather admire her for making such an effort, in despite of all conventionalities, in behalf of literature & two aspiring lovers of it. I really admired her benevolence & her boldness. Something of the sort too, I said in my reply—explaining the truth that I had ten brothers & sisters, was no heiress; & observing—which at that time was literally true—that if she had asked me for a thousand half-pence I c.^d not have given them to her. Can you believe in the fact of her writing again, to desire me to collect forty pounds *among my friends*—I a stranger to her, among them strangers to her, for others strangers to both parties?—and in the worst fact of all (discovered by me long afterwards) that the two aspiring geniuses were related to her benevolence very closely—the one being her son & the other about to be her son in law?—!- And she a lady—in family—education—& position in society! This does beat the three volumes!—— Yield the palm to me!——

People who are not "ladies" say sometimes .. "I am afraid you are not agreeable". Well!—in that sense of the word (& also, perhaps in worse senses) I cant be agreeable to *you* today—no, not at all, dearest dearest Miss Mitford!- Dear Dr Mitford is a magistrate & a country gentleman, & my own dear Papa was both all his life until the last very few years[12]—but still a country gentleman & a magistrate *per se* I cannot say much eloquent praise of- I have known a good many—& ... I leave the species to *you*. You shall be laureate to them—and I will hide myself somewhere behind Ma^{dme} de Staels'[13] petticoats at the other side of the room-

> Blessings be on them & eternal praise
> The poets!-[14]

How can you write such blasphemies!- Dont you see the advertisement of a new edition of the Tales of the Genii with alterations & additions[15]— & is'nt it by *me*?- And isn't a "needle" used for mending stockings, and a "pen" for making demigods?-[16] Are spirits finely touched but to fine uses?[17] And if Wordsworth had no divinity, sh^d we talk & sigh, any of us, over his humanity?-

And, what *is* the cockney school?[18] I never c^d make out. Hazzlitt Leigh Hunt Keats Charles Lamb, Barry Cornwall—. What is *common* to these gifted writers, that we sh^d make a school with it? Is it not their locality which gave the name—& still less resonably than the Lakes gave another?[19] And are any of us the worse for living in London, if we dont roll in the dust of the streets? And altho' there have been & are among these writers, sins of coarseness & affectation & latitudinarianism,[20] did any one of them all ever perpetrate such an enormity as Mr Ainsworth's Jack Shepherd,[21] he, who for aught I know, may keep sheep in the wilderness—with a crook on one side & Burns's Justice on the other?[22]

And then .. to crown my not being agreeable .. I cant agree about the Legend. I read the whole of it—& although your remark upon the versification seems to me not without its verity—I do think it a beautiful & most touching play.[23] Ginevra is Griselda[24] with a "touch of nature";[25] & tho bursting of natural emotion thro' the meshes of her sweet patience, quite overcame me. Surely there must be pathos & power in whatever makes our tears flow & pulses beat! I *think* there must.

The "ill humour" if unheroical & unpoetical in itself as a *tragic power*, proves the faculty of the author who c^d turn it to such tragic uses. Do read the whole play when you have an opportunity. I struggle, you see, to be agreeable.

Did you ever read Leigh Hunt[']s stanzas to his sick child—

> "Sleep breathes at last from out thee
> My little patient boy-"?-[26]

And will you ever forgive all my disagreeableness—my impertinen[c]es, my contrariousness?- Here are contradictions enough for a lifetime—even a woman's!- But I am always *sincere* in writing to you—& none the less in assuring you, dearest dearest Miss Mitford of my true & grateful & *uplooking* affection of

Your

E B Barrett—

My thankful love to dear D.ʳ Mitford— May you be better *still*— I fear tho' improvement has not been regularly progressive.

What can the Findens mean? Are the three months expired yet?— I have asked a thousand & one questions in this letter. It is a catechism of a letter—but dont, if you are busy (& you must be) say *M* or *N* to it.[27]

Publication: EBB-MRM, I, 184–189.
Manuscript: Wellesley College.

1. In a letter of 19 February 1840 (L'Estrange (2), III, 106–107), Miss Mitford speaks of being encouraged to publish her letters, written years before, to Sir William Elford (1749–1837), the banker and politician. However, EBB's apologies for being unable to help with notes of her reading suggest that Miss Mitford was contemplating something of broader scope. Whatever her plan, nothing came of it.
2. See letter 709, note 3.
3. Currently Robert Southey (1774–1843).
4. A play on the title of Jonson's *Every Man in His Humour* (1598).
5. Emanuel Swedenborg (1688–1772), the Swedish theologian, philosopher and mystic, in whose teachings EBB maintained a life-long interest. Of the several notebooks listed in *Reconstruction*, D1415 refers to Swedenborg.
6. Thomas Fuller (1608–61), divine, whose book, *The Historie of the Holy Warre* (3rd edn., 1647) is listed in *Reconstruction* (A1006). He is also known for his *Good Thoughts in Bad Times* (1645). The notebook mentioned in note 5 also includes EBB's comments on Fuller's work.
7. Wordsworth's verses "Composed upon Westminster Bridge, September 3, 1802" (1807), line 12.
8. In the memoir included in *The Zenana and Minor Poems of L.E.L.* (1839), Emma Roberts said that Miss Landon "rushed fearlessly into print, not dreaming for a moment, that verses which were poured forth like the waters from a fountain, gushing, as she has beautifully expressed it, of their own sweet will, could ever provoke stern or harsh criticism" (p. 9).
9. Dryden, "The Cock and the Fox" (*Fables Ancient and Modern*, 1700), lines 659–670: "Ye Princes rais'd by Poets to the Gods, / And Alexander'd up in lying Odes." "Perpetual sunshine" refers back to EBB's earlier comment about Alexander and Diogenes (see letter 360, note 1).
10. *Macbeth*, IV, 1, 1.
11. Mrs. Mushet; see letters 362 and 364.
12. As far as is known, Edward Moulton-Barrett only served as a magistrate during his years at Hope End.
13. Anne Louise Germaine de Staël (*née* Necker, 1766–1817), whose *Corinne* was thought by EBB to be "an immortal book" (letter 453).
14. Cf. Wordsworth, "Personal Talk" (1807), 51–53.
15. *The Athenæum* of 18 January 1840 (no. 638, p. 58) had advertised a new edition "revised, and in part rewritten, by a Lover of the Marvellous and the True." For details of the original edition, see letter 733, note 11.
16. This foreshadows a recurrent theme: the relative merits of "needle and thread" (i.e., domestic) and "pen and ink" (i.e., professional) writers.
17. Cf. *Measure for Measure*, I, 1, 35–36.
18. An article "On the Cockney School of Poetry" in *Blackwood's Edinburgh Magazine*, October 1817 (pp. 38–41), described Leigh Hunt as its "chief Doctor and Professor." The appellation was pejorative, denoting, in the words of the writer, absolute ignorance of Greek literature, and no more than a smattering of Latin, Italian and French writers, coupled with "extreme moral depravity."

19. The Lake poets included Wordsworth, Coleridge and Southey, from their residing in the Lake District of England. This label was also used pejoratively at first, but soon lost all hint of disparagement.
20. Latitudinarians favoured latitude in thought, action, or conduct, especially in religious matters (*OED*).
21. See letter 730, notes 2 and 4.
22. As Justice figures in several of Burns's poems, it is not possible to interpret EBB's reference with certainty. She may have had in mind the lines: "Dame Justice fu' brawly has sped: / She's gotten the heart of a Bushby, / But Lord! what's become o' the head?" ("Ballads on Mr. Heron's Election, 1795," no. 2, verse 3, lines 2–4).
23. Leigh Hunt's just-published *A Legend of Florence*, mentioned in letter 733.
24. In Hunt's play, Ginevra is the wife of a Florentine noble. Griselda was the patient heroine in the final story in Boccaccio's *The Decameron*, tested and tested again by her husband. She was also depicted by Chaucer in "The Clerk's Tale."
25. *Troilus and Cressida*, III, 3, 175.
26. "To T.L.H., Six Years Old, During a Sickness" (1816), 1–2. Thornton Leigh Hunt (1810–73) was Leigh Hunt's eldest son.
27. See letter 727, note 17.

738. EBB TO JOHN KENYON

Torquay
March 7 1840.

My dear cousin & friend,

I am disheartened in beginning to write to you & as insecure of my letter's reaching you as if it were to go by the via lactea[1] where I c^d learn nothing of the foreign postage. Your own was dated November & did not reach me until the close of February. I just waited to ask Miss Mitford for a message—& she replying that she w^d write herself to you at Rome if she did not expect you in England immediately, makes me really hesitate whether to write myself or not. But you may be at Rome still– You ask me to write—I will run the risk of it.

Thank you most earnestly for so kindly thinking of me at Florence! Only why did you go to Mr Fisher instead of to the post.[2] 'Patience & shuffle the cards'[3] always must be after those dealings with private hands!– And Papa says that I have a particular taste for paying postages—so that, .. particularly in these barren days of Rowland Hill,[4] .. it is a pity you did'nt indulge me. Here you will find us all thinking like Parliamentary dignitaries—prepaying "a penny for our thoughts",[5] & wondering in the high sublime of our vanities & the deep obscure of our ignorances as to *cheapness!*——

But indeed & indeed I was delighted to see your writing. I had begun taking my state with yours, by being still with your wanderings afar, to fancy that I never again was to see so much of you! Thank you for the pleasure of the undoing of that fancifulness as well as for the other pleasurablenesses of your letter—ending as was fitting, in those close clear classical stanzas which brought you before me at once.[6] You left behind you, by the way, a song for the Tableaux—& while you were praising Florence we were praising you. It was extracted in the Athenæum & elsewhere[7]—& worthily—although inferior to that Immortal who floated away on wine to his immortality!–[8] The Tableaux Annual prospered this year, above any annual. Well, it might– The engravings rise far above their predecessors,—& dear Miss Mitford's stories are more than usually full of interest & character. Mr Horne too, the Cosmo de' Medici Horne, vouchsafed what he called a "tragic brevity" which c^d not, being his, fail in power & imagination. As for me I only sate in the chimney corner & told a ghost story. Miss Mitford sends you her kindest regards,—and I am able, thank God, to tell you that she is better than she has been. At one time she was so ill as to make me quite uncomfortable,—her fathers illness having tried & worn her more than appeared at first!. He is quite well again now.

You desire to know all about us– Papa is in London!– He left me a fortnight before Christmas intending & promising to return very soon. And I have not seen him yet!– Well—there is nothing for it but patience & endurance ... & an inward vow that if I can leave Torquay before next winter, I will– He has so much London occupation, that it is next to impossible, his being with me much, at this distance of two hundred miles. But in his kindness—which touches me even to pain sometimes in thinking of—he lets me keep with me both my sisters & my eldest brother—so many comforts stripped away from him for my sake!– All this human love is tender & beautiful of itself, & none the less for that secret meaning of pathos in which it shadows forth the Divine. I have been confined to my bed since October, & am pretty nearly as weak as a baby—only I can write you see, & can*not* make a noise!– My voice has quite failed– But I recovered it last year in the warm weather, & my physician thinks it will return to me now. I am not, he assures me, essentially worse since October—(when the colder weather came on, & poor Dr Barry's sudden death by fever affected me naturally & deeply—) and it is considered "both possible & probable" that in the case of my passing a favorable summer, the next winter may be an improvement upon the present. In fact I *may* (although the case is very precarious) recover *in a measure*—but never to an ordinary degree of strength & health.

Papa dear Papa is quite well. He gave me his picture when I saw him last,[9] & it hangs just opposite to my eyes all day & night. George is on *circuit!* From my brothers in Jamaica, comes nothing but good news—both of them being perfectly well satisfied with a sugar cane life. But oh Mr Kenyon, what pain it gave me to think of their going without a farewell!– God's will be done– May He bless *you!*– There must be much to enjoy & triumph in where you are—but dont forget England. Your friends the Garrows are quite well. I hear of them. I see nobody except my physician—but I *shall*. And I did see Miss Garrow three times during the summer. She is full of talent & enthusiasm—but I confess myself disappointed in her poetry. It is feeling & graceful- *Is* IT MORE? There is too much conventionalism in the poetry of the day.

I have much to say—but I cannot fancy that you will read it—that it will reach you!-

With united kindest regards, believe me
Ever affectionately yours
Elizabeth B Barrett.

Do let me hear from you now & then—if only by a few lines. It is so pleasant to me.

Publication: None traced.
Manuscript: Berg Collection.

1. "Milky Way."
2. Probably William Fisher (1817–95), an Irishman who had studied in Italy and who exhibited at the Royal Academy, the Dublin Academy, the British Institute and the New Water-colour Society. He painted portraits of Landor and Kenyon, and RB later (1854) sat for him.
3. Cervantes, *The Ingenious Gentleman Don Quixote of La Mancha*, pt. II, ch. 23.
4. A reference to the newly-introduced, prepaid penny postage, the brain-child of Rowland Hill (1795–1879).
5. One of the proverbs listed in Morris Palmer Tilley's *Dictionary of the Proverbs in England in the Sixteenth and Seventeenth Centuries* (1950). No derivation is given.
6. i.e., the stanzas quoted by EBB to Miss Mitford in letter 734.
7. *The Athenæum* of 26 October 1839 (no. 626, pp. 809–810), in its review of the 1840 *Findens' Tableaux*, quoted four verses of Kenyon's "To an Æolian Harp."
8. A reference to Kenyon's "Champagne Rose," embodied in Miss Mitford's "The Wager" in the 1838 *Findens' Tableaux*.
9. Presumably painted by the man referred to as "Papa's artist, Mr. Mills" in letter 731.

---

739. RB TO ALFRED DOMETT[1]

[London]
[7 March 1840][2]

My Dear Domett,

Pray accept the book,[3] and do not reject me. However, I hope you will like it a little, and beat it famously yourself[4] ere the season is out.

Ever yours most truly,
R Browning.

Sat.^y Night.
St Perpetua's Day!! (see Almanack)

Publication: RB-AD, pp. 27–28.
Manuscript: British Library.

1. For details of RB's friendship with Domett, see pp. 315–317. See also "Robert Browning and Alfred Domett," by W. Hall Griffin, in *The Contemporary Review*, January 1905 (pp. 95–115).
2. Dated by reference to St. Perpetua's Day.
3. *Sordello*.
4. A pencil note by Alfred Domett appears at the foot of the page of the album in which he preserved this letter: "A little bit of playful affection this, taken as such and perfectly understood on both sides.—A.D."

740. RB TO WALTER SAVAGE LANDOR[1]

Hanover Cottage, Southampton S.[t]
Camberwell, London.
March 7. 1840.

My dear Sir,
May I beg you will accept the accompanying little book published to-day?[2] I had rather you praised it than anybody else now in the world.

Faithfully yours,
Rob.[t] Browning.

W. S. Landor Esq

Publication: None traced.
Manuscript: R.H. Taylor Collection.

1. For details of RB's friendship with Landor, see pp. 323–325.
2. The volume, *Sordello*, is also in the R.H. Taylor Collection. It is inscribed: "Walter S. Landor, / from R.B–" (see *Reconstruction*, C566).

741. EDWARD MOULTON-BARRETT (FATHER) TO EBB

[London]
March 9. 1840–

My beloved Ba
As I am sending off a note to dear Bell, I must just put one line in the envelope for you, to tell you the old tale, how you live in my affections, & the many anxieties I suffer on your account, in Consequence of the long continuance of this inexorable wind sparing neither man or beast– But I trust that He Who holdeth the wind in his hand, will moderate it & temper it to you the shorn lamb–[1]

Alfred Domett

Walter Savage Landor

No. 742 9 March [1840] 255

We have heard nothing of the learned gentleman[2] since he left but I suppose that he is well, & looking on the engagements of others in the very opposite spirit of the tenth commandment—[3]

What a poor miserable attempt of an apology for Southey has Landor made in the Examiner of Saturday & to my mind as poor or nearly so a mention of the Queen's marriage.[4]

I fear that I have been very remiss in not having returned Arabel my best thanks for her work, which is intended to grace my feet, pray give them for me with my warmest affections—

Were you not amused with Sette's immense assurance in going up with the Oxford Address, not knowing an individual in the Train;[5] it beats every thing I ever heard, but it seems to sit very long upon him, & to be thought nothing out of the common way— He is however a dear good kind fellow, both my right & left hand. Whilst you are my *head*—

Dearest Ba
Y^{rs} most affectly—
E M Barrett

Address, on integral page: For my Ba.
Publication: None traced.
Manuscript: Berg Collection.

1. "Maria," in Laurence Sterne's *A Sentimental Journey Through France and Italy* (1768), II, 175–176.
2. i.e., George Moulton-Barrett.
3. "Thou shalt not covet thy neighbour's house," etc.
4. *The Examiner* of 8 March (no. 1675, p. 147) printed an ode by Landor in defence of Southey. A note explained that the ode was "Suggested by verses in the *Globe* of Thursday the 27th ult., grossly reproaching the Laureate for his silence on the occasion of the Royal Marriage."
5. The Duke of Wellington, as Chancellor of the University of Oxford, together with a deputation of officials and "several hundred members of the University," had presented to the Queen on 3 March an "address of cordial congratulations" on the occasion of her marriage (*The Times*, 4 March 1840). *The Times* of 2 March had given details of the forthcoming ceremony, together with the time and place of assembly, and Sette (with no association with the University) had borrowed his brother's dress coat and insinuated himself into the delegation (see letter 748).

---

742. RB TO ELIZA FLOWER

[London]
Monday Night. March 9. [1840][1]

My dear Miss Flower,

I have this moment received your very kind note—of course, I understand your objections .. how else? But they are somewhat lightened already (confess—nay, "confess" is vile—you will be rejoiced to holla from the house-top)—will go on, or rather go off, lightening, and will be .. oh, where *will* they be half a dozen years hence? Meantime praise what you can praise, do me all the good you can, you and Mr Fox (as if you will not!)—for I have a headful of projects—mean to song-write, play-write forthwith,—and, believe me, dear Miss Flower,

Yours ever faithfully,
Robert Browning.

By the way, you speak of "Pippa"[2]—could we not make some arrangement about it,—the lyrics *want* your music—five or six in all—how say you? When these three plays are out I hope to "build" a huge Ode—but "all goeth but God's will!"[3]

Publication: LRB, p. 4.
Manuscript: Michael Meredith.

    1. 9 March fell on Monday in 1840.
    2. *Pippa Passes* was published in April 1841, but DeVane (p. 91) conjectures that it was written in the late spring and early summer of 1839.
    3. EBB used this quotation as the motto for "An Island" in *The Seraphim*. It was "a line from an old poet whose antiquity has buried his name" (letter 619).

743. RB TO RICHARD MONCKTON MILNES

Camberwell
Tuesday M^g [?10] [March 1840][1]

My dear Milnes,
    I shall be delighted to breakfast with you on Thursday.
    I hope Sordello may please you, I am sure.

Yours most truly,
R Browning.

Publication: None traced.
Manuscript: Trinity College, Cambridge.

    1. Dated by the publication of *Sordello* and RB's residence at Camberwell, from which he moved in December 1840. It is not known when he first met Milnes.

744. RB TO ANDRÉ VICTOR AMÉDÉE DE RIPERT-MONCLAR

Londres,
10 Mars. 1840.

Mon cher Amédée,

Est-a que je n'aurai jamais de vos nouvelles? Voici enfin ce pauvre Sordello[1] dont nous avons tant causé dans le tem[p]s[2]—qu'il me soit bon à quelque chose en me procurant l'occasion de vous rappeler que je suis
toujours à vous de cœur et
d'âme,
Robert Browning.

Publication: None traced.
Manuscript: Yale University.

Translation: My dear Amédée, / Shall I never hear from you? Here at long last is that poor Sordello[1] about which we talked so much in the past—may it serve a good purpose in providing me the opportunity to remind you that I am / still yours with heart and soul, / Robert Browning.

1. This copy of *Sordello* is now at Yale (see *Reconstruction*, C571).
2. For a comment on RB's spelling of French words, see letter 509, note 15.

745. WALTER SAVAGE LANDOR TO RB

[Bath]
[*Postmark:* 18 March 1840]

My dear Sir

Three days have nearly slipped by since I received your poem,[1] and a family which came to Bath about the same time, claiming all the rights of old acquaintance, has prevented me from enjoying it. You much overrate my judgement: but, whatever it is, you shall have it, before I have redd it so often as I redd Paracelsus—

With many thanks, I remain, My dear Sir,

Your very obliged
W S Landor

Address: Robert Browning Esqr. / Hanover Cottage / Southampton S!. / Camberwell.
Publication: BBIS-5, p. 17 (as 19 March 1840).
Manuscript: Armstrong Browning Library.

1. Landor's copy of *Sordello* is now in the R.H. Taylor Collection at Princeton (see *Reconstruction*, C566).

746. EBB TO MARY RUSSELL MITFORD

[Torquay]
Saturday. March 21. 1840

My beloved friend,

I waited to see if Howel's letters w^d come to me as I expected.[1] They have not—but in the case of your not having access to them, they *shall*. Let me know by a word. W^d this do for a motto

> "I find you all record and prophecie"
> *Donne*.[2]

or Ford's

> Thoughts fly away– Time hath passed them;
> Wake now, awake! See and taste them[3]

or perhaps better than the rest Ben Jonson's

> "It hath been your ill fortune to be taken out of the nest young."
> *Masque of* AUGURS[4]

The hint at the augury does'nt seem much amiss—but you may think of more pregnant sentences, mine being quite dismissible "at your pleasure, Lady".[5] Pray do tell me the whole story long about the letters[6]--I mean, how they succeed in London, & when they are to appear. And yet—dont! You must have so much to do. Only in writing the yea or nay about Howel, you might let fall one upon this subject also. I think very very much about you!–

Thank you for your wonderful tales of blunderful people—people without knowledge & feeling, or *tact*, to fill the place of either. The penny post[7] must let in a flood upon you, over & above your & Noah's old one. Dearest, dearest Miss Mitford—there is the effect, you see, of wearing your heart upon your sleeve & walking through the village with it!– Daws will be daws![8]

The only apparent way of deliverance for you is to set up a scarecrow—to set about writing something savage directly (the letters wont do), grinning horrible a ghastly smile[9] in the notes. Not that you c^d do it by yourself—but you have friends who c^d help you. I for instance c^d tomahawk plenty of commonplaces for you, from ... There! that will do! ——

But now—(oh these obstinate people!—but we call ourselves firm!) be sure dearest dearest Miss Mitford that you dont convince me even against my will. I cant be convinced. I wont be convinced. I am in/con/vincible.[10] Your tales are very amusing tales, but have nothing to do with my geniuses. My genii dont wear velvet pelisses. Indeed they are generally in wings. My genii may be very idle people, & are in fact by no means as steady & regular & rational as Mrs Hoffland w^d approve of[11]—but the besetting sin with *them* is very seldom meanness & dirtiness, such as the lady of the very clean pelisse displayed toward you. My firm conviction is, that the world is the world & a very dirty place at the cleanest—but still that the pure (to use a strange word) the pure, neat, unadulterated ladies & gentlemen in it are apt to be dirtier, by a very considerable degree, than all the "pen & ink" you revile,[12] c^d make the fingers of others. Is it not that we unconsciously, & properly, & justly enough, measure high imagination with actions not high enough to touch that height—& that we are *shocked* by the contrast of the ideal & real, in the case of certain distinguished persons?. Oh—am I not firm?– And moreover—oyez oyez[13]—if I were to see you & hear you ever so much, you never could succeed in *"disenchanting"* me! How sh^d you, when your forte is, *enchanting*?

But lest you sh^d seriously suppose me capable of treating grave subjects with absolute levity, do let me gravely assure you that "I hate" & as Donne says, "I thank God for it—*perfectly*"[14] all these coteries, (as far as I guess their character) all these menials of literature, all these putters of noble things to vile uses, these desecrators of wisdom & greatness in the very eyes of the wise & the great. Here however I stop. Do let me! For I cannot choose but hold with rare Ben,[15] that "there goeth more to the making of a good poet than of a sheriff"[16] .. albeit the sheriff sh^d be Mr Sheriff Evans!–[17] By the way, the lion, the great lion of the Zoological gardens is said to have a bilious attack, and I am going to petition the House of Commons to let him out. Absolute freedom will be necessary—& we can have his picture afterwards—such of us as survive.

Did I tell you that I am going to write sometimes for the Monthly Chronicle. Mr Horne asked me. Not that he is editor– By the way, I must try to find the message which I received from him for you, the very day I sent away my last letter. Here it is "*I received the same from the kind Miss Mitford. I never thanked her for it at the time—I had no time: and when it became too late, I did'nt know what to say "altogether". When you next write to her pray tell her of my grateful predicament*".

I believe there is to be a new tragedy soon, but not for the stage. But it will be better perhaps not to mention this immediately.[18]

I am as well today as is possible after a sleepless night. The weather is very trying—& I have not been suffered by my Liege Lord physician, to have my bed made, for above a month. But altogether I bear up tolerably. What they mean to do with me this summer is matter of fidgetting. Here, I am sure not to stay, if I can move,—my own longing being for London—& my physician's I see too plainly, for the torrid zone. Do not mention this to anybody, dearest Miss Mitford. May God bless you, & dear Dr Mitford!— May God bless you in health & strength & dearer blessings—& prosper you in those honorable & exalting labours which involve in them a happier means than rest, & a sweeter & prouder end than fame. In the truest esteem & attachment,

your EBB—

It has amused me to think of the assurance of the Athenæum: Be certain that it will never be looked at.[19] *I* am! At any rate you have given me the best "introduction to court" I c^d have, in calling me your friend—a name & fame in one, & dear & grateful to me. *Thank you.*

Mr Merry has sent me a kind interesting letter which I am under a temptation, from a kind word, to answer. Not angry with me at all. Tell me about Howel.

Address: Miss Mitford / Three Mile Cross / near Reading / Prep^d
Publication: EBB-MRM, I, 189–192.
Manuscript: Wellesley College.

1. *Epistolæ Ho-Elianæ: Familiar Letters domestic and forren* (1645–47) by James Howell (1594?–1666) author and Historiographer Royal to King Charles II. He also wrote Δενδρολογια. *Dodona's Grove, or the vocall forrest* (1640). Later editions of both these works formed lots 772 and 773 of *Browning Collections* (see *Reconstruction*, A1260 and A1261).
2. "To the Countess of Bedford" (no. 2, 1633), line 52.
3. *The Sun's Darling* (1657), I, 1, 11–12.
4. Lines 50–51.
5. Cf. Byron, *Marino Faliero, Doge of Venice* (1820), V, 1, 329.
6. Miss Mitford's projected edition of letters (see letter 737, note 1). It seems probable that her request to borrow Howell's *Letters* was connected in some way with this project.
7. See letters 719, note 2 and 738, note 4.
8. "Daws" used here in its figurative sense, meaning "simpleton" or "sluggard" (*OED*).
9. *Paradise Lost*, II, 846.
10. A play on "thou art invincible," the answer given to Alexander the Great by the Oracle of Delphi.
11. Barbara Hofland (*née* Wreaks, 1770–1844) was the author of the popular novel *The Son of a Genius; a tale, for the use of youth* (1816).
12. See letter 737, note 16.
13. "Hear ye, hear ye," the call to attention used by Town Criers.
14. Cf. Donne's "Satyres" (1633), II, 1–2.
15. See letter 706, note 14.
16. *Every Man in His Humour*, V, 5, 39–40 (revised text of 1616).
17. A reference to a celebrated case involving parliamentary privilege. To help defray the cost of printing papers and reports for Parliament, Messrs. Hansard, the parliamentary printers, had been given authority to sell copies to the public. One such report, by the Inspector of Prisons, stated that "improper books" were finding their way into Newgate and mentioned in particular "a book of a most disgusting nature" published by Stockdale in 1827. Stockdale brought an action against Messrs. Hansard for libel, but the Attorney-General claimed that the publication, having been sold by order of the House of Commons, was privileged. A Select Committee took up the question, and held that no

other tribunal could define parliamentary privilege, directly or incidentally. Because Hansard, on instructions from the Commons, did not appear in court, Stockdale was awarded £600 damages, and the Sheriffs of London and Middlesex levied that amount on Hansard's goods. Ordered by the Commons to return the money, the sheriffs refused to comply, holding that, as officers of the court, they were bound to do the court's bidding, whereupon they were committed to the custody of the Sergeant-at-Arms for breach of privilege. Apart from the matter of defining the relative powers of the courts and Parliament, the case attracted much attention, as it was felt by many that innocent parties were being punished for doing their duty. Evans was kept in custody for several weeks, and was finally released because his health was suffering.

18. These two paragraphs reveal the two secrets mentioned by EBB in letter 735. She provided two contributions to *The Monthly Chronicle*; "A Night-Watch by the Sea" appeared in the issue of April 1840 (p. 297) and "A Lay of the Rose" in the July number (pp. 13–17). The latter was included in *Poems* (1844) with its title changed to "A Lay of the Early Rose."

Horne's new tragedy was *Gregory VII*.

19. A reference to Miss Mitford's plan of sending a copy of *The Athenæum*, containing EBB's "The Crowned and Wedded Queen," to her friend Miss Skerrett, in the hope that it might reach the Queen (see letter 735, note 6).

747. RB TO ALFRED DOMETT

[London]
Monday M^g [23 March 1840][1]

My dear Domett,

I was a little way out of Town when your letter arrived—how much it gratified me, blame as well as praise,[2] I cannot tell you, nor need, I hope. The one point that wants correcting is where you surmise that I am "difficult on system"– *No*, really—the fact is I live by myself, write with no better company, and forget that the "lovers" you mention are part & parcel of that self, and their choosing to comprehend *my* comprehensions—but an indifferent testimony to their value: whence it happens, that precisely when "lovers," one and all, bow themselves out at the book's conclusion ... enter (according to an old stage-direction) two fishermen to the one angel, Stokes and Nokes[3] to the Author of "Venice"[4] (who *should* have been there, *comme de droit*,[5] had I known him earlier)— and ask, reasonably enough, why the publication is not confined to the aforesaid brilliant folks, and what do hard boards and soft paper solicit if not *their* intelligence, such as it may be? I wish I had thought of this before—meantime I am busy on some plays (those advertised)[6] that shall be plain enough if my pains are not thrown away—and, in lieu of Sir Philip[7] & his like, Stokes may assure himself that I see *him*—(first row of the pit, under the second Oboe, hat between legs, play-bill on a spike, and a "comforter" round his throat "because of the draught from the stage"—) and unless *he* leaves off sucking his orange at the pathetic morsels of my play—I hold them naught.

I have just received a note from Chr. Dowson—a piece of himself, so kind is it—and must try to thank him forthwith: after all, writing unintelligible metaphy⟨si⟩cs, is not voted as bad as murder—some murders—this Islington affair, for instance:[8] Nay, Bell's Life in London, of yesterday week, after exposing the malice of a report "that the long and earnestly expected set-to between the Snuffy Seedsman and Bermondsey George was *off*"—and setting an anxious correspondent ("Alligris") right on "Grab the black tan crop-eared dog's mother's pedigree,["] assured its readers "Browning" was "a lofty poet"—somebody must have vouched to the Editor for my being seven feet high.[9]

I must get Dowson's assent ere I try to tempt you here, for the quietest of dinners, ere long: will you much mind the walk, this odd weather? Snow fell a minute since, and now a sun (after a sort) shines merrily– Don't you feel a touch of the *vagabond*, in early spring-time? How do the lines go—

"ηλιβατοις υπο κευθμωσι γενοιμαν
ινα με πτερουσσαν ορνιν
θεος εν πταναις αγελαισι θειη–
αρθειην δε επι ποντιον,
κυμα τας Αδριηνας ακτας,
Ηριδανου θ' 'υδωρ.["][10]

and so would you, I fancy–

Ever yours most truly,
R Browning.–

Docket, in hand of Domett: R.d March 1840. AD.
Publication: RB-AD, pp. 28–31.
Manuscript: British Library.

1. Dated by the docket and the references to *Bell's Life in London*.
2. The "blame as well as praise" would have been in response to RB's gift of *Sordello* (letter 739).
3. Fictitious names, the equivalent of the impersonal "A" and "B," used for illustrative purposes.
4. i.e., Domett himself. RB's copy of this 1839 work formed part of lot 1063 in *Browning Collections* (see *Reconstruction*, A810).
5. "By right."
6. These were *Pippa Passes, King Victor and King Charles*, and *Mansoor the Hierophant* (later called *The Return of the Druses*). An advertisement at the end of *Sordello* announced them as "nearly ready." However, as letter 754 indicates, not all copies of the book contained this notice.
7. The context suggests that RB's reference is to Sir Philip Sidney (1554–86), who discussed the use of fictitious names ("John a noakes" and "John a stile") by poets and lawyers in *An Apologie for Poetrie* (1595).
8. *Bell's Life in London and Sporting Chronicle*, 22 March 1840, carried an account of the brutal murder in Islington the previous Tuesday of John Templeman: "The forehead was completely dashed in by a blow from some heavy instrument; the nose and both jaw-bones were smashed, and the mouth was severely bruised and mutilated. It is the opinion that the violence must have been inflicted by a hatchet. Three of the deceased's teeth were found lying about. . . ."

9. *Bell's Life in London*, 15 March, contained a short review of *Sordello* (see p. 416). RB's reference to his being called "a lofty poet" is perhaps a paraphrase of "the vision and the faculty divine" ascribed to him. However, a careful search of all the issues for March and April failed to disclose anything about "Snuffy Seedsman" *et al.*, so we must assume that, tongue-in-cheek, RB was parodying the paper's style.

10. Euripides, *Hippolytus*, 732–737: "Under the arched cliffs O were I lying, / That there to a bird might a God change me, / And afar mid the flocks of the winged things flying / Over the swell of the Adrian sea / I might soar—and soar,—upon poised wings dreaming, / O'er the strand where Eridanus' waters be" (trans. Arthur S. Way, 1980). The Eridanus was one of the tributaries of what is now known as the Po.

---

748. EBB TO MARY RUSSELL MITFORD

[Torquay]
Saturday [28] March 1840.[1]

My ever beloved friend,

I am grieved past words, at this new sorrow .. the accident to dear D.[r] Mitford & the accumulation of anxiety to yourself.[2] Dearest Miss Mitford, how it must have shocked you. Looking around us in this world, even where our horizon is rounded to the faces of the most loving & beloved, is a mournful thing– Oh for help & grace to look UP more earnestly & perpetually, where the Fountain of Love is also the source of joy!– May the God of all comfort,[3] comfort you in all ways!–

After all, he is *doing well*––you must think of *that*, my beloved friend, & take courage. Will you fold up one word of information now & then, directing it to me? I mean, literally, as little in the inside of a note .. as the post-people are at liberty to read outside. I w.[d] not for the world press upon your time—& yet I do want to know how he goes on to be.

But the arm will be strong again & everything well again! I have good hope! I love you & pray for you—be sure of *that*. And dont neglect yourself– Dont forget to sleep & rest when you should,—I do not say for *your* sake—which w.[d] be a vain adjuration .. but for *his* sake .. for the sake of the health & life of one, to whom you are, in a sense, health & life. Think of this, dearest Miss Mitford.

When everything is right again, I shall be delighted to see M.[r] Darley's play, if you keep your kind promise of trusting it with me.[4] Happy M.[r] Darley, to be so *prosylytable*– Everybody is'nt so!– Oh yes—I *have* Sylvia or the May Queen among my books in London.[5] Dont you remember telling me to read it, & did'nt I obey you & buy it directly? It overflows with poetry, in the Aminta, Guarini, Sad Shepherd, Faithful Shepherdess way:[6] but does as pastorals can scarcely choose but do, hold on to one by the skirts of one's fancy rather than by the imagination in a high sense, or by the *heart poetical*,[7] in any—I mean with the hands of passion & sentiment. Oh but it is true, lovely, fantastical poetry .. & there is besides, power of language & metrical skilfulness. I saw Thomas á Becket, praised, altho' something coldly as I fancied, in the Athenæum[8]—to which I knew before that M! Darley contributed. *He* wrote the able *guilty* article upon Ion[9]—& he is to be traced very often by his ability. Disinherited for being a poet!! There is an alderman for you!–[10] Consistent, after his kind. "Blame not the cobbler for his black thumbs".[11] People *may* have black thumbs you see, without "pen & ink"!–

As to Buckingham Palace, dearest dearest Miss Mitford, I never dreamt of anything beyond silence—or at least if I dreamt, I *dreamt*.[12] I never *thought* it. Sette is more successful in making his way to court than I—even with your presentation! Think of Sette's assurance in costuming himself in a long tailed coat belonging to his elder brother, & squeezing himself into St James's Palace, with the *address from Oxford!*[13] of course at the momently risk of being turned out, long coat & all!– But he saw the Queen & Prince Albert .. & thinks no more of the *means*, Papa says,—than if he had done the most natural thing possible. So when I want to go to court, I shall go with Set!– What nonsense to teaze you with!– I am very anxious about you notwithstanding–

Your ever attached
EBB.

I am so sorry to hear of M! Kenyon's having been unwell: was it a rheumatic attack? Did you hear? I am tolerable, assailed by feverishness though towards night more than usual, from that eternal wind. You don't mention *Howell*.[14]

Address: Miss Mitford / Three Mile Cross / near Reading / Prepaid.
Publication: EBB-MRM, I, 192–194.
Manuscript: Wellesley College.

1. Dated by the reference to Dr. Mitford's accident.
2. In a letter to Miss Anderdon of 26 March 1840, Miss Mitford said "one rib was broken, if not more, and the right arm. All this at eighty makes a sad amount of suffering. At present the being totally disabled, and the loss of sleep and appetite caused by his confinement, have had a very bad effect upon his spirits—he won't see any one, and is very much depressed indeed" (Chorley, I, 174).
3. II Corinthians, 1:3.
4. *Thomas à Becket* (1840) by George Darley (1795–1846), poet and writer for *The Athenæum*.
5. Published in 1827, Darley's *Sylvia; or, The May Queen* formed part of *Browning Collections* (see *Reconstruction*, A760).
6. *Aminta* (1573), by Torquato Tasso (1544–95), first appeared in English translation in 1591. Giovanni Battista Guarini (1538–1612) was the author of *Il Pastor Fido* (1590), modelled on *Aminta*, which also provided the basis of the plot of Fletcher's *The Faithful Shepherdess* (1609?). Jonson's play, *The Sad Shepherd*, was left unfinished at the time of his death in 1637 and was published posthumously.

7. Cf. *The Christian Year* (1827), XXX, by John Keble (1792–1866), divine and poet.
8. *The Athenæum* of 14 March 1840 (no. 646, pp. 204–205), in reviewing *Thomas à Becket*, spoke of its "unsuitability to the stage" and said "we are half-inclined to regret the form which ... his work has taken."
9. A negative review of Talfourd's *Ion*, in *The Athenæum* of 28 May 1836 (no. 448, pp. 371–373), generally attributed to Chorley, was, in fact, written by Darley.
10. According to Miss Mitford, Darley was the "son of a rich alderman of Dublin, who disinherited him because he would write poetry" (L'Estrange (2), III, 56).
11. A variation on the old proverb, "the richer the cobbler, the blacker his thumbs."
12. See letter 735, note 6.
13. See letter 741, note 5.
14. i.e., whether she did need the loan of EBB's copy of Howell's *Letters* (see letter 746).

---

749. Bryan Waller Procter to RB

5 Grove End Place[,] St Johns Wood
1840 March 30.th

My dear Browning

All thanks for the Sordello—which I have this Instant (11 o'Clock Monday Evening) received—& which I acknowledge thus early, that you may not deem me remiss. The book has remained at Storeys Gate ever since you left it there.

The *out*side is admirable, for its simplicity & elegance. *Now* for the *In*side!——

Wishing you (& it) all success & pleasure.

I am very sincerely yours
B W Procter

Address, on integral page: To / Robert Browning / Hanover Cottage / Camberwell.
Publication: None traced.
Manuscript: Armstrong Browning Library.

---

750. EBB to Mary Russell Mitford

[Torquay]
April 4.th [1840]¹

My beloved friend,

It came into my head a day or two since, that dear Dr Mitford might like some of our cream with his coffee just now—& the people promised to have it ready to go, tonight.

A slip of paper may go with it, doing no dishonor to Rowland Hill[2]—& your letter has just come in time to be thanked by the same opportunity.

I am very very glad to hear the better news of D! Mitford .. & pray that it may wax better & better. The weather is unbending—& altho' the east wind returned yesterday, we are not likely to be long molested. By favor of its absence I had my bed made three days ago—the first time for six weeks—but the moving to the sofa produced great faintness & exhaustion—to which however I shall not yield the point *about trying again*. Indeed *we*—D! Scully & I—are beginning to talk of transferring me by the said sofa, & additional wheels, thro' the one intervening door into the drawing room—let but the weather be settled, & one of us something stronger.

Thank you again & again for your endeavour to insinuate my poetry into Dionysius's ear![3] The failure "came as nat'ral"[4] as the kindness—albeit the last was YOURS. Thank you again & again dearest Miss Mitford.

I am not as severe as you—oh nothing like it—for the rest. Royalty does not sit in an elbow chair—& is forced to wear a backboard—& we sh! make allowances—*we* who loll at ease!- A more than commonly strong soul is requisite in order to burst thro' the cerements of the ceremonies of that unhappy condition—& there may be a want of the right degree of *magnanimous peculiarity*, without absolute 'hardness' or 'coldness'. May there not? Miss Skerrett must indeed be a prize in the acquaintanceship of anyone[5]—but I believe I cannot claim it even by hereditary right. The family she refers to,[6] is not connected with mine on either side .. May it not be, & partly from the character of her office,—that the Queen suspects nothing of her height above it?- But oh—I am growing afraid of you-

       Your most obstinate . . . ly affectionate
       EBB—

I have written to M! Merry—'Merry & wise'[7]- Is'nt he?

Address: Miss Mitford / Three Mile Cross / near Reading.
Publication: EBB-MRM, I, 194–195.
Manuscript: Wellesley College.

1. Year provided by internal references.
2. Under the new Postal Duties Act (effective January 1840) formulated by Hill, postage was assessed only by weight; under the prior regulations the number of sheets was also a factor affecting the postage due. EBB was, therefore, now able to send an enclosure without additional payment.
3. Dionysius the Elder, King of Sicily, caused to be made a subterranean room in the form of a human ear; a communication with an adjoining room enabled Dionysius to overhear what was said by those he had confined in the cave. The workmen who had constructed the chamber were all put to death to prevent them from revealing its purpose.
 EBB is referring to Miss Mitford's attempt to bring "The Crowned and Wedded Queen" to Victoria's attention (see letter 735).

4. We have not located the source of this quotation.
5. T.A. Trollope believed that "of all those in the immediate service of Her Majesty, it is probable that there was not one, whether menial or other, equal to Miss Skerret [sic] in native power of intellect, extent of reading, and linguistic accomplishment. And this the Queen very speedily discovered" (*What I Remember*, 1887, I, 362–363).
6. Possibly that of the poet Andrew Marvell, from whom Miss Skerrett claimed descent.
7. The original derivation of this is obscure; it occurs in old ballads (e.g., "The Good Fellow's Advice" and "The Father's Wholesome Admonition") and Burns uses it in "Here's a Health to Them That's Awa" (1792), line 5.

751. RB TO WILLIAM SMITH[1]

Hanover Cottage, Southampton S^t., Camberwell.
[*Postmark:* 7 April 1840]

Sir,

Mr Moxon has just published a long Poem of mine, "Sordello", meant for a limited class of readers—and I am on the point of following it up by three new Dramas, written in a more popular style, and addressed to the Public at large:—a friend has called my notice to your handsome Reprints and suggested the proposal I am about to make. Would it answer your purpose to try the experiment of coming out with a *new* work as part of your series?- As in that case I will give you the 1st Edition for nothing—for the sake of your large circulation among a body to which my works have little access at present. Of course I mean that these Dramas should form one publication, of the same size and at the same low price as your other pamphlets.[2]

Yours truly,
Robert Browning.

Be so kind as to answer at your earliest convenience.

Mr W. Smith.

Address, on integral page: Mr William Smith, / 113 Fleet-Street.
Publication: None traced.
Manuscript: Pierpont Morgan Library.

1. *London Publishers and Printers c. 1800–1870*, comp. Philip A.H. Brown (1982) shows Smith to have been active from 1830 to 1849, both at the address given by RB and at 2 Saville Place, Burlington Gardens.
2. On an advertisement, torn from a copy of *Sordello* and enclosed with this letter, RB has indicated the three works (see letter 747, note 6). When published, they were brought out by Moxon.

752. HARRIET MARTINEAU TO RB

12. Front S^t. Tynemouth. Northumberland.
April 8th [1840][1]

Dear Mr Browning

Your book & kind note have reached me. I meant to have delayed this acknowledgment, & my hearty thanks for your gift, till I had read

"Sordello", & could thank you for *it*, as well as for remembering me: but your note shows such kind anxiety & concern for my health & comfort, that I cannot but write at once to tell you that my friends must not be unhappy about me. I cannot say that I am better; nor do I anticipate being better for a very long time to come: but I am not quite idle, & I am perfectly happy.

I removed hither 3 weeks ago, for the sake of a fine sea-view, & fresh air,—very important things to one who is confined to the house. Another object gained is perfect leisure & quiet. While I have no other call upon my strength, I can write a little; & I do it with a delight I never experienced before. A multitude of relations are only half an hour distant, by rail-road; & one welcome face or another is frequently looking in upon me; & I am taken the very best care of. Then I have letters innumerable, from kind friends who do not wait for answers. I assure you I am not at all to be pitied. At the same time, I admit that I am not better, & that there is no anticipating the time of my return to town.

Have you heard that we have lost my kind, dear aunt Lee. Little as you saw of her, you will be able to believe that hers was a *faultless* old age. We shall miss & mourn her long. My mother has been too ill herself to arrange the plans rendered necessary by this event, & by the pulling down of poor old Fludyer S^t., of w^h. we have received notice.[2] We hope the first thing she will do will be to visit us in the North.

If you see the Macreadys, pray give my kindest remembrances to them.

I hope "Sordello," with w^h. you have taken so much pains, will be a crown to you. I long to sit down to it.

Believe me very truly yours
H. Martineau.

Publication: None traced.
Manuscript: Berg Collection.

1. Dated by her acknowledgement of *Sordello*.
2. Until illness forced her to leave London, Miss Martineau and her mother had occupied a house at 17 Fludyer Street, Westminster. *Robson's Royal Court Guide for 1840* lists Mrs. Lee, Miss Martineau's late aunt, as residing there also.

---

753. RB TO WILLIAM CHARLES MACREADY

[London]
Thursday [April/May 1840][1]

My dear Macready,

What you say puts fresh heart into me– I am sure you will like this last labour of mine, and mean therefore to spend a day or two in making a fair copy of it, the M.S. I should have read being a portentous scribble.[2] Most likely you will receive it on Saturday Night.

Ever yours most faithfully,
R Browning.

My best regards to Mrs & Miss Macready—shall I not see them at the Lecture next week?[3]

Publication: None traced.
Manuscript: University of Kentucky.

1. Dated by the reference to "the Lecture."
2. RB refers to his work-in-progress, *The Return of the Druses.*
3. Carlyle's Lectures on "Heroes and Hero-Worship" were given on 5, 8, 12, 15, 19 and 22 May. RB's reference to "next week" means that the letter could have been written on 30 April, 7 May or 14 May.

---

754. RB TO EUPHRASIA FANNY HAWORTH

[London]
Thursday Night. [May 1840][1]

My dear Miss Haworth,

Yours received some five minutes since—fancy! But the truth is I am glad to find you have not been indisposed—as I feared. As to Sordello—enfoncé![2] You say roses and lilies and lilac-bunches and lemon-flowers about it while every body else pelts cabbage stump after potato-paring—nay, not every body—for Carlyle .. but I won't tell you what Milnes told me Carlyle told him the other day: (thus I make you believe it was something singular in the way of praise—connu![3]) All I need remark on in your note is the passage you want cleared up: "What are you to be glad of?" Why that as I stopped my task awhile, left off my versewriting one sunny June day with a notion of not taking to it again in a hurry, the sad disheveled form I had just been talking of, that plucked and pointed, wherein I put, comprize, typify and figure to myself Mankind, the whole poor-devildom one sees cuffed and huffed from morn to midnight, that, so typified, she may come at times and keep my pact in mind, prick up my republicanism and remind me of certain engagements I have entered into with myself about that same, renewed me, gave me fresh spirit, made me after finishing Book 3^d commence Book 4th, what is involved here? Only one does not like serving oneself as a certain "Watson" served Horace in a translation I have: e.g. Book 1. Ode 1. Lines 1 & 2: "O Mæcenas, descended from Kings (*Tuscan, that is Etrurian*) your Ancestors, (*O you who have proved yourself to be*) both my patron (*since you kindly reconciled me with Augustus*) and a sweet honor to me (*by your Quality and politeness to poor me whose father was nothing but a Freedman*) &c.&c.&[c][4]

You don't know, it seems, that I have announced Three Dramas?[5]—I see—the fly-leaf was left out of your copy; I am in treaty with Macready about one of these—which I am going to send him, I should say rather[6]—which I think clever and he will think stupid. Don't fear, however, any more unintelligible writing--

Carlyle is lecturing with éclât[7]—the Macreadys go, & the Bishop of Salisbury, and the three Miss Styles[8] that began German last week: I have still your Tieck, remember.[9]

Ever yours faithfully,
R Browning.

Publication: NL, pp. 18-19.
Manuscript: Huntington Library.

1. Dated by the reference to Carlyle's lectures.
2. "Done for!" The reception accorded *Sordello* was almost entirely negative, with it acquiring a reputation of being "the least comprehensible poem written in the English language" (DeVane, p. 85). RB himself, in letter 771, spoke of its being "praised by the units, cursed by the tens, and unmeddled with by the hundreds!"
Miss Haworth's copy was offered for sale in 1971 (see *Reconstruction*, C565).
3. "That's an old story!" (colloquial).
4. RB refers to *The Works of Horace* (1741), translated by David Watson (1710-56). The passage he criticizes occurs on p. 2.
5. See letter 747, note 6. As RB's comment indicates, apparently some copies of the book lacked the advertisement.
6. One of the works announced as "nearly ready" was *Mansoor the Hierophant*; this was renamed *The Return of the Druses*, a revised text of which RB promised Macready in letter 761.
7. Carlyle was delivering six lectures, on 5, 8, 12, 15, 19 and 22 May, on "Heroes and Hero-Worship."
8. Edward Denison (1801-54) was consecrated Bishop of Salisbury in 1837, at the unusually early age of 36. In 1835, he had violently opposed proposals for the admission of Dissenters to Oxford University. The Misses Styles have not been identified.
9. Johann Ludwig Tieck (1773-1853), novelist and playwright, translated Shakespeare into German (*Shakespeare's dramatische Werke*, 1825). As RB makes mention of this work in a letter to Domett on 5 March 1843, it is quite probable that this is the book borrowed from Miss Haworth.

---

755. EBB to George Goodin Moulton-Barrett

Torquay.
Thursday. [14 May 1840][1]

My own dearest Georgie,

Your two letters—or are there more which your kindness sent to me?—must not be unrecognized any longer—altho' I know you w^d tell me not to write if I c^d hear your voice. But indeed it can do no harm to

No. 755 [14 May 1840] 271

any part of me, this relief of heart in writing—& I want to tell you dearest Georgie & all of you how I love you & think of you & how grateful I am for every thought of yours— Of the past there is no need to speak. What is done, is done—& we, knowing that God did it, know in that knowledge the extremity of love & mercy involved in the doing.[2] Oh may the great Doer teach us to bow low in unmitigated apprehension of Him as the Supreme in will—and in mercy also. Dearest Georgie, we do not know the meaning of the things we suffer, more than of the things we see; but we "shall know hereafter"—[3] In the meantime let it be enough that God doeth all.

May He bless & keep you every one. Be sure that I am a great deal better—rather weak still certainly—but shaking off more & more of the weakness— It is my earnest wish to get home,—& if I cannot do that, to *get nearer*— Dearest Minny cant wish it half so much as *I*, tell her. Yet I am afraid they wont let me even try to get home. On "getting nearer" I shall insist upon in all events. Even you c^{dnt} blame me for that obstinacy—but, as they all say, there will be a more becoming time for such speculations when I am out of bed—& I hope to be on the sofa soon again. My dear dear Papa's being here is an inexpressible comfort—& he never seems to DREAM OF GOING AWAY, they say— We lost Jane & uncle Hedley this morning—regarding their past visit, as indeed every detail of their conduct to us, with grateful affection. If you go—any of you—to Richmond—DO[4] take care, & take the waterman.

Now mind you believe me to be a GREAT DEAL[4] better. I am REALLY *so*. And if the writing goes up & down, that is nothing but *want of* use. Bro is sailing with Mr Vaneck at this moment[5]—& Henrietta & Arabel walking out in the sun—& Papa reading on the other side of the green door.

How I love you all!— May God in Christ Jesus bless you— Give my affectionate love to dearest Trippy—& ever do you love

Your

Ba—

Address: George Goodin Barrett Esqr / 50. Wimpole Street / London.
Publication: B-GB, pp. 44–46.
Manuscript: Pierpont Morgan Library.

1. Dated by postmark, 15 May. Thursday fell on the previous day.
2. Their brother Sam had died of a tropical fever in Jamaica on 17 February, although the news did not reach London until April.
3. Cf. John, 13:7.
4. Underscored three times.
5. Mr. Vanneck was the owner of the boat in which Bro was sailing when he met his death later in the year. Vanneck also died, his body never being recovered.

756. EBB to Richard Hengist Horne

Torquay
Friday May 15.th [1840]¹

I shall be more at ease when I have thanked you—my dear M! Horne, for your assurance of sympathy² which in its feeling & considerate expression, a few days since, touched me so nearly & deeply. Without it, I sh.^d have written when I was able .. I mean physically able—for in the exhaustion consequent upon fever I have been too weak to hold a pen– As to reluctancy of *feeling* .. believe me that I must change more than illness or grief can change me, before it becomes "a painful effort" to communicate with one so very very kind as you have been to me. Kindness & sympathy are not such common things. And as to the strangership—why a friend is proved by remaining one in adversity. You BEGAN to be one in mine—and FOR THAT REASON—a peculiarity which in separating you from the class of ordinary friends, removes you still farther from that of strangers– It is easier for you to forget this, than for me, dear M! Horne.

Besides the appreciated sympathy, I have to acknowledge four proofs of your remembrance, the seals of which lay unbroken for a fortnight or more, after their arrival here. In one letter, was something about "neglect"—you told me never to fancy a silence into a neglect. Was I likely to do it? Was there any room for even fancy to try? That w.^d be still more surprising than the fact of *your* making room for a thought of *me* in the multitude of your occupations.

You have been in the fields, I know by the *flowers*—& found there I suppose, between the flowers & the life & dear Mrs Orme, that pleasant-dream (for *me!*) about my going to London at Easter!– *I*³ never dreamt it– And while you wrote, what a mournful contrary was going on here!– It was a heavy blow—(May God keep you from such!—I knew you w.^d be sorry for me when you heard—) it was a heavy blow for all of us—& I, being weak you see, was struck down as by a *bodily* blow, in a moment, without having time for tears. I did not think indeed to be better any more—but I have quite rallied now—except as to strength—& they say that on essential points I shall not suffer permanently—and this is a comfort to poor Papa. But oh M! Horne– God's will—so high above humanity, that its goodness & perfectness cannot be scanned at a glance,—w.^d be very terrible if it were not for His manifested Love—manifested in Jesus Christ. Only *that* holds our hearts together when He shatters the world.

Saturday.

I had finished Napoleon & was about to write to you on the subject⁴— & I will still write. Now .. GREGORY!!–⁵

'His large hands sway the air about my head.'[6]

I have read but little lately & not at all until very lately; but two or three days ago Papa held up Gregory before my eyes as something sure to bring pleasure into them. [']'Ah! I knew that *that* w^d move you". After all I have scarcely been long enough face to face with him to apprehend the full grandeur of his countenance. There *are* very grand things—& expounded in y^r characteristic massiveness of diction—but it does so far appear to me that for the tragic heights & for that passionate singleness of purpose in which you surpass the poets of our time, "we shall revert to Cosmo & Marlowe.["][7] Well—it may be very *wrong*—I must think over my thoughts. And at any rate the Essay on Tragic Influence is full of noble philosophy & poetry.[8] Only you do more honor to the stage & the actorship than I c^d do. Tragedy is a high form of poetry—perhaps the highest—& absolutely independent in its own essence, of stages—which involve to my mind little more than its translation into a grosser form, in order to its apprehension by the vulgar. What Macready can touch Lear?- In brief, if the union between Tragedy & the gas lights be less incongruous & absurd than the union between Church & State, is it less desecrative of the divine Theory?- In the clashing of my no against your yes, I must write goodbye.

Do believe me, under all circumstances, truly & gratefully yours,
E B Barrett.

Will you tell me when there is any criticism upon Gregory made by the συνετοι[9]—in case I sh^d miss any. I am anxious for the laurels. And you will not be angry that I revert to Cosmo? Cosmo is . . *Cosmo*——& the precedence (were it granted) is only *you* of *you*. You wont be angry?

Publication: EBB-RHH, I, 13-18.
Manuscript: Pierpont Morgan Library.

1. Year provided by the reference to *Gregory VII*. Its publication date had been announced as 20 April 1840 (*The Athenæum*, 18 April 1840).
2. On Sam's death.
3. Underscored twice.
4. *The History of Napoleon*, 2 vols., 1840.
5. *Gregory VII*. EBB's copy is now in the Berg Collection (see *Reconstruction*, A1250).
6. *Gregory VII*, act IV, sc. 3 (p. 65).
7. The reviewers had reservations also. *The Athenæum* (no. 671, 5 September 1840, p. 699) said: "Mr. Horne is a clever man; but cleverness may run into conceit, thought into mysticism, and poetry mistake its way" and found in the play "a perversity and want of judgment, which must hinder Mr. Horne from attaining the honours he so much desires."
8. This precedes the play.
9. "Sagacious ones."

757. EBB TO MARY RUSSELL MITFORD

[Torquay]
May 17 [1840][1]

My beloved friend, I must try to write a few lines to you today, lest you sh^d. in y^r. kindness turn my long silence into sad thoughts for y^{r}self. There have been many many for me—worse than sad—lately. Dearest Miss Mitford, I have been very unhappy—& very ill besides or you sh^d. have heard before. Dreadful news came from the West Indies five weeks ago—& I have lost one of my beloved brothers .. lost him while I was thinking of him as being in health & joyousness & with a long earthly futurity before his feet!– God's will be done—but it has worked of course much bitter suffering to all of us—worked it *in love*—I w^d. not forget *that*. But I was weak you see, & was struck down instantaneously as by a bodily blow. I have been very ill with fever—passing from delirium at nights to such extreme exhaustion by day, that I never thought to write to you any more– It w^d have been very melancholy for poor Papa, if he had lost two children by one stroke—w^d it not?

But I am much better now, & have been able to read for these ten day's past—& for a whole month my dear dear Papa has been with me– I ought to be better .. with *him*. We are all better now– I am sure you will feel for us .. my beloved friend. Write to me & say how you are, & how dear D^r. Mitford is– Dont say much about me– I w^d rather hear of *you*– I love you continually. Is it true that you
⟨...⟩[2]

I w^d. not let my sisters tell you any bad news & make you uneasy about me & so sent the 'mute fish'[3]—to reassure you. I am glad you liked to receive them– You shall hear again soon—of M^r. Darley &c. The book came quite safe.[4]

Publication: EBB-MRM, I, 195–196.
Manuscript: Wellesley College.

1. Year provided by Sam's death.
2. The conclusion of the letter is missing, except for the following sentences, cross-written on the first page.
3. William Congreve (1670–1729), *The Way of the World* (1700), IV, 9, 4.
4. i.e., Darley's play, *Thomas à Becket.*

758. EBB TO RICHARD HENGIST HORNE

Torquay.
Thursday morng. [?21] [May 1840][1]

It requires some moral courage dear M:̲ Horne, to send you such a present as this cream: but it is of "Britannia's Pastorals"[2] & the only fit tribute from Devonshire—& people do like it sometimes in their coffee or tea, or with their fruit– Therefore I pre-forgive your laughing at me–

Gregory enlarges while you gaze– Indeed it is a grand production, & one upon which I congratulate both you & our literature. Oh no!– It was not merely 'for *you*'– You know you told me you were working for yourself–

At the same time there is a vacillation of incident & opinion & character—& we want room for our sympathies to stand upright in; Matilda's madness,[3] exquisite as it is, seems (as well as Gregory's remorse) to want a ["]parceque"[4]—she being cold as a stone from the beginning & apparently hard enough to receive & rebound a hundred such trifling incidents as Godfrey's murder–[5] I admit the sudden revi[vi]fication to be fine—but then it w:̲d̲ in my fancy, have been finer, at least more moving,—had you suffered us to look, tho' by a glance, at some heart of love before. We never guessed at such a thing. She was a cold hearted woman & a very bad wife—until she lost her senses: & we want the 'parceque' for the loss–

The returning upon Gregory's words about 'wasting himself upon her', in the madness, is very fine.[6]

The whole of the fourth & fifth acts lies in masses before my admiration,—with short interventions– How sublime is the prayer—that one epithet "the *insufficient* sea["][7] .. ! & how much besides, which I cant write of this morning, is not to be forgotten while day follows day. Your Elizabethan fashion of malleting down your metaphors into the groundwork, produces a diction of extraordinary power– It is concentrated language– *Can* you read a word?[8]

Most truly yours.
Elizabeth B Barrett–

Address: R H Horne Esqr. / 2– Gray's Inn Square / Gray's Inn.
Publication: EBB-RHH, I, 18–19 (in part).
Manuscript: Pierpont Morgan Library.

1. Dated by the references to *Gregory VII*, which EBB had received as a gift earlier in the month (see letter 756).
2. William Browne (1591–1643?), the author of *Britannia's Pastorals* (1613–16), was a Devonshire man.
3. Matilda, Countess of Tuscany, loses her mind in act V of Horne's play, after the murder of her husband, Godfrey, Duke of Bouillon.
4. "Reason."

5. Matilda's madness does seem improbable, given her earlier lack of feeling towards her husband, who said he was dying "In the palace of a most unloving wife, / Abetting my arch-foe! Most hated Gregory!" (act V, sc. 1). EBB's reservations were shared by the reviewer in *The Examiner* (no. 1686, 24 May 1840, pp. 323–324), who wrote: "The failure of the sketch of Matilda is a necessary part of what we hold to be the failure in the conception of Gregory himself."

6. In act IV, sc. 4, Gregory says to Matilda "Retire, retire!—I waste myself upon you." Matilda echoes his words in act V, sc. 1, when she says "He wastes himself upon me!—this the reward / Of sympathies that reached from heaven to hell"; her final lines also reflect them: "Woe and alas! / The sun doth waste himself upon me!"

7. "And to behold / A shadowy portion of Thy Countenance / Reflected o'er the insufficient sea!" (IV, 2, 1–3).

8. Even by EBB's normal standards, this letter is particularly difficult to read.

759. EBB TO MARY RUSSELL MITFORD

[Torquay]
[late May 1840][1]

⟨✱✱✱⟩[2] Have you heard at all of Mr Kenyon? I hear nothing. Sh.^d you see Mr Merry, will you thank him for his kind letter to whc I shall reply—soon– I gratefully felt all your sympathy– Oh yes!—much is left—very much!—& what is taken serves to endear with human love the Heavenly places. I, standing on the threshold of two worlds, see love in each!–

I open my letter to announce ⟨the⟩ arrival of a note from dear Mr Kenyon conveyed here by Mr Bezzi who travelled with him as far as Paris– He does not mention his health—and as to other news you are to hear in a few days–

Address: Miss Mitford / Three Mile Cross / near Reading.
Publication: EBB-MRM, I, 196–197.
Manuscript: Edward R. Moulton-Barrett.

1. EBB's thanks for Miss Mitford's expressions of sympathy suggest that this is an acknowledgement of Miss Mitford's response to letter 757, announcing Sam's death.
2. The letter itself is missing; what appears here was written on the envelope.

760. EBB TO MARY RUSSELL MITFORD

Torquay.
Saturday [?30 May] [1840][1]

My beloved friend,
    I w^d willingly, gladly, thankfully, hear something of you & dear Dr Mitford—the last account being, for all the promise, at the close, so unsatisfying. It grieves me very much that your anxieties sh^d last. Perhaps the *season* & the confinement in which his accident resulted,[2] may have induced the temporary disposition towards the head. May it prove to be temporary—the good, lasting!– God bless & keep you both– I sh^d like so much to hear.

    Let me put first, lest I forget it, one question. When did you send—at what time last year—the geranium plants to Wimpole St.?– I never heard of their arrival, & Arabel says she is sure they never did arrive unless it were late in the autumn,—& if they had done so *at all*, I cant fancy that (what with Set's triumph & his knowledge of the things I care to be told) I shoul'nt have 'heard the fame thereof with my ears'.[3] In the case of your remembering, do answer,—because you see we cant afford to lose them.

    I have learnt a little about Mr Bezzi's marriage and a great deal about him personally. Mr Kenyon's estimation of him in all possible ways appears of the highest—and indeed in the note which he brought me there was a request that if I saw anybody at Torquay it sh^d be Mr Bezzi. I cant however do it, till at least I get into a dressing gown & the next room— which I shall be more particularly anxious to do soon from the circumstance of dear Mr Kenyon coming here his very own self .. intending to come .. in the autumn– Nay!—I understand Mr Bezzi to be holding the office of house hunter for him—hunter of a *permanent* house which he means to occupy a portion of the year, retaining his house in London. It surprised me a good deal in the hearing. The place is very lovely, a gathering of hills & waters wrapped in silken snoods for atmosphere: but Mr Kenyon couldnt go on anywhere without society,—& the worst of the society here is that there is such plenty of it. Dining, dancing, cardplaying society (—into the depth of which one is thrust, if solitude be not chosen at first for the better & the worse,—) will scarcely suit him—& he cant or wont do without it. Mr Landor comes too, I understand, but only for a short time.

    Tell me if you hear of Mr Horne's Gregory VII. There are magnificent things in it. His power of *language* as well as thought, seems to me less masculine than gigantic—& his whole mind to partake of that distinctive

& originating character, properly called genius,—to at least the degree of any writing of the day. Gregory w.^d scarcely do I sh.^d think for the ⟨...⟩[4]

I gain strength I think—but very slowly– Do tell me what you are doing, dear dearest Miss Mitford! Where are the LETTERS?–[5]

Say how you are—& tell me of dear Dr Mitford. My affectionate remembrances to him—& many from hence to *you*–

God bless you!

Ever your attached
EBB–

Address: Miss Mitford / Three Mile Cross.
Publication: EBB-MRM, I, 199–200 as [June? 1840].
Manuscript: Wellesley College.

1. This letter obviously follows no. 759, in which EBB mentions Bezzi's arrival in Torquay.
2. See letter 748, note 2.
3. Job, 28:22.
4. The remainder of the letter is missing, except for the concluding sentences written across the top of the first page and on the flap of the envelope.
5. See letter 737, note 1.

761. RB TO WILLIAM CHARLES MACREADY

Camb.^ll
Monday M.^g [June 1840][1]

Dear Macready,

Since I saw you I have considerably altered and, I hope, improved my play;[2] the three acts are now five, as you advised, and *go* the better for it—such as they are I will send them as soon as I can—but I am not in the best health, and my copyist is from home.[3] —this I mention lest you should think me sleepy or sulky this wondrous June-weather .. while I am, with best regards to Mrs and Miss Macready,

Ever yours
R Browning.

Publication: NL, p. 20.
Manuscript: Yale University.

1. The month is provided by RB; the year by reference to his play.
2. *The Return of the Druses.*
3. His sister Sarianna.

762. EBB TO RICHARD HENGIST HORNE

Torquay
June 1, 1840

My dear Mr Horne,

I have doubted about writing altho' at last I do write—by a venture—rather than leave myself heavily beneath your ban in relation to Matilda.[1] I doubted about writing because the letter after the one 'sub tempore fugi'[2] seemed to throw a shadow in another way, benighting me as to where you were. The [illegible word] of York for a postmark & a ship for a seal seemed to make a total of New York. You trampled out your own footsteps either by accident or sagacity so I doubted.

Under the circumstances, however, a little note may be cast upon the waters *mutis piscatus*[3] perhaps.

No question about Matilda, of course, after your adjuration. Only forgive me if I took a mistaken view, as I must have done, in relation to her in it, if I still fancy there is something too twofold about her[4] & not the character—[illegible word] be more effective if more clearly developed. He [illegible word] who considers her cold & calm self possession through the former scenes or self vindicated by her very first words, "Let us be calm & wait"[5]—is pardonable perhaps for starting & looking round for the major "parceque"[6] when she goes mad just like a common woman.[7] You know she says herself that her sympathies had reached from Heaven to hell before,[8] without asking any questions. Well!—but there was said quite enough to make her mad;—& I was wrong. Only there is something abrupt as also in Gregory's remorse "And where are now my hopes?"[9] It seems transition time with every body. But you who work by grand masses are the very person to produce this sort of hard outline occasionally tho' you contrasted adjacencies—and we should be ungrateful people to complain of them. However 'foreheads' may ache with gazing on your foot—"puzzling its breadth & purpose."[10] The critic in the examiner made a worse mistake than I (which is a comfort) in—puzzling about Gregory himself whose delineation is to my mind wonderfully fine and perfect in all its parts—the delineation of that sort of intellect which is best expressed by the epithet *physical*.[11] There are such in the world. Nothing subtle or dreamy about it—nothing fitted to |side| the angels or the saints going straight to its ends & means with a ferocious & bestial energy. While its very end[s] are *physical*[12] after their kind—visible tangible *power*[—]Gregory is self contradictory in nothing at all. His is the [illegible transcription] of the physical intellect- The [illegible word] is ethereal & knew absolutely nothing of Christ's sublime, the sublime of Love—& of evil testifying to it—the Father of Spirits crowning it.

His end is visible, tangible power even in his praying that is the 'end'. Thou givest us prayer to reach the stars and the thrones of the remote. Oh—I am sure you never meant to admit the ideal of Christianity into Gregory and are absolutely guiltless of inconsistency in regard to him.

Napoleon interested me very much.[13] What I estimated was that we are not suffered in this as in some other animated narratives to be separated from our higher feelings without our consciousness. I like the tone of solemn thought distinguishable through it from the cannonading—the half sarcasm dropped as unaware among the pseudo glories which are the subjects of description. "The dead say nothing."[14] There are fine things too—more than I can count particularly with the book out of[15] sight. The Duc d'Enghien's death has haunted me—with the concluding words on human power—that "effluence of mortality already beginning to decay".[16] The book's fault is its inequality of style—in fact that you did'nt write it all[17]—and I am consistent enough not to complain of that. Did you ever see M! Landor's epigram upon Napoleon? He was so kind as to give it to me—the only evening I ever spent in his company—& here it is.

> Τις ποτε, Ναπολεον, τα σα πρωτα και υστατα
> Εργα; Χρονος τεκνων αιματι γραψει τερπομενος.[18]

to which be now added another tragic person!

Who—or rather to put the question I was going to ask, less personally & directly—WHAT is the "impertinent book"– So you say dear M! Horne, in your character of *Oates*,[19] that I shall be "so well"– Well, perhaps I may. That is considered possible—, altho' my actual condition is precarious—, & when a vessel has broken upon the chest, which was my case two years ago, there is always danger of recurrence,—particularly where the effects linger– Therefore it is wise to temper quite a sufficient eagerness to recover, with a willingness to go—and this is rendered the easier for me from the circumstance of there being objects of my love on each side the grave.

Most truly yours
E B Barrett.

Address: R H Horne Esq! / 2: Gray's Inn Square / Gray's Inn / London.
Publication: EBB-RHH, II, 26–28 (in part).
Source: Transcript and partial manuscript at Yale University.

1. One of the major characters in *Gregory VII*.
2. "At the time."
3. "Fishing in still waters."
4. For EBB's earlier comments, see letter 758.
5. On her first entrance, in act I, sc. 2, she says "We must be calm, and wait."

6. "Reason."
7. At the conclusion of the play, after the murder of her husband.
8. See letter 758, note 6.
9. Act V, sc. 2, spoken after the murder of Matilda's husband.
10. *Gregory VII*, act IV, sc. 3 (p. 65).
11. The review in *The Examiner* (no. 1686, 24 May 1840, pp. 323–324) included this passage: "For what is Mr Horne's purpose in the delineation of Gregory? It is not to give us the ordinary figure of a great and unscrupulous man of action, but to express that thing in his person before which action commonly quails and the conventional strengths of the world fall prostrate. . . . The lesson of Gregory's life, howsoever written, should be the triumph of the spiritual nature"; further comments question Horne's characterization. The reviewer in *The Monthly Chronicle* (July 1840, pp. 17–32) supported EBB's view: "Gregory, as here delineated, is eminently a man of action, with strong physical capabilities, indomitable energy, unquenchable pride and self-reliance."
12. The transcript offers "material" as a possible alternative reading.
13. *The History of Napoleon*.
14. Cf. "Dead men tell no tales" (Dryden, *The Spanish Friar; or, The Double Discovery*, act IV, sc. 1).
15. Up to this point, we reproduce the transcript made by Catharine Tinker Patterson; from here on, we transcribe the two pages remaining of EBB's manuscript, which, together with the envelope, accompany Mrs. Patterson's transcript.
16. Louis Antoine Henri de Bourbon Condé, Duc d'Enghien (1772–1804) fled from France after the fall of the Bastille in 1789. He worked for the restoration of the monarchy, receiving a pension from the English, and took part in the Duke of Brunswick's unsuccessful invasion of France in 1792. He was suspected of complicity in the Cadoudal-Pichegru conspiracy to oust Napoleon and place Louis XVIII on the throne, and was arrested on 15 March 1804 on the orders of Napoleon, then First Consul. When it proved impossible to link him with the plot, he was charged instead with bearing arms against France in the late war. A speedy military trial found him guilty, his request for an interview with Napoleon was refused, and he was shot in the moat of the castle of Vincennes. Horne dealt with this incident in chapter XXIII of his book.
17. Horne had a collaborator, Mary Gillies.
18. "Who then, Napoleon, writes about your earliest and your latest deeds? Time, delighting, writes them with the blood of children." Horne made a paraphrastic translation of this epigram, as follows: "Napoleon! thy deeds beyond compeers, / Who shall write, thrillingly?— / The Father of Years! / And—with the blood of children—willingly" (*EBB-RHH*, II, 28). Landor's original manuscript, given to EBB on 27 May 1836, is listed as L147 in *Reconstruction*.
19. Titus Oates (1649–1705) was the perjurer who fabricated the "Popish Plot," alleging that Catholics were conspiring to assassinate Charles II and put the Duke of York on the throne.

---

763. EBB to Mary Russell Mitford

Torquay.
June 3^d 1840.

Ever dearest Miss Mitford,

I long to hear about you– May I? I am gathering strength (stick by stick) myself—but the movement to the sofa from the bed for the first time last sunday produced such fainting & exhaustion that it is not to be repeated immediately. Still the strength comes—*however* slowly—& I am able to write & read pretty much as usual—& Papa is here still—so that there is nothing to repine about. Dreaming of going to London which is my dream, whenever my spirits rise into sight, in relation to myself, is a dream unpartaken I fear by my physician. I do long, naturally & fervently to be at home—but he says there are two reasons against it—one being that I could'nt go, & the other, that Dr Chambers w^d send me back again if I c^d.– Well! I dream.

And my dreams involve much of you my beloved friend & dear Dr Mitford! Oh do let me hear of you. It seems lately as if the mountains & rivers between us had grown higher & broader. Whose fault is this? I dont feel as if it possibly c^d be *mine*. How are you? How is he? How are the LETTERS?—in the press?–[1] How is the garden?—& Flush?– And what summer plans have you all taken up?–

Thank you for the beautiful geranium which held its colors fast, and let me look at them entire! So that is *I!* Bearing my name, its bloom put me to shame,—in my thinness & ghastliness! The contrast suggested a very "pretty moral"[2]—only I chose rather to think of the graceful compliment implying the dear kindness!–

Have you given up the idea of ever seeing Mr Darley's book again?–[3] It chaperons or is chaperoned by some Devonshire cream—but I beg you to remember that the stains upon its back came to me as they go, & proceeded from neither cream nor me– The chronicle is very clever & spirited—picturesque & racy—& the character of Becket appears to me developped with no ordinary power: at the same time I confess myself disappointed in the absence of tragic passion & concentration, & in the baldness as to poetry generally. Is it a work of talent merely—or of genius? Of high talent, I sh^d say .. if I might. The want of imagination rather than its exuberance is manifest in Dwerga who is simply *nasty*. I sh^d like to lift her out of the book with a pair of tongs![4] Not without them—notwithstanding my earnest wish for the triumphant speeding of Mr Darley's indubitable powers–

Oh yes! I have often attended religious branch meetings, in country towns, whose *roots* are in Exeter Hall. I never was at a meeting in *Exeter Hall*,[5] on account of the crowds—& never read the book you speak of. The book may be vulgar enough—but surely there is nothing vulgar in that gathering of mighty sympathies in order to a mighty end—God's end as well as man's—which we find embodied in our Bible society & the various missionary societies. Dont let anybody prejudice you, dearest dearest Miss Mitford. Some of those exposition books whether in relation to religious views in the abstract or habits founded upon such, often do the very greatest harm with the very best intentions. Save me from friends of that class—

Have you seen Mr Horne's Gregory VII? It is a work of surprising power—altho' it does not, to my mind, reach the tragic heights of his Cosmo.

Love to dear Dr Mitford— Forgive my abruptnesses. I have written myself quite tired.

Your ever attached
EBB—

Publication: EBB-MRM, I, 197–198.
Manuscript: Wellesley College.

1. A further enquiry about the progress of Miss Mitford's project to publish some of her letters (see letter 737, note 1).
2. Shakespeare, *Pericles, Prince of Tyre*, II, 1, 35.
3. Miss Mitford's copy of *Thomas à Becket*, the loan of which EBB acknowledged in letter 757.
4. In Darley's play, Dwerga was Queen Eleanor's female dwarf. As EBB indicates, she was not a pleasant character; in act I, sc. 2, she says "Have I not eat live mandrakes, screaming torn / From their warm churchyard-bed, out of thy hand?" Queen Eleanor, well aware of the dwarf's evil nature, apostrophizes her in act I, sc. 2: "Venomous spider! I could pierce it through / With a witch's bodkin, but it does me service."
5. Exeter Hall, erected in 1831, with accommodation for over 4,000, was largely used for annual meetings of religious and philantropical organizations. The Strand Palace Hotel now occupies its site.

764. EBB TO MISS HOOKER

Torquay.
June 12.th 1840—

In consequence of sudden affliction & increased illness, Miss Barrett has not been able to receive Miss Hooker's pleasing verses[1] until some time after they were written, nor to acknowledge them until some time after they were received. May she now express, in imperfect words yet a true gratitude, her sense of the kindness & sympathy with which the face of the unknown has been turned towards her? That before the face so turned, all the goodness of God may pass, remains her prayer.

Publication: None traced.
Manuscript: Armstrong Browning Library.

1. Unless anonymously published, these verses must have been either in manuscript or privately printed, as there is no formal record of any publication by Miss Hooker at this date. It is assumed that the recipient was Mary Ann Hooker, the author of *Sketches from the Bible* (1842).

765. EBB TO RICHARD HENGIST HORNE

Torquay.
[*Postmark:* 14 June 1840]

Thank you dear M.ʳ Horne for the Statesman which is returned by the present post. So dramatists cant originate under the Guelphs—cant 'call their souls th.ʳ own'—and nothing *is* originated in your tragedies. Such nonsense sh.ᵈⁿᵗ provoke us as it does—BUT it does.[1]

Now there is that M.ʳ Darley who has written a Dramatic Chronicle (Tho.ˢ a Becket) to prove that Nature being exhausted, there can be no more tragedies!– No!—the *Chronicle* was'nt written to prove it—the *preface* was![2] But he might more safely have left it to the Chronicle. Q E D– A clever picturesque composition—powerful in a certain way, tho' not in the tragic. If M.ʳ Darley stood alone as a tragedian, his proposition w.ᵈ be irrefragable– Not that I dis-esteem him. He wrote a beautiful fanciful pastoral once—Sylvia or the May Queen[3]—but the missing thing is *passion*—pathos—if not a *besides*.

How wonderful that such ideas sh.ᵈ be taken up by people with one!– You know he is a spirit of the Athenæum.[4] I care for the Athenæum—but as to poetry, they are all sitting (in mistake) just now, upon Caucasus for Parnassus—& wondering why they dont see the Muses.[5] He has'nt a heart even for Bea[u]mont & Fletcher! And to his mind—the CAUSE of the abundance of poetical genius in the old times, was .. the difficulty they had in writing!– We spell too well for anything!!——– There's a discovery!–

It comes to this. If poetry under any form be exhaustible, Nature is—and if Nature be––we are near a blasphemy. I, for one, c.ᵈ not believe in the immortality of the soul.

> Si l'ame est immortelle,
> L'amour ne l'est il pas?[6]

extending '*l'amour*' into all love of the ideal, & attendant power of idealising.

But—ah—there *may* be another mistake!– Dear M.ʳ Horne, do you fancy that directly you have opened the minor theatres, Cosmos & Gregories unsent by you, will pour through the doors?– *I* dont—tho' the present system is iniquitous, & everything involving a patent odious, & your reformation is all ways desirable.[7] I dont believe in mute inglorious Miltons[8]—& far far less in mute inglorious Shakespeares. Van Amburgh's new elephant will take turns with Gregory the Seventh—you will see.

Which reminds me of another sort of taking turns—the sort you propose––in cruel jest as I must *suppose*. You think it w.ᵈ be a good joke to take the "click of small machinery" into y.ʳ Gregorian chaunt!– Well—I can only answer in sober sadness—that I sh^d like to do anything with you—both for the pleasure's sake & the honor's sake—but I am afraid of you. You w^d tread on me if I were so near, with the great Gregory foot[9]—& everybody w^d talk of want of proportion.

Where do you go in July? For *me*, I cant answer. I am *longing* to go to London, & hoping to the last. That is all. For the present, . . certainly the window has been opened twice—an inch,—but I cant be lifted even to the sofa without fainting—and my physician shakes his head or changes the conversation (which is worse) whenever London is mentioned. But I do grow stronger; and if it becomes possible, I shall go—WILL go! *That* sounds better—does'nt it?– Putting it off to another summer is like a never.

Oh I was so glad to have your note. I really thought you had gone to America[10]—or were tired of *me*—worse still. I never thought of "*neglect*"—that being such a wrong word—but otherwise, I lie here fancying all sorts of things in Heaven & earth–

It is a shame to expect all this stuff to be read by any person with their time filled as yours must be– Never mind throwing aside what I write for your leisure. Never let me be in the way. Pray dont. To prove myself not quite inconsiderate, . . I wanted (sh^d have preferred it) to send you something meant for the M^{thly} Chronicle—to know from you whether it sh^d be *some*thing or another thing—but I enclose it by this post to the editor,[11]—that I may not wear you quite away. Now if you are tired you are avenged––for *I am too*!

Ever & truly yours
EBB.

Address: R H Horne Esqr– / 2– Gray's Inn Square / Gray's Inn / London.
Publication: EBB-RHH, I, 49–54 (in part).
Manuscript: Pierpont Morgan Library.

1. *The Statesman* (10 May 1840, p. 10), in a review of *Gregory VII*, said: "Mr. Horne is unlucky not to have lived in the reign of Queen Elizabeth. He might only have been admired by about the same number of persons as at present; but then that number would have been a much larger and more commanding portion of the reading public. . . . His dramas then would have been acted. And they might now have been . . . revived, with a little softening of the language or situations . . . No critic in that case, would have objected that his language was so like that of the old dramatists . . . But if Mr. Horne *will* live under the Guelphs, instead of the Tudors, he must take the consequences. . . . Forbidden to originate, he may still emulate. . . . 'Gregory the Seventh' is a tragedy of colossal structure; but, to our apprehension, with defects and flaws proportionate to the vastness of the design."
2. In the preface to his play, Darley said: "Being impressed with an idea that the age of legitimate Acting Drama has long gone by,—that the means to reproduce such a species of literature do not exist in our present cast of mind, manners, and language,—I have under this persuasion spent no vain time upon attempts to fit 'Thomas à Becket' for the public scene." The play's full title was *Thomas à Becket. A Dramatic Chronicle. In Five Acts* (1840).

3. EBB's copy of Darley's 1827 work is now at the Brighton Area Library (see *Reconstruction*, A760).
4. Darley was on *The Athenæum*'s staff.
5. In classical literature, the Caucasus was inhabited by savages, while Parnassus was sacred to the Muses.
6. "If the soul is immortal, is not love also?"
7. See letter 767, note 3.
8. Gray, "Elegy in a Country Churchyard" (1751), 59.
9. Cf. "Before thy mediating feet," *Gregory VII*, act IV, sc. 3 (p. 67).
10. See letter 762.
11. "A Lay of the Rose," printed in the July number (VI, 13–17).

---

766. EBB TO GEORGE GOODIN MOULTON-BARRETT

Torquay.
Wednesday. [17 June 1840][1]

My ever dearest Georgie,

When you are measuring the length & breadth of my ingratitude, do make allowances for the time during which 'Glencoe'[2] lingered upon the seas. It never reached me until last week—& every day since has found me on the edge of a letter to you– Thank you my dearest Georgie!– If you think as stedfastly of the rights of your clients as of my pleasures, you will be *sacked*[3] in no time. It was, as you well knew it w^d be, a great pleasure to me to look into Glencoe—and yet the play is to my mind, a failure, even without thinking of *Ion*. The newspapers seemed however to speak well of its reception[4]—the consequence perhaps of some melodramatic capability. Otherwise the feebleness & want of concentrative power w^d be as obvious, I sh^d suppose, upon the stage as elsewhere. High & tender thoughts there are, gracefully & harmoniously expressed— which is not *being tragic!* Thank you my dearest Georgie. *Your* part is more perfect than the Serjeant's.

Thank you too for two notes—are there not two?—& for the *advices* in both. Bro is of opinion that I "move my legs & arms" (which was in y^r prescription) "quite enough for anything"—and in regard to other movements, be patient & you shall hear of them. In the meantime deduct from your fancies about me that I am lying in bed, from *fear* of the exertion of getting up. When a medical man stands by saying,—"Dont do it—you will throw yourself back again—it always does you harm—" it is rather difficult to take the other side of the question. Nevertheless, Papa being evidently anxious about it, I urged a repetition of the experiment upon Dr Scully yesterday,—& he agrees to its being made tomorrow or next day, when the wind subsides. At the same time his reluctance was tolerably evident,—& his words to Crow when he left the house were—"If Miss Barrett does'nt take care, she will make herself ill again".

When I was up last, there was not merely *fainting*,—the consequences were agitation of the pulse for some days, & tendency to fever. D.̲ Scully says "I am as anxious as anybody can be for you to be *able* to move—but I do wish you to gain a little strength, (which you are doing slowly) before too much is attempted– The case is of such a nature, that it is far easier to make you much worse than at all better."– So now pray acquit *me*. I am afraid of nothing except of not seeing you this summer—& it is'nt altogether as agreeable to lie here half in the dark as you might possibly *fancy*– The real truth is that the fever in April induced a degree of weakness from which it is only surprising, considering my previous debility, that I sh.ͩ have rallied so far. I never was so ill or weak at anytime in my life, to my own remembrance—& now all is past, by divine mercy, I may tell you that I myself did not suppose it *humanly possible* for me to be better anymore. Indeed D.̲ Scully told me at the time, that if I were an older person he sh.ͩ despond, but that he trusted to the elasticity remaining in the constitution. This accounts for my not reviving as quickly with the present summer as with the former one,—& since the strength is really & gradually though slowly coming, it sh.ͩ do so *satisfactorily* to all of you—even to you, my dearest learnedest George with your latent genius for *MD-city*.

You have heard of Arabel's & Brozie's separate romances.[5] The latter has discarded his green blind, & indeed ventures to show his whole face out of doors by twilight instead of waiting for the very pitch dark. As to Arabel, was'nt it an adventure? Poor dearest Bella! With the scolding after the perils!—& after that ideal drowning & assassination, the real thorough fatigue of half running nearly eight miles! But two days *stiffness* was all the harm done—& she & the Mackintoshes continue great friends, & I encourage her being with them as much as possible because their happy spirits & love of fresh air & country excursions are both exhilarating & advantageous to her—forming breaks upon the monotony & gloom which her kindness to me necessarily produces– She was so kind when I was ill– 〈...〉[6] It was all D.̲ Scully c.ͩ do to keep her from sitting up night after night—which w.ͩ never have done. They were all of them very very kind.

I wish we c.ͩ hear more of what you all do. Has Henry made up his mind to some occupation which is *not* insurmountably objectionable to Papa? I am sure he is too kind, & I hope he is too wise, to cleave any longer to military or naval fancies, the fulfilment of which w.ͩ entail such anxiety & pain upon many of us– And to anything else, there is a plain way– Why does'nt he think *hard* about it?– Affec.ͭᵉ love to him. Dearest Joc's[7] first vol. of Napoleon shall go back in a better state than it came here. I like it very much. You know M.̲ Horne is editor. He sent me a ballad yesterday—& we continue fast-sworn friends. Did you see any extracts from Gregory? I have the tragedy.– Very fine—but not as overwhelming as the Cosmo. Set writes nothing but business. My best love to dearest Trippy who ought to write to me. Make her stay in for a good deal. Bummy writes very seldom, always talks of coming when she does– *But she wont come*. Poor little Mary [Hunter] has terrible sick headaches—but the rest of us are well enough to administer the emetics. Her father left Cork yesterday for Dublin & Liverpool whence he goes to Leicester on his way homewards. It seems almost certain that he will enter into a temporary engagement with the Kingsbridge people. God bless you all. I long to see you beyond all things—feeling it hard to be patient. God bless you my beloved George.

Your own Ba.

Love to my dearest Minny, whose kind letters I shall soon reply to. I am ordered to be raised to "an angle of 45" today with pillows. Will THAT please you? My thoughts day & night wander round about you– Oh you *dont* know how I love you all. Everybody's best love.

Address: George Goodin Barrett Esq.r / 50. Wimpole Street/ London.
Publication: B-GB, pp. 46–50.
Manuscript: Pierpont Morgan Library.

1. Dated by postmark, 18 June 1840. 17 June fell on Wednesday.
2. Thomas Noon Talfourd's new play (1840). George sent EBB a copy of the second edition (see *Reconstruction*, A2242).
3. A play on words, the Woolsack being the Lord Chancellor's seat in the House of Lords.
4. *The Morning Chronicle* of 25 May, reviewing the play's première on 23 May, said "not till the third act did general attention seem fairly seized, and then, through the fourth and fifth acts, there was one decisive triumph. The curtain fell to successive bursts of genuine applause." *The Times* of 25 May said "the last two acts were triumphant ... we have little doubt that it will prove attractive."
5. No specific details of these romances survive. Obviously, parental opposition was involved—EBB later recounted to RB (letter of 12 December 1845) that she wished to assist Bro by making over to him her financial interests, but that her "hands were seized & tied."
6. About half a line obliterated, apparently by EBB.
7. i.e., Octavius.

---

767. EBB TO MARY RUSSELL MITFORD

Torquay.
June 24.th '40

Ever dearest Miss Mitford,

Really you want me?[1] Then I am ready. I have been writing again for the last week or two & without detriment. Surely I may, for *you*. Only be sure of the prudence of it on your own account—& dont be beguiled, 'all for love of me'[2] into monotonizing the work, if you sh^d have any sudden access to contributive novelty. That is my 'advice'– Moreover .. the more *prose* the better. Do remember *that*.

As to Mr Horne, oh I wish you had him safely harnessed—he is a courser of the sun!—but to the *catching*, I dont know what 'advice' to give. You must ask him yourself dearest Miss Mitford this time—& feel certain that he wont say 'no' if the other word is sayable– I do know that his time is occupied in a manner which renders his unceasing kindnesses to me the more moving to my grateful sense of them. Literary engagements, to be counted (perhaps) upon the fingers,—besides the present campaign against the theatrical monopolists[3]—which by the way, you will care for,—and towards which he says that he has Ld Lyndhurst's support, in promise.[4]

Still these night-&-day energetically laborious people, stretch 'their times' to almost any extent—particularly when they mean to be kind. Do ask him. If the 'no' comes, the reason will be evident. And any proposition of the sort from YOU, will imply a compliment to balance this requested grace–

He did *not send* me the Gregory—and has not sent it even to the critics, in the usual way. So he told me. Certainly he does put 'a spirit into leaves',[5] which lifts them up by breathing between, in a fashion so contrary to annual pneumatics in general, as to be desirable for any.

I am very glad (per Mr Kenyon) to hear of Mr Harness's prosperity.[6] Dear Mr Kenyon has changed his intention about purchasing a house here—but he means to come.

Thank God for the happy account, comparatively speaking, of dear Dr Mitford & y^r anxieties. I have borne raising in my bed to a half sitting posture, half an hour at a time, for several day⟨s now⟩ & am pretty well–

Ever your affec^{te}
EBB

My sisters will be so glad to see M^{rs} & Miss Anderdon– I fear I shall not be fit for it—if they come *very* soon. Think of the geraniums! & thank you for our next year's prospect, dear dear Miss Mitford.

Address: Miss Mitford / Three Mile Cross / near Reading.
Publication: EBB-MRM, I, 200–201.
Manuscript: Wellesley College.

    1. As a contributor to the 1841 *Findens' Tableaux*.
    2. Tennyson, "The Mermaid" (last line of verses two and three).
    3. By an Act of 1737, the performance of legitimate drama was restricted to nominated "patent theatres," of which there were only three in London: Covent Garden, Drury Lane, and the Haymarket. Horne was organizing a petition, urging amended legislation, but it was not until the Theatre Act of 1843 that dramatic "free trade" was established.
    4. John Singleton Copley, 1st Baron Lyndhurst (1772–1863), had held a number of ministerial posts from 1819, when he was appointed Solicitor-General. He was raised to the peerage in 1826, and appointed Lord Chancellor in Canning's administration; he

was currently High Steward of the University of Cambridge, but again became Lord Chancellor when Peel returned to office in 1841. He had undertaken to sponsor Horne's petition in the House of Lords.

5. EBB apparently refers to Christopher North's *Recreations*, which substitutes "leaves" for "woods" in Wordsworth's line "Touch—for there is a spirit in the woods" ("Nutting," 1799, line 56).

6. Henry Petty-Fitzmaurice, 3rd Marquis of Lansdowne (1780–1863), was Lord President of the Council in Melbourne's administration. He had just appointed Harness as Registrar to the Privy Council, at a salary of £420 per annum. Kenyon wrote to Mary Harness that "the news has made me quite buoyant, and it will make scores of others buoyant too" (*Miss Mitford and Mr Harness: Records of a Friendship*, Caroline M. Duncan-Jones, 1955, pp. 42–43).

768. EBB to Richard Hengist Horne

Torquay.
Saturday– [?27 June] [1840][1]

So you were afraid of a conspiracy dear M!˙ Horne! Let me explain our innocency!– After my last note had gone to you I received a letter from Miss Mitford mentioning the annual for the first time; (the Mess.ʳˢ Finden having just made th!˙ proposition)—to find out if I myself were alive enough to help her, & what my 'advice' was about M!˙ Horne—whether an application to him might be dared or not.

Immediately came the thought of your labors & of the moral tale among them .. "Do this for me, or past kindnesses are thrown away". No! *I*[2] w.ᵈ not ask you– That was certain! But then Miss Mitford need not be quite, altogether, so magnanimous, & I said in 'my advice' .. "Just ask! you can but ask—you will ask yourself this time"—telling her however how over-occupied I understood you to be.. to prevent the least pressing beyond a bare question, & also any disappointment on her own side afterwards– I am so glad you sent the "backwork". It is more than my hope, & very very kind of you. I w.ᵈ not have teazed you in any case–

The truth is that "annualizing" brings an important part of dear Miss Mitford's income .. or to put the word in the sense which it assumes to her anxieties .. of her father's support—he being eighty & subject to attacks which render medical expenses only too necessary. She works upon the very roads of literature, in heavy stone-breaking labor, for hire & his sake. "Composition is no pleasure to *me*", said she to me once .. [']'it is too forced & incessant—but I work for my father." There never was a more womanly woman .. in the supreme womanliness of *devotion*.

I tell you this partly for the pleasure of telling it, & partly to make you glad of your past kindness. There never was one more womanly––or more instinct with generous sympathies in all things good & true. I love her very much—few in the world more—yet I have only seen her four times—& *this* in one week & three years ago in London– She can make anybody love her she pleases, & she pleased to make me.

I do hope you may know Miss Mitford some day.

But perhaps you will be satisfied *today* with my coming to an end quickly. *That* will be good luck enough for once–

Truly yours
Elizabeth B Barrett.

Have just been considering .. what an admirable preparation this "annualizing" will be to me, for the Greek Tragedy??[3] The Chorus will have their thymele-attitudes[4] perfect!

You "think you see that I intend" not to go to London!! I wish my intention had any power. I w^d intend most intently directly. As it is I do hold by the *power* of the hope of it—but the weakness *is so* great! Think of Mrs Orme being in Germany. I never heard she even thought of such a thing, until she was gone.

Publication: None traced.
Manuscript: Armstrong Browning Library.

1. The references to Miss Mitford's asking EBB about approaching Horne for a contribution to the 1841 *Findens' Tableaux* show that this follows the previous letter. It could have been written the following Saturday, but thereafter EBB was prostrated by Bro's death.
2. Underscored twice.
3. This is the first recorded reference to the projected collaboration of EBB and Horne on "Psyche Apocalypté."
4. In the ancient Greek theatre, the thymele was a Dionysian altar, near which the chorus was generally grouped.

---

769. EBB TO HUGH STUART BOYD

Torquay. 1. Beacon Terrace
July 8.th 40.

My ever dear friend,

I must write to you, although it is so very long, or at least seems so, since you wrote to me! But you say to Arabel in speaking of me that I "*used* to care for what is poetical"—therefore perhaps you say to yourself sometimes that I USED[1] to care for YOU!– I am anxious to vindicate my identity to you, in that respect above all.

It is a long dreary time since I wrote to you. I admit the pause on my own part, while I charge you with another. But *your* silence has embraced more pleasantness & less suffering to you than mine has to me—and I thank God for a prosperity in which my unchangeable regard for you, causes me to share indirectly. Indeed it is, & always must be very pleasant for me to hear of your being well & appearing well, & enjoying any sort of gladness from Greek to bell-ringing, from the majores to the Bobs major—& I perceive that the latter 'bears the bell'[2] just now. I congratulate you on your bell neighbourhood. The *caste* seems excellent. And the *clappers*, according to Swift's Laputa,[3] augur understanding.

"Bells on your fingers & rings on your toes
And you will have music wherever you *goes*"[4]

in your walks round the monastery. May other people have rings on their *fingers*, to give you the benefit of their marriage bells. I know your politics, and that you always liked a Peel[5]—excepting those three weeks when you wore the cap & bells & *wear* a radical "for love of me".[6] But you dont write to me now—only to AraBEL.

You see you have made me write nonsense once more, my dear friend. Indeed it seems almost time for me to pause from such work, & that I have had almost enough to wear out my laughters. I have not rallied this summer, as soon & well as I did last. I was very ill early in April at the time of our becoming conscious to our great affliction[7]—so ill, as to believe it utterly improbable, speaking humanly, that I ever should be any better. I am however a very great deal better, & gain strength by sensible degrees, however slowly—& do hope for the best—"the best" meaning one sight more of London. In the meantime I have not yet been able to leave my bed.

To prove to you that I who "used to care" for poetry, do so still, & that I have not been absolutely idle lately, an Athenæum shall be sent to you containing a poem on the subject of the removal of Napoleon's ashes.[8] It is a fitter subject for you than for me. Napoleon is no idol of *mine*. I[9] never made a 'setting-sun' of him. But my physician suggested the subject as a noble one,—& then there was something suggestive in the consideration that the Bellerophon lay on those very bay-waters, opposite to my bed.[10]

Another poem (which you wont like, I dare say) is called 'The Lay of the Rose' & appeared lately in a magazine. Arabel is going to write it out for you, she desires me to tell you, with her best love.[11] Indeed I have written lately (as far as manuscript goes) a good deal—only on all sorts of subjects & in as many shapes.

Lazarus w^d make a fine poem—w^{dnt} he?–[12] I lie here, weaving a great many schemes– I am seldom at a loss for thread.

Do write some times to me—& tell me if you do anything besides hearing the clocks strike & bells ring. My beloved Papa is with me still.

No. 770 [?27 July] [1840] 293

There are so many mercies close around me, (and his presence, far from the least),—that God's BEING seems proved to me, *demonstrated* to me, by His manifested love– May His blessing in the full lovingness, rest upon you always. Never fancy I can forget or think of you coldly.

Your affectionate & grateful
Elizabeth B Barrett.

Address: H S Boyd Esq.ʳ / 21. Downshire Hill / Hampstead / London.
Publication: EBB-HSB, pp. 237–239.
Manuscript: Wellesley College.

1. Underscored three times.
2. Chaucer, *Troilus and Criseyde* (1379), III, 198.
3. A play on "flappers," servants on Swift's island in the air, who each carried a bladder in which was "a small Quantity of dryed Pease or little Pebbles. . . . With these Bladders they now and then flapped the Mouths and Ears of those who stood near them" in order to rouse them from the "intense Speculations" occupying their minds (*Gulliver's Travels*, 1726, pt. III, ch. 2).
4. Cf. the anonymous nursery rhyme, "Ride a Cockhorse to Banbury Cross" (lines 3 and 4).
5. A play on Boyd's interest in campanology and his political views.
6. Tennyson, "The Mermaid" (last line of verses two and three).
7. i.e., Sam's death.
8. As a gesture of reconciliation, the Government had agreed to allow the repatriation of Napoleon's remains, and Louis Philippe had ordered the Prince de Joinville to go to St. Helena and escort the body back to Paris. EBB's poem, "Napoleon's Return," was printed in *The Athenæum* of 4 July (no. 662, p. 532). It was reprinted in a modified form in *Poems* (1844) as "Crowned and Buried."
9. Underscored twice.
10. H.M.S. *Bellerophon*, under the command of Capt. Frederick Lewis Maitland (1777–1839) had brought Napoleon to England after his surrender; the ship arrived at Tor Bay on 24 July 1815.
11. "A Lay of the Rose" was printed in *The Monthly Chronicle* for July (pp. 13–17). Arabel's handwritten copy is now at Wellesley (see *Reconstruction*, D454).
12. i.e., the story told in John, 11. No poem by EBB on this subject is extant.

---

770. RB TO WILLIAM CHARLES MACREADY

Hanover Cottage, Southhampton St.C.ⁱⁱ
Monday Mg [?27 July] [1840]¹

My dear Macready,

"The luck of the third adventure" is proverbial– I have written a spick & span new Tragedy—(a sort of compromise between my own notion & yours—as I understand it, at least—) and will read it to you if you care to be bothered so far—there is *action* in it, drabbing, stabbing, et autres gentillesses,²—who knows but the Gods may mean me good even yet?– Only, make no scruple of saying flatly that you cannot spare the time, if engagements of which I know nothing but fancy a great deal, should claim every couple of hours in the course of this week.³

Yours ever truly,
Robᵗ Browning.

294 [?27 July] [1840] *No. 770*

Publication: LRB, p. 5 (as ca. 1840).
Manuscript: Armstrong Browning Library.

  1. Dated by the reference to RB's play.
  2. "Other pretty tricks."
  3. *Mansoor the Hierophant* was one of the works advertised as "nearly ready" when *Sordello* was published in February 1840. Re-named *The Return of the Druses*, RB's first version was promised to Macready in letter 753. As a result of Macready's comments, the play was expanded to five acts and was the subject of letter 761. Further changes were made, and RB was now hoping "third time lucky"; however, as the following letter shows, Macready was still not enthusiastic about the play. He recorded in his diary on 3 August: "Read Browning's play, and with the deepest concern I yield to the belief that he will *never write again*—to any purpose. I fear his intellect is not quite clear. I do not know how to write to Browning" (*Macready*, II, 72).

---

771. RB to William Charles Macready

Camberwell
Sunday Night. [9 August 1840][1]

So once again, dear Macready, I have failed to please you! The Druzes *return*, in another sense than I had hoped;[2] for though, to confess a truth, I have worked from the beginning somewhat in the spirit of the cucumber-dresser in the old story (the doctor, you remember, bids such an one "slice a plate full—salt it, pepper it, add oil, vinegar &c &c and then .. throw all behind the fire")—spite of this, I *did* rather fancy that you would have "sympathized" with Djabal in the main scenes of my play; and your failing to do so is the more decisive against it, that I really had you *here*, in this little room of mine, while I wrote bravely away—*here* were you, propping the weak, pushing the strong parts (such I thought there might be!)—now majestically motionless, and now "laying about as busily, as the Amazonian dame Penthesilé"[3]—and *here*, please the fates, shall you again & again give breath and blood to some thin creation of mine yet unevoked—but *elsewhere—enfoncé!*[4] Your other objections I think less material—that the auditory, for instance, know nothing of the Druzes and their doings *until I tell them* (which is the very office I take on myself) that they are men & women oppressed and outraged in such and such ways and desirous of being rid of their oppressor and outrager: if the auditory thus far instructed (and I considered that point sufficiently made out) call for a previous acquaintance with the Druzes before they will go along with such a desire .. are they not worthy compatriots of the Hyde-park gentleman who "could not think of pulling a man out of the Serpentine to whom he had not been previously introduced"?

    I intend to be with you in a day or two under the greenwood at Arden[5]—but, ask me whence the "banished Duke"[6] comes, why they

My dear Macready,

"The luck of the third adventure" is proverbial — I have written a spick & span new Tragedy — (a sort of compromise between my own notion & yours — as I understand it, at least) and will read it to you if you care to be bothered so far — there is action in it, "stabbing, stabbing, et autres gentillesses,"— who knows but the Gods may make me good even yet? — Only, make no

Letter 770

scruple of saying flatly that you cannot spare the time, if engagements of which I know nothing but fancy a great deal, should claim every couple of hours in the course of this week.

Yours wishfully,
Robt Browning.

Hanover Cottage,
South Hampstead, N.
Monday N.

banish him and how,—and you confound me .. who yet shall rejoice from my heart when Duke Frederick makes restitution at the end[6]—so much can "that one word, banished" (as Juliet says) effect![7] Surely such matters are the *"donnés,"* the given quantities, the logical "be it conceded"-s, without which there is no working problem or deducing an *ergo*,[8]— and so it has been from the very dawn & cock-crow-time of the drama (—for it is edifying to observe how in some primitive Mystery (Johan à Tadcastre's or Robert Leicestensis'[9] essay in King John's reign) the courtship of the Sultan of Mesopotamia's daughter by the "King of Port's" nephew shall have rivetted the attention of all London or St Albans for six hours together—) —And so I could remark on your other "misgivings"—the sole and simple point, let me say, on which I find you, to my judging, attackable: this note (written "on a spurt" at midnight and with a sad headache) is from me to you, and for no third overlookers: to the devil all flattery! with the exception of Miss Horton[10] there is not an actor or actress on the stage I can look at without loathing (that's the word) beside yourself: they vulgarize, and bestialize—no matter, you will not comprehend me: Charles Kean I never saw (he talks about "these: HANGMEN's hands"—"with a fine burst" (says a paper of yesterday)—and sees "gouts of BLOOD" "with even a finer—." I never saw him)[11]—why don't you force the whole herd to run violently down a steep place into the sea?[12] Kean wants to be Macbeth three times a week .. people go to see if he can manage it; *you are* & have been this—how many years?— Macbeth—as everybody knows: why not be something else? Were *I you* (save the mark!)—it should be my first condition with a playwright that his piece should be new, essentially new for better or for worse: if it failed .. who that has seen you perform in some forty or fifty parts I could name, would impute the failure to you who were Iago on Thursday and Virginius[13] on Saturday? If it did not fail .. were it even some poor Return of the Druzes, it would be something yet unseen, in however poor a degree—something, therefore, to go and see. Laugh at all this—I write, indeed, that you may .. for is it not the characteristic of those who withdraw from "the scene" to "take on us the mystery of things, as if [we] were God's spies"?- "And we'll wear out, in a walled prison" (my room here) "sects & packs of great ones that ebb and flow by the moon"![14]—for tomorrow will I betimes break new ground with So & So—an epic in so many books ... let it but do me half the good "Sordello" has done—be praised by the units, cursed by the tens, and unmeddled with by the hundreds! God bless you, dear Macready, send you the Man and the Tragedy and *how* both of you will be hailed from the back of the boxes, by,

Yours ever
R Browning

I have left out the essential amid this chatter—and have not thanked you for your offer to forward my play to Webster:[15] He knows by this, I should say, another mode in which performances he ought to approve of, reach him! "I will rather sue to be despised!"[16]—or send it to Madame Vestris[17] leaving your name out by a pure oversight! Keep it safe, please, till I call on you some morning this week.

Publication: NL, pp. 20–23 (as [23 August 1840]).
Manuscript: Yale University.

1. Dated by reference to the newspaper article on Kean.
2. Despite Macready's negative comments, RB did not abandon hopes of having the play staged. Macready recorded in his diary for 27 August that RB "really *wearied* me ... with his self-opinionated persuasions upon his *Return of the Druses*. I fear he is for ever gone" (*Macready*, II, 76). After a second reading of the latest version, Macready's final judgement was that the play was "mystical, strange and heavy" (*Macready*, II, 80). The play was not published until 1843, and, as far as is known, was never performed in RB's lifetime.
3. Penthesilea, Queen of the Amazons, assisted Priam in the Trojan Wars and was slain by Achilles. RB's quotation is a paraphrase of Spenser's lines: "Full fiercely layde the Amazon about, / And dealt her blowes unmercifully sore" (*The Faerie Queene*, bk. V, 7, 31, 1–2).
4. "Done for!"
5. The setting for *As You Like It*, here intended as a poetic reference to Macready's home at Elstree.
6. In *As You Like It*.
7. *Romeo and Juliet*, III, 2, 113.
8. "Therefore."
9. John of Tadcaster, Robert of Leicester—names invented by RB to make a point.
10. Priscilla Horton, a young actress whose range extended from the Fool in *Lear* to Juliet.
11. Charles John Kean (1811?–68) was sharing the season at the Haymarket with Macready, and was his principal rival. Perhaps because of this, RB's assertion "I never saw him" may be taken as an expression of loyalty to Macready. The article referred to was a review of Kean's final performance of the season, in the role of Macbeth; it appeared in *The Times* of 8 August 1840.
12. Matthew, 8:32.
13. In the play of that name by James Sheridan Knowles, first produced in 1820, and one of Macready's favourite roles.
14. *King Lear*, V, 3, 16–19.
15. In his diary for 12 August, Macready recorded: "Browning called, and ... talked of his play and of *Sordello*, and I most honestly told him my opinion on both ... He wished me to have his play done for nothing. I explained to him that Mr. Webster *would not* do it" (*Macready*, II, 73).
16. *Othello*, II, 3, 277.
17. Lucia Elizabeth Mathews (*née* Bartolozzi, 1797–1856), professionally known as Mme. Vestris, had a career as a singer and actress from 1815 until 1828. In 1831 she became "the first female lessee the stage had known" when she assumed the management of the Olympic Theatre (*DNB*). Under the constraints of the Act of 1737 (see letter 767, note 3) the programmes she mounted were perforce less weighty than those at the Haymarket.

772. EBB TO MARY RUSSELL MITFORD

[Torquay]
[early October 1840][1]

My ever beloved friend,

I never once thought of your thanking [us] for such a thing—nor could any of us—although it seems to me that no hand can so rightly express this as the one which trembles so in doing it. You are always among the most affectionate & disinterested. *I* supposed it to be a duty on my part to give up the trust into your hand.[2]

I am better you see—& thankful for being so, on ONE account (as far as concerns myself) for it gives me hope that they will soon let me go away from this dreadful dreadful place. The physician said I sh^d die in going if they took me—but nearly three months' anguish here has been the worse killing. Oh my beloved friend!— These walls—& the sound of what is very fearful a few yards from them—that perpetual dashing sound, have preyed on me. I have been crushed trodden down. God's will is terrible!—[3]

But they are well—those who are *left*. I thank God. I pray for you beloved friend & yours—loving you truly & to the *end*.

Your EBB.

I am very much better. Arabel's affect^e thanks! *Write to me.*

Publication: EBB-MRM, I, 202.
Manuscript: Wellesley College.

1. Dated by EBB's reference to "nearly three months' anguish" after Bro's death.
2. EBB's prostration after her brother's death made it impossible for her to fulfil her promise to contribute to the 1841 *Findens' Tableaux.* As she was unable to write herself, it is apparent that some member of her family wrote to Miss Mitford on her behalf.
3. "Bro," the closest to EBB of all the family and "always the adytum of all her secrets & plans" (SD1131), had died on 11 July while out sailing, when a sudden squall capsized the boat (see SD1129 and vol. 1, pp. 289–290). Because he had been allowed to remain in Torquay through her pleading, she felt herself to blame for the tragedy; she was scarcely able to bring herself ever to mention it, even to RB.

---

773. EBB TO MARY RUSSELL MITFORD

[Torquay]
Monday— [November 1840][1]

My beloved friend,

You have not thought me ill or—worse still—unkind, for not writing?— I feel bound more than I ever remember having felt, in chains, heavy & cold enough to be iron—& which have indeed entered into the soul.² But I do love you still—& am rather better than worse—likely, I do suppose to live on. In the meantime, thank you thank you for your letter, & *both* of you dear Dr Mitford, & my beloved friend, for your affectionate sympathy. Months roll over months. I know it is for good— but *very hard to bear*. And now—at least a week ago—my kind physician, after having held out hope from time to time, for the sake I do suspect now of drawing me onward, brought me his ultimatum—that he cannot sanction my attempting to leave this dreadful place before the spring– He told me he had wished & prayed it might be otherwise, but he was convinced now that in the case of my removing even to another house *here* much less to London, the consequences w^d be fatal.

After all, I suffer so in staying that I w^d dare it & go– But my saying this is quite vain, with Papa & my sisters looking on– They wont hear of it. So I stay– They are well I thank God.

You wont miss me dearest Miss Mitford in the Tableaux– I know & knew you w^{dnt}—except in your illogical affectionateness. Then Mr Horne does not contribute? Mind you dont think of sending *me* a copy– I shall try to see it—& such a largesse w^d be quite out of place considering the circumstances.

May God bless you always– My sisters['] love to you—& mine to Dr Mitford. *Can* you read?³

Your unchangingly affectionate
EBB–

Notwithstanding this trembling hand, I am better & stronger—& more tranquil as to my thoughts. I suffered from what was called *congestion of the heart*—& was in so singular & frightful a state of weakness as not to be able to sleep for five minutes together without *fainting*. For weeks they watched me in their kindness night after night—only ascertaining the transition by a sigh, or the sudden coldness of cheek & forehead. And now I can sleep for an hour or more at a time—& the faintings are almost quite gone. Dearest Miss Mitford—I do truly love you. Love me a little. You understand so well—& will—besides—that I want them all to go & leave me here with my maid for the winter. I sh^d be far easier & happier if they w^d—*far easier*. But I fear they wont go,—dear things!–

So far I had written—& now I hear thro' Mr Kenyon that dear Dr Mitford has not been well & that you are in distress. Oh do do, write—if you can—when you can– I must not lay a straw's further weight on you my beloved friend. May God bless you *both*–

Your ever attached
EBB.

M.ʳ Kenyon talks of remaining here a fortnight longer,—& of buying, moreover, a house to live in occasionally—not to the exclusion of his London one. Papa does *not believe* ⟨the r⟩umour.[4]

Address: Miss Mitford / Three Mile Cross / near Reading.
Publication: EBB-MRM, I, 202–204.
Manuscript: Wellesley College.

1. Dated by Kenyon's being in Torquay. He had arrived at the end of October (SD1137).
2. Cf. *The Book of Common Prayer*, Psalm 105:18.
3. EBB's handwriting still reflected her distress over Bro's death.
4. i.e., that Kenyon's house-hunting foreshadowed his marriage: "It is all stuff about Kenyon's marriage" (SD1133).

---

774. EBB TO MARY RUSSELL MITFORD

Torquay–
Nov.ʳ 26.ᵗʰ– [1840][1]

Ever my dearest Miss Mitford—
Let my silences express as well as my words the unchangeable affection with which I regard you, & which, bearing as it does just now, an anxious character, suggests a beseeching for a few more words from you– The last account of dear D.ʳ Mitford & your own dearest self will not let me rest satisfied with a silence from you, suiting mine. As for mine—oh you must pardon it & me my beloved friend. I fall into silences now, both of voice & writing, & lie in them too—when unawakened. Forgive me. It is not the LOVE'S fault–

Well!—but may you *both* be quite well & cheerful by this time!– I hoped dear D.ʳ Mitford might be inclined to the Devonshire cream with his coffee—& not be less so because I sent it—that is—because a person sent it, who cares with her whole heart for *you*.

How anxious you must have been!– Those mustard applications are very useful & safe. I had them for three months & more *every* day, upon the region of the heart, when I was so ill lately with congestion there as they called it. They give their scientific names even to our agonies!–

Will you, when you next see Miss Anderdon give her my regards with the expression of my thankfulness for the kind interest & enquiries you tell me of.

Dear M.ʳ Kenyon left Torquay a few days ago without my seeing him. When I heard that he was *gone unseen*, it struck me something painfully, & with another thought,—that I might not recover that rejected or lost opportunity of seeing him. But I am quite confined to bed—he w.^{d} have thought the admission strange!—and my voice is gone, & all else besides—at least so much,—that I shrink away from the very *idea* of a human face. Well—not to speak such sadnesses for your sake—I think I may assure you that Mr Kenyon is not going to be married,—with any present prospect of the same. He went away with no other than the half intention of purchasing a residence here—"a house" he said to my sister "to which he might come occasionally as a lodging, *not* a home, because he did not mean to give up his London house,—& one home was quite enough for a single man." Now this is decisive, & exclusive of Miss Mackenzie![2]

Mr Bezzi, the whole world being witness,—& myself besides—for whose use he brought down a great book the other day thro' wind rain & twilight,—is an incarnate benevolence. There is no romance,—I mean romantic fallacy,—in the estimate of it & him.

No!—I never saw Mr Horne. I thought you knew— Thank you for your little sketch.

May the Heavenly blessing be eternally with you dearest dearest Miss Mitford!–

                        Your attached & grateful
                        Elizabeth B Barrett–

Never forget my love to Dr Mitford .. WHENEVER *he will take it*. I am going on better–

Oh yes!– I shall like to hear about Sir Lytton Bulwer—only not to tire *you*. A few words about your own self & yours is all I ask for.

I have not yet seen the Tableaux. Are the *Letters* to appear & when?–[3]

Publication: EBB-MRM, I, 204–205.
Manuscript: Wellesley College.

  1. Dated by Kenyon's leaving Torquay.
  2. EBB's comment suggests that Miss Mackenzie may have been Kenyon's presumptive bride.
  3. See letter 737, note 1.

775. EBB to Thomas Powell[1]

[Torquay]
9th December 1840

Offered for sale in North's December 1907 catalogue, item 38. 1½ pp., 12mo. "Miss Barrett begs to offer Mr. Powell ... her thanks for the cordiality of his expression towards her ..."

  1. For details of EBB's friendship with Powell, see pp. 330–331.

776. EBB TO MARY RUSSELL MITFORD

[Torquay]
Decr 10.th 1840

Day after day my beloved friend, have I been meaning & dreaming to write to you. Here at last & now, I begin. Thanks oh thanks for your delightful gleams of letters. They bring light to me,—& if it goes again, that is, because I cannot think of you & your kindness always–

Another little note today. I almost feel *guilty*– But I lean for rest upon a pleasanter feeling, . . one of gladness at hearing of the amendment in dear Dr Mitford's health, & your consequent relief from immediate anxieties. The note makes me glad too, in a secondary way,—to think of his caring for my cream . . & me. Give my love to him—will you, dearest Miss Mitford?–

You cant guess what my business has been lately. Chaucer?– No!— not Chaucer. Chaucer was done with some time since, & I received him the evening before last, with a vernally green back like "a sweet new poem".[1] No—my business has been retracing my steps in the Village, your village,—step by step, up & down, & never feeling tired. You cannot realize,—you the writer—cannot,—the peculiar effect of that delightful book, upon one in a prison like me, shut up from air & light, & to whom even the captive of Chillon's bird does not come to sing–[2] It is not sadness—it is not regret. On the contrary. It frees me at once, for the moment—shows me the flowers & the grass they grow by, & pours into my face the sweetness & freshness & refreshment of the whole summer in a breath.

Oh do tell me whatever more may be decided in respect to *Otto*.[3] I care so much.

You were in London!– When I read *that* I began to dream what joy your going w.^{d} have been to me if I had been in London too! But perhaps my turn may come to take joy in your being in London. Perhaps. If such a word as joy is ever to come to my lips again with a meaning in it—for indeed the three letters in that word, seemed to mock me as I wrote them. And yet, I have thanked God tonight for a deeply-felt mercy—, for the safe arrival of my beloved brother Charles John from the West Indies.[4] I thank God for his abundant mercies. Abundant, past my deserts, they are always. Only hearts in a manner broken, do not hold the right & full sense of them—I fear, not.

Papa wrote this news to me–

But dearest dearest Miss Mitford, what have you thought of my dumb tongue in regard to the Tableaux? Dont think that I am not pleased—not very pleased. It w.^{d} be 'foul & unnatural'[5] of me, not to be very very pleased. Your stories are delightful[6]—pass all your old Tableaux stories, with a turn-the-corner & out-of-sight passing,—& w.^{d} win the obduratest heart of the best annual hater in her Majesty's dominions—win or bewitch, I wont be sure which. And then Mr Darley's poem– It is very very beautiful—poetry in the full word.–[7] There can be no room for hoping anything about the work's success, because none for fearing. So I wont hope. I'll be sure. I *am* sure.

Mr Kenyon is likely after all to purchase a house here, although not for a bride. At least Dr Scully told me yesterday that things were in progress as to purchase—or rather that the purchase remains a probability,—for I dont know that a step upon solid ground has been actually taking [*sic*]. And the object of the purchase is said to be—a home for his brother—who is, you know, a great invalid, & about, as you may not know, to settle in England. This solves the problem,—of the WHY of dear Mr Kenyon's turning his face towards Torquay.

Can you tell me if Mrs Jamieson is married—I mean—if her husband lives, & lives with her. There is a strangeness in her Canada-book which makes me curious, & inclined to be gossiped *to*.[8]

In such haste, dearest dearest Miss Mitford!– You see it, without my saying it!! If besides you see Chaucer anywhere tell me what you think of US!– Mr Horne's Introduction has delighted me– I am tolerably well—&

ever your attached
EBB.

Publication: EBB-MRM, I, 205–207.
Manuscript: Wellesley College.

1. *The Poems of Geoffrey Chaucer, Modernized*. Horne, believing that Chaucer was unjustly neglected owing to his archaic language, had invited several poets, including Wordsworth, Leigh Hunt, and EBB, to produce a modern version of *The Canterbury Tales*. EBB contributed "Queen Annelida and False Arcite" and "The Complaint of Annelida to False Arcite."

2. The captive was François de Bonivard (1493–1571), whose imprisonment was the subject of Byron's *The Prisoner of Chillon* (1816). The episode of the bird occurs at lines 251–270.

3. The hope that Miss Mitford's play would be produced in April (see letter 729, note 4) came to nothing. Apparently, Miss Mitford still was optimistic that it might be staged.

4. SD1142 reports his safe arrival after a 60-day passage. He had gone to Jamaica with Sam in July 1839.

5. Cf. *Hamlet*, I, 5, 25.

6. The 1841 *Findens' Tableaux*, published on 2 November 1840, contained six prose stories by Miss Mitford.

7. George Darley had contributed "Harvest-Home."

8. Anna Brownell Jameson (*née* Murphy, 1794–1860) had been living apart from her husband, Robert Jameson, since she returned to England in 1838, leaving him in Canada, where he was Vice-Chancellor of Upper Canada.

Her book, *Winter Studies and Summer Rambles in Canada* (3 vols.), had been published in 1838.

777. EBB TO JULIA MARTIN

[Torquay]
Decr 11.th 1840

My ever dearest Mrs Martin,

I should have written to you, without this last proof of your remembrance—this cape, which, warm & pretty as it is, I value so much more as the work of your hands and gift of y.^r affection towards me. Thank you, dearest Mrs Martin—and thank you too for *all the rest*—for all your sympathy & love. And do believe that although grief had so changed me from myself, & warped me from my old instincts, as to prevent my looking forwards with pleasure to seeing you again, yet that full amends are made in the looking back, with a pleasure more true because more tender than any old retrospections. Do give my love to dear Mr Martin, & say—what I c.^d not have said even if I had seen him.

Shall you really, dearest Mrs Martin, come again? Dont think we do not think of the hope you left us. Because we do indeed.

A note from Papa has brought the comforting news that my dear dear Stormie is in England again, in London, & looking perfectly well. It is a mercy which makes me very thankful—& would make me joyful if anything could. But the meaning of some words change as we live on. Papa's note is hurried– It was a sixty day passage—& that is all he tells us. Yes—there is something besides about Sette and Occy being either unknown or misknown, through the fault of their growing.[1] Papa is not near returning I think. He has so much to do & see, & so much cause to be enlivened & renewed as to spirits, that I begged him not to think about me & stay away as long as he pleased. And the accounts of him & of all at home are satisfying I thank God.

How soon you were in London![2] May you come here in a proportionate velocity to your dreams ... & ours, dearest Mrs Martin.

We have heard from Bummy, who speaks of our Cousin John Clarke's marriage being *imminent*—immediately after Christmas—& of his having left his father's house by mutual declaration *'for ever'*. I wonder how people can use such expressions—& from such motives. For ever is a word for God. John & Miss Eagles[3] are both at Clifton—or near Clifton. Dear Bummy, quite well–

Henrietta will be too glad—be sure of that—to make herself in any way useful to Mrs Hanford—& I only hope that the latter may be as sure of as many good reasons for liking to remain here. There is an east wind just now, which I feel– Nevertheless Dr Scully has said, a few minutes since, that I am as well as he c.^d hope, considering the season.

May God bless you ever—

Your gratefully attached
Ba.

Henrietta's & Arabel's best love—

Publication: LEBB, I, 85–86 (in part).
Manuscript: Wellesley College.

1. In SD1142, telling Henrietta of Charles John's return, Edward Moulton-Barrett wrote that Storm "made some strange mistake about the two younger boys, Ockey he knew nothing of, & Sette he took for Harry."
2. Presumably a reference to the spreading network of railways, making travel so much faster than by stage-coach.
3. EBB's cousin's prospective bride was the daughter of John Eagles, the Curate of Kinnersley; Kinnersley Castle was the home of the parents of John Altham Graham-Clarke the younger, which EBB says he had left *"for ever."* The marriage took place on 29 December.

---

778. RB TO WILLIAM CHARLES MACREADY

[London]
Tuesday night. [15 December 1840][1]

Dear Macready,

"My friends—do they now and then send"—and so on. Have you divined, arch-diviner as you are, that I have been sick, and doctored, and slowly convales[c]ent, and enforcedly quiescent, and all and everything except indifferent to you and yours—new play included?[2] I may go out on mornings already—(loquitur Medicus)[3]—on evenings, Haymarket-ward, next week—and have to get as far as Clarence Terrace through a few more bottles-full of Tonic: what motives are here for getting strong! (I ought to have said that something is, or was, wrong in my circulation and that it nearly stopped of a sudden). Will you do me the favour to remember me to Mrs and Miss Macready?— But I must call myself,—for we remove into a new house, the week after next,[4]—a place really not impossible to be got at—and monstrously ambitious thoughts begin to rise like clouds within me: "By that sin, fell the angels"[5] . . . noun—no use!

Ever yours, and ambitious
of *that*,
R Browning.

Publication: LRB, pp. 4–5.
Manuscript: Browning Settlement.

1. Dated by the impending move to New Cross.

2. Macready's new play was Bulwer-Lytton's *Money*, first performed on 8 December.
3. "Says the Doctor."
4. At the end of December, the Brownings moved from Camberwell to a larger house in New Cross. In a letter dated 31 [sic] April 1841 to Laman Blanchard, RB described it as "resembling a goose-pie—only a crooked hasty and rash goose-pie."
5. *Henry VIII*, III, 2, 441.

779. EBB TO MARY RUSSELL MITFORD

[Torquay]
[mid-December 1840][1]

Ever ever dearest Miss Mitford & dear D! Mitford,

May I say so? May I thank both of you for letting me & liking me to have Flush the second? I do, you see—if I may or not. I must. No dog in the world c^d please me so—and if really & truly I dare accept him, that is if you are quite unrepentant of your kind proposal, why there is nothing to be done but to be ready to receive him at the earliest moment, & to love him at all moments, for your sake, until we reach the 'inherent merit,' the loveability for his own.

But dearest Miss Mitford, we have considered, & enquiries have been made for me at the Hotel here,—& it is matter of assurance that there is no room for fear, if you send him directly hither through Basingstoke. Send him by the railroad to Basingstoke, with a direction on the card .. 'to be forwarded by the first Exeter coach'—& the coachman both there & at Exeter will be commissioned to feed him & see to his comfort generally. There is no danger M! Webb[2] assured my councillor—that is, if he is packed carefully in a *hamper*.

But then comes my dread– Is it not a robbery?—or rather shall you not miss him?– Will D! Mitford miss him? Will Flush (the first) miss him? Now I trust to you not to *grieve* me by suffering such things to be.

And if the kindness says '*no*', will you write to mention the very day he sets out—so that the coachman may be prepared? And oh thank you .. for your first thoughts at least.

If Flush the second comes, he is sure to be loved. The logic is so strong!– There is no escape from the conclusion of *love*.

My dearest Miss Mitford! do you know your letter this morning made me quite smile—quite amused—I mean the part of it relating to the country gentlemen versus the poets—more especially, to that poor 'neutralized poet'—the *cross* between poet & sportsman. Dearest Miss Mitford! And I so obstinate all the time!! And none of the eternized great spirits,[3] who were poets & were never country gentlemen, haunting *you!!*

When there is an opportunity I will lend you *my* Chaucer to read[4]—so dont think of getting it. Mr Horne's Indroduction [*sic*] has both beauty & wisdom—although I secede from one or two of his sayings—that is, I think I do, while he thinks I dont.[5] After all, I fear the book is sure to be left, for the most part, in the publisher's hands, & that no second volume will be called for.[6]

In regard to the Tableaux, I compassionate with you, [about] Mr Townsend's daughter—or would, if that feeling were not too soft for the occasion. Such things always make me angry—not at their delicacy, but *indelicacy*[7]. I do assure you most seriously & sincerely, that one suspicion of

⟨...⟩[8]

Does Miss Niven write as well as ride?–[9] or have you converted her? Do tell me of your own writing. Do my beloved friend. I love you always.

Publication: EBB-MRM, I, 208–209.
Manuscript: Folger Shakespeare Library and Wellesley College.

1. Dated by the impending arrival of Flush, the first offspring of Miss Mitford's Flush.
2. E. Webb was the proprietor of the Royal Hotel, whence coaches ran daily between Torquay and Exeter.
3. Cf. Keats, "Addressed to Haydon" (1816), line 1.
4. EBB's copy of *The Poems of Geoffrey Chaucer, Modernized* formed lot 568 of *Browning Collections* (see *Reconstruction*, A628).
5. EBB had reservations about some of the current usages substituted for Chaucer's words. They are noted in *EBB-RHH*, I, 110–114.
6. There was no second volume.
7. The significance of EBB's remark is not known. Townsend had contributed a poem, "Home," to the recently-published *Findens' Tableaux*.
8. The conclusion of the letter is missing, except for the following sentences written across the top of the first page.
9. The formal mode of address suggests that the reference is to Mrs. Niven's sister-in-law, rather than to Miss Mitford's protégée, Agnes Niven.

---

780. EBB TO RICHARD HENGIST HORNE

[Torquay]
Decr 17.th 1840.

I did not say half—not half—enough about the 'Introduction'– The Apotheosis of Chaucer, or rather your witness to his poetic divineness, is very beautiful—that passage for instance about the greenness of his green leaves & the whiteness of his daisies (so true that is!) & above all a noble paragraph nearer the end, close to the end, testifying to the devotional verity of every veritable poet. I have read it again & again.[1]

Notwithstanding all the merit & the grace, do not some of the poems militate against the principle you set out with? I venture to think that the refashioners stand,—some of them & in a measure,—too far from Chaucer's side—however graceful the attitudes. You yourself & Wordsworth are devoutly near, & most devoutly. *Most*—for even M[r] Leigh Hunt is sometimes satisfied with being with Chaucer in the spirit, & spurns the accidents of body[2]—while M[r] Bell's Mars & Venus is too smooth & varnished & redolent of the 19th century, as appears to me, for spirit or body.[3] I think people will say 'you might keep nearer Chaucer'—but however .. they may'nt: and if they are not (say what they please) delighted with this volume, this breathing of sweet souths[4] over the bank of deathless violets, there can be no room for delight in their souls.

No—are you in earnest about liking Psyche?[5] And after that huge mass of spiritual matter hight Gregory?– Perhaps after all, the passion you throw into everything w[d] exhale too dimly in the allegorical twilight of such a subject. But I will think as you tell me. Only dear M[r] Horne, how do you know that I shall think effectively? And indeed you do me "an infinite deal"[6] of superfluous credit, when you suffer my providence of poetry to predestinate habitually the whole future of every poetic subject. I always struggle for a purpose—& mold a beginning middle & end part *in my mind* before writing a line! No—nothing can be done towards unity without wholeness—& the one purpose, is the soul of the composition,—the proof of life, the *puto* ergo *sum*.[7] So I do struggle for the purpose—but not for a 'plan' implying I suppose details. Oh but I do not wonder at *your* doing so—& indeed with so artistic a developper of high dramatic designs, it c[d] scarcely be otherwise.

You see how the inequalities begin to manifest themselves at the first step!——

M[r] Powell's question was about a stanza in "Cowper's Grave", my little poem, which he said M[r] Leigh Hunt & himself did not understand in the same way.[8] That was all.

Papa has ventured to leave his card upon you. So he tells me. He is a very bad visitor, or w[d] have done it long ago,—with his strong impression of all your kindness towards one of his family. Do go and see them in Wimpole Street, dear M[r] Horne some day when you are in the neighbourhood—do—before *I* am there—if really it is not out of all order in me to say such a thing. But it w[d] give them real pleasure to know you, *I* am very sure—& besides, I shall like to think that they do–

Ever & truly yours
EBB—

No, we dont agree—& I want to set up not the contrariety but the *identity* of the principle[s] of Greek versification & ours.

Address: R H Horne, Esq.ʳ / 2. Gray's Inn Square / Gray's Inn / London.
Publication: EBB-RHH, I, 107–110 (in part).
Manuscript: Pierpont Morgan Library.

1. In the introduction to *The Poems of Geoffrey Chaucer, Modernized*, Horne said of him, "he is so graphic, so sure of eye and hand, so rich in the power of conveying objects of sense to the imaginations of others, that his words have almost the effect of substances and colours ... Certainly, the *green leaves* of Chaucer are among the very *greenest* we ever saw, the coolest and freshest; his *white* and *red*, the utmost realities the mind, apart from sensuous contact, can possibly apprehend of those colours" (p. xcvi). "His garlands of daisies are so white and full of fresh fragrance in the loveliest mornings in May, that we can scarcely leave them to look at the troop of knights and ladies in various attire, who ride forth" (p. xcvii). At the end, he says, "As every true poet 'has a song in his mind,' yet more certainly has every great poet a religious passion in his soul" (p. civ).
2. Horne's own contributions were the "Prologue to the Canterbury Tales," "The Reve's Tale," and "The Franklin's Tale." Wordsworth's were "The Cuckoo and the Nightingale" and "Extract from Troilus and Cresida." Leigh Hunt supplied "The Manciple's Tale," "The Friar's Tale," and "The Squire's Tale."
3. "The Complaint of Mars and Venus," by Robert Bell, pp. 211–234.
4. See letter 668, note 3.
5. The subject of a projected drama, for which EBB would prepare the outline and Horne the dialogue. As subsequent letters show, a considerable amount of work was done by both during the spring and summer of 1841, but after her return to London in September, she lost interest. Horne never entertained the idea of completing the drama alone, feeling that it would be "like treading upon sacred ground" (*EBB-RHH*, II, 110). Accounts of the genesis and history of "Psyche Apocalypté" can be found in *EBB-RHH* (II, 61–110), *The St. James's Magazine and United Empire Review* (February 1876, pp. 478–492) and *HUP* (II, 201–221).
6. *The Merchant of Venice*, I, 1, 114.
7. "I think therefore I am."
8. This question was presumably answered in letter 775.

---

781. RB TO RACHEL TALFOURD

Camberwell
18 December 1840

Offered for sale in Sotheby's 27 July 1905 Catalogue, lot 1072. 1 p., 8vo. "I have I am sure many more regrets than may be put into a note that your kind invitation finds me engaged for next Sunday past all hope of release. My Xmas week opens but ominously. I hope, however, to call on you one of these mornings and to console myself."

782. EBB TO THOMAS POWELL

[Torquay]
Decr 24.th 1840.

Dear Sir,

I prefer sending you my first thanks, to keeping them back even a day,—although doing so w.^d enable me to read through what your kindness sent, & this most probably, suggest[s] still better reasons for thanking you. But it is right to apprize you of the safe arrival—& the reasons are good enough already—seeing that—this kind attention wins quite *unprovoked*, & proceeded, besides, from a friend of Mr Horne's, & a writer neither unknown nor unesteemed by the obliged. For I see the Monthly Chronicle—& had read some of the poems which accompanied the book.[1]

Of the rest, it has not yet of course been possible for me to do more than read a little with my eyes & a little with my fingers—but poetical thoughts "sweetly spoken"[2] have been recognized & felt notwithstanding the haste—for instance in page 12, that mutual intertexture of sound & light—& the stanza in '*Stanzas*' p 22, beginning "The moonlight sleepeth on the grave"—& the true, touching words at the bottom of p 25

> 'The memory of the storm may cease,
> But not of those who smiled the peace'.

Then I like 'the Hills'. But the 'Chaunt' comes nearer to me than anything—notwithstanding that beautiful stanza in the Dirge,

> 'As a young child from her sleep
> Is wakened by the song she sings &c['][3]

That appears to me a new & beautiful thought.

Believe me, I estimate the high & graceful finishing of the Flower & the Leaf—which indeed is, in my mind .. if I may dare to say so, .. almost excessive—for does not its polish occasion us sometimes to slide over Chaucer?—to very soft sounds, I admit?[4]

I am glad you like anything done by me, whether in the Chaucer or elsewhere—& will readily, if you continue to wish it, work as well as I can for the second volume. You mean I think the *second Nun's tale*, instead of the Nun's Priest's[5]—altho' you *say* the latter—(the 2.^d Nun's *Cecilia*)[6],—& I do trust Mr Wordsworth will not deny himself to it after all. Poets *never grow old!*– I knew an individual once, Sir Uvedale Price, who was not a poet,—only poetical,—yet a very young man, at eighty one. By which sign, the great poet of our times must be in his very prime of youthfulness,—surely not too old for Cecilia!

With my repeated thanks for your obliging present & words, I remain
faithfully yrs
Elizabeth B Barrett.

Publication: None traced.
Manuscript: Armstrong Browning Library.

1. Powell was a prolific contributor of poems to *The Monthly Chronicle* (19 appeared between July and December 1840). From the context it appears that he had now sent EBB a volume of his poems, but we have been unable to trace such a work; the earliest listed in the British Library Catalogue is his *Poems* (1842).
2. We have not located the source of this quotation.
3. Of these quotations, only this last comes from a poem printed in *The Monthly Chronicle* (VI, 434–435). A poem entitled "Stanzas" did appear there (p. 470), but did not contain the phrase quoted by EBB. Another poem in the magazine was entitled "The Grave! A Chaunt!" (pp. 381–384); this may be the same as the 'Chaunt' that EBB admired.
4. "The Flower and the Leaf" was one of Powell's two contributions to *The Poems of Geoffrey Chaucer, Modernized*. The second was "The Legends of Ariadne, Philomene, and Phillis."
5. As previously noted, nothing came of the plans for a second volume. Powell published "The Nun's Priest's Tale; or, The Cock and the Fox" in *The Monthly Chronicle*, February 1841, pp. 119–133.
6. "The Second Nonnes Tale" refers to the "maid and martir Seinte Cecilie" (verse 4).

783. EBB TO MARY RUSSELL MITFORD

[Torquay]
Dec. 28.th 40.

My ever dearest Miss Mitford,

When you first 'thrust the honor'[1] of your little Flush upon me, I clasped it by the first impulse, as I think I told you, 'with both hands'![2] But now I stand perplexed—(oh, dont wonder at me!) & loose my hold. Because you see, my beloved friend, with all my thankfulness to you & dear D.r Mitford for wishing me the space of a minute, to have y.r Flush, I could not be comfortable in going farther than the thankfulness, into an acceptance. Oh no! LET me say 'oh no' without building up a character for capriciousness!– I keep the thankfulness– I thank you both cordially— but I let little Flush go–

In the first place, the dog is of far too great value; wh.ch objection I never thought of at first––knowing, you see, so little about dogs!– The price *I* set upon him, was his having been near *you*: the inherent value was overlooked. And indeed, a very small, quiet little dog was the limit of my dog-ambition—and a larger one, a valuable one, & fit *for sporting* purposes w.d be thrown away upon me, & exposed to a martyrdom, whether in this room, or hereafter, in London. You will understand how it is dearest kindest Miss Mitford!– You will understand how foolish, almost cruel, I sh.d be, to introduce a sporting valuable spaniel into the London Streets prison, for ever & ever. D.r Mitford will agree with me, that it w^dnt do at all. But I thank you—both of you—none the less—& shall hope, to greet the paternal Flush some day at Three Mile Cross, in lieu of the earlier greeting of his son!–

And perhaps no dog w^d quite suit me, with my present habits, except a certain Mayfair one of which I once heard--given, whenever exposed to the cold air, to faint away & be revived with hartshorn. Until I meet with its counterpart, I must try to do "without a velvet gown or a little dog or a gentleman usher, or anything befitting a lady."[3]

You say nothing about the *Letter*-book[4] or other books—& I am so anxious to hear. Do you know I half wish the last Finden stories out of the Finden annual. They are too good for the annual Fairy circle where, however sweet the music, no *green grows*. Dont you think that a volume of your delightful stories might be hazarded next year at annual time with some annual splendor of binding, so as to be bought by annual buyers, yet not desecrated in the estimation of the 'higher orders' by *being* actually an annual. The very name is poison strong enough to dissolve—with many persons,—I observe—even the spell of your's.

Think of dear Mr Kenyon's kindness in sending me a box of sulphuric casts[5] ⟨★★★⟩

Publication: EBB-MRM, I, 209–211.
Manuscript: Wellesley College.

1. *Twelfth Night*, II, 5, 146.
2. Micah, 7:3.
3. We have not located the source of this quotation.
4. Yet another enquiry about the progress of Miss Mitford's projected edition of letters (see letter 737, note 1).
5. "An impression taken of a seal, medallion, etc. in a composition consisting of sulphur and wax" (*OED*).

Appendices

APPENDIX I

Biographical Sketches of Principal Correspondents and Persons Frequently Mentioned

ALFRED DOMETT (1811–87)

The close friendship between RB and Alfred Domett began during their years in the Camberwell area, where both were born, and continued until Domett's death. Alfred was born a year ahead of RB, on 20 May 1811, son of Nathaniel and Elizabeth (*née* Curling) Domett. Nathaniel had served as a midshipman in the Navy after going to sea at age 12 (Maynard, p. 100 and n. 112) and later had turned to merchant shipping. The son seemingly inherited his spirit of restlessness. Alfred Domett attended school at Stockwell, then spent four years at St. John's College, Cambridge, without taking a degree. His life in the 1830's included visits to North America and Italy, and the publication of some poetry: *Poems* (1833), various pieces for *Blackwood's Edinburgh Magazine*, and *Venice* (1839). For a while he looked toward law as a career, becoming a barrister of the Middle Temple in 1841. Restlessness prevailed, however, prompting him in 1842 to emigrate to New Zealand, where he remained for the next three decades. He held important positions in the colonial government, including that of Prime Minister in 1862–63. As Commissioner of Crown Lands in the province of Hawke's Bay he laid out the town of Napier—naming streets after Tennyson, Carlyle, and RB. Domett dealt sympathetically with native Maori culture in his long poem *Ranolf and Amohia, a South Sea Day Dream* (1872), but as a colonial official he came down on the side of toughness toward the Maoris. He married a widow, Mrs. George; they had a son, Alfred, plus children from her previous marriage. Domett reappeared in England in early 1872 and renewed his association with the Brownings—RB and Sarianna. Upon his return he began keeping a diary, available as *The Diary of Alfred Domett: 1872–1885*, ed. E.A. Horsman (1953). This journal is important to Browning biographers not only for its accounts of contacts with RB at the time it was written, but also for reminiscences about the poet in earlier times. Domett received a knighthood in 1880, and died on 2 November 1887.

Since RB and Domett grew up in the same London suburban area, biographers' uncertainty over just when they first met is understandable. There is a copy of *Paracelsus* (1835) in which Domett wrote: "Alfred Domett from Robt. Browning 1835" (*Reconstruction*, C428), but this may not mean that the book actually was presented in the year of publication. The earliest known letter between RB and Domett was written by RB on 7 March 1840 (no. 739) saying: "Pray accept the book ..."—an inscribed copy of *Sordello* (*Reconstruction*, C562). W. Hall Griffin, writing in *The Contemporary Review* (January 1905, pp. 95–115), said that "no real intimacy seems to have existed until at least 1840." In any case, Griffin's biography of RB, which was completed by H.C. Minchin and published in 1910, refers to Domett as an early friend of RB "beyond all other men" (G & M, p. 79). Frequently mentioned is the participation of RB and Domett in a loosely organized club or "set" of suburban men, mostly quite young, that flourished ca. 1835–40 (G & M, p. 80). Among other members were Christopher and Joseph Dowson, Frederick and William Curling Young, Joseph Arnould, and an older man—Captain Pritchard (see letter 497). Getting together frequently for discussions and arguments about history, politics, etc., the members called their meetings—and frequently themselves—"colloquials." Clearly this group had a significant influence on RB and Domett in their formative years. Domett was among the people to whom RB wrote intimate and somewhat playful letters, such as no. 747, dated 23 March 1840. RB valued Domett's careful attention to his works and frank criticism of them. He remarked to Joseph Arnould about one Domett critique, for instance: "Now this is what one wants; how few men there are who will give you this" (*RB-AD*, p.78). RB's first letter after Domett's departure for New Zealand, written 22 May 1842, spoke of "my real love for you—better love than I had supposed I was fit for." He wrote a tribute to Domett in the form of his poem "Waring," published as part of *Dramatic Lyrics* (1842). Domett also crops up in RB's "The Guardian-Angel," published in *Men and Women* (1855), and seemingly (DeVane, p. 180) in "Time's Revenges," which appeared in *Dramatic Romances and Lyrics* (1845). RB kept up a stream of letters to Domett in New Zealand until 1846, the year of his own marriage to EBB and departure for Italy. Then a lapse occurred, partly because of RB's changed situation, no doubt, and partly because of the "five-months' inevitable voyage" between England and New Zealand which he mentioned in his last known letter to Domett for a quarter of a century, dated 13 July 1846. Domett, on 20 August of the same year, thanked RB "for the book," obviously *Dramatic Romances and Lyrics* (1845) and said: "Your Lyrics have delighted me." So far as is known, that was all from either side until 6 May 1864, when Domett wrote of endeavouring "to renew our old familiarity"; reported that he had been "sticking your poems 'into the entrails' of the *better* sort of *folk* out here"; and said of RB's "lost wife": "How I should have liked to have known her both for your sake & her own!" RB did not reply. Despite this neglect, Domett called at the Browning residence upon his return to England in 1872 and was greeted by Sarianna. RB was not at home, but promptly wrote (on 1 March): "How very happy I am that I shall see you again! I never could bear to answer the letter you wrote to me years ago ... it was too hard to begin ... But come & let us begin all over again." Domett came, and contacts were thus resumed. Domett continued his old custom of expressing honest opinions about RB's poetry. He questioned the wisdom of RB's attack on poet and critic Alfred Austin in *Pacchiarotto* (1876), writing to RB on 27 October 1876 that "*he was utterly beneath your notice.*" Domett's reaction, in his diary, to RB's *Jocoseria* (1883)

Biographical Sketches 317

is described by G & M (p. 273) as "a prolonged growl." Domett became a vice-president of the London Browning Society when it was established in 1881; but, like most of the other vice-presidents, he played no major role in its activities. His poetical work *Flotsam and Jetsam* (1877) was dedicated to RB (see *Reconstruction*, A806). RB sent a copy of his *Parleyings* (1887) to Domett (*Reconstruction*, C446), and it clearly was the book cited in the last known letter to pass between these two friends. On 30 January 1887, Domett thanked RB for "your new book of Poems" and went on to say: "I have only as yet *run* through the Prologue—and you as you know, are not exactly a poet whom one may read as he runs." Later in 1887, on 12 November, RB wrote to Pen and Fannie Browning: "Poor Domett died last week, to my surprise and sorrow. I was hindered, by the distance and much else, from seeing him of late years ... There are notices of him in the Papers, and he proves to have been not other than successful in his life, though not so thoroughly and conspicuously as he might have been."

RICHARD HENGIST HORNE (1802?–84)

In view of all the eccentricities later exhibited by R.H. Horne, it almost seems that he planned the moment of his own birth for the eventual befuddlement of biographers. This Browning friend and correspondent was born near the midnight which divided 1802 from 1803, and therefore the year of his birth is uncertain; the official register gives 31 December 1802, *DNB* 1 January 1803. The son of James and Maria (*née* Partridge) Horne, he was born at Edmonton, near London. When Horne wrote in *A New Spirit of the Age* (1844) about EBB's secluded way of life, perhaps he mentally contrasted it with his own life of adventure. He grew up in the same locality as did John Keats and attended the same school, that of Dr. John Clarke at Enfield. Keats was older, however, so the two would not have been schoolmates for long, if at all. Later Horne went to the Royal Military College at Sandhurst in the hope of eventually entering service with the East India Company, but did not succeed there. In the mid-1820's, as a midshipman with the Mexican Navy, he took part in a closing phase of the Mexican war of independence against Spain. Biographer Cyril Pearl, in *Always Morning: The Life of Richard Henry "Orion" Horne* (1960, p. 11), gives this sidelight: "Horne learned to play the guitar, and to sing Spanish and Mexican songs. His devotion to the guitar lasted all his life and sometimes made his friends regret that he had been to Mexico." Moving northward, he visited Indians near the U.S.-Canadian border, was shipwrecked in the Gulf of St. Lawrence, and reputedly broke two ribs swimming in the turbulent waters at Niagara Falls. He returned to England on a timber vessel, surviving a mutiny and a fire en route. In England after his North American wanderings, Horne turned to journalism and literature. He wrote in *The Monthly Repository* of his adventures (with the signature "M.I.D.") and edited that magazine for about a year starting in mid-1836. His tragedies *Cosmo de' Medici* and *The Death of Marlowe* appeared in 1837, *The History of Napoleon* in 1841. Horne's epic *Orion* (1843) is the work for which he is best known as a writer, and his rules for its distribution strengthened his reputation as an eccentric. He initially priced it at a farthing per copy, strictly limited sales to one copy per customer, and decreed that *none* should be sold to any person who mispronounced the title (correctly: Orīon). EBB commented to Horne in a letter dated 14 June 1843: "Papa says—'Perhaps he is going to shoot the Queen, & is preparing

318 Appendix I

evidence of monomania'." *A New Spirit of the Age* (1844), on which he received EBB's help, is discussed below. Horne also published some volumes of poetry: *The Ballad of Delora* (1836), *Regrets of Memory* (1840) and *Ballad Romances* (1846), together with two children's books, *The Good-Natured Bear* (1846) and *Memoirs of a London Doll* (1846). In 1847 Horne married Miss Catherine Foggo, whose age was considerably below his own. EBB, in a letter written to Mary Russell Mitford on 15? September 1847, referred to her as being nineteen. By 1852, despite employment as a writer for Charles Dickens' periodical *Household Words*, Horne had grown deeply discouraged with his life in England. Lured by gold discoveries on the other side of the world, he departed for Australia. His wife was left behind, and their separation became permanent. In Australia, Horne sold the elaborate equipment he had brought along for gold-digging and got into a succession of other pursuits, including government service, lecture tours, and the publication of several literary works. His financial condition was generally precarious. It was while in Australia, in 1867, that Horne substituted "Hengist" for his original middle name, "Henry." He claimed to have done so in honour of a Mr. Hengist who saved his life there, but Ann Blainey, in *The Farthing Poet* (1968, p. 235), says: "Of the alleged Mr. Hengist nothing is known; it is not even certain that he existed." Horne returned to England in 1869, continued his writing career, and was granted a Civil List pension in 1874 for his services in Australia. He died at Margate on 13 March 1884 and was buried there.

Horne was among the literary people with whom RB began mingling in the mid-1830's. According to G & M (p. 76), they first met at the home of William Johnson Fox. Publication of Horne's *The Death of Marlowe* (1837) put an end to RB's plan of writing on the same subject (letter 575 and G & M, p. 112). Though RB and Horne were friends, seemingly not much correspondence passed between them until both were back in England after RB's long stay in Italy and Horne's in Australia. EBB, on the other hand, corresponded with Horne frequently and intimately before her 1846 marriage to RB. They became acquainted in about 1839 through a mutual friend, Mrs. Orme, a former Hope End governess. Horne, in *EBB-RHH*, I, 7–8, wrote: "My first introduction to Miss Barrett was by a note from Mrs. Orme, enclosing one from the young lady, containing a short poem, with the modest request to be frankly told whether it might be ranked as poetry or merely verse." EBB gave her account of the introduction in a letter to Miss Mitford dated 18 July 1841, saying that Horne had learned from the mutual friend "the straightness of my prison" and had written his "first kind little note ... to ask me to allow him to help in amusing me." Letter 717 dated 20 November 1839 is the first extant letter between the two, though not the first ever written. Horne had already expressed a low opinion of most annuals, as reported by EBB to Miss Mitford in letter 705, but he did contribute to the 1840 edition of *Findens'* as requested—a piece entitled "The Fetches." Not long afterward, EBB was able to return the favour by helping Horne with *The Poems of Geoffrey Chaucer, Modernized* (1841), which he was editing. She contributed "Queen Annelida and False Arcite" and "The Complaint of Annelida to False Arcite" (*Reconstruction*, D757–758). (See also *Reconstruction*, A628, for EBB's copy of the Chaucer work.) The year 1841 saw EBB and Horne grappling with a project which never reached completion: a poetic drama, discussed in *EBB-RHH*, II, 61–110, as "Psyche Apocalypté." EBB, in a letter written to Miss Mitford on 30 May 1841, described it as "balancing itself between the high fantastical & the high philosophical." She explained that the project had been suggested by Horne "more than a year ago," and that after a pause (during which interval the drowning of EBB's beloved "Bro" occurred) it had been resumed in the spring of 1841. By about the end of that year it was quietly dropped. For details of preliminary drafts, etc., and their publication long after EBB's death, see *Reconstruction*, A1994 and D754–756. A noteworthy social contribution by Horne in the early 1840's was his work with a Royal Commission which investigated the employment of children in mines and factories. Putting his considerable descriptive talents to work, he joined other commissioners in scathing reports which exposed horrible working conditions, led to some protective measures, and prompted EBB's "The Cry of the Children," first published in the August 1843 issue of *Blackwood's Edinburgh Magazine*. In 1843 EBB became deeply involved in the preparation of Horne's *A New Spirit of the Age* (1844), which was to include essays on a number of great and not-so-great contemporary writers. Her association with the project was not widely known until long afterward (nor did she herself know that her future husband also was involved, selecting mottoes). Writing to RB on 25 July 1845 about her own role, EBB said: "It was simply a writing of notes .. of slips of paper .. now on one subject, & now on another .. which were thrown into the great cauldron & boiled up with other matter." Nevertheless Elvan Kintner, editor of *RB-EBB*, says that "particularly in the papers on Carlyle, Landor, and Tennyson, Horne drew heavily on her contributions" (p. 134). (See *Reconstruction*, D1282, 1310–13, 1374.) Included were essays on RB and on EBB. Kintner wrote of the latter: "A modern press agent could hardly have aroused more interest than Horne's picture of her as a fabulous invalid of great learning who corresponded with many important people but lived in an 'almost hermetically sealed' apartment and saw no one" (*RB-EBB*, p. xxxiii). Among the people whom she did not see was Horne himself. During the entire period of their close relationship prior to her departure for Italy, and despite her admiration for Horne, she only once consented to let him visit her, and on that occasion he failed to appear. Writing to RB of this episode in a letter postmarked 4 December 1845, she said: "I clapped my hands for joy when I felt my danger to be passed." Not until she returned to London with RB did EBB actually meet Horne, at which time she also met his wife. To Miss Mitford on 12 November 1851 she wrote: "One evening he had the kindness to bring his wife miles upon miles just to drink tea with us ... She is less pretty, & more interesting than I expected—looking very young ... with deep earnest eyes, & a silent listening manner. He ... seems to write articles together with Dickens." Undoubtedly Miss Mitford was interested in this report, though Horne had long been a source of disagreement between her and EBB. More than once, Horne had visited Miss Mitford's home at Three Mile Cross, the first occasion having been in August 1843, and Miss Mitford was much annoyed by his conduct. Among other things, she accused him of taking three baths per day (a serious problem for a hostess in the era before modern plumbing) and of courting neighbourhood heiresses on a grand scale. Deeply upset, EBB tried desperately to defend Horne. On 5 September 1843 she wrote to Miss Mitford: "After all, vexed as I am, I am conscious of a regard for him—a strong sense of all the interest he has shown towards me, .. & a high respect for his powers of mind." She later told RB of Miss Mitford's complaints, and he likewise vigorously defended Horne, asserting that the latter's characteristics had been "grossly misrepresented" (RB to EBB, 11 February 1846). Earlier, after reading some of EBB's comments, he had written: "Now, let me never pass occasion of speaking well of Horne, who deserves your opinion of him,—it is my own, too" (13 May 1845). There was a friendly exchange of letters between Horne and the Brownings just after the couple's marriage in 1846, but not a great deal of further correspondence during EBB's lifetime. RB did write to Horne on 3 December 1848 to seek help in retrieving some of his own juvenilia that had been in the possession of Eliza Flower (see vol. 3, p. 312). During the 1870's, after both men had returned to England from overseas, Horne peppered RB with letters about his countless worries and distresses. His strenuous efforts to obtain a government pension, which eventually he received in 1874, were supported by RB and numerous other friends—including Tennyson and Carlyle. Horne sought and obtained RB's permission to publish the letters he had received from EBB many years earlier. Despite reluctance to see his wife's privacy invaded, RB yielded in this case, partly out of sympathy for Horne and partly for reasons given to John H. Ingram in a letter dated 5 May 1882: "The correspondence was literary only, between persons who had never seen each other, and before I could pretend to any sort of guardianship." The eventual result was Horne's 1877 publication of *EBB-RHH*, which gave the public its first good look at EBB as a letter writer. Horne inscribed to RB a copy of this work, which is listed in *Reconstruction* as item A343. The last known letter to pass between Horne and RB was written by Horne on 3 August 1883 and was typical. In it he wrote of his near-blindness, and cited the inadequacy of his government pension, which at the time amounted to £100 per year. He asked RB to approach the Prime Minister, William Gladstone, "touch his elbow," and point out that "the *burthen* upon the country would not be great if he *doubled* my present Pension." Horne died, with no increase, about seven months later.

ANNA BROWNELL JAMESON (1794–1860)

This long-time correspondent ranks near John Kenyon as a benefactor of the Brownings, because of the assistance she gave during their strenuous flight to Italy at the beginning of their marriage. She was born in Dublin on 17 May 1794, daughter of Denis Brownell Murphy, who was an accomplished painter of miniatures. Anna became a governess, accompanied an English family to France and Italy, and wrote a fictionalized account of her experiences. This attracted much attention when published in 1826 as *The Diary of an Ennuyée*, and was one of the books that EBB enjoyed while living at Hope End. Anna married Robert Jameson in 1825, but the match proved unsatisfactory. (EBB told a gossipy story of the circumstances in a letter to Mary Russell Mitford, written 23–25 December 1841.) The couple separated in 1829, at about the time of Mr. Jameson's appointment to a minor judgeship in the British West Indies. She briefly rejoined him in Canada when he received a governmental position there in 1836. Upon final separation, and before returning to England, she made a tour of remote areas, thus acquiring material for her *Winter Studies and Summer Rambles in Canada* (1838). In the 1840's, Mrs. Jameson pursued her interest in art appreciation, the literary field in which she became best known, and published among other works *A Handbook to the Public Galleries of Art* (1842) and *Memoirs of the Early Italian Painters* (1845). She also increasingly developed a concern for social welfare problems. Over a number of years, starting in 1834, Mrs. Jameson was a close friend of Lady Byron, widow of the famous poet. This was a point of difference between Mrs. Jameson and EBB, since EBB idolized the poet, from whom Lady Byron had been estranged. The Jameson-Byron friendship terminated with a quarrel in 1852. During most of her life, Mrs. Jameson faced financial difficulties, though assisted by a government pension starting in 1851. She died at her home in Ealing on 17 March 1860.

Mrs. Jameson was among the literary people whom RB met soon after publishing *Paracelsus* (1835). His first known letter to her is no. 722, written in 1840 or earlier. EBB's sisters met the prominent authoress in 1842, as reported by EBB in a letter to Miss Mitford on 6 April of that year. EBB herself may have assisted with the section on Mrs. Jameson in R.H. Horne's *A New Spirit of the Age* (1844), but was not yet personally acquainted with her. On 1 September 1844, referring to her newly published *Poems*, EBB wrote to Miss Mitford: "Mrs. Jameson used strong language of praise to Mr. Kenyon, & said that she meant to write to me—but she has not yet written." On 3 September, still hoping for a letter from Mrs. Jameson, EBB wrote to Miss Mitford: "She has the very genius of criticism, in fact,—& adds to her fine sense of Beauty, a most subtle apprehension & most exercised power of analysis of the Art which produces Beauty." On 20 September she reported having received "a very kind letter," though apparently it did not contain such detailed analysis as she had desired. Finally, in November, while staying as a guest at the house next door, Mrs. Jameson received permission to visit EBB at 50 Wimpole Street. Discussing the new friend in a letter to Miss Mitford on 28 January 1845, EBB wrote: "I like her very much—but I have not fallen in love with her at first sight, as you know, I did with *you*."

By this time, EBB had started to correspond with RB, and their courtship was under way. In this episode, Mrs. Jameson's role was at first somewhat comical and later of vast importance. The comical aspect: Mrs. Jameson was a friend both of EBB and of RB, was seeing each of them frequently, but showed no awareness that they were seeing *each other*. Concerned—like numerous other people—about EBB's health in the London climate, Mrs. Jameson was generously offering to take her to Italy, while the younger woman was already plotting an escape to that country with RB. On 17 June 1846 EBB reported to her lover: "I told her [Mrs. Jameson] .. told her .. what might be told." This apparently included the fact of the EBB-RB friendship, but nothing of the wedding plans. Mrs. Jameson, knowing that EBB wanted to go to Italy, kept pressing for details on how this might be accomplished. Meanwhile, Mrs. Jameson had been making plans for an Italian trip of her own (via France) regardless of EBB's intentions. EBB mentioned this to RB in a letter of 29 May 1846. Mrs. Jameson's purpose was to conduct research for her *Sacred and Legendary Art* (1848–52). She would take along her young niece, Gerardine Bate, for "an 'artistical education'," as EBB wrote in her 29 May letter. Mrs. Jameson and Gerardine were already in Paris when the newly-married Brownings arrived there on 21 September 1846. RB went immediately to her hotel, leaving a message about recent developments. Gerardine (later Mrs. Macpherson) reported in her *Memoirs of the Life of Anna Jameson* (1878, p. 230), that her aunt's astonishment was "almost comical." For some time thereafter they travelled as a party of six: the two Brownings, EBB's maid Elizabeth Wilson, Mrs. Jameson, Gerardine, and the dog Flush. Leaving Paris on 28 September they went to southern France, then by steamer to Italy, finally arriving in Pisa on 14 October. There the Brownings were to remain until the next spring. Mrs. Jameson and Gerardine stayed near them until 4 November, then moved on to Florence. Interesting commentary on the Brownings by Mrs. Jameson is provided by George K. Boyce in "From Paris to Pisa with the Brownings"—*New Colophon*, 3 (1950), 110–119. Boyce's article presents five letters sent by Mrs. Jameson to her friend Lady Byron. On 22–23 September 1846 she wrote of the Brownings just after their arrival in Paris: "Robert Browning, my poet, is here—& with a wife he has run off with—& who, think you, is this wife?—no other than Elizabeth Barrett, my poetess—a pretty pair to go thro this prosaic world together! . . . I have sympathized, scolded, rallied, cried & helped, & now they want me to join them on the road to the South." Mrs. Jameson persuaded EBB to rest in Paris for a few days, and she wrote on 24 September that "I really believe I have saved her life" by so doing. On 29 September, from Orleans, she wrote of the Brownings: "They have thrown themselves upon me with such an entire & undoubting confidence, that to have refused help & comfort, or even hesitated, would have been like a brute or a stone." On 15 October, from Pisa, she wrote: "They are really excellent . . . *He* is full of spirit & good humour and his unselfishness, & his turn for making the best of every thing & his bright intelligence & his rare acquirements of every kind rendered him the very prince of travelling companions. *But* (always *buts!!*) he is in all the common things of this life the most impractical of men, the most uncalculating, rash, in short the worst *manager* I ever met with. *She*, in her present state, & from her long seclusion almost helpless. Now only conceive the ménage that is likely to ensue & without FAULT on either side!" Apparently Mrs. Jameson soon took a more optimistic view. In a letter of 5 November to Julia Martin, EBB was able to report: "Mrs. Jameson laughs outright at our miraculous prudence & economy, & declares that it is past belief & precedent that we shd. not burn the candles at both ends." Mrs. Jameson feared that Gerardine would develop romantic notions through close association with the honeymooning couple, and it is possible that she did. Though failing to meet Mrs. Jameson's expectations as an art student herself, she soon fell in love with an impecunious artist in Rome, a Mr. Robert Macpherson, and eventually—despite Mrs. Jameson's efforts—married him. In the mid-1850's they were living in Rome and he had become a photographer. On 20 April 1847 the Brownings moved from Pisa to Florence. Mrs. Jameson (still accompanied by Gerardine) soon visited them in that city before returning to London. After that, meetings between the Brownings and Mrs. Jameson became less frequent, although they saw her occasionally in London in the 1850's, in Paris in 1852, and in Florence in 1858. EBB remained devoted to this friend until the latter's death, often calling her "Mona Nina," and more than 80 letters that passed between the Brownings and Mrs. Jameson after the marriage still exist. EBB's interest in the great 1851 International Exhibition in London was undoubtedly heightened by Mrs. Jameson's contribution, a *Guide to the Court of Modern Sculpture*. The poem "Clive" in RB's *Dramatic Idyls, Second Series* (1880) was credited by him to a tale he had heard from Mrs. Jameson long before. There were, as might be expected among strong-minded people, differences of opinion. Mrs. Jameson, for instance, did not approve of EBB's devotion to spiritualism. In a letter to her brother George dated 13-14 May 1852, from Paris, EBB gave this amusing account: "We had Lady Elgin here last saturday evening again, and the evening did not go off half as well as usual,—because of a decided dyspathy between her & Mrs. Jameson. Lady Elgin is a great spiritualist, with . . . a belief in every sort of incredible thing. While she talked of a communion of souls, Mrs. Jameson began to talk of private madhouses . . in a way which made my blood run cold." Later, writing from Italy to her sister Henrietta on 1 August 1857, EBB referred to some apparent jealousy between Mrs. Jameson and another close friend, Isabella Blagden. "I feel a little, a little, uncomfortable," she said. Learning of Mrs. Jameson's death, 17 March 1860, EBB wrote on the 27th to the niece, Gerardine Bate Macpherson: "You know, but perhaps not *all*, how I feel in losing (as far as the loving can lose those whom they love——as far as death brings loss) that great heart, that noble human creature–" A little later, some friends undertook a subscription for the benefit of Mrs. Jameson's sisters, and EBB would have liked to participate; she wrote to Isabella Blagden on 21? January 1861: "I am seriously vexed about the subscription—but Robert .. you know him .. he is like a rock– He is wrong, I think. We see differently. He looks at the claim of the sisters—while I look entirely to the memory of my dear friend Mrs. Jameson– It would be a token of love to her ... Robert thinks the sisters weighed her down while she lived—therefore *his* regard expresses itself in a sort of indignation— which is a natural mode of love with him– I am sorry–"

Reconstruction lists numerous gifts of books and other materials that passed between the Brownings and Mrs. Jameson, or that were related to their friendship. There are, for instance, a music album (A32) given by Mrs. Jameson to Pen Browning in 1858, two of her books (A1301–02) inscribed to the Brownings, and one (A1303) inscribed to "Miss E B Barrett." (This last item is an 1846 book of memoirs and essays on which EBB assisted her—see D1226.) EBB presented a copy of her *Poems* (1844) to Mrs. Jameson (C74), and RB did likewise with several of his books (C396, 432, and 465). The Brownings presumably treasured item H73, a sketch of Avignon by moonlight which Mrs. Jameson made while travelling with them through France just after their marriage.

WALTER SAVAGE LANDOR (1775–1864)

Landor was one of the first major literary figures whom EBB actually met, but he conducted far more correspondence with RB than with her. His bad temper eventually imposed a heavy burden on RB's patience. Elvan Kintner, editor of *RB-EBB*, describes him as "a literary rebel admired by a small but discriminating audience" (p. 1095). Born at Warwick on 30 January 1775, he was the eldest son of Walter and Elizabeth (*née* Savage) Landor. His father was a physician who retired after receiving a large inheritance, and the son never had to worry about earning a living. Removed from Rugby school after various offenses, young Landor spent some time in private study, and then—in 1793—entered Trinity College, Oxford. Suspended for firing a gun in connection with a political dispute, he refused to return even when given a chance to do so. A quarrel with his father ensued, but matters were patched up sufficiently for him to receive an allowance of £150 per year, with freedom to travel as he pleased. He began publishing poems in 1795. At an early age he met the scholar Samuel Parr, whose name often crops up in EBB's correspondence. Their friendship continued until Parr's death in 1825. Becoming independently wealthy upon the death of his father in 1805, Landor settled in Bath. Three years later he went to Spain, raising and financing a volunteer force to fight against Napoleon. The adventure soon ended, and Landor returned to England. In 1811 he married Miss Julia Thuillier, a woman considerably younger than himself. The marriage was troubled, and the couple eventually separated. For about three years, starting in 1811, Landor lived on his Llanthony Abbey estate in Monmouthshire, and was constantly involved in disputes while trying to upgrade the land's productivity and the local people's living conditions. He next went to France and then to Italy, residing in Florence from 1821 until 1835, at which time he left his wife and returned to Britain. He went back to Italy in 1858 for the final, unhappy six years of his life. Landor produced a vast quantity of poetry and prose—in English, Latin, and Italian. His works included the long narrative poem *Gebir* (1798); the tragedy *Count Julian*

(1812), prompted by his war experiences in Spain; *Imaginary Conversations* (1824–29); and various lyrics, including "Rose Aylmer" (1806). *Last Fruit off an Old Tree*, not actually his final work, appeared in 1853. He died in Florence on 17 September 1864 and was buried in the English Cemetery near the tomb of EBB.

Landor was among the literary people with whom RB became acquainted upon publication of his *Paracelsus* (1835), and was among those present at Thomas Noon Talfourd's *Ion* supper (vol. 3, p. 324), likewise attended by RB. EBB saw Landor two nights later, on 28 May 1836, at the home of John Kenyon. On 7 December of that year she wrote to Julia Martin (letter 546) of this meeting with "Landor, the brilliant Landor!" On 24 May 1843 she wrote of him in a letter to Mary Russell Mitford: "Mr. Landor is a man of fine genius, & not far (if far at all) from being the noblest prose writer of the day." The first known letter between one of the Brownings and Landor was no. 740, sent by RB on 7 March 1840 to accompany a gift copy of *Sordello* (*Reconstruction*, C566). Landor wrote to EBB about her *Poems* (1844), and in a letter of 5 July 1846 he complained of being unable to "decypher" her signature. He continued: "Do you write your name in such a manner, that nobody may attempt a forgery? There are higher and better things in which you ought to be contented to be inimitable." Meanwhile, EBB had contributed substantially to the portion dealing with Landor in R.H. Horne's *A New Spirit of the Age* (1844). (See *Reconstruction*, D1310–13.) In 1845, Landor was sufficiently impressed by RB's *Dramatic Romances and Lyrics* to write a poem including the following passage (as quoted by EBB to Miss Mitford on 21 November of that year):

"Since Chaucer was alive & hale
No man hath walked along our roads with step
So active, so inquiring eye, or tongue
So varied in discourse."

(See *Reconstruction*, D1446 and L159–160.) In 1846, RB published *Luria* and *A Soul's Tragedy* together as No. VIII of his *Bells and Pomegranates* series, and dedicated the booklet to Landor, who thanked him on 15 April: "And now accept my thanks for the richest of Easter offerings made to anyone for many years.... Go on and pass *us* poor devils! If you do not go far ahead of me, I will crack my whip at you and make you spring forward." Shortly afterward, on the night of 2 June, RB was with Landor at John Kenyon's house. EBB, knowing of this and of a headache from which RB had been suffering, wrote to him that night: "But your head ... is it ringing & aching even, under the crashing throat-peals of Mr. Landor's laughter? He laughs, I remember, like an ogre—he laughs as if laughter could kill, & he knew it" (EBB to RB, 2 June 1846).

The Brownings, for some years after their marriage, apparently had little contact with Landor, though they did see him during their 1852 visit to London. In 1858, Landor's quarrelsome nature made him the target of a libel suit, and he was persuaded to assign his property and leave England. In Italy for the final six years of his life, he was dependent on his family and on RB, who served as an unofficial guardian. For most of that period Landor was in Florence under the care of Elizabeth Wilson Romagnoli, EBB's former maid. Around 10 October 1859, when the arrangement was being worked out, EBB wrote about it to RB's sister Sarianna: "Robert must see Mr. Landor (his adopted son, Sarianna) settled in his new apartment, with Wilson for a Duenna.... Dear darling Robert amuses me by talking of his 'gentleness & sweetness.' A most courteous & refined gentleman he is of course, & very affectionate to Robert (as he ought to be)—but of self-restraint, he has not a grain, & of suspiciousness, many.... What do you say to dashing down a plate on the floor when you dont like what's on it?" In London after EBB's death, RB had to endure a continual bombardment of letters in which Landor complained of everything imaginable, but on 19 October 1864, about a month after Landor's death, RB wrote to Isabella Blagden: "I have been more than rewarded for my poor pains by being of use for five years to the grand old ruin of a genius, such as I don't expect to see again."

Listed in *Reconstruction* are numerous items relating to Landor. RB and his son received many books from the older man. A good example is item A165, vol. 1 of Jean Jacques Barthélemy's *Voyage du Jeune Anacharsis en Grèce*, published in 1796, and inscribed by RB: "Given by Walter Savage Landor to Robert Wiedemann Barrett Browning, in 1863." Listed as items A1388–1416 are many of Landor's own works, some inscribed by him. A photograph of his birthplace in Warwick, with pencil notation by RB, is cited as item H222. Items L139–160 include numerous Landor manuscripts.

Harriet Martineau (1802–76)

This prominent and controversial writer, a frequent correspondent of EBB in the 1840's, was born in Norwich on 12 June 1802, daughter of Thomas and Elizabeth (*née* Rankin) Martineau. Her younger brother James became well known as a Unitarian minister and religious philosopher. Her father was a textile manufacturer. In a self-written obituary published by *The Daily News* at the time of her death, Miss Martineau stated that her parents "gave their children the best education which they could, by all honourable means, command." Harriet was hard of hearing as a child, and in later years resorted to an ear-trumpet. She began writing for *The Monthly Repository* while still in her teens. After her father died, in 1826, Miss Martineau helped with family finances not only through writing but also by doing needlework. Conditions were eased somewhat when she won three substantial prizes, offered by the Unitarian Association, for religious essays. In 1832–34 she achieved public recognition through a set of stories entitled *Illustrations of Political Economy*, relating to the sufferings of Britain's poor and the need for social and economic reforms. Later writings covered a wide range, even including children's stories. In 1834–36 she visited the United States, where—siding with the abolitionists—she became much involved in the conflict over slavery. In 1839 began the most publicized episode of her life, the struggle with an abdominal tumor. She underwent treatment by mesmerism, crediting it with a seemingly miraculous cure. Her controversial series of *Letters on Mesmerism* began in 1844 and appeared as a collected edition in 1845. Not until after Miss Martineau's death was it known that the apparent recovery came from a shift in the position of the tumor (see Theodora Bosanquet, *Harriet Martineau*, 1927, p. 202). In any case, she celebrated her return to good health by making a strenuous trip to the Middle East (1846–47) and subsequently writing *Eastern Life, Present and Past* (1848). During her illness she was offered a government pension, which she rejected on grounds that it would tend to stifle her freedom as a writer. In 1843, however, a group of friends raised a fund for her, amounting to about £1,300. Having left London on account of her health in April 1839, in the mid-1840's she acquired property at Ambleside in the Lake District near William Wordsworth's home, and had a house built. There she continued her literary work and engaged in efforts to help the community. Miss

Martineau died at her Ambleside residence, "The Knoll," on 27 June 1876, and her body was taken to a family burial site at Birmingham.

Miss Martineau was so well acquainted with RB's friends the Flower sisters that she placed them—thinly disguised—in her 1831 novel *Five Years of Youth; or, Sense and Sentiment* (see vol. 3, p. 311). RB is mentioned in G & M (p. 136) as being acquainted with Miss Martineau as early as 1837, and in that year she inscribed to him a copy of Thomas Carlyle's *Sartor Resartus* (*Reconstruction*, A574). Her *Autobiography*—ed. Maria Weston Chapman (1877), I, 417-418—refers to her strong interest in *Paracelsus* (1835). She goes on to say: "The unbounded expectation I formed from that poem was sadly disappointed when 'Sordello' came out [in 1840]. I was so wholly unable to understand it that I supposed myself ill. But in conversation no speaker could be more absolutely clear and purpose-like.... A real genius was Robert Browning, assuredly; and how good a man, how wise and morally strong, is proved by the successful issue of the perilous experiment of the marriage of two poets." She then said of EBB: "I ... think her poetry wonderfully beautiful in its way, while wishing that she was more familiar with the external realities which are needed to balance her ideal conceptions." The earliest extant piece of correspondence between either of the Brownings and Miss Martineau is letter 622, by RB, thought to have been written on 9 April 1838. Most of the further known correspondence, however, consists of letters from Miss Martineau to EBB—preserved despite the fact that Miss Martineau pleaded with her acquaintances to destroy all letters they received from her. The first letter to EBB was written on 1 August 1843. Miss Martineau expressed admiration for "your very noble poem, Pan Departed" ("The Dead Pan," which was to be printed in *Poems* the following year and was already being seen in manuscript by various individuals). After commenting further on the poem she wrote: "These few words may perhaps not come amiss from one who has for friends some who are yours,—who has, like you, lost health, & become inured to the want of it, & who, like you, almost forgets to wish for ease & vigour in the keen sense of enjoyments which bear no relation to the body & its welfare." EBB reported this to Mary Russell Mitford on 12? August 1843, and wrote of Miss Martineau: "She is a very noble woman—& her least word wd. give honor to me." On 31 August of the same year, EBB wrote to R.H. Horne: "I have had a great pleasure lately in some correspondence with Miss Martineau, the noblest female intelligence between the seas." A portrait of Miss Martineau was one of five from Horne's *A New Spirit of the Age* (1844) which EBB placed on the wall of her room at 50 Wimpole Street—"because," as was explained to RB on 4 December 1845, "she was a woman & admirable, & had written me some kind letters." EBB's interest in Miss Martineau was predictably intensified when the latter underwent mesmerism and supposedly thereby recovered from disease— mesmerism being a subject which both frightened and intrigued EBB. She admired Miss Martineau's willingness to sacrifice privacy in publishing the full story of her treatment. Miss Martineau discussed this sacrifice in a letter to EBB dated 10 December 1844: "I took my part deliberately,—*knowing privacy to be impossible*, & making up my mind to *entail* publicity as the only course faithful to truth & human welfare. I cannot tell you how the thought of *Godiva* has sustained & inspired me." The 1845-46 letters between EBB and RB are liberally sprinkled with references to Miss Martineau. It becomes clear that RB was not deeply enthusiastic about her, and both writers disagreed with her on at least one point. Miss Martineau believed that women should be allowed to serve in Parliament; RB and EBB did not. EBB, even before she began corresponding with her future husband, was considerably shaken by a scolding she received from Miss Martineau in a letter of 22 August 1844. In it, EBB was accused of having written to Miss Martineau in excessively flattering terms: "Your estimate of me seemed almost absurd,—& your expression of it such as never ought to pass between sincere & humble Christians." After taking some time to recover from her "humiliation," EBB wrote to Miss Mitford on 28 September: "I really felt abashed. . . . I thought everybody wd. think as even Papa did, 'WHY WHAT CAN YOU HAVE BEEN SAYING?'" By this time, however, Miss Martineau had already apologized (in a letter of 16 September 1844) and had commented at length, for the most part very favourably, on EBB's new *Poems* (see *Reconstruction*, C76, for Miss Martineau's copy of this work). Correspondence continued, as already indicated, about Miss Martineau's mesmeric treatments plus other topics. The exchange of letters does not appear to have continued much beyond the time of EBB's departure for Italy, though in writing to Miss Mitford from Florence on 20 August 1847 she mentioned receiving "a few kind lines yesterday from Miss Martineau." In 1860 Miss Martineau wrote to an American paper harshly criticizing EBB's views on Napoleon III as expressed in *Poems Before Congress*, published that year. EBB apparently did not make a direct reply to Miss Martineau, but in writing to Arabella Moulton-Barrett on 11 June she called the criticism "monstrously unjust & absurd." EBB died just over a year later; Harriet Martineau survived her by 15 years—minus two days.

MARY MINTO

Her extant correspondence with EBB runs from 1839 to 1856. From this correspondence and secondary documents, one knows that Mary Minto and her family were acquainted with the Moulton-Barretts and their circle as early as 1837. In particular, Mary was a friend of Ann Eliza Moulton-Barrett, widow of EBB's uncle Sam (1787–1837), and she served as a bridesmaid when Ann Eliza remarried in 1840. Miss Minto was in Paris when EBB wrote to her from Torquay in January 1839 (letter 682). This letter accompanied one from EBB's sister Henrietta (SD979), who mentioned two of the Moulton-Barrett brothers: "Bro remains with us, indeed he is quite essential to us—perhaps you will be inclined to disbelieve this, for I know *he* is not your favorite– Georgie was very pleased to hear that you are going on with your singing . . ." In a letter to Mary Russell Mitford dated 3 August 1843, EBB referred to Miss Minto as "a very accomplished & intelligent young woman." EBB wrote too of Mary's interest in mesmerism—also known at that time as "magnetism." "Mary Minto . . . thinks of nothing but Mesmer," she wrote to Miss Mitford on 12? August 1843. EBB herself was curious about mesmerism but not enthusiastic, and she did not plunge into the subject in her known letters to Miss Minto. As reported in a letter to Miss Mitford on 22? November 1843, the persistently-ailing EBB resisted an effort by Mary to obtain a lock of her hair so that "a chief Rabbi of the Magnetisers in Paris" could "declare straightway the nature of & remedy for my complaint." Most of EBB's letters to Mary include greetings to Mrs. Minto, the recipient's mother, and various instances of contact between the Minto and Moulton-Barrett families can be cited. EBB, writing to her brother George on 1 August 1843, mentioned a possible visit by their brother Henry to Mrs. Minto in Dover. On 3 April 1844 EBB told George that the "Bells & Mintos are coming here [50 Wimpole Street] today, either to dinner or to tea." On 4 August of the same year she reported to George: "Mr.

Minto has sailed for the West Indies,—& Mary & her mother for Germany." A sketchbook that belonged to EBB's brother Alfred (*Reconstruction*, H100) contains a sketch inscribed: "Mary Minto Nov 15 1843." On 30 June 1846 EBB, who was within a few months of fleeing to Italy with RB, asked Miss Minto about climatic conditions there, especially in La Cava and Salerno. Miss Minto apparently forwarded the query to another acquaintance, who provided a rather dismal response. This answer was relayed to EBB. She passed it along to RB on 9 July with accompanying comments which raise doubts about the closeness of her relationship with Mary Minto—though allowance must be made for her unsettled state of mind at the time. She wrote: "I feel disappointed.... I dont at all see why we should receive the responses of this friend of my friend *who is not so very much my friend*, as if they were oracular & final" [our italics]. On 21 May 1852 EBB wrote from Paris to Miss Minto, who was in London and was soon to be married. She included comments about spiritualism, a subject that was starting to interest her, and presumably Mary too. By 10 June of the same year EBB had learned that the future husband was a Mr. Ruxton; but on 4 March 1853 she wrote to Henrietta: "I wonder if anybody has heard of Mary Minto .. once so called .. I forget her present name at this moment." The editor of *B-GB* wrote in 1958 that at this point "Mary fades tantalizingly from the picture" (p. 110). There are, nevertheless, letters received by her as Mrs. Ruxton from EBB in 1856, when both women were in London. In them, EBB gives evidence of their mutual interest in the philosopher Swedenborg, and refers cordially to Mary's husband and children.

Edward Moxon (1801–58)

He was a poet in his own right, a prominent London publisher, and a friend of the Brownings even after they turned elsewhere for the publication of their works. Born at Wakefield in 1801 and apprenticed to a bookseller at age nine, Moxon successfully educated himself, especially in contemporary literature. In 1821 he began work with the London publishing firm of Messrs. Longman. In 1826 he produced a volume of verse entitled *The Prospect, and other Poems*, which, according to *The Encyclopædia Britannica*, "was received with some favour." He dedicated it to banker-poet Samuel Rogers, who, in 1830, backed Moxon in the establishment of his own publishing firm. This firm's first production was *Album Verses* (1830) by Charles Lamb, whose adopted daughter, Emma Isola, married Moxon in 1833. Prominent Moxon friends and clients, besides Lamb and the Brownings, included William Wordsworth, Alfred Tennyson, Bryan Waller Procter, Walter Savage Landor, and Harriet Martineau. Moxon eventually moved his firm from its original New Bond Street location to 44 Dover Street, an address which became famous in the publishing world. In November 1839 Moxon issued an edition of Shelley's poetry containing the full text and notes of the controversial *Queen Mab*, and was consequently prosecuted for blasphemous libel. Although Thomas Noon Talfourd argued eloquently in defense of Moxon's right to publish such materials, a "guilty" verdict was rendered. The prosecution being satisfied with this pronouncement, Moxon suffered no further serious consequences.

Moxon's relationship with the Brownings began in the mid-1830's. On 27 March 1835 (letter 500), RB wrote to his friend William Johnson Fox to seek help in finding a publisher for *Paracelsus*. After recounting earlier woes with the publication of *Pauline*, he proceeded: "Now I would ascertain whether it is possible for you to procure me an introduction to a good publisher,—Moxon for instance, who seems a superlative fellow . . . can you do this?" Fox did procure the introduction—through another literary figure, Charles Cowden Clarke—and soon RB wrote again to Fox (letter 503), saying that "the Moxonian visage" had "loured exceedingly" at Clarke's letter of introduction. Discouraged over poor sales of recent publications, including some of Tennyson's poetry, Moxon "in short begs to decline even inspecting" *Paracelsus*. The work was published in August 1835 by Effingham Wilson, at the expense of RB's father. *Sordello* (1840) was the first of RB's works to be published by Moxon, but, again, RB's father had to bear the expense. Next came *Bells and Pomegranates* (1841–46), likewise published by Moxon, but financed by RB, Sr. It was Moxon who suggested a series of pamphlets as an economical means of publication. As all Browning fans know, eight pamphlets eventually appeared. No. V, *A Blot in the 'Scutcheon*, is of special interest. RB was quarrelling bitterly with theatre manager William Charles Macready over the production of this play (see vol. 3, p. 319) and had Moxon publish it hastily on 11 February 1843 to prevent Macready from "mutilating" it in that night's stage presentation.

EBB's dealings with Moxon began in 1842 when she approached him through her brother George to see if he would publish a set of poems that she had accumulated. He was "infinitely civil," EBB wrote to Mary Russell Mitford on 30 December 1842, but he turned her down for the same reason that had made him reject RB's *Paracelsus* in 1835: poetry wasn't selling well. Later though, through her ubiquitous friend John Kenyon she secured Moxon's agreement to publish what became *Poems* (1844). On 13 March 1843 she wrote to her brother George that Moxon had asked Kenyon "to take a message from him to me, offering to ruin himself for me, & me alone, by accepting any MS. I might please to send him." Moxon advised that the book be issued in two volumes (as it was) and that the title be simply "Poems," instead of "New Poems" as EBB had suggested. After considerable flurrying, the book was published on 14 August. Just prior to that, on 9 August 1844, EBB noted with pleasure in a letter to Mary Russell Mitford that Moxon was going to send a copy to Tennyson, though she had "never said a word" about his doing so. EBB's reference to "Browning" in *Poems* (see vol. 3, p. 317) triggered the RB-EBB correspondence and courtship. Thus, Moxon was involved with both poets before they became directly acquainted with each other. The letters they exchanged in 1845 and 1846 show much evidence of their connections with the prominent publisher. For instance, in a letter of 2–3 July 1845, EBB said that someone in America had sent her a piece of mail "addressed to—just my name .. *poetess, London!*" and that it had reached her via Moxon. Also, Moxon's name often crops up in RB's letters. G & M (p. 124) mentions RB as "a frequent visitor" at Moxon's place of business, "listening to the gossip" about Tennyson, Wordsworth, and others. Moxon presented numerous books to RB and EBB. For instance, he inscribed a copy of his *Sonnets*, second edition (1837) to RB (*Reconstruction*, A1685). The two volumes of Mary Wollstonecraft Shelley's *Rambles in Germany and Italy* . . . (1844) went to EBB with inscriptions by Moxon (*Reconstruction*, A2091). As early as 1846, however, RB was becoming critical of his publisher. On 28 August of that year he wrote to EBB: "Moxon is the 'slowest' of publishers, and if one of his books can only contrive to pay its expenses, you may be sure that a more enterprising brother of the craft would have sent it into a second or third edition." Moxon never took any risk in publishing RB's works. All that he handled were subsidized by RB,

Sr. After marrying, RB looked for a company which would bear the costs of publication. The firm of Chapman & Hall did so, producing his *Poems* (1849) and many items thereafter. EBB likewise switched to Chapman & Hall, who published her *Poems* (1850). Dorothy Hewlett speculated in *Elizabeth Barrett Browning* (1953, p. 346), that they may have insisted on handling EBB's works as a prerequisite to taking those of the less-popular RB. Despite the changeover, the Brownings seemingly remained friendly with Moxon. In 1851 he was preparing to print a set of letters, hitherto unpublished, supposedly written by Shelley. He asked RB to furnish an introductory essay, which the latter did. The book (see *Reconstruction*, M258), published in 1852, was withdrawn from distribution when most of the letters were found to be forgeries, but RB's introductory essay has many times been reprinted. RB wrote the essay in Paris in late 1851, and on 17 December of that year he also wrote to Moxon: "Do you ever run over to Paris? Our little band box apartment has not even the *hole in the wall*, that I had hoped never to be without, when the question was where to stow a friend for a night: but accommodations abound, and we would have a merry evening, at all hazards." A copy of *Men and Women* (*Reconstruction*, C401), published for RB in 1855 by Chapman & Hall, was sent to Moxon at RB's request. Moxon continued in the publishing business until his death on 3 June 1858. In a letter to Frederick Locker-Lampson on 20 February 1874, RB wrote: "Moxon was kind & civil, made no profit by me, I am sure, and never tried to help me to any, he would have assured you."

Thomas Powell (1809–87)

Born in London on 3 September 1809, this Browning acquaintance is described by G & M (p. 53, note 1) as "an admitted scamp, by whom Browning and some of his early friends were taken in." By Maynard (p. 165) he is called "the poet's scalawag acquaintance." RB, in a letter to John H. Ingram dated 24 November 1886, discussed the origin of his relationship with Powell: "He obtained credit with [Thomas Noon] Talfourd, who introduced him to various friends and myself." RB, in turn, introduced Powell to his set of friends in the Camberwell area, sometimes known as the Colloquials. Powell published a book entitled *Poems* in 1842, with a new edition appearing in 1844. (See *Reconstruction*, A1889, for a copy of the early version inscribed to RB; and E565, concerning suggested changes by RB which were incorporated into the 1844 edition.) A frequent contributor of poems to *The Monthly Chronicle*, Powell also published *The Count de Foix* (1842) and *True at Last* (1844), a copy of the latter being given to RB (see *Reconstruction*, A1890). It appears that Powell was among the first persons to know the secret of RB's authorship of the anonymously-published *Pauline* (1833). RB's father was to some degree acquainted with Powell and wrote to him on 11 March 1843 about RB's efforts to destroy as much of his own juvenilia as possible (Orr, pp. 32–33). It was at the home of Powell in the mid-1840's that RB met George Murray Smith, who was eventually to become his publisher. Powell borrowed from RB a copy of the Pisa edition (1821) of Shelley's *Adonais* (*Reconstruction*, A2092)—which RB valued considerably—and sold it (*LRB*, p. 373, note 86:4–2).

In a biography of R.H. Horne, *The Farthing Poet* (1968, pp. 114–115), Ann Blainey relates that it was Powell who interested Horne in a modernization of Chaucer's poems. Horne became editor of the project, with Powell as a collaborator (although, as Ms. Blainey observes, one wonders why Powell did not undertake the editorship himself). Another collaborator was EBB, with two contributions (*Reconstruction*, D757–758). The Chaucer work was published in 1841. When EBB felt it necessary to defend Horne in a letter to Mary Russell Mitford (18 July 1841), she cited Powell as one of his friends, and as "a very dear friend also of Wordsworth's." She went on to say: "Mr. Powell has written to me two or three times, & sent me his poems, which are marked by poetical sentiment & pure devotional feeling, but by no remarkable power." On 21 March 1842 she mentioned him to Miss Mitford as "a friend of all the poets."

By 1846, some of the poets were changing their opinions of Powell. In a letter to EBB on 11 January of that year, RB called him "a *buyer* of other men's verses, to be printed as his own." He also told of an attempt by Powell, who was a joint proprietor of *The New Quarterly*, to defraud a writer, presumably RB's friend Joseph Arnould. Then, after expressing curiosity as to what EBB knew "of this Mr Powell," RB said: "Do not write one word in answer to me .. the name of such a miserable nullity, and husk of a man, ought not to have place in your letters." A few months later, writing to EBB on 16 May, RB commented that their mutual friend R.H. Horne was saying "kind things about my plays—and unkind things of Mr Powell 'a dog he repudiates for ever'." When Powell was on friendly terms with RB and numerous other English writers he often imitated their signatures, supposedly just for amusement. It later became clear that he was putting his imitative skill to more serious uses. By 1849 he was deeply involved in charges of forgery and embezzlement. Escaping criminal prosecution through a claim of insanity, he fled to New York and there continued his literary career. In *The Living Authors of England* (1849), he superlatively praised EBB—at a time when she probably no longer cared much about his opinion. Stanley J. Kunitz and Howard Haycraft, in *American Authors 1600–1900* (1938), discuss his literary activities on both sides of the Atlantic without any reference to blots on the British portion of his career, and cite him as "a lively 'John Bull' member of the coterie of 'lions' that gathered at the famous Pfaff's." He died on 14 January 1887. Writing to F.J. Furnivall on 15 October 1883, RB referred to Powell as "a person of infamous character,—an unparall[el]ed forger, who only escaped transporation thro' the ill-deserved kindness of his employers,—and who, premeditating a defence of 'inborn and ineradicable dishonesty', actually practised forging on every possible occasion,—would send you, for instance, a letter signed 'Dickens' or 'Thackeray.'" RB then added: "I heard he had libelled me—who found him out earlier than most of his dupes."

For more details of his criminal activities, see Wilfred Partington, *Should a Biographer Tell?* [1947].

Appendix II

Checklist of Supporting Documents

IN EDITING THIS volume of the Brownings' collected correspondence, we have studied all known original items of Browningiana during the period it covers. Besides primary sources (listed in *The Browning Collections: A Reconstruction*) there exists an extensive body of significant secondary source material, most of it relating to the Barrett and Moulton-Barrett families.

These supporting documents have been invaluable in editing the correspondence which appears in this volume. In numerous cases they helped us assign dates; and, even more, they have helped with notes to enhance the meaning of the letters. We have decided, therefore, to provide a listing of such items—thus sharing them with others contemplating in-depth Browning studies.

Listed below is the supporting material for the period covered by this volume. Subsequent volumes will carry similar appendices of material parallel to their primary-correspondence contents.

Relevant extracts are given where the material includes comments directly pertaining to EBB or RB, or comments impinging on events covered in the primary correspondence.

Following the practice established for our *Checklist*, in all cases where the writer, recipient, or any part of the date is conjectured, we give the first phrase, for positive identification. This is also done in cases where there are two letters of the same date to the same recipient. Location of the document is given, as a cue title or abbreviation, in square brackets at the right-hand margin.

SD845] [1838]. A.L.s. Mary Russell Mitford to Don Boyne. ... *I think the poetry—especially Mr. Kenyon's, Miss Barrett's, Mr. Forster's, & Mr. John Chorley's remarkably beautiful– Miss Barrett's ballad is certainly the finest poem I ever saw in an annual, & she herself (she is still very young) will be probably the most distinguished woman of the age—she has made a translation of the*

Prometheus bound the most difficult of the Greek plays which is said by eminent scholars to be the finest version of a Greek Tragedy in the language. I should like her name—but I fear we must be content with her Initials— May I entreat your particular attention to the corrections . . . about which I am of course more than usually anxious. . . . [Brown]

SD846] [1838]. A.L.s. Anna Jameson to Mary Russell Mitford. *. . . I have written to Miss Barrett, expressing the gratitude I felt, without volunteering any uncalled-for, uninvited criticism. . . .* L'Estrange (1), II, 34. [ ]

SD847] [?1838]. A.L.s. James Phillpotts to Samuel Moulton-Barrett (brother). *I waited for Mr Knowles's . . .* Enclosing estimate for building a house. [ERM-B]

SD848] [ca. 1838]. A.D. unsigned. Notes on points of Law, headed "Storys Equity Pleading." [MM-B & RAM-B]

SD849] [ca. 1838]. A.D. unsigned. Statement to Mary Scarlett, concerning hire of Negroes on Cornwall Estate from 1 April 1834 to 1 August 1838. [ERM-B]

SD850] [ca. 1838]. Exercise. Translation of Latin and Greek verses in unidentified hand. *Terra Salutiferas . . .* [ERM-B]

SD851] [ca. 1838]. A.D. unsigned. Inventory and appraisement of Estate of Samuel Moulton-Barrett (uncle), with valuation at £17,276.11.0. [ERM-B]

SD852] [ca. 1838]. A.D. unsigned. Statement of crops in Trelawney Parish for 1836 and 1837. [ERM-B]

SD853] [ca. 1838]. A.D. unsigned. *The equitable side of the Courts of Westminster . . .* In an unidentified hand. [MM-B & RAM-B]

SD854] 1838. A.D. unsigned. List of consignment of wine to Edward Moulton-Barrett (father) from [Samuel Moulton-Barrett (brother)] [ERM-B]

SD855] [ca. 1838]. A.L.s. Samuel Goodin Barrett to Samuel Moulton-Barrett (brother). *I hope this may find you . . .* [ERM-B]

SD856] [ca. 1838]. A.L.s. Samuel Goodin Barrett to Samuel Moulton-Barrett (brother). *We were much dissapointed . . .* [ERM-B]

SD857] [ca. January 1838]. A.D. unsigned. Statement of stock on Retreat Penn on 15 January 1838. [ERM-B]

SD858] [January 1838]. A.D. unsigned. Inventory of household effects of Samuel Moulton-Barrett (uncle) at Retreat Penn and Cinnamon Hill on 1 January 1838. Verified by Samuel Moulton-Barrett (brother) and sent on 9 January 1838 to Edward Moulton-Barrett (father). [ERM-B]

SD859] 1 January 1837 [*sic* for 1838]. A.L.s. Edward Moulton-Barrett (father) to Samuel Moulton-Barrett (uncle). [ERM-B]

SD860] 2 January 1838. Diary entry of Charles Dickens. *With Ainsworth all day, at Macrone's place on business . . . and afterwards to Covent Garden where we met Browning. . . . Letters of Charles Dickens*, eds. Madeline House and Graham Storey, I, 629–630. [V&A]

SD861] 9 January 1838. A.L.s. Samuel Moulton-Barrett (brother) to Unidentified Correspondent. *I cannot sufficient thank you . . .* [ERM-B]

SD862] 10 January 1838. A.L.s. J. Tennison to Samuel Moulton-Barrett (brother). [ERM-B]

SD863] 12 January 1838. A.L. signed with initials. Joshua Rowe to Samuel Moulton-Barrett (brother). [ERM-B]

SD864] 13 January 1838. A.L.s. Alex W. Aikman to Samuel Moulton-Barrett (brother). [ERM-B]

SD864.1] 15 January 1838. A.L.s. Edward Moulton-Barrett (father) to Samuel Moulton-Barrett (uncle). [ERM-B]

SD865] 16 January 1838. A.L.s. Boddington & Co. to Samuel Moulton-Barrett (uncle). . . . *We also send a Bill of Sale for the transfer of your ⅛th part of the David Lyon to Miss Barrett, which you will be so good as to execute in the presence of two Witnesses, one of whom had better be Capt Selby, that he may be able to do what is necessary, in case of a formal proof of the execution be required by the Custom House here– As this share will not be the property of Miss Barrett legally, until it has been transferred to her by the Bill of Sale, we shall make the usual Insurance upon it, to guard against any accident by which your intention in her favour may possibly be defeated– . . .* [ERM-B]

SD866] 20 January 1838. A.L.s. Alex W. Aikman to Samuel Moulton-Barrett (brother). [ERM-B]

SD867] 23 January 1838. A.L.s. Matthew Farquaharson to Samuel Moulton-Barrett (brother). [ERM-B]

SD868] 23 January 1838. A.L.s. Samuel Moulton-Barrett (brother) to Edward Moulton-Barrett (father). [ERM-B]

SD869] 25 January 1838. A.L.s. J.R. Vermont to Samuel Moulton-Barrett (brother). [ERM-B]

SD870] 26 January 1838. A.L.s. William Tinkler to Samuel Moulton-Barrett (brother). [ERM-B]

SD871] 1 February 1838. A.L.s. Edward Moulton-Barrett (father) to Samuel Moulton-Barrett (uncle). . . . *I delivered your message to Ba who with the rest of my Children deeply sympathize in your sufferings– She has had & indeed still has a terrible cough that racks her, but I am told she is all sound, & that fine weather will restore her—God grant it– . . .* [ERM-B]

SD872] 1 February 1838. A.L. signed with initials. Joshua Rowe to Samuel Moulton-Barrett (brother). [ERM-B]

SD873] 10 February 1838. A.L.s. Alex W. Aikman to Samuel Moulton-Barrett (brother). [ERM-B]

SD874] 14 February 1838. A.L.s. Edward Moulton-Barrett (father) to Samuel Moulton-Barrett (brother). *Your afflicting communication found me as little prepared to receive it as though I had never heard of the illness of my dearest, my most beloved Brother, so much had he gone through, & such nobility had he displayed, that I could not believe he was so soon after his most affectionate letter to me, dated the 8th Decemr. to be removed from me for ever in time. . . . Annie has been dreadfully cut down, but I trust is resigned– Dear Ba feels it most severely, her weakened state was little calculated to bear up against the shock, but I trust in the Lord & she will get well, & that soon. . . .* [ERM-B]

SD875] 17 February 1838. A.L.s. Alex W. Aikman to Samuel Moulton-Barrett (brother). [ERM-B]

SD876] 17 February 1838. A.L. signed with initials. Joshua Rowe to Samuel Moulton-Barrett (brother). [ERM-B]

SD877] 18 February 1838. A.L.s. J. Tennison to Samuel Moulton-Barrett (brother). [ERM-B]

SD878] 28 February 1838. A.L.s. Anne Eliza Moulton-Barrett to Samuel Moulton-Barrett (brother). . . . *Dear Ba is still very poorly, with a sad cough, to cure which we look anxiously for the Spring: What a sweet creature she is!* . . .
[ERM-B]

SD879] 28 February 1838. Incomplete Copy of Letter. [Edward Moulton-Barrett (father)] to Mr. Anderson. *There is but one circumstance attending* . . .
[ERM-B]

SD880] [March 1838]. A.L. signed with initials. Joshua Rowe to Samuel Moulton-Barrett (brother). *I am sorry we are not* . . . [ERM-B]

SD881] 1 March 1838. A.L.s. Edward Moulton-Barrett (father) to Samuel Moulton-Barrett (brother). . . . *I am sorry to say that dear Ba has got a sad cough but I hope the warm weather may help her–* . . . [ERM-B]

SD882] 1 March 1838. A.L.s. J. G[?resham] to Samuel Moulton-Barrett (brother). [ERM-B]

SD883] 1 March 1838. A.L.s. J. G[?resham] to Joshua Rowe. [ERM-B]

SD884] 4 March 1838. A.L.s. W.K. Hyatt to Samuel Moulton-Barrett (brother). [ERM-B]

SD885] 15 March 1838. A.L.s. Edward Moulton-Barrett (father) to Samuel Moulton-Barrett (brother). [ERM-B]

SD886] 30 March 1838. A.L.s. Mr. Anderson to Samuel Moulton-Barrett (brother). [ERM-B]

SD887] 30 March 1838. Receipt. Samuel Flemming to Samuel Moulton-Barrett (brother). [ERM-B]

SD888] [31 March 1838]. A.L.s. Mr. Anderson to [Joshua Rowe]. Forwarded to Samuel Moulton-Barrett (brother). *I regret that indisposition prevents my waiting upon you* . . . [ERM-B]

SD889] [ca. May 1838]. Receipt. J.M. Clarke to Samuel Moulton-Barrett (brother), for transactions on 27 April 1838 to 29 April 1838. [ERM-B]

SD890] 4 April 1838. A.L.s. Anderson & Kemble to Edward Moulton-Barrett (father). [ERM-B]

SD891] 5 April 1838. A.L.s. Richard Barrett to John F. Badley. [ERM-B]

SD892] 6 April 1838. Receipt. Edward A. Smith to Samuel Moulton-Barrett (brother). [ERM-B]

SD893] 10 April 1838. A.D.s. Supreme Court of Jamaica to Samuel Moulton-Barrett (brother), concerning case against William Weld. [ERM-B]

SD894] 14 April 1838. A.L.s. P. Redwood to Samuel Moulton-Barrett (brother). [ERM-B]

SD895] 18 April 1838. A.D.s. Mason Estimate from William Lace to Samuel Moulton-Barrett (brother). With second receipted copy. [ERM-B]

SD896] 20 April 1838. Cover sheet. Unknown to Henrietta Moulton-Barrett. Franked by S. Colingsbroke and directed to 74 Gloucester Place. Redirected to 50 Wimpole Street. [MM-B & RAM-B]

SD897] 21 April [1838]. A.L.s. Henriette Willoughby Barrett to George Goodin Barrett (1792–1854). *I have great pleasure in announcing to you* . . .
[ERM-B]

SD898] 21 April [1838]. A.L. signed with initials. Joshua Rowe to Samuel Moulton-Barrett (brother). *I am only this morning* . . . [ERM-B]

Appendix II

SD899] 25 April 1838. A.L.s. Richard Barrett to John F. Badley.
[ERM-B]

SD900] 26 April 1838. A.L.s. Mr. Anderson to Edward Moulton-Barrett (father). [ERM-B]

SD901] 27 April 1838. A.D.s. Permission from Christopher, Bishop of Jamaica, to Samuel Moulton-Barrett (brother) to exhume the body of Samuel Moulton-Barrett (uncle) for reburial at Cinnamon Hill. [ERM-B]

SD902] 27 April 1838. A.L.s. Anderson & Kemble to Edward Moulton-Barrett (father). Enclosing A.D.s. giving advice and opinions on the Barrett vs Barrett suit. [ERM-B]

SD903] 27 April 1838. A.L.s. Jacob Bravo to Samuel Moulton-Barrett (brother). [ERM-B]

SD904] 28 April 1838. Receipt. J. Soulette to Samuel Moulton-Barrett (brother). [ERM-B]

SD905] 1 May 1838. A.L.s. Edward Barrett (of Oxford Estate) to Edward Moulton-Barrett (father). [ERM-B]

SD906] 4 May 1838. A.L.s. J. MacIntyre to Samuel Moulton-Barrett (brother). [ERM-B]

SD907] 4 May 1838. A.L. signed with initials. Joshua Rowe to Samuel Moulton-Barrett (brother). [ERM-B]

SD908] 7 May 1838. A.L.s. J.R. K[?itchin] to Samuel Moulton-Barrett (brother). [ERM-B]

SD909] 11 May 1838. A.L.s. Vestry of Trelawney to Samuel Moulton-Barrett (brother). With Resolution by the Committee, dated 23 April 1838.
[ERM-B]

SD910] 12 May 1838. A.L.s. James Room to Samuel Moulton-Barrett (brother). [ERM-B]

SD911] 18 May 1838. A.L. signed with initials. Joshua Rowe to Samuel Moulton-Barrett (brother). [ERM-B]

SD912] 19 May 1838. Receipt. John Clayton & Co. to Samuel Moulton-Barrett (brother). [ERM-B]

SD913] 21 May 1838. A.D.s. Memorandum of Agreement between Samuel Moulton-Barrett (brother) and the Justices and Vestry of Trelawney. [ERM-B]

SD914] 2 June 1838. Receipt. Robert Chapman to Cinnamon Hill Estate.
[ERM-B]

SD915] 6 June 1838. Cover sheet. Charles Drake and Co. to Samuel Moulton-Barrett (brother), enclosing three A.Ds.s. relating to Sam's trip to America. [ERM-B]

SD916] 9 June [?1838]. A.L.s. Richard Barrett to John F. Badley. *I have just got out of* ... [ERM-B]

SD917] [28 June 1838]. A.L.s. Lady Dacre to Mary Russell Mitford. ... *I have sent my book to Miss Barrett, and have a sweet note from her. I shall try to* niggle *on with her; but I am too deaf and old, I fear, to scrape acquaintance with a young person.* ... L'Estrange (1), II, 21. [   ]

SD918] [ca. July 1838]. A.D. unsigned. Statement of condition and size of labourers Cottages on Retreat Penn, with list of occupants for each, as of 12 July 1838. [ERM-B]

SD919] 2 July 1838. Draft of Letter, signed with initials. Edward Moulton-

Barrett (father) to [?Anderson and Kemble]. *Barrett* vs *Vermont– Still I have heard* . . . [ERM-B]

SD920] 3 July 1838. Receipt. William Lace to Samuel Moulton-Barrett (brother). [ERM-B]

SD921] 5 July 1838. Copy of Document. Republication of last Will with Codicils of Richard Barrett. Signed for as a true copy by Samuel Goodin Barrett and George Goodin Barrett (1792–1854). [ERM-B]

SD922] [14 July 1838]. A.L. signed with initials. Joshua Rowe to Samuel Moulton-Barrett (brother). *I have only a few minutes* . . . [ERM-B]

SD922.1] [ca. 15 July 1838]. A.L.s. Arabella Moulton-Barrett to H.S. Boyd. . . . *My* angelic *sister is tolerably well this morning.* . . . [Eton]

SD923] 16 July 1838. A.L.s. Edward Moulton-Barrett (father) to Samuel Moulton-Barrett (brother). [ERM-B]

SD924] [ca. August 1838]. A.D. unsigned. Statement of expenses incurred in America from 24 May 1838 to 2 August 1838, in the hand of Samuel Moulton-Barrett (brother). [ERM-B]

SD925] [ca. August 1838]. A.D. unsigned. Statement of size of Labourers Grounds on Retreat Penn and the occupant of each, on 1 August 1838. [ERM-B]

SD926] 1 August 1838. A.L.s. Henrietta Moulton-Barrett to Samuel Moulton-Barrett (brother). . . . *I have scribb[l]ed all this without saying anything to you of our dearest Ba, who I am grieved to say still remains on the Invalid list—but my beloved Sam don't let me make you uneasy about her. I do not think it right to conceal altogether her illness from you, you know that she has always been delicate, & the unhappy cold she caught last winter has not left her chest—but every means has been taken, & is taking, & we trust with the blessing of Him she will soon be restored. Dr. Chambers who attends her has ordered her to Torquay for the winter. Papa has given his consent to her going, & Dr. Chambers says she has* every *hope that she will return from thence quite well. She goes to the Hedleys for a week or two (they have a house there) & very soon our dearest Bummy who is now returned to Frocester goes to Torquay & she & Ba are thinking of taking a cottage between them for the winter—so she will be as happy & as well taken care of as if she were at home. Bro goes down with her & will return & we are very anxious that Papa may allow Arabel & me to take it by turns to be with her. I think he* cannot *refuse. Our plan is that one of us should be with her until Christmas & then that the other should go– We are in great suspense about it. Not only on our own accounts, but we have the vanity to suppose that she would not be comfortable without one of us to nurse her. She likes the idea of going much—she goes by sea– Her new Poem "The Seraphim" is come out & has been most favorably received in the literary world. Almost all the Reviews have taken notice of it, & in the most flattering way– As you are coming home so soon, there will be no use in sending it to you, but I know you will be enchanted with it. Her name is attached to it—& in one of the Reviews she is mentioned as the "fair Elizabeth"– Indeed we have every reason to be proud of this beloved sister of ours. May God in His mercy soon restore her health to us—don't my beloved Sam be uneasy about her. You shall hear constantly of her, & we will tell you faithfully.* . . . *We continue to like our new home extremely, the drawing rooms are even not yet finished & James Mathews is still working in the house. I am sure you will be pleased with it.* . . . *Trippy is quite* *well—but unhappily not so her temper– She has not even yet received Bummy's being here so long– What a misfortune her temper is to her! She says that when Ba goes to Torquay she will never come here—but I think her better heart will not permit her to keep this resolution....* [ERM-B]

SD927] 1 August 1838. Receipt. Robert Coal to Samuel Moulton-Barrett (brother). [ERM-B]

SD928] 2 August 1838. A.L.s. Joshua Rowe to Samuel Moulton-Barrett (brother). [ERM-B]

SD929] 11 August 1838. A.L.s. Hill Davies and M. Neil to Samuel Moulton-Barrett (brother), enclosing Statement of Account. [ERM-B]

SD930] 11 August [1838]. A.L.s. Joshua Rowe to Samuel Moulton-Barrett (brother). *Being about to negociate ...* [ERM-B]

SD931] 15 August 1838. A.L.s. Edward Moulton-Barrett (father) to Samuel Moulton-Barrett (brother). *... Our dear Ba continues much in the same State, she is going to Torquay for the Winter & under the blessing of God, I trust she will improve– All the rest are quite well....* [ERM-B]

SD932] 17 August [1838]. A.L.s. William and Mary Wordsworth to John Kenyon. *I have been so much pleased with the power & knowledge displayed in Miss Barret's* [sic] *vol of Poems which you were so kind as to send Mr W. some time ago, that I am desirous to see her translation of Eschylus– cd you send me a copy thro' Mr Moxon—& tell me also where it is to be bought—as two of my acquaintances wish to purchase it....* [Berg]

SD933] 17 August [1838]. A.L. signed with initials. Joshua Rowe to Samuel Moulton-Barrett (brother). *I was going to have ...* [ERM-B]

SD934] 18 August 1838. A.L.s. Mr. Anderson to Samuel Moulton-Barrett (brother). [ERM-B]

SD935] 20 August 1838. A.L.s. William Knibb to Edward Moulton-Barrett (father). [ERM-B]

SD936] [ca. September 1838]. Copy of Document. Proposal for a Scale of Wages for Labourers on Retreat Penn dated 17 August 1838, and Statement of Stock on Retreat Penn as of 20 September 1838. [ERM-B]

SD937] [ca. September 1838]. Receipt. Joseph G. Jump to Samuel Moulton-Barrett (brother) for purchases from 4 August 1838 to 11 September 1838. [ERM-B]

SD938] 6 September 1838. A.L.s. Anderson & Kemble to Samuel Moulton-Barrett (brother). [ERM-B]

SD939] 7 September 1838. A.L. signed with initials. Joshua Rowe to Samuel Moulton-Barrett (brother). [ERM-B]

SD940] [10 September 1838]. Cover sheet. Addressed to Edward Moulton-Barrett (father), with docket in his hand indicating the contents (missing) as "The Will of SMB & S.M.B. Junr." [ERM-B]

SD941] 15 September 1838. A.L.s. Edward Moulton-Barrett (father) to Samuel Moulton-Barrett (brother). *... Our precious Ba, who you know is at Torquay & where she is to remain during the winter, is much the same, but is sensible that the Climate is much more agreeable to her, than that of this Town, & that there she gets air & exercise, one day going out in a Boat & the next in a Chair, without exertion or labor. She is in God's Hands, & being assured that she is an handmaid of the Lords, He will order all things aright for her good. She is a blessed one, the most beautiful of Characters, of the highest attainments*

& possessed of the noblest Mind, she esteems herself little & would always take the lowest place– God has truly blessed me in her, & thanks be to His Grace, has evidently blessed her for himself.... [ERM-B]

SD942] 15 September 1838. A.L.s. Harvey & Daniel to Samuel Moulton-Barrett (brother). [ERM-B]

SD943] 15 September [1838]. A.L.s. Henrietta Moulton-Barrett to Samuel Moulton-Barrett (brother). *What will you say when you see where I am my beloved Sam—it does indeed seem strange to me to feel myself once more in Devonshire– I believe when I wrote last to you, I was in a most terrible state of inquietude & anxiety about the probability that existed of not obtaining permission of accompanying our dearest Ba to these genial shores, but Papa very kindly gave it to me at last & here I am seated in Jane's pretty drawing room with a most lovely view of woods & sea before me going to tell you all that will be most likely to interest you & first of all on the subject of our present anxieties, our dear Ba's health– We have been here nearly three weeks, in that short time much improvement will hardly be expected, but I do think there* is *an improvement, you can believe my beloved Sam how great an invalid she has been lately, it would not be right to conceal the truth from you, but I cannot express to you how thankful I feel that she is out of that horrible London where air and everything else combined to retard the recovery—& in this lovely & genial climate when with God's blessing, all will tend to restore her precious health– Indeed we had every reason to fear another winter for her in London after the last, & after Doctor Chamber's opinion, that her recovery there would be running a* risk *Papa at first made some objections to her coming, but happily for us all, it appeared to him in the right light at last, & I am sure he must feel satisfied &* glad *now that he made the sacrifice in parting with her, it was a great sacrifice to make for him & when the day of our departure came, I really almost feared that the parting would not have been effected– but after all, she is only here for the winter & I hope Papa may often come to see her. We came by sea, the* we *consists of Ba, Bro, George & myself—Bro & George I fear will be obliged to return soon, at least they talk of doing so, & I am to remain during half the time of Ba's sojourn in Torquay, I suppose about the end of December or the beginning of Janry I shall return to London & change places with dearest Arabel who I can assure you I left with a heavy heart, but we could not have both left home together, she bore our coming away most heroically—& now I am much more comfortable about her than I was for little Mary Hunter is gone to be her companion, as long as she remains* sisterless– *You know what a favorite she is, & therefore I hope she will make Arabel forget our absences it was very kind in Mr. Hunter giving her up– Ba bore her voyage wonderfully well, she was the only lady on board who did not suffer from sea sickness (poor George & I were in a most terrible condition). We left London very early on a Saturday morng, & arrived here on Monday Eveng– We are now dearest Jane's & uncle Hedley's visitors who really seem glad to have us, their kindness is not to be* expressed– *Ba was only able to get out I think not more than three times during the course of the last year in London, & now* here *she goes out almost every day, either in a chair or in a sailing boat– Being out in the air as much as possible is recommended to her—in London she could not bear it, here thank God she can– Jane's house is some distance from the sea, & at present it is rather a fatigue to her getting down to it, but from the first of October she has taken a small house where she will be* *in a partnership with our dearest Bummy—who about that time promises us to leave Frocester where she at present is & come here for the winter, so you see how comfortable we shall be my beloved Sam & how well Ba will be taken care of with so many whom she loves with her if we only have the blessing of seeing her getting well soon how happy we shall be! & I have indeed every hope it may be so. Should it be God's will— There is a very clever & most attentive medical man here who attends her— You know that her complaint is connected with the* chest *& now my dearest Sam my candour & openess with regard to her must not make you uneasy, I did not like to keep you in the dark about her, as I should not like you to have done so by me, but do not be unhappy or anxious for she is most advantageously situated here, she could not be in a better climate, & with it she has* every *other advantage— She seems delighted with the place, & is in very good spirits which is really a proof of her improvement— She & I, with* Crow *our maid, took a most delightful sail yesterday for more than an hour, & enjoyed it extremely.... Ba is every day, getting more & more in repute among the Literati— I wish you could see all the very favorable reviews that have come out of the Seraphim—two days [ago] she received a most flattering letter from an editor of one of the annuals, entreating her to contribute to his— She is certainly beginning not only to be known, but* appreciated— *... The house is taken here at the rate of a £180 a year, the rent is high but we took it in best situation on Ba's account & this she talks of paying out of her* own *pocket leaving the rest of the household expenditure to Bummy—the latter we expect* will bring dear Little Arlette & Cissy & their French governess with her—*they are I hear sweet little girls, I am quite anxious to see them.... I hope I may find some opportunity of going to Sidmouth—old Mr.* [Thomas] *Mogridge talks of coming here to see dear Ba but I rather hope he may not.... Harvey has sold five copies of Ba's Seraphim in Sidmouth. Now dearest Sam, I must think of sealing up this sheet, which I hope you may not find* too well filled— *Pray do not make yourself uneasy about Ba, for she is now really going on well, & I trust it may please God to restore her* entirely— *She desires her affecte. love with Bro George James uncle Hedley &c &c....* [ERM-B]

SD944] 15 September 1838. A.L. signed with initials. Joshua Rowe to Samuel Moulton-Barrett (brother). [ERM-B]

SD945] [28 September 1838]. A.L.s. Arabella Moulton-Barrett to Hugh Stuart Boyd. *... We heard yesterday from Ba,—& although she says she is better in some respects, yet I did not think it altogether a satisfactory account. She is very much weaker than she was, but this is occasioned by the violent remedies her medical man makes use of— She says she has corrected & returned the proof sheet of the poem she has written for the Amaranth— The title of the poem is "A Sabbath on the Sea"— We were told the other day by Mrs. Orme, that the author of the review in the Sunbeam is a Mr.* Frank—*a person of no* great *celebrity— At any rate, we ought to be much obliged to him for puffing Ba as he does....*
[ABL]

SD946] 1 October 1838. A.L.s. James Graham-Clarke to Samuel Moulton-Barrett (brother). [ERM-B]

SD947] 1 October 1838. Statement of Account. Estate of Samuel Moulton-Barrett (uncle) in account with Matthew Farquaharson, from 23 December 1837. Posted to Samuel Moulton-Barrett (brother) on 5 October 1838. [ERM-B]

SD948] 2 October 1838. A.L.s. Matthew Farquaharson to Samuel Moulton-Barrett (brother). [ERM-B]

SD948.1] 6 October 1838. A.L.s. Arabella Moulton-Barrett to H.S.

Boyd. ... *Ba is* rather better.... [Eton]

SD949] 13 October 1838. A.L.s. Anderson & Kemble to Edward Moulton-Barrett (father). [ERM-B]

SD950] 16 October 1838. A.L.s. William Tinkler to Samuel Moulton-Barrett (brother). [ERM-B]

SD951] 18 October 1838. A.L.s. Matthew Farquaharson to James Phillpotts. [ERM-B]

SD952] 23 October 1838. A.L.s. James Phillpotts to Samuel Moulton-Barrett (brother). [ERM-B]

SD953] 5 November 1838. A.L.s. John Forster to Leigh Hunt. ... *Will you oblige me my dear Hunt by sending a line to Browning—"Robert Browning, Hanover Cottage, South Hampton Street, Camberwell." ... to say that our dinner is deferred till the Thursday after—and to express with the delay our regrets and affectionate regard....* [ ]

SD954] 13 November 1838. A.L.s. Mr. Anderson to Edward Moulton-Barrett (father). [ERM-B]

SD955] [21 November 1838]. A.L.s. Arabella Moulton-Barrett to Henrietta Moulton-Barrett. ... *I can tell you I often get a scold from all of them here for writing so often to you, and when I told George last Wednesday that I had been writing to Ba, he said "What a strange fancy, why you wrote only the other day–" You see we have much more regard for yr pockets than you have yrselves– How I wish your account of our dearest Ba could have been more satisfactory– I cannot bear to think of the return of that hoarseness, but I trust it has gone now. You did not say anything of it– May the God of all soon rejoice our hearts, in granting us what we all so ardently desire & pray for– I did not say anything of Sam's arrival in the* P.S. *I wrote to Ba the other day, as I concluded of course that Papa has done so.... We had a dinner party of 15 people.... Papa was walking about the drawing room all the morning making such preparations, as if at ⟨six the⟩ royal family were coming! Tell Ba he placed her busts of Dante & Tasso on the pillars on the stair case. I suppose to meet Capt. Selby's taste for the fine arts! But he says he is going to buy busts to place there!... I am going to write a line to Ba upon some private business & as it is nothing that will give any interest to any one but to herself, I have begged her not to show my letter. I assure you it does not concern any of us excepting herself—so you need none of you in the least care about seeing it....* [Altham]

SD956] 21 November 1838. A.L.s. Samuel Moulton-Barrett (brother) to Henrietta Moulton-Barrett. ... *The house I am as well pleased with as the inhabitants, but am in some measure disappointed at the width of the Street; to this however I am reconciled for the house is delightful in every respect, & my room as warm as I could wish it when in bed, but as cold as my* bitterest *enemy could desire when out. I like the first drawing room the best & is I think very hand⟨s⟩ome, all the others are excellent especially the Bed Rooms, but the Library is smaller than I expected; I will be more explan⟨a⟩tory when we meet for time just now will ⟨n⟩ot allow, as I am about to go into the city⟨.⟩ My best love to all your party, I am in ⟨ho⟩pes from your account that dear Ba is ⟨gr⟩adual[l]y improving I trust she has better r⟨e⟩ason to be satisfied with Dr. Barry; My best love to her Jane & party ...* [Altham]

SD957] [24 November 1838]. A.L.s. Henrietta Moulton-Barrett to Samuel Moulton-Barrett (brother). *Thank you much for your letter which was long in coming but very welcome when it did come—as you are a man of so much business I suppose I must forgive the delay—& before I say more endeavor in some measure* *to satisfy your anxieties about our beloved Ba– She put on the blister last night, but this is not to say that she is any worse for thank God she passed a comfortable day yesterday, & slept well last night, & consequently appears comfortable this morning. I told you that Dr. Barry has been for some days passed threatening her with a blister, I feared she would not escape it, but if it does her good in the end, it is worth while feeling uncomfortable for a day or so with it– She has only kept it on for six hours so subsequently it will not be so bad to bear– Tell dearest Arabel that she has had no encrease of hoarseness lately so I know not exactly to what she alludes—indeed I think I may say that the cough sounds less hoarse than it did– She is beginning to walk a little every day—as Dr. Barry seems to fear the* habit *of always lying– He gave her a close examination yesterday morng. when I went up to see Jane, I did not hear the result– She of course feels her weakness very much when she tries to walk, & cannot do a great deal in that way yet—but Dr. Barry saw her make the attempt the other day & so expressed himself satisfied with it– ... I am so glad that you like our new house—indeed I believe we shall find it a very comfortable one, & a happy one if it only pleases God to restore our dearest Ba soon to us.... All before this was written in the morng dearest Sam I must only add a very few words now– Dearest Ba has not passed quite so comfortable a day as yesterday—owing to the blister I dare say in great measure—& partly to be attributed to the encrease of coldness in the air—which always affects her—but we keep her rooms as high as 63 or 64 by Papas thermometer– The rain is gone but it is not nearly so warm today as it has been– Ba was pleased by the arrival of the Literary Gazette yesterday Eveg directed by Papa– ...* [ERM-B]

SD958] 24 November [1838]. A.L.s. H.M. Waddell to Samuel Moulton-Barrett (brother). *Your favour of Wednesday morning* ... [ERM-B]

SD959] 27 November 1838. A.L.s. John Altham Graham-Clarke Jr. to Samuel Moulton-Barrett (brother). [ERM-B]

SD960] 30 November 1838. File Copy of Letter. Edward Moulton-Barrett (father) to [Anderson & Kemble]. *Having heard from my Son* ... [ERM-B]

SD961] December 1838. A.L.s. Anderson & Kemble to Edward Moulton-Barrett (father). Appended to a Legal Opinion by B. Middleton. [ERM-B]

SD962] 2 December [1838]. A.L.s. Samuel Goodin Barrett to Samuel Moulton-Barrett (brother). *I recd your most amusing letter* ... [ERM-B]

SD962.1] [7 December 1838]. Arabella Moulton-Barrett to H.S. Boyd. *I have written out the poem* [EBB's "A Sabbath on the Sea"] ... [Eton]

SD963] 9 December 1838. A.L.s. W.K. Hyatt to Samuel Moulton-Barrett (brother). [ERM-B]

SD964] 10 December 1838. A.L.s. William Tinkler to Samuel Moulton-Barrett (brother). [ERM-B]

SD965] [15 December 1838]. A.L.s. Henrietta Moulton-Barrett to Samuel Moulton-Barrett (brother). ... *Our dear Ba is about the same as she was the day before yesterday, if there be* any *alteration in her, it is for the better, & she this instant desires me to say that she* does *feel better today, in spite of her not having slept so well last night as she did the night before– She looks comfortable & cheerful just now, & promises to behave better tonight. I trust there may be no more decision for any more blisters, but I think the last was of use to her upon the whole—the pulsation which she has suffered most from lately, has been better* *today– dearest Arabel's letter pleased her very much, & she did not complain of the shortness of it this time, I hope that tomorrow being Sunday another may arrive for her. She has just been talking very confidently of its arrival, therefore I hope she may not be disappointed– Tell Arabel from her that she ought not to expect me to write such lengthy letters as she does. When mine are so much more frequent—& I often think that you must sometimes find them too long. . . . Whilst we were absent Ba (knowing from past experiences that boys were very fond of cakes thought that girls might be so too) sent out & bought some buns for our tea which we have done ample justice to. . . . Ba had a most melancholy letter from her friend Miss Mitford a day or two ago, giving a most lamentable account of the illness of her father– Three months ago a wheel went over his leg—& the other day he caught cold & that part was effected by it. She was very much alarmed at his illness—& on the outside of her note she writes "there is very great danger, but still some little hope"– Poor Ba is terribly distressed about it, the communication arrived just at her breakfast time, it quite took away her appetite. I do hope she may have a better account soon. . . . I think I had better tell Papa that the coffee is all gone. Ba will be angry with me I know for doing so—but what she gets here she does not like half so much, as that that he bought in London—& as it is the principal thing she takes, & what she most enjoys—it is a pity she should not have it good– When Papa comes, he may like to bring some with him. . . . Ba has received dear Henry's German paper for which she thanks him with an affecte. kiss. . . . Our dearest Ba slept better last night, & has only just opened her eyes to tell me so–* . . .   [ERM-B]

SD966] 23 December [1838]. A.L.s. Samuel Goodin Barrett to Samuel Moulton-Barrett (brother), enclosing copy of Heads of Agreement for case of Barrett *vs* Plummer. *I received by last Packt.* . . .   [ERM-B]

SD967] 26 December 1838. A.L.s. Samuel Moulton-Barrett (brother) to Henrietta Moulton-Barrett. *We recieved your letter about an hour since & though you evidently were half asleep when you wrote the latter part of it, or perhaps rather mystified by your over nights indulgence; we are still tha⟨n⟩kful to you for your account of dear Ba w⟨h⟩ich we all flatter ourselves is rather of passable description: we all feel, & I think, the* Governor *amongst the number, that dear Ba has greater confidence in her Medical adviser, if this be so in reality a great point is gained without the aid of either your detestable drugs or Bro's sanguin recommendations. . . . Mr. Kenyon has just been here to enquire about Ba, who I trust will feel duly honoured; he looks exceedingly well & in good spirits.* . . .
[Altham]

SD968] [?1839]. A.L.s. W. Carey to Samuel Moulton-Barrett (brother). *I came here yesterday Evening* . . .   [ERM-B]

SD969] [?1839]. A.L.s. H.M. Waddell to Samuel Moulton-Barrett (brother). *I received your favour* . . .   [ERM-B]

SD970] [ca. 1839]. A.L.s. W. Carey to Samuel Moulton-Barrett (brother). *Finding Mr. G. Gordons* . . .   [ERM-B]

SD971] [ca. 1839]. A.L. signed with initials. Edward Moulton-Barrett (father) to Henrietta Moulton-Barrett. *The Bearer will I doubt not* . . .   [Altham]

SD972] [ca. 1839]. Broadside. Rules & Orders of an Association, at Leamington Priors, concerning apprehension and prosecution of offenders.
[ERM-B]

SD973] [ca. 1839]. Copy of Document. Statement on Estate of Samuel Moulton-Barrett (uncle) from 27 December 1837 to 28 October 1838, with later entries up to 11 February 1840. [ERM-B]

SD974] [ca. 1839]. Statement of Account. Cinnamon Hill Estate with R.Y. Scott. [ERM-B]

SD975] [1839]. A.D. unsigned. Statement of acreages and total numbers of Negroes and stock on each estate in Jamaica, for March Quarter 1839. [ERM-B]

SD976] [2 January 1839]. A.L.s. Henriette Willoughby Barrett to Samuel Moulton-Barrett (brother). *Thanks for so kindly writing ...* [ERM-B]

SD977] [3 January 1839]. A.L.s. Henrietta Moulton-Barrett to Samuel Moulton-Barrett (brother). *You may guess our disappointment when the Exeter coach came in yesterday eveng, without dearest Papa, & the only substitute we had for him was a paper directed by him, had it not been for it we should have been expecting him again at nine o'clock when the last coach was to arrive– You might at least have sent us a letter to say what had prevented him. Poor Ba was terribly disappointed, however I think he must ⟨co⟩me today or we shall hear from you.... Ba is* tolerable *today, in spite of her disappointment she did not pass a* bad *night, altho' it might have been better—but I do not think she looks her* best *today which I am sorry for as Papa will see her– ... Pray thank Mary for me for her beautiful little present– I shall value it very much for her sake—& dear Minny for her cakes which are now on the table before me, they look so good that I long for the breakfast hour tomorrow morning when we may make an* incision– *Papa thought Ba had better not have any tonight lest it might prevent her from sleeping– I will tell you what he thinks of her when I write again– ... To dearest Stormie for the* valuable *book Ba desires me to tell him how* pleased *how* grateful, *how* angry *she is with him for buying it for her. It was very* kind of him, *& I think he could not have given her a* more *acceptable present. She says she will say more on the subject* herself– *... I have forgotten to say how delighted Ba is with dear Marys pretty little book– I dare say she will see it well fil[l]ed some day, as Mary has given her so many good subjects to write upon....* [ERM-B]

SD978] 11 January 1839. A.L.s. Edward Moulton-Barrett (father) to Samuel Moulton-Barrett (brother). *I was happy to receive your letter, first as communicating the happy intelligence that you had escaped the two returns which the fever had considered to have been his; & now that you have made such inroads on his supposed rights, I trust that you will bold[l]y maintain them, & fairly rout the ......– I suppose Ba is recommending the use of Arsenic, did it upon the known fact of its efficiency in destroying all vermin, dont mistake, she did not mean to class you with the breed, but your assailant. However she has the authority of the Doctor that arsenic is a specific for the ague fever. Your letter was satisfactory also in letting us know that you were all well, long may you continue so.... Our dear Patient has had three good, good for her, nights, & I trust under the blessing of our Lord is going on well, altho no symptom has ceased of an unpleasant nature....* [ERM-B]

SD979] 15 January [1839]. A.L.s. Henrietta Moulton-Barrett to Mary Minto. *... I would much rather tell you dearest Mary how grateful to you I feel for all the anxiety you express, & for the sincerity of those expressions about our beloved Ba. The winter thank God has hitherto done her no harm, indeed in* *spite of it, I think we have reason to hope that there is a gradual improvement going on. We could not at this season expect a very rapid one but her being even a* little *better now, excites us to hope for a much greater improvement when the warm weather comes back to us again– God grant that such a blessing may be ours. We could not have a greater one!—but* He *will do what is best for us– She is not of course able to go out, this you must be aware of. Nor does she often leave her sofa, altho' she can walk– She looks nicely, & her spirits are generally good– It is a blessing that her happy disposition enables her to bear up so well– I am very fortunate to be allowed so long to be her companion here—it is as you may suppose a great comfort to me but altho' the pleasure is so great, I am beginning to wish to relinquish it in favor of poor Arabel– We cannot both enjoy it together, but as I have been here so long it is only fair she should have her turn, & I know she must be dreadfully anxious to come, altho' in the kindness of her heart she refrains from telling me so, but the movements of both of us, depend upon* Papa, *& not on ourselves, therefore we can only* wish *on the subject....* [BL]

SD980] 15 January [1839]. A.L.s. Samuel Goodin Barrett to Samuel Moulton-Barrett (brother). *I fully intended to have written ...* [ERM-B]

SD981] [19 January 1839]. A.L.s. Henrietta Moulton-Barrett to Samuel Moulton-Barrett (brother). ... *We really had begun to think you had forgotten us altogether—but guessing how it was that we did not receive letters from any of you, we could not be* angry *with you, which* Ba *considered the most provoking part of the business– It is such a relief to scold, when angry fires are burning within– Ba had not heard from Arabel or any of you for* ten *days, notwithstanding the debt of gratitude you owed her for her* lengthy *letter—but you need not be uneasy now, you know she can forgive—& after all, she quite feels that you are not* very *much to blame, excepting for the Sunday omission, & I trust dearest Arabel will not forget it again– I do not mean to say to say* [sic] *forget, for I am sure that is an accusation she* never *deserves. But I am loitering– The box arrived late last night after two walks that Papa & Mr. Hunter had to enquire for it—in the rain—it came after Ba had gone to bed– Consequently Papa would not allow her to be instructed of its arrival, lest the letters should disturb her slumbers—it was quite a mistaken notion* I *think– However she was not told of it, nor was the box opened until this morng—between prayers & breakfast time, just before Mr. Hunter's departure—so that he had just time to read Mary's notes—& to* look *at, but not to* taste *the cake– He remained with us longer than I thought he would, & (tell Mary) made himself as agreeable as he always does—he promises to come here again at Easter—but in spite of Ba's entreaties I think he will* not *accept Dr. Pye Smith's invitation until* Midsummer– *Then he will, if he be alive, & at the same time promises to pay us a visit in Wimpole Street, where if it pleases God we shall* ALL *be assembled then– Ba had great pleasure in his society, it has induced her to sit up an hour later at night, & to talk more than she* ought *to have done so that Dr. Barry threatened either to lock Ba up in her room, or to send Mr. Hunter to Coventry—which so incensed the latter, that I really began to fear nothing less than a* duel—*however all these unlawful doings have not made our beloved Ba any worse. She did not sleep well last night, but she was a little excited before she went to bed in taking leave of Mr. Hunter, & she looks frightly this morng—the hoarseness is better– Mr.*

Hunter thought her improved in appearance– It is my belief that she really is a little better– May God in his mercy continue the improvement!! She was as pleased with her letters as I was with mine– Thank dearest Arabel for writing to me, & you too– We are so grateful to hear that that horrible ague is going away from ⟨you.⟩ . . . Ba is very desirous to see Arabel & Arabel must be so anxious to come here—but even if I were desirous to remain, in spite of my gay propensities, Minny ought to know if she does not, that they would be very secondary objects under present circumstances– To leave my beloved Ba, whether it is to be now, or in the Spring, of course I shall always feel the same degree of pain—but notwithstanding I am willing & desirous to relinquish my place– Minny need not fear that I shall injure Ba with my gaieties, the injury to myself I will give her leave to fear—with all the dreadful results she anticipates from it—but I can assure her they would soon cease altogether—were they to affect our dear Ba in any way– I sleep on a sofa in her room, & I have a dressing room to myself, therefore I make no noise whatever in her room—besides our parties are always very early ones generally– Minny's sayings I know were all MEANT *in kindness—& give her my love–* . . . [ERM-B]

SD982] [28 January 1839]. Arabella Moulton-Barrett to Hugh Stuart Boyd. *You may fancy our surprise when, upon opening the Athenæum, on Saturday, the first thing Papa saw, was these lines ["L.E.L.'s Last Question"] of Ba's,— who had written them & sent them to the editor, unknown to any one. I supposed that you wd. care about seeing them, therefore I have written them out for you. I dare say you heard of Miss Landon's last letter that she wrote to some friend in England, a day or two before her death—supposing it may not have been in yr. newspaper, I must tell you, that* the question *upon wh. these lines are written, were the last words of her letter. I shall be anxious to know what you think of Ba's lines. Papa returned last Friday, but did not bring an improved account of Ba. He thinks her much the same as when he last saw her.* . . .

[Wellesley]

SD983] [29 January 1839]. A.L.s. Edward Moulton-Barrett (brother) to Samuel Moulton-Barrett (brother). *Here goes for a very* . . . [ERM-B]

SD984] 31 January 1839. A.L.s. Samuel Moulton-Barrett (brother) to Henrietta Moulton-Barrett. . . . *To night I dine at the Cunninghams, & tomorrow at Mr. Benzons; the latter is quite well, he called here a few days since making very* delicate *enquiries about Ba. Tell Ba in reference to her lines on L.E.L., "If a Planter in her opinion can justly estimate poetry" that I do so most sincerely & admire them very much indeed; give my most affectionate love to her & say that I have prevailed on Treppy to present me with Ba's picture, & with a few alterations for which Arabella sat, have succeeded in obtaining a very good likeness; this I shall value much as a companion when in Jamaica.* . . . [Altham]

SD985] 14 February 1839. A.L.s. M. Williams to George Goodin Barrett (1792–1854). [ERM-B]

SD986] [18 February 1839]. A.L.s. Henrietta Moulton-Barrett to Samuel Moulton-Barrett (brother). *You shall break the seal today my own dearest Sam & read that Ba is a* little *better– I must not say a great deal, since she suffers yet considerably from lowness & weakness, & this I fear she will do for some days—she slept better last night, & does not complain of pain this morng, she has a feeling of restlessness, which is very wearying to her, but she is better.*

She is of course still confined to her bed—& we keep her perfectly quiet—indeed she has not even read during this day or two, except dearest Arabel's letter last night, however the reading I trust she will soon be able to do with pleasure to herself—these two last nights we have persuaded her to take a melted jelly for her supper, but her appetite remains very bad, & as long as it is so, how can we expect the weakness to diminish— All she has gone through lately from the billious attack alone, *would have effected the strength of the* strongest *of us—& how much more must it effect her!! However thank God the worst really seems to have passed now—& I trust I may have the unexpressible blessing of* seeing, *& of being able to tell you of her encreasing health & strength— God is the hearer of prayer, & will He not hear our prayers in her behalf? I am* sure *He will, if it be good for us— She is now* trying *to take her Beef tea but I am sorry to say, she often makes many vain efforts— She was asking me yesterday when I thought dearest Papa would come— I told her that as he had been gone from here a* month, *I thought that we had every reason to hope he would soon be here— I hope it may be so, for I think it would do her a great deal of good to see him with a few more of you— Such remedies are very pleasant ones, & more effectual I believe in many instances than even medicine— She took white wine ..... twice yesterday, a table spoonful of wine at a time, she is to repeat the dose today again— I really think it does her good— She still speaks in a whisper but believe me upon the whole, she is* better, *so do not give yourselves more uneasiness than there is occasion for— I have just given to her Zenana Miss Landon's last book, which she ordered Elliott to get for her— So you see, she has already begun to read—uncle Hedley gave her the other day the Bijou Almanack for this year, edited by Miss Landon—the same as Papa gave her last—but when he sent for it from London he expected it was a large & expensive book, & told me what he had done as a great secret—he was terribly disappointed when he saw the diminutive size of it, as I* thought *he could be— Ba has put it with Papa's, & values them both. . . . Bummy had a letter from Miss Price this morng—she is at Aberystworth* [sic] *complains of the cold & is very sorry she left Mansel— She wrote to make further enquiries about Ba— She is a kind person, & never forgets us— . . . Ba says she is very glad that Papa was on a Grand Jury— Why, I cannot quite make out— I hope at any rate that he was soon released from it— Arabel's letter was as welcome yesterday as it* always *is— I hope you are soon going to write to me dearest Sam—but do not write* instead *of Ba's letter—let it be an* additional *pleasure— Now I remember it, will you tell Papa that all Ba's Ode de Cologne is gone—& if he could bring a bottle or two with him when he comes, I think it would be very acceptable— . . . Tuesday Morng. / Dearest Sam, Ba has told me that last night was worth the two nights before put together, she slept so comfortably—there is a bonne bouche for you, & this will make you swallow all the indigestable part of this sheet— I am thankful for it, & I dare say it will be the means of making her feel better today— Oh! I trust she will go on improving now* every *day—I have not time for more let us hear from you frequently . . .*

[ERM-B]

SD986.1] 26 February 1839. A.L.s. William Wordsworth to John Kenyon. *. . . Mrs Wordsworth begs me to thank you cordially for your Lady-friend, Miss Barrett's Poems which you sent her some time ago. Miss B. appears to be a very interesting person, both for Genius and attainments. . . .* [Lilly]

SD987] 26 February 1839. A.L.s. Samuel Moulton-Barrett (brother) to Henrietta Moulton-Barrett. ... *I earnestly trust now the Spring is rapidly approaching our dear Ba may as rapidly rally, my kind affectionate love to her Bell Arlette Cissy Jane* ... [Altham]

SD988] 26 February 1839. A.L.s. Mr. Anderson to Edward Moulton-Barrett (father). [ERM-B]

SD989] 26 February 1839. A.L.s. Anderson & Kemble to Edward Moulton-Barrett (father). [ERM-B]

SD990] 9 March 1839. A.L.s. Edward Moulton-Barrett (father) to Samuel Moulton-Barrett (brother). With a continuation by Henrietta Moulton-Barrett. ... *This terrible illness of my beloved Ba, has unhinged every thing with me, my mind, my time &c ... Our beloved one is much the same, she had not a good night, but less expectoration. I trust to-morrow morning will find her much refreshed from a good sleep this night.... Papa has just sent me his letter dearest Sam to tell you how Ba is this morning. She is nicely but has not had a good night but this must not make you uneasy for her good nights at the best are only occasional. The expectoration is better....* [ERM-B]

SD991] 9 March [1839]. A.L.s. Ann C. Gordon to [Samuel Moulton-Barrett (brother)]. *What ever has given rise* ... [ERM-B]

SD992] 14 March 1839. A.L.s. Mary Russell Mitford to Arabella Moulton-Barrett. *I cannot write as a stranger to the Sister of my dear & honoured friend Miss Barrett—the woman of all the world whom I love & admire & revere–* ...
[MM-B & RAM-B]

SD993] [30–31 March 1839]. A.L.s. Henrietta Moulton-Barrett to Samuel Moulton-Barrett (brother). *Here I am beginning to answer your kind letter which Arabel says you wrote to me quite* unintentionally, *I hope the kindness of it was not unintentional too—if I thought it was so I should not intentionally sit down to reply to it but I believe Arabel has libelled you– Her letter yesterday eveng. was received with many acclamations of contentment—it had been my* private *opinion that as Thursday had passed without hearing from her, that she was going to cheat us again, & so she would have done according to her own confessions, had it not been for you– I am glad you exerted your authority in so good a cause, & she would have been glad that she had submitted had she been able to forsee the good it was to do to my dearest Ba, for it could not have arrived at a more opportune time, when she had undergone all the fatigue of being brought* downstairs, *carried up again, undressed & put to bed, she was exhausted, as we had every reason to suppose she would be, I tried to relieve her, but even my eloquence failed, when dearest Arabel's letter came to brighten her eyes, & cheer her heart—it quite rallied her again– After this, I need not thank her for it she will thank herself that it was better– But to return to Ba—she is in no way worse for her expedition yesterday—altho it caused her so much fatigue at the time– She was down about two hours, Dr. Barry is going to give her a holiday today, & tomorrow she comes down again. I am afraid she likes her own room much better than this—but as she gains strength I dare say she will like ours better– We should be thankful dearest Sam, to think that she had been downstairs, & that it has done her no harm– May God in His mercy continue to answer our prayers, & restore her precious health to us—what greater blessing for* this *world can we ask for?! ... Ba received a long letter from Miss Mitford this morning—she says that Arabel's note* "charmed her"—*she hopes that* "those *dear boys seeds may flourish" not the boys– . . . You will receive no letter from me on Wednesday morng– Don't get into a passion but wait for my reasons—which cannot fail to restore to you your accustomed equanimity of temper– They are these, on the afternoon of that day, a parcel will arrive from* Ba *containing a turkey for you all & a goose for Treppy–* Court *will arrive in London on that day, & will be the bearer of it– I think it is likely Ba will write* a line—or two in it, *therefore for that day I may spare you some of my scribblings the stupidity of which I am sure you must be so tired of!!– . . . Sunday Morng. I am happy to be able to add dearest Sam that Ba slept better last night—"more sleep" she says– She desires me to give you her love & to tell you that you are to expect the turkey, & Treppy the goose on Wednesday (which I have already done) i.e. if in this* wise *place Torquay, a goose* can *be found—but I can assure the |hen| is nearly extinct here– She also says that she is in the midst of the composition of sundry Notes– I think I shall let Dr. Barry into this secret today . . .* [ERM-B]

SD994] [ca. April 1839]. A.L.s. Edward Moulton-Barrett (brother) to Samuel Moulton-Barrett (brother). . . . *I cannot tell you how great a disappointment it is to me to find myself unable to come to Town even for a day or two before you sail, because I have much to talk over with you which I cannot conveniently discuss excepting by word of mouth. If however the least ill is to arise to dearest Ba from your coming down here (which might possibly be the case) or I can be of the slightest service to her in remaining where I am, I am sure you will agree with me in acquiescing most cheerfully in any plan which may be considered the most advisable under such circumstances. . . . These winds are so mild & genial that I think that spring must be floating in them, if it had not been for that unfortunate bilious attack I think dearest Ba must have derived advantage from them. That is however I trust now quite removed, & hope that the accounts which you are now to receive of her will be accounts of increasing strength. . . .* [ERM-B]

SD995] [ca. April 1839]. Incomplete A.L. [Samuel Moulton-Barrett (brother)] to Henrietta Moulton-Barrett. *I have been, I very much fear . . .*
[Altham]

SD996] [1 April 1839]. A.L.s. Arabella Graham-Clarke (aunt) to Samuel Moulton-Barrett (brother). . . . *I am sure you will all rejoice that dearest Ba is so nicely & that Dr Barry pronounced her yesterday to be improving during the last fortnight, but Henrietta is writing so I will not say more on the subject of dearest Ba in case by comparing our bulletins any variation might cause* doubts . . .
[ERM-B]

SD997] 15 April 1839. File Copy of Letter. Edward Moulton-Barrett (father) to [Anderson & Co.]. *I was not disappointed . . .* [ERM-B]

SD998] [18–19 April 1839]. A.L.s. Henrietta Moulton-Barrett to Samuel Moulton-Barrett (brother). . . . *Our beloved Ba did not feel yesterday quite as comfortable as usual, she felt rather low & weak & went to bed sooner than she generally does– When Dr. Barry came at night he ordered her to discontinue the Styptic, & gave her something as a substitute, she had not a very good night but she appears much better this morning—perhaps it was only the result of the Styptic, it has certainly done good in one way in decreasing the expectoration— when may I have the blessing of telling you that it has passed away?– May God grant it– I am sorry to say the appetite does not improve—the asses milk & the soup at eleven o'clock are the most nutritious things she takes—she seems to* *have taken dislike to chicken or any sort of animal food, & for her dinner she either takes oysters or maccaroni, but do not say any thing of it, as she does not like to be teased about it—& after all, it is much better that she should have what she can take most of– We have had a great deal of rain these two last days, & when it stops I do hope we shall have warm settled weather, & then I trust our dear Ba may be able to benefit from it– The first step will be to bring her downstairs & then she may begin her sailing expeditions, & when you once hear of us in a boat you may expect next, to hear of our cruising about among the Islands in the Mediterranean or maybe somewhat nearer to you in some of the London dock yards. I think we shall find our load stone to be there—but joking apart, I do hope that "La bella donna" may be soon & often in our service, the getting to it now, will not be half as fatiguing as it used to be when we were at the Braddons & I trust much strength may be obtained in this way– Jane & uncle Hedley seem determined upon their London expedition, & I think it will be very shortly—it is very selfish to have* any *regrets about it, but Ba & all of us will miss them so sadly. . . . tell Arabel that both Ba & I were very much shocked by the confession of such* unnatural *sentiments contained in her letter– She may well fear the exposure of them. However she need not make herself very uneasy, our sisterly affection will induce us to keep them in obscurity. . . . Mr. Hunter most* GENEROUSLY *recommended Ba to give him Phillips Geology, telling her where it was to be bought in Torquay—& Ba almost as generously made the purchase of it & gave it to him– . . . Friday Morng– You will be sorry to hear dearest Sam that when Dr. Barry came last night he ordered a blister, a* small *one— perhaps it was* precautionary, *but do not any of you be uneasy– She complained yesterday of a slight pain in the chest but she says it really was very little—& she has had a better night which she will tell you perhaps herself, as in spite of the blister she says she must write a little in this– . . . This lovely morning I am sure* must *do Ba good . . .* [ERM-B]

SD999] [20 April 1839]. A.L.s. Edward Moulton-Barrett (brother) to [John Biddulph]. *It does appear to me . . .* [Hereford]

SD999.1] 29 April 1839. A.L.s. Henriette Willoughby Barrett to Maria and Samuel Goodin Barrett. [Brims]

SD1000] 30 April 1839. A.L.s. John Hornby to Samuel Moulton-Barrett (brother). [ERM-B]

SD1001] [4 May 1839]. A.L.s. Henrietta Moulton-Barrett to Samuel Moulton-Barrett (brother). *People do meet occasionally with much more than they deserve, & this must be your case today dearest Sam, for I am seized with a sudden &* unaccountable *inclination to write to you—it is extraordinary that it should be so considering all circumstances, but so it is, & now for the benefit of not only you but all around you I must tell you about our beloved Ba, that she was pretty well all day yesterday & down stairs from two o'clock to six. She slept tolerably not as well as we could wish for her, & she is tolerable this morning– You must content yourselves with such for today– I trust on Monday I may have brighter tidings to tell you but these must not make you look grave, for Dr. Barry seems to think she is going on comfortably, & yesterday he allowed the window to remain open when she was in the drawing room, the first breath of external air she has breathed for many months—this is* another *step towards the boat—but where is the bonnet & the shawl? She really talks very seriously of going out & Dr. Barry told us yesterday that he was beginning to think of the boat instead of* *the chair, so do not be surprised to hear of a christen some day soon!! . . . Bummy & all very much pleased with our expedition, & found our dearest Ba equally pleased to see us, looking very comfortable & amusing herself by reading the magazines– . . . We shall hear from dearest Arabel or one of you today– Ba was so unreasonable as to expect a letter from her on Friday, in spite of dearest Papa's the day before—the pleasure of hearing from you is the greatest she has—therefore it should not be given grudgingly to her—but Arabel deserves great credit for her punctuality in writing—& know how her letters please Ba, is her best reward—knowing the time & the nature of your Sunday engagements, perhaps we think of you more on this day than on any other– May both yours & ours be blessed to us today dearest Sam– Ba is still sleeping, & I have nothing more to send to you until she awakes– . . . I forgot in my last letter to ask Papa to get for Ba a black* elastic *band for her* waist—*she has been long trying here to procure it, but in vain– I hope you understand what I mean—remember it is to wear over her gown– She has just awoke, & glad can I tell you that she slept better last night & is comfortable this morning– She sends her very best love with mine to dearest Papa Arabel yourself & every body.* . . . [ERM-B]

SD1002] 6 May 1839. Copy of Letter. H.M. Waddell to W. Carey.
[ERM-B]

SD1003] 14 May 1839. Copy of Letter. Mr. Knibb to [Mr. Anderson]. *As a matter of duty* . . . [ERM-B]

SD1004] 20 May 1839. Copy of Letter. W. Carey to H.M. Waddell.
[ERM-B]

SD1005] 23 May 1839. Copy of Letter. Samuel Goodin Barrett to R.W. Appleton. [ERM-B]

SD1006] [30 May 1839]. A.L.s. Henrietta Moulton-Barrett to Samuel Moulton-Barrett (brother). . . . *as my reports have not been quite as good of our dearest Ba lately, I must hasten to tell you of her & that I can do with more satisfaction today, for thank God she is better than she has been the last day or two—although she was without her nightly draught, last night she slept very comfortably, & she looks nicely this morning—the expectoration has been but little these last two nights & the cough I think is certainly very quiet—next week I trust nothing may prevent her going out, but even had she been well enough, she would not have been able to have done so this on account of the northeasterly wind, that enemy of hers—but in spite of it, it is beginning to be very hot– Mr. & Mrs. Weale say it is much hotter than Plymouth.* . . . *Ba heard from Lady Margaret a day or two ago, she says she missed her very much when she was in London she expresses a great deal anxiety to be acquainted with Arabel– Ba complains of her coldness, but all are not of the same warm affectionate temperament as she herself is–* . . . *Friday Morng– Not a good night dearest Sam I am sorry to say– She was very restless, but nothing is the matter this morng it might have been occasioned by the fatigue of the warm bath which Dr. Barry ordered for her yesterday eveng– She went downstairs, & saw Mr. & Mrs. Weale– She seems very well pleased with the former—he talked to her a good deal about poetry & her friend Wordsworth & promised to send her a picture from Plymouth of Spencer's window– Whilst he was talking to Ba he did a beautiful little drawing in water colors for Bummy to copy* . . . [ERM-B]

SD1007] 3 June [1839]. A.L.s. John Altham Graham-Clarke Jr. to Samuel Moulton-Barrett (brother). *It was a matter of a* . . . [ERM-B]

SD1008] 14 June 1839. A.D.s. Appointment of Samuel Moulton-Barrett (brother) as Attorney by John Altham Graham-Clarke, his Wife and their Son, with two enclosures. [ERM-B]

SD1009] 14 June 1839. A.L.s. Samuel Moulton-Barrett (brother) to Henrietta Moulton-Barrett. ... *Your continued good accounts of dear Ba are very cheering to us all, we hope ere this she may have ventured on the Sea. The weather here having been delightfully warm & I take it for granted you are not much farther to the Northard– Our gaieties here have been rather limited, my having few friends in Town to afford an opportunity: Tell Ba I met "Dickens" alias ["]Sam Weller" —& a number of other Lions & Lionessess at Mr. Kenyons the other night, & I assure her I enjoyed myself very much; Dickens is my height exact, rather darker, about my age & wears his hair "à la Brosy", very animated but I should not have given him credit for so much real fun & talent, he did not stay long; I also met Mr. & Mrs. Bradford, four or five Americans & a society of fashion & beauty....* [Altham]

SD1010] 17 June 1839. A.L.s. Edward Moulton-Barrett (brother) to Samuel Moulton-Barrett (brother). ... *Before I say much more on my own account—I have a heavy case of messages to deliver from Ba & Henrietta which is now swinging upon the wave of my memory & had better be landed before it slips into the water– Ba in the first place desires me to fill up a slight hiatus which she accidentally left in what she calls her very businesslike communication of the other day. The price of the house which she proposes to purchase is £1200 mind that last blotted naught goes for* nothing. *She begs likewise to apologise to Papa for her ingratitude in writing to him the* savage *letter which she did about the box & to thank him for sending it* at last– *Henrietta & I send likewise our united thanks for that portion of its contents addressed to us– Ba does not seem to be as much consternated as I should be about the vignettes round her illustration. I think often nothing short of mere impertinences, for if they are not meant to assist a weak imagination & suggest the story they are irrelevant encumbrances– Ba at Miss Mitford's direction intends to consider them in this last light & make no further allusion to them than she may find quite convenient to herself in the course of her story– Today's bulletin of our dearest Ba is though in no* material respect *the least worse, not quite so good as yesterday's—she had not a very good night & has (perhaps in consequence) not been quite so comfortable today. Yesterday she had the sofa placed immediately in front of the open window which was pretty nearly the same thing as being out of doors, & remained there for a considerable time, enjoying both the air & the scene extremely. She certainly regains her strength slowly, but is as certainly regaining it, & I think we have reason to believe that with God's help she will continue mending more rapidly as the summer advances– Before this time you will have seen Dr. Barry & heard all the particulars of her care. Well did you find him to be the kind of medicine monster which Arabel, Stormy, & some of the more imaginative of you must have considered him to be, going about with a bottle of Laudanum peeking out of one pocket & a bottle of Prusic acid out of the other seeking whom he might poison? Poor little man; if he knew half that Arabel has said of him & was half as bad as she thought him, I would recommend her to avoid eating in his society—or if she were guilty of so great an act of rashness, to have a stomach pump put upon the sideboard as a weapon of defense. By the bye tell Arabel that since the departure of Mr. Weale I have been making sundry ungainly efforts at watercolours ... Ba most unartistically criticises the dresses of the figures as too brilliant—*

forgetting that all artists have or ought to have some object to gain by the introduction of strong colours into the foreground– ... *I really mean to work hard & try to mend, & would wish to imitate Mr. Weale, in every thing, excepting in swallowing paint & water by the pint* ... [ERM-B]

SD1011] 17 June 1839. A.L.s. Mr. Anderson to Edward Moulton-Barrett (father). [ERM-B]

SD1012] 18 June 1839. A.L.s. Mary Elizabeth Graham-Clarke to Samuel Moulton-Barrett (brother). ... *I was glad to learn you were all well & I hope this warm weather is favorable to Elizabeth's going out on the Sea as I hear she is so much better–*.... [ERM-B]

SD1013] [18 June 1839]. A.L.s. John Altham Graham-Clarke to Samuel Moulton-Barrett (brother). *I have only this moment* ... [ERM-B]

SD1014] 19 June 1839. Receipt. To Samuel Moulton-Barrett (brother) for £71.16.6. [ERM-B]

SD1015] 22–26 June 1839. A.L.s. Samuel Moulton-Barrett (brother) to Henrietta Moulton-Barrett. ... *I have deeply felt my absence from you all at Torquay; but when I know how painful a parting scene would be to us all & how injurious it might be to dear Ba, I rather rejoice we have escaped it.... My most affectionate love to dear Ba who I am sure will bear this temporary separation with patience for our sakes* ... *Write to me regularly about Ba once a fortnight & commence on the* 1st of July *you wh. know my anxiety will I am sure not disappoint me–* ... / *June 26th. Once more my own dearest Henrietta & Ba, God bless you both, we sail in two hours from this: That God in his mercy may protect & return our dear Ba is the earnest prayer of yr. fondly attached Sam.*
[Altham]

SD1015.1] [ca. 24 June 1839]. A.L.s. Arabella Moulton-Barrett to H.S. Boyd. ... *Saunders told Papa the other day that the Seraphim was selling very well.*... [Eton]

SD1016] 1 July 1839. A.L.s. Arabella Moulton-Barrett to Samuel Moulton-Barrett (brother). ... *But you will skip over all that I have written to find out something of Ba, & I think it was very inconsiderate of me not to begin my letter with intelligence of her. Last Saturday's letter was from her to Papa. A very long letter, filled with plans. She knew nothing then of yr. departure. Today, the letter is from Henrietta. Bro had received yr. letter the day before & had told them. They are both of course very much distressed. Henrietta says much of having seen you only for one fortnight, & desires me to write immediately & tell them every particular about yr. going "Our dear Ba was very much grieved about it last night, & did not sleep very well but is quite comfortable this morning". It was very grievous indeed, dearest Sam, that you were not able to spend more of yr. time with them, but perhaps after all, it is as well as it has happened. Ba could* not *have borne the parting from you. When you return, may this affliction be taken from us. If so, what a happy meeting it will be! All this pain & trouble will only make it the happier. But to tell you of all the news contained in Henrietta's letters, Uncle Hedley is still at Torquay packing up his books & furniture wh. is to be removed directly to Southampton, when he is to follow, with the boys. Arabel & Ibbet went last Wednesday. I am so sorry for it for their sakes. Poor Ba is very much distressed about it. She will indeed miss all their kindness. Ba has taken a great dislike for Southampton, & she has written to Papa to tell him she is afraid to go there, on account of the dampness of the place, occasioned by all the wet mud of the river, & to propose at the same time remaining at Torquay this summer & the next winter, as it is certainly now doing her good.*

She begs Papa to let us all go there for the summer. Without he gives his consent, she says she will come either to Southampton or to Hastings, where she may be able to see us. I fear there is little chance of Papa's thinking of taking us such a distance—but we shall see! . . . [ERM-B]

SD1017] 12 July 1839. A.L.s. R.W. Appleton to George Goodin Barrett (1792–1854). [ERM-B]

SD1018] 14–15 July 1839. A.L.s. Henrietta Moulton-Barrett to Samuel Moulton-Barrett (brother). . . . *The letter that came to tell us of your departure did not arrive until the Saturday after you went– . . . for Ba after examining the exterior of it had terrible forebodings that it was going to bring us some bad news, which forebodings I tried to laugh & scold her out of—as the subject had never been hinted at for so long a time, we did not think such bad news would have come to us– . . . It seemed hard upon us indeed that during all the time you were in England—you should only have spent one short fortnight with us—I did not think when we parted with you here, that we should not have seen you again– I have been very angry about it, but I find it of no use—as to you & dearest Stormie just coming here to wish us good bye—it would have been a very painful pleasure & it was better for Ba that it should not be—therefore we must not repine—she expressed many regrets when she first heard it that she had not obliged me to leave her to go to London to be with you– I felt very sorry she shd. have had any feeling of the sort—for that, under such circumstances I could not have done, no, not even to see you– We sometimes very selfishly wish, that your visit had been postponed, until next year but it has been all arranged for the best we may be assured of– You have been a great comfort to dearest Arabel & all dear to us at home—who at this time separated from Ba had need of cheering! Thank you a thousand times for your letter, they did not send it to me till it was too late to obey your order contained in it that I was to write to you by the 1st. Arabel tells me she did so, therefore I hope you did not miss my pen—you may depend on my regularity in future, for I can measure your anxiety about our beloved Ba, by what my own would be. Since you left us, she has been out on the sea several times, & lately has performed it with less fatigue to herself—it is still of course attended with much exertion for you know how weak she is—but this is the means, shd. it please God for her to gain strength, so I hope she may be able to continue it– Papa hearing how very tired it made her, wrote a day or two ago to Bro to beg that she might not go out two days consecutively—now I hardly know how this is to be arranged for Dr. Barry does not like her to miss a fine day, & when we tell him of this order, I fear he will not approve of the interference– Dr. Barry has treated her well & the least we can do I think is now to confide in him– . . . This was a very kind arrangement both for us, & her—& she evidently wrote to Papa to tell him of it, that the want of accomodation here might be no excuse to him to bring them—to this letter she has had no reply—& when he wrote to Ba he took no notice of it, therefore I sometimes doubt (tho' I would not say so to Ba) that he does not mean to bring them. But he told Jane he would take them to Southampton to meet us—but what would be the use of giving Ba the fatigue of going there for this short remainder of the summer– Dr. Barry says she cd. not possibly be there in the winter—for that reason Hastings & Torquay are the only places for her & the latter much better than the former—besides I do not think on many accounts that she wd. be happy at Hastings, & here she has Dr. Barry who she really likes & has confidence* in– Oh I hope Papa may not think *of moving her—the distance from London ought not to be considered in such a case– There would be no difficulty in their all coming by the steam packet—on such an expedition Arabel would not care about being a little sick– I think Bummy intends to remain with us the winter—we have sometimes thought she would not & Ba had determined not to ask her—for a little deficiency in* temper *(not in heart) has now & then given us reason to think she was discontented here– I did not mention it in any of my letters, & be careful that you do not dearest Sam, but she has sometimes been disposed to scold me a little & sometimes to look coldly upon Ba which has made her feel nervous & fidgity, but I hope that has quite gone by now—since dear Jane left us we have seen nothing of it, & all is going on in a very sunshiny way– There might have been a little jealousy!! but we all know the warmth of dearest Bummy's heart towards us– We shd. be ungrateful were we to doubt it. . . . we miss uncle Hedley's horses, as well as himself– It is very provoking for me—when the Gardens were here, & while there were so many riding parties going on, it was a great distress to me often that I had no habit of my own & could only join them, when I was able to* borrow *one—when the Hedley's were in London our* dear kind *Ba surprised me one day very much by presenting me with a new habit– I had not many rides in it, when I was obliged thus to give up my little pony—however I trust some day or other the pony & habit will meet again– I did not mention it in Wimpole St. as it was Ba's particular request that I should not– She has finished her Ballad for Miss Mitford– It is* most *beautiful– Bro who is a much better judge than I am is delighted with it—very melancholy & about 3 pages in length– I hope it may not be too long for Finden– It was dispatched this morning to Miss Mitford, accompanied by some* clouted cream– *The title is "The Legend of the Brown Rosary"– I will write it out some day for you & send it in one of the ships– The composition of it has done our beloved Ba no harm—but Dr. Barry was very indignant when he heard of it—her cough I really think is better than it was—the expectoration the same—*not much– *Her spirits generally are cheerful & good– I am just going to take another sail with her today—neither Crow nor I can boast of being very good sailors– Bummy has not ventured to accompany us since the first time when she was in such terrible trepidation–* . . .

[ERM-B]

SD1019] 15 July 1839. A.L.s. Edward Moulton-Barrett (father) to Samuel Moulton-Barrett (brother). . . . *Our dear Ba is much the same she has been four times out, which has fatigued her very much. I am happy to say that she has finished her poem for the Tableaux—which she says she is happy in the thought that no one will be able to read by Candle light, still less by rush light. She says it consists of 350 lines for the most part of fourteen syllables—& in apology for its length, she says when you begin a story you cant bring it to end all in a moment, & what with nuns & devils & orgies & marriages & deaths & little boys, she couldn't get out of the mud without a great deal of splashing. She writes in great spirits, & I trust in the Lord that she is going on tolerably– But I hope Bro or Henrietta will have consideration enough to send you the latest intelligence by writing from Torquay by this Packet– The Rest are as usual quite well.* . . . [ERM-B]

SD1020] 8 August 1839. A.L.s. R.W. Appleton to George Goodin Barrett (1792–1854). [ERM-B]

SD1021] 12 August 1839. A.L.s. John Altham Graham-Clarke Jr. to Samuel Moulton-Barrett (brother). [ERM-B]

SD1022] [12 August 1839]. A.L.s. Mary Elizabeth Graham-Clarke to Samuel Moulton-Barrett (brother). *John has left me this* . . . [ERM-B]

SD1023] 15 August [1839]. A.L.s. Arabella Moulton-Barrett to Samuel Moulton-Barrett (brother). . . . *But now to tell you of our dearest Ba. She is going on very nicely, & she speaks most confidently of the certainty in her own mind, of her being much better than she was last summer in London. She acknowledges that she is weaker, but that the disease is very much reduced—& that is the great thing after all. The disease being once overcome, her strength wd. soon return. And this will be in God's time. Although we cannot pray* together *now for her, let our prayers meet together for her at the throne of grace. There is no distance that can separate us there. I am going almost immediately to Torquay. I am as pleased in consequence as I can be & I shd. be completely happy if we were all going together.* . . . *Georgie is still at Torquay, & he wrote out & sent to me the other day, Ba's ballad, unknown to her—& by doing so, Papa says he has committed a breach of morality & he refuses to read it until Ba knows & has given him permission to read it. I, not being quite so strict, have read it & I am quite overflowing with gratitude to George for being so very* IMMORAL– *It is most beautiful, very superior to the "Romaunt of the Page"—but* SO *horrible. I was prepared in some way for the horrors there, having been told by Ba "that no one cd. read it by candlelight, far less by rush light"—but in spite of this preparation &* my *natural bravery, my hair felt inclined to turn* upward *as I read it! As soon as the book comes out, it will be sent to you & Stormie—* . . . [ERM-B]

SD1024] 16 August 1839. A.L.s. Edward Moulton-Barrett (brother) to Samuel Moulton-Barrett (brother). . . . *Our dear Ba, although I cannot report any very material change for the better, is I think certainly stronger than when you left us, & bears her excursions upon the water (which are as frequent as the weather will permit,) with less fatigue to herself–* . . . [ERM-B]

SD1025] 22 August 1839. A.L.s. John G. Nidal to Samuel Moulton-Barrett (brother). [ERM-B]

SD1026] 25 August 1839. A.L.s. Joseph G. Jump to Samuel Moulton-Barrett (brother). [ERM-B]

SD1027] 25 August 1839. A.L.s. Mr. Ricketts to M. Hawes. [ERM-B]

SD1028] 26 August 1839. File Copy of Letter. Samuel Moulton-Barrett (brother) to James Graham-Clarke. [ERM-B]

SD1029] 26 August 1839. File Copy of Letter. Samuel Moulton-Barrett (brother) to M. Hawes. [ERM-B]

SD1030] 26 August 1839. File Copy of Letter. Samuel Moulton-Barrett (brother) to Joseph G. Jump. [ERM-B]

SD1031] [ca. 30 August 1839]. File Copy of Letter. [Samuel Moulton-Barrett (brother)] to Edward Moulton-Barrett (father). *The above is a copy* . . . [ERM-B]

SD1032] 31 August 1839. A.L. signed with initials. Joshua Rowe to Samuel Moulton-Barrett (brother). [ERM-B]

SD1033] 1 September 1839. A.L.s. Mary Elizabeth Graham-Clarke to Samuel Moulton-Barrett (brother). . . . *I hear that Elizabeth intends remaining at Torquay another winter finding that it has been of service to her, and I am glad that she is so much better—but whether Bell & the little Butlers are to continue with her I have not been informed.* . . . [ERM-B]

SD1034] 1 September [1839]. File Copy of Letter. Samuel Moulton-Barrett (brother) to Mr. Chambers. *Having only just returned* ... [ERM-B]

SD1035] 2 September 1839. File Copy of Letter. Edward Moulton-Barrett (father) to William W. Anderson. [ERM-B]

SD1036] 3 September 1839. File Copy of Letter. Samuel Moulton-Barrett (brother) to Alex W. Aikman. [ERM-B]

SD1037] 3 September 1839. File Copy of Letter. Samuel Moulton-Barrett (brother) to Edward Moulton-Barrett (father). [ERM-B]

SD1038] 3 September 1839. File Copy of Letter. Samuel Moulton-Barrett (brother) to Joshua Rowe. [ERM-B]

SD1039] 4 September 1839. Two A.Ds.s. Appointing Samuel Moulton-Barrett (brother) as Justice of the Peace and Assistant Judge of Court of Common Pleas in the Parish of St. James. With his appointment as the Ensign of a Company in St. Elizabeth's Regiment on 25 October 1837. [ERM-B]

SD1040] 7 September 1839. A.L.s. Anderson & Kemble to Edward Moulton-Barrett (father). With Statement of Account for 1838. [ERM-B]

SD1041] 12 September 1839. A.L. signed with initials. Joshua Rowe to Samuel Moulton-Barrett (brother). [ERM-B]

SD1042] 14 September [1839]. A.L.s. Henrietta Moulton-Barrett to Samuel Moulton-Barrett (brother). ... *Our dearest Ba (for she must be first & foremost in all our thoughts) continues about the same, as when you last heard from me, certainly not worse, if not better, the arrival of our dear Arabel has appeared to instil new life into her, & she looks, & is quite happy, & this I hope may be the means of advancing her recovery—the cough I do think is better, & so has the expectoration been until these last few days, when it has been rather encreased, owing it may be to the non-attendance of Dr. Barry, he has been so ill with nervous fever, that he has been confined to his bed for some days, but he is better again I am happy to say, & I trust both for his own sake (last tho' not least) that of our beloved Ba he may soon again be able to renew his visits—for altho' he has been, & still is sometimes so unjustifiably abused, she feels his absense very much—there cannot be a more attentive medical man than he is, & I think we have every reason to be satisfied with his abilities in our dear Ba's case—he has taken a great interest in her which is also very much in his favor—as he has not received as yet a farthing for his attendance. She wrote to him the other day requesting he would let her know "the pecuniary part of her obligations to him" he sent in his account £125— A moderate charge I think for so long a time, then she has the druggists bill to defray £50. so that with this expensive house to boot, I fear that her finances will hardly bear it, it is almost settled that we are to move from this one to No 1. on the same Terrace, it is somewhat cheaper than this & the bedrooms more in number, it is not in my opinion so cheerful looking as this, but I will tell you presently, whether we have it or not—they reckon that Ba will be saved £17 by going to it—they are talking so much about it now, whether it shall be taken or not, that I really can hardly write. Bummy seems uncertain whether she will remain the winter with us. She talks of the necessity of her returning to Frocester. Now really I cannot make out what tie she has there—however she will stay I think at any rate a part of the winter, & she very kindly says she would not leave Ba were she not so well— If she remains I only hope she will remain happily—but say nothing of her* *movements when you write– As Georgie talks of going away from here, I wrote to Papa the other day to propose returning to London with him as Arabel is now here to take my place near our dearest Ba, & as Papa was without one of us, I thought it right to do so. I waited with some anxiety for his answer, it came at last, to say that George was not to go home as soon as he intended as it would disarrange all his plans, & that I was not to go until he sent for me. I was very glad of this respite for you know (in spite of the pleasure of going home) how I shall lament leaving my dearest Ba, but this time is not come yet altho' I expect it to do so before the winter.... It seems decided now that we go to No. 1. & I hope it will be all for the best, the situation of Ba's bedroom is delightful, opening into the drawing room– So that she will have no cold passages to pass during the winter time—if it only agrees with her, I am sure I shall like it– ... Ba's letter is gone to Stormie. I kept this to you that you might have the latest intelligence. Our dearest Ba is nicely & sends you with all others her best affections.... Ba had a letter from Mary Minto the other day, she seems quite reconciled to Brighton. I know you were a great admirer of her's therefore I tell you this. God bless you– ...* [ERM-B]

SD1043] 18 September 1839. A.L.s. W. Carey to Samuel Moulton-Barrett (brother). [ERM-B]

SD1044] 18 September 1839. File Copy of Letter. Samuel Moulton-Barrett (brother) to W. Carey. [ERM-B]

SD1045] 21 September 1839. A.L.s. Alex W. Aikman to Samuel Moulton-Barrett (brother). [ERM-B]

SD1046] 21 September 1839. A.L.s. Rich Chambers to Samuel Moulton-Barrett (brother). [ERM-B]

SD1047] 24 September 1839. A.L.s. H.M. Waddell to Samuel Moulton-Barrett (brother). [ERM-B]

SD1048] 27 September [?1839]. A.L.s. H.M. Waddell to Samuel Moulton-Barrett (brother). *I am sorry I have not ...* [ERM-B]

SD1049] 28 September 1839. A.L.s. Alex W. Aikman to Samuel Moulton-Barrett (brother). [ERM-B]

SD1050] 29 September [1839]. File Copy of Letter. Samuel Moulton-Barrett (brother) to Edward Moulton-Barrett (father). *Mr. Carey yesterday placed me ...* [ERM-B]

SD1051] 30 September 1839. A.L.s. Edward Moulton-Barrett (father) to Samuel Moulton-Barrett (brother). ... *Ba, our most precious Ba, is much the same, but you will have the latest information, for some one will write to Stormie from Torquay, the Bulletin to-day was rather more favorable than it had been for some little time, she has been left much to herself, I mean medically, for Dr. Barry has been desperately ill, & she would not see another Physician; he is however I am happy to say better, & I suppose will ere long resume his attendance on her. We have had a sad summer for her—I am sorry to inform you that poor Newdick is in Exeter Gaol, arrested for debt, & I hear that he is not likely to be released without passing through the Insolvent Court–* ... [ERM-B]

SD1052] 1 [*sic*, for 2] October 1839. Edward Moulton-Barrett (brother) to Charles John Moulton-Barrett. ... *I write to you from our new house into which we moved yesterday; it is taken for eight months, & is I think likely to suit us better than the one we last occupied with the additional recommendation of the reduction of a guinea per week in the rent. Its great advantage is that dearest*

Ba's room is I think larger & more sheltered from the violent westerly winds, besides being separated from the drawing room only by a door, so that she can be easily transferred to it for change of air during the winter without being exposed to the draught of staircases & passages. Poor dear Ba is this morning in a state of deep affliction at the death of Dr. Barry which occurred about 2 hours since—he had been suffering for some time from a violent fever proceeding from cold, but until within the last three days was suffered to be in an almost convalescent state, a relapse however took place, inflammation in the bowels supervened & he died this morning to the great sorrow of all who knew him either in his professional or private capacity— Every one is lamenting this event both rich & poor particularly the latter to whom Dr. Barry was a kind & generous friend, one old woman has walked a distance of five miles every day during his illness to enquire after him—& at this moment the flags of all the vessels in the harbour are hoisted at half mast— Dearest Ba to whom Dr. Barry's attention has been most unremitting, is sadly afflicted & I fear will suffer much both in mind & body at first— She is I think much as she was when you left England not worse, but I cannot say that I think she has gained much in strength— This rainy ungenial summer has thrown insuperable impediments in the way of her being as much in the open air as it was desirable she should have been—& it is now too late to look forward to the possibility of much more boating this year. Arabel is now with us & adds much to dearest Ba's happiness, Henrietta is not to go away, & George who intended to have left us some three weeks past has received an injunction to remain where he is for the present—so that with Uncle Richd. who still vegetates amongst us we form a goodly company.... [ERM-B]

SD1053] 3 October 1839. A.L.s. Samuel Simmons to Samuel Moulton-Barrett (brother), enclosing Receipt. [ERM-B]

SD1054] 5 October 1839. A.L.s. Alex W. Aikman to Samuel Moulton-Barrett (brother). [ERM-B]

SD1055] 8 October 1839. A.L.s. Rich Chambers to William Tinkler. [ERM-B]

SD1056] 9 October 1839. A.L.s. Edward George Barrett to George Goodin Barrett (1792–1854). [ERM-B]

SD1057] 13 October 1839. A.L.s. S. Newdick to Samuel Moulton-Barrett (brother). [ERM-B]

SD1058] 15 October [1839]. A.L.s Arabella Moulton-Barrett to Samuel Moulton-Barrett (brother). ... *But to tell you of our dearest Ba before I go any farther, I dare say Bro told Stormie both of our change of house—from No. 3 to 1 of this Terrace—and also of the sudden death of poor Dr. Barry. This latter event was indeed a great shock for dearest Ba, & for a time, threw her back a good deal—but she is now, I am thankful to say, much better again, & is daily improving & regaining her strength & spirits. It was indeed a very afflicting circumstance; both as it concerns the patients & the poor widow & child that Dr. Barry left. But it was God's doing, & therefore wisely done— Ba was persuaded by us, but with some difficulty, to call in Dr. Scully, who is allowed to be by all, a very clever man, & from his age & his long standing in this place, must consequently have had more experience in complaints of the chest than Dr. Barry had, & we may feel assured that she is safe in his hands. She appears to have confidence in him & to like him, wh. is a great thing. His opinion entirely coincides in every respect with that of Dr. Barry's, which is satisfactory, & he does not* *seem to be inclined to make any changes in his mode of treatment of her. Let us pray that he may be made a blessing in the hands of God for doing her good. This house is a delightful one for her, as her bedroom is not only a warmer one than her last, but it is contiguous to the drawing room, & therefore there will be no risk incurred in carrying her up & down stairs during the winter.... Ba has heard today from Mrs. Martin, who tells her of a bazaar that has been held at Hope End, for the purpose of building a church on Wellington Heath, & they collected an immense sum at it....* [ERM-B]

SD1059] [17–18 October 1839]. A.L.s. Arabella Moulton-Barrett to Septimus Moulton-Barrett, with note by Arabella Graham-Clarke (aunt). ... *But I know you will not like to have read so far of the letter without hearing something of Ba—& as what I have to tell you is* good news, *I am rather surprised at myself not to have told you of it before. Dr. Scully pronounced her to be better to day. He said the respiration was much more tranquil—the pulse calmer—her countenance looked better, & to use his own words "the storm is almost passed".- Now is not this very delightful news, Sette, & is it not a mercy for which we should be very thankful? Dr. Scully talks of removing her to the drawing room next week,* if possible; *& for that purpose, has desired her to remain longer on the sofa today than usual, which has fatigued her a little, but that is of no consequence! She looks & is* much more cheerful than when Georgie left, so that every thing is beginning to look bright again.... [MM-B & RAM-B]

SD1060] 19 October 1839. A.L.s. W. Carey to Samuel Moulton-Barrett (brother). [ERM-B]

SD1061] 19 October 1839. A.L. signed with initials. Joshua Rowe to Samuel Moulton-Barrett (brother). [ERM-B]

SD1062] 23 October 1839. A.D.s. Promissory Note from George Goodin Barrett (1792–1854) to Edward Moulton-Barrett (father). [ERM-B]

SD1063] 23 October 1839. A.L.s. R. Sydney Lambert to Samuel Moulton-Barrett (brother). [ERM-B]

SD1064] 24 October 1839. File Copy of Letter. Samuel Moulton-Barrett (brother) to Edward Moulton-Barrett (father). [ERM-B]

SD1065] 24 October 1839. A.L.s. Samuel Moulton-Barrett (brother) to Henrietta Moulton-Barrett. ... *We are delighted to hear that dearest Ba is so much better, & trust she may not leave a place that has so much profited her: you who* knew *how anxious we were to hear* twice a week *when in London of our dear invalid, might suppose that the climate has not diminished my anxiety, & have written me one letter the last two Packets, indeed dearest Henrietta you must write oftener to me....* [Altham]

SD1066] 31 October 1839. A.L. unsigned. [George Goodin Barrett (1792–1854)] to Samuel Goodin Barrett. *I am sorry that rumours ...* [ERM-B]

SD1067] 31 October [–1 November] 1839. A.L.s. Edward Moulton-Barrett (brother) to Septimus Moulton-Barrett, with note in the hand of Edward Moulton-Barrett (father). ... *Dearest Ba feels this cold weather sadly she is however not worse & I hope a change has taken place this morning in the temperature, for it is raining most perseveringly, snowing I suppose with you.... Precious Ba slept pretty well last night & is tolerable this morng.* [MM-B & RAM-B]

SD1068] November 1839. File Copy of Letter. Samuel Moulton-Barrett (brother) and Joseph G. Jump to Mr. Holden. [ERM-B]

SD1069] 9 November 1839. A.L.s. Alex W. Aikman to Samuel Moulton-Barrett (brother). [ERM-B]

SD1070] 9 November 1839. A.L.s. H.M. Waddell to Samuel Moulton-Barrett (brother). [ERM-B]

SD1071] 10 [–11] November 1839. A.L.s. Edward Moulton-Barrett (father) to Septimus Moulton-Barrett. *As all the rest of the Party are gone to bed, I shall employ my first moments of solitude in writing to you, and as I am sure that your first enquiry will be, how is Ba; I will reply to it before passing on to other topics. Yesterday as compared with the preceding one, she was not so well, but to-day she has been better, & if she should have a good night, I hope to see her to-morrow better still; as regards the disease itself, I suppose I must say, that it is much the same– I hope & trust that God has His own time, when He will answer the many prayers which have been offered up for her restoration to us in health & strength, & it becomes us to wait with patience the manifestation of His Will concerning her, of this I am certain we have a brilliant example of humble submission, & pious resignation in the dear sufferer, which it becomes us to study & follow– I believe that you all love her, as who does not, who knows her, then why not, inasmuch as you all can, contribute to the very few enjoyments she has, & no one she estimates more than hearing frequently from one or other of you; I will not do you the injustice to think that any one would consider it a trouble to give her occasionally an hours conversation on paper, therefore I beg that you will display, in the only way, you now have the affection you bear her by writing, & if it were in turn, it would prove, all thought of her, all loved her & hence all desired to contribute to her pleasure for it is her love for you all, that constitutes her pleasure– I must say however that you are out of the reproach, for you have written several letters to her, & to your kindness in doing so, I assure you she is very elaborate in her expressions.... 1 ½ after 9 Monday Morng– Our dear Ba has had for her a good night & Arabel says that she is nicely this Morning. By the bye in respect to her, in what snug nook has she obtained all the vast learning & wisdom she posesses—hard work & determined perseverance were her nooks, many a Professor could she dumbfound & what were her advantages—keep her in view & you will go point blank to Helicons Stream–* ... [MM-B & RAM-B]

SD1072] 11 November 1839. A.L.s. W. Carey to Samuel Moulton-Barrett (brother). [ERM-B]

SD1073] 13 November 1839. A.L.s. Mary Russell Mitford to Arabella Moulton-Barrett or Henrietta Moulton-Barrett. *Three Mile Cross / My dear Miss Barrett– / Will whichever of my fair unknown friends remains in Wimpole Street have the goodness to transmit the one Volume of Tableaux, with its little note to Mr. Horne? & the other copy to that dear friend at Torquay to whom the book owes its chiefest charm?– I earnestly trust that she is better, & that the new physician will, so far as is possible replace the old– Kindest regards to you all. Ever dear Miss Barrett / Very faithfully yours / M R Mitford.* [MM-B & RAM-B]

SD1074] 14 November 1839. 3 A.Ds.s. Power of Attorney from George Goodin Barrett (1792–1854) to Edward George Barrett and James Geddes, with two documents authenticating the signatures. [ERM-B]

SD1075] 15 November 1839. A.L.s. Edward Moulton-Barrett (father) to Samuel Moulton-Barrett (brother). *You will see from the date that I am still with* *our dear Ba, who is, I am happy to say somewhat better than when I came down, suffering as she then was & had been for some time from the loss of poor Dr. Barry: you know how exquisitely acute her feelings are by nature, & now disease has weakened her frame these feelings are painfully severe when the least called into play; but she is in the Hands of One Who loves her, & altho his dealings are oftimes very misterious, yet we know all are founded in mercy & goodness, & there we must leave her, yes rejoicingly leave her, for He has promised his own "I will never leave or forsake you" Thanks be to His Grace for this record for his abiding care—* ... [ERM-B]

SD1076] 16 November 1839. File Copy of Letter. Samuel Moulton-Barrett (brother) to H.M. Waddell. [ERM-B]

SD1077] 19 November 1839. File Copy of Letter. Samuel Moulton-Barrett (brother) to Edward Moulton-Barrett (father). [ERM-B]

SD1078] 25 November 1839. A.L.s. H.M. Waddell to Samuel Moulton-Barrett (brother). [ERM-B]

SD1079] 26 November 1839. File Copy of Letter. Samuel Moulton-Barrett (brother) to Samuel Goodin Barrett. [ERM-B]

SD1080] 30 November 1839. A.L.s. John Altham Graham-Clarke to Samuel Moulton-Barrett (brother). [ERM-B]

SD1081] 30 November 1839. A.L.s. Mary Elizabeth Graham-Clarke to Samuel Moulton-Barrett (brother). ... *Bell is still at Torquay & intends I believe to remain a great part of the winter— Elizabeth was rallying her spirits for the loss of her Physician when Bell last wrote & your father was then staying with them but I shd. suppose he cannot long absent himself from his family in Town.* ... [ERM-B]

SD1082] 4 December 1839. Copy of Letter. J. Edwards to [Samuel Goodin Barrett]. *You may remember* ... [ERM-B]

SD1083] [7 December 1839]. A.L.s. Maria Barrett to Samuel Moulton-Barrett (brother). *I have often thought* ... [ERM-B]

SD1084] 7 December [1839]. A.L.s. Samuel Goodin Barrett to Samuel Moulton-Barrett (brother). *I did not write in answer* ... [ERM-B]

SD1085] 7 December 1839. File Copy of Letter. [Samuel Moulton-Barrett (brother)] to The Deputy Collector of Customs. *Understanding you have at present* ... [ERM-B]

SD1086] 10 December 1839. File Copy of Letter. Samuel Moulton-Barrett (brother) to Edward Moulton-Barrett (father). [ERM-B]

SD1087] 11 December 1839. A.L.s. Allan Kennedy to Samuel Moulton-Barrett (brother), enclosing four receipts. [ERM-B]

SD1088] [14 December 1839]. A.L.s. Arabella Moulton-Barrett to Samuel Moulton-Barrett (brother). *I have begged for this corner* ... [ERM-B]

SD1089] 18 December 1839. A.L.s. Edward George Barrett to George Goodin Barrett (1792–1854). [ERM-B]

SD1090] 14 December 1839. A.L.s. Henrietta Moulton-Barrett to Samuel Moulton-Barrett (brother). ... *I can only say now dearest Sam, that I am very sorry you should have been thus disappointed but it does appear to me that you could not have received* all *our letters, we have sent either you or Stormie one by almost* every *packet. However as now that postage is not so ruinous, you shall hear more regularly, for I know you will be glad to pay a* shilling *a fortnight to hear of our beloved Ba—& particularly as it appears that you are beginning to* *prosper so well in the world—& before I say any thing less interesting to you, I must tell you that she continues about the same as when I last wrote to you—she has not been made worse by the badness of the weather, which we should be thankful for, as it always affects her so much—as long as it lasts we must not expect much improvement but if we can only pass the coldest part of the winter pretty well, we shall hope in the Mercy of God for better things as the Spring advances– She is carried to her sofa for a short time every day, but her coming into the drawing room has not been thought of yet—nor will it be I suppose for the next month at least! You must not think dearest Sam that she has not the power to do so, but Dr. Scully is so very prudent & cautious in all his proceedings with her, that he will not allow her to exert herself in any way, or to run any risks!—it is quite right it shd. be so– He comes to see her every day not only medically it appears, but to chat. He seldom leaves her under an hour & tells her all the news & the scandal of the neighbourhood, but not* ill naturedly– *She has not recovered her voice, but that I trust will come in time & I really think her cough is better than it was. She is not any thinner, altho' perhaps not* fatter, *& I hope she is a little stronger than she was about a month ago– The expectoration remains about the same, not very bad dearest Sam, & her spirits are cheerful, there are many who have health, & without her deprivations who are not half so happy as she—it is her contentedness & power of mind that makes her so—& it is a blessing both to herself & all around her– She is indeed dear to us! Oh! may it please God to give us back our happiness in the restoration of her precious health– Papa left us not a week ago, he promised Ba to come back as quickly as possible, he said something about a fortnight, but I do not expect him so soon as that—he must have quite exhausted poor Capt. Selby's patience....* [ERM-B]

SD1091] 18 December 1839. File Copy of Letter [Samuel Moulton-Barrett (brother)] to [Joshua Rowe]. *Your being appointed by his Excellency* . . . [ERM-B]

SD1092] 20 December [1839]. A.L. signed with initials. Joshua Rowe to Samuel Moulton-Barrett (brother). *I have spoken to* . . . [ERM-B]

SD1093] 21 December [1839]. A.L.s. Samuel Goodin Barrett to Samuel Moulton-Barrett (brother). *The House is adjourned* . . . [ERM-B]

SD1094] 22 December 1839. A.L.s. Samuel Goodin Barrett to George Goodin Barrett (1792–1854). [ERM-B]

SD1095] [?1840]. Copy of Document. Account for Landing Cargo of an American Vessel, with Sketch of the Plat of Trelawney Wharf. [ERM-B]

SD1096] [ca. 1840]. A.L.s. Charles John Moulton-Barrett to Samuel Moulton-Barrett (brother). *Acknowledgments of money are most necessary* . . . [ERM-B]

SD1097] [1840]. A.D. unsigned. List of Houses and Occupants on Cinnamon Hill Estate. [ERM-B]

SD1098] [1840]. A.D. unsigned. List of Houses and Occupants on Cornwall Estate. [ERM-B]

SD1099] [1840]. A.D. unsigned. Weekly Rental Rates of Houses on Cambridge and Oxford Estates. [ERM-B]

SD1100] [1840]. A.D. unsigned. Weekly Rental Rates of Houses on Cinnamon Hill and Cornwall Estates. [ERM-B]

SD1101] 1840. A.D. unsigned. Extent and Yield of cane fields on Cambridge and Oxford Estates. [ERM-B]

SD1102] 1 January 1840. File Copy of Letter. Samuel Moulton-Barrett (brother) to Edward Moulton-Barrett (father). [ERM-B]

SD1103] 4 January 1840. A.L.s. Samuel Goodin Barrett to Samuel Moulton-Barrett (brother). [ERM-B]

SD1104] 8 January 1840. Mary Howitt to Mary Russell Mitford. . . . *I have just got your "Findens' Tableaux." I have not yet had time to read your articles, nor even Miss Barrett's, but I have looked it through. Is it not a glorious book?* . . . L'Estrange (1), II, 59–60. [ ]

SD1105] 15 January 1840. File Copy of Letter. Edward Moulton-Barrett (father) to Messrs. Anderson & Kemble. [ERM-B]

SD1106] 15 January 1840. Copy of Letter. Pownall & Cross to Messrs. Anderson & Co. [ERM-B]

SD1107] 26 January 1840. A.L.s. Samuel Moulton-Barrett (brother) to Henrietta Moulton-Barrett. . . . *I was glad to hear from Papa last Packet & to receive so good an account of dearest Bas state of health. I trust the convenience of her new bedroom & your sheltered corner house will tend much to relieve her of much of the pain she suffered last winter. I hope she may have as much faith in her new medical adviser as she had in poor Dr. Barry.* . . . [Altham]

SD1108] 27 January 1840. File Copy of Letter. Samuel Moulton-Barrett (brother) to John Altham Graham-Clarke. [ERM-B]

SD1109] 30 January 1840. A.L.s. Robert Dewar to Samuel Moulton-Barrett (brother). [ERM-B]

SD1110] 9 February 1840. A.L. signed with initials. Joshua Rowe to Samuel Moulton-Barrett (brother). [ERM-B]

SD1111] 10 February 1840. Three A.Ds.s. Appointing Samuel Moulton-Barrett (brother) as Justice of the Peace, Magistrate and Assistant Judge of Court of Common Pleas for the Parish of Trelawney. [ERM-B]

SD1112] 10 February 1840. A.L.s. W. & R. Dewar & Co. to William Tinkler. [ERM-B]

SD1113] 11 February 1840. File Copy of Letter. [Samuel Moulton-Barrett (brother)] to Edward Moulton-Barrett (father). *I should hardly write to you* . . . [ERM-B]

SD1114] 11 February 1840. Copy of Letter. [William Tinkler] to Unidentified Correspondent. *From the tone of your reply* . . . [ERM-B]

SD1115] 15 February 1840. A.L.s. George Goodin Barrett (1792–1854) to John Edwards. [ERM-B]

SD1115.1] [17 February 1840]. A.L.s. Mary Russell Mitford to Miss Yates. *I send the Athenæum with Miss Barrett's fine verses my dear Miss Yates, & must trouble you to return it when your family party have read them because it is just possible that that very copy may go to Miss Skerrett to be put into her Majesty's or Prince Albert's hands by the Baroness Lehzen– It certainly shall, unless Miss Barrett tells me that it has been shown to them by Miss Cocks whose Aunt Lady Barbara* [sic, for Margaret] *is her correspondent & friend. I am quite sure that Mr. Giles & Miss Lorham will like these stanzas as well as yourself—although it is possible that my love for the writer may a little influence my estimate of their merit.* . . . [Duke]

SD1116] 20 February 1840. A.L.s. H.M. Waddell to Edward Moulton-Barrett (father). [ERM-B]

SD1117] 24 February 1840. A.L.s. James Whitehorne to Edward Moulton-Barrett (father). [ERM-B]

SD1118] 26 February 1840. File Copy of Letter. Edward Moulton-Barrett (father) to James Whitehorne. [ERM-B]

SD1119] 20 March 1840. A.L.s. W.W. Anderson to Edward Moulton-Barrett (father). [ERM-B]

SD1120] [11 April 1840]. A.L.s. Edward Moulton-Barrett (father) to Henrietta Moulton-Barrett. *God is our Refuge ...* [Altham]

SD1120.1] 26 April 1840. A.M.s. "A Vision at Berry Pomeray," by Edward Moulton-Barrett (brother). [MM-B]

SD1121] [4 May 1840]. A.L.s. Edward Moulton-Barrett (father) to Septimus Moulton-Barrett. ... *Our precious Ba, has certainly rallied a little since my arrival. When I saw her she appeared crushed by the intelligence, she has never wept, nor has ever alluded to the distressing subject– But what a Creature she is, I reverence her for the beauty of her character, so happy a specimen of christian submission & devotional feeling never was surpassed– No murmur is ever heard to escape her, no wish uttered to be better, only once or twice I have heard her say, as to any future plan, if it should please God that I should be better &c– Humanly speaking I should say, her health & strength are desirable for the Chest, but I thank God, that I know, she is loved by one, far more than any can love her here, for He gave his life a ransom for hers, & He will order all things aright for her happiness & best interests– But let us never cease importuning the Most High to spare her to us, & "who knows but that He may return & leave a blessing behind"– Nothing is impossible to Him, either as regards Power, or the exhibition of His Love, with whom we have to do– ...*
[MM-B & RAM-B]

SD1122] 12 May 1840. File Copy of Letter. Edward Moulton-Barrett (father) to Mr. Kemble. [ERM-B]

SD1123] 13 May 1840. A.L.s. Edward Moulton-Barrett (father) to Septimus Moulton-Barrett. ... *The Hedleys go to-morrow! Our precious Ba has had a better day than yesterday, & has been I fear exerting herself to write a few lines to George, to whom she said she owed two letters. ...* [MM-B & RAM-B]

SD1124] [22 May 1840]. A.L.s. Charles Dickens to T.N. Talfourd. ... *Not content with telling Tom Hill, Wordsworth, Browning, and Heaven knows who besides, this traitorous publisher* [Moxon] *told (yesterday) Knowles ... Letters of Charles Dickens*, eds. Madeline House and Graham Storey, 2, 71.
[   ]

SD1125] 26 May [1840]. A.L.s. Samuel Goodin Barrett to George Goodin Barrett (1792–1854). *I have received both your notes ...* [ERM-B]

SD1126] 30 May 1840. A.L.s. Edward Moulton-Barrett (father) to Septimus Moulton-Barrett. ... *Our beloved Ba is much the same; I cannot add any thing to this report. ...* [MM-B & RAM-B]

SD1127] 24 June 1840. A.L.s. Edward Moulton-Barrett (father) to Septimus Moulton-Barrett. ... *To return to your letter, it is a monstrous time since I left you, and I am wanted very much in London, but how to leave my beloved Ba, I know not, I fear the very mention of it, for she is indeed lamentably weak, & yet it is absolutely necessary I should go; I really know not how to act. She is today much as usual, & she has this week sent a Poem, very short, to the*

Athenæum for insertion upon Napoleon's Bones; & when some one goes to buy my number on Saturday, just let him look into it, & if the verses are there, send one to Bell at Frocester, & another to me here, independent of the one for Wimpole St.... [MM-B & RAM-B]

SD1128] [?2] [July 1840]. A.L.s. Edward Moulton-Barrett (father) to Septimus Moulton-Barrett. ... *There will be a Poem of Bas in the next Athenæum I expect, & if so, send one to Bell, one to Annie, one to Jane, Barnsfield House, Ryde, Isle of Wight, give one to Minny, & send me an extra one, besides that for Wimpole St. which subsequently goes to Stormie.... You may buy a Monthly Chronicle, which contains Ba's poem of the Bones for the use of the House.... Thank God Ba has had a rather nice day upon the whole. Love to all....*

[MM-B & RAM-B]

SD1129] 13 July 1840. A.L.s. Edward Moulton-Barrett (father) to George Goodin Moulton-Barrett. *Ba is as well as one could expect, for indeed it is a most distressing communication I have to make, & altho there may be the most distant possibility that our fears are unnecessary, still the facts & circumstances are so much against our entertaining such a hope, that it is right in my mind that you, my dear Boys, should be prepared for the worse. Our dear Bro & two of his friends Mr. Vanneck & Captn. Clarke with a Sailor went on Saturday last in Mr. Vanneck's Boat on an excursion; they left at a little of the 12 o'clock it seems, & up to this time 11 o'clock Monday Night, they have not been heard of, further than that on Saturday afternoon about ½ after 3 o'clock, a Gentleman in his Yatch, about 4 miles to the East of Teignmouth, saw a Boat exactly corresponding to the one they went in, which it appear is rigged out of the customary way, carrying a great deal of Sail—about a mile from him, when he observed it go down; He set sail immediately to the spot, which he says he reached in 4 or 5 minutes, but nothing whatever could he see belo[n]ging to her or the Party in her ... altho he remained about the place for nearly four hours—& what is extraordinary it does not appear that she upset, for he saw the point of her mast above the water last so that I cannot understand, how some one did not keep upon the surface, until the Yatch came up, the more particularly, as all could swim excepting the sailor— But it would appear, that it has pleased God, & vain is all that is a man, when the Lord ordereth it otherwise; supposing these to have been our beloved Bro & his companions.... Up to the arrival of the Mail we caught as a straw at the possibility of their having gone to the Land Slip near Lyme or the Weymouth ... but if it had been so, we should surely have heard this evening of their being there; & besides dear Bro whenever he went out for Ba's sake, always let her know previously, & if any plan had been formed after they sailed he would have taken assuredly the earliest opportunity of acquainting her where he was.... Henrietta, I think, scarcely can believe it, but weeps, Arabel does, & weeps, but her faith bears her up well—our beloved Ba is scarcely conscious, her mind wanders, but if I can once get her to fix it on her Lord, all will be well; her state of body is all against her, but we must trust & pray & call upon God for the needful support. For myself I am supported, blessed be the Lord, and as billow upon billow pass over me, I desire to praise Him in the midst of it all— ... Pray for us all, especially our beloved Ba, she wants it— But her Lord loves her, altho she has indeed been tried; as if by fire....* [Berg]

SD1130] 14 July [1840]. A.L.s. Edward Moulton-Barrett (father) to Septimus Moulton-Barrett. ... *Our beloved Ba has felt it to the very core, & what may be the result with her I know not, but considering every thing she is wonderful; she knows in whom she has believed, & she feels the truth doubtless of the promise I will never leave or forsake thee. Indeed she has for many years been tried in the fire of affliction both personally & relatively, & the Lord will eventually bring her out as gold, fine gold....* [MM-B & RAM-B]

SD1131] 1 August 1840. A.L.s. Edward Moulton-Barrett (father) to Septimus Moulton-Barrett. *Through the blessing of God we are going on a little better, the pulse stronger but still dreadfully exhausted, the nervous energy being as low as possible to keep life in its dwelling place. We must wait the Lord's time, for His counsels shall stand. The rest are tolerable.... It had been my intention on my return to Town, to have sent you all down here a little after this time, but this is out of the question now, for among other objections Ba could not bear it— She cannot hear of any one coming near her, indeed she would have us all to leave her, as she associates in her mind every one & every thing with her loss.... I think to-night that our dearest Ba is certainly improved, the pulse indicates more power, & she did not appear so low, nay she even asked me to remain longer with her, & certainly her mind has acquired a more healthy tone— Oh, may the Lord carry on the good work, & after manifold trials of our faith, receive our many prayers. But I confess, knowing all I did, it is a wonder to me that she lives, for her love for him, we mourn, was truely great, & in addition their friendship was uninterrupted, it began in infancy & has gone on growing with their growth— He was always the adytum of all her secrets & plans— It has been indeed an aweful dispensation. One that oftimes I can scarcely believe, for continually my mind is impressed that somehow, he has been providentialy preserved & will present himself, & then I proceed to make my arrangements as to the best method in which I shall communicate the blessed intelligence to the rest, & particularly to our suffering one, but I am roused out of my happy reverie by the astounding fact, that he cannot come to me, but I must go to him for the meeting; well, God's Will be done, sooner or later this may be, in the mean time May He enable me to rest satisfied, that it is all for the best, because He has ruled it....* [MM-B & RAM-B]

SD1132] 26 August [1840]. A.L.s. Edward Moulton-Barrett (father) to Septimus Moulton-Barrett. ... *Your mistake is not half so good as dear Bas who thought the £800 came for my acceptance, were really for the purpose of putting them into my pocket, instead of taking so much out— Whilst upon business, tell Stormy I want him to go again to the Marine Office for the purpose of insuring Ba's & my shares in the ship David Lyon from London to Jamaica with liberty to call at Madeira & to dock & undock—but as there is some little difficulty about this, he must call at the Jamaica Coffee House on Friday & Captn. Selby will go with him— the value of the shares are to be taken at what he has put on his own, & for this purpose I have written to him. It must be done on friday, as on Saturday the Ship goes into Dock as Selby expresses it to have her bottom looked at, & I would run no risk in her going there & back, particularly as no difference is made in the amount of insurance, further than the loss of the little interest on the premium between this & the time she commences her voyage— ... Oh that our precious one was so much better, that I could, with any satisfaction,* *leave her; if only for a fortnight. She is much the same, altho as Scully said to-day certainly better than she was 10 days ago—at the same time the least excitement would throw her back. Can you get the Advertiser which alludes to her & Southey, or has Pick filled up the* TWO *poets with the names– Write to her, to be sure, write every one of you, she will be glad to read all your sayings and doings. It will alleviate if only for a short time, but that is worth something– After all her real & only permanent comfort must be from above, & it has come I think in a measure & will come in God's time in amplitude....*

[MM-B & RAM-B]

SD1133] 12 September 1840. A.L.s. Edward Moulton-Barrett (father) to Septimus Moulton-Barrett. *I must first tell you what I know you are all most anxious about, the state of our dear Ba: yesterday she was really very nicely, the pulse being down to 84, & this morning when Scully was here it had only risen one beat 85, but in consequence of her being taken up to-day & placed upon the sofa for a quarter of an hour, it went off at a countless pace, & the exertion, slight as it was, produced very great exhaustion. It was however to be expected in a measure; & I trust she may get some sleep to-night, which will do great things for her. The spasmodic action in the throat, upon swallowing, is certainly very much diminished, as well as the fainting upon falling asleep; this is good, & for which we should be thankful, as they were very distressing to her. What God's purposes may be concerning her we know not; it is for us to wait in patience & watch unto prayer–– ...* [MM-B & RAM-B]

SD1134] 16 September 1840. A.L.s. Edward Barrett (former slave) to Edward Moulton-Barrett (father). [ERM-B]

SD1135] 25 September 1840. A.L.s. Edward Moulton-Barrett (father) to Septimus Moulton-Barrett. *... Now I must tell you our dear Ba was very tolerable this morning, but the exertion of getting up to-day, which by the bye is only being removed from the bed to the sofa close by, brought on a very bad head-ache & great exhaustion,—tho not worse than when she made the last effort, & to-day she was out of her bed half an hour. They are all gone to bed, or I would have told some one to give you an account of her night's rest in the morning– You must hope the best– You will see from my letter to Henry that we found out the intended criticism in the Quarterly before your scratches indicated that you had– Ba expects to be well trimmed in it, but she is proof against all they might say, & means to think as little of the important We, as she would of I– However I dont think that it will be very unfriendly, altho her evident politics will of course be looked at with a jaundice-eye. The Writer will I dare say most kindly give advice, & recommend this or that, when if the truth were known, peradventure he may not be worthy to hold a candle to her– But Critics must live, altho Authors cannot, by their writings....* [MM-B & RAM-B]

SD1136] October 1840. A.L.s. John Forster to W.J. Fox. *... Ask Miss Flower this question for me. If friendly relations are to be resumed between myself and Browning, on whom, in her judgment, and taking into account my obvious motive in all that passed, rests the propriety of making the first advance? I think I know what her answer will be, but yet there will be much satisfaction in having it from herself. You had not seen her to speak of the matter yesterday before we met; and though, if I sought a man's judgment, I would never ask beyond your own, you will forgive the anxiety I have, in such a case as this, to* *be right in Miss Flower's opinion. Her "roman-nosed grandeur" is the only thing that mars my self-approving recollections of the foolish quarrel. Nevertheless, it was not grandeur. I leave town to-night for a few days, and wish to be quite clear in conscience before I go. I have not heard from Browning. He waits, it is clear, till I break his "pet" for him. It would be mortifying to me if I were not justified in letting him continue to wait; but it would mortify me more to interrupt or suspend, by anything I could blame myself for hereafter, a friendship on which I placed no indifferent value.* . . . Garnett, p. 195. [   ]

SD1137] [?20] October 1840. A.L.s. Edward Moulton-Barrett (father) to Septimus Moulton-Barrett. . . . *Mr. Kenyon arrived on Saturday, & I saw him yesterday. He is looking very well, but how long he stays I know not. Our dearest sufferer is much the same; Horne has written to her giving her 10 days to modernise a portion of Chaucer, which he is going to publish. I hope it may not excite her too much.* . . . [MM-B & RAM-B]

SD1138] 3 November 1840. A.L.s. William Tinkler to Edward Moulton-Barrett (father). [ERM-B]

SD1139] 5 November 1840. A.L.s. Edward Moulton-Barrett (father) to Septimus Moulton-Barrett. . . . *I want you to execute the following commissions for me, & have the articles packed up & sent to the London Wharf before 12 o'clock on Saturday, to come in the Steam Boat, I think City of Glasgow– 4 Copies of the Essay on Mind which you will get at Dawson's Corner of Paternoster Row– 4 Prometheus, under the Table in my Bed Room, & 4 Seraphim at Saunders & Co, & ask them when there, if the 6 Copies or 12, which was it of the Prometheus I sent are sold; & if so perhaps they would take more—a few quires of note paper similar to this, & 100 Envelopes something like what this is enclosed in, but not longer– Near Duncan's at Groombridge's Panyer Alley, Paternoster Row, get me the Sept Octr & Novr. Nos of the Inquirer—at Proctor's 6 oz of Cuba snuff & 2 oz of Paraguy mixed, & at Chabonniers, Regent St. a pair of strong walking boots for Henrietta. No. 51.* . . . [MM-B & RAM-B]

SD1140] 14 November 1840. A.L.s. J. G[?resham] to [Edward Moulton-Barrett (father)]. *With reference to the condition of the proceedings* . . . [ERM-B]

SD1141] 16 November 1840. File Copy of Letter. Edward Moulton-Barrett (father) to Messrs. Anderson & Kemble. [ERM-B]

SD1142] [December 1840]. A.L.s. Edward Moulton-Barrett (father) to Henrietta Moulton-Barrett. *I have just returned home & find that the boys not knowing my mind have omitted to write to inform you of a circumstance, that I know will afford you very great happiness; it is the safe arrival of our dear Storm about a 60 Days passage.* . . . *Communicate this intellegence to our dear Ba, as best you may, & tell her she must pardon me, for the motive, for not communicating the possibility of his return, as I feared giving her any uneasiness, & I would not unnecessarily disturb either of you further than telling you of his inclination to come back– I thank God, all anxiety respecting him on this point is at an end–* . . . [Altham]

SD1143] 12 December 1840. Printed Document. Legacy Duty on Residues of personal Estate of Samuel Moulton-Barrett (uncle). [ERM-B]

SD1144] 28 December 1840. A.L.s. Anderson & Kemble to Edward Moulton-Barrett (father). [ERM-B]

Appendix II

SUPPORTING DOCUMENTS: INDEX OF CORRESPONDENTS

(References are to SD number, not page number.)

Aikman, Alex W., 864, 866, 873, 875, 1036, 1045, 1049, 1054, 1069
Anderson, Mr., 879, 886, 888, 900, 934, 954, 988, 1003, 1011
Anderson & Co., 997, 1106
Anderson & Kemble, Messrs., 890, 902, 919, 938, 949, 960, 961, 989, 1040, 1105, 1141, 1144
Anderson, William W., 1035, 1119
Appleton, R.W., 1005, 1017, 1020
Badley, John F., 891, 899, 916
Barrett, Anne Eliza Moulton-, 878
Barrett, Arabella Moulton-, 922.1, 945, 948.1, 955, 962.1, 982, 992, 1015.1, 1016, 1023, 1058, 1059, 1073, 1088
Barrett, Charles John Moulton-, 1052, 1096
Barrett, Edward (former slave), 1134
Barrett, Edward (of Oxford Estate), 905
Barrett, Edward George, 1056, 1074, 1089
Barrett, Edward Moulton- (brother), 983, 994, 999, 1010, 1024, 1052, 1067, 1120.1
Barrett, Edward Moulton- (father), 854, 858, 859, 864.1, 868, 871, 874, 879, 881, 885, 890, 900, 902, 905, 919, 923, 931, 935, 940, 941, 949, 954, 960, 961, 971, 978, 988, 989, 990, 997, 1011, 1019, 1031, 1035, 1037, 1040, 1050, 1051, 1062, 1064, 1067, 1071, 1075, 1077, 1086, 1102, 1105, 1113, 1116, 1117–1120, 1121–1123, 1126–1135, 1137–1142, 1144
Barrett, George Goodin, 897, 921, 985, 1017, 1020, 1056, 1062, 1066, 1074, 1089, 1094, 1115, 1125
Barrett, George Goodin Moulton-, 1129
Barrett, Henrietta Moulton-, 896, 926, 943, 955–957, 965, 967, 971, 977, 979, 981, 984, 986, 987, 990, 993, 995, 998, 1001, 1006, 1009, 1015, 1018, 1042, 1065, 1073, 1090, 1107, 1120, 1142
Barrett, Henriette Willoughby, 897, 976, 999.1
Barrett, Maria, 999.1, 1083
Barrett, Richard, 891, 899, 916, 921
Barrett, Samuel Goodin, 855, 856, 921, 962, 966, 980, 999.1, 1005, 1066, 1079, 1082, 1084, 1093, 1094, 1103, 1125

Barrett, Samuel Moulton- (brother), 847, 854–856, 858, 861–864, 866–870, 872–878, 880–882, 884–889, 892–895, 898, 901, 903, 904, 906–913, 915, 920, 922, 923, 924, 926–931, 933, 934, 937–939, 941–944, 946–948, 950, 952, 956–959, 962, 963–970, 976–978, 980, 981, 983, 984, 986, 987, 990, 991, 993–996, 998, 1000, 1001, 1006–1010, 1012–1015, 1016, 1018, 1019, 1021–1026, 1028–1034, 1036–1039, 1041–1051, 1053, 1054, 1057, 1058, 1060, 1061, 1063–1065, 1068–1070, 1072, 1075–1081, 1083–1088, 1090–1093, 1096, 1102, 1103, 1107–1111, 1113
Barrett, Samuel Moulton- (uncle), 851, 858, 859, 864.1, 865, 871, 901, 947, 973, 1143
Barrett, Septimus Moulton-, 1059, 1067, 1071, 1121, 1123, 1126–1128, 1130–1133, 1135, 1137, 1139
Biddulph, John, 999
Boddington & Co., 865
Boyd, Hugh Stuart, 922.1, 945, 948.1, 962.1, 982, 1015.1
Boyne, Don, 845
Bravo, Jacob, 903
Carey, W., 968, 970, 1002, 1004, 1043, 1044, 1060, 1072
Chambers, Mr., 1034
Chambers, Rich, 1046, 1055
Chapman, Robert, 914
Clarke, Arabella Graham- (aunt), 996, 1059
Clarke, J. M., 889
Clarke, James Graham-, 946, 1028
Clarke, John Altham Graham-, Jr., 959, 1007, 1021
Clarke, John Altham Graham-, Sr., 1008, 1013, 1080, 1108
Clarke, Mary Elizabeth Graham-, 1012, 1022, 1033, 1081
Clayton, John, & Co., 912
Coal, Robert, 927
Dacre, Lady, 917
Davies, Hill, 929
Dewar, Robert, 1109
Dewar, W. & R., & Co., 1112
Dickens, Charles, 860, 1124
Drake, Charles, & Co., 915

Supporting Documents 371

Edwards, J., 1082, 1115
Farquaharson, Matthew, 867, 947, 948, 951
Fleming, Samuel, 887
Forster, John, 953, 1136
Fox, W.J., 1136
Geddes, James, 1074
Gordon, Ann C., 991
G[?resham], J., 882, 883, 1140
Harvey & Daniel, Messrs., 942
Hawes, M., 1027, 1029
Holden, Mr., 1068
Hornby, John, 1000
Howitt, Mary, 1104
Hunt, Leigh, 953
Hyatt, W.K., 884, 963
Jamaica, Bishop of, 901
Jameson, Anna, 846
Jump, Joseph G., 937, 1026, 1030, 1068
Kemble, Mr., 1122
Kennedy, Allan, 1087
Kenyon, John, 932, 986.1
K[?itchin], J.R., 908
Knibb, Mr., 1003
Knibb, William, 935
Lace, William, 895, 920
Lambert, Sydney, 1063
MacIntyre, J., 906
Minto, Mary, 979
Mitford, Mary Russell, 845, 846, 917, 992, 1073, 1104, 1115.1

Neil, M., 929
Newdick, S., 1057
Nidal, John G., 1025
Phillpotts, James, 847, 951, 952
Pownall & Gross, Messrs., 1106
Redwood, P., 894
Ricketts, Mr., 1027
Room, James, 910
Rowe, Joshua, 863, 872, 876, 880, 883, 888, 898, 907, 911, 922, 928, 930, 933, 939, 944, 1032, 1038, 1041, 1061, 1091, 1092, 1110
Scarlett, Mary, 849
Scott, R.Y., 974
Simmons, Samuel, 1053
Smith, Edward A., 892
Soulette, J., 904
Talfourd, T.N., 1124
Tennison, J., 862, 877
Tinkler, William, 870, 950, 964, 1055, 1112, 1114, 1138
Trelawney, Vestry of, 909, 913
Vermont, J.R., 869
Waddell, H.M., 958, 969, 1002, 1004, 1047, 1048, 1070, 1076, 1078, 1116
Whitehorne, James, 1117, 1118
Williams, M., 985
Wordsworth, Mary, 932
Wordsworth, William, 932, 986.1
Yates, Miss, 1115.1

Appendix III

Contemporary Reviews of The Brownings' Works

RB AND EBB, understandably, showed much interest in the reviews—favourable and otherwise—which their works received. Frequently mentioned in their correspondence, the criticisms unquestionably influenced their subsequent writings. Because it is difficult to convey the full impact of the reviews through brief quotes, and since many of them would be hard for readers to locate, we here reproduce—in chronological order for each poet—all reviews whose publication we have traced for the period covered by this volume.

We have, however, excluded reviews of *The Amaranth* in *The Literary Gazette* (20 October 1838, p. 660), *The Metropolitan Magazine* (November 1838, pp. 85–86), and *The Monthly Chronicle* (November 1838, p. 466), because no mention is made of EBB's contribution. For the same reason, we have excluded a review of *Findens' Tableaux* (1840) in *The Morning Chronicle* (26 November 1839, p.3).

WORKS BY EBB

THE SERAPHIM. The Atlas, 23 June 1838, p. 395.

THE SUBJECT of the poem called *The Seraphim*, was suggested to the author while she was engaged upon her translations of the *Prometheus* of ESCHYLUS; and she observes in her preface that had ESCHYLUS lived after the incarnation and crucifixion of the Saviour, he would have recognized in that sublime history a loftier and grander theme than the *Prometheus*. There cannot be fairly instituted a comparison between these subjects, although the extreme agony embraced in both, and the character of the noble poem of the Greek, would naturally lead the mind from the consideration of the Titanic conception to the awful mystery of the Christian atonement. Miss BARRETT's treatment of the theme is in keeping with the humility which she expresses in approaching it; she merely gives us a distant glimpse of the crucifixion, and throws a poetical obscurity over it which may probably impress her readers more solemnly than if she had ventured to delineate it with a bolder hand. In the poem of *The Seraphim* there are but two persons, and they are of the angelic nature. The time is that of the crucifixion, and the Creator has directed the angelic host towards the earth, but these two angels linger at the closed gates of Heaven in the First Part of the poem, and mid-way in the air over Judæa, in the Second Part, communing with each other on the events that are taking place on Earth, and the causes that produced them. The form of the dialogue is irregular, and it constitutes, as the author justly describes it, a dramatic lyric, rather than a lyrical drama. In this conception there is not much power, nor does it admit of that breadth and force in the treatment of which the subject is susceptible, and, indeed, which it demands. But we have hardly any right to expect a more elaborate structure, for the author deprecates such criticism by declaring that she has "not written a book

[372]

but a suggestion." The suggestion is sufficiently striking to excite the imagination, and, although in some parts the poem is feeble and obscure, there are occasional passages of great beauty, and full of deep poetical feeling. Take, for an example, the following description of the descent of the angelic host through the air—the speakers being still hestitating at the gate of Heaven.

> *Ador.* Thus, now, beloved! unpausingly
> Beneath us sinks the pomp angelical—
> The roar of whose descent hath died
> To a still sound, as thunder into rain!
> Th' immeasurable space seems magnified
> With that thick life; whereof we nought retain
> *In vision, save the pale and eddying fall*
> *Of wings innumerous, brightly crossed*
> *By lines of hair that hath not lost*
> *The glitter of the God-smile shed*
> *Last, on bowed angel's head!*
> And gleamed between by hands that fling
> Homages like upward rays,
> From constant habitude of praise
> And high instinct of worshipping.
> *Zerah.* Rapidly they drop below us.
> *Pointed palm and wing and hair,*
> *Indistinguishable show us*
> *Only pulses in the air*
> *Throbbing with a fiery beat—*
> As if a new creation heard
> (Late unhearing, still unseeing)
> Some divine and plastic word;
> And trembling at its proper being
> Did waken at our feet.

We have put some of these lines in *italics*, to direct the attention of the reader more emphatically to the exquisite beauty of the picture they bring before us. The effect of these descriptions is rendered still more vivid and complete by the contrast between *Ador*, the elder angel, who is strong and somewhat saddened by his experiences, and *Zerah*, the younger, who is weak and full of love and natural fear. Thus *Zerah* appeals to his brother to impart his knowledge to him concerning the earth, and the changes that have been wrought in it by the sin of man.

> *Ador.* Hast thou seen it since—the change?
> *Zerah.* Askest thou? I fear—I fear—
> To look upon it now!
> I have beheld the ruined things
> Only in the picturings
> Of angels sent on earthward mission!
> Strong one, e'en upon thy brow—
> When with task completed, given
> Back to us from earthly vision,
> I have beheld thee silent stand,
> Abstracted in the seraph band—
> *Without a smile in heaven!*

In the second part, going down upon the earth they behold the cross—the figure at its foot is described with touching truth.

> *Ador.* The cross—the cross!
> *Zerah.* A woman doth
> Kneel the mid cross under—
> Meekly with her lips asunder,
> And a motion upon each,
> Too fast to show or suffer speech—
> With folded lids as close as sleep—
> Yet not as tranquil—for the eyes
> That dream within, have room to weep
> Drop after drop—

A variety of poems follow in the volume, in some of which—where the subject comes more easily within the scope of the author's powers—she is more successful: but in none do we find such flashes of imagination as in the *Seraphim*. From a poem called the *Romaunt of Margret*, we will give one extract, as a specimen of the shorter pieces. The portrait of *Margret*, sitting by the river's side, will recall some of the fanciful images of TENNYSON.

> The night is in her hair,
> And giveth shade to shade;
> And the pale moonlight, on her forehead white,
> Like a spirit's hand is laid:—
> Her lips part with a smile,
> Instead of speakings done—
> I ween she thinketh of a voice,
> Albeit uttering none!
> Margaret, Margaret! [sic]
> * * *
> The ladye's shadow lies
> Upon the running river.
> It lieth no less in its quietness,
> For that which resteth never:
> Most like a trusting heart
> Upon a passing faith—
> Or as upon the course of life,
> The stedfast doom of death!
> Margaret, Margaret.
> The ladye doth not move—
> The ladye doth not dream—
> Yet she seeth her shade no longer laid
> In rest upon the stream!
> It shaketh without wind—
> It parteth from the tide—
> It standeth upright in the cleft moonlight—
> It sitteth at her side.
> Margaret, Margaret!

Miss BARRETT is sometimes chargeable with affectation. She overworks the tints, and, if we may employ the figure, the tapestry has consequently a cumbrous appearance, here and there, from the excessive weight of the colouring. But she possesses a fine poetical temperament, and has given to the public, in this volume, a work of considerable merit.

THE SERAPHIM. The Examiner, 24 June 1838, pp. 387–388.

THIS BOOK opens with a preface which is very remarkable for power and beauty of expression. After intimating that the subject of the principal poem in the volume was suggested by the *Prometheus Bound* of Æschylus, Miss Barrett proceeds—

"I thought, that, had Æschylus lived after the incarnation and crucifixion of our Lord Jesus Christ, he might have turned, if not in moral and intellectual, yet in poetic faith, from the solitude of Caucasus to the deeper desertness of that crowded Jerusalem where none had any pity; from the 'faded white flower' of the Titanic brow, to the 'withered grass' of a Heart trampled on by its own beloved; from the glorying of him who gloried that he could not die, to the sublimer meekness of the taster of death for every man; from the taunt stung into being by the torment, to HIS more awful silence, when the agony stood dumb before the love! And I thought, how, 'from the height of this great argument,' the scenery of the Prometheus would have dwarfed itself even in the eyes of its poet,—how the fissures of his rocks and the innumerable smiles of his ocean would have closed and waned into blankness,—and his demigod stood confest, so human a conception as to fall below the aspiration of his own humanity. He would have turned from such to the rent rocks and darkened sun—rent and darkened by a sympathy thrilling through nature, but leaving man's heart untouched—to the multitudes, whose victim was their Saviour—to the Victim, whose sustaining thought beneath an unexampled agony, was not the Titanic 'I can revenge,' but the celestial 'I can forgive!'

* * * *

"I have worn no shoes upon this holy ground: I have stood there, but have not walked. I have drawn no copy of the statue of this GREAT PAN,—but have caught its shadow,—shortened in the dawn of my imperfect knowledge, and distorted and broken by the unevenness of our earthly ground. I have written no work, but a suggestion. Nor has even so little been attempted, without as deep a consciousness of weakness as the severest critic and the humblest Christian could desire to impress upon me. I have felt in the midst of my own thoughts upon my own theme, like Homer's 'children in a battle.'

"The agents in this poem of imperfect form—a dramatic lyric, rather than a lyrical drama—are those mystic beings who are designated in Scripture the Seraphim. The subject has thus assumed a character of exaggerated difficulty, the full sense of which I have tried to express in my Epilogue. But my desire was, to gather some vision of the supreme spectacle under a less usual aspect,—to glance at it, as dilated in seraphic eyes, and darkened and deepened by the near association with blessedness and Heaven. Are we not too apt to measure the depth of the Saviour's humiliation from the common estate of man, instead of from His own peculiar and primeval one? To avoid which error, I have endeavoured to count some steps of the ladder at Bethel,—a very few steps, and as seen between the clouds.

"And thus I have endeavoured to mark in my two Seraphic personages, distinctly and predominantly, that shrinking from, and repugnance to, evil, which, in my weaker Seraph, is expressed by *fear*, and, in my stronger one, by a more complex passion; in order to contrast with such, the voluntary debasement of Him who became lower than the angels, and touched in His own sinless being, sin, and sorrow, and death. In my attempted production of such a contrast, I have been true to at least my own idea of angelic excellence, as well as to that of His perfection. For one holiness differs from another holiness in glory. To recoil from evil, is according to the stature of an angel; to subdue it, is according to the infinitude of a God."

We should have done a great injustice to an extremely fine writer, had we attempted to describe her purpose in other words than these, her own.

Our readers will also be glad to receive from the poem itself, before any remarks of our's which we may venture to think it calls for, a few of its striking and brilliant bursts of fancy and of passion.

The poem opens as the two Seraphim, Ador and Zerah, stand on the outer side of the shut heavenly gate, on the eve of their passage to the mid-air, above Judæa. Beneath them

sinks the pomp angelical—
The roar of whose descent hath died
To a still sound, as thunder into rain—
and as they arrive nearer and nearer earth, the fear of Zerah, so bright and yet so timid, increases more and more. "Well beloved! what fearest thou?" asks the strong and passionate Ador—
    Zerah. I fear, I fear—
    Ador.   What fear?
    Zerah.   The fear of *earth.*
    Ador. Of earth, the God-create, the beautiful?
From whence the sweet sea music hath its birth,
And vernal forests lift their leaves in tune,
Beneath the gracious, water-leading moon?
Where every night, the stars do put away
    Meekly its darkness dull,
And look their spirit-light into the clay?
Where every day, the kingly sun doth bless
    More lovingly than kings,
And stir to such harmonious happiness
    All leafed and reeded things,
It seems as if the joyous shout which burst
    From angel lips to see him first,
Had left a silent echo in his ray?
Still trembles Zerah as he thinks of the curse the earth has inherited, of Death, and the yet fearfuller Evil—
    the cursed thing that moved
    Its shadow of ill, long time ago,
    Across our heaven's own shining floor.
Then Ador tells to Zerah (from whom it has till now been concealed) the mission which had carried "peace on earth—goodwill to man," and upon himself there falls, at the instant, the terrible thought of the human agonies then inflicting on the Divine One—
    O heart of man—of God! which God hath ta'en
    From out the dust, *with its humanity*
    Mournful and weak and soft yet holy round it—
    And bade its many pulses beating lie
    Beside that incommunicable stir
    Of Deity wherewith he interwound it!
With like thoughts, awakened thus by Ador, Zerah is then filled, and with the hope of seeing "His loving smile through his woeful clay," becomes strong for earth—
    Were I never to see my heaven again,
    I would wheel to earth like the tempest-rain
    Which sweeps there with exultant sound
    To lose its life in the reachëd ground!
The second part sees the Seraphim in mid-air, above Judæa, somewhat apart from the visible angelic hosts. The opening is indeed masterly—
    Ador. Belovëd! dost thou see?—
    Zerah. Thee,—thee!
    Thy burning eyes already are
    Grown wild and mournful as a star,
    Whose occupation is for aye
    To look upon the place of clay,
        Whereon thou lookest now!
    The crown is fainting on thy brow
    To the likeness of a cloud—
    Thy forehead's self, a little bowed
    From its aspect high and holy,—
    As it would in meekness meet
    Some seraphic melancholy!
    Thy very wings that lately flung
    In heavenly airs, an outline clear,
    Flicker in their glory here;
    And wear to each a shadow hung,
        Dropped across thy feet.

The weights of earth around us lying,
Our breath comes heavily like sighing;
And in these strange contrasting glooms,
Stagnant with the scent of tombs,
Seraph faces, O my brother,
Show awfully to one another!
  Ador. Dost thou see? dost thou see?
  Zerah. Yea! our heaven's bright company—
Alone the memory of their brightness
  Left in them, as in thee!
The circle upon circle, tier on tier—
The perpendicular sea whose rampant whiteness
Stands fixed, because the sudden wind drops low—
The sea of living Ones, afar, anear,
  Above us, and around!
Their songful lips divorcëd from all sound;
A darkness gliding down their silvery glances,—
Bowing their steadfast solemn countenances,
As if they heard God speak, and could not glow!
  Ador. Look downward! dost thou see?—
For Ador already looks upon what Zerah is not strong
enough to see, and strives to prepare him for the sight—
  Unto Him whose forming word
  Gave to Nature flower and sward,
  She hath given back again,
    Instead of flowers, the thorn;
Instead of sylvan calms, the human scorn.
At last, straining downward, downward, Zerah beholds—
    I see
  Beyond the city, crosses three,
  And mortals three that hang thereon,
  'Ghast and silent to the sun!
  And round about them sweep and press
    Living multitudes.
We pass the descriptions which succeed, up to the coming
on of the Supernatural Darkness—
  Ador. The pathos hath the day undone!
  The death-look of His eyes
  Hath overcome the sun,
And made it sicken in its narrow skies—
But not to death!——
  Zerah.   He dieth! Through the dark,
He still, He only, is discernible—
The barëd hands and feet transfixëd stark,—
The countenance of patient anguish white,—
Do make, themselves, a light
More dreadful than the glooms which round them
  dwell,
And therein do they shine.

Who will deny to the writer of such verses as these
(and they are not sparingly met with in the volume) the
possession of many of the highest qualities of the divine
art? We regret to have some restriction to add to an
admission we make so gladly.

Miss Barrett is indeed a genuine poetess, of no common order; yet is she in danger of being spoiled by over-ambition, and of realising no greater or more final reputation than a hectical one, like Crashaw's. She has fancy, feeling, imagination, expression; but for want of some just equipoise or other between the material and spiritual, she aims at flights which have done no good to the strongest, and therefore falls infinitely short,rt, except in such detached passages as we have extracted above, of what a proper exercise of her genius would infallibly reach. In a word, the subject of her present poem has been chosen with an unhappy want of judgment.

For, let us add, notwithstanding the sneer (a thing that never sits well on a woman's face) in Miss Barrett's admirable preface, at the unlucky critic who was "*not* Longinus" (Doctor Johnson, we presume), we venture to be of opinion that religion, or what is exclusively understood by "sacred subjects," is not fit for poetry, except on very rare and brief occasions; and that such of the greatest poets as have thought otherwise, have proved themselves mistaken in the very midst of their greatness. Milton degraded the Deity, not only into a "school-divine," but something worse; and the presumption of Dante is at least equal to his genius. How indeed can the Infinite, which Time itself can never arrive at,—the Ineffable, of which the visible stars do but express a few atoms,—be a proper subject for the faculties of the mere dwellers upon one of those atoms? The greatest do but show their littleness, and not a very humble littleness (for all their talk of humility), in approaching such themes, and the weakest (among whom we do *not* place Miss Barrett) are in danger, moth like, of doing worse than singe their wings.

We find that we must give one extract more. We had determined to resist the temptation of selecting from among the minor poems in the volume, but we cannot withstand this noble picture of the Poet in the "Poet's Vow"—

  Nor wore the dead a stiller face
    Beneath the cerement's roll:
  His lip seemed carved to an endless thought
    No language dared controul;
  And his steadfast eye burnt inwardly,
    As gazing on his soul.

  You would not deem that brow could e'er
    Ungentle moods express:
  Yet seemed it in this troubled world,
    Too calm for gentleness!
  The very star that shines from far,
    Shines trembling ne'ertheless.

Very various, and in the main beautiful and true, are these minor poems. But the entire volume deserves more than ordinary attention.

The Seraphim. The Athenæum, 7 July 1838, pp. 466–468.

This is an extraordinary volume—especially welcome as an evidence of female genius and accomplishment—but it is hardly less disappointing than extraordinary. Miss Barrett's genius is of a high order; active, vigorous, and versatile, but unaccompanied by discriminating taste. A thousand strange and beautiful visions flit across her mind, but she cannot look on them with steady gaze;—her descriptions, therefore, are often shadowy and indistinct, and her language wanting in the simplicity of unaffected earnestness. She addresses herself to sacred song with a devotional ecstacy suiting rather the Sister Celestines and Angelicas of Port-Royal, than the religious poets of our sober protestant communities; yet we are constantly drawn downwards from ecstatic visions by the fantastic spirit which clothes them,—from the loftiest contemplations, to consider some peculiarity of attitude and utterance—the tinkling of the bells of the priest's garment, as it were, distracting our attention from the divine wisdom issuing from his lips. Though personally we may not much regard these things,—though we may be content, ourselves, to catch glimpses of genius and of power, and of fancies "chaste and noble," even though revealed to us from behind a quaint Isis-like veil,—the case is different as concerns the public. We hold that those whose mission it is to declare

Oracles divine, and wisdom golden,

act unfaithfully, if they allow themselves to interpose between the Divinity and their less imaginative audience.

In offering a few specimens to justify our praise, we are quite sure, that, select where we may, they will prove that the strain of our remarks was not uncalled for. The first, and principal poem gives the work its title. In its manner it occupies, as it were, an intermediate ground between an ancient Greek tragedy and a Christian mystery: as regards its matter,—we shall allow Miss Barrett to explain her own intentions:—

"The subject of the principal poem in the present collection having suggested itself to me, though very faintly and imperfectly, when I was engaged upon my translation of the 'Prometheus Bound' of Æschylus, I thought, that, had Æschylus lived after the incarnation and crucifixion of our Lord Jesus Christ, he might have turned, if not in moral and intellectual yet in poetic faith, from the solitude of Caucasus to the deeper desertness of that crowded Jerusalem where none had any pity: from the 'faded white flower' of the Titanic brow, to the 'withered grass' of a Heart trampled on by its own beloved; from the glorying of him who gloried that he could not die, to the sublimer meekness of the Taster of death for every man; from the taunt stung into being by the torment, that HIS more awful silence, when the agony stood dumb before the love! And I thought, how, 'from the height of this great argument,' the scenery of the Prometheus would have dwarfed itself even in the eyes of its poet,—how the fissures of his rocks and the innumerous smiles of his ocean would have closed and waned into blankness,—and his demigod stood confest, so human a conception as to fall below the aspiration of his own humanity. He would have turned from such to the rent rocks and darkened sun—rent and darkened by a sympathy thrilling through nature, but leaving man's heart untouched—to the multitudes, whose victim was their Saviour—to the Victim, whose sustaining thought beneath an unexampled agony, was not the Titanic 'I can revenge,' but the celestial 'I can forgive!'"

An extrinsic interest attaches to this preface, independently of its great and original merit, from a remarkable coincidence in its spirit with some observations—probably not known to the writer—by Edgar Quinet, in his prelude to the 'Prométhée,' in which the lofty-thoughted but wild genius also proposes to himself the completion of the Pagan fable. We shall translate one passage, by way of drawing the attention of our readers to a subject, which—though far from the circuit of everyday contemplation—is increasingly attracting the meditation of the poets and thinkers of Europe.

"In completing, by Christianity, the tradition of Prometheus," says M. Quinet, "we conform ourselves to the natural progress of religious revolutions. We finish this divine tragedy after the very plan which has been marked out in history by Providence, and, in fact, followed by humanity. The poems thus become the image of the same reality. Besides, in this idea, we meet with the imagining of many fathers of the church. Long before me, an ancient commentator upon Eschylus—the Englishman, Stanley, remarked that the founders of Christianity addressed themselves in this manner to interpret the allegory of Prometheus. In spite of the horror which paganism inspired in them, they have not ceased to associate this tradition with the spirit of the most sacred mysteries of the church. They have often compared the torture upon Caucasus with the passion upon Calvary,—thus making of Prometheus a Christ before *the* Christ. Among these authorities that of Tertullian is, above the rest, striking. Twice, in proclaiming to the Gentiles, the God of the martyrs, he exclaims, '*Behold the real Prometheus—the omnipotent God! transpierced by blasphemy!*' Elsewhere, and conformably with the same idea, he speaks of the '*Cross of Caucasus.*' Although expressed in other terms, the sentiment of the Greek and Latin apologists is the same as that of the African. Nor is it, perhaps, useless to observe that the most remarkable bas-relief of Prometheus was discovered in the crypts of a church, among the tombs of bishops and catholic sculptures, with which it was confounded during many ages. But, without attaching to this circumstance more importance than belongs to it, the testimonies just adverted to, will suffice to prove that the connexion which I have established between the antique fable, and the spirit of Christianity, is no artifice of modern fantasy: that, on the contrary, it reposes, in some sort, upon tradition, and, I may dare to say, upon the inmost nature of things."

Enough has been quoted to indicate a parallel singular and worthy of examination: to trace it further,—to illustrate at length the several and national preponderances of the artist and the devotee, in the respective works of the French and English writers, would lead us too far, and through speculations for which the many have but little appetite. Let us, therefore, return to Miss Barrett's volume, and in particular to the division containing her miscellaneous poems. Each of these is tinctured with one prevailing purpose and idea: among them are 'The Romaunt of Margret,' which appeared in the *New Monthly*—and which is not improved by sundry verbal changes its authoress has made in it. Here, too, is its companion, 'The Poet's Vow.' 'Isobel's Child,' the next lyric, has never been published before: we shall therefore make our principal selections from it. The idea is simple:—a young mother is watching by the side of her baby, cheating herself with hopes, and pouring forth prayers for its recovery:—

> Motionless she sate!—
> The hair had fallen by its weight
> On either side the smile, and lay
> Very blackly on the arm
> Where the baby nestled warm!—
> Pale as baby carved in stone
> And seen by glimpses of the moon
> In a dark cathedral aisle!—
> But through the storm no moonbeam fell
> Upon the child of Isobel—
> I ween you saw it by the ray
> Alone of her still smile.
>
> 'Tis aye a solemn thing to me
> To look upon a babe that sleeps—
> Wearing in its spirit-deeps
> The unrevealëd mystery
> Of its Adam's taint and woe,
> Which, when they revealëd be,
> Will not let it slumber so!
> Lying new in life beneath
> The shadow of the coming death,
> With that soft low quiet breath,
> As if it felt the sun!—

Knowing all things by their blooms,
Not their roots!—yea!—sun and sky,
Only by the warmth that comes
Out of each!—earth, only by
The pleasant hues that o'er it run!—
And human love, by drops of sweet
White nourishment still hanging round
The little mouth so slumber-bound!—
All which broken sentiency
Will gather and unite and climb
To an immortality
Good or evil, each sublime,
Through life and death to life again!—
O little lids, now closèd fast!
Must ye learn to drop at last
Our large and burning tears?—
O warm quick body! must thou lie,
When is done the round of years,
Bare of all the joy and pain,
Dust in dust—thy place upgiving
To creeping worms in sentient living?—
   *   *   *   *

More soft, less solemn images
Drifted o'er the lady's heart,
 Silently as snow;
She had seen eight days depart,
Hour by hour, on bended knees,
With pale-wrung hands and prayings low
And broken—through which came the sound
Of tears that fell against the ground,
Making sad stops! "Dear Lord, dear Lord!"
She aye had prayed—(the heavenly word,
Broken by an earthly sigh!)
"Thou who didst not erst deny
The mother-joy to Mary mild
Blessèd in the blessèd child—
Hearkening in meek babyhood
Her cradle-hymn, albeit used
To all that music interfused
In breasts of angels high and good!
Oh, take not, Lord, my babe away:
Oh, take not to thy songful heaven,
The pretty baby thou hast given;
Or ere that I have seen him play
Around his father's knees, and known
That *he* knew how my love hath gone
 From all the world to him!
And how that I shall shiver, dim.
In the sunshine, thinking e'er
The grave-grass keeps it from his fair
Still cheeks! and feel at every tread
His little body which is dead
And hidden in the turfy fold,
Doth make the whole warm earth a'cold!
O God! I am so young, so young—
I am not used to tears at nights
Instead of slumber—nor to prayer
With shaken lips and hands out-wrung!
Thou knowest all my prayings were
'I bless thee, God, for past delights—
Thank God!' I am not used to bear
Hard thoughts of death! The earth doth cover
No face from me of friend or lover!
And must the first who teacheth me
The form of shrouds and funerals, be
Mine own first-born belovèd? he
Who taught me first this mother-love?
Dear Lord, who spreadest out above

Thy loving piercèd hands to meet
All lifted hearts with blessing sweet,—
Pierce not my heart, my tender heart,
Thou madest tender! Thou who art
So happy in thy heaven alway,
Take not mine only bliss away!"
Her prayer—how beautiful and simple in its agony!—appears to be answered; the infant drops into slumber, and—the mother's heart running over with an exulting and thoughtful hopefulness,—she begins, with a fond prescience, to question her darling as to its wishes for the future,—little dreaming that the Angel of Death is about to answer her upbraidingly at the mouth of her child! She has asked it, as if the fulness of her pride and love gave her the power of endowment, whether it will have the crown and the glory appertaining to knowledge and genius. The following is a part of the Spirit's reply, put into the mouth of the expiring infant:—

Is your wisdom very wise,
 Mother, on the narrow earth?
Very happy, very worth
 That I should stay to learn?
Are these air-corrupting sighs
 Fashioned by unlearnèd breath?
Do the students' lamps that burn
 All night, illumine death?
Mother! albeit this be so,
 Loose thy prayer, and let me go
Where that bright chief angel stands
Apart from all his brother bands,
 Too glad for smiling! having bent
 In angelic wilderment
O'er the depths of God, and brought
Reeling, thence, one only thought
To fill his whole eternity!
He the teacher is for me!—
He can teach what I would know—
 Mother, mother, let me go!
Can your poet make an Eden
 No winter will undo?
And light a starry fire, in heeding
 His hearth's is burning too?
Drown in music, earthly din?—
And keep his own wild soul within
The law of his own harmony?—
 Mother! albeit this be so,
 Let me to mine Heaven go!
A little harp me waits thereby—
A harp whose strings are golden all,
And tuned to music spherical,
Hanging on the green life-tree,
Where no willows ever be.
Shall I miss that harp of mine?
 Mother, no!—the Eye divine
Turned upon it, makes it shine—
And when I touch it, poems sweet
Like separate souls shall fly from it,
Each to an immortal fytte!
 We shall all be poets there,
 Gazing on the chiefest Fair!

With all the beauty of this passage, the interwoven conceit, against which we have protested, cannot but be felt; and the extracts given, are by no means so remarkable for far-fetched allusion, as many we could select from the more ambitious poems. Some among the minor verses have appeared in our columns. We should like to have given the 'Deserted Garden' complete, because it shows its authoress in her simplest, and, to our thinking, most becoming garb. A few stanzas, however, may be linked together, for the sake of their fresh and graceful beauty:

 The trees were interwoven wild,
 And spread their boughs enough about
 To keep both sheep and shepherd out,
  But not a happy child.

 Adventurous joy it was for me!
 I crept beneath the boughs, and found
 A circle smooth of mossy ground
  Beneath a poplar tree.

 Old garden rose-trees hedged it in—
 Bedropt with roses waxen-white,
 Well satisfied with dew and light,
  And careless to be seen.

 Long years ago it might befall,
 When all the garden flowers were trim,
 The grave old gardener prided him
  On these the most of all;

 And Lady stately overmuch,
 Who movëd with a silken noise,
 Blushed near them, dreaming of the voice
  That likened her to such!

 And these to make a diadem,
 She may have often plucked and twined;
 Half smiling as it came to mind,
  That few would look at *them*.

 Oh! little thought that Lady proud,
 A child would watch her fair white rose,
 When buried lay her whiter brows,
  And silk was changed for shroud!—

 Nor thought that gardener, full of scorns
 For men unlearn'd and simple phrase,
 A child would bring it all its praise,
  By creeping through the thorns!
   * * * *

 My childhood from my life is parted;
 My footstep from the moss which drew
 Its fairy circle round: anew
  The garden is deserted!

 Another thrush may there rehearse
 The madrigals which sweetest are—
 No more for me!—myself afar
  Do sing a sadder verse;—

 Ah me! ah me! when erst I lay
 In that child's-nest so greenly wrought,
 I laughëd to myself and thought
  'The time will pass away!'
   * * * *

 The time *is* past!—and now that grows
 The cypress high among the trees,
 And I behold white sepulchres
  As well as the white rose—

 When wiser, meeker thoughts are given,—
 And I have learnt to lift my face,
 Remembering earth's greenest place
  The colour draws from heaven—

 It something saith for earthly pain,
 But more for Heavenly promise free,
 That I who was, would shrink to be
  That happy child again!

We must still add another extract from the fugitive pieces:—

   The Sea-Mew.

 How joyously the young sea-mew
 Lay dreaming on the waters blue,
 Whereon our little bark had thrown
 A forward shade—the only one—
 (But shadows aye will man pursue!)

 Familiar with the waves, and free,
 As if their own white foam were he:
 His heart upon the heart of ocean,
 Learning all its mystic motion,
 And throbbing to the throbbing sea!

 And such a brightness in his eye,
 As if the ocean and the sky,
 Within him had lit up and nurst
 A soul God gave him not at first,
 To comprehend their majesty.

 We were not cruel, yet did sunder
 His white wing from the blue waves under,
 And bound it—while his fearless eyes
 Shone up to ours in calm surprise,
 As deeming us some ocean wonder!

 We bore our ocean bird unto
 A grassy place where he might view
 The flowërs bending to the bees,
 The waving of the tall green trees,
 The falling of the silver dew.

 But flowers of earth were pale to him
 Who had seen the rainbow fishes swim;
 And when earth's dew around him lay,
 He thought of ocean's wingëd spray,
 And his eye waxëd sad and dim.

 The green trees round him only made
 A prison, with their darksome shade:
 And drooped his wing, and mournëd he
 For his own boundless glittering sea—
 Albeit he knew not they could fade!

 Then One her gladsome face did bring,
 Her gentle voice's murmuring,
 In ocean's stead his heart to move,
 And teach him what was human love—
 He thought it a strange, mournful thing!

 He lay down in his grief to die,
 (First looking to the sea-like sky,
 That hath no waves!) because, alas!
 Our human touch did on him pass,
 And with our touch, our agony.

  And here we must take leave of the poetess: well pleased if our notice shall make a way for her book into the hands of those who seek in literature for the spirit rather than the letter,—well pleased, if any of our words,—which, however hastily said, have not been hastily conceived,—sink into her mind, and like "bread cast upon the waters" be found again "after many days," in a strengthened resolution on her part to give her fancy, and her strength, and her learning, the only assistance they require to become widely as well as warmly recognized,—that is, a simpler and less mannered clothing than they at present wear.

      [Henry Fothergill Chorley]

The Seraphim. *Blackwood's Edinburgh Magazine*, August 1838, pp. 279–284.
Christopher in his Cave.

[This review of *The Seraphim* is preceded by a review of Richard Monckton Milnes's *Poems of Many Years*.]

What other pretty book is this? "The Seraphim, and other Poems, by Elizabeth Barrett, author of a Translation of Prometheus Bound." High adventure for a Lady—implying a knowledge of Hebrew—or if not—of Greek. No common mind displays itself in this Preface pregnant with lofty thoughts. Yet is her heart humble withal—and she wins her way into ours by these words—"I assume no power of art, except that power of love towards it, which has remained with me from my childhood until now. In the power of such a love, and in the event of my life being prolonged, I would fain hope to write hereafter better verses; but I never can feel more intensely than at this moment—nor can it be needful that any should—the sublime uses of poetry, and the solemn responsibilities of the poet."

We have read much of the volume, and glanced it all through, not without certain regrets almost amounting to blame, but far more with love and admiration. In "The Seraphim" there is poetry and piety—genius and devotion; but the awful Idea of the Poem—the Crucifixion—is not sustained—and we almost wish it unwritten. The gifted writer says—"I thought that, had Æschylus lived after the incarnation and crucifixion of our Lord Jesus Christ, he might have turned, if not in moral and intellectual, yet in poetic faith, from the solitude of Caucasus to the deeper desertness of that crowded Jerusalem where none had any pity; from the 'faded white flower' of the Titanic brow, to the 'withered grass' of a Heart trampled on by its own beloved; from the glorying of him who gloried that he could not die, to the sublimer meekness of the Taster of death for every man; from the taunt stung into being by the torment, to His more awful silence, when the agony stood dumb before the love! And I thought how, 'from the height of this great argument,' he scenery of the Prometheus would have dwarfed itself even in the eyes of its poet—how the fissures of his rocks and the innumerous smiles of his ocean would have closed and waned into blankness,—and his demigod stood confest, so human a conception as to fall below the aspiration of his own humanity. He would have turned from such to the rent rocks and darkened sun—rent and darkened by a sympathy thrilling through nature, but leaving man's heart untouched—to the multitudes, whose victim was their Saviour—to the Victim, whose sustaining thought beneath an unexampled agony, was not the Titanic 'I can revenge,' but the celestial 'I can forgive!'"

The poems that follow are on subjects within the compass of her powers—there is beauty in them all—and some of them, we think, are altogether beautiful. From the "Poet's Vow," "The Romaunt of Margaret," "Isobel's Child," compositions of considerable length, might be selected passages of deep pathos—especially from the last, in which the workings of a mother's love through all the phases of fear, and hope, and despair, and heavenly consolation, are given with extraordinary power, while there is an originality in the whole cast and conception of the strain that beyond all dispute proves the possession of genius. But they are all disfigured by much imperfect and some bad writing—and the fair author is too often seen struggling in vain to give due expression to the feelings that beset her, and entangled in a web of words. "I would fain hope to write hereafter better verses"—and we do not fear that her hopes will not be fulfilled—for she "hath that within which passeth show," but will, we predict, some day shine forth with conspicuous splendour.

Some of the shorter compositions are almost all we could desire—and let us murmur some of them to ourselves in our Cave.

MY DOVES.

My little doves have left a nest
  Upon an Indian tree,
Whose leaves fantastic take their rest
  Or motion from the sea:
For, ever there, the sea-winds go
With sunlit paces, to and fro.

The tropic flowers looked up to it,
  The tropic stars looked down;
And there my little doves did sit,
  With feathers softly brown,
And glittering eyes that showed their right
To general Nature's deep delight.

And God them taught, at every close
  Of water far, and wind
And lifted leaf, to interpose
  Their chanting voices kind;
Interpreting that love must be
The meaning of the earth and sea.

Fit ministers! Of living loves,
  Their's hath the calmest sound—
Their living voice the likest moves
  To lifeless noises round—
In such sweet monotone as clings
To music of insensate things!

My little doves were ta'en away
  From that glad nest of theirs,
Across an ocean foaming aye,
  And tempest-clouded airs.
My little doves!—who lately knew
The sky and wave, by warmth and blue!

And now within the city prison,
  In mist and chillness pent,
With sudden upward look they listen
  For sounds of past content—
For lapse of water, swell of breeze,
Or nut-fruit falling from the trees!

The stir without the glow of passion—
  The triumph of the mart—
The gold and silver's dreary clashing
  With man's metallic heart—
The wheeled pomp, the pauper tread—
These only sounds are heard instead.

Yet still, as on my human hand
  Their fearless heads they lean,
And almost seem to understand
  What human musings mean—
(With such a plaintive gaze their eyne
Are fastened upwardly to mine!)

Their chant is soft as on the nest,
  Beneath the sunny sky;
For love that stirred it in their breast,
  Remains undyingly,
And 'neath the city's shade, can keep
The well of music clear and deep.

And love that keeps the music, fills
  With pastoral memories!
All echoings from out the hills,
  All droppings from the skies,
All flowings from the wave and wind,
  Remembered in their chant I find.

So teach ye me the wisest part,
  My little doves! to move
Along the city ways, with heart
  Assured by holy love,
And vocal with such songs as own
  A fountain to the world unknown.

T'was hard to sing by Babel's stream—
  More hard, in Babel's street!
But if the soulless creatures deem
  Their music not unmeet
For sunless walls—let *us* begin,
  Who wear immortal wings, within!

To me, fair memories belong
  Of scenes that erst did bless;
For no regret—but present song,
  And lasting thankfulness—
And very soon to break away,
  Like types, in purer things than they!

I will have hopes that cannot fade,
  For flowers the valley yields—
I will have humble thoughts, instead
  Of silent, dewy fields!
My spirit and my God shall be
My sea-ward hill, my boundless sea.

Unambitious verses these—and haply the fair Elizabeth sets no great store by them—recurring in her day-dreams of fame to "The Seraphim." But they will live in the memory of many a gentle girl—and mothers will ask their daughters to recite them, that they may watch the workings of nature in the eyes loving innocence—and even fathers looking on and listening—
  May from their eyelids wipe the tear
    That sacred pity had engendered.
  Surely Poetesses (is there such a word?) are very happy, in spite of all the "natural sorrows, griefs, and pains," to which their exquisitely sensitive being must be perpetually alive. Tighe suffered woman's worst—wounded affections; nor was Hemans without a like affliction—but she who died first had a cheerful genius, and fancy led her heart into lands of enchantment, where her human life was lulled in repose, and its woes must have often and long been forgotten in the midst of visionary bliss. That other Sweetest Singer had children round her knees, and sufficient happiness it must have been for her, in that long desertion, to see
    How like a new existence to her heart
  Uprose those living flowers beneath her eyes,
now flourishing, when she is gone, in the light of Heaven. Lætitia Landon—a name not to be merged—is a joyous spirit not unacquainted with grief—her genius was invigorated by duty—now it is guarded by love—and in good time—may gentler suns shine again on her laurelled head—returning to us from the "far countrie," that may even now be inspiring into her startled imagination the beauty of "a New Song."
  And our Elizabeth—she too is happy—though in her happiness she loveth to veil with a melancholy haze the brightness of her childhood—and of her maidenhood—but the clouds we raise we can ourselves dispel—and far away yet beyond the horizon are those that may gather round the decline of her life.

THE DESERTED GARDEN.

I mind me in the days departed,
  How often underneath the sun,
With childish bounds I used to run
  To a garden long deserted.

The beds and walks were vanished quite;
  And wheresoe'er had fallen the spade,
The greenest grasses Nature led,
  To sanctify her right.

I called it my wilderness,
  For no one entered there but I.
The sheep looked in, the grass t' espy,
  And passed ne'ertheless.

The trees were interwoven wild,
  And spread their boughs enough about
To keep both sheep and shepherd out,
  But not a happy child.

Adventurous joy it was for me!
  I crept beneath the boughs, and found
A circle smooth of mossy ground
  Beneath a poplar tree.

Old garden rose-trees hedged it in—
  Bedropt with roses waxen-white,
Well satisfied with dew and light,
  And careless to be seen.

Long years ago it might befall,
  When all the garden flowers were trim,
The grave old gardener prided him
  On these the most of all;

And Lady stately overmuch,
  Who moved with a silken noise,
Blushed near them, dreaming of the voice
  That likened her to such!

And these to make a diadem,
  She may have often plucked and twined;
Half smiling as it came to mind,
  That few would look at *them*.

Oh! little thought that Lady proud,
  A child would watch her fair white rose,
When buried lay her whiter brows,
  And silk was changed for shroud!—

Nor thought that gardener, full of scorns
  For men unlearn'd and simple phrase,
A child would bring it all its praise,
  By creeping through the thorns:

To me upon my low moss seat,
  Though never a dream the roses sent
Of science or love's compliment,
  I ween they smelt as sweet.

Nor ever a grief was mine, to see
  The trace of human step departed—
Because the garden was deserted,
  The blyther place for me!

Friends, blame me not! a narrow ken
  Hath childhood 'twixt the sun and sward!
We draw the moral afterward—
  We feel the gladness then!

And gladdest hours for me did glide
In silence at the rose-tree wall:
A thrush made gladness musical
    Upon the other side.

Nor he nor I did e'er incline
To mar or pluck the blossoms white—
How should I know but that they might
    Lead lives as glad as mine?

To make my hermit-home complete,
I brought clear water from the spring
Praised in its own low murmuring,—
    And cresses glossy wet.

And so, I thought my likeness grew
(Without the melancholy tale)
To gentle hermit of the dale,
    And Angelina too!

For oft I read within my nook
Such minstrel stories! till the breeze
Made sounds poetic in the trees,—
    And then I shut the book.

If I shut this wherein I write,
I hear no more the wind athwart
Those trees!—nor feel that childish heart
    Delighting in delight!

My childhood from my life is parted;
My footstep from the moss which drew
Its fairy circle round: anew
    The garden is deserted!

Another thrush may there rehearse
The madrigals which sweetest are—
No more for me!—myself afar
    Do sing a sadder verse!—

Ah me! ah me! when erst I lay
In that child's-nest so greenly wrought,
I laughed to myself and thought
    'The time will pass away!'

I laughed still, and did not fear
But that, whene'er was past away
The childish time, some happier play
    My womanhood would cheer.

I knew the time would pass away—
And yet beside the rose-tree wall,
Dear God!—how seldom, if at all,
    I looked up to pray!

The time *is* past—and now that grows
The cypress high among the trees,
And I behold white sepulchres
    As well as the white rose.

When wiser, meeker thoughts are given,
And I have learnt to lift my face,
Remembering earth's greenest place
    The colour draws from heaven—

It something saith for earthly pain,
But more for Heavenly promise free,
That I who was, would shrink to be
    That happy child again.

"Has not love," says Elizabeth in her Preface, "a deeper mystery than wisdom, and a more ineffable lustre than power? I believe it has. I venture to believe those beautiful and often-quoted words, 'God is Love,' to be even less an expression of condescension towards the finite, than an assertion of essential dignity in Him, who is infinite." To illustrate that attribute she wrote "The Seraphim." But there is nothing in that poem so affecting as the following simple lines. They cannot be read without bringing to mind the sum of all consolation, "Come unto me all ye who labour and are heavy laden, and I will give you rest."

THE SLEEP.

Of all the thoughts of God that are
Borne inward unto souls afar,
Along the Psalmist's music deep—
Now tell me if that any is,
For gift or grace, surpassing this—
"He giveth His beloved, sleep?"

What would we give to our beloved?
The hero's heart, to be unmoved—
The poet's star-tuned harp, to sweep—
The senate's shout to patriot vows—
The monarch's crown, to light the brows?
"He giveth *His* beloved, sleep."

What do we give to our beloved?
A little faith, all undisproved—
A little dust, to overweep—
And bitter memories, to make
The whole earth blasted for our sake!
"He giveth *His* beloved, sleep."

"Sleep soft beloved!" we sometimes say,
But have no tune to charm away,
Sad dreams that through the eyelids creep;
But never doleful dream again
Shall break the happy slumber, when
"He giveth *His* beloved, sleep!"

O earth, so full of dreary noises!
O men, with wailing in your voices!
O delved gold, the wailer's heap!
O strife, O curse, that o'er it fall!
God makes a silence through you all,
And giveth His beloved, sleep!

His dews drop mutely on the hill;
His cloud above it saileth still,
Though on its slope men toil and reap!
More softly than the dew is shed,
Or cloud is floated overhead,
"He giveth His beloved, sleep."

Yea! men may wonder while they scan
A living, thinking, feeling man,
In such a rest his heart to keep;
But angels say—and through the word
I ween their blessed smile is *heard*—
"He giveth His beloved, sleep!"

For me my heart that erst did go
Most like a tired child at a show,
That sees through tears the jugglers leap,
Would now its wearied vision close,
Would childlike on *His* love repose,
Who giveth His beloved, sleep!

And friends!—dear friends!—when it shall be
That this low breath is gone from me,
And round my bier ye come to weep—
Let one, most loving of you all,
Say, "Not a tear must o'er her fall—
He giveth His beloved, sleep!"

Cowper has found at last the best of biographers in Southey; and Southey—should he see them—and surely he will—though we think he has somewhere said that he seldom reads the verses of the day—will not withhold his praise from the affecting and beautiful lines on Cowper's Grave. Had they been anonymous, we should have attributed them to Caroline Bowles.

COWPER'S GRAVE.

It is a place where poets crowned
    May feel the heart's decaying—
It is a place where happy saints
    May weep amid their praying—
Yet let the grief and humbleness,
    As low as silence, languish;
Earth surely now may give her calm
    To whom she gave her anguish.

O poets! from a maniac's tongue
    Was poured the deathless singing!
O Christians! at your cross of hope
    A hopeless hand was clinging!
O men! this man, in brotherhood,
    Your weary paths beguiling,
Groaned inly while he taught you peace,
    And died while ye were smiling!

And now, what time ye all may read
    Through dimming tears his story—
How discord on the music fell,
    And darkness on the glory—
And how, when one by one, sweet sounds
    And wandering lights departed,
He wore no less a loving face,
    Because so broken-hearted—

He shall be strong to sanctify
    The poet's high vocation,
And bow the meekest Christian down
    In meeker adoration:
Nor ever shall he be in praise,
    By wise or good forsaken;
Named softly, as the household name
    Of one whom God hath taken!

With sadness that is calm, not gloom,
    I learn to think upon him;
With meekness that is gratefulness,
    On God whose heaven hath won him—
Who suffered once the madness-cloud,
    Toward His love to blind him;
But gently led the blind along
    Where breath and bird could find him;

And wrought within his shattered brain,
    Such quick poetic senses,
As hills have language for, and stars,
    Harmonious influences!
The pulse of dew upon the grass,
    His own did calmly number;
And silent shadow from the trees
    Fell o'er him like a slumber.

The very world, by God's constraint,
    From falsehood's chill removing,
Its women and its men became
    Beside him, true and loving!—

And timid hares were drawn from woods
    To share his home caresses,
Uplooking to his human eyes
    With silvan tendernesses.
But while, in blindness he remained
    Unconscious of the guiding,
And things provided came without
    The sweet sense of providing,
He testified this solemn truth,
    Though frenzy desolated—
Nor man, nor nature satisfy,
    When only God created!

Like a sick child that knoweth not
    His mother while she blesses,
And droppeth on his burning brow
    The coolness of her kisses;
That turns his fevered eyes around—
    "My mother! where's my mother?"
As if such tender words and looks
    Could come from any other!

The fever gone, with leaps of heart
    He sees her bending o'er him;
Her face all pale from watchful love,
    Th' unweary love she bore him!
Thus, woke the poet from the dream
    His life's long fever gave him,
Beneath these deep pathetic eyes
    Which closed in death, to save him!

Thus! oh, not *thus!* no type of earth
    Could image that awaking,
Wherein he scarcely heard the chant
    Of seraphs, round him breaking—
Or felt the new immortal throb
    Of soul from body parted;
But felt *those eyes alone*, and knew
    "*My* Saviour! *not* deserted!"

Deserted! who hath dreamt that when
    The cross in darkness rested,
Upon the Victim's hidden face
    No love was manifested?
What frantic hands outstretched have e'er
    Th' atoning drops averted—
What tears have washed them from the soul—
    That *one* should be deserted?

Deserted! God could separate
    From His own essence rather:
And Adam's sins *have* swept between
    The righteous Son and Father—
Yea! once, Immanuel's orphaned cry,
    His universe hath shaken—
It went up single, echoless,
    "My God, I am forsaken!"

It went up from the Holy's lips
    Amid his lost creation,
That of the lost, no son should use
    Those words of desolation;
That earth's worst frenzies, marring hope,
    Should mar not hope's fruition;
And I, on Cowper's grave, should see
    His rapture, in a vision!

                                    [John Wilson]

The Seraphim. *The Metropolitan Magazine*, August 1838, pp. 97-101.

AT OUR FIRST glance at this extraordinary little book, we were singularly struck with the originality, ideality, earnestness, and masterly power of expression and execution; and a more careful examination has deepened its first impression, and awakened in us a great respect for the fair author's uncommon learning. Whether she be qualified to split critical straws with a Parr or a Porson we know not, but she seems well read in the Greek poets, and perfectly imbued with their spirit. We should also infer that she is as familiar with German as with Grecian poetry—or at least we fancy that we trace in many passages a half inspiration derived from the immortal Goethe. With the old poets of England, from Spenser downwards, she has evidently a most perfect acquaintance, and a truly scholar-like familiarity. The style and manner resulting from this combination remind us more of Shelley than of any other recent English writer. But there is a devotional glow, an almost seraph-like enthusiasm in this lady, which the unfortunate Shelley never reached,—though, be it said, that much misunderstood man—that generous and glorious intellect—had a wonderful devotion in his very unbelief. With him it was only a mistake about names. He worshipped God with a soul-exalting worship in the mountains and seas, in the blue sky, the green forest, in the veriest stock and stone around him; and everything in his imagination was sublime and godlike. There is also here and there a happily reflected light from the great and good Wordsworth; and one or two of Miss Barrett's minor pieces might be mistaken for the productions of the greatest of our poets since Milton. Now and then a conception, the hint of a great thought, is taken up and expanded. This seems to be the case, for example, in the following beautiful lines, which will recall to every worshipper of Wordsworth the "Sonnet on London," and the expression of "mighty heart" applied to the great city.

I dwell amid the city.
The great humanity which beats
 Its life along the stony streets,
Like a strong unsunned river
 In a self-made course, is ever
 Rolling on, rolling on!

We cannot quite agree with this truly-gifted writer that the awful mysteries of the christian faith are suited to mortal verse—we remember that even a Milton could here make the sublime ridiculous, or something worse—but we admire with a heart-warm admiration her *intentions* in this way; and the all-absorbing enthusiasm with which she advocates the cause of devotional poetry. The following passages are magnificently expressed: they are specimens of poetry of the highest order without its rhythm.

"'An irreligious poet,' says Burns, meaning an undevotional one, 'is a monster.' An irreligious poet, he might have said, is no poet at all. The gravitation of poetry is upwards. The poetic wing, if it move, ascends. What did even the heathen Greeks—Homer, Æschylus, Sophocles, Pindar? Sublimely, because born poets; darkly, because born of Adam, and unrenewed in Christ, their spirits wandered like the rushing chariots and winged horses, black and white, of their brother poet Plato, through the universe of Deity, seeking if haply they might find him: and as that universe closed around the seekers, not with the transparency in which it flowed first from his hand, but opaquely, as double-dyed with the transgression of its sons; they felt, though they could not discern, the God beyond, and used the gesture, though ignorant of the language of worshipping. The blind eagle missed the sun, but soared towards its sphere. Shall the blind eagle soar, and the seeing eagle peck chaff? Surely it should be the gladness and the gratitude of such as are poets among us, that in turning towards the beautiful, they may behold the true face of God."

After mentioning that the subject of the principal poem (*The Seraphim*) in this collection was suggested to her when she was engaged upon her translation of the "Prometheus Bound," Miss Barrett continues in this lofty strain—

"I thought that had Æschylus lived after the incarnation and crucifixion of our Lord Jesus Christ, he might have turned, if not in moral and intellectual, yet in poetic faith, from the solitude of Caucasus to the deeper desertness of that crowded Jerusalem where none had any pity; from the 'faded white flower' of the Titanic brow, to the 'withered grass' of a Heart trampled on by its own beloved; from the glorying of him who gloried that he could not die, to the sublimer meekness of the taster of death for every man; from the taunt stung into being from the torment, to HIS more awful silence, when the agony stood dumb before the love! And I thought how, 'from the height of this great argument,' the scenery of the Prometheus would have dwarfed itself even in the eyes of its poet,—how the fissures of his rocks and the innumerous smiles of his ocean would have closed and waned into blankness,—and his demigod stood confest, so human a conception as to fall below the aspiration of his own humanity. He would have turned from such to the rent rocks and darkened sun—rent and darkened by a sympathy thrilling through nature, but leaving man's heart untouched—to the multitudes, whose victim was their Saviour—to the Victim, whose sustaining thought beneath an unexampled agony was not the Titanic 'I can revenge,' but the celestial 'I can forgive?'

* * * * *

"I have worn no shoes upon this holy ground: I have stood there, but have not walked. I have drawn no copy of the statue of this GREAT PAN,—but have caught its shadow,—shortened in the dawn of my imperfect knowledge, and distorted and broken by the unevenness of our earthly ground. I have written no work, but a suggestion. Nor has even so little been attempted, without as deep a consciousness of weakness as the severest critic and the humblest Christian could desire to impress upon me. I have felt, in the midst of my own thoughts upon my own theme, like Homer's 'children in a battle.'

"The agents in this poem of imperfect form—a dramatic lyric, rather than a lyrical drama—are those mystic beings who are designated in Scripture the Seraphim. The subject has thus assumed a character of exaggerated difficulty, the full sense of which I have tried to express in my Epilogue. But my desire was, to gather some vision of the supreme spectacle under a less usual aspect,—to glance at it, as dilated in seraphic eyes, and darkened and deepened by the near association with blessedness and heaven. Are we not too apt to measure the depth of the Saviour's humiliation from the common estate of man, instead of from his own peculiar and primeval one? To avoid which error, I have endeavoured to count some steps of the ladder at Bethel,—a very few steps, and as seen between the clouds.

"And thus I have endeavoured to mark in my two seraphic personages, distinctly and predominantly, that shrinking from and repugnance to, evil, which, in my weaker Seraph, is expressed by *fear*, and, in my stronger one, by a more complex passion; in order to contrast with such, the voluntary debasement of him who became lower than the angels, and touched in his own sinless being, sin, and sorrow, and death. In my attempted production of such a contrast, I have been true to at least my own idea of angelic excellence, as well as to that of his perfection. For one holiness differs from another holiness in glory. To recoil from evil, is according to the stature of an angel; to subdue it, is according to the infinitude of a God."

Coleridge might have written or *spoken* these words in one of his rapt moments, when he was three parts in heaven. The poem to which they refer, though the longest and most substantial in the book, is not, to our tastes, the best. It contains, however, passages of feeling and lofty imagination which, perhaps, no two, certainly no *three* of our living poets could surpass. We regret to say that the last line of all is a striking specimen of bathos—a negligence, or a slip, calculated to excite a familiar, mean, and ridiculous idea. The earthly garment of the Saviour was rolled 'in *red blood*,' in order that the feeble, the frail, and the faint, according to this unhappy expression,

Before his heavenly throne should walk *in white*.

The next piece in the volume, entitled the "Poet's Vow," is exquisite, and all but perfect; and the same may be said of the "Romaunt of Margaret," "Isobel's Child," "The Devoted Garden," [*sic*] "The Soul's Travelling," and the "Stanzas on the Death of Mrs. Hemans."

As our extracts must be of the shortest, we have chosen the following, to give some faint idea of a truly original and gifted author, whose works, we trust, will soon be as well known and as warmly admired as they deserve to be.

MEMORY AND HOPE.

Back-looking Memory
And Hope prophetic sprang from out the ground!
One, where the flashing of cherubic sword
Fell downward, sad and broad;
And one, from Eden earth, within the sound
Of the four rivers lapsing pleasantly,
What time the promise after curse was said—
"Thy seed shall bruise his head."

Memory is very wild,
As moon-struck by cherubic flashings near,
When she was born! Her deep eyes shine and shone
With light that conquereth sun,
And stars to wanner paleness year by year.
With sweetest scents, she mixeth things defiled—
She trampleth down earth's grasses green and sweet,
With her far-wandering feet.

She plucketh many flowers,
Their beauty on her bosom's coldness killing;
She teacheth every melancholy sound
To winds and waters round;
She droppeth tears with seed, where man is tilling
The rugged soil in yet more rugged hours;
She smileth—ah me! in her smile doth go
A mood of deeper woe!

Hope seemed of happier sprite.
Crowned with an Eden wreath she saw not fade,
She went a nodding through the wilderness—

With brow that shone no less
Than sea-bird wings, by storm more frequent made—
Searching the treeless rock for fruits of light;
Her white feet being armed from stones and cold
By slippers all of gold!

And Memory did her wrong,
And, while she dreamed, her slippers stole away!
But still she wended on, with mirth unheeding,
The while her feet were bleeding;
Until she met her on a certain day,
And with her evil eyes did search her long
And cruelly, whereat she sank to ground
In a stark deadly swound.

And so my Hope were slain,
Had it not been that thou wert standing near,
O Thou! who saidst "live" to spirits lying
In thine own blood, and dying!
For Thou her forehead to thine heart didst rear,
And make its silent pulses sing again,—
Pouring a new light o'er her darkened eyne,
With tender tears from Thine!

Therefore my Hope arose
From out her swound, and gazed upon Thy face!
And meeting there that soft subduing look
Which Peter's spirit shook,
Sank downwards in a rapture to embrace
Thy pierced hands and feet with kisses close,
And prayed Thee to assist her evermore
To "reach the things before."

Then gavest Thou the smile
Whence angel wings thrill quick like summer lightning;
Vouchsafing rest beside Thee, where she never
From Love and Faith may sever!
Whereat the Eden crown she saw not whitening,
A time ago, though whitening all the while,
Reddened with life, to hear the voice which talked
To Adam as he walked!

VICTORIA'S TEARS.

Hark! the reiterated clangour sounds!
Now mariners, like the sea or like the storm,
Or like the flames on forests, move and mount
From rank to rank, and loud and louder roll;
Till all the people is one vast applause.
                         LANDOR'S GEBIR.

O maiden! heir of kings!
A king has left his place!
The majesty of Death has swept
All other from his face!
And thou upon thy mother's breast,
No longer lean adown,
But take the glory for the rest,
And rule the land that loves thee best!
She heard and wept—
She wept, to wear a crown!

They decked her courtly halls;
They reined her hundred steeds;
They shouted at her palace gate,
A noble Queen succeeds!
Her name has stirred the mountain's sleep,
Her praise has filled the town!

And mourners God had stricken deep,
Looked hearkening up, and did not weep.
Alone she wept—
Who wept to wear a crown!

She saw no purple shine,
For tears had dimmed her eyes;
She only knew her childhood's flowers
Were happier pageantries!
And while her heralds played the part,
For million shouts to drown—
"God save the Queen!" from hill to mart,
She heard through all her beating heart,
And turned and wept—
She wept, to wear a crown!

God save thee, weeping Queen!
Thou shalt be well beloved!
The tyrant's sceptre cannot move,
As those pure tears have moved!
The nature in thine eyes we see,
That tyrants cannot own—
The love that guardeth liberties;
Strange blessing in the nation lies,
Whose sovereign wept—
Yea! wept to wear its crown!

God bless thee, weeping Queen,
With blessing more divine!
And fill with happier love than earth's
That tender heart of thine!
That when the thrones of earth shall be
As low as graves brought down;
A pierced hand may give to thee
The crown which angels shout to see!
Thou wilt not *weep*
To wear that heavenly crown!

THE SERAPHIM. *The Monthly Chronicle*, August 1838, p. 195.

A POEM of high excellence, but still higher promise, by Miss Barrett, called "The Seraphim," may be described as a bold attempt to catch some of the points of a subject, the whole scope of which could hardly be compassed by the loftiest powers. The structure of the poem is lyrical—the form is in some sort dramatic. The action described is that of the Crucifixion, which is supposed to be witnessed by two of the seraphim, as they are winging earthward. The dialogue that takes place between these spirits furnishes the *materiel* of the verse. The combination of sublimity—suggested, but not developed—of natural grace and ethereal beauty in this production, may be at once admitted as a favourable evidence of the poetical temperament of the writer. There are some passages in this sketch of unusual delicacy, and, on the other hand, many feeble and affected lines. In the same volume there are several minor pieces, which, though less ambitious in design, are more perfect in execution. The more simple of these are indeed gems equally pure and lustrous; and in them every lover of poetry must find delight, and every student of poetry a model.

[Edward Bulwer-Lytton]

THE SERAPHIM. *The Monthly Review*, September 1838, pp. 125–130.

"THE SERAPHIM, and other Poems," by Miss Barrett, the able translator of no less a work of genius than the "Prometheus Bound" of Æschylus, is by far the most remarkable and promising work of the four.* These pieces are in various respects extraordinary productions, and especially, when considered as the compositions of a female, must they command admiration and awaken hope. Still it is rather on account of the promise they give than their own positive qualities that we admire the author; for while they afford ample evidence of a singularly original mind, yet the peculiarities of that mind, which must be carefully directed and forcibly controuled to render them advantageously available, seem to be so strongly interwoven with the beauties and powers of her genius, that we almost make ourselves sure of witnessing its shipwreck. Sacred subjects are her themes, and Miss Barrett can soar aloft and happily seize upon them. But, alas! such is her flightiness and such the indulgence of a vigorous and restless wing, that she is constantly putting our complacency to a severe test, and alarming us or making us conscious that we are upon the verge of what will precipitate herself and her readers to an offensive or irrecoverable condition. We have not room for doing critical justice or even showing to proper advantage any of the special beauties of the main poem; and finding ourselves at present thus precluded, we shall merely have recourse to one or two of the miscellaneous pieces, which, however, are sufficiently characteristic to bear out any general opinion we have offered. But to show that Miss Barrett's mind and genius are after no ordinary stamp, and that the "Seraphim" aims at no mean or common object, let us present a specimen of what she can do in prose, that specimen, besides, explaining her own intentions in the principal poem before us:—

"The subject of the principal poem in the present collection having suggested itself to me, though very faintly and imperfectly, when I was engaged upon my translation of the 'Prometheus Bound' of Æschylus, I thought, that, had Æschylus lived after the incarnation and crucifixion of our Lord Jesus Christ, he might have turned, if not in moral and intellectual yet in poetic faith, from the solitude of Caucasus to the deeper desertness of that crowded Jerusalem where none had any pity; from the 'faded white flower' of the Titanic brow, to the 'withered grass' of a Heart trampled on by its own beloved; from the glorying of him who gloried that he could not die, to the sublimer meekness of the Taster of death for every man; from the taunt stung into being by the torment, to HIS more awful silence, when the agony stood dumb before the love! And I thought, how, 'from the height of this great argument,' the scenery of the Prometheus would have dwarfed itself even in the eyes of its poet—how the fissures of his rocks and the innumerous smiles of his ocean would have closed and waned into blankness—and his demigod stood confest, so human a conception as to fall below the aspiration of his own humanity. He would have turned from such to the

---

*Reviewed with *The Seraphim*, under the title "Minor Books of Poetry," were three other titles, here omitted.

darkened sun—rent and darkened by a sympathy thrilling through nature, but leaving man's heart untouched—to the multitudes, whose victim was their Saviour—to the Victim, whose sustaining thought beneath an unexampled agony, was not the Titanic 'I can revenge,' but the celestial 'I can forgive!'"

Our first selections from her smaller pieces shall belong to "Isobel's Child," a lyric founded upon the simple idea of a young mother keeping her vigils over her sick babe, and uttering yearning love-prayers for its restoration to health:—

    Motionless she sate!—
The hair had fallen by its weight
On either side the smile, and lay
Very blackly on the arm
Where the baby nestled warm!—
Pale as baby carved in stone
And seen by glimpses of the moon
    In a dark cathedral aisle!—
But through the storm no moonbeam fell
Upon the child of Isobel!—
I ween you saw it by the ray
    Alone of her still smile.
'Tis aye a solemn thing to me
To look upon a babe that sleeps—
Wearing in its spirit-deeps
The unrevealëd mystery
Of its Adam's taint and woe,
Which, when they revealëd be,
Will not let it slumber so!
Lying new in Life beneath
The shadow of the coming death,
With that soft low quiet breath,
    As if it felt the sun!—
Knowing all things by their blooms,
Not their roots!—yea!—sun and sky,
Only by the warmth that comes
Out of each!—earth, only by
The pleasant hues that o'er it run!—
And human love, by drops of sweet
White nourishment still hanging round
The little mouth so slumber-bound!—
All which broken sentiency
Will gather and unite and climb
To an immortality
Good or evil, each sublime,
Through life and death to life again!—
O little lids, now closëd fast!
Must ye learn to drop at last
Our large and burning tears?—
O warm quick body! must thou lie,
When is done the round of years,
Bare of all the joy and pain,
Dust in dust—thy place upgiving
To creeping worms in sentient living?—
She had seen eight days depart,
Hour by hour, on bended knees,
With pale-wrung hands and prayings low
And broken—through which came the sound
Of tears that fell against the ground,
Making sad stops! "Dear Lord, dear Lord!"
She aye had prayed—(the heavenly word,
Broken by an earthly sigh!)
"Thou who didst not erst deny
The mother-joy to Mary mild
Blessëd in the blessëd child—
Hearkening in meek babyhood

Her cradle-hymn, albeit used
To all that music interfused
In breasts of angels high and good!
Oh, take not, Lord, my babe away:
Oh, take not to thy songful heaven,
The pretty baby thou hast given;
Or ere that I have seen him play
Around his father's knees, and known
That *he* knew how my love hath gone
    From all the world to him!
And how that I shall shiver, dim
In the sunshine, thinking e'er
The grave-grass keeps it from his fair
Still cheeks! and feel at every tread
His little body which is dead
And hidden in the turfy fold,
Doth make the whole warm earth a'cold!
O God! I am so young, so young—
I am not used to tears at nights
Instead of slumber—nor to prayer
With shaken lips and hands out-wrung!
Thou knowest all my prayings were
'I bless thee, God, for past delights—
Thank God!' I am not used to bear
Hard thoughts of death? The earth doth cover
No face from me of friend or lover!
And must the first who teacheth me
The form of shrouds and funerals, be
Mine own first-born beloved? he
Who taught me first this mother-love?
Dear Lord, who spreadest out above
Thy loving pierced hands to meet
All lifted hearts with blessing sweet,—
Pierce not my heart, my tender heart,
Thou madest tender! Thou who art
So happy in thy heaven alway,
Take not mine only bliss away!"

Our readers are to imagine that the child drops into a gentle sleep, as if in answer to the importunate and agonizing uncertainty of the watcher. She begins to indulge careering and bright hopes, and in her exultation cannot but be led to prophesy, to gaze into the future regarding the powers, the doings, and the destinies of her son. But alas the Angel of Death is at hand, and the response of the Spirit, coming miraculously from the lips of the child, informs her that it is not the mortal glory or fame which genius earns on earth that she so passionately longs to witness that is worthy of such ecstacies of hope:—

    "Is your wisdom wise
Mother, on the narrow earth?
Very happy, very worth
That I should stay to learn?
Are these air-corrupting sighs
Fashioned by unlearned breath?
Do the student's lamps that burn
All night, illumine?
Mother! albeit this be so,
Loose thy prayer and let me go
Where that bright chief angel stands
Apart from all his brother bands
Too glad for smiling! having bent
In angelic wilderment
O'er the depths of God, and brought
Reeling, thence, one only thought
To fill his whole eternity!
He the teacher is for me!—

He can teach what I would know—
Mother, mother let me go!
Can your poet make an Eden
No winter will undo?
And light a starry fire, in heeding
His hearth's is burning too?
Drown in music, earthly din?—
And keep his own wild soul within
The law of his own harmony?—
Mother! albeit this be so,
Let me to mine Heaven go!
A little harp me waits thereby—
A harp whose strings are golden all,
And tuned to music spherical,
Hanging on the green life-tree,
Where no willows ever be.
Shall I miss that harp of mine?
Mother, no!—the Eye divine
Turned upon it makes its shine—
And when I touch it poems sweet,
Like separate souls shall fly from it,
Each to an immortal fytte!
We shall all be poets there,
Gazing on the chiefest Fair!"

There is something not very remote from a trenching on debateable ground in more than one portion of these remarkable extracts. It will be seen also that the fair writer is easily led into the pursuit of fantastic images and overwrought conceits, when the nature of the topic and the solemnity of concomitant thoughts demand a sustained and straightforward simplicity. But the beauty and the power of the poetess are, nevertheless, so apparent in these lines, that the reader must feel she has only to set her mind to the task and she will perform still more admirable things. We present another specimen, in which imagination and depth of sentiment are finely blended.

The Sea-Mew.

How joyously the young sea-mew
Lay dreaming on the waters blue,
Whereon our little bark had thrown
A forward shade—the only one—
(But shadows aye will man pursue!)

Familiar with the waves, and free,
As if their own white foam were he:
His heart upon the heart of ocean,
Learning all its mystic motion,
And throbbing to the throbbing sea!

And such a brightness in his eye,
As if the ocean, and the sky,
Within him had lit up and nurst
A soul God gave him not at first,
To comprehend their majesty.

We were not cruel, yet did sunder
His white wing from the blue waves under,
And bound it—while his fearless eyes
Shone up to ours in calm surprise,
As deeming us some ocean wonder!

We bore our ocean bird into
A grassy place where he might view
The flowers bending to the bees,
The waving of the tall green trees,
The falling of the silver dew.

But flowers of earth were pale to him
Who had seen the rainbow fishes swim;
And when earth's dew around him lay,
He thought of ocean's wingèd spray;
And his eye waxèd sad and dim.

The green trees round him only made
A prison, with their darksome shade:
And drooped his wing, and mournèd he
For his own boundless glittering sea—
Albeit he knew not they could fade!

Then One her gladsome face did bring,
Her gentle voice's murmuring,
In ocean's stead his heart to move,
And teach him what was human love—
He thought it a strange, mournful thing!

He lay down in his grief to die,
(First looking to the sea-like sky,
That hath no waves!) because, alas!
Our human touch did on him pass!
And with our touch, our agony.

An Essay on Mind; Prometheus Bound; and *The Seraphim. The Sunbeam,*
1 September 1838, pp. 243, 245; 8 September, pp. 254–255;
22 September, pp. 269–270; 6 October, p. 287; 13 October, pp. 293–295.

WE THIS week give the commencement of a review on Miss Barrett's poems, and of another on Mr. Thomas Carlyle's *Sartor Resartus;* for both which we expect the reasonable thanks of our readers. Each of these works has been before the public for some weeks, and has doubtless received such notice as the ordinary publications afford. But something more is wanted by the present state of literature; and therefore, we mean to adopt, in our reviewing department, a very different system from that which is now only too common.

In illustration of our proposed method, we beg to refer to the practice of some portion of the French press, in relation to the stage. Unlike ourselves, our neighbours are not solicitous of inserting an *ad captandum* notice in the next morning's paper, in review of the over-night's performance; but wait for days, or weeks, until the critic has had ample means of judging of a new piece—a new actor—or a new part; and then, duly prepared and informed, the writer proceeds to the composition of an elaborate essay upon the subject. Thus, the decision is well-weighed, before it is pronounced, and the review is worthy of its subject and its author.

In like manner, it is our intention to deal with all possible matters, that in our opinions there may be always something of permanent value, however temporary may seem to be the topic dealt with. We shall continue both the subjects we have alluded to, until we extract the heart and soul from them, and present to the reader the very concentrated essence of their virtue. There is enough of weekly reviewing, and reviewing of all kinds, which is only meant to be read for the day and then thrown aside for ever. We shall select the worthiest works, and hold them up in a mirror which the reader shall prize both for ornament and use. We will give, in "The Sunbeam," a standard for criticism, such as has seldom if ever been witnessed. We have the means of doing it, and it shall be done.

THE POETRY OF ELIZABETH B. BARRETT.

We have already, as our readers well know, noticed in terms of great commendation the poems of Elizabeth B. Barrett.* But it is not by means of a cursory notice that poetic merit like hers should be rewarded. Perceiving of what *calibre* her genius was, we determined, pursuant to a design more particularly announced in our leading article of the present number, to give this lady a prominent place on the first opportunity, in our reviewing department. That opportunity now occurs, and we proceed in our promise.

The title-page of *The Seraphim*, and other poems, mentions the authoress as a translator of Æschylus' *Prometheus Bound*. Her version of this splendid drama we had not seen, but desired much to read. When we succeeded in obtaining a sight of it, we found it to be anonymous,—we were again referred on to an *Essay of Mind and other Poems*, by the same writer. This last work we were lucky enough to possess, by some chance, in our own library. We have, therefore, now before us ample materials for judging of this new and prerogative appearance in the arena of poetic endeavour.

It is not with a slight and cursory notice, as we have before intimated, that a true poet should be greeted. Here is one, who has previously made two attempts on the public mind, from which no impression has been received—worthy attempts, too; and in the meanwhile, a cry was raised that the fountains of poesy had been dried-up at its source, that the tree of poesy had been withered branch and bole and root, that the time for the singing of birds had utterly gone, and that the turtle should no more be heard in our land for ever and ever.

Never, perhaps, was a more profane and impious assertion made than this. Do the raisers of such a cry know what poetry is, and why it was granted as a gift by God to man? Do they know that it is one of the highest and holiest of things, and never can cease while piety and religion are dwellers of man's bosom?—never while hope and fear and memory and love are the elements of man's life? Little they know, and less they feel, who dream of the possibility of poetry decaying. Let it be no less esteemed than a perpetual inspiration, for the supply of truth and goodness, and beauty, as oracular utterances, even when they cease to be visibly exhibited in the character and conduct of men, in their daily walk and conversation.

The poet Southey, says rightly in his *Colloquies*, that in these days, there is, and will be, more verse written than ever. He adds, "but that there will be less printed." Now, we say, that more poetry will be written undoubtedly; and we believe more printed too; but perhaps not more in proportion to the quantity produced. Much of what has been written of the kind implied by Southey, has fallen under the eye of the present writer; and all bespeaks to his apprehension an increased susceptibility to poetical influences, and an originality and a facility in expressing them, peculiar to the present age in England, and giving promise of her at length rivalling Greece in the truthfulness and abundance of the poetical harvest.

The tendencies that he remarks are chiefly of a lyrical kind, and the feeling and experiences embodied of a personal character. Self-introspections—mystical speculations—spiritual aspirations—remote and interior analogies—these are the subjects mostly of poetic argument, with the increasing number of minds who are seeking now to pour themselves forth in the media of verses; and thereby to get rid of the haunting thoughts—the air drawn daggers that float before the heat-oppressed brain—the over-stimulated nerves—and the excited states of being, that education induces in the mind which it instructs and awakens into consciousness of power and desire of action.

One of this class evidently is ELIZABETH BARRETT, and one who has been for some period endeavouring to procure audience for the communications which her bosom was throbbing to deliver. For a long time she must have been accustomed to self-investigation, and have qualified herself for looking into the essences of things about her, by forming a previous acquaintance with that essential thing which she herself was, and is, and will be. The fact of her commencing with an Essay upon Mind, is of itself a sufficient ostent and indication of psychological habits. She repudiated the notion that poetry is not a proper vehicle for abstract ideas;—she disdained to believe that the imaginative is incompatible with the philosophic. With the name of Bacon upon her lips, she demands finely, why should we expel the argumentative from the limits of the poetic? She beheld in poetry, the inspiritings to political feeling—the *monumentum ære perennius* of buried nations; and therefore had faith in poetry being on a level with any walk of intellect however high, and in the poetic spirit being equal to the loftiest exercises of ratiocination. With the works before her of the great though erring Lucretius, the sublime Dante, the syllogistic Pope,—corroborated by a Quintillian's acknowledgment of submission due from philosophers to poets—and a Gibbon's declaration that Homer was the lawgiver, the theologian, and the philosopher of the ancients—poetry to her was nothing less than the enthusiasm of the understanding; and, with Milton, she burned to confess "the high reason" that must ever be recognized "in her fancies," by whoso is capable, and apt to finely perceive the fine issues whereto heaven itself has touched some hearts and lips, for the illustration of its own mysteries.

Such an one was precisely the spirit to attempt an Essay on Mind in immortal verse. She had no need to wish that it had fallen to the lot of one more familiar than herself with the dwelling-place of mind;—one who could better search her secret chambers, and call forth those that sleep;—one who could fitlier enter into her temples and cast out the iniquitous who buy and sell, profaning the sanctuary of God; one who could wiselier try the golden links of that chain which hangs from heaven to earth, and show that it is not placed there for man to covet for lucre's sake, or for him to weigh his puny strength at one end against omnipotence at the other, but that it is placed there to join in mysterious union the natural and the spiritual, the mortal and the eternal, the creature and the Creator. Still, with the modesty of true genius, she did wish this—and only reconciled herself to the task to which she was appointed, by the reflection that if she had failed in representing, she had never ceased to love Truth. What capacity would not be narrow as opposed to the infinite object that she sought to embrace? To us, the illustrations that she has rendered are dear for the sake of their subject, and receive elevation from having been identified with an argument so exalted. Thus, (to use her own exquisite language) the waters of Halys acquire a peculiar taste from the soil over which they flow.

With trembling steps she might well adventure on the field of endeavour which her muse has best delighted to cultivate. It will be our part, in our next number, to trace her print-marks,—to follow her in her wanderings—to mark her progress—and to declare the station where

---

*On 11 August 1838, p. 219, *The Seraphim* was described as "beautiful exceedingly."

we find her at present to have arrived. Nor will our readers be less delighted than ourselves, by partaking of this enchanting pursuit, to which we heartily invite them all this day week.

[Continued in the issue of 8 September 1838.]

It is now twelve years ago since Miss Barrett's *Essay on Mind* was published, yet new to the world, (is it not?) as if it appeared only yesterday. Well! it was with trembling steps, as we have said, that she ventured on the mighty argument; for clear enough it is that her mind was then less developed than it is now. This might have been expected. She seems to have considered, at that time, that Byron was the chief of poets, and Jeffrey the chief of critics. In this, the gifted one shared the error of the multitude. In the same degree she depreciated the merits of Southey; nor did his hexameters meet with much favour at her hands. We believe that there is no reference to Wordsworth, or to Coleridge, in the whole two books, of which her poem consists. Scott, and Moore, and Rogers, and Campbell, were evidently overestimated by her in this part of her progress. Indicative these omissions and commissions, of immature judgment and defective experience. Time was evidently wanted to perfect the fruit which was but as yet green.

On the other hand, we find her capable of admiring Irving's *pierian* eloquence, which, at the time she speaks of, was certainly captivating, soul-stirring, and instructive, yet infected with certain taints and spots that prophesied the possible fall one day of the mighty in speech and action! Historical scepticism, as illustrated in the Gibbons and Humes, and Mitfords, falls in for condemnation; and indeed, to the historical spirit in itself, she shows but little quarter. For the philosophical, she manifests some esteem, and for the poetical, much love. Sometimes, however, she wanders into the vulgar hypothesis that poetry draws from nature. We like her better when exclaiming,

> All poetry is beauty, but exprest
> In inward essence, not in outward vest.
> Hence lovely scenes, reflective poets find,
> Awake their lovelier images in Mind;
> Nor doth the pictur'd earth, the bard invite,
> The lake of azure, or the heav'n of light,
> But that his swelling breast arouses there,
> Something less visible, and much more fair!
> There is a music in the landscape round,—
> A silent voice, that speaks without a sound—
> A witching spirit, that reposing near,
> Breathes to the heart, but comes not to the ear!
> These softly steal, his kindling soul t' embrace,
> And natural beauty, gild with moral grace.
> Think not, when summer breezes tell their tale,
> The poet's thoughts are with the summer gale;
> Think not his Fancy builds her elfin dream
> On painted flowret, or on sighing stream:
> No single objects cause his raptured starts,
> For Mind is narrow'd, not inspir'd by parts;
> But o'er the scene the poet's spirit broods,
> To warm the thoughts that form his noblest moods;
> Peopling his solitude with faëry play,
> And beckoning shapes that whisper him away,—
> While lilied fields, and hedge-row blossoms white,
> And hills, and glittering streams, are full in sight—
> The forests wave, the joyous sun beguiles,
> And all the poetry of Nature smiles!

> Such poetry is formed by Mind, and not
> By scenic grace of one peculiar spot.
> The artist lingers in the moon-lit glade,
> And light and shade, with him, are—light and shade.
> The philosophic chymist wandering there,
> Dreams of the soil, and nature of the air.
> The rustic marks the young herbs' fresh'ning hue,
> And only thinks—his scythe may soon pass through!
> None "muse on nature with a Poet's eye,"
> None read, but Poets, Nature's poetry!
> Its characters are trac'd in mystic hand,
> And all may gaze, but few can understand.

The conclusion of the poem is fine:—

> I love my own dear land—it doth rejoice
> The soul, to stretch my arms, and lift my voice,
> To tell her of my love! I love her green,
> And bowery woods, her hills in mossy sheen,
> Her silver running waters—there's no spot
> In all her dwelling, which my breast loves not—
> No place not heart-enchanted! Sunnier skies,
> And calmer waves, may meet another's eyes;
> I love the sullen mist, the stormy sea,
> The winds of rushing strength which,
>   like the land, are free!
> Such is my love—yet turning thus to thee,
> Oh Græcia! I must hail with hardly less
> Of joy, and pride, and deepening tenderness,
> And feelings wild, I know not to contrioul,
> My other country—country of my soul!
> For so, to me, thou art! my lips have sung
> *Of* thee with childhood's lisp, and harp unstrung!
> *In* thee, my Fancy's pleasant walks have been,
> Telling her tales, while Memory wept between!
> And now *for* thee I joy, with heart beguiled,
> As if a dying friend looked up, and smiled.

>   Lo! o'er Ægæa's waves, the shout hath ris'n!
> Lo! Hope hath burst the fetters of her prison!
> And Glory sounds the trump along the shore,
> And Freedom walks where Freedom walk'd before!
> Ipsara glimmers with heroic light,
> Redd'ning the waves that lash her flaming height;
> And Ægypt hurries from that dark blue sea!
> Lo! o'er the cliffs of famed Thermopylæ
> And voiceful Marathon, the wild winds sweep,
> Bearing this message to the brave who sleep—
> "They come! they come! with their embattled shock,
> From Pelion's steep and Paros' foam-dash'd rock!
> They come from Tempe's vale, and Helicon's spring,
> And proud Eurotas' banks, the river king!
> They come from Leuctra, from the waves that kiss
> Athena—from the shores of Salamis,
> From Sparta, Thebes, Eubœa's hills of blue—
> To live with Hellas—or to sleep with you!"

>   Smile—smile, beloved land! and though no lay
> From Doric pipe, may charm thy glades to day—
> Though dear Ionic music murmur not
> Adown the vale—its echo all forgot!
> Yet smile, beloved land! for soon, around,
> Thy silent earth shall utter forth a sound,
> As whilom—and, its pleasant groves among,
> The Grecian voice shall breathe the Grecian song,
> While the exiled muse shall 'habit still
> The happy haunts of her Parnassian hill.

Till then, behold the cold dumb sepulchre—
The ruin'd column—ocean, earth, and air,
Man, and his wrongs—thou has Tyrtæus there!

And pardon, if across the heaving main,
Sound the far melody of minstrel strain,
In wild and fitful gust from England's shore,
For *his* immortal sake, who never more
Shall tread with living foot, and spirit free,
Her fields, or breathe her passionate poetry—
The pilgrim bard, who lived, and died for thee,
Oh land of Memory! loving thee no less
Than parent—with the filial tenderness,
And holy ardour of the Argive son,
Straining each nerve to bear thy chariot on—
Till when its wheels the place of glory swept,
He laid him down before the shrine—and slept.

So be it! at his cold unconscious bier,
We fondly sate, and dropp'd the natural tear—
Yet wept not wisely, for he sank to rest
On the dear earth his waking thoughts loved best,
And gently life's last pulses stole away!
No Moschus sang a requiem o'er his clay,
But Greece was sad! and breathed above, below,
The warrior's sigh, the silence, and the woe!

The remaining thirty or forty lines are of inferior merit.

The versification of the poems in this volume is far more mechanical than in the author's later publications. The lyric verses have not the same freedom and flow—that mastery had not yet been won which should be ultimately—nevertheless, it was winning—and though thought and feeling were struggling with expression, thought and feeling were there to struggle. Clear enough there was hope.

Eight years had passed, and their immaterial suns had ripened her soul with the light of light, and the fruit of psychological experience, growing on that tree of life, had proved for the healing of opinion and taste, wherever they had suffered from the world's contact and accident. Æschylus presents difficulties to the manliest Greek scholar—think of these rugged obstacles to a woman's mind!—then think that they have been conquered, and then esteem Elizabeth Barrett as ye ought!

It has been stated that the drama of Greece was unlike our own, in not having ascended to excellence by slow steps. In our own, there are many names of the illustrious obscure, previous to that of Shakspere. Æschylus stood alone; having only his country's legends for quarry, out of which the dramatic sculptor shaped those stately groups which, by their stern beauty, gave his fellow men a love for dramatic representation. Stern, indeed, was the beauty in which he delighted—austere—sublime—terrible. It was like that of the antediluvian Amazarah:—

——Whose beauty was so terrible,
Whose courage wooed her merited reward
Of ample realm and huge metropolis;
Ay, for surpassing bravery, merited
Power and all adoration, like a god.

What with a masculine genius like this was a woman to do. To her, the beauty so extravagant, must have been as sublimity, and the sublimity!—why—even as the ineffably divine! Nay, had not even a man signally failed in rendering this great poet? Who can endure to read Potter's version? With a boldness only to be accounted for by the rightful consciousness of power, Elizabeth Barrett felt that, even relative to this mighty mind as

manifested in his mightiest work, *The Prometheus,* "a mirror may be held in different lights by different hands; and, according to the position of those hands, will the light fall. A picture may be imitated in different ways,—by steel engraving, or stone engraving; and according to the vocation of the artist will the copy be." But it is desirable, as the translator justly opines, that the same composition should be conveyed by different minds, that the character of the medium may not be necessarily associated with the thing conveyed.

The would-be originality of the present age, operates against the success of translations, however excellent; nor would Elizabeth Barrett nor would we repine at this. Let it dream its undreamt of dreams—let it glow with unearthly frenzy. If its dreams be noble dreams, may they, exclaim we both, be dreamt on; if its frenzy be the evidence of inspiration, may we, as Prometheus said, be mad! But let the age take heed, warns the muse before us, "There is one step from dreaming nobly to sleeping inertly; and one from frenzy to imbecility."

"I do not ask," she continues, "I would not obtain, that our age should be servilely imitative of any former age. Surely it may think its own thoughts and speak its own words, yet turn not away from those who *have* thought and spoken well. The contemplation of excellence produces excellence, if not similar, yet parallel. We do not turn from green hills and waving forests, because we build and inhabit palaces; nor do we turn towards them, that we may model them in painted wax. We make them subjects of contemplation, in order to abstract from them those ideas of beauty, afterwards embodied in our own productions; and, above all, in order to consider their and our Creator under every manifestation of his goodness and his power. All beauties, whether in nature or art, whether in physics or morals, whether in composition or abstract reasoning, are multiplied reflections, visible in different distances and under different positions, of one archetypal beauty. If we owe gratitude to Him, who created and unveiled its form, should we refuse to gaze upon those reflections? Because they rest even upon heathen scrolls, should we turn away from those scrolls? Because thorns and briers are the product of the earth, should we avert our eyes from that earth? The mind of man and the earth of man are cursed alike.

"But the age would not be 'classical.' 'O, that profaned name!' What does it mean, and what is it made to mean? It does not mean what it is made to mean: it does not mean what is necessarily regular, and polished, and unimpassioned. The ancients, especially the ancient Greeks, felt, and thought, and wrote antecedently to rules: they felt passionately, and thought daringly; and wrote because they felt and thought. Shakspeare is a more classical writer than Racine."

How qualified to judge of the character of *Prometheus,* was the author before us, no other evidence is required than that of the passage which we gave in the Family Circle of No. 28, under the title of "Prometheus." We say, that that passage gives sufficient evidence, that Elizabeth Barrett is qualified to estimate Æschylus' claims, for his Conception of Character, as worked out in this dramatic person. It would seem as if he himself had been desirous of resting his ambition on even such fulcrum, and none other in this tragedy.

For, as our author justly observes, it is not in Æschylus' usual manner to produce upon his canvass any very prominent figure, to which every other is made subordinate, and to which the interest of the spectator is very strongly and almost exclusively attached. Agamemnon's πληγὴν ἔχω we do not feel within our hearts. In the Seven Chiefs, there is a clear division of interest; and the reader willingly agrees with Antigone, that Polynices should be as honourably buried as Eteocles. In the Supplices, we are called upon to exercise universal charity towards fifty heroines. In the Persæ, we cannot weep with Atossa over the misfortunes of Xerxes; not even over what she must femininely considers to be his greatest misfortune—μάλιστα δ᾽ ἥδε συμφορὰ δάκνει—his wearing a tattered garment. Perhaps we know more of Orestes than of any personage, always excepting Prometheus, introduced by Æschylus: and yet both in the Choëphorœ and Eumenides, we are interested in his calamities, rather from their being calamities than from their being his. But Prometheus stands eminent and alone; one of the most original, and grand, and attaching characters ever conceived by the mind of man. That conception sank deeply into the soul of Milton, and, as has been observed, rose from thence in the likeness of his Satan. But the Satan of Milton and the Prometheus of Æschylus stand upon ground as unequal, as do the sublime of sin and the sublime of virtue. Satan suffered from his ambition; Prometheus from his humanity; Satan for himself; Prometheus for mankind: Satan dared perils which he had not weighed; Prometheus devoted himself to sorrows which he had foreknown. 'Better to reign in hell,' said Satan; 'Better to serve this rock,' said Prometheus. But in his hell, Satan yearned to associate man; while Prometheus preferred a solitary agony: nay, he even permitted his zeal and tenderness for the peace of others, to abstract him from that agony's intenseness.

[Continued in the issue of 22 September 1838.]

Not as he deserved was Æschylus rewarded by his country; even Athens could be unjust to the merits of her greatest tragic poet, indeed, the father of her tragedy. Miss Barrett dwells on the bitter feeling with which the conceiver of Prometheus must have regarded this treatment. "Are you not ashamed," said Menander to Philemon, "to conquer me in comedy?" "Such a reproach," she exclaims, "might Æschylus have used to his dramatic rival, and extracted as deep a blush as ever stained Philemon's cheek. But he did not. Silent as his own Prometheus, he left for ever the Athens on whom he had conferred the immortality of his name and works; and went to Sicily to die." Notwithstanding our love for Æschylus, we fear that Miss Barrett has forgotten that this dramatic rival was none other than Sophocles. Could Æschylus *envy* a younger poet? Let us not think it; if we would not have him now contract his divine brows into a frown amid the gardens of Elysium, where haply he may have power of knowing, (for is not Hades the realm of soul?) all that passes respecting himself in the minds of the dwellers on earth. Who shall say that the Fame-immortality which some have substituted for the personal may not be in addition instead, and be even such a privilege as this? Were it not indeed to *live* in human memory? But to quit this pleasant reflection.

There are considerable doubts on the historical point. If Sophocles was only a few years younger than Æschylus—seven or seventeen—he was not very young when his master was sixty-four. Take seventeen from sixty-four and there remains forty-seven; add to this, the circumstance that the prize was adjudged to the last exhibition of "the Father,"—and which exhibition consisted of the *Agamemnon*, the *Choephorœ*, the *Furies*, and a satyric piece. But the tragedy of the *Furies*, we are told, gave great umbrage to the city; and the poet, whether for that or on some other pretence, was accused of impiety. His brother Amynias having pleaded his cause, and thus impressed his audience with a spectacle of fraternal affection; the Athenians reverenced their maimed veteran, and Æschylus was acquitted.

However all this be, certain it is, that the poet quitted his native city indignant. In his place of exile, says Miss Barrett, "he wrote his epitaph instead of tragedies, calling with his dying voice on the grove of Marathon and the conquered Persians, as the only witnesses of his glory."

Marathon and Platæa! ye witnessed what martial spirit could inspire the bosom of a poet. We read not that Æschylus ran away, as a celebrated orator did afterwards when in the shock of fight. The poet is a braver man than the rhetorician. We cannot help thinking here of Glover's *Athenaid*, a neglected poem, superior to the *Leonidas* of the same author, and which ought always to be bound up with the rest of his works. In this poem Æschylus is a prominent person; and thus opens it:—

> A burning ray the summer solstice cast,
> Th' Olympiad was proclaim'd; when Xerxes pour'd
> His millions through Thermopylæ, new-stain'd
> With blood. From Athens Æschylus divine
> In genius, arts, and valour, musing deep
> On his endanger'd country's future doom,
> Repairs, invited by an evening still,
> To clear Ilissus, Attic stream renown'd.
> Beneath on oak, in solitary state
> Apart, itself a wood, the hero's limbs
> On tufted moss repose. He grasps the lyre;
> Unfolded scrolls voluminous he spreads
> Along the ground: high lays repeating thence,
> Leonidas the Spartan he extols,
> And sweeps th' accordant strings. To closing day
> He bade farewell, and hail'd th' ascending stars
> In music long continued; till the stream
> With drowsy murmur won his eye to sleep,
> But left his fancy waking, In a dream,
> The god of day, with full meridian blaze,
> Seem'd to assume his function o'er the skies;
> When, lo! the earth divided: through the cleft
> A gush of radiance dimm'd the noon-tide sun.
> In structure all of diamond, self pois'd,
> Amid redundant light a chariot hung
> Triumphal. Twelve transparent horses breath'd
> Beams from their nostrils, dancing beams of day
> Shook from their manes. In lineaments of man,
> Chang'd to immortal, there the mighty soul
> Of Sparta's king apparent shone. His wounds
> Shot forth a splendour like the clust'ring stars,
> Which on Orion's chest and limbs proclaim
> Him first of constellations. Round in cars
> Of triumph too arrang'd, the stately forms
> Of those whom virtue led to share his doom,
> And consecrate Thermopylæ to fame.
> Pines tipp'd with lightning seem'd their spears; their shields
> Broad like Minerva's ægis: from their helms
> An empyreal brightness stream'd abroad:
> Ineffable felicity their eyes,
> Their fronts the majesty of gods display'd.

He is charged by the awful and honoured shade to alarm the Olympian concourse; and, being thereto further advised by Themistocles, sets out accordingly, not unaccompanied, on a journey to "Phœbean Delphi, seated on a rock abrupt, sublime." There he meets Timon, the priest of Phœbus, whose daughter Amarantha had even that very hour been captured by the barbarians, and who tells his sad story to the tragic bard. The following lines present a grand image.

He scarce had finish'd, when the earth beneath
Rock'd from her centre in convulsive throes;
From pole to pole th' ethereal concave groan'd:
Night from her cavern with gigantic steps
Bestrode the region, lifting high as heav'n
Her broad, infernal palm, whose umbrage hides
The throne of light; while, glancing through the rifts
Of her black mantle, overlaid with clouds,
Blue vapours trail'd their fires. The double head
Of tall Parnassus reeling, from the crag
Unloos'd two fragments; mountainous in bulk,
They roll to Delphi with a crashing sound,
Like thunder nigh whose burst of ruin strikes
The shatter'd ear with horror.

Æschylus advises the priest to arm himself and turn soldier awhile for his daughter's sake; and the party proceed to attack the wrongous invaders, whom, from the suddenness of their onset, they defeat. Then follows the bard's ablution in Castalia's fount and grove; his prayer to Phœbus in his own temple; the prophecy of the Pythian maid—his departure for Elis.

Ready are the barks——
These with extended canvas quit the port,
And, doubling round Achaia, cut the main
To sacred Pisa. On their way the harp
Of Æschylus, preluding to the strain
Which on his banks Alpheus was to hear,
Relieves the sailor toiling at his oar,
Enchants the wind retentive of the sounds
Which harmonize his breath. If round the keel
Of sweet Arion dolphins ever play'd,
Or blithsome Nereids to the pleasing mood
Of Orpheus danc'd, while Argo plough'd the deep;
They now had felt controulment as in bonds,
Not on their pliant, azure-glossy fins
Disporting light, but rigid with amaze
At this majestic muse. Yet sounding verse,
In solemn cadence to the deep-ton'd lyre,
Which could the boist'rous mariner subdue,
The ear of Timon, languid by despair,
Rejects, attentive to his grief alone,
Which sighs within. Society is pain,
Ev'n with his friend.

Timon thought only of his daughter—what to him was the voice of Æschylus, singing on the waters! what is it *not* to us? Honour awaited the bard's landing at Elis—the victor's chaplet—the processional car—the Elean judgment—and Greece's awakening, as one man, in resistance of invasion.

But we must pass from the Glover to the Barrett, who has "brave translunary things" in her of which he had no notion. It is from her deep sympathy with Æschylus that she writes indignantly of his supposed wrongs. But not to dwell on these; his memory has suffered real ones enough to exhaust the stock of a translator's patience. According to Suidas, the Athenians "brake down the benches," on the occasion which gave offence to the poet, and caused his departure for Sicily. This according to Scaliger, would seem to be their mode of condemning the poet. But this violent proceeding, in the Barrett's estimation, is preferable to the "faint-praise" of succeeding Grecian commentators, which damns more surely, or would do, if, after all, truth were not omnipotent, even in this world of deceptive shadows.

The fact is that the game that has been played with Shakspere, and is now, happily, almost played out, was played with Æschylus. Acknowledge, by all means, the poet's genius; but show the *acumen* of the critic, by censuring his taste. The world is slow to admit that the greatest genius involves the correctest judgment.

All comparison of Æschylus with Sophocles and Euripides, is, without question, invidiously meant—and the father of tragedy has suffered much from this kind of abusive opposition, on the part of the ancient critics. It is quite evident that too frequently they render him churlish mention. Of the three great critics of antiquity,— Longinus, Dionysius of Halicarnassus, and Quintilian,— Dionysius alone does not measure his criticism to twice the length of his commendation. Quintilian calls him "rudis in plerisque et incompositus," which the authoress's sense of justice almost gives her courage to call a false criticism. "Longinus," she exclaims, "—Longinus!! uses similar language:—ἐνίοτε μέντοι ἀκατεργάστους καὶ οἱονεὶ ποκοειδεῖς τὰς ἐννοίας καὶ ἀμαλάκτους φέροντος. Now there are, undeniably, some things in Æschylus, which, like the expressions of Callisthenes, would properly fall under the censure of Longinus, as being οὐχ ὑψηλά, ἀλλὰ μετέωρα. But according to every principle by which he himself could urge his immortal claim upon posterity, the Homer of criticism should have named with less of coldness and more of rapture, the Homer of dramatic poetry."

From the poet, let us turn to his poem, and its hero— that powerful portraiture of which the dramatic bard felt the force in its weight and fulness. In sign of this—mark, that he never removes Prometheus from the spectator's sight. Nor do the readers of Æschylus fail to feel its engrossing interest. They are impatient at Io's long narrations; not because those narrations are otherwise than beautiful, but because they would hear Prometheus speak again: they are impatient even at Prometheus's prophetic replies to Io, because they would hear him speak only of Prometheus. From the moment of the first dawning of his character upon their minds, its effect is electrifying. He is silent: he disdains as much to answer the impotent and selfish compassion of Vulcan, as to murmur beneath the brutal cruelty of strength. It was not thus that *he* pitied in the days of his joy: it was not thus that *he* acted in the days of his power: and his spirit is above them, and recks not of them; and when their pity and their scoffs pollute his ears no more, he pours out his impassioned sorrows to the air, and winds, and waters, and earth and sun, whom he had never visited with benefits, and "taxed not with unkindness." The striking nature of these, our first ideas of Prometheus, is not enfeebled by any subsequent ones. We see him daring and unflinching beneath the torturing and dishonouring hand, yet keenly alive to the torture and dishonour; for himself fearless and rash, yet for others considerate and wary; himself unpitied, yet to others pitiful. And when, at the last, he calls no longer upon the sun, and earth, and waters, from whom the Avenger is secluding him; but demands of Æther, who is rolling light to all eyes excepting his, whether he beholds how he suffers by injustice;—our hearts rise up within us, and bear witness that the suffering is indeed unjust.

Now then suppose that Vulcan, Strength, and Force have chained the Providence of God (such is the meaning of *Prometheus*) to the rock of the *World's Necessity*: then under the dominion of "the Prince of the Power of the Air," who was and is "the god of this world;"—and that the sufferer is left alone. Thus he pours out his anguish—

> O holy æther, and swift-winged winds,
> And river founts, and dimples numberless
> Of oceanic waves—all-fostering earth,
> And, all-beholding sun, on thee I call,
> Behold me, what I bear—a god, from gods.
> Behold me, by what anguish worn,
> These eyes of mine shall weary turn
>   Unto time's myriad years.
> So harsh a chain of suffering,
> Hath form'd for me heav'n's new-made king!
>   Alas! alas! my tears
> Alike for present and for future flow!—
> Where lies the bound'ry of my mighty woe?
> What do I say? all things, all future things,
> I view unclouded; nor can sorrow come
> Strange to my soul. It doth behove to bear
> Calmly what Fate ordaineth, knowing that
> Necessity hath force impugnable.
> Yet can I not be silent, or unsilent,
> Of these my woes. To these necessities,
> Because I gave to man a glorious gift,
> I have been yoked—because I stole away
> The ferule-treasured secret fount of fire,
> Teacher of every art, high help to mortals—
> For such sin I endure such punishment!
> Rock-fixëd, in the desert air, in chains.
>   Ah me! ah me! ah me! what sound,
> What viewless odour hovers round?
> From god or man, or half divine
> Being, who nears this rock of mine,
> This limit of the earth, to see
> My woes, or seek—whate'er it be?
> View me a bound and sorrowing god,
> The foe of Jove, the hate of such
> As Jove's imperial courts have trod;
> Because I lovëd man too much.
>   Ah me; ah me! what sound I hear
> Of coming birds! Air murmuring sings,
> Beneath the soft light stroke of wings—
> And all society is fear.

PROMETHEUS *and* CHORUS

Chorus.

> Fear nothing. Lo! This friendly train
> On the fast-flashing oar of pinions,
> Draws nigh; but scarce such boon could gain
> From him who holdeth sea dominions.
> Me too the rapid winds have borne afar.
> Deep thro' our caves the clank of iron came—
> Forth from my cheek was struck the blush of shame—
> And rush'd I shoonless on my wingëd car.

Prometheus.

>   Ah me! ah me! ah me!
> Children of Tethys, who hath given birth
> To many, and involveth all the earth
>   With an unsleeping sea!
> Daughters of old Oceanus,
> Behold, look on me, how constrainëd thus
> By chains to this exalted rocky steep,
>   Sad vigil I must keep.

Chorus.

> Prometheus, I *do* look on thee!—but now
>   A cloud is o'er mine eyes,
> A trembling cloud surcharged with many tears;
> When I would gaze where rock-constrainëd thou
> Hangest consumed by iron miseries—
> Because new gods th' Olympian hill obtaineth,
> And by new laws the son of Saturn reigneth–
> And past the mighty things of former years.

Prometheus.

> Would that under earth, beneath
>   Haïdes, the host of death,
> Into baseless Tartarus,
>   He had hurled me shackled thus
> Cruelly, infrangibly!
> Then, neither god nor man could be
> Rejoicer o'er Prometheus' woes:
> Now, motion'd by each wind that blows,
> I gladden—wretched me!—my foes.

Chorus.

> Who of the gods so stern as to be gladden'd?
>   Who by thy fate unsadden'd?
> Who of the gods save Jove? He ever lending
>   To wrath his soul unbending,
> Ruleth the heav'ns, nor e'er shall cease from ill,
> Until his heart be satiate, or until
> By fraud the sceptre's strength be wrested from his will.

Prometheus.

> Yea! even me, albeit indeed
> By fetter strong consumed I lie,
> The ruler of the blest shall need—
> To show that counsel new whereby
> He loseth honour, sov'reignty.
> And honey'd, suasive words shall be,
> Though charmed, no spell to soften me;
> Nor iron threats shall move me e'er
> By fear this counsel to declare,
> Before he break my cruel chain,
> And pay the price of all this pain.

Chorus.

> Daring thou art, nor aught to bitter woe
>   Dost yield, but speakest words too free—
> And fear doth vex and pierce my spirit thro'!
>   I fear the fate attending thee,
> Where thou shalt voyage ere thou see
> The shore of grief; for none can move
> The will or melt the heart of Jove.

Prometheus.

> I know that Jove is cruel; that he hath
>   For his sole justice, his own will.
> Yet shall he soft and tender be,
>   Moved by this threaten'd ill;
> And calming his unconquerable wrath,
>   He shall not hasten less than I,
>   To concord and to amity.

Cho. Remove the veil from all things, and narrate
In what offences Jove detecting thee,
Imposed such cruel and dishon'ring woe.
Instruct us, if th' instruction grieve thee not.

Pro. Grievous to me to speak of what is past:
Grievous to speak not—each way miserable!—
What time the gods their primal wrath began,
And 'mid their ranks arose the mutual strife,
Some eager to thrust Saturn from his throne,
That Jove forsooth should fill it; some averse,
Resolved that Jove should never rule the gods—
Did I by wisest counsel seek to move
The Titans, children of the heav'ns and earth;
But failed in power. For all my courteous guile,
Contemning with inexorable mind,
They thought to lord it, without toil, by force.
Oft had my mother Themis, yea, and Gaia,
(Albeit one, she beareth many names)
Foretold to me what future was to come;
That not by fortitude or force, but fraud,
The victors were to vanquish. Such decree
When I unfolded in mine arguments,
They deignëd not to view the whole! what time
Meseem'd it best of every ancient ill,
That having won my mother to my side,
I willing should assist the willing Jove—
And by my counsel the Tartarean pit,
Basëd in darkness, covers ancient Saturn,
And with him his allies. The King of gods,
Being by me so benefited, now
Hath paid me back with this ill recompense;
Because there lies inbred in royalty,
A rank disease—distrustfulness of friends.
But that which ye demand, the cause wherefrom
He doth afflict me, I will render clear.
What time he sate upon his father's throne,
First, unto various deities he gave
Gifts various, and arranged his government;
But reck'd he nothing of unhappy man,
Eager to rase his universal kind,
And generate another; which desire
None dared resist, save I: but I, with daring
Interposition, rescued mortal man
From sinking into hell, exterminate.
Wherefrom beneath this anguish am I bent,
Grievous to suffer, piteous to behold;
And I who pitied man, am deem'd myself
Unmeet for pity; but am harped on thus
By Jove's fell hand, dishonour'd spectacle!
   Cho. Oh, iron-hearted, formëd from the rock,
Is he, Prometheus, who lamenteth not
Thy woes. I yearned, not to look on them,
And, having looked, mine heart was anguished.
   Pro.   Yea:
To friends I am a piteous spectacle.
   Cho. But didst thou not offend in more than this?
   Pro. I smote with blindness man's prophetic sight.
   Cho. What drug devising for their malady?
   Pro. Blind hopes I sent among them.
   Cho.   Mighty help
Thereby thou didst afford to men.
   Pro.   Besides,
I yielded them the gift of fire—
   Cho.   And now
Th' ephemerals possess the red-eyed fire—
   Pro. By which they shall be learn'd in many arts.
   Cho. For such crimes doth the hand of Jove afflict,
And loosen not the chain of chastisement?
Is there prescribed no limit to thy woe?
   Pro. No limit—none; save what seems good to him.
   Cho. And how will it seem good? What hope remains?
Seest thou not, thou hast sinn'd? To say, thou hast,
Gives me no joy, and may increase thy grief;
So let that pass, and seek out thy deliv'rance.
   Pro. Easy for him, whose foot is free from toils
Of grief, to counsel and reproach the grieved!
But all these things I knew. By mine own will—
By mine own will I sinn'd—and will confess—
And, aiding mortals, met with woe myself,
Indeed I thought not, by such chastisement,
Attenuate, against the lofty rocks,
To guard this tenantless and lonely hill—
Nathless bewail not o'er my present woes,
But on the plain descending, what shall come,
Attend, that ye may learn the perfect whole.
Obey me, nymphs, obey me; labour with
Him who is toiling now; for wand'ring Woe
Sits at the feet of every one by turns.

Deferring to some specific essay, an entire dissertation on Æschylus' Prometheus, we must now pass on (having given this specimen of her powers as a translator) to the author's original poems.

[Continued in the issue of 6 October 1838.]

It is in her own poetry that we must trace the progress of the Poet's own mind. A powerful poem entitled THE TEMPEST succeeds her version of *Prometheus*, marked with Byronic energy. There is in it much of his spirit which we could well spare—the following, for instance; vigorous and bold as it is—

> All hail unto the lightning! hurriedly
> His lurid arms are glaring through the air,
> Making the face of heav'n to show like hell!
> Let him go breathe his sulphur stench about,
> And, pale with death's own mission, lord the storm!
> Again the gleam—the glare: I turn'd to hail
> Death's mission: at my feet there lay the dead!
> The dead—the dead lay there! I could not view
> (For Night espoused the storm, and made all dark)
> Its features, but the lightning in its course
> Shiver'd above a white and corpse-like heap,
> Stretch'd in the path, as if to show his prey,
> And have a triumph ere he passed. Then I
> Crouch'd down upon the ground, and groped about
> Until I touch'd that thing of flesh, rain-drench'd,
> And chill, and soft. Nathless, I did refrain
> My soul from natural horror! I did lift
> The heavy head, half-bedded in the clay,
> Unto my knee; and passed my fingers o'er
> The wet face, touching every lineament,
> Until I found the brow; and chafed its chill,
> To know if life yet linger'd in its pulse.
> And while I was so busied, there did leap
> From out the entrails of the firmament,
> The lightning, who his white unblenching breath
> Blew in the dead man's face, discov'ring it,
> As by a staring day. I knew that face—
> His, who did hate me—his, whom I did hate!

Take now a fine image:

I no longer knew
Silence from sounds, but wander'd far away
Into the *deep Eleusis* of mine heart,
To learn its secret things.

And these verses are of indubitable excellence:

Oh Death—Oh crownëd Death—pale-steedëd
    Death!
Whose name doth make our respiration brief,
Muffling the spirit's drum! Thou, whom men know
Alone by charnel-houses, and the dark
Sweeping of funeral feathers, and the scath
Of happy days,—love deem'd inviolate!—
Thou of the shrouded face, which to have seen
Is to be very awful, like thyself!—
Thou, whom all flesh shall see!—thou, who
    dost call,
And there is none to answer!—thou, whose call
Changeth all beauty into what we fear,
Changeth all glory into what we dread,
Genius to silence, wrath to nothingness,
And love—not love!—thou hast no change for love!
Thou, who art Life's betroth'd, and bear'st her forth
To scare her with sad sights,—who hast thy joy
Where'er the peopled towns are dumb with
    plague,—
Where'er the battle and the vulture meet,—
Where'er the deep sea writhes like Laocoon
Beneath the serpent winds, and vessels split
On secret rocks, and men go gurgling down,
Down, down, to lose their shriekings in the depth!
Oh universal thou! who comest aye
Among the minstrels, and their tongue is tied;—
Among the sophists, and their brain is still;—
Among the mourners, and their wail is done;—
Among the dancers, and their tinkling feet
No more make echoes on the tombing earth;—
Among the wassail rout, and all the lamps
Are quench'd; and wither'd the wine-pouring
    hands!

A SEA-MEDITATION is unequal:—but what thinks the reader of the following reflection?

I have read
Of that Athenian, who, when ocean raged,
Unchain'd the prison'd music of his lips,
By shouting to the billows, sound for sound.
I marvel how his mind would let his tongue
Affront thereby the ocean's solemnness.
Are we not mute, or speak restrainedly,
When overhead the trampling tempests go,
Dashing their lightning from their hoofs? and when
We stand beside the bier? and when we see
The strong bow down to weep—and stray among
Places which dust or mind hath sanctified?
Yea! for such sights and acts do tear apart
The close and subtle clasping of a chain,
Form'd not of gold, but of corroded brass,
Whose links are furnish'd from the common mine
Of every day's event, and want, and wish;
From work-times, diet-times, and sleeping-times:
And thence constructed, mean and heavy links
Within the pandemonic walls of sense,
Enchain our deathless part, constrain our strength,
And waste the goodly stature of our soul.

Howbeit, we love this bondage; we do cleave
Unto the sordid and unholy thing,
Fearing the sudden wrench required to break
Those claspëd links. Behold! all sights and sounds
In air, and sea, and earth, and under earth,
All flesh, all life, all ends, are mysteries;
And all that is mysterious dreadful seems,
And all we cannot understand we fear.
Ourselves do scare ourselves: we hide our sight
In artificial nature from the true,
And throw sensation's veil associative
On God's creation, man's intelligence;
Bowing our high imaginings to eat
Dust, like the serpent, once erect as they;
Binding conspicuous on our reason's brow
Phylacteries of shame; learning to feel
By rote, and act by rule, (man's rule, not God's!)
Until our words grow echoes, and our thoughts
A mechanism of spirit.

Her patriotic APPEAL to British men is full of devotion as well as of poetry.

CHILDREN of our England! stand
On the shores that girt our land;
The ægis of whose cloud-white rock
Braveth Time's own battle-shock.
Look above the wide, wide world;
Where the northern blasts have furl'd
Their numbëd wings amid the snows,
Mutt'ring in a forced repose—
Or where the madden'd sun on high
Shakes his torch athwart the sky,
Till within their prison sere,
Chainëd earthquakes groan for fear!
Look above the wide, wide world,
Where a gauntlet Sin hath hurl'd
To astonied Life; and where
Death's gladiatorial smile doth glare,
On making the arena bare.
Shout aloud the words that show
Jesus in the sands and snow;—
Shout aloud the words that free,
Over the perpetual sea.

Speak ye. As a breath will sweep
Avalanche from Alpine steep,
So the spoken word shall roll
Fear and darkness from the soul.
Are ye men, and love not man?
Love ye, and permit his ban?
Can ye, dare ye, rend the chain
Wrought of common joy and pain,
Clasping with its links of gold,
Man to man in one strong hold?
Lo! if the golden links ye sever,
Ye shall make your heart's flesh quiver;
And wheresoe'er the links are reft,
There, shall be a blood-stain left.
To earth's remotest rock repair,
Ye shall find a vulture there:
Though for others sorrowing not,
Your own tears shall still be hot:
Though ye play a lonely part;
Though ye bear an iron heart;—
Woe, like Echetus, still must
Grind your iron into dust.

[Continued in the issue of 13 October 1838.]

A Vision of Life and Death is ballad-like, and touching. A blank verse poem called Earth, bespeaks an advance in the art of composition. The Picture Gallery at Penhurst is in Spenserian stanzas, which are managed with skill and effect. The lines To a Poet's Child are sweet; as is also the following poem:—

MINSTRELSY.

> One asked her once the resun why
> She hadde delyte in minstrelsie,
> She answerëd on this manère.
> Robert de Brunne.

> For ever, since my childish looks
> Could rest on Nature's pictured books;
> For ever, since my childish tongue
> Could name the themes our bards have sung;
> So long, the sweetness of their singing
> Hath been to me a rapture bringing!—
> Yet ask me not the reason why
> I have delight in minstrelsy.

> I know that much whereof I sing,
> Is shapen but for vanishing;
> I know that summer's flower and leaf,
> And shine and shade are very brief,
> And that the heart they brighten, may,
> Before them all, be sheathed in clay?—
> I do not know the reason why
> I have delight in minstrelsy.

> A few there are, whose smile and praise
> My minstrel hope, would kindly raise:
> But, of those few—Death may impress
> The lips of some with silentness;
> While some may friendship's faith resign,
> And heed no more a song of mine.—
> Ask not, ask not the reason why
> I have delight in minstrelsy.

> The sweetest song that minstrels sing,
> Will charm not Joy to tarrying;
> The greenest bay that earth can grow,
> Will shelter not in burning woe;
> A thousand voices will not cheer,
> When one is mute that aye is dear!—
> Is there, alas! no reason why
> I have delight in minstrelsy?

> I do not know! The turf is green
> Beneath the rain's fast-dropping sheen,
> Yet asks not why that deeper hue
> Doth all its tender leaves renew;—
> And I, like-minded, am content,
> While music to my soul is sent,
> To question not the reason why
> I have delight in minstrelsy.

> Years pass—my life with them shall pass:
> And soon, the cricket in the grass
> And summer bird, shall louder sing
> Than she who owns a minstrel's string.
> Oh then may some, the dear and few,
> Recall her love, whose truth they knew;
> When all forget to question why
> She had delight in minstrelsy!

The elegiac lines to the memory of Sir Uvedale Price, Bart., are pathetic and striking. But, in The Death-bed of Teresa del Riego, we trace some imitation of Barry Cornwall's manner: yet is the matter original and of so much merit, that we cannot resist quoting the entire poem:—

THE DEATH-BED OF TERESA DEL RIEGO.

> —Si fia muta ogni altra cosa, al fine
> Parlerà il mio morire,
> E ti dirà la morte il moio martie.
> Guarini.

> The room was darken'd; but a wan lamp shed
> Its light upon a half-uncurtain'd bed,
> Whereon the widow'd sate. Blackly as death
> Her veiling hair hung round her, and no breath
> Came from her lips to motion it. Between
> Its parted clouds, the calm fair face was seen
> In a snow paleness, and snow silentness,
> With eyes unquenchable, whereon did press
> A little, their white lids, so taught to lie,
> By weights of frequent tears wept secretly.
> Her hands were clasp'd and raised—the lamp did fling
> A glory on her brow's meek suffering.

> Beautiful form of woman! seeming made
> Alone to shine in mirrors, there to braid
> The hair and zone the waist—to garland flowers—
> To walk like sunshine through the orange bowers—
> To strike her land's guitar—and often see
> In other eyes how lovely hers must be—
> Grew she acquaint with anguish? Did she sever
> For ever from the one she loved for ever,
> To dwell among the strangers? Ay! and she,
> Who shone most brightly in that festive glee,
> Sate down in this despair most patiently.

> Some hearts are Niobes! In grief's down-sweeping
> They turn to every stone from over-weeping,
> And after, feel no more. Hers did remain
> In life, which is the power of feeling pain,
> Till pain consumed the life so call'd below.
> She heard that he was dead!—she ask'd not how—
> For he was dead! She wail'd not o'er his urn,
> For he was dead—and in her hands, should burn
> His vestal flame of honour radiantly.
> Sighing would dim its light—she did not sigh.

> She only died. They laid her in the ground,
> Whereon th' unloving tread, and accents sound
> Which are not of her Spain. She left behind,
> For those among the strangers who were kind
> Unto the poor heart-broken, her dark hair.
> It once was gauded out with jewels rare;
> It swept her dying pillow—it doth lie
> Beside me, (thank the giver) droopingly,
> And very long and bright! Its tale doth go
> Half to the dumb grave, half to life-time woe,
> Making the heart of man, if manly, ring
> Like Dodonæan brass, with echoing.

But what shall we say to this lyric addressed to a Boy? Wordsworth might almost envy it.

TO A BOY.

> When my last song was said for thee,
> The golden hair swept, long and free,
> Around thee; and a dove-like tone
> Was on thy voice—or Nature's own:
> And every phrase and word of thine
> Went out in lispings infantine!

Thy small steps faltering round our hearth—
Thine een out-peering in their mirth—
Blue een! that, like thine heart, seem'd given
To be, for ever, full of heaven!
Wert thou, in sooth, made up of glee,
When my last song was said for thee?
And now more years are finished,—
For thee another song is said.
Thy voice hath lost its coming tone;
The lisping of thy words is gone;
Thy step treads firm—thine hair not flings
Round thee its length of golden rings—
Departed, like all lovely things!
Yet art thou still made up of glee,
When my *now* song is said for thee.

Wisely and well responded they,
Who cut thy golden hair away,
What time I made the bootless prayer,
That they should pause awhile, and spare.
The[y] said, 'its sheen did less agree
With boyhood than with infancy.'
And thus I know it aye must be.
Before the revel noise is done,
The revel lamps pale one by one.
Ah! Nature loveth not to bring
Crown'd victims to life's labouring.
The mirth-effulgent eye appears
Less sparkling—to make room for tears:
After the heart's quick throbs depart,
We lose the gladness of the heart:
And, after we have lost awhile
The rose o' the lip, we lose its smile;
As Beauty could not bear to press
Near the death-pyre of Happiness.

This seemeth but a sombre dream?
It hath more pleasant thoughts than seem.
The older a young tree doth grow,
The deeper shade it sheds below;
But makes the grass more green—the air
More fresh, than had the sun been there.
And thus our human life is found,
Albeit a darkness gather round:
For patient virtues, that their light
May shine to all men, want the night:
And holy Peace, unused to cope,
Sits meekly at the tomb of Hope,
Saying that 'she is risen!'

          Then I
Will sorrow not at destiny,—
Though from thine eyes, and from thine heart,
The glory of their light depart;
Though on thy voice, and on thy brow,
Should come a fiercer change than now;
Though thou no more be made of glee,
When my next song is said for thee.

That is beautiful—what follows is sublime.

THE IMAGE OF GOD.

I am God, and there is none like me.
                    Isaiah xlvi. 9.
   Christ, who is the image of God.
                    2 Cor. iv. 4.

Thou! art thou like to God?
(I ask'd this question of the glorious sun)
Thou high unwearied one,
Whose course in heat, and light, and life is run?
Eagles may view thy face—clouds can assuage
Thy fiery wrath—the sage
Can mete thy stature—thou shalt fade with age.
Thou art not like to God.

Thou! art thou like to God?
(I ask'd this question of the bounteous earth)
Oh thou, who givest birth
To forms of beauty and to sounds of mirth?
In all thy glory lurks the worm decay—
Thy golden harvests stay
For seed and toil—thy power shall pass away.
Thou art not like to God.

Thou: art thou like to God?
(I ask'd this question of my deathless soul)
Oh thou, whose musings roll
Above the thunder, o'er creation's whole?

Thou art not. Sin, and shame, and agony
Within thy deepness lie:
They utter forth their voice in thee, and cry
"*Thou* art not like to God."

Then art Thou like to God?
Thou, who didst bear the sin, and shame, and woe—
Oh Thou, whose sweat did flow—
Whose tears did gush—whose brow was dead and
    low?

No grief is like thy grief; no heart can prove
Love like unto thy love;
And none, save only Thou,—below, above,—
Oh God, is like to God!

A poem entitled Idols admits as within the veil of the Poet's soul. Three times had she been deluded, she says, by Idols. "Natural Beauty" once beguiled her—next, "Moloch Fame"—and subsequently, "Human Love." Alas!—she has known sorrow—but in her sorrow she has lifted up her eyes to Heaven, to Him who abideth ever with his creatures in weal or in woe.

   In woe,—that, while to drowning tears
      Our hearts their joys resign,
   We may remember *who* can turn
      Such water into wine.

This is an exquisite use of the miracle!

Well prepared was she for her great effort that commences her last published volume—The Seraphim. In the mind of the Poet the subject of the dramatic lyric was associated, in tone and object, with the Æschylean *Prometheus*. "The great tragic Soul," writes Miss Barrett, "though untaught directly of Deity, brooded over His creation with exhaustless faculties, until it gave back to her a thought—vast, melancholy, beneficent, malign—the Titan on the rock, the reflected image of her own fallen immortality; rejoicing in bounty, agonizing in wrong, and triumphant in revenge. This was all. 'Then,' said He, 'Lo I come!' and we knew love, in that He laid down His life for us. 'By this we know love'—love in its intense meaning. 'The splendour in the grass and fragrance in the flower' are the splendour and fragrance of a love beyond them. 'All thoughts, all passions, all delights,' are 'ministers' of love around us. All citizenship, all brotherhood, all things for which men bless us, saying, 'Surely this is good,'—are manifestations of a love within us. All exaltations of our inward nature, in which we bless ourselves, saying, 'Surely this is great,'—are yearnings to a love above us. And thus among the fragments of our fallen state, we may guess at LOVE even as Plato guessed at God: but by this, and this only, can we *know* it,—that Christ laid down His life for us. Has not LOVE a deeper mystery than wisdom, and a more ineffable lustre than power? I believe it has. I venture to believe those beautiful and often quoted words 'God is love,' to be even less an expression of condescension towards the finite, than an assertion of essential dignity in Him who is infinite.

"But if my dream be true that Æschylus might have turned to the subject before us, in poetic instinct; and if in such a case—and here is no dream—its terror and its pathos would have shattered into weakness the strong Greek tongue, and caused the conscious chorus to tremble round the thymele,—how much more may *I* turn from it, in the instinct of incompetence! In a manner I have done so. I have worn no shoes upon this holy ground: I have stood there, but have not walked. I have drawn no copy of the statue of this GREAT PAN,—but have caught its shadow,—shortened in the dawn of my imperfect knowledge, and distorted and broken by the unevenness of our earthly ground. I have written no work, but a suggestion. Nor has even so little been attempted, without as deep a consciousness of weakness as the severest critic and the humblest Christian could desire to impress upon me. I have felt in the midst of my own thoughts upon my own theme, like Homer's 'children in a battle.'

"The agents in this poem of imperfect form—a dramatic lyric, rather than a lyrical drama—are those mystic beings who are designated in Scripture the Seraphim. The subject has thus assumed a character of exaggerated difficulty, the full sense of which I have tried to express in my Epilogue. But my desire was, to gather some vision of the supreme spectacle under a less usual aspect,—to glance at it, as dilated in seraphic eyes, and darkened and deepened by the near association with blessedness and Heaven. Are we not too apt to measure the depth of the Saviour's humiliation from the common estate of man, instead of from His own peculiar and primæval one? To avoid which error, I have endeavoured to count some steps of the ladder at Bethel,—a very few steps, and as seen between the clouds.

"And thus I have endeavoured to mark in my two Seraphic personages, distinctly and predominantly, that shrinking from, and repugnance to, evil, which, in my weaker Seraph, is expressed by *fear*, and, in my stronger one, by a more complex passion; in order to contrast with such, the voluntary debasement of Him who became lower than the angels, and touched in His own sinless being, sin and sorrow and death. In my attempted production of such a contrast, I have been true to at least my own idea of angelic excellence, as well as to that of His perfection. For one holiness differs from another holiness in glory. To recoil from evil, is according to the stature of an angel; to subdue it, is according to the infinitude of a God."

We may now be sure, that our Poet has been utterly delivered from Byronic passion; the spirit of Wordsworth has evidently been with her, bearing witness with her spirit, that the law of conscience is the voice of Deity. Quarles and Wither too, are mentioned by her with thoughtful reverence. And we believe her when she says, "I assume no power of art, except that power of love towards it, which has remained with me from my childhood until now. In the power of such a love, and in the event of my life being prolonged, I would fain hope to write hereafter better verses; but I never can feel more intensely than at this moment—nor can it be needful that any should—the sublime uses of poetry, and the solemn responsibilities of the poet."

We tremble as we approach her great poem; and, having read it once, reperuse it that we may do justice to its ambitious order and its not unsuccessful execution.

Ador the Strong and Zerah the Bright One are the two dramatic persons, who hold angelic commune outside the shut heavenly gate. Their brethren have departed at the command of the Father, on a mission to the earth at the time of the Crucifixion. The Strong One has unfurled the thunder cloud of his wing, ready for speed. The Bright One lingers on celestial ground, and looking into his companion's face asks sympathy for those emotions that "stir too deeply his soul's secret springs." But the Strong One thus urges the Bright One to prompt departure.

  Beneath us sinks the pomp angelical—
   The roar of whose descent hath died
  To a still sound, as thunder into rain!
  Th' immeasurable space seems magnified
  With that thick life; whereof we nought retain
  In vision, save the pale and eddying fall
   Of wings innumerous, brightly crossed
   By lines of hair that hath not lost
   The glitter of the God-smile shed
  Last, on bowëd angel's head!
  And gleamed between by hands that fling
   Homages like upward rays,
  From constant habitude of praise
  And high instinct of worshipping.

Zerah. Rapidly they drop below us.
  Pointed palm and wing and hair,
  Indistinguishable, show us
  Only pulses in the air
  Throbbing with a fiery beat—
  As if a new creation heard
  (Late unhearing, still unseeing)
  Some divine and plastic word;
  And trembling at its proper being,
   Did waken at our feet.

Ador. Zerah! stand not lingeringly:
  His voice—the voice that thrills us so
  As we our harpstrings—uttered *Go*,
  Behold the Holy in his woe—
  And all are gone, save thee and—

Zerah.   Thee!

Ador. I stood the nearest to the throne,
   What time the Voice said *Go*.
  And whether I was shook
  By the storm-pathos of the tone
  Which swept thro' Heaven the alien name of woe;
  Or that the subtle glory broke
  Thro' my strong and shielding wings,
  Bearing to my finite essence
   Incapacious of their presence,
    Infinite imaginings—
  None knoweth save the Throned who spoke!
  But I who years agone
  Stood upright while th' eternal Breath did move,
  Shaping the words that lightened—"Let light be"—
   Nor trembled but with love;
  Now fell down tremblingly,
  My face upon the pavement floor,
  Without the praise that evermore
   In music gusheth there!
  As if mine immortality

O'erpowered by God's eternal were!
Thou—wherefore dost thou wait?
Oh! gaze not backward, brother mine;
The deep love in thy mystic eyne
Deepening inward, till is made
A copy of the earth-love shade—
Oh! gaze not thro' the gate!
God filleth heaven with God's own solitude
Till all its pavements glow!
His Godhead being no more subdued
By itself, to glories low
Which seraphs can sustain,
What if thou in gazing so,
Should behold but only one
Attribute, the veil undone—
And that the one to which we press
Nearest, for its gentleness—
Ay! His love!
How the deep ecstatic pain
Thy being's strength would capture!
Without a language for the rapture,
Without a music strong to come
And set th' adoring free:
For ever, ever, wouldst thou be
Amid the general chorus dumb,—
God-stricken, in seraphic agony!—
Or, brother, what if on thine eyes
In vision bare should rise
The life-fount whence His hand did gather
With solitary force
Our immortalities!—
Straightway how thine own would wither,
Falter like a human breath,—
And *shrink into a point like death,*
By gazing on its source!

My words have mirrored dread!
Meekly hast thou bent thine head,
And o'er each droppëd lid, hast bowed
Another broader silver cloud,
A languid wing—as if the glory
Of the God-throne were before thee!

Yet not—not so,
O loving spirit and meek, dost thou fulfil
All motions of the one pre-eminent Will
Which stirreth unto will and act our natures
As human souls do stir the fleshly creatures!
Not for obeisance, but obedience,
Give motion to thy wings? Depart from hence—
The voice said 'Go.'

Zerah. Belovëd! I depart!
His will is as a spirit within my spirit;
A portion of the being I inherit—
His will is mine obedience! I resemble
A flame all undefilëd tho' it tremble—
I go and tremble! Love me, O beloved!
O thou, who stronger art,
And standest ever near the Infinite,
Pale with excelling light!
Love me, belovëd! me, more newly made,
More feeble, more afraid—
And let me hear with mine thy pinions moved,
As close and gentle as the loving are;
That love being near, heaven may not seem so far!

Compare these verses with the best passages in Moore's *Loves of the Angels,* and acknowledge the superiority of the Seraphic Poet, and her school of song. Here are Ideas—Thoughts—Images; glorious, beautiful, and divine. But we must proceed. Zerah suffers under the "Fear of Earth"—"Of Earth," exclaims Ador:

Of earth, the God-create, the beautiful?
From whence the sweet sea-music hath its birth,
And vernal forests lift their leaves in tune
Beneath the gracious, water-leading moon;
Where every night, the stars do put away
Meekly its darkness dull,
And look their spirit-light into the clay?
Where every day, the kingly sun doth bless
More lovingly than kings,
And stir to such harmonious happiness
All leafed and reeded things,
It seems as if the joyous shout which burst
From angel lips to see him first,
Had left a silent echo in his ray?

Both spirits then unite in lamenting the wickedness and weakness of Earth. The intractability of matter—the war of the flesh against the spirit—the mystery of Death—the primeval innocence of earth—the fall of man—fill them with awful meditations. Zerah dreads to look upon the wreck which time has made of this world.

Zerah. I fear—I fear—
To look upon it now!
I have beheld the ruined things
Only in the picturings
Of angels sent on earthward mission!
Strong one, e'en upon thy brow—
When with task completed, given
Back to us from earthly vision,
I have beheld thee silent stand,
Abstracted in the seraph band—
Without a smile in heaven!

They proceed to more consolatory themes, such as the Angel-Song of Peace on Earth to the shepherds watching at night, when the Redeemer of Men was born: soon however rebuked by more melancholy thoughts of a Shadow laid on Light, and of Death to the Everliving. Nor scarcely less perplexing the mystery of the Incarnation itself—"The crownëd Son—walking in the clay which He created." Indeed, the contemplation seizes on Ador with a divine frenzy. He exclaims:—

What do I utter? what, conceive? Did breath
Of demon howl it in a blasphemy?
Or was it mine own voice, informed, dilated,
By the seven confluent Spirits?—Speak—answer me!
Who said man's victim was his deity?

Zerah. Beloved, beloved! the word came forth from thee!
Thine eyes are rolling in tempestuous light,
Above, below, around—
As putting thunder-questions without cloud,
Reverberate without sound,
To universal nature's depth and height.
The tremor of an unexpressëd thought
Too self-amazed to shape itself aloud,
O'erruns the awful curving of thy lips:
And while thine hands are stretched above,
As newly they had caught
Some lightning from the Throne—or flashed abroad

Some Eden-guarding sword—
Thy brows do alternate with wild eclipse
And radiance—with contrasted wrath and love—
As God had called thee to a seraph's part,
With a man's quailing heart!

Ador. O heart—O heart of man!
O ta'en from human clay,
To be no seraph's, but Jehovah's own;
Made holy in the taking,
And yet unseparate
From death's perpetual ban,
And human feelings sad and passionate!
Still subject to the treacherous forsaking
Of other hearts, and its own stedfast pain!
O heart of man—of God! which God hath ta'en
From out the dust, with its humanity
Mournful and weak and soft yet holy round it—
And bade its many pulses beating lie
Beside that incommunicable stir
Of Deity wherewith He interwound it!
O man! and is thy nature so defiled,
That all that holy Heart's devout law-keeping,
And low pathetic beat in deserts wild,
And gushings pitiful of tender weeping
For cruel ones who smote it into woe—
That all could cleanse thee not—without the flow
Of blood—the life-blood—*His*—and streaming *so!*
O earth, the thundercleft, windshaken!—where
The louder voice of 'blood and blood' doth rise—
Hast thou an altar for this sacrifice?—
O heaven—O vacant throne!
O crownëd hierarchies, that wear your crown
When His is put away!
Are ye unshamëd, that ye cannot dim
Your alien brightness to be liker Him,—
Assume a human passion—and down-lay
Your sweet secureness for congenial fears—
And teach your cloudless ever-burning eyes
The mystery of His tears?

Zerah. I am strong, I am strong!
Were I never to see my heaven again,
I would wheel to earth like the tempest rain
Which sweeps there with exultant sound
To lose its life in the reachëd ground!
I am strong, I am strong!
To mine inward vision waxeth dim
The shining seat of my heavenly birth—
I see but His, I see but Him—
The Maker's steps on His cruel earth!
Will the bitter herbs of earth grow sweet
To me, as touchëd by His feet?
Will the vexed, curst humanity,
A blessed—yea! a holy thing,
For love, and awe, and minist'ring?
I am strong, I am strong!
By our angel ken, shall we survey
His loving smile through his woeful clay?
I am swift, I am strong—
The love is bearing me along.——

Ador. My wings with thine! At once we go
To see the Holy in his woe!

The reader must pursue the rest of this divine poem for himself; in which he will be taught to hear the voice of all things groaning in pain to be delivered, together with the victorious agony of the deliverer. These themes were wonderful to be spoken of by men—by an Æschylus and a Shelley; how much more wonderful thus uttered by a woman?

After this can we criticise the Barrett's remaining poems? No! we can but learn from them what mystic oracles there are in earth and heaven, and in the heart of man—and her's!

On the POET'S VOW, and THE ROMAUNT OF MARGARET, the Poet has been her own critic, nor have we a word to add. She teaches two truths—first, that the creature cannot be *isolated* from the creature, and second, that the creature cannot be *sustained* by the creature. The other poems are characterised by the distant—the profound and the sublime—by remote analogies, by deep analysis, and by lofty aspirations—all, however, moderated by a spirit of piety and restrained within the scheme of the Christian dispensation. In her style of diction and verse, Elizabeth Barrett is frequently like Alfred Tennyson, but she is capable of sustaining a more prolonged flight, and pours herself out with greater emotion, enthusiasm and more intense feeling. Great as are her merits, however, she has not yet attained those pure intuitions of true philosophy which leave no place for doubt, but is still struggling for light. A smouldering fire is consuming her, which, if it do not quickly blaze into radiance, will slay her in the flesh, that, uncontrolled, she may rise to glory in the spirit. There is something that is preternatural, but not supernatural, in the poems before us—beautiful they are, but pensive in their beauty;—ideal, yet not ideal enough—more speculative than practical. Eternity, in them, meditates on the time-element, in which it hovers, not in its own. Awake, soul of song, and contemplate the immortal in the infinite. Look not downward—but upward and inward—from the sinning to the sinless—from the suffering to the triumphant—from the partly dim to the all-glorious! Equally possible this, to the Perfect Poet and the Perfect Christian. Such an one was the Sainted JOHN; but the meagre religionists of this age shrink from this theology, or contract it by interpretation within the narrow limits of private system, and reduce by accommodation its sublime verities to the standard of modern belief.

FINDENS' TABLEAUX (1839). *The Athenæum*, 20 October 1838, pp. 757–758.

THE PLATES of this volume, though still overcharged with sentiment and prettiness, in place of that feeling which pervades legitimate works of art,—appear to us more carefully finished than those of last year. Among the best groups are, 'The Greek Wife,' and 'The Novice,' both from Mr. Perring's designs. As regards the letter-press, Miss Mitford has acted wisely in giving the poetical portion of her book a greater prominence and space than has hitherto been customary. There are few capable of writing such stories as 'The Buccaneer,' and 'The Cartel,' who would have been content to exhibit so self-denying a good taste. We must, however, rest content with a general acknowledgment of the literary merit of the volume, as we wish to make some extracts from Miss Barrett's 'Romaunt of the Page.' Thus it begins:—

A knight upon a battle-steed,
  And a page on a steed beside,
From the holy war in Palestine
  As slow and thoughtful ride,
As each were a palmer, and told for bead
  The dew of the eventide.

"O young Page," said the knight,
  "A noble page art thou;
And fearing not to steep in blood
  The curls upon thy brow
Anon in the tent, and anon in the fight,
  Didst ward me a mortal blow?"

"O brave Knight," said the page,
  "A while since talkëd we
In tent and field; and then we talked
  Of the deadly chivalry;—
But I have not a breath of that battle-rage
  To breathe betwixt grass and tree!

"Our friends are far behind;
  The calm is very new;
Our steeds, with slow grass-muffled hoofs,
  Tread deep the shadows through;
And from leaf to leaf the soul o' the wind
  Is sliding with the dew.

"Twice, when a pause was won,
  I heard my mother pray!
I heard, Sir Knight, the prayer for *me*,
  Wherein she passed away;
And I know the Heavens are leaning down,
  To hear what I shall say!"

The page spake calm and high
  As of no mean degree;
Perhaps he felt in nature's broad
  Full heart, his own was free!
And the knight looked up to his lifted eye,
  Then answered smilingly:—

"Sir Page, I pray your grace;
  Certes, I meant not so
To cross your pastoral mood, Sir Page,
  With the crook of the battle-bow;
But a knight may speak of a lady's face,
  If the grasses die or grow!

"And this I meant to say,—
  My ladye's face shall shine,
As ladyes' faces use, to see
  My page from Palestine;
Or, speak she fair or prank she gay,
  She is no lady of mine!

"And this I meant to fear—
  Her bower may suit thee ill;
For, sooth, in that same field and tent,
  Thy *talk* was very still;
And fitter thine hand for my knightly spear,
  Than thy tongue for my ladye's will."

Slowly and thankfully
  The young page bowed his head;
His large eyes seemed to muse a smile,
  Until he blushed instead:
And I ween no lady in her bower
  Could blush more sudden-red!
"Sir Knight, the bower of thy ladye
  Will suit me well," he said.

Beati, beati, mortui!
  From the convent on the sea,
Which they pass not very nigh,
  Swells the dirge as clear and high,
As over brake and over lea
  Bodily the wind did carry
The great altar of St. Mary,
  And the fifty tapers burning o'er it,
And the Lady Abbess dead before it,
  And the nuns she yester-week did bless,
Chanting with their steady breath,
  Palely chanting,—because less
They think upon the dead than death!
Beati, beati, mortui!
  Now they wander back—away—
The uplands will not let them stay
  To dark the western sun—
Mortui!—away at last,
  Or ere the page's blush is past!
And the knight heard all, and the page heard none.

The page then tremulously questions his master as to the history of his marriage, and the latter replies but coldly. He had been compelled to wed from a sense of honour—he had wedded his bride in a dark chamber, and parted from her at the altar's foot, without seeing her face. Then the ballad continues:—

"My Page, my Page, what grieves thee so,
  That the tears run down thy face?"
"Alas! what if my own sister
  Was in thy ladye's case!
But *she* lay down the silks she wore,
  And followed him she wed before,
Disguised as his true servitor,
  To the very battle-place."

And wept the page, and laughed the knight,
  A gay laugh laughëd he:
"Well done it were for thy sistèr,
  But not for my ladyè!
No woman bright, my loves requite,
  Unwomaned if she be."

The page wept not—he smilëd cold—
  "Some wisdoms may declare
That womanhood is provëd best
  By golden brooch and glossy vest,
The mincing ladies wear.
  Yet almost is it proved as well,
By truth,—or by despair."

No more he smiled, no more he wept,
  But passionate he spake,—
"Oh womanly she prayed in tent,
  When none beside did wake!
Oh womanly she paled in fight,
  For one belovëd's sake!
And her little hand defiled with blood,
  Her tender tears of womanhood,
Most woman-pure did make!

"Well done it were for thy sistèr,—
  Thou tellest well her tale;
But for my lady she shall pray
  I' the kirk of Nydersdale—
No dread for me, but love for me
  Shall make my lady pale—
No casque shall hide her woman's tear—
  It shall have room to trickle clear
Behind her woman's veil."

"But what if she mistook thy mind,
  And followed thee to strife;
Then kneeling askëd thee for love,
  As Paynims ask for life?"
"I would forgive; and evermore
Would love her as my servitor,
  But little as my wife.

"Look up—there is a small bright cloud
  Alone amid the skies!
So high, so pure, and so apart
  A woman's glory lies."
The page looked up,—the cloud was sheen—
A sadder cloud did rush, I ween,
  Betwixt it and his eyes.

The lord and his disguised page, ride onward, till the latter perceiving an enemy near at hand, whom his master does not see, finds an excuse, and loiters behind. Thus closes the ballad:—

He clenched his hands, as if to hold
  His soul's great agony—
"Have I renounced my womanhood,
  For wifehood unto *thee*—
And is this the last last look of thine
  That ever I shall see?—

"Yet God thee save,—and mayst thou have
  A ladye to thy mind—
More woman-proud, not faithfuller,
  Than one thou leav'st behind!
And God me take with HIM to dwell,—
For HIM I cannot love too well,
  As I have loved my kind."

She looketh up in earth's despair,
  The hopeful Heavens to seek—
There floateth still the little cloud,
  Whereof her loved did speak!
How bright the little cloud appears!
Her eyelids fall upon the tears,
  And the tears fall down her cheek.

*   *   *   *   *

The stroke of hoof, the flash of steel—
  The Paynims round her coming!
The sound and sight have made her calm,
  False page, but truthful woman:
She stands amid them all unmoved—
The heart once broken by the loved,
  Is strong toward the foeman.

"Ho! Christian Page! art keeping sheep,
  From pouring wine cups, resting?"
"I keep my master's noble name,
  For warring, not for feasting.

And if that here Sir Hubert were,
  My master brave, my master dear,
    Ye would not stay to question."

"Where is thy master, scornful Page,
  That we may seize and bind him?"
"Now search the lea, and search the wood,
  And see if ye can find him!
Nathless, as hath been often tried,
Your Paynim heroes faster ride
  Before him than behind him."

"Give smoother answers, lying Page,
  Or perish in the lying."
"I trow, an if the warrior brand
Beside my feet, were in my hand,
  'Twere better at replying."—
They cursed her deep, they smote her low,
They cleft her golden ringlets through,—
  The loving is the dying!

She felt the scimetar gleam down,
  And met it from beneath
With smile more bright in victory
  Than any steel from sheath,—
Which glanced across her lip serene,
Most like the spirit-flash between
  The darks of life and death!

  Ingemisco ingemisco!
From the convent on the sea!
As over wood and over lea,
  Bodily the wind did carry
The great altar of St. Mary,
And the fifty tapers paling o'er it,
And the Lady Abbess stark before it,
And the weary nuns with hearts that faintly
  Beat along their voices saintly.
  Ingemisco ingemisco!
That dirge for Abbess laid in shroud,
  Sweepeth o'er the shroudless dead
With the dews upon her head,
  All as sad, if not as loud.
  Ingemisco ingemisco!
Is ever a lament begun
By mourner underneath the sun,
Which, ere it end, will suit but *one?*

Besides this, which seems to us one of the most beautiful things from a woman's hand which has appeared for many a day, there are poems by Mr. John R. Chorley, Mr. Kenyon, and the author of 'Provence and the Rhone.' We can only further add, that Miss Mitford's prose is pleasantly varied by a contribution from one who has been some time missing from the world of fact or fiction—we mean, Amelia Opie.

Findens' Tableaux (1839). *The Literary Gazette*, 20 October 1838, pp. 661–662.

This well-conceived series embrace a subject replete with interest for every human heart. The virtues and affections of woman; the moral sustenance and balm of life. What circle do they not brighten and cheer, what individual breast do they not warm and solace? The *Tableaux* are of sufficient variety to illustrate the excellence of young and old; of matron, wife, widow, and maiden, under many straits and trials, and in positions of danger and difficulty, as well as of happiness and sunshine. The "Cartel," the "Romaunt of the Page," the "Buccaneer," the "Greek Wife," the "Novice," the "Sister of Charity," &c. indicate the nature of the subjects which the painter has embodied, and of the poems or prose stories which have been framed to illustrate them. The engravings do honour to the *burin* of the Messrs. Finden, and those artists whom they have associated with them in this task,—the Messrs. Holl, Egleton, Freeman, Hall, Scriven, and Hollis.

The literary contributions are by Miss Mitford, Miss E. Barrett, J.R. and H.F. Chorley, J. Hughes, J. Kenyon, F.A. Osgood, R.E. Townsend, and Amelia Opie. They all possess merit, and we are sorry that we can only select one example of them; and, in so doing, be directed as much by the eligible length of the piece, as by any superiority, though it reflects no disgrace on the name of Mr. Kenyon.

[The review concludes with "The Greek Wife" by John Kenyon; this we omit.]

FINDENS' TABLEAUX (1839). *The United Service Gazette*, 20 October 1838, p. 7.

WE HAVE ALREADY borne our testimony to the beauty and interest of the series to which this volume belongs; and, although we prefer the variety of styles with its corresponding competition for supremacy, which characterises works in which several artists are employed, we are bound to admit that Mr. Perring's tableaux are, most of them, very graceful and elegant. The figure (somewhat absurdly) designated "The Coronation," but which is, in fact, intended for Madame Cottin's Elizabeth, kneeling before a shrine, is extremely simple and beautiful. "The Buccaneer," similarly misnamed, by the way, "a Mexican Girl contemplating a Portrait[,]," "Treason of Gomez Arias," "a Moorish Lady flying from her Pursuers with a Page," "The Greek Wife," "A Story of the Woods," and the "Novice," are pleasing and graceful compositions. "The Minstrel of Provence" would also be worthy of mention were it not too palpable a plagiarism from Middleton's "Dorothea." In our review of the last volume of this work we took occasion to complain of the harsh, and, as we thought, unjust spirit in which its literature was criticised by some of our would-be cynical contemporaries. It is now pretty notorious that, unless the proprietors of such works will invoke the assistance of certain "ladies" and "gentlemen of the press," the collaborateurs of newspapers and magazines, and reward them in an inverse ratio to the merits of their contributions, they must expect to be demolished without mercy. Let them, however, but pay the accustomed black mail, and the affair is arranged in the most agreeable manner possible. Not content, however, with drafting them into her pages, Miss Mitford has felt it necessary to offer them the most extravagant compliments in her preface:—

It would gratify me to particularise each separate production (says the fair editress) whether in prose or verse; but that may hardly be; and only naming Mr. Chorley and Mr. Kenyon, whom it must always be honour to name; Mrs. Osgood, our fair American; and Amelia Opie, that truest *friend;* I cannot but be proud that my book should contain such poems as Mr. Townsend's pure and high-souled "Elizabeth;" Mr. Hughes's "Minstrel of Provence," a fine old feudal tale, in whose chivalrous friend his friend Sir Walter would have delighted; and last, because best and dearest, Miss Barrett's "Romaunt of the Page," a ballad, which seems to me worthy even the genius of the translatress of the "Prometheus Bound," and the authoress of the "Seraphim." Can I say more?

Now, putting the bad English of this glowing coruscation of eulogiums wholly aside, and even that is hardly excusable in so practised a writer as Miss Mitford, what option does she leave, either to her readers or critics, of judging of her work for themselves, without dissenting somewhat ungallantly from her opinions. Had her literature been from the pens of Shakspeare, Milton, Scott, Southey, Wordsworth, Coleridge, &c., she could hardly have complimented them in a higher strain. Living, however, in the midst of the world of letters, and constantly on the look-out for any new star that may arise in the literary hemisphere, we are yet ignorant of the immortal works of the Chorleys, the Kenyons, the Osgoods, the Hughess, the Townshends, and the Barretts of her contributory heaven. Not deeming it safe, however, to dissent from such high authority as we here have, for their genius, we shall take the liberty of quoting a few passages from their works, leaving it to our readers to estimate their value. To begin with the "best and dearest." We have a ballad, occupying, in double columns, five folio pages, by Miss Barrett, entitled "The Romaunt of the Page," which opens with the following stanza:—

  A knight upon a battle steed
    And a page on a steed *beside,*
  From the holy war in Palestine
    As *slow* and thoughtful ride,
  As each were a palmer *and told for bead*
    The dew *of eventide.*

The story is the very old one of a ladye love, or wife, we hardly know which, following her knight in page's attire. The authoress, who appears to have muddled her brains at the hippocrene of the poet Coleridge, makes a discovery worthy of the gold medal of the British Association, namely—that the wind is a sentient creature, with a "soul." *Ex gra.*

  From leaf to leaf the soul of the wind
    Is sliding with the dew.

She then gives us a parody upon one of Coleridge's fine Invocations, of which, perhaps, the following will suffice:—

  From the convent on the sea,
    As over wood and over lea,
  Bodily the wind did carry
    The great altar of St. Mary,
  And the fifty tapers paling* o'er it,
    And the Lady Abbess stark before it.

Of a superfine sketch, entitled the "Sister of Charity," by one of those gentlemen, "whom it must always be an honour to name," the following exquisite piece of bombast is the exordium:—

"*Avant pendant et apres,*" I have often thought, is the motto most suitable to any scene in Paris of moderate extent—to any *gathered score* of its motley inhabitants. La Madelene and the Luxor Obelisk, for instance, how harmonious in effect, but how odd, in reality, is their juxta position. The Louvre, and the Palais de Justice, come into the same picture; the Pont D'Arcole, and Notre Dame, made even more ancient to the eye by the magical associations gathered round it—thanks to Victor Hugo! So too the *right eye* will take in some republican artist of *jeune* France, in his melo-dramatic *toilette* of low-crowned Spanish hat and Spalatro moustache, as he hurries on "*violent* and smoking" to finish his frightful copy of his frightful original, Gericault's Medusa, perhaps, in the Louvre; while the *left* (eye) is more

*Query *swaling.*—Printer's Devil.

pleasantly busied with the pretty coquettish grisette—Sterne's grisette unchanged—not so wholly absorbed in the little *orison she is about to deposit* in St. Germain L'Auxerrois, but that she will turn back as she enters its time-eaten porch with a smile, and a look for the passing stranger. We have nothing in London, save the occasional pageant of *Punch in the Quadrant*, to match this "jumble of times, dynasties, and creeds."

To what an amiable squint must this immortal writer have coined his countenance, to have been enabled to look to the right with one eye, and the left with the other; to "take in" with his "right eye" the republican artist, and with his left the "grisette," who is about to "*deposit her little orison*" in the church of St. Germain L'Auxerrois! But this is all, we dare say, very possible and practicable. The author of this sublime passage is, we are told, a leading contributor to a popular weekly newspaper, in which capacity he will probably have to sit in judgment on this very volume. But we have said enough, we trust, to impress Miss Mitford with the absurdity of calling her geese swans; and will now turn to the pleasanter part of our task. Her own pleasing and graceful lines are all more or less good of their kind. Mr. R. Townshend's poem, entitled "The Coronation," is also a chaste and beautiful production, and almost the only poem that does not discredit the fair editress's *couleur-de-rose* eulogiums. We had almost forgotten to say, that the engravings are carefully executed, as are, we believe, most of the works under Messrs. Findens' superintendence.

THE AMARANTH. *The Athenæum*, 27 October 1838, pp. 775–776.

IN THIS splendid book, the literary contents, for their excellence and variety are the leading attraction. Mr. Hervey numbers hardly one insignificant name among his contributors, and, what is more to the purpose, he has hardly one insignificant contribution. The prose,—by Mr. Harrison, Mr. Sheridan Knowles, Mr. Poole, Mary Howitt, the Author of 'Conti,' and the Editor himself—is beyond our limits for extract. Nor dare we attack Mr. Jerrold's 'Prodigal's Farewell,' nor its companion dramatic scene, 'The Cousins,' by Barry Cornwall; for we must steal a few pages from the poets—who are singing so loudly and so well as to warrant a notion that *their* spring is coming round, after a long and wintry pause.

[The review continues with extracts from four poems; these we omit.]

Mr. Praed's charades—graceful and piquant enough to set all poets at work to dress up "*My first, my second, and my whole*,"—Mr. Graham's 'Fleta,'—two touching Sonnets by the Rev. T. Dale,—Miss Barrett's 'Sabbath on the Sea,' and Mr. Whitehead's 'Death of Chatterton,' must be left untouched, though reluctantly. Our last extract shall be a sprightly one.

[The review concludes with an extract from "Reasons for Risibility" by E.M. Fitzgerald and comments on the illustrations; these we omit.]

THE AMARANTH. *The Atlas*, 27 October 1838, p. 681.

[After some remarks about annuals in general, this review dealt with three of them; we reproduce only the comments relating to The Amaranth, to which EBB contributed.]

The *Amaranth* appears for the first time—a volume of costly dimensions, but, except in size and grandeur of pretension, not distinguished from the rest of the annuals. The articles are all of the same class—stories so airy, brief, and graphic, as to make us feel, while we are reading them, as if we were looking at a vignette—little poems, some legendary, some of the class called "occasional," and some as fantastic as the dance of idle phantasies can make them. Of the pieces that deserve special enumeration, we may particularly point out an exquisite dramatic scene by DOUGLAS JERROLD, called "The Prodigal's Farewell," exceedingly touching, and full of beauty, of a kind which is not often to be traced in Mr. JERROLD'S writings—a very tender and sweet dramatic sketch by BARRY CORNWALL, called "The Cousins"—a poem of an elevated and spiritual cast by Miss BARRETT, entitled "A Sabbath on the Sea"—and "The Sculptor of Cyprus," by JOHN GRAHAM, whose muse, we were afraid, had fallen asleep in the sunshine of praise, but is here revived in all her original vigour. We have enumerated only four pieces, and these all poetical, out of a collection of probably fifty articles; but it must not be supposed that there are not many others of considerable, and some, perhaps, even of a higher order of merit. It is out of the question, however, in our cabined confines, to discuss special claims in a catalogue of this description, and, as these poems struck us in running through the volume more immediately than any of the others, we are disposed to think that a close examination would only confirm our first impressions. The prose tales, as usual, exhibit the least skill; there is not room in such short narratives to vary the incidents very materially; love, disappointment, revenge, all shown in glimpses of circumstantial evidence, rather than in complete development, constitute the staple of these inventions; and they seem to us exactly like a row of faces with pretty much the same family lineaments, modified merely enough to stamp upon each a separate individuality. Mr. HERVEY is too good a poet himself not to be a judge of poetry in others; and he has, therefore, not only contributed well himself to this volume, but drawn able contributions from other quarters. We cannot quote prose, so we will give a snatch of verse. The worthier poems in the collection are too long for extract, but we will take something that will amuse a part of our readers, at least, even more.

[The review concludes with "A Charade" by Winthrop Mackworth Praed; this we omit.]

FINDENS' TABLEAUX (1839). *The Morning Chronicle*, 27 October 1838, p. 3.

THIS IS a title which much awaken the sympathies of every man having a spark of domestic feeling in his composition. The "Womanly Virtues"—how excellent, how pure-toned, how never-failing are they! and sad indeed must be his heart or his lot in life who does not confess with enthusiasm their charming and beneficial influence in one or other of the relations of mother, wife, sister, or daughter, to say nothing of the more distant and casual spheres in which these fairest and best of God's creatures cross our every-day path, to enrich its joys and temper its acerbities? The theme is indeed a mine of rich materials for the artist, the poet, and the philosopher, and one at the same time so homely and comforting in its endless fireside associations, that in congratulating the proprietors of the present very handsome volume in having adopted it, we can only express our surprise that it had never been thought of before amongst the endless projects for annuals and drawing room scrapbooks with which the town has been so inundated of late. Delays, however, are not always "dangerous," and when they bring the hand of the authoress of "Our Village" to bear upon a subject in every way so well adapted to her genius, the result is one for congratulation. There is no living writer who tells with more persuasive truthfulness, in the absence of all maudlin affectation of sentiment, a tale of real life than Miss Mitford—there is no one who can point a homely moral with more terseness and elegance—and none, we are sure, who can paint with a more graceful colouring the lights and shadows, the virtues, the passions, and the weaknesses of her own sex. Miss Mitford is ably assisted in the present work by several writers whose productions deserve a more lasting reputation than that afforded by the generality of annuals, amongst which, however, we cannot class the work before us, inasmuch as it puts forth pretensions to completeness and design which is at once an original and enhancing feature. Prose and poetry—romance and fact—domestic life and chivalrous adventure—the grave, the gay, the pathetic, and the terrible are happily blended to give illustration to the various impulses of female character; and although the tales, twelve in number, are for the most part short, there are none of them devoid of point, whilst some of them exhibit much dramatic interest. "The Romaunt of the Page," by Miss Barrett, is full of fancy and originality, and, with a pathetic termination, highly picturesque. "The Minstrel of Provence," by the author of "Provence and the Rhone," is a poem of considerable length, and no slight merits. It contains many very beautiful passages, and its general style is pure and elegant. "The Novice," by Amelia Opie, is an interesting story of a young lady's narrow escape from the black veil. There are three pieces by the accomplished editor, namely, "The Buccaneer," a tale of crime and blood; "The Baron's Daughter," a sketch of a light and satirical character; and a "Story of the Woods," a striking incident of Indian gratitude in the back woods of the American settlements. From the first-mentioned of these we extract the following prettily written passage.

[The review continues with an extract from "The Buccaneer" by Mary Russell Mitford; this we omit.]

We have now to speak of the embellishments to this handsome volume. They are, like the stories, twelve in number; and graceful, soft, and exquisite are the various forms of female beauty which they portray. We will not stop to make selections from so much intellectual loveliness, and sure we are that our readers will excuse us from the task when by trying it themselves they prove its difficulty. We will only add that the artist has well and worthily studied his subjects, and that the engravers have done him and them full justice. The binding, moreover, is about the most rich and beautiful we have ever seen; and altogether a more fascinating or acceptable present we could hardly offer to any of our fair friends than the volume which we now commend to their hands.

Findens' Tableaux (1839). *The Examiner*, 28 October 1838, p. 677.

Our heart failed us for a moment as our eye glanced at the title of this beautiful annual. Here, we thought, is another batch of the young ladies, manufactured of blancmange and white sugar—things whose rightful position is the top of a Twelfth cake—another bevy of "Beauties," or "Flowers," or "Gems," or "Shells," or "Pearls of Loveliness," caricaturing good wholesome flesh and blood, and making it look like a confectioner's journey-work, and not a thing of pulse and thought. Happy are we to say that we were in some sort agreeably disappointed; Mr Perring's ladies—"women" is vulgar—are for the most part pleasing enough damsels, with varying character in their forms and faces; although, in one or two instances, he appears to have laboured under the "Beauty"-phobia. Miss Mitford has supplied several papers, in that attractive style which has won for her the admiration of those who love nature in its most graceful form; but she seems to have curtailed their fair proportions, to give "ample room and verge enough" for poems of higher tone and aim than are usually to be found in embellished publications. "The Romaunt of the Page," by Elizabeth Barrett, is a poem with the spirit of the elder and better day of poetry in every line of it—in truth, a very sweet and noble composition, not unworthy of the author of the "Seraphim." There is fine energy with high poetic power in "The Greek Wife," by Mr Kenyon. Mrs Opie contributes a tale in her very best manner. We have no doubt, then, that *Finden's Tableaux* will "be ordered to lie upon the table" of very many drawing-rooms. The engravings are certainly an improvement on the absurd collections of eyes, noses, and mouths, huddled up and called faces, and not only faces, but "Beauties" of the season; and the letter-press of the work is enriched by papers, both in prose and verse, worthy to outlive the short and brilliant day of the class to which it belongs.

[John Forster]

Findens' Tableaux (1839). *The Monthly Chronicle*, November 1838, pp. 465–466.

A new species of Annual has appeared this year transcending the older series in size and costliness. Of this class we have three specimens—"The Diadem," edited by Miss Sheridan; Finden's "Tableaux of the Affections," edited by Miss Mitford; and "The Amaranth," edited by Mr. T.K. Hervey. These volumes are of equally imperial dimensions, but not of equal merit. "The Diadem," in point of literary excellence, may perhaps be permitted to take the first place, while Finden's "Tableaux" surpasses "The Diadem" in the beauty of its embellishments; and "The Amaranth" is inferior to both in both respects.

Miss Sheridan's anthology of prose and verse deserves great commendation, and not the less that its contributors are chiefly selected from the higher circles—an evidence of cordiality in the pursuit of letters that must be gratifying to the reading public. With the exception of a few puerilities and ephemeral verses that might have been spared with advantage, the pieces generally are elegant in construction, and indicative of cultivated taste. In addition to the usual variety of matter, there are some stanzas by Lord Chesterfield, now published for the first time, and a song by Congreve, both of which are strikingly characteristic of their authors; and a story of the feudal times, preserved by the late Duchess of St. Albans, as it was related by Sir Walter Scott to a party of friends on a visit at Abbotsford. These novelties considerably enhance the attractions of the volume.

It would be difficult to divine the meaning or application of the title of Miss Mitford's Annual. If the volume were intended to suggest by engravings some of those noble conceptions that are occasionally, but not often, realised by sculpture, there might be some excuse for so affected a designation; but the engravings, exquisite as they are, make no pretensions to be considered as representatives of the affections, or "womanly virtues" as they are oddly called in the second title of the book; in fact, they might as reasonably be described as the tableaux of the sun, moon, and stars, for all the separate passions that are expressed in them. But the reader will find in this volume two or three felicitous compositions that, taken alone, are worth all the literature of the rest of the Annuals; notwithstanding that we think, for the general purpose of such publications, Miss Sheridan has catered better. Two poems, one by Miss Barrett, and the other by Mr. Hughes, are works distinguished by poetical qualities of the highest order. They are both dipped in the hues of ballad minstrelsy. The "Romaunt of the Page," by Miss Barrett, is full of the early spirit of English poetry—quaint, simple, and pathetic: and in "The Minstrel of Provence," Mr. Hughes has given us a very perfect specimen of a style which is now but little cultivated, but which can never lose its fascination, wherever the romantic costume and high-hearted chivalry of the middle ages are regarded with enthusiasm. The rest of the pieces hardly demand special notice. The prose tales are slight, and not very striking either in subject or treatment.

FINDENS' TABLEAUX (1839). *Tait's Edinburgh Magazine*, November 1838, pp. 682–684.

THE ANNUALS may now be regarded as a staple literary manufacture, quite as much as the supplies of the circulating library. Like these, they are a symptom of the progressive refinement of taste in society, if our theory hold, that they have taken the place of the savoury and substantial *tokens* of Christmas cakes, turkeys, and chines, and of the flimsy and tinsel perishing gifts of tawdry millinery and coarse jewellery. No one will question that this change is for the better. A book at worst is a book—a picture a picture; both endure, and are capable of diffusion; and these are but the smallest of their claims to superiority; for there is something to give intellectual pleasure, something to admire and to profit by, in the humblest Annual; while among them are embodied some of the most finished performances of living artists and authors. And this in addition to their value as gifts, as

—— the beads of Memory's rosary,
Whereon she reckons kind remembrances
Of friends and old affections.

The competition of publishers, and the becoming pride of artists and literary contributors, but, above all, the ambition, and by'r lady, the *interest* of all concerned, is every season improving the new literary manufacture in one respect or another, and sometimes in all. Each in its own sphere, so far as we have yet seen them, maintains its character and its claim on public patronage.

And first among the first comes Miss Mitford's special charge, FINDEN'S TABLEAUX, again "regally gorgeous" in its garniture of green and gold, and containing gems worthy of so rich a casket. Miss Mitford has herself praised her friendly contributors so cordially and handsomely, that she has left us nothing to say. The "Tableaux" are this year illustrative of the "Womanly *Virtues* and *Affections*"; the designs are chiefly by Perring. They are all fine things enough in their way; but *Zuliete* and *The Greek Wife* are something more; and the *Coronation* is exquisite, and beautifully engraved. It is not the Coronation of Queen Victoria, nor indeed any vulgarity of the sort, but the picture of a lovely young girl, half reclining, half kneeling at a way-side chapel, in the attitude of devotion. It is the *Elizabeth* of Madame Cottin's "Exiles of Siberia," which is "done into" flowing and mellifluous verse by Richard E. Townsend, Esq., for Miss Mitford's superb book. But the literary gem of this poetic volume is the "Romaunt of the Page," by Miss Barrett. It is not without the peculiar blemishes of that lady's style—haziness, and an occasional quaint simplicity, verging on something very like affectation; but, at the same time, it is rich in all the higher beauties of her poetry—a graceful and deep-toned composition, shewing true and original genius, and of a fine order:—

A knight upon a battle-steed,
    And a page on a steed beside,
From the holy war in Palestine,
    As slow and thoughtful ride
As each were a palmer, and told for bead
    The dew of the even-tide.

"O young page," said the knight,
    "A noble page art thou;
And fearing not to steep in blood
    The curls upon thy brow;
Anon in the tent, and anon in the fight,
    Didst ward me a mortal blow."

"O brave knight," said the page,
    "A while since talked we
In tent and field, and then we talked
    Of the deadly chivalry;
But I have not a breath of that battle-rage
    To breathe betwixt grass and tree."

As they ride on, the knight speaks of his lady as of one whose bower might ill suit her silent page.

Slowly and thankfully
    The young page bowed his head;
His large eyes seemed to muse a smile,
    Until he blushed instead;
And, I ween, no lady in her bower
    Could blush more sudden-red!
"Sir Knight, the bower of thy lady
    Will suit me well," he said.

A beautiful descriptive passage intervenes, and heightens the dramatic effect of the scene; but all passes unheeded by the musing page.

"A boon, thou noble knight,
    If ever I served thee—
Though thou art a knight, and I am page,
    Now grant this boon to me.
Now, tell me sooth, if dark or bright,
    If little loved, or loved aright,
    Be the face of thy ladye."

Gloomily looked the knight—
    "As a son thou has served me;
And, oh, that I never had granted boon
    To another, saving thee!

For haply then I should love aright;
For then I should know if dark or bright
  Were the face of my ladye.
"Yet ill befits it knightly tongue
  To mourn that granted boon;
For her Baron-sire avenged the wrong
To the fame of mine, sepulchred long,
  By a lying caitiff done,
Who looked up the minster nave,
And *dared* to lie; for my father's glaive
  Was changed from steel to stone."

The baron fell in this quarrel, and his dying wife, recovering from her swoon, as the knight relates, summoned him in haste, and demanded the boon that he should marry "the sweet child" made an orphan, for his father's sake. He proceeds:—

"I said, my steed neighs in the court,
  My bark rocks on the brine;
And the warrior's vow I am under now,
  To free the pilgrim's shrine;
But fetch the ring, and call the priest,
  And call that daughter of thine;
And rule she wide, from my castle of Nyde,
  While I am in Palestine.

["]In the dark chambère, if the bride were fair,
  Ye wis I could not see;
But the steed thrice neighed,
  And the priest fast prayed,
  And wedded fast were we:
Her mother smiled in her bed,
  As at its side we knelt to wed.
When the bride rose from her knee,
She kissed the smile of her mother dead
  Or ere she kissed me.

"My page, my page, what grieves thee so,
  That the tears run down thy face?"
"Alas! what if mine own sister
  Was in that lady's case!
But *she* laid down the silks she wore,
And followed him she wed before,
  Disguised as his true servitor,
    To the very battle-place."

And wept the page, and laughed the knight,
  A gay laugh laughed he:—
"Well done it were for thy sister,
  But not for my ladye!
No woman bright my loves requite,
  Unwomaned if she be."

The page wept not—he smiled cold.
  "Some wisdoms may declare
That womanhood is proved best
By the golden brooch and glossy vest
  The mincing ladies wear;
Yet almost is it proved as well
  By truth or by despair."

No more he smiled, no more he wept,
  But passionate he spake:—
"Oh, womanly she prayed in tent,
  When none beside did wake!
Oh, womanly she paled in fight,
  For one beloved sake.
And her little hand, defiled with blood,
Her tender tears of womanhood

Most woman-pure did make."
"Well done it were for thy sister,
  Thou tellest well her tale;
But, for *my* lady, she shall pray
  I' the kirk of Nydersdale.
No dread for me, but love for me,
  Shall make my lady pale—
No casque shall hide her woman's tear—
It shall have room to trickle clear
  Behind her woman's veil."

"But what if she mistook thy mind,
  And followed thee to strife;
Then, kneeling, ask thee for thy love,
  As Paynims ask for life?"
"I would forgive; and evermore
Would love her as my servitor,
  But never as my wife.

"Look up—there is a small bright cloud
  Alone amid the skies:
So high, so pure, and so apart,
  A woman's glory lies."
The page looked up—the cloud was sheen—
A sudden cloud did rush, I ween,
  Betwixt it and his eyes.

And so his eyes did drop away
  From welkin to the hill.
Ha! who rode there? the page is 'ware,
Though the cry at his heart is still!
The page seeth all, the knight seeth none,
Though banner and spear do fleck the sun,
  And the Paynims ride at will.

He speaketh calm, he speaketh low—
  "Now ride, my master, ride,
Or ere, within the broadening dark,
  The narrow shadows hide!"
["]Yes, fast—yes, fast—thou zealous page,
  And keep thou by my side."

The page prays to remain behind—he has a vow, and again urges his master to ride on—

——Who smiled free at the fantasy,
  And adown the dell did ride.

Had the knight looked up to the page's face,
  No smile his words had won;
Had the knight looked up to the page's face,
  I ween he had never gone;
Had the knight looked back to the page's geste,
  I ween he had turned anon.
For dread was the wo in the face so young,
And wild was the geste wherewith he flung
Casque, sword, to earth, and downward sprung,
  And stood alone, alone.

He clenched his hands, as if to hold
  His soul's great agony:—
"Have I renounced my womanhood,
  For wifehood unto *thee*?—
And is this the last look of thine
  That ever I shall see?"

"Yet God thee save—and mayst thou have
  A ladye to thy mind,
More woman-proud, not faithfuller,
  Than one thou leav'st behind!
And God me take with Hɪᴍ to dwell,

For HIM I cannot love too well,
  As I have loved my kind."

She looked up in earth's despair,
  The hopeful heaven to seek—
There floateth still the little cloud
  Whereof her love did speak!
How bright the little cloud appears!
  Her eyelids falls upon the tears,
  And the tears fall down her cheek.

. . . . .

The Paynims ride up; and the faithful page refuses to tell of his master, and answers them proudly;—
  They cursed her deep, they smote her low,
  They cleft her golden ringlets through—

The loving is the dying!

. . . . .

A pathetic dirge closes this exquisite tragic ballad.

We have to complain of Miss Mitford giving way so much to her contributors as to have left little room to herself; though there are several gem-like stories from her own pen; one in particular, of which the scene is laid in the Imperial Court, and in which Napoleon, as well as Josephine, is made amiable. This little story is a sweet specimen of the pathos of the domestic affections.

Mrs. Opie, Mr Kenyon, the brothers Chorley, and others, have brought tribute to the gifted Editress: but we turn from temptation, as we can go no farther with the "Tableaux."

THE AMARANTH. The Examiner, 4 November 1838, p. 692.

A VERY handsome Annual of the folio size, the text portion of which excels the graphic. What Goldsmith's connoisseurs said of *every* work of art, would correctly apply to this work—"The artists would have done better if they had taken more pains." And "this effect defective comes by cause," which the Editor very candidly and very properly explains; for Mr T.K. Hervey has an established reputation, and so great a likelihood of extending it that he should not risk anything by the unpromising issue of a literary and pictorial race against time; and such he announces this to have been. The elegant and graceful poetry of the Editor himself, of Mr Whitehead, and of Miss Barrett; the first contribution by Mr Jerrold, a dramatic scene of great power and beauty; the *second* one of Mr Horace Smith (entitled "A New Nightmare"); the tale by the author of *Virginius*; a dramatic sketch ("The Cousins") by Barry Cornwall [and] the "Charades," by W. M. Praed; Mr Hood's and Mr Fitzgerald's pleasant verses; and, though last not least, Mr Douglas Jerrold's second article—"Epitaph of Sir Hugh Evans—'There's pippins and cheese to come'"—stand in no need of the shelter which such an apology offers, for they are all as good as possible in their way.

[The review continues with an extract of the last mentioned article and comments on the illustrations; these we omit.]

As to the ensuing number, assuming Mr T.K. Hervey to have the proper management, with plenty of time before him, and his present auxiliaries, we think it safe to predict that he may render it, in so far as Annuals are concerned, the *primus inter pares*.

FINDENS' TABLEAUX (1839). *Chambers's Edinburgh Journal*, 24 November 1838, p. 349.

FINDEN'S TABLEAUX OF THE AFFECTIONS is the title of a magnificent volume, of which the Editor, Miss Mitford, has kindly sent us a copy. It is one of the annuals for the year 1839, and of the superior class of those fair but fleeting publications. A thin folio in shape, and splendidly bound, it contains sixty pages of print, and twelve large engravings, these being after pictures, all of which, except two, are by Mr W. Perring. The virtues and affections of woman constitute the subjects of these fine drawings, and of the accompanying letter-press, which consists partly of prose and partly of poetry, the writers being Miss Mitford, Mrs Opie, Miss Barrett, Mr Townsend (American), and others of less note.

Of the more important portion of this volume—the engravings—it is unfortunately out of our power to convey an adequate idea, for this only the exhibition of a specimen could do. They are dazzlingly beautiful, and show the female form in an ideality of perfection exceeding all we have before seen. Of them we can say no more. The letter-press forms so unimportant a portion of this, as of all similar volumes, that it almost seems absurd to speak of it. Yet the Romaunt of the Page, and the Minstrel of Provence, respectively by Miss Barrett and Mr John Hughes, are pleasing metrical tales. Most of the other articles are too slight and shadowy to stand undetached from the pictures which they are designed to illustrate: perhaps it is thought best that such pieces should not be qualified to distract attention from the cardinal part of the work. There is, however, a French story by Miss Mitford, which may be tagged to our notice, by way of giving it weight, and as an apology to our readers for intruding upon them the description of a book, which but a few of them have any chance of seeing:—

[The review concludes with "The Cartel" by Miss Mitford; this we omit.]

THE SERAPHIM. The Literary Gazette, 1 December 1838, pp. 759–760.

ALTHOUGH THIS volume contains much delightful poetry, still we cannot let it pass without censuring the many antiquated and affected phrases with which it abounds. Our authoress seems to have modelled herself upon the very worst portion of Keats and Tennyson, in labouring for outlandish compound words, picking up obsolete phrases, and accenting every unnecessary syllable. Then we have such expressions as "a low shadowy laughter," "the night is in her hair," "ranks of solemnities," "the silentnesses," "putting thunder-questions," "mournful as a star," eyes that "gaze most starry kind," &c. &c. Now we object to such expressions as these, a few of them may be looked over, and in many instances the author has struck out several new and beautiful epithets, such as we have never before seen surpassed, but we do think that her coinages are sometimes too mysterious. Besides, she has no need to have recourse to the worst examples of this school of poetry, for she has that within her soul which is far above all forced and false art. Her poetry is of a very high order, and, in numerous instances, will bear comparison with the best portions of Shelley. But she also seems to have caught that wild, dreamy spirit, which too prominently pervades the writings of that author. We know no modern writer in whose works we could point out so many imperfections as in Miss Barrett's: neither do we know one possessing more genuine excellences; there is a feeling and a flow of true poetry in her pages that seem to know no bounds; heart and soul are borne away by her power; she showers down her wealth of song without let or hinderance; and it is only the cold, experienced critic, that will dwell upon what she herself might poetically call her "beautiful errors." We are late in the field with our remarks, but from us they come in sincerity; her works need no praise, all she requires is a little honest censure, to make her one of the bright literary ornaments of the present day. We have only to accompany these observations with the following extract, which needs not a word of commendation.

My dream is of an island place
   The distant seas are folding;
And over which, the only watch
   Those trooped stars are holding.
Those bright still stars! they need not seem
   Brighter or stiller in my dream!

Hills questioning the heavens for light—
   Ravines too deep to scan!
As if the wild earth mimicked there
   The wilder heart of man:
Only it shall be greener far
   And gladder than hearts ever are.

More like, perhaps, some mount sublime
   Of starry paradise,
Disrupted to a hundred hills,
   In falling from the skies—
Bringing within it, all the roots
   Of heavenly trees, and flowers, and fruits.

For saving where yon spectral heights
   Denude their rocky whiteness,
Or ragged fissures, miser-like,
   Hoard up some fountain brightness—
(And e'en in them—stoop down and hear—
   Leaf sounds with water in your ear!)

Around, above, the plumed trees
   Their gracious shadows throw;
Through whose clear fruit and blossoming,
   Whene'er the sun may go,
The ground beneath he deeply stains,
   As shining through cathedral panes.

But little needs the ground beneath,
   That shining from above her,
When many Pleiades of flowers
   (Not one lost) star her over:
The rays of their unnumbered hues
   Being refracted by the dews.

Wide-petalled plants, that boldly drink
   Th' Amreeta of the sky;
Shut bells, all heavy with delight,
   Whose faces earthward lie—
I cannot count them: but between,
   Is room for grass, and mosses green,

And rapid brooks, that bear all hues
   Reflected in disorder;
Or, gathering up their silver lengths
   Beside their winding border,
Sleep, haunted through the slumber hidden
   By lilies white as dreams in Eden.

Nor think each arched tree with each
   Too closely interlaces,
T' admit of vistas opening broad,
   And sweet sun-basking places,
Upon whose sward the antlered deer
   View their own image long and clear.

Unless they fainer would behold
   That image on the seas,
Whene'er's a way through shelving rocks
   And over-branching trees,
Whose doves from half-closed lids espy
   The green and purple fish go by.

One mateless dove is answering
   The water every minute,
Thinking such music could not be
   Without his cooing in it!
So softly doth earth's beauty round
   Infuse itself in ocean's sound.

My soul in love bounds forwarder
   To meet the bounding waves!
Beside them is the home for me,
   Within the coral caves—
And near me two or three may dwell
   Whom dreams fantastic please as well.

High winding caverns! not uncleft
   In all their sparry ceilings;
Through which may shine the earnest stars
   In prophet-like revealings,
And down their slanted glory, move
Scents from the flowers that grow above.

Findens' Tableaux (1840). *The Athenæum*, 26 October 1839, pp. 809–810.

THE DESIGNS in *Findens' Tableaux* are after the fashion of their class; but some of them are very beautifully engraved—the Beacon, as it is called, is deserving of especial mention for its brilliant effect. The novelty to which we have alluded is the encircling these designs with a sort of arabesque border, in which a series of small groups illustrates the principal points in the story. Miss Mitford, the editor, is also the principal contributor: and where shall we find a pleasanter narrator of a short healthy, racy, story, just such a one as is sure to be the gem of an Annual! She has, however, secured some worthy assistants in Miss Barrett, Barry Cornwall, Mr. Kenyon, Mr. J.R. Chorley, Mr. Horne, and others. Tales require more space than we can afford, and are not exactly suited to our purpose. We shall therefore steal a few verses from a wild legend, entitled 'The Brown Rosarie,' by Miss Barrett. The reader must understand that our extract is but a fragment of the poem:

   'Tis a morn for a bridal. The merry bride-bell
     Ringeth clear through the greenwood that skirts the chapelle;

And the priest at the altar awaiteth the bride,
And the grave young sacristans jest slyly aside
   At the work shall be doing.
While down through the wood rides that fair companie,
The youths with the courtship, the maids with the glee,
Till the chapel-cross opens to sight, and at once
All the maids sigh demurely, and think, for the nonce,
   So endeth a wooing!

And the bride and the bridegroom are leading the way,
With his hand on her rein, and a word yet to say;
Her dropped lids suggest the replyings beneath,
And the little quick smiles come and go with her breath
   If she sigheth or speaketh.

And the tender bride-mother breaks off unaware,
From an Ave to trow that her daughter is fair;
But, in nearing the chapel, and glancing before,
She seeth her little son stand at the door—
   Is it play that he seeketh?

Is it play? when his eyes wander innocent, wild,
Yet sublimed with a sadness unfitting a child.
He trembles not, weeps not, his passion is done,
And meekly he kneels in their midst, with the sun
   On his head like a glory.

"O merry fair maids, ye are many," he cried,
"But in fairness and vileness who matcheth the bride?
O merry brave youths, ye are many, but whom
For courage and woe can ye match with the groom,
   As ye see them before ye?"

Outspake the bride's mother—"The vileness is thine,
Who would'st shame thine own sister, a bride at the shrine!"
Outspake the bride's lover, "The vileness is mine,
If he shame mine own wife at the hearth or the shrine!
   And his charge be unproved."

"Bring the charge, prove the charge, brother! speak it aloud,
That thy father and hers hear it deep in the shroud!"
—"O father, thou seest—for dead eyes can see—
How she wears on her bosom *a brown rosarie*,
   O father beloved."

Outlaughed the bridegroom, and outlaughed all
The maidens and youths by that old chapel wall—
"So she weareth no love-gift, kind brother," quoth he,
"She may wear an she listeth a brown rosarie,
   Like a pure-hearted lady."

Then swept through the chapel the long bridal train,
Though he spake to the bride she replied not again;
On, as one in a dream, pale and stately she went
Where the altar lamps burn o'er the great sacrament,
   Faint with daylight, but steady!

But her brother had passed between them and her,
And calmly knelt down on the high altar stair—
Of an infantine aspect so stern to the view
That the priest could not smile as he used to do
   When a child knelt before him.

He knelt like a child, marble-carved and white,
That appeareth to pray on the tomb of a knight;
With a look taken up to each iris of stone,
From the greatness and death where he kneeleth, and none
   From the mother who bore him!

"In your chapel, O priest, ye have wedded and shriven
Fair wives for the hearth, and fair sinners for heaven!
But this fairest, my sister, ye think now to wed,
Bid her kneel where she standeth, and shrive her instead.
   Oh shrive her, and wed not![")

In tears, the bride's mother, "O priest, unto thee
Would he lie, as he lied to this fair companie!"
In wrath, the bride's lover, "This lie shall be clear,
Speak it out, boy! The saints in their niches shall hear!
   Be the charge proved or said not![")

Serene in his childhood he lifted his face,
And his voice sounded holy and fit for the place,
"Look down from your niches, ye still saints, and see
How she wears on her bosom a *brown rosarie*.
   Doth she wear it for praying?"

The youths looked aside—to laugh *there* were a sin,
And the maidens' lips trembled with smiles shut within;
Quoth the priest, "Thou art wild, pretty boy! blessed she
Who prefers at her bridal a brown rosarie
   To a worldly arraying."

The bridegroom spake low, and led onward the bride,
And before the high altar they kneel side by side;
The rite book is opened, the rite is begun—
They have knelt down together to rise up as one!
   Who laughed by the altar?

The maidens looked upward, the youths looked around,
The bridegroom's eye flashed from his prayer at the sound;
And each saw the bride as if no bride she were,
Gazing cold at the priest without gesture of prayer
   As he read from the psalter.

The priest never knew that she did so, but still
He felt a power on him too strong for his will;
And whenever the great NAME was there to be read,
His voice sunk to silence—THAT could not be said,
   Or the air could not hold it!

"I have sinned," quoth he, "I have sinned I wot;"
And the tears ran adown his old cheeks at the thought:
They dropped on the book, but he read on the same,
And aye was the silence where should be the NAME,
   The sacristans have told it.

The rite book is closed, the rite being done—
They who knelt down together have risen as one;
Fair riseth the bride—Oh, a fair bride is she,
But for all (think the maidens) that brown rosarie,
   No saint at her praying!

What aileth the bridegroom? he stands stony-eyed;
Then suddenly turning he kisseth the bride—
Cold, cold. He glanced upward, fear-stricken and mute:
"Mine own wife," he said, and fell stark at her foot
   In the word he was saying.

They have lifted him up, but his head sinks away,
And his face showeth bleak in the sunlight and grey;
Leave him now where he lieth, for oh, nevermore
Will he kneel at an altar or stand on a floor,
    With that wife gazing on him!

Long and still was her gaze, while they chafed him
    there
And breathed in the mouth whose last life kissed her!
But when they stood up—only *they!* with a start,
The shriek from her soul struck her pale lips apart,
    She hath loved and foregone him.

And low on his body she sinketh adown:
"Didst call me thine own wife, beloved, thine own?
Then take thine own with thee! Thy coldness is warm
To the world's cold without thee! Come, teach me
    thy calm,
      I would learn it, beloved!"

She looked in his face earnest, long, as in sooth
There were hope of an answer, then kissed his mouth,
And with head on his bosom, wept, wept bitterly,

"Now, O God, take pity,—take pity on me.
    Let the sin be removed!"

She was ware of a shadow that crossed where she lay,
She was ware of a presence that curdled the day,
Wild she sprang to her feet. "I surrender to thee,
The broken vows witness the foul rosarie,
    I am ready for dying!"

She dashed it in scorn to the hollow-paved ground,
Where it fell mute as snow; and a weird music sound
Crept up—like a chill—up the aisles long and dim,
As the fiends tried to mock at the choristers' hymn
    But moaned in the trying.

We are much tempted to steal a little Spanish song, by Mr. H.F. Chorley, and, indeed, the whole tale, into which it has been so gracefully woven by Miss Mitford; but we must have the following, by Mr. Kenyon, and be content with it.

[The review concludes with an extract from "To an Æolian Harp" by John Kenyon; this we omit.]

Findens' Tableaux (1840). *The Atlas*, 26 October 1839, pp. 684–685.

WE KNOW not in what terms to commend the whole design and execution of this magnificent work. To say that it is the most splendid of all the annuals we have yet seen, and that it is not unlikely, when they shall all have been published, to be pronounced the most splendid among them, would be merely to decide upon it as a work of art; but we allude more expressly to its great and unusual merits as a literary production. Miss MITFORD—whose judgment in such matters has been already tested in former publications of this description—appears to have taken extraordinary pains on this occasion to render her book worthy of the patronage of the most fastidious critics in prose and verse, and not only to keep mediocrity out of her pages, but to secure the highest order of talent that could be rendered available in a production of this class.

The contributions are not numerous, a circumstance which has ensured to the writers ample scope for the full development of their subjects. The prose tales are by Miss MITFORD and they may be reckoned amongst the most felicitous of her fictions—especially "The Proud Ladye" and the "Roundhead's Daughter." Upon a rapid perusal, these stories strike us as the most successful, but if any one should be disposed to prefer the "King's Page," "The Beacon," "The Bride" or "The Woodcutter," we confess we should be at a loss to assign any satisfactory grounds for maintaining a different opinion. They all possess attractions of some kind, and are so varied in form, matter, and treatment that each may become a special favourite with some readers without casting any reproach upon the taste of others who detect more fascinating qualities elsewhere. The poetical articles are furnished by Miss BARRETT, J.R. CHORLEY, JOHN HUGHES, BARRY CORNWALL, and R.H. HORNE. Of all these pieces "The Fetches," a German trilogy, illustrative of a familiar superstition, common to Germany and Ireland, is the most remarkable, and presents on many accounts the highest claims to precedence.

[Following are several passages from "The Fetches."]

We have given so much space to this poem—but not more than it deserves—that we must briefly dispose of the remainder. Miss BARRETT's "Legend of the Brown Rosarie," "The King's Forester," by Mr. HUGHES, and "Venice," by BARRY CORNWALL, are each of its kind admirable. "The Maid's Trial," by Mr. CHORLEY, is also cleverly imagined and skilfully treated, and the opening piece, by Miss BARRETT, called "The Dream," forms a very appropriate and poetical introduction to the whole. The nature of these poems precludes us, for the most part, from making extracts from them, as we cannot find any passages capable of being severed without injury from the context:—but the following snatch from the lines on Venice, taking apart from the little legend that runs like a thread of light through them, will not suffer by standing alone.

[Following are three verses of the poem.]

Findens' Tableaux (1840). *The Literary Gazette*, 26 October 1839, p. 676.

"THE DREAM," which graces the title-page of this elegant volume, is a beautiful specimen of the whole plan, which consists of twelve plates of human groups, by Mr. Browne. It represents a lovely boy sleeping, and his dream shews many small groups of figures (such as surround the other engravings), invented with great taste, and drawn with infinite grace and spirit. All these bear reference to the principal, and serve as a framework commentary on the subject. We have not seen more appropriate and characteristic accompaniments. With regard to the principal designs, they are generally well conceived; but, perhaps, upon the whole, too smooth and pretty. The young men (such as the Woodcutter) are peculiarly liable to the remark of being effeminate, and like handsome girls in male attire. The females are much better—we expect the Roundhead's daughter with her round shoulders, and almost the beacon, with its indifferent foreshortening. Wherever there are children introduced, they are deliciously painted; and most of the subjects are of a touching nature. Of the letterpress, we cannot say much: "Venice," a poem, by Barry Cornwall; and "The Bride," and "The Woodcutter," two of the editor's neat little prose narratives, being the only essays to be noticed with praise as literary productions. But, after all, such publications must rely chiefly on the Arts; and in this respect the *Tableaux* are worthy of the high names of the Findens.

FINDENS' TABLEAUX (1840). *The Metropolitan Magazine*, November 1839, pp. 91–92.

HERE WE have twelve compositions by J. Browne, which have all very considerable merit, with indications of higher power than is usually employed in this way. The artist seems to have been an attentive student of Retzsch and the other modern Germans. The little groups in outline arranged round the centre figure, and illustrating different points of the same story, are clever, graceful, and imaginative; but the cutting of the corners, and making the main picture an octagon, has, to our eyes, somewhat of an artificial effect. The engraving, in most of the plates, is exceedingly delicate and beautiful. The size of the plates is a great advantage.

The literature of the volume is far superior in quality to any that we have lately seen in Annuals, and does infinite credit to Miss Mitford's taste. She herself, always industrious and conscientious, contributes no fewer than six tales and sketches in prose—her own graceful and unaffected prose, which is worth a great deal more than most other people's poetry. Yet here she has given us some poetry, the productions of her friends, of a very high quality indeed. "The Fetches," by Mr. Horne, the original-minded author of "Cosmo de' Medici," and "The Death of Marlowe," (the latter a wonderful fragment, which has not yet attracted a tithe of the attention it merits,) is an exquisite specimen of dramatic poetry. The whole plan of the piece, which is founded on the old German superstition of the Death Fetch, is novel, wild, and most impressive. There are in it some snatches of song. The following lyric might be fathered upon some of the Shaksperian men.

[Following are sixteen lines from "The Fetches."]

"The Dream," by E.B. Barrett; "Venice," by Barry Cornwall; and "The King's Forrester," by J.Hughes, are beautiful little poems. The "Legend of the Brown Rosarie," also by Miss Barrett, seems to have been inspired by a part of that genius which suggested Goethe's Faust. Each and all of these things give a rare value to the book.

The binding of the volume is in excellent taste.

FINDENS' TABLEAUX (1840). *The United Service Gazette*, 2 November 1839, p. 6.

THIS IS certainly the most attractive of all the publications of its class which have yet reached us. It comprises twelve magnificent engravings, from designs by Mr. S. Browne, the greater part of which are full of grace and beauty. Of this description are the following, viz.,—"The Legend of the Brown Rosary," "The Roundhead's Daughter," "The Pilgrim," "The Beacon," "The Death of Luath," "The Warning," and "The Wood Cutter." By some obliquity of taste a series of designs are introduced around each plate, which completely destroy its effect, and which will not, we trust, be persisted in another year. The literature, such of it at least, as is from the pen of the editress, Miss Mitford, is of a very superior order. We must confess, however, that there is nothing about Miss E.B. Barrett's productions to warrant the great pretence they evince. A more sickening farrago of stilted trash we never perused than her unconscionably long ballad of "The Legend of the Brown Rosary;" nor are the opening verses from her pen much better. The fault of nearly all the pieces in this volume is, that they are too long. Taken as a whole, however, it is one of the most (in fact *the* most) attractive annuals of the season. The binding is superb.

FINDENS' TABLEAUX (1840). *The New Monthly Magazine*, December 1839, p. 559.

[We omit the commencement of this review which praises the binding and illustrations.]

The literature is chiefly by the two most exquisite female writers we have for this species of composition: Miss Mitford (the editor) and Miss E.B. Barrett;—and the entire result is the most readable as well as the most rich and attractive gift-book of the season that we have yet seen.

FINDENS' TABLEAUX (1840). *Tait's Edinburgh Magazine*, December 1839, pp. 813–814.

HOW ENCHANTING a combination—Prose, Poetry, and Art! Over the three united graces, Miss Mitford presides, as in former years, imparting to the TABLEAUX whatever is most charming and characteristic in her peculiar style of thought, invention, and expression. One is glad to find that the ennobling genius of old romance—rudely exorcised from the three volume fictions of the day, whose elements are either wild and extravagant passion, or the stern and coarse realities of vulgar life—obtains refuge in the Annuals. Miss Barrett is once more the tuneful auxiliary of her friend, the Editor. And among her allies of the nobler sex, as they call themselves, are Barry Cornwall, H. Chorley, and R.H. Horne. The latter contributes a slight dramatic sketch *The Death-Fetch*, imbued with poetry. Miss Mitford, however, as well beseems her, plays the principal part in her own entertainment. The nature of her five prose tales (each brief, though graceful and felicitous) may be divined from the prints they illustrate. The *King's Page* is a pretty picture, illustrated by a pretty dramatic incident, the personages of which are Frederick the Great, and the page and his sister. It turns upon sisterly affection, though a little incidental *true love* gives zest to the narrative. *The Proud Ladye*—of which the scene is also Germany, though in the olden time—and *The Roundhead's Daughter* are both love stories; the latter is the gem of the volume. Our Miss Mitford is much more at home on the wolds and among the villages of Kent, Hampshire, and Berkshire, than in the Highlands of Scotland; and so her *Woodcutter* much excels *The Death of Luath*, though it is a neatly-turned clan fragment. A great deal of the poetry of the Tableaux is legendary—a style which is peculiarly suited to the work. Miss Barrett's supernatural legend of the *Brown Rosarie*, is inferior to her beautiful and pathetic poem of last year, but still a wildly imaginative performance. Our only extract must be this graceful opening of Part Third; as it is difficult, within moderate bounds, to convey any idea of how passionate love, and the fear of death tempted Leonora to the deadly sin of sorcery, and how love and faith finally redeemed her from the power of the fiends:—

'Tis a morn for bridal. The merry bride-bell
Ringeth clear through the greenwood that skirts the chapelle,
And the priest at the altar awaiteth the bride,
And the grave young sacristans jest slyly aside,
    At the work shall be doing;
When down through the wood rides that fair companie—
The youths with the courtship, the maids with the glee—
Till the chapel-cross opens to sight, and at once
All the maids sigh demurely, and think for the nonce.
    So endeth the wooing!

And the bride and the bridegroom are leading the way,
With his hand on her rein, and a word yet to say;
Her dropped lids suggest the replyings beneath,
And the little quick smiles come and go with her breath,
    If she sigheth or speaketh.
And the tender bride-mother breaks off unaware
From an Ave, to trow that her daughter is fair;
But in nearing the chapel, and before,
She seeth her little son stand
    Is it play that he

Is it play when his eyes wander in
Yet sublimed with a sadness unfitting a child,
He trembles not, weeps not, his passion;
And meekly he kneels in their midst, wane,
    On his head like a glory sun
"O merry fair maids! ye are many," he cri
"But in fairness and vileness who matcheth
O merry brave youths! ye are many, but who ride?
For courage and wo can ye match with the gro
    As ye see them before ye?"

The pure-minded and pious child is aware of the dealings of his sister with the Fiend. But we cannot follow the legend, which, without its poetical dress, were comparatively tame. In the opening poem, *The Dream*, Miss Barrett, as many ladies have, wittingly or unwittingly, done before her, chooses to mistake a Sleeping Cupid—a very palpable boy-god—for a dreaming child. This plate, which forms the frontispiece to "The Tableaux," is peculiarly rich and delicate, and also gorgeous in those accessary embellishments which this year give a new feature to the prints. These are a series of smaller groups, which "illustrate some point of the story"—according to Miss Mitford—and are so arranged as to form a frame-work round the central figures. Those who see "Knight's Illustrated Shakspere," and other works of the same nature, will be already familiar with the plan. The execution of those dainty, Ariel-like groups is fanciful and delicate. The designs are all by J. Browne; and if somewhat theatrical in character, we may presume the artist meant it so, as the style best adapted to the "Tableaux," such groups always consisting of stage-dressed or masquerading figures. Although it greatly impairs the effect of Mr Kenyon's elegant verses, not to present them with Miss Mitford's ingenious dramatic introduction, as found in the tale of the *Roundhead's Daughter*, we venture this poem in its simple state.

[The review is concluded with Kenyon's "To an Æolian Harp"; this we omit.]

THE SERAPHIM. *The Quarterly Review*, September 1840, pp. 382–389.

MISS ELIZABETH BARRETT, who stands next in our list,* may justly claim to stand alone anywhere else, as well for her extraordinary acquaintance with ancient classic literature, as for the boldness of her poetic attempts. In our judgment, however, her success has not been in proportion to her daring. Her early enthusiasm for Æschylus has sensibly aggravated the tendency to the overstrained and violent, which seems natural to her mind, and irretrievably precluded, we fear, that discipline of art and sense of beauty which a warmer study of Sophocles might probably have imparted. The αὐθαδία of her hero, Prometheus, communicates itself to Miss Barrett's prefaces and notes; she is something too dogmatic in her criticism, and a world too positive in her philosophy. A little more reverence of expression upon all subjects would be more becoming, and not less energetic. The awful name of God is used throughout her

---
*EBB was one of nine writers whose work was examined in an article entitled "Modern English Poetesses"; we include only the remarks pertaining to her.

volumes with such reckless repetition, that we really cannot describe the pain it gave us in perusal, although of course we notice it on the score of ill taste alone. And on the same ground, likewise, we mention and denounce the strange trick, for which Miss Barrett is conspicuous, but not singular, of converting the received monosyllables *called, bowed, vowed*, and the like, into dissyllables, *bowëd, vowëd,*—this not as the usage of solemn emphasis, and the exception, but familiarly and as the rule:—

'And wailing like a kissëd child,
    Kissëd soft against his will.'

Kiss'd, or perhaps correctly *kist*, is what English children have for the last three centuries at least agreed to call the infliction in question, and Shakspeare and Milton, when they grew up, followed the custom. It is really scarcely credible how much the effect of Miss Barrett's poems is injured by this single piece of mannerism alone. These two-dotted words star her pages as if they were written in German, and, to say the least of it, are a very poor compliment to the ears of her readers.

, although less than this would have
But enough.* We proceed with much more
been short ie or two specimens of Miss Barrett's
pleasure tore and better style, and we make the
poetry in er minor miscellaneous poems. The following paratively free from the stiffness of most
of her bl rse, and surely a powerful composition:—

EARTH.

beautiful is Earth! My starry thoughts
 k down on it from their unearthly sphere,
 d sing symphonious—Beautiful is Earth!
 ne lights and shadows of her myriad hills;
The branching greenness of her myriad woods;
Her sky-affecting rocks; her zoning sea;
Her rushing, gleaming cataracts; her streams
That race below, the winged clouds on high;
Her pleasantness of vale and meadow!—
                      Hush!
Meseemeth through the leafy trees to ring
A chime of bells to falling waters tuned,
Whereat comes heathen Zephyrus, out of breath
With running up the hills, and shakes his hair
From off his gleesome forehead, bold and glad
With keeping blithe Dan Phœbus company;—
And throws him on the grass, though half afraid;
First glancing round, lest tempests should be nigh;
And lays close to the ground his ruddy lips,
And shapes their beauty into sound, and calls
On all the petall'd flowers that sit beneath
In hiding-places from the rain and snow,
To loosen the hard soil, and leave their cold
Sad idlesse, and betake them up to him.
They straightway hear his voice.—
                A thought did come,
And press from out my soul the heathen dream.
Mine eyes were purged. Straightway did I bind
Round me the garment of my strength, and heard
Nature's death-shrieking—the hereafter cry,
When He of the lion voice, the rainbow-crown'd,
Shall stand upon the mountains and the sea,
And swear by earth, by heaven's throne, and Him
Who sitteth on the throne, there shall be time
No more, no more! Then veil'd Eternity
Shall straight unveil her awful countenance
Unto the reeling worlds, and take the place
Of seasons, years, and ages. Age and age
Shall be the time of the day. The wrinkled heaven
Shall yield her silent sun, made blind and white
With an exterminating light: the wind,
Unchained from the poles, nor having charge
Of cloud or ocean, with a sobbing wail
Shall rush among the stars, and swoon to death.
Yea, the shrunk earth, appearing livid pale,
Beneath the red-tongued flame, shall shudder by
From out her ancient place, and leave a void.
Yet haply by that void the saints redeem'd
May sometimes stray; when memory of sin,
Ghost-like, shall rise upon their holy souls;
And on their lips shall lie the name of earth

In paleness and in silentness, until
Each looking on his brother, face to face,
And bursting into sudden happy tears,
(The only tears undried) shall murmur—"Christ!"

The following poem is in a very different style, and,
in our judgment, one of the best and most finished of
Miss Barrett's productions. Indeed it is a beautiful
poem:—

COWPER'S GRAVE.

It is a place where poets crown'd
  May feel the heart's decaying—
It is a place where happy saints
  May weep amid their praying—
Yet let the grief and humbleness,
  As low as silence languish;
Earth surely now may give her calm
  To whom she gave her anguish.

O poets! from a maniac's tongue
  Was pour'd the deathless singing!
O Christians! at your cross of hope
  A hopeless hand was clinging!
O men! this man in brotherhood,
  Your weary paths beguiling,
Groan'd inly while he taught you peace,
  And died while ye were smiling.

And now, what time ye all may read
  Through dimming tears his story—
How discord on the music fell,
  And darkness on the glory—
And how, when, one by one, sweet sounds
  And wand'ring lights departed,
He wore no less a loving face,
  Because so broken-hearted.

He shall be strong to sanctify
  The poet's high vocation,
And bow the meekest Christian down
  In meeker adoration;
Nor ever shall he be in praise
  By wise or good forsaken;
Named softly as the household name
  Of one whom God hath taken!

With sadness that is calm, not gloom,
  I learn to think upon him;
With meekness that is gratefulness,
  On God, whose heaven hath won him.
Who suffer'd once the madness-cloud
  Towards his love to blind him;
But gently led the blind along,
  Where breath and bird could find him;

And wrought within his shatter'd brain
  Such quick poetic senses,
As hills have language for, and stars
  Harmonious influences!
The pulse of dew upon the grass
  His own did calmly number;
And silent shadow from the trees
  Fell o'er him like a slumber.

The very world, by God's constraint,
  From falsehood's chill removing,
Its women and its men became
  Beside him true and loving!
And timid hares were drawn from woods
  To share his home-caresses,
Uplooking in his human eyes,
  With sylvan tendernesses.

---

*Upon second thoughts, however, we will also
notice another trick, equally caught, as it seems to
us, from Mr. Tennyson's writings—we mean the
reiterated usage of *very κατ' ἔμφασιν*. 'The hair
had fallen by its weight on *either side the smile*, and
lay *very* blackly on the arm,' &c. &c. &c.—This
is a mere affectation, and totally unidiomatic.

But while in darkness he remain'd,
  Unconscious of the guiding,
And things provided came without
  The sweet sense of providing,
He testified this solemn truth,
  Though frenzy desolated,—
Nor man nor nature satisfy
  Whom only God created.

And the remainder is equally excellent. Miss Barrett's version of the 'Prometheus' is a remarkable performance for a young lady; but it is not a good translation in and by itself. It is too frequently uncouth, without being faithful, and, under a pile of sounding words, lets the fire go out. Thus, to take a single instance within twenty-five lines from the beginning of the drama. Æschylus says:—

σταθευτὸς δ' ἡλίου φοίβῃ φλογὶ
χροιῦς ἀμείψεις ἄνθος.

That is, 'and thou (Prometheus) *toasted* (slowly burnt) by the shining fire of the sun, shalt change the flower (beauty) of your colour (complexion).' Miss Barrett renders this simple passage thus:—

'where '*stablished*
'Neath the fierce sun thy *brow's white flower* shall fade;'

which, beside the mistake of σταθευτὸς, is really mere nonsense. Again, scarcely anything can be finer than the accelerated movement given to the speeches in the last sixty lines of the drama, beginning with,—

εἰδότι τοι μοὶ τάσδ' ἀγγελίας
ὅδ' ἐθώϋξεν, κ.τ.λ.

It is like the preparatory rapid of Niagara, which you see not till you feel the whirl. The play goes off, like the great Titan himself, in a flash of fire, and skilfully compensates to the reader now, as it did once to the auditor, the slow narrative march of so much of that which has preceded. Miss Barrett has not attempted to reproduce this grand effect of the anapæstic systems of the Greek, for which, nevertheless, there are great facilities in English; and instead of the fullest and completest close in the whole range of the Greek drama, the English 'Prometheus' comes to an end before you expect it.*

'The Seraphim,' a dramatic lyric poem, represents the converse of two Seraphs, Ador and Zerah, the strong and the weak, whilst hovering, aloof from the rest of the Seraphic host, over Calvary during the Passion; a subject from which Milton would have shrunk, and which Miss Barrett would not have attempted, if she had more seriously considered its absolute unapproachableness. In the first place, there is not, in the proper critical sense, any human interest in such a subject; and in the next place, the awful narrative of the Evangelist exterminates all parallel or supplement. The least unsuccessful attempt upon the 'guarded mount,' in our day, is to be found in some parts of Mr. Heraud's 'Descent into Hell,' a remarkable poem, and worthy of the studious perusal which indeed it requires. We give Miss Barrett, however, the full credit of a lofty purpose, and admit, moreover, that several particular passages in her poem are extremely fine; equally profound in thought, and striking in expression. But we prefer concluding our hasty notice of this lady's writings with an extract from her somewhat fantastic poem, 'Isobel's Child,' which may be considered a fair specimen of Miss Barrett's general manner and power:—

'Tis aye a solemn thing to me
To look upon a babe that sleeps;
Wearing in its spirit-deeps
The unrevealed mystery
Of its Adam's taint and woe,
Which, when they revealed be,
Will not let it slumber so!
Lying new in life beneath
The shadow of the coming death,
With that soft low quiet breath,
  As if it felt the sun!
Knowing all things by their blooms,
Not their roots! Yea! sun and sky
Only by the warmth that comes
Out of each!—earth, only by
The pleasant hues that o'er it run!
And human love, by drops of sweet
White nourishment still hanging round
The little mouth so slumber-bound!
All which broken sentiency
Will gather, and unite, and climb,
  To an immortality,
Good or evil, each sublime,
Through life and death to life again.
O little lids, now closed fast,
Must ye learn to drop at last
Over large and burning tears?
O warm quick body! must thou lie,
When is the round of years,
Bare of all the joy and pain,
Dust in dust—thy place upgiving
To creeping worms in sentient living?
O small frail being! wilt thou stand
  At God's right hand,
Lifting up those sleeping eyes,
Dilated by sublimest destinies,
In endless waking? Thrones and Seraphim,

---

*We have lately been favoured with the perusal of a very free version, or rather imitation of this great poem, from the manuscript of which we are permitted to make the following quotation; and we think our readers will agree with us that such poetry ought not always to remain unpublished:—

CHORUS.—μηδὲν φοβηθῆς. φιλία γὰρ ἥδε τάξις
πτερύγων θοαῖς ἁμίλλαις
προσέβα, κ.τ.λ.—v. 128, &c.

'O fear not us!
A long, long way we come to visit thee;
  To this extreme of earth,
  On clipping pinions borne.

For the grating of fetters,
  The voice of upbraiding,
The deep earthly groan
  Of anguish half stifled;
The ear-piercing shriek
  Of pain in its sharpness,

A concert, all tuneless, came ruffling the rose-buds,
Where sweetly we slumber'd the sultry hours;
So with pinions unsmooth'd, and tresses unbraided,
Our bright feet unsandall'd, we leap'd on the air;
Like the sound of a trumpet we shook the wide ether;
A moment we quiver'd—then glancing on high,
Ascended a sun-ray, light pillar of silver,
And seem'd the gay spangles that danced in the beam.'

Through the long ranks of their solemnities,
Sunning thee with calm looks of heaven's surprise—
Thy look alone on *Him?*
Or else, self-willed, to the Godless place—
(God keep thy will!)—feel thine own energies,
Cold, strong, objectless, like a dead man's clasp,
The sleepless, deathless life within thee, grasp,—
While myriad faces, like one changeless face,
With woe, not love's, shall glass thee everywhere,
And overcome thee with thine own despair?
  In a word, we consider Miss Barrett to be a woman of undoubted genius, and most unusual learning; but that she has indulged her inclination for themes of sublime mystery, not certainly without displaying great power, yet at the expense of that clearness, truth, and proportion, which are essential to beauty; and has most unfortunately fallen into the trammels of a school or manner of writing, which of all that ever existed—Lycophron, Lucan, and Gongora not forgotten—is the most open to the charge of being *vitiis imitabile exemplar.*

[Editors' note: At the end of the article (p. 416), each of the nine poetesses was compared to a flower: "Miss Barrett must be *Greek Valerian,* or *Ladder to Heaven*; or, if she pleases, *Wild Angelica.*"
  This review was reprinted in full in *The Museum of Foreign Literature, Science, and Art,* Vol. 41, February 1841, pp. 195–197.]

WORKS BY RB

SORDELLO. The Spectator, 14 March 1840, p. 257.

WHAT THIS poem may be in its extent we are unable to say, for we *cannot* read it. Whatever may be the poetical spirit of Mr. BROWNING, it is so overlaid in *Sordello* by digression, affectation, obscurity, and all the faults that spring, it would seem, from crudity of plan and a self-opinion which will neither cull thoughts nor revise composition, that the reader—at least a reader of our stamp—turns away. The scene is laid in Italy, during the age of Frederick the Second, when the country was in its palmy state, and the contest of the Guelphs and Ghibellines in full vigour.

SORDELLO. Bell's Life in London and Sporting Chronicle, 15 March 1840, p. 4.

IN THE NAME of Browning, many of our readers will recognize the author of "Paracelsus," a work of extraordinary power and promise. The poem before us is of a higher and more ambitious tendency, and cast in a maturer mould. It requires, and will, we believe, richly repay a careful, and patient [s]tudy. This we have not yet been able to afford it, and the little space necessarily allotted to this department of our journal will not admit of our attempting an analysis at all adequate to its merits and importance. It may be described as the psyc[h]ological biography of Sordello, a provençal poet of the twelfth century, an exposition of the sensations, aspirations, and progress of the poetic mind and character. There are many and rare beauties throughout the book, from which we select the following address to Dante, showing, we think, the impress and true cunning of a master-hand—"the vision and the faculty divine."
              Florentine!
  A herald star* I know thou did'st absorb

*Sordello

Relentless into the consummate orb
That scared it from its right to roll along
A sempiternal path, with dance and song,
Fulfilling its allotted period,
Serenest of the progeny of God,
Who yet resigns it not, his darling stoops
With no quenched lights, desponds with no blank troops
Of disenfranchised brilliances, for, blest
Utterly with thee, its shy element
Like thine upburneth prosperous and clear—
* * Dante, pacer of the shore
Where glutted hell disgorgeth dithiest gloom,
Unbitten by its whirring sulphur spume—
Or whence the grieved and obscure waters slope
Into a darkness quieted by hope—
Plucker of amaranths grown beneath God's eye
In gracious twilights where his chosen lie.

SORDELLO. The Atlas, 28 March 1840, p. 203.

WE ARE disappointed in this poem, and have no inclination to dwell at length upon the causes of what we must consider a descent from the high promise of *Paracelsus.* The faults of that production were obvious—rugged and abrupt lines—strange turns of expression—want of fullness and completeness. Its merits were equally striking—intense enthusiasm—rich imagery—profound feeling—strong delineation. In the poem of *Sordello,* all the faults recur in exaggerated shapes, without being relieved or compensated for by an equal amount of excellence in any single point of view.
  The subject is one of deep and extraordinary interest. The readers of DANTE need not be reminded of it, nor need it be suggested to them as a theme pregnant with capabilities. Mr. BROWNING has treated it in the narrative form; and an odd, fantastic narrative he has made of it—sometimes starting off into a mood of scoffing humour, anon melting into pathos, and then bursting out into passion, but fulfilling none of the conditions of any of these fits, and producing a mosaic of bits and tints

which it is difficult to trace with satisfaction or coherency. Nor does he make amends to us even by occasional fragments of the beautiful, such as we believe his genius to be able to accomplish. The whole structure is faulty, not only in its entire outline, but in its minutest details. One example, long enough to include samples of most of the peculiarities of the writer, will suffice as an illustration:—

> Is it the same Sordello in the dusk
> As at the dawn? merely a perished husk
> Now, that arose a power like to build
> Up Rome again? The proud conception chilled
> So soon? Ay, watch that latest dream of thine
> —A Rome indebted to no Palatine,
> Drop arch by arch, Sordello! Art possest
> Of thy wish now?—rewarded for thy quest
> To-day among Ferrara's squalid sons?—
> Are this, and this, and this the shining ones
> Meet for the Shining City? Sooth to say
> Our favoured tenantry pursue their way
> After a fashion? This companion slips
> On the smooth causey, t'other blinkard trips
> At his mooned sandal. Leave to lead the brawls
> Here i' the atria? No, friend. He that sprawls
> On aught but a stibadium suffers . . . . goose,
> Puttest our lustral vase to such an use?
> Oh, huddle up the day's disasters—march
> Ye runagates, and drop thou, arch by arch,
> Rome!
>
> Yet before they quite disband—a whim—
> Study a shelter, now, for him, and him,
> Nay, even him, to house them! any cave
> Suffices—throw out earth. A loophole! Brave!
> They ask to feel the sun shine, see the grass
> Grow, hear the larks sing? Dead art thou, alas,
> And I am dead! But here's our son excels
> At hurdle-weaving any Scythian, fells
> Oak and devises rafters, dreams and shapes
> That dream into a door-post, just escapes
> The mystery of hinges. Lie we both
> Perdue another age. The goodly growth
> Of brick and stone! Our building-pelt was rough
> But that descendant's garb suits well enough
> A portico-contriver. Speed the years—
> What's time to us? and lo, a city rears
> Itself! nay, enter—what's the grave to us?
> So our forlorn acquaintance carry thus
> A head! successively sewer, forum, cirque—
> Last age that aqueduct was counted work,
> And now they tire the artificer upon
> Blank alabaster, black obsidion,
> —Careful Jove's face be duly fulgurant,
> And mother Venus' kiss-creased nipples pant
> Back into pristine pulpiness, ere fixed
> Above the baths. What difference betwixt
> This Rome and ours?

Here we have the same pitching, hysterical, and broken sobs of sentences—the same excisions of words—the same *indications* of power—imperfect grouping of thoughts and images—and hurried, exclamatory, and obscure utterance of things that would, probably, be very fine if we could get them in their full meaning, but which, in this bubbling and tumult of the verse, are hardly intelligible—the same idiosyncrasy of mind and manner that was first exhibited in *Paracelsus*, and that was afterwards carried to still greater excess in *Strafford*. We looked for an improvement upon all this in *Sordello*. We expected that the poet would have shaken off these crudities, and emerged a natural and free man, disenchanted out of his youthful heresies, and prepared to exhibit a sound and vigorous maturity. But we are disappointed. *Sordello* is worse than *Strafford*, with less excuse, for what might be tolerated in the clamour and heat of action in a drama, is intolerable in a narrative; and it is further chargeable with betraying the disagreeable truth that the author has not only benefited nothing from experience, but that the sins of his verse are premeditated, wilful, and incurable.

SORDELLO. *The Metropolitan Magazine*, April 1840, pp. 108–109.

IF IT WERE possible to understand the meaning of the writer of this poem, we should be delighted to impart the information to our readers. It is full of hard words and mysterious sentences, but what they allude to, it would puzzle a conjuror to tell. In this dilemma, what can we do better than let Mr. Browning speak for himself?

> —Meantime, just meditate my madrigal
> O' the mugwort that conceals a dewdrop safe!
> What, dullard? We and you in smothery chafe,
> Babes, baldheads, stumbled thus far into Zin
> The Horrid, getting neither out nor in,
> A *hungry* sun above us, *sands among*
> Our throats, each dromedary lolls a tongue,
> Each camel churns a sick and frothy chap,
> And you, 'twixt tales of Potiphar's mishap,
> And sonnets on the *earliest ass that spoke*,
> Remark you wonder any one needs choak
> With founts about! Potsherd him Gibeonites,
> While awkwardly enough your Moses smites
> The rock, though he forego the Promised Land,
> Thereby, have Satan claim his carcass, and
> Dance, forsooth, Metaphysic Poet . . . . ah
> Mark ye the dim first oozings?

This is a fair specimen of the poem throughout. We had rather write sonnets on the *latest*, as well as the earliest *speaking ass*, than be doomed to read such unintelligible oozings of nonsense.

SORDELLO. *The New Monthly Belle Assemblée*, April 1840, p. 214.

IF MR. BROWNING will write, we wish he would write something comprehensible. Sordello is full of hard names, and nonsense. He calls it poetry, we term it trash of the very worst description.

PARACELSUS (1835). *La Revue Des Deux Mondes*, April 1840, pp. 127–133.

DU THÉÂTRE EN ANGLETERRE. *Paracelse* (*Paracelsus, a drama*) est d'autant plus digne de remarque, que son mérite a passé à peu près inaperçu en Angleterre. Rarement un poète a perdu plus de pensée, d'éclat, de pathétique et de profondeur dans une création sans avenir, mais non sans puissance. Comme essai dramatique, c'est le néant même. A peine éclos, vite oublié, noyé dans les dissertations d'une esthétique nuageuse et dans les périphrases d'un style prolixe, ce livre doit être signalé cependant comme une très belle analyse psychologique et morale.

L'auteur a voulu mettre en scène un révolutionnaire de la science et intéresser le lecteur aux vicissitudes de sa pensée. Le personnage de Paracelse était bien choisi; il représente tout un mouvement de civilisation. Fils du XIXe siècle, nous sommes étonnés de celui qui s'opère sous nos yeux; au commencement du XVIe, il s'en fit un bien plus étrange dont le nôtre n'est que le développement, et dont nous suivons encore l'impulsion. Alors paraissent en même temps Cardan, rédacteur de magnifiques formules géométriques; Copernic, qui dit au soleil comme Josué: *Arrête-toi!* Corneille Agrippa, qui soutenait en 1510 la même thèse que Jean-Jacques en 1750; Luther, Calvin et Melancthon. Par eux, toute la vieille autorité est ébranlée. Les évolutions du monde nouveau vont s'opérer sur un nouvel axe. Je ne pardonne pas à Voltaire de s'être moqué de Cardan et d'avoir abaissé Luther. Qu'était-il, Voltaire, qui cultivait le doute; qu'était-il, auprès de ceux qui en avaient hardiment jeté le premier germe dans le sol de l'Europe? Le plus original de ces personnages étranges fut, sans aucun doute, Paracelse, qui renouvela la médecine et créa la chimie moderne, nécromant, sorcier, alchimiste, charlatan; Paracelse, qui se vanta d'avoir trouvé la pierre philosophale et la quadrature du cercle, et qui enfermait le démon dans le pommeau de son épée. L'ardeur de la science, la fièvre de connaître, le besoin de la gloire, précipitèrent à travers toutes les folies, tous les voyages, tous les ridicules, cette intelligence enflammée. C'est Faust réduit à la réalité, n'écoutant d'autre Méphistophélès que ses passions et son amour-propre, entouré d'ennemis, d'envieux et d'admirateurs, plein de mépris pour l'espèce humaine, qui est si facile à tromper, irrité jusqu'au délire de notre impuissance à pénétrer les secrets de la vie; aux yeux des uns, ange de lumière; aux yeux des autres, fils de l'enfer; à ses propres yeux, être incomplet et impuissant; pour l'histoire et l'avenir, énigme.

La beauté et la difficulté de cette analyse ont séduit l'imagination de Robert Browning. Le drame intérieur, qui se joue chez tous les hommes célèbres et grands, et qui prend un caractère de frénétique beauté chez un personnage tel que Paracelse, moitié sublime et moitié fou, a exercé sur le jeune poète, dont l'intelligence est évidemment subtile et profonde, une fascination irrésistible; il a tenté d'en faire l'œuvre précisément la plus opposée à la nature même de ses pensées et de son sujet, une pièce de théâtre. Il n'y a pas de plus étrange petit livre que le sien. Descendant en ligne directe de Wordsworth pour la dissection métaphysique des idées, de Goethe pour la poésie plastique et extérieure, et de Byron pour le scepticisme, l'auteur a cru que ces élémens, précieux d'ailleurs, feraient un drame. Ce sont des scènes, et il n'y manque, pour que l'œuvre soit dramatique, qu'une toute petite chose, le drame. Au premier acte, Paracelse déclare à ses amis qu'il veut chercher, au péril de son bonheur, la science et la gloire. Au second acte, ayant beaucoup voyagé, il découvre que la science n'est pas tout, qu'elle tue l'amour, et que sans l'union des deux facultés, amour et intelligence, l'ame humaine languit et meurt. Au troisième acte, il revient en Europe, professe la médecine à Bâle, atteint la gloire, augmente son crédit en mystifiant les hommes, et retombant sur lui-même avec plus de douleur que jamais, reconnaît la misère de ces trois ruines dont il est possesseur, science incomplète, amour impuissant, gloire menteuse. Au quatrième acte, il redescend de ses sublimes inspirations, demande à la volupté terrestre l'oubli de son ennui et de ses peines, retrouve quelque paix et quelque espérance dans la foi vulgaire et dans l'abnégation de l'orgueil, et finit par mourir à l'hôpital de Salzburg. Tout cela se passe entre quatre personnes, ou plutôt ce n'est qu'un monologue en deux mille vers, interrompu par quelques questions incidentes. Festus, l'homme simple et l'ami dévoué; Michal, sa femme; Aprile, jeune homme beau comme Apollon, symbole de la poésie et des arts, ne prennent la parole de temps en temps que pour donner à Paracelse l'occasion de plonger le scalpel dans sa propre pensée, d'interroger l'immensité de ses désirs, le désespoir de ses efforts et le dédain que lui inspirent son succès et l'admiration du genre humain. Voilà tout. Jamais drame n'osa se présenter avec de tels élémens. Nul mouvement, nulle péripétie, nulle catastrophe; rien qu'une élégie éloquente, suivant dans son cours tortueux la vie de Paracelse, comme le soleil et les nuages marquent d'ombre et de lumière le Rhin tombant en nappes bouillonnantes, disparaissant sous les rochers, ou se développant comme un large miroir qui étincelle. Par un renversement singulier de l'art dramatique, vous n'apercevez plus dans cette œuvre aucune action visible. Le phénomène extérieur des passions et des caractères humains s'évanouit. Il fait place au phénomène intérieur d'une pensée qui s'étudie et d'une ame qui se creuse.

Nous signalons ce résultat bizarre comme le dernier terme de l'abus métaphysique si naturel à la muse du Nord. Le drame d'escamotage habile que les Français ont adopté récemment, le drame d'incidents et de passion que les Espagnols ont porté si haut vers le commencement du XVIIe siècle, occupent l'extrémité opposée du diamètre. Shakspeare penche, mais sans excès, vers l'observation métaphysique du Nord; Calderon, sacrifiant au contraire la pensée à l'action et à la couleur, gravite aussi d'un autre côté vers le point central et vers la perfection de l'art. Quant à l'auteur nouveau dont nous parlons, philosophe et poète remarquable, il faut le nier comme dramaturge.

Prenons-le donc pour ce qu'il est, non pour ce qu'il croit être. Comme œuvre d'analyse philosophique, son prétendu drame est rempli de talent. La poésie des images y est jetée à pleines mains sur la subtilité des pensées. *Manfred* et *Faust* ne renferment pas de plus beaux passages que certains fragmens de ce *Paracelse*, obscurci par tant de divagations inutiles et construit sur un plan insoutenable. Nous donnerons pour exemple la rencontre et le dialogue de Paracelse et d'Aprile, symboles, l'un de la science, l'autre de l'amour, du besoin de connaître qui veut pénétrer tous les secrets du monde visible et invisible, de l'amour s'assimilant à tous les genres de beauté, et produisant la poésie, la musique et les arts.

—Qui es-tu (demande Aprile à Paracelse), homme profond et inconnu?

PARACELSE.—Je suis le mortel qui aspire à CONNAITRE.—Et toi?

APRILE.—Je voudrais AIMER infiniment et être AIMÉ.
PARACELSE.—Esclave! je suis ton roi.
APRILE.—Ah! Dieu t'a bien partagé. L'idéal que je poursuis me fuit sans cesse. Mon désir est immense, et le feu qui me brûle me consume sans me satisfaire. Toi, génie attentif et patient, tu acquiers toujours, tu amasses sans cesse. Ah! malheureux! malheureux que je suis!
PARACELSE.—Calme-toi, je te l'ordonne au nom de la puissance que j'ai sur toi. Je veux te connaître, je veux savoir ce que tu désires.
APRILE.—Ne te l'ai-je pas dit? Je n'ai qu'un but, qu'un désir: aimer! Toutes les belles formes du monde, je voudrais les reproduire dans le marbre, dans la pierre et dans le bronze. Ah! si je pouvais! si je pouvais! rien n'échapperait à ma sympathie; la nymphe, ame secrète des chênes séculaires, le majestueux vieillard à longue barbe, le jeune homme dans sa première beauté, l'athlète aux muscles nerveux, la femme plus souple, plus moelleuse et plus blanche que le cygne; toutes les passions, tous les désirs, toutes les idées; la laideur même et sa beauté, qui est l'énergie, voilà ce que je voudrais saisir et créer d'un mot. O Dieu! permets-moi de les reproduire, ces beautés que poursuit mon inutile amour, forêts, vallées, miroir de l'Océan, lacs étincelans sous le soleil qui naît, et vous, labyrinthes de bronze, pyramides de pierre, villes peuplées d'hommes, et vous, agitations, passions, cruautés, ambitions, dont le cœur se nourrit et dont il meurt! Qui me donnera des couleurs pour tout exprimer, et des paroles pour tout reproduire, et des notes musicales pour imiter les mouvemens mystérieux de l'ame et les inconnus balancemens des planètes! qui me permettra d'épuiser tout ce que le monde et la vie offrent à l'admiration et à l'amour, jusqu'à ce que Dieu me reprenne à lui, lui l'éternel amour! (Paracelse soupire.)
APRILE.—Tu soupires? Tu n'es donc pas mon roi! Tu n'as point passé par mes épreuves; tu n'as pas souffert de mes souffrances.
PARACELSE.—Continue.
APRILE.—Tu n'as pas, comme moi, arrêté ton regard sur le soleil idéal jusqu'à devenir aveugle. Tu as cherché la cause de tout, et non la sympathie et l'amour des choses divines. On prétend qu'il y a partout des squelettes, dans les fleurs, dans les arbres, dans les étoiles même qui resplendissent là-haut. Ces squelettes, tu les a cherchés. En es-tu plus heureux?
PARACELSE.—Non.
APRILE.—Tu t'occupes à démeubler la nature, moi je la meuble. Cette société des hommes avec leurs lois et leurs coutumes est pour moi une île déserte. J'y bâtis mon palais comme je puis. La réalité est vulgaire, je la transforme. Les coquillages amassés au bord de la mer sont mes diamans, les branches des arbres sont les arcades de mon palais, le jonc tressé remplace le tapis de pourpre, l'imagination est ma servante, et l'opulente fée obéit à toutes mes volontés. Amour universel, sympathie sans bornes! Dans le cœur du paysan et du berger, je découvre une pensée qui est l'essence de la poésie; et ce qu'il y a de plus vulgaire au monde, la branche desséchée qui tombe dans les cavernes de ma poésie, en sort parée de cristaux qui brillent au soleil. O maître orgueilleux, as-tu ce pouvoir? N'as-tu jamais senti cette ivresse? N'as-tu jamais été conduit au désespoir par l'aspiration vers la beauté, et des milliers de fantômes n'ont-ils pas flotté devant toi pour te mener au précipice? N'as-tu pas compris l'impuissance des sons pour reproduire les accens de l'ame, celle des couleurs et des formes, celle des rythmes et des mots? N'as-tu pas vu que plus la pensée grandit et s'élève, plus la parole devient faible et débile? Dis-moi cela, mon seigneur?
PARACELSE.—Le désir de *connaitre* a son impuissance; l'homme n'est que faible poussière!
APRILE.—Tu pleures! toi, des larmes! toi, le maître! toi, le roi!
PARACELSE.—Nous sommes misérables tous deux. Apprends à CONNAITRE, et que Dieu m'apprenne à AIMER. Qu'il nous pardonne à tous deux, êtres ambitieux et impuissans! Nous avons rêvé, Aprile, et nous nous éveillons. Nous sommes deux voyageurs transportés dans un monde de féerie et qui se retrouvent tout à coup auprès de leur foyer. Nous portons les cicatrices du voyage, mais nous avons aussi les bracelets d'or et les colliers de perles dont nos bras ont été parés. J'ai cherché la *science*, comme tu as cherché l'*amour;* aveugle comme toi! L'amour n'est rien sans la science, ni la science sans l'amour. Cependant nos conquêtes nous restent; j'ai la puissance; tu as la beauté. Hélas! nous nous éveillons cependant, et l'expiation nous attend l'un et l'autre.
APRILE.—Je le vois, Dieu est la poésie complète.
PARACELSE.—Dieu est la science parfaite. Les deux moitiés de l'idéal se réunissent en lui seul. Faibles et fous que nous sommes! mortels débiles! nous avons voulu les atteindre en les isolant. Nous sommes trop punis!

Ce qu'il y a d'élévation et de profondeur dans ces pages n'a pas besoin de commentaire. Paracelse, représentant l'ardeur de connaître au commencement du XVIe siècle, c'est-à-dire à une époque de renouvellement total où la pensée humaine changeait de peau comme le serpent, offre au philosophe un spectacle d'un intérêt immense. C'est, je l'ai dit, un révolutionnaire de la pensée; il ne voit que l'avenir, il n'a foi qu'aux nouvelles espérances qui animent le genre humain. Il veut savoir, non le passé qu'il rejette, mais ce qui est et ce qui sera. Il veut *connaitre*, non les livres, non l'érudition proprement dite, mais le présent, mais l'avenir, mais l'essence des êtres. Il rompt à jamais avec les connaissances acquises par les autres nations et les autres temps, avec les maximes et les conquêtes des sages d'autrefois.

«La vérité n'est-elle pas en nous-mêmes? (dit-il dans le poème). Il y a en nous tous un point central où l'intime vérité réside dans sa plénitude. Autour d'elle, s'élèvent des remparts qui l'environnent et l'obstruent; la chair et les sens dérobent la flamme de la vérité à nos propres yeux. *Connaitre*, c'est délivrer la vérité captive; c'est ouvrir une issue au rayon secret et caché qui est en nous.»

Paracelse n'admettra donc rien de ce qui est convenu; plein de courage et de foi en lui-même, chevalier d'aventure, rejetant tous les anciens naturalistes et tous les vieux philosophes, il n'est là que pour courir le monde pour dégager, au moyen de l'expérience active, cette vérité cachée. Plus il avance, plus cette soif de savoir s'augmente et s'irrite; à mesure qu'elle s'abreuve, elle devient plus ardente. Paracelse rit des hommes qui l'admirent, il rit de les voir redoubler d'enthousiasme quand il les trompe; il prend en pitié sa gloire et son école:

«Vous avez vu ce matin, dit-il à Festus son ami, la foule qui se pressait autour de ma chaire! Parbleu! ce n'est pas merveille d'exciter leurs bravos et de faire battre leurs cœurs. Mes principes sont simples; je détruis et je nie. Toutes les fois qu'on nie ce que la foule et les âges ont accepté, la foule est là béante, sans haleine, l'œil hagard, les cheveux hérissés, attendant le tonnerre qui va frapper ses idoles. Comptons un peu mes admirateurs:

voyons! D'abord ceux qu'attirent la curiosité, l'étonnement, la nouveauté, rien de plus; puis la race nombreuse des sots qui veulent des miracles; je leur en donne. Ensuite vient le nombreux bataillon de ceux qui haïssent les institutions établies et les écoles adoptées, toujours prêts à seconder l'homme qui attaque, jusqu'à ce que, victorieux à son tour, ayant planté le drapeau de sa doctrine, il les voie se retourner contre lui. Jetez sur cette cohue une infusion considérable d'indifférens qui profitent de la circonstance; esprits madrés, trop habiles pour s'opposer au courant des opinions, flatteurs adroits qui caresseront et protégeront mon système, charmés de lui donner un développement absurde qui le tuera!

«Pourquoi grossir la liste? Tous ces gens ont leur intérêt à servir, et la vérité leur importe peu. Restent peut-être douze ou quinze pauvres hères qui aiment sincèrement la science, qui ont foi au pouvoir de la vérité; ceux-là méritent ma sympathie et mes efforts: ce n'est pas la peine d'en parler!»

Voilà comment le réformateur apprécie ceux qui l'admirent. Ainsi se juge lui-même, au milieu de sa gloire, ce révolutionnaire et ce novateur. Il n'a pas touché le but qu'il voulait atteindre; il n'a pas découvert le grand mystère de la vie et du monde. La couronne qu'il a obtenue, c'est la réputation, et il la méprise. L'ombre de sa gloire lui fait peur et pitié:

«Je la sais bien, dit-il, je suis en avant de mon siècle. Je suis un de ces flots précurseurs qui viennent battre le rivage, long-temps avant que la multitude des vagues le suive et recouvre la côte. Je sais bien quelle sera ma destinée. On usera de ma pensée en la niant, on montera sur mon cadavre en le déshonorant. Orgueil ou vanité, je n'ai rien voulu devoir à mes ancêtres; on ne voudra rien me devoir. J'ai détruit, on me détruira; c'est juste. J'ai élevé un échafaudage sur lequel on montera pour découvrir de nouvelles régions de la science. Que m'importe après tout? J'aurai accompli mon destin, Dieu fera le reste!»

Convaincu de la vanité de la science et de celle de la gloire, Paracelse cherche enfin le plaisir; il se plonge dans les délices sensuelles et trouve en échange de sa dernière tentative le mépris des hommes qui se vengent ainsi de ses dédains. Lorsque, malade et mourant sur son grabat de l'hôpital, à Salzburg, Paracelse retrouve auprès de lui Festus, le cordial et simple ami qui ne l'a jamais abandonné, l'auteur touche tout à coup à l'effet dramatique, et l'atteint naïvement par une invention très simple et très belle.

PARACELSE, sur son lit de mort.—Parle-moi! Que j'entende ta voix! Chante quelque vieille ballade. Je ne veux point songer au passé, je ne veux point rêver!... Parle-moi.

FESTUS, chantant.—«Le Mein est un fleuve charmant dont les flots coulent doucement, à travers les vallons, à travers les prairies; et ses petits flots qui bruissent font la musique la plus douce. Il coule, il coule paresseux sous le soleil qui brille, au milieu des gazons, au milieu des joncs et des charmantes primevères; et de temps à autre l'abeille rase ses vagues en bourdonnant, et le martin-pêcheur qui plane, avec son plumage de feu, baigne le bout de son aile quand midi sonne au clocher des hameaux...»

PARACELSE.—Mon cœur, mon cœur s'éveille et se desserre lorsque j'entends cette chanson de la jeunesse; les ténèbres passent, le serpent noir qui me pressait l'ame se déroule enfin et me quitte. Ah! Festus, je respire! c'est toi, c'est toi!

Après cet admirable mouvement, Festus console son ami, dont l'agonie s'éclaire d'un rayon d'espoir sublime:

«Esprit souverain (lui dit son ami), maître, créateur, inventeur, ceux qui raillent les convulsions de ta vie se moqueront de l'Etna dont les profondeurs bouillonnent. Je t'ai connu, moi! je te comprends, je te suis fidèle. Je t'ai vu surgir et lutter. Je te vois mourir. O Dieu puissant, que je sois traité comme il le sera. Si tu m'avais créé fort comme lui, j'aurais failli comme lui; advienne que pourra, je suis avec lui, je suis pour lui!... Dieu! nous nous présentons ensemble devant toi: punis-nous, ou récompense-nous ensemble!»

Paracelse, œuvre qui porte, comme on le voit, toutes les traces d'un esprit supérieur, mais que déparent la diffusion, l'incohérence, le vague des détails et le défaut de concentration dans la forme, ne se rapproche du drame que par son titre.

SORDELLO. *The Dublin Review*, May 1840, pp. 551–553.

THIS IS A work by the author of Paracelsus, and one not likely to exalt his reputation, or to produce any adipose tendency in the exchequer of his respectable publisher. The title page is brief, not defining its character. This brevity may be studied, to enhance curiosity, or forced, from the difficulty of selecting the most appropriate description of the production issued. We have noted down several definitions, out of many that have struck us in the perusal, as being fitted to characterise it; such as "Sordello a conundrum," from the difficulty of making out the meaning or object of the author. "Sordello, couplets illustrative of the interrogative system;" from the profuse use made of the contorted marks of interrogation, which are spread in great numbers through the pages, standing like so many Scarrons, Popes and Æsops, but not contributing their wit, melody or wisdom. "Sordello, or exercises for the asthmatics," from the wheezy, spasmodic, sobbing nature of the verse. These are but a few specimens which the perusal has suggested to us; but as the determination, seeing their conflicting pretensions, is difficult, we must imitate a late chancellor, and postpone our final judgment.

We remember perusing the *Paracelsus* with some gratification, as a work of promise, which, despite its many defects, led us to hope that ultimately, we should be able to hail the author as one deserving of taking his seat among the crowned poets of the age, and whose productions would hereafter contribute fresh stores of beauty, strength, philosophic insight, and harmonious thought, appareled in majestic and melodious numbers, to the literature of our country. The play of *Strafford* somewhat checked that expectation. Although in it there was no insignificant dexterity in the construction, and language occasionally exhibited power and richness, and somewhat of an artistic eye, there was a meanness in the working out of his conceptions, a want of dignity and

List of Absent Letters

DURING THE COURSE of our research in editing the Brownings' correspondence, brief references have been found, principally in sale catalogues, to additional letters. All attempts to locate these documents have failed. In addition, some letters are in known locations, but access to them has been denied. Following is a list of letters which, for such reasons, are absent from this volume. Those that are located and become available will be presented in a supplementary volume.

[1838]. John Kenyon to EBB. In the private collection of Aurelia Brooks Harlan.

[ca. May 1838]. John Kenyon to EBB. In the private collection of Aurelia Brooks Harlan.

[ca. June 1838]. John Kenyon to EBB. In the private collection of Aurelia Brooks Harlan.

[June 1838]. John Kenyon to EBB. In the private collection of Aurelia Brooks Harlan.

[June 1838]. John Kenyon to EBB. A second letter. In the private collection of Aurelia Brooks Harlan.

15 July 1838. John Kenyon to EBB. In the private collection of Aurelia Brooks Harlan.

11 November 1838. John Kenyon to EBB. In the private collection of Aurelia Brooks Harlan.

5 July 1840. EBB to William Cox Bennett. Offered for sale by Sotheby's, 27 February 1896, lot 271. 4pp., 12mo. Discusses literary matters.

List of Collections

(References are to letter number, not page number.)

Armstrong Browning Library, Baylor University, Waco, Texas, 604, 608, 613, 616, 624, 628, 643, 646, 657, 676, 708, 722, 723, 745, 749, 764, 768, 770, 782

Barrett, Edward R. Moulton-, Platt, England, 631, 662, 688, 692, 759

Barrett, Myrtle Moulton-, Ringwood, England, 610, 714, 731

Barrett, Ronald A. Moulton-, Aberdeenshire, Scotland, 610, 714, 731

Berg Collection, The Henry W. & Albert A., The New York Public Library, Astor, Lenox and Tilden Foundations, 603, 666, 686, 690, 695, 703, 738, 741, 752

Boston Public Library, Boston, Massachusetts, 681, 702

British Library, Department of Manuscripts, London, 656, 682, 739, 747

Browning Settlement, London, 778

Columbia University, New York, 634

Dunedin Public Library, Dunedin, New Zealand, 711

Fitzwilliam Museum, Cambridge, England, 614

Folger Shakespeare Library, Washington, D.C., 779

Harvard University, Cambridge, Massachusetts, 622

Hervey-Bathurst, Hon. Mrs. Elizabeth, Ledbury, England, 611, 619, 644, 658, 699, 707

Huntington Library, The Henry E., San Marino, California, 635, 642, 659, 663, 678, 689, 754

Iowa, University of, Iowa City, Iowa, 637

Kentucky, University of, Lexington, Kentucky, 753

Meredith, Michael, Eton, England, 602, 724, 742

Mills College Library, Oakland, California, 639

Morgan Library, The Pierpont, New York, 633, 665, 672, 679, 726, 751, 755, 756, 758, 765, 766, 780

New York Public Library, Manuscript Division, 654

Ray, Gordon N., New York, 674

Southwark Central Reference Library, London, 675

Taylor Collection, R.H., Princeton, New Jersey, 717, 740

Trinity College, Cambridge, England, 743

Wellesley College Library, The English Poetry Collection, Wellesley, Massachusetts, 605, 606, 609, 615, 618, 620, 621, 626, 627, 629, 630, 632, 636, 638, 640, 641, 645, 647–651, 653, 655, 660–662, 664, 668, 669, 683, 684, 687, 691–694, 696, 700–702, 705, 706, 709, 710, 712, 713, 715, 716, 718–721, 727–729, 732–735, 737, 746, 748, 750, 757, 760, 763, 767, 769, 772–774, 776, 777, 779, 783

Yale University, The Beinecke Rare Book and Manuscript Library, New Haven, Connecticut, 652, 744, 761, 762, 771

Index

Index

(For frequently-mentioned persons not covered by the biographical sketches in Appendix I, or for places frequently named, the principal identifying note, if in this volume, is italicized. If the principal identifying note occurs in a prior volume, its page reference is given in square brackets at the beginning of the entry.)

Abernethy, John, 82
Abydos, 36
Adam, 53, 140, 191, 383
Adams, Sarah (née Flower), [vol. 3: 311–312], 326
Addison, Joseph
   quotation from, 158
Admiral's Daughter, The, 189
Admiralty, Lords of the, 245
Æschylus, 15, 18, 372, 373–374, 376, 379, 383, 385–386, 390–392, 397–398, 400, 413, 415
   EBB's *Prometheus Bound*, 13n, 15, 18, 21, 35n, 194, 332–333, 338, 369, 372, 373, 376, 385
      reviews of, 96n, 99, 387, 415
   quotation from, 72
Æsculapius, 114
Agamemnon, 72
Ainsworth, William Harrison, 232, 333
   Jack Sheppard, 232, 249
Aix-la-Chapelle, 68
Albany Chapel, 129
Albert, Prince, 212, 264, 364
Alexander the Great, 248, 260n
Alfieri, Vittorio, 109
Alford, Henry, 16
Algiers, 67
Alice, or the Mysteries, 23
Almack's Assembly Rooms, 194
Amaranth, The, 96, 405
   EBB's contribution to, 84, 99, 340
   reviews of, 372, 404, 408
America, 206, 285
Aminta, 263
Ancient Mariner, The Rime of the, 207
Anderdon, Lucy Olivia Hobart, 78, 85, 134n, 166, 167, 195, 289, 299
   Costanza of Mistra, 168n, 180, 185–186, 195
   letter from, 204
   letters to, 103n, 186, 226n
Anderdon, Mrs. Oliver, 78, 166, 289
Andral, Gabriel, 158, 159
Andrewes, Lancelot (Bishop of Winchester), 131
Animal magnetism, 4, 23
   see also Mesmerism
Antwerp, 68
Aphrodite, 223
Apollo, 237
"Appeal, The," 395
Arden, 294
Ariosto, Lodovico, 123
Arlette, *see* Butler, Charlotte Mary
Arnould, Joseph, 316, 331
Asolo, 68
Athanasian Creed, 219, 223
"Atheist's Tragedy, The," 113
Athenæum, The, 13, 25, 48n, 50, 60, 61, 65, 73, 102, 132, 144, 154, 158, 165n, 167, 187n, 189n, 190n, 194, 204, 205, 216n, 232n, 242n, 250n, 252, 260, 264, 273n, 284, 375, 404, 409, 422
   EBB's contributions to, 116, 121n, 153n, 183n, 237, 244, 261n, 292, 346, 364, 365–366
   letter to the Editor, 116
Athenian Captive, The, 42, 47, 69
Athens, 227
Atherton, 132
Atlas, The, 59, 60, 65, 88, 213, 372, 404, 411, 416

[433]

Index

Attwood, C., 197
Augustus, 269
Austen, Jane
  Persuasion, 124
Austin, Alfred, 316
Austin, Sarah (*née* Taylor), 76
Avicenna (horse), 197
Axminster, 221
Aylmer, St., 151

Babel, 144
Bacon, Francis (Lord Bacon), 388
Baillie, Joanna, 97, 132, 146n, 160
Balzac, Honoré de
  Béatrix, 138
Barham Lodge, 138
Barker, Edmund Henry, [vol. 2: 109n], 167
  death, 153, 167
  letters from, 167
"Baron's Daughter, The," 102, 104, 405
Barrett, Alfred Price Barrett Moulton- ("Daisy"), (brother), [vol. 1: 293–294], 95, 248, 328
  health, 14
Barrett, Ann Eliza Moulton- (*née* Gordon), (aunt), 327, 334, 366
Barrett, Arabella Barrett Moulton- (sister), [vol. 1: 291], 1, 18, 19, 28, 30, 41, 42, 46, 49–50, 63, 64, 65, 69, 70, 71, 73, 75, 79, 80, 89, 95, 104, 109, 136, 147, 149, 150, 151, 152, 163, 166, 167, 171, 183, 186, 188, 195, 202, 217, 219, 220, 221, 228, 230, 239, 248, 252, 255, 271, 274, 277, 287, 289, 291, 292, 297, 298, 304, 321, 337, 339, 342, 345, 346, 351, 352, 355, 358, 361, 366
  at Torquay with EBB, 188n, 191, 210, 211, 357, 359
  letters from, 92, 93, 94, 104, 107, 124, 126, 140, 142, 152, 155, 172, 202, 343, 346, 347, 348, 351
  letters to, 91, 122, 124, 133, 139, 154, 168, 173, 292, 327
Barrett, Charles John Barrett Moulton- ("Storm"), (brother), [vol. 1: 292], 95, 114, 129, 248, 303, 344, 352, 354, 356, 359, 362, 366, 367, 369
  in Jamaica, 171, 252, 301
  letter to, 358
Barrett, Edward Barrett Moulton- ("Bro"), (brother), [vol. 1: 289–290], 15, 44, 61, 71, 77, 79, 80, 88, 91, 92, 94, 98, 127, 132, 136, 139, 154, 155, 156, 157, 163, 175, 176, 177, 201, 202, 210, 211, 220, 221, 248, 252, 271, 286, 287, 327, 337, 339, 343, 355, 359

  death, 190n, 271n, 297n, 318–319, 366, 367
  letter from, 190n
  letters to, 89, 90, 93, 95, 353, 354
Barrett, Edward Barrett Moulton- (father), [vol. 1: 286–288], 3, 5, 13, 17, 18, 20, 21, 28, 30, 34, 39, 40, 42, 46, 51, 52, 58, 60, 64, 69, 70, 72, 74, 75, 78, 80, 88, 92, 94, 95, 96, 98, 99, 101, 104–105, 109, 115, 116, 117, 124, 125, 129, 137, 142, 147, 154, 163, 165, 171, 173, 174, 178, 183, 187–188, 203, 206, 220, 234, 239, 249, 251, 252, 264, 272, 273, 274, 286, 287, 299, 303, 307, 327, 337, 339, 341, 342, 343, 344, 345, 346, 347, 351, 354, 355, 356
  a Dissenter, 234
  at Torquay with EBB, 102, 104, 115, 116, 117, 119, 122, 152, 163, 204, 210, 212, 214, 271, 274, 282, 292, 298, 361–362, 363, 365, 367
  health, 252
  letters from, 95, 154, 155, 159, 178n, 233, 254, 301, 303, 304n, 351, 354
  letters to, 91, 352, 353, 354, 358
  likeness of, 235n, 252
Barrett, Elizabeth Barrett Moulton- ("Ba"), [vol. 1: xxvi–xxxiv], 316ff, 332ff
  dreams, 137
  health, 5, 6, 7, 8, 9, 13, 16, 17, 18, 19, 20, 22, 23, 26, 28, 31, 32, 33, 34, 37, 39, 45, 47, 49, 50, 51, 52, 53, 55, 57–58, 61, 64, 65, 70–71, 72, 74, 77, 82, 83, 87, 89, 91–92, 94, 95, 98, 102, 104–105, 106, 112, 116, 117, 118, 120, 124–125, 127–128, 133, 136, 137, 141, 142, 144–145, 147, 150, 151, 154, 156, 157–158, 161, 162–163, 164, 167, 169, 170, 174, 175, 177, 186, 187, 195, 199, 201, 203, 204, 207, 210, 211–212, 214, 220, 222–223, 227, 228, 230, 234, 239, 240, 245, 252, 259, 264, 266, 271, 272, 274, 278, 280, 281–282, 283, 285, 286–287, 289, 292, 297, 298, 299–300, 302, 303, 321, 326, 327, 334, 335, 337–369 *passim*
  hæmorrhages, 70, 82, 122, 222, 230
  medical consultants, *see* Barry, Robert Fitzwilliam de Barry; Chambers, William Frederick; Scully, William
  use of opium, 236–237
  languages
    German, 144
    Greek, 63, 77

Index

Hebrew, 144
likeness of, 346
literary opinions, 3, 4, 5, 7, 12, 15, 16, 17, 18, 26, 27–28, 30, 35–36, 39, 40, 48, 52, 58, 61, 63–64, 75, 83, 84, 85, 101, 102, 104, 105, 106, 108, 109, 119, 120, 131, 132, 133–134, 144, 147–148, 170, 171, 175, 184–185, 186, 188, 191, 195, 199, 207, 208–209, 214, 228, 230, 233, 240, 241, 242, 249, 252, 253, 263–264, 273, 275, 277–278, 279–280, 282, 283, 284, 286, 288, 302, 306–307, 309, 321, 324, 331
pets, 2, 6, 28, 40, 89, 95, 96, 129
see also Flush; "My Doves"
political opinions, 109–110, 152, 368
reading
  Greek, 77
  history, 230
  novels/stories, 18, 23, 61, 85, 147, 184, 185, 189, 230
  philosophy, 239
  plays, 47, 114, 120, 249, 263, 273, 286
  poetry, 5, 16, 17, 36–37, 52, 58, 63, 129, 133, 181, 214–215, 309
  religious works, 131
    Bible, 144, 157
religious opinions, 181, 234
works, 44, 52, 60, 107, 151, 307
"A Flower in a Letter," 196n, 209n
"A Lay of the Rose," 261n, 285, 292
"A Night-Watch by the Sea," 261n
"A Romance of the Ganges," 22–23, 41n
"A Sabbath on the Sea," 84, 88, 340, 342, 404
"A Sea-Side Meditation," 395
"A Song Against Singing," 86n
"A Vision of Life and Death," 396
"A Vision of Poets," 135n
An Essay on Mind, 21, 65, 72, 369
  reviews of, 96n, 387–390
"Cowper's Grave," 72, 78n, 307, 382, 414–415
"Earth," 396, 414
Hunt's comments on, 151
"Idols," 397
"Isobel's Child," 47n, 72, 77, 78n, 376–377, 379, 384, 386–387, 415–416
Kenyon's comments on, 181–182
"L.E.L.'s Last Question," 116n, 119, 151, 181–182, 346
"Memory and Hope," 384
"Minstrelsy," 396
Miss Mitford's comments on, 10, 181, 182, 332–333
"My Doves," 88, 379–380
"Napoleon's Return," 292, 366
"Night and the Merry Man," 72
"On laying Hooker under my pillow," 134n
Poems (1844), 135n, 172n, 178n, 183n, 192n, 196n, 209n, 261n, 293n, 321, 323, 324, 326, 327, 329
Poems (1850), 330
Poems Before Congress, 327
Prometheus Bound, 13n, 15, 18, 21, 35n, 194, 332–333, 338, 369, 372, 373, 376, 385
  reviews of, 96n, 99, 387, 415
"Psyche Apocalypté," 291, 307, 318–319
"Queen Annelida and False Arcite," 302n, 318
"Sounds," 34, 73n
stanzas on the death of Mrs. Hemans, 384
"The Appeal," 395
"The Complaint of Annelida," 302n, 318
"The Crowned and Wedded Queen," 237, 244, 261n, 266n, 364
"The Cry of the Children," 319
"The Cry of the Human," 195, 209
"The Death-Bed of Teresa del Riego," 396
"The Deserted Garden," 377–378, 380–381, 384
"The Dream," 190, 192, 193, 198, 208n, 214, 411, 412, 413
"The Image of God," 397
"The Legend of the Browne Rosarie," 168n, 169–170, 171, 174–175, 186, 191, 192, 193, 198, 205n, 208n, 211, 212, 213, 252, 355, 356, 364
  reviews of, 409–411, 412, 413
"The Madrigal of Flowers," 195, 209
"The Picture Gallery at Penshurst," 396
"The Poet's Vow," 15, 30, 375, 376, 379, 384, 400
"The Romaunt of Margret," 15, 63, 74, 373, 376, 379, 384, 400
"The Romaunt of the Page," 29n, 33, 35, 38, 40, 41, 42, 43–44, 52, 74, 79, 80, 88, 101, 103n, 170, 175, 213, 356, 403, 406
  reviews of, 103n, 104, 400–402, 405, 406–408
"The Sea-Mew," 34, 88, 378, 387
The Seraphim, 15, 18, 20, 21, 22, 23, 25, 27, 29n, 30, 31, 32–33,

Barrett, Elizabeth Barrett Moulton-
works (cont.)
    34, 38, 41, 42, 45, 49, 52, 55, 59, 62–63, 71, 72, 81, 86n, 88, 120, 157, 178n, 181, 188, 193, 337, 338, 353, 369
    reviews of, 50n, 53, 59–60, 65, 69, 71, 72, 73, 74–75, 93, 96n, 99, 337, 340, 372–387, 397–400, 408–409, 413–416
    "The Sleep," 381
    "The Soul's Travelling," 384
    "The Tempest," 394–395
    "The Virgin Mary to the Child Jesus," 53–54, 78n
    "To a Boy," 396–397
    "To a Poet's Child," 396
    "To the Memory of Sir Uvedale Price," 396
    "Victoria's Tears," 384–385
    see also *Chaucer, Modernized*
Barrett, George Goodin Barrett Moulton- (brother), [vol. 1: 292–293], 30, 79, 80, 89, 91, 94, 95, 166, 172, 176, 233, 248, 327, 329, 360
    at Torquay with EBB, 171, 183, 188, 202, 339, 358, 359
    letters from, 219, 220, 270, 286, 356
    letters to, 106, 114, 219, 270, 286, 322, 327, 329, 365
    studying/practising law, 107, 166, 188, 210, 212, 220, 252, 255
Barrett, Henrietta Barrett Moulton- (sister), [vol. 1: 290], 1, 18, 22, 26, 28, 30, 41, 46, 64, 70, 71, 75, 76, 79, 80, 85, 88, 89, 92, 93, 98, 119, 125, 127, 129, 135n, 136, 141, 142, 146, 155, 156, 159, 163, 164, 171, 174, 177, 178, 185, 188, 195, 209, 210, 217, 221, 230, 239, 248, 252, 271, 274, 289, 298, 303, 304, 321, 337, 339, 352, 355, 359, 366, 369
    health, 127, 129
    letters from, 98, 115, 118n, 126–127, 136, 142, 159n, 173, 178n, 215n, 349, 353
    letters to, 155, 165, 209, 322, 328
Barrett, Henry Barrett Moulton- (brother), [vol. 1: 293], 91, 95, 96, 173, 248, 287, 327, 343
    letter to, 368
Barrett, Mary Moulton- (*née* Graham-Clarke), (mother)
    death, 199
Barrett, Octavius Butler Barrett Moulton- ("Ocky"), (brother), [vol. 1: 295–296], 3, 16, 23, 33, 52, 95, 103, 128, 141, 248, 287, 303

Barrett, Samuel Barrett Moulton- (brother), [vol. 1: 290–291], 20, 140, 248
    death, 172n, 190n, 271, 272, 274, 276n, 292, 365
    in Jamaica, 171, 252
    letters from, 124, 126, 136, 353, 354
    letters to, 129, 136, 159n, 178n, 190n
Barrett, Samuel Barrett Moulton- (uncle), [vol. 1: 288–289], 327
    death, 13, 17, 20, 334, 336
Barrett, Septimus Barrett Moulton- (brother), [vol. 1: 294–295], 3, 16, 23, 33, 52, 58, 95, 102, 103, 114, 122–123, 124, 126, 128, 141, 176, 237, 248, 255, 264, 277, 303
    at Torquay with EBB, 119, 122
    letters from, 202, 213, 233, 288, 365
    letters to, 202, 233
Barrett, Wisdom, 85
Barrow, Isaac, 131
Barry, Robert Fitzwilliam de Barry, 81, 82, 85n, 91, 92, 93, 94, 98, 117, 122, 125, 127, 128, 129, 131, 133, 136, 137, 141, 147, 148, 151, 154, 156, 157, 158, 163, 164, 174–175, 176, 177, 186, 187, 340, 341, 342, 343, 345, 348, 349, 350, 351, 352, 354, 355, 364
    illness and death, 193, 198–199, 203–204, 210, 227, 252, 357, 358, 359
Barry, Mrs. Robert, 157, 193, 204, 210, 359
    letter from, 198
Basingstoke, 305
Bassano, 68
Bastille, The, 108
Bate, Gerardine, 321, 322
Bath, 145, 154, 160, 190, 257, 323
Baxter, Richard, 21
Bazalgettes, The, 93
Beacon Hill, 95, 98
Beacon Terrace, 84, 92, 95, 98, 195, 201, 223, 239
Béatrix ou les Amours Forcés, 138
Beattie, James, 185
    quotation from, 185
Beaumont, Francis, 109, 284
    Dramatic Works, 107
Beauty, The Book of, 105, 106, 170
Becken, Dr., 25
Belford Regis, 40, 147, 166
Bell, *see* Clarke, Arabella Graham-Bell, Robert, 307
"Bella Donna, La" (boat), 177, 350
"Bellerophon" (ship), 292
Bells and Pomegranates, 324, 329
Bell's Life in London, 262, 416
Bendemeer (river), 129

Bentham, Jeremy, 148
Bentley, Samuel, 32
Berkeley, George (Bishop of Cloyne), [vol. 2: 58n], 62
Bezzi, Giovanni Aubrey, 100, 276, 277, 300
Bezzi, Mrs. Giovanni Aubrey, 100
Bible, The
   Cranmer's, 13
   Hebrew, 144
   King James's, 134n
   quotations from, 83, 89, 103, 104, 115, 117, 120, 122, 131, 136, 138, 176, 178, 181, 185, 219, 227, 228, 237, 242, 263, 271, 277, 295, 310
Bible Society, The, 282
Blackwood's Edinburgh Magazine, 69, 71, 72, 74–75, 90n, 143, 149, 183, 315, 379
   EBB's contribution to, 319
Blagden, Isabella, 322
   letters to, 323, 325
Blake, William
   quotation from, 151
Blessington, Marguerite, Countess of, 171
   The Book of Beauty, 105, 106, 170
Blot in the 'Scutcheon, A, 329
Boileau Despréaux, Nicolas, 10, 54n
Book of Common Prayer, The, 223, 226n
   quotation from, 298
Bordeaux, 138
Bordman, Eleanor Page, [vol. 3: 177n], 45, 53, 54, 56, 65, 72
   letters from, 31, 129, 136, 227
Boswell, James, 167
Botany Bay, 96
Bottom the Weaver, 132
Boulogne, 96
Boyd, Miss
   death, 19, 31
Boyd, Hugh Stuart, [vol. 2: 339–341], 5, 30, 63, 90, 93, 95, 155, 193, 240
   letters from, 45, 49, 72, 77, 81, 150, 168, 211, 226, 227, 291, 292
   letters to, 7, 13, 19, 21, 25, 31, 32, 42, 45, 49, 53, 55, 65, 72, 77, 80, 150, 168, 211, 226, 291
   works, 212, 228
Boyle, Mary Louisa, 189
Braddons, The, 98
Britannia's Pastorals, 131, 162, 275
British Museum, The, 3
Brittany, 138
Brixham, 118
Bro, *see* Barrett, Edward Barrett Moulton- (brother)
Broomfield, 64n
"———— Churchyard," 12
Browne, J., 222, 412, 413

Browne, William
   Britannia's Pastorals, 131, 162, 275
Browning, Robert, [vol. 1: xxiv–xxvi], 315ff, 365, 368–369
   health, 217, 278, 304
   languages
      French
         letter in, 257
   political opinions, 269
   reading
      French, 138
   works, 256
      A Blot in the 'Scutcheon, 329
      Bells and Pomegranates, 324, 329
      Dramatic Idyls, 322
      Dramatic Lyrics, 316
      Dramatic Romances and Lyrics, 316, 324
      essay on Shelley, 330
      Jocoseria, 316–317
      King Victor and King Charles, 261, 267, 270
      Men and Women, 316, 330
      Pacchiarotto, 316
      Paracelsus, 24n, 257, 316, 321, 324, 326, 328–329, 416, 417, 420, 421
         review of, 418–420
      Parleyings with Certain People, 317
      Pauline, 329, 330
      Pippa Passes, 256, 261, 267, 270
      Poems (1849), 330
      Sordello, 24, 67, 253, 254, 256, 257, 261, 265, 267, 268, 269, 295, 296n, 316, 324, 326, 329
         reviews of, 263n, 416–417, 420–424
      Strafford, 417, 420, 421
      The Return of the Druses, 261, 267, 268–269, 270, 278, 293, 294, 295, 296
Browning, Robert, Sr. (father), [vol. 3: 307–309], 7, 329
   letter from, 330
Browning, Sarianna (sister), [vol. 3: 310–311], 67, 278, 315, 316
   letter to, 324
Browning Collections, 30n, 47n, 113n, 135n, 146n, 190n, 241n, 260n, 262n, 264n, 306n
Brozie, *see* Barrett, Edward Barrett Moulton- (brother)
Brucciani, Lewis, 40
"Buccaneer, The," 102, 119, 400, 405
Buckingham Palace, 264
Buckland, William, 97, 169
Bulwer-Lytton, *see* Lytton, Bulwer-
Bum/Bummy, *see* Clarke, Arabella Sarah Graham-

Burns, Robert, 249
  quotations from, 236, 383
Butler, Charlotte Mary ("Arlette"), (EBB's cousin), 142, 235, 340, 356
Butler, Cissy (EBB's cousin), 142, 235, 340, 356
Butler, Frances (née Graham-Clarke), (EBB's aunt), [vol. 1: 298–299], 159
Butler, Richard Pierce (EBB's uncle), [vol. 1: 199n], 177, 359
Butler, Samuel
  quotation from, 144
Byron, Lady (née Milbanke), 148, 320, 321
Byron, Lord, 121n, 320, 389, 394, 398, 418
  Cain, 186
  Childe Harold's Pilgrimage, 48, 133, 186
  Heaven and Earth, 186
  Lara, 191
  Manfred, 418
  quotations from, 23, 189, 200, 258
  The Corsair, 191
  The Prisoner of Chillon, 301

Cæsar, Julius, 122–123, 135n
Cain, the Wanderer, 186
Calais, 130
Caldecott, William Marriott, 228, 239
Calderón de la Barca y Henao, Pedro, 418
Campanology, 292
Campbell, Robert Calder, 151
Campbell, Thomas, 185, 389
Canada, 302, 320
Canova, Antonio, 67
Capitol, The, 132
Carlyle, Thomas, 269, 315, 319, 320, 326
  lectures, 269, 270
  quotation from, 191
"Cartel, The," 102, 400
Cary, Henry Francis, 3, 28, 131
Cassandra, 131
Catiline, 186
Caucasus, The, 284
Cave, Mr., 141
Cecilia, St., 309
Ceracchi, 134, 147, 168n, 175
Chambers, William Frederick, [vol. 3: 299n], 6, 8, 9, 16, 17, 18, 20, 21, 22, 26, 27, 28, 31, 33, 34, 39, 45, 49, 50, 52, 53, 54, 55, 57, 64, 70, 71, 74, 82, 91, 92, 94, 142, 187, 282, 337, 339
Chambers's Edinburgh Journal, 408
"Champagne Rose," 252
Chapman & Hall, Messrs., 330
Chartists, The, 221, 232
Chaucer, Geoffrey, 129, 162, 324
  EBB's bust of, 40
  Modernized, 301, 302, 306–307, 309, 318, 330–331, 369
  quotations from, 154, 292
  "The Knight's Tale," 242
  "The Nun's Priest's Tale," 309
Cheltenham, 61
Chesterfield Street, 51
Cheveley, or the Man of Honour, 138, 145, 147–148, 154
Childe Harold's Pilgrimage, 48, 133, 186
Chillon, The Prisoner of, 301
Chiron, 138
Cholera, 158, 179
Chorley, Henry Fothergill, [vol. 3: 185n], 50, 60, 64, 75, 102, 148, 171, 378, 408, 411, 412
  health, 28, 100, 145, 149
  Sketches of a Sea Port Town, 185
  The Authors of England, 9
  The Lion, 184
  "The Sister of Charity," 76n, 101
Chorley, John Rutter, 101, 408, 409
  "The Maid's Trial," 207, 411
Christ, Jesus, 20, 122, 133, 142, 159, 178, 182, 203, 226, 271, 272, 279, 383
  crucifixion, 372, 373, 376, 379, 385, 398
  "The Virgin Mary to the Child Jesus," 53–54, 78n
"Christopher's Cave," 71, 88
Chrysostom, St. John, [vol. 2: 85n], 22
  Homilies, 25
Circe, 227
Clapton, 176
Clarence Terrace, 304
Clark, James, 172n, 200, 201
Clarke, Arabella Sarah Graham- ("Bummy"), (EBB's aunt), [vol. 1: 297–298], 70, 74, 85, 127, 155, 156, 157, 163, 164, 173, 202, 206, 210, 217, 221, 234, 235, 337, 340, 351, 355, 356, 357, 362, 366
  health, 127, 142
  letters from, 92, 95, 203n, 288, 303
  letters to, 126, 254, 347
Clarke, Charles Cowden, 329
Clarke, Charles Mansfield, 202n
Clarke, John Altham Graham- (EBB's cousin), 235n, 303
Clarke, John Altham Graham- (EBB's uncle), [vol. 1: 297], 126, 303
Clemanthe, 67
Cliffes, The, 65
Clifton, 303
Cockney School, The, 249
Cocks, Caroline Margaret, 244, 364
Cocks, Isabella Jemima, 20
Cocks, Lady Margaret Maria, [vol. 2: 341–342], 244, 364
  letters from, 8, 162, 163, 187, 351

letters to, 9, 20, 49, 70, 162, 187
poems, 49
Coke, Edward, 166
Colburn, Henry, [vol. 1: 160n], 15
Coleridge, Samuel Taylor, 251n, 384, 389, 403, 421
quotation from, 236
The Rime of the Ancient Mariner, 207
Coleridge, Sara, 63
Coliseum, 93
Collas, Achille, 10n
Collier, John Payne, 121n
letter to, 113
Cologne, 68
Colwall, 165, 211
Commeline, James, Jr., [vol 2: 34n], 188
Commelines, The, 188
"Complaint of Annelida to False Arcite, The," 302n, 318
Congreve, William
quotations from, 143, 274
Constant, Benjamin de, 12
Constantinople, 218
Cook, Eliza, 213, 214, 215, 225
Corelli, Arcangelo, 25
Cork, 288
Corn Laws, 148
Cornwall, Barry (pseud.), *see* Procter, Bryan Waller
Corsair, The, 191
Cosmo de' Medici, 181, 228, 252, 273, 283, 284, 288, 317, 412
Costanza of Mistra, 168n, 180, 185–186, 195
Covent Garden Theatre, 111, 138, 289n
Cowper, William, 5
"Cowper's Grave," 72, 78n, 307, 382, 414–415
Crabbe, George, 191
Crashaw, Richard, 375
Crawford Street, 28
Creon, 18
Critic, The, 11
Crosse, Andrew, [vol. 3: 243n], 46, 54, 55, 57, 63
Crow, Miss, 79, *80n*, 92, 121, 125, 126, 127, 141, 157, 158, 159, 173, 174, 177, 186, 203, 234, 239, 286, 298, 340, 355
"Cry of the Children, The," 319
"Cry of the Human, The," 195, 209
Cumberland Terrace, 218
Cummings, William Fullerton, 158–159
Cupid, 36
Curzon, Eliza Roper- (née Joynes), 13
Curzon, George Henry Roper-, [vol. 2: 189n], 13
Curzon, Henry George Roper-, 13

Dacre, Lady (née Ogle), [vol. 3: 245n], 11, 52, 55, 56–57, 119, 120, 124, 132, 215
letter from, 51, 52
letter to, 50, 52
Translations from the Italian, 51
Dante Alighieri, 3, 375, 388, 416, 421
Darley, George, 264, 274
"Harvest-Home," 302
Sylvia, 263, 284
Thomas à Becket, 263, 264, 274, 282, 284
Dash (dog), 48
"David Lyon" (ship), 334, 367
Deerbrook, 132
Deffell, John Henry, 75, 76
Deluge, The, 120, 238n
"Deserted Garden, The," 377–378, 380–381, 384
"Destiny," 12
Devonport, 81
Devonshire, 15, 73, 74, 131, 132, 162, 211, 230
—— cream, 79, 85, 95, 96, 99, 102, 111–112, 116, 129, 171, 172, 183, 184, 265, 275, 282, 299, 301
Dickens, Charles, 166, 318, 319, 331, 333, 352
Oliver Twist, 232
Dilke, Charles Wentworth
letter to, 116
Dionysius, King of Sicily, 266
Dionysius Halicarnassus, 392
Dispensary, The, 17
Dissenters (Non-Conformists), 221, 223, 224, 270n
EBB one, 234
Djabal, 294
Domett, Alfred
biographical sketch, 315–317
letters from, 261, 316, 317
letters to, 253, 261, 270n, 316
Venice, 261, 315
Don Giovanni, 37
Don Quixote, 191
quotations from, 103, 251
Donne, John
quotations from, 258, 259
"Dorchester Amphitheatre," 15
Dow, William Alexander, [vol. 3: 252n], 67
Dowson, Christopher, Jr., [vol. 3: 124n], 262, 316
letter from, 262
Dowson, Joseph, 316
Dramatic Idyls, 322
Dramatic Lyrics, 316
Dramatic Romances and Lyrics, 316, 324
Drayton, Michael
Poly-olbion, 131
"Dream, The," 190, 192, 193, 198, 208n, 214, 411, 412, 413

440 Index

Dresden, 25
Drury Lane Theatre, 289n
Dryden, John, 152
   quotations from, 82, 102, 125, 248, 280
Dublin, 288
Dublin Review, The, 420
Dudevant, Amantine Lucile Aurore (*née* Dupin), *see* Sand, George
Duke, Richard, 17
Dulcinea del Toboso, 191
Dupuy, Mrs. J.P., 149
Duty and Inclination, 85
Dwerga, 282

Eagles, Emma Jane, 235n, 303
Eagles, John, 235n, 304n
"Earth," 396, 414
East Indies, 42
Eastnor, Lady, [vol. 2: 79n], 20
Eastnor, Lord, [vol. 2: 79n], 20
Eastnor Castle, [vol. 1: 43n], 187
"Eclipse" (ship), 183n, 185
Eden, 140, 178
Edinburgh Review, The, 56n
Egypt, 158
Elgin, Lady, 322
Elliotson, John, 129, 136
Elliott, Mr., 219, 223
Elstree, 68
Enghien, Duc d', 280
England, 20, 55, 61, 70, 117, 136, 149, 152, 167, 169, 175, 188, 215, 251, 253, 302, 303
   Church of, 224
      catechism, 224, 250
   The Authors of, 9
Epicurus, 126
Eridanus (river), 262
Essay on Mind, An, 21, 65, 72, 369
   reviews of, 96n, 387–390
"Essay on Tragic Influence," 273
Euripides, 18, 392
   quotation from, 262
Evans, Sheriff, 259
Eve, 140, 141
Examiner, The, 53, 54, 58, 65, 233n, 255, 279, 373
Exeter, 88, 220, 221, 222, 227, 305
   Bishop of, 109–110, 219, 223
   ——— Hall, 282
"Exile, The," 18
"Eyebright" (Miss Haworth), 67
Eyre, 88

"Familiar Love," 75
Fates, The, 36
Father and Daughter, 61
Faust, 144, 418
Faust, 120, 208n, 412, 418

Feast of the Poets, The, 241, 242
"Feast of Violets, The," 237, 241, 242
"Fetches, The," 172n, 183n, 195, 207, 208, 212, 228, 252, 318
   reviews of, 411, 412
Finden, Edward Francis & William, 192, 193, 206, 214, 229, 250, 290
Findens' Tableaux (1838), 6, 9, 20, 41n, 160
   EBB's contribution to, 22, 186
   Kenyon's contribution to, 252
   Miss Mitford's contribution to, 102
Findens' Tableaux (1839), 37n, 38, 59n, 99, 100, 101, 102, 160
   Chorley's contribution to, 76n, 101, 402, 408
   EBB's contribution to, 27, 33, 35, 38, 40, 41, 42, 43–44, 74, 79, 80, 101, 103n, 170, 175, 186, 213, 356, 403, 406
   Hughes's contribution to, 101, 403, 405, 406, 408
   Kenyon's contribution to, 37n, 104, 402, 403, 405, 408
   Miss Mitford's contribution to, 39, 79, 101, 102, 402, 404, 405, 406, 408
   reviews of, 102, 400–404, 404–408
   Townsend's contribution to, 101, 408
Findens' Tableaux (1840), 109, 131, 171, 180, 192, 195, 201, 204, 206, 212, 213, 225n, 242, 252, 361, 364
   Chorley's contribution to, 207, 409, 411
   EBB's contribution to, 160, 164, 165–166, 169, 174–175, 186, 190, 191, 192, 193, 198, 211, 212, 252, 355, 356, 361, 364, 409–411, 412
   Horne's contribution to, 172n, 180, 183n, 195, 207, 208, 212, 228, 237, 252, 318, 411
   Hughes's contribution to, 208n, 214
   Miss Mitford's contribution to, 161n, 164, 170, 201, 205n, 206, 208, 212, 213, 214, 252, 409, 411, 412–413
   Procter's contribution to, 161n, 183n, 187n, 411
   reviews of, 205, 206, 213–214, 372, 409–413
Findens' Tableaux (1841), 288–289, 290, 297n, 298, 300, 301–302, 306, 311
Fisher, Harriet, 106, 110, 177, 189
Fisher, William, 243n, 251
Fitzgerald, Hamilton, 200, 201
Five Years of Youth, 326
Fletcher, John, 109, 162, 284
   Dramatic Works, 107
   quotation from, 15
   The Faithful Shepherdess, 263

Index

"Flight of Youth, The," 75
Florence, 242, 251
   The Legend of, 241, 242, 249
Flower, Eliza, [vol. 3: 311–312], 320, 326, 368–369
   letter from, 255
   letter to, 255
"Flower in a Letter, A," 196n, 209n
Fludyer Street, 268
Flush (EBB's dog), 53n, 305, 310–311, 321
Flush (Miss Mitford's dog), 52, 96, 238, 282, 305, 311
Foley, Captain, 221
Foley, Mrs., 221
Foote, Samuel, 10–11
Ford, John
   quotation from, 258
Forster, John, [vol. 3: 169n], 67, 102
   quarrel with RB, 368–369
Fortescues, The, 157
Fox, William Johnson, [vol. 3: 313–314], 138, 256, 318
   letters to, 328, 329
France, 117
Franconia, 68
Frank, Mr., 96n, 340
Frankfurt, 68
Fraser's Magazine, 237
Frederick, Duke, 294–295
French language & literature, 17, 123, 144
Fridolin, 119
Frocester, 85, 142
Fulham, 13
Fuller, Thomas, 247
Furnivall, Frederick James
   letter to, 331

"Ganges, A Romance of the," 22–23, 41n
Garden, Henrietta, 155
Garden, Monti, 155
Garrow, Joseph, 153, 154
Garrow, Theodosia, *105n*, 161, 170, 177, 253
   letters to, 106, 110, 189
   poems, 105, 106
Garrows, The, 253
Garth, Samuel
   The Dispensary, 17
Gascoigne, George, 63
Geneva, 29
Geraldine, 215, 230
German language & literature, 120
Germany, 291
Gibraltar, 67
Gillies, Mary, 229n, 281n
Ginevra, 249
Gladstone, William Ewart, 320

Glencoe, 286
Gloucester, 20, 221
—— Place, 10, 28
Gloucestershire, 70, 74
Glover, Richard, 391–392
God, 3, 5, 8, 9, 13, 14, 17, 19, 20, 21, 26, 27, 28, 31, 33, 39, 45, 49, 50, 52, 54, 58, 64, 71, 72, 74, 75, 78, 79, 81, 85, 89, 92, 94, 95, 98, 100, 104, 105, 107, 111, 112, 115, 117, 118, 119, 122, 127, 128, 133, 142, 145, 146, 148, 151–152, 157, 159, 161, 163, 164, 167, 171, 173, 176, 181, 182, 184, 186, 188, 191, 193, 198, 199, 201, 203, 204, 205, 207, 210, 211, 212, 215, 216, 221, 222, 223, 225, 226, 230, 231, 234, 235, 237, 239, 243, 245, 252, 254, 256, 260, 263, 271, 272, 274, 277, 278, 282, 283, 288, 289, 292, 293, 295, 297, 298, 301, 303, 304
"The Image of," 397
Godfrey, Duke of Bouillon, 275
Goethe, Johann Wolfgang von, 120, 383, 418
   Faust, 120, 208n, 412, 418
Golding, The Misses, 195
Goodrich Castle, 64
Gore, Catherine Grace Frances (*née* Moody), 148
   Preferment, 230
Gosset, Allen Ralph, [vol. 3: 207n], 2–3, 5, 86n
Gosset, Arabella Sarah (*née* Butler), (EBB's cousin), [vol. 1: 21n], 2, 86n, 142
Gosset, William, [vol. 3: 207n], 2, 3
Gower, Francis Leveson-, 120
Graham-Clarke, *see* Clarke, Graham-
Gray, Thomas, 169
   quotations from, 207, 284
Greece,
   The History of, 240
"Greek Wife, The," 104, 403, 405
Greeks, The, 7, 18, 240
Gregory VII, 245n, 259, 272–273, 275, 277–278, 279–280, 283, 284, 285, 288, 289, 307
   reviews of, 273n, 281n, 285n
Griselda, 249
Grote, George, 57
Guarini, Giovanni Battista, 263
Guelphs, The, 284
Guérande, 138

Hall, Mr., 139
Hall, Anna Maria (*née* Fielding), 9
Hamilton, Mr., 142
Hampstead, 140, 151, 152, 227

Hanford, Miss, 216
Hanford, Mrs. C., [vol. 2: 79n], 303
Harding, Emily, 42, 81
Harley Place, 46
Harley Street, 76
Harness, William James, 115, 197, 289
   letter to, 208n
   Welcome and Farewell, 18
Harold, Le Dernier Chant du Pèlerinage d', 17
Harpocrates, 147
Harrow, 88
Hastings, Lady Flora Elizabeth, 171, 200–201
Haworth, Euphrasia Fanny, [vol. 3: 314–315]
   letters from, 67, 197, 269
   letters to, 66, 137, 197, 269
Hayes, Ann Henrietta (*née* Boyd), [vol. 2: 339], 240, 243
Hayley, William, 5
Haymarket Theatre, 289n, 304
Hazlitt, William, 249
   quotation from, 17
Heaven and Earth, 186
Hedley, Elizabeth Jane ("Ibbit"), (EBB's cousin), 84, 104, 155, 200, 223, 240, 353
Hedley, Jane (*née* Graham-Clarke), (EBB's aunt), [vol. 1: 299–300], 74, 84, 93, 94, 110, 142, 158, 159, 271, 339, 341, 342, 350, 354, 355, 366
   letter from, 177
Hedley, Robert ("Robin"), (EBB's cousin), 84
Hedley, Robert (EBB's uncle), [vol. 1: 299–300], 70, 71, 74, 110, 177, 271, 339, 347, 350, 353, 355
   health, 74
Hedleys, The, 139, 171, 202n, 219n, 337, 355, 365
Hemans, Felicia Dorothea (*née* Browne), 224, 246, 380
   stanzas on the death of, 384
   Works of, 167
Herefordshire, 144
Hero and Leander, 36
Hervey, Thomas Kibble, 86n, 92, 99, 404, 408
   letters from, 84, 99
Hill, Rowland, 251, 266
   see also Penny postage
Hippocrene, 17
Hobhouse, John Cam, 149
Hofland, Barbara (*née* Wreaks), 259
Holland, 67
Holland, Elizabeth, Lady, 82
Holland House, 82
Holliday, Miss, 14

Holmes, Miss, 22, 26, 31, 32, 33
Holy Ghost, The, 227
Homer, 77, 164, 374, 383, 388, 392
   EBB's bust of, 40
   Iliad, 151
Honiton, 155
Hooker, Mary Ann
   letter to, 283
Hooker, Richard, 131
   EBB's verse on, 134n
Hope End, 193, 360
"Hopeful" (ship), 234
Horace, 269
Horne, Richard Hengist, 180–181, 182, 186, 191, 195, 213, 237, 289, 298, 300, 309, 331, 361, 409
   A New Spirit of the Age, 317, 318, 319, 321, 324, 326
   biographical sketch, 317–320
   Chaucer, Modernized, 301, 302, 306–307, 309, 318, 330–331, 369
   Cosmo de' Medici, 181, 228, 252, 273, 283, 284, 288, 317, 412
   "Essay on Tragic Influence," 273
   Gregory VII, 245n, 259, 272–273, 275, 277–278, 279–280, 283, 284, 285, 288, 289, 307
   reviews of, 273n, 281n, 285n
   letters from, 180, 195, 228, 237, 241, 244, 259, 272, 279, 285, 319, 320, 369
   letters to, 208, 272, 275, 279, 284, 290, 306, 317, 318, 319, 320, 326
   Orion, 317
   petition to Parliament, 284, 289
   poetry, 171, 181, 318
   "Psyche Apocalypté," 291, 307, 318–319
   The Death of Marlowe, 195, 228, 241, 273, 317, 318, 412
   "The Fetches," 172n, 183n, 195, 207, 208, 212, 228, 252, 318
   reviews of, 411, 412
   The History of Napoleon, 228, 272, 280, 287, 317
Horton, Priscilla, 295
Howell, James, 260, 264
   Familiar Letters, 258
Howitt, Mary (*née* Botham), 39, 160, 222, 404
   letter from, 225n
Hubbard, Mother, 210
Hughes, John, 74, 80, 101, 232, 403, 405, 406, 408
   "The King's Forester," 208n, 214, 411, 412
Hugo, Victor, 17, 144
Hume, David, [vol. 2: 58n], 36, 389

Index

Hume, Joseph, 2
Hunt, Leigh, 151, 249, 302n, 307
  Hero and Leander, 36
  letter from, 25
  The Feast of the Poets, 241, 242
  "The Feast of Violets," 237, 241, 242
  The Legend of Florence, 241, 242, 249
  The Story of Rimini, 242
  "To T.L.H., Six Years Old," 249
Hunt, Thornton Leigh, 249
Hunter, George Barrett, [vol. 3: 315–316], 127, 129, 137, 176, 177, 221, 288, 339, 345–346, 350
  letters from, 86, 93, 95, 126, 140, 221
  letters to, 95, 126–127, 140
Hunter, Mary, [vol. 3: 87n], 44, 88–89, 90, 93, 95, 128, 137, 139, 140, 159, 221, 224, 288, 339, 344
  letters from, 88, 221, 345
  letter to, 91
Hyde Park, 294
Hymen, 36

Iago, 295
Ianthe, 67
"Ibbit," *see* Hedley, Elizabeth Jane
"Idols," 397
Iliad, The, 151
Illustrations of Political Economy, 132, 325
"In laudem virginitatis," 212
Inglise, Mrs., 221
Ingram, John H.
  letters to, 320, 330
Inner Temple, The, 210, 212
Innsbruck, 68
Ion, 207, 264, 286, 324
Ireland, 3, 157, 220
Irving, Edward, 389
Islington, 262
"Isobel's Child," 47n, 72, 77, 78n, 376–377, 379, 384, 386–387, 415–416
Italian language & literature, 123
Italy, 158, 215, 242
  Kenyon's poem on, 243, 251–252
  RB goes to, xi–xiii
Italy, 44, 48, 133, 238n

Jack Sheppard, 232, 249
Jamaica, 234, 252
"James" (ship), 185
James, George Payne Rainsford, 189
Jameson, Anna Brownell (*née* Murphy), 302
  biographical sketch, 320–323
  letters from, 321, 322
  letters to, 217, 321
  Winter Studies and Summer Rambles, 302, 320
Jameson, Robert, 302, 320

Janin, Jules, 144
Jeffrey, Francis (Lord Jeffrey), 389
Jephthah, 36–37
Jerdan, William, 213, 214, 215, 225
Jericho, 140
Jerusalem, 243
Jessica, 207
Joc, *see* Barrett, Octavius Barrett Moulton-
Jocoseria, 316–317
John, King, 295
Johnson, Samuel, 53, 375
  Boswell's Life of, 41n
  quotation from, 62
  Lives of the English Poets, 17
Jones, William, 3
Jonson, Ben
  Catiline His Conspiracy, 186
  quotations from, 17, 148, 149, 166, 224, 258, 259
  The Sad Shepherd, 263
  The Works of, 114, 166
Jove, 15, 164
Juliet, 295
Jupiter, 45

Kate, 227
Kean, Charles John, 295
Keats, John, 317, 408
  quotation from, 305–306
Keble, John
  quotation from, 263
Kenyon, Caroline (*née* Curteis), 1n
Kenyon, Edward, [vol. 3: 229n], 144, 302
Kenyon, John, [vol. 3: 316–318], 2, 3, 6, 18, 22, 26, 38, 39, 40, 46, 52, 54, 55, 56, 57, 60, 61, 74, 75, 80, 85, 95, 100, 102, 104, 105, 109, 132, 160, 166, 171, 180, 185, 186n, 201, 215, 229, 232, 236, 243, 244, 276, 277, 289, 298, 299–300, 302, 311, 320, 321, 324, 329, 343, 352, 369, 403, 408, 409
  "Champagne Rose," 252
  comments on EBB's poetry, 181–182
  health, 3, 14, 16, 34, 39, 112, 115, 120, 142, 144, 149, 264
  "Italy," 243, 251–252
  letters from, 14, 44, 62, 110, 183, 242, 251, 276, 277, 290n
  letters to, 1, 6, 7, 11, 12, 14, 30, 33, 34, 35, 43, 47, 62, 69, 161, 251
  Poems, 11, 12, 15, 22, 26, 27–28, 30, 62
  review of, 44
  resemblance to Pickwick, 3
  Rhymed Plea for Tolerance, 12
  "The Greek Wife," 104, 403, 405
  "The Shrine of the Virgin," 104
  "To an Æolian Harp," 204, 252, 411

King, William, 17
King Lear, 273
King Victor and King Charles, 261, 267, 270
"King's Page, The," 206, 411, 413
Kingsbridge, 221, 288
Kitely, 68
"Knight's Tale, The," 242
Kock, Charles Paul de, 144

Lady Cheveley, or the Woman of Honour, 145, 154n
Lake Poets, The, 249
Lamartine de Prat, Alphonse Marie Louis de, 144
  Le Dernier Chant du Pèlerinage d'Harold, 17
Lamb, Charles, 249, 328
Lampson, Frederick Locker-, 330
Landon, Letitia Elizabeth, 61, 85, 119, 128, 142, 215, 224, 226n, 247, 347, 380
  death, 116, 164, 170, 197
  "L.E.L.'s Last Question," 116n, 119, 151, 181–182, 346
  marriage, 58, 97
  memoir of, 132
Landor, Walter Savage, 6, 7, 24, 56n, 75, 102n, 105, 121n, 153–154, 160, 166, 171, 189, 255, 277, 319, 328
  Andrea of Hungary and Giovanna of Naples, 190n, 195
  biographical sketch, 323–325
  epigram on Napoleon, 280
  letters from, 257, 323, 324, 325
  letters to, 190, 254, 324
  The Pentameron and Pentalogia, 6, 15
  Pericles and Aspasia, 7n
Langland, William, 131
Laputa, 292
Lara, 191
Latitudinarianism, 249
"Lay of the Humble, The," 75
"Lay of the Rose, A," 261n, 285, 292
Lazarus, 292
Ledbury, St. Catherine of, 131
Lediard, John, 93, 147
Lee, Mrs., 268
Lee, Samuel, 144
"Legend of the Browne Rosarie, The," 168n, 169–170, 171, 174–175, 186, 191, 192, 193, 198, 205n, 208n, 211, 212, 213, 252, 355, 356, 364
  reviews of, 409–411, 412, 413
Leicester, 288
Leipzig, 25
Lenora, 171, 175
Lewis, John, 13

Liège, 68
Lion, The, 184
Lister, Thomas, 3
Literary Gazette, The, 213, 226n, 342, 372, 408, 411
Liverpool, 288
Liverpool Association, Poems on the, 61
Locker-Lampson, *see* Lampson, Locker-
Log, King, 200
London, 9, 13, 29, 46, 75, 80, 81, 89, 92, 98, 99, 102, 104, 117, 127, 129, 139, 141, 144, 145, 148, 149, 152, 163, 171, 175, 179, 185, 187, 194, 220, 221, 222, 224, 229, 237, 239, 249, 252, 258, 260, 263, 272, 277, 282, 285, 291, 292, 295, 298, 299, 300, 301, 303, 310
  see also specific places and streets
Londonderry, Lady, 194
"Long-Ago, The," 75
Longinus, Dionysius Cassius, 53, 375, 392
Louis XIV, King, 10
Lucretius (Titus Lucretius Carus), 388
Ludlow, 220
Luther, Martin, 228
Lying, Illustrations of, 61
Lyme Regis, 122, 123–124
Lyndhurst, Lord, 289
Lytton, Edward George Bulwer- [vol. 3: 54n], 88, 145, 148, 154, 300, 385
  Alice, or the Mysteries, 23
  Money, 304
  Richelieu, 111
Lytton, Rosina Bulwer- (*née* Wheeler), 145, 148, 154

McAdam, John Loudon, [vol. 1: 196n], 33
Macbeth, 295
Macedonia, 138
Mackenzie, Miss, 157, 300
Mackintoshes, The, 287
Maclean, George, 59n, 85, 97, 116n, 165n
Macpherson, Robert, 322
Macready, Catherine Frances (*née* Atkins), [vol. 3: 183], 138, 269, 278, 304
  letter from, 218
  letter to, 218
Macready, Letitia Margaret, 269, 278, 304
Macready, William Charles, [vol. 3: 318–319], 67, 68, 139n, 270, 273, 329
  letter from, 111
  letters to, 268, 278, 293, 294, 304
Macreadys, The, 268, 270
McSwiney, Daniel, [vol. 1: 300–301], 77
Madagascar, 90

Index

"Madrigal of Flowers, The," 195, 209
Mæcenas, Gaius Cilnius, 269
Maintenon, Mme. de, 10
Malvern, 61, 131, 193, 199, 200, 240, 243
Manfred, 418
Mann, Mr., 139
"Mansoor the Hierophant," see *Return of the Druses, The*
"Marion Campbell," 18
Marlowe, The Death of, 195, 228, 241, 273, 317, 318, 412
Marryat, Frederick, 245
"Mars and Venus, The Complaint of," 307
Martha (maid), 80n, 83, 93, 100, 112n, 147
Martin, James, [vol. 2: 342–343], 211, 216, 303
Martin, Joseph, 164
Martin, Julia (*née* Vignoles), [vol. 2: 342–343], 188
   letters from, 165, 209–210, 217, 360
   letters to, 209, 216, 303, 322, 324
Martineau, Elizabeth (*née* Rankin), 23, 268
Martineau, Harriet, 24n, 68, 137, 197, 328
   biographical sketch, 325–327
   Deerbrook, 132
   Five Years of Youth, 326
   health, 4n, 268, 325
   Illustrations of Political Economy, 132, 325
   letters from, 267, 326, 327
   letters to, 23, 267, 268, 326, 327
Mary, The Virgin, 54
   "The Shrine of," 104
   "_____ to the Child Jesus," 53–54, 78n
Mary Anne (maid), 112
Matilda, Countess of Tuscany, 275, 279
May, George, *111*, 148, 199, 205–206, 222
Mayence, 68
Mayfair, 311
"Medusa," 113
"Memory and Hope," 384
Men and Women, 316, 330
"Mermaid, The," 79
   quotations from, 131, 186
"Merman, The," 79
Merry, William, 225
   letters from, 240, 260, 276
   letters to, 239, 240, 266
   The Philosophy of a Happy Futurity, 226n, 229, 239, 240
Merry Oak, 171, 177
Mesmerism, 130n, 325, 326, 327
   Letters on, 325
Mesopotamia, Sultan of, 295
Methuen, Lord, 134, 149

Metropolitan Magazine, The, 74, 206, 372, 383, 412, 417
Michael Armstrong, The Life and Adventures of, 232
Miller, Dr., 220, 222, 227
Mills, John, 234
Milnes, Richard Monckton, 29n, 39, 69, 71, 72, 74, 188, 191, 269
   letter to, 256
   Memorials, 28, 63
   Poems of Many Years, 39, 70n, 75, 138
Milton, John, 48, 76n, 188, 284, 375, 383, 388, 391, 413
   quotations from, 57, 180, 188, 237, 242, 258
Minny, see Robinson, Mary
"Minstrelsy," 396
Minto, Mrs., 117, 327, 328
Minto, Mary
   biographical sketch, 327–328
   letters from, 117, 327, 358
   letters to, 117, 327, 328
Mitford, George, [vol. 3: 176], 3, 18, 28, 32, 52, 53, 57, 75, 79, 85, 96, 99, 102, 111, 115, 116, 119, 121, 122, 133, 145, 147, 149, 153, 166, 171, 183, 191, 195, 201, 204, 207, 215, 222, 225, 230, 231, 236, 239, 241, 243, 244, 245, 248, 250, 260, 265, 274, 278, 282, 283, 290, 298, 300, 305, 310
   health, 27, 30, 38, 39, 58, 61, 80n, 108, 111, 112, 115, 117, 126, 143, 146, 161, 179, 184, 229, 252, 263, 266, 277, 289, 298, 299, 301, 343
   portrait of, 41
Mitford, Henry, 240
Mitford, Mary Russell, [vol. 3: 319–321], 9, 30, 33, 37n, 42, 43, 51, 53, 62, 63, 73, 88, 93, 128, 164, 169, 175, 212, 251, 290–291, 352, 403, 404, 405, 411
   government pension, 4n, 5, 29n, 57
   health, 2, 3, 6, 16, 23, 27, 32, 38, 39, 58, 83, 122, 146–147, 190, 192, 197, 199, 205–206, 213, 222, 229, 245, 246, 250, 252
   languages, 123
   letters from, 3, 10, 16, 17, 20, 27, 28–29, 30, 37, 39, 48, 52, 56, 60, 64, 74, 78, 81, 82, 93, 96, 98, 99, 102, 104, 108, 111, 114, 115, 117, 118, 119, 122, 123, 126, 130, 133, 146, 149, 165, 170, 179, 180, 181, 184, 186, 203, 204, 205, 208n, 222, 225n, 226n, 229, 231, 236, 238, 239, 243, 244, 245, 246, 250n, 264n, 290, 298, 301, 305,

Mitford, Mary Russell
  letters from (cont.)
    343, 348
    plan to publish, 246–247, 258, 278, 282, 300, 311
  letters to, 2, 5, 17, 22, 26, 32, 37, 46, 51, 55, 56, 59, 73, 78, 81, 98, 100, 103, 108, 111, 115, 118, 121, 126, 130, 143, 146, 153, 160, 165, 169, 173, 179, 184, 190, 192, 197, 198, 203, 205, 213, 222, 229, 236, 238, 244, 246, 258, 263, 265, 274, 276, 277, 281, 288, 297, 299, 301, 305, 310, 318, 319, 320, 321, 324, 326, 327, 329, 331, 355
  likeness of, 9
  literary opinions, 10–11, 191, 193, 207, 232, 245, 249
    comments on EBB's poetry, 10, 181, 182, 332–333
  political opinions, 232
  reading
    biographies/letters, 10
    French, 123, 144
    Italian, 123
    novels, 232
  works, 130–131, 164, 190, 290, 311
    "A Story of the Woods," 103n, 405
    Atherton, 132
    "Marion Campbell," 18
    Otto of Wittelsbach, 229, 241, 301
    Our Village, 248, 301
    Rienzi, 213
    "The Baron's Daughter," 102, 104, 405
    "The Buccaneer," 102, 119, 400, 405
    "The Cartel," 102, 400
    "The Exile," 18
    "The King's Page," 206, 411, 413
    "The Roundhead's Daughter," 214, 411, 413
    "Wedding Slippers," 40, 44
    see also *Findens' Tableaux*
Mitford, William, 240, 389
Moile, Nicholas T. (pseud.)
  State Trials, 188, 191
Molière (Jean Baptiste Poquelin), 10
Monclar, André Victor Amedée de Ripert-, [vol. 3: 321–322]
  letter to, 257
Montaigne, Michel de
  quotation from, 169
Monthly Chronicle, The, 90n, 104, 195, 245n, 259, 309, 385, 405, 421
  EBB's contributions to, 261n, 285, 292, 366
Monthly Review, The, 385, 422
Monument, The, 139
Moody, Mr., 141
"Moonlight," 12, 27–28

Moore, Thomas, 389
  "The Meeting of the Waters," 104
  "The Pilgrim's Rest," 104
Morgan, Lady (Sydney Owenson), 57
Morning Chronicle, The, 213, 372, 404
Motherwell, William
  quotation from, 206
Moulton-Barrett, *see* Barrett, Moulton-
Moxon, Edward, 267, 338, 365
  biographical sketch, 328–330
  letters to, 113, 330
Munich, 68
Murphy, Patrick, 8, 23
Musæus Grammaticus, [vol. 3: 171n], 36
Muses, The, 165, 284
Mushet, Agnes (*née* Wilson)
  letter from, 248
"Music," 12
"My Doves," 88, 379–380

Naiades, The, 155
Nantes, 138
Napoleon I, Emperor, 246n, 292, 323
  Landor's epigram on, 280
  "Napoleon's Return," 292, 366
  The History of, 228, 272, 280, 287, 317
Napoleon III, Emperor, 327
Naylor, Samuel, *135n*, 166, 172
  Ceracchi, 134, 147, 168n, 175
  letter to, 175
Nazianzen, St. Gregory, [vol. 2: 39n], 25, 152, 212
  "In laudem virginitatis," 212
"Neglected Wife, The," 12
New Monthly Belle Assemblée, The, 417
New Monthly Magazine, The, 195, 213, 238n, 376, 412
New Spirit of the Age, A, 317, 318, 319, 321, 324, 326
New York, 279
Newcastle-upon-Tyne, 88
Newman, Francis William, 83
"Night and the Merry Man," 72
"Night-Watch by the Sea, A," 261n
Nile (river), 158
Niven, Miss, 306
Niven, Mrs. (*née* Vardill), 231
Niven, Agnes, 223, 231, 236
Noah, 258
Nokes, 261
Nominalism, 224
Normandy, 34, 39, 57
North Pole, 71
Nuttall, Mrs., 95, 129, 137

Oates, Titus, 280
Ocky, *see* Barrett, Octavius Barrett Moulton-
O'Connell, Daniel, [vol. 3: 221n], 129, 152, 169, 184

Index

Œdipus Tyrannos, 18
Oliver Twist, 232
One Fault, 230
Ophelia, 67
Opie, Amelia (*née* Alderson), *61*, 402, 403, 405, 408
Orange, J., 176–177, 234
Orestes, 3
Origen, 28
Orion, 317
Orme, Mrs. C., [vol. 1: 115n], 129, 171, 241, 272, 291, 318, 340
  letters from, 180, 318
  letter to, 180, 181
Orpheus, Caius Valerius Flaccus, 22
Osgood, Frances Sargent (*née* Locke), 58, 403
Otto of Wittelsbach, 229, 241, 301
Our Village, 248, 301
Oxford, 10, 255, 264

Pacchiarotto, 316
Paddington, 93
Padua, 68
Painting, Epistle on, 5
Palestine, 42, 243
Paracelsus (horse), 197
Paracelsus, 24n, 257, 316, 321, 324, 326, 328–329, 416, 417, 420, 421
  review of, 418–420
Paris, 61, 138, 158
Parkhurst, John, 144
Parleyings with Certain People of Importance, 317
Parliament, 3, 260n, 326
  Horne's petition to, 284, 289
  House of Commons, 259
Parnassus, Mt., 284
Parr, Samuel, [vol. 2: 100n], 167, 228, 323, 383
Parriana, 167
Parry, Dr., 246
Pascal, Blaise, 144
  quotation from, 238
Patagonia, 169
Patch, Mr., 95
Patience, 226
Patten (servant), 141
Pauline, 329, 330
Payne, George, [vol. 3: 149n]
  letter to, 129
Pedro of Castile, 193, 194, 207, 222, 229
Peel, Robert, 149, 292
Penny postage, 212, 233, 251, 258, 266n
"Penshurst, The Picture Gallery at," 396
Pentameron and Pentalogia, The, 6, 15
Penthesilea, 294
Pepoli, Carlo, 68
Percy, Thomas
  quotation from, 38

Pericles and Aspasia, 7n
Persuasion, 124
Peter, St., 5
Peyton, Charlotte Lea, [vol. 3: 68n], 188
Philips, John, 148
Phillpotts, Henry (Bishop of Exeter), 109–110, *219*, 223
Philoctetes, 18
Philosophy of a Happy Futurity, The, 226n, 229, 239, 240
Pickwick, Mr., 3
Pierce, Mrs., 235
Piers Plowman, 131
"Pilgrimage," 17
"Pilgrim's Rest, The," 104
Pindar, 3, 17, 383
Pinhay Cliffs, 122, 124
Pippa Passes, 256, 261, 267, 270
Plato, 117, 131, 193, 233
  quotation from, 108
Pleiades, The, 46
Pluto, 57
Plymouth, 13, 79, 81
Poems (1844—EBB), 135n, 172n, 178n, 183n, 192n, 196n, 209n, 261n, 293n, 321, 323, 324, 326, 327, 329
Poems (1849—RB), 330
Poems (1850—EBB), 330
Poems Before Congress, 327
Poetical Epistle on Epic Poetry, 5
"Poet's Vow, The," 15, 30, 375, 376, 379, 384, 400
Poly-olbion, 131
Pomfret, John, 17
  quotation from, 17
Pope, Alexander, 388
  quotations from, 132, 139, 170, 234, 240
Pope, The, 133, 152, 169
Porson, Richard, [vol. 2: 57n], 383
Port Royal, 75, 78, 375
  Select Memoirs of, 230
Potter, John (Archbishop of Canterbury), 390
Powell, Thomas, 307
  biographical sketch, 330–331
  letters from, 309, 331
  letters to, 300, 309, 330
  poems, 309, 330
Preferment, 230
"Pretence," 27
Price, Uvedale, [vol. 1: 301], 131, 247, 309
  "To the Memory of," 396
Prior, Matthew, 162
Pritchard, James, 316
Procter, Bryan Waller ("Barry Cornwall"), [vol. 3: 322–323], 39, 75, 161, 166, 181, 186, 249, 328, 396, 404, 408, 409
  letter from, 265

Procter, Bryan Waller (cont.)
  quotation from, 197
  The Works of Ben. Jonson, 114, 166
  "Venice," 161n, 183n, 208n, 411, 412
Prometheus Bound, 13n, 15, 18, 21, 35n, 194, 332–333, 338, 369, 372, 373, 376, 385
  reviews of, 96n, 99, 387, 415
Prussia, 67
  King of, 205
"Psyche Apocalypté," 291, 307, 318–319
Punch (dog), 122, 123
Pylades, 3
Pyrenees, The, 158

Quantock Hills, 63
Quarles, Francis, 398
Quarterly Review, The, 188, 368, 413
"Queen Annelida and False Arcite," 302n, 318
Quietism, 115
Quinet, Edgar, 61, 144, 376
Quintilian (Marcus Fabius Quintilianus), 388, 392

Racine, Jean, 10, 390
Raleigh, Walter,
  quotation from, 170
Reade, John Edmund, *45n*, 134, 237
  Catiline, 186
  Italy, 44, 48, 133, 238n
  The Deluge, 120, 238n
Reading, 43, 243
  ⸺ Quarter Sessions, 30
Regent's Park, 103
  ⸺ Canal, 15
Reigate, 9, 21
Reliques of Ancient English Poetry
  quotation from, 38
"Reminiscence," 12
Resolute (dog), 91
Return of the Druses, The, 261, 267, 268–269, 270, 278, 293, 294, 295, 296
Retzsch, Maritz, 119, 412
Revue des Deux Mondes, La, 418
Rhine (river), 68
Ricardo, Harriet (née Mallory), 210
Ricardo, Osman, 210
Rice, Thomas Spring-, 28
Richelieu, 111
Richmond, 271
Rienzi, 213
Rimini, The Story of, 242
Ripert-Monclar, *see* Monclar, Ripert-
Robbers, The (Die Räuber), 120
Roberts, Emma, 132, 247
Robertson, John
  letter to, 24
Robinson, Henry Crabb, 39

Robinson, Mary ("Minny"), [vol. 1: 47n], 58, 94, 95, 137, 159, 173, 178, 203, 271, 344, 346, 366
  letters from, 158, 235, 288
Robinson Crusoe, 17
Rogers, Samuel, 149, 328, 389
"Romaunt of Margret, The," 15, 63, 74, 373, 376, 379, 384, 400
"Romaunt of the Page, The," 29n, 33, 35, 38, 40, 41, 42, 43–44, 52, 74, 79, 80, 88, 101, 103n, 170, 175, 213, 356, 403, 406
  reviews of, 103n, 104, 400–402, 405, 406–408
Rome, 229, 242, 243, 251
  Church of, 230
Roper-Curzon, *see* Curzon, Roper-
Ross-on-Wye, 64, 139
"Roundhead's Daughter, The," 214, 411, 413
Rousseau, Jean-Jacques
  quotations from, 191, 246
Royal Academy, The, 41
Russell Square, 218
Russells, The, 95, 129
Ruxton, Mr., 328

"Sabbath on the Sea, A," 84, 88, 340, 342, 404
St. Albans, 295
St. James's Palace, 264
St. John's Wood, 169
St. Leger, 197
St. Petersburg, 180
Salisbury, Bishop of, 270
Sand, George (Amantine Lucile Aurore Dudevant, née Dupin), 144
Satan, 157
Saunders & Otley, Messrs., [vol. 3: 74n], 32, 120
  letter to, 59
Scarlett, Miss, 117
Schiller, Friedrich von, 120
  Fridolin, 119
  The Robbers, 120
Schimmelpenninck, Mary Ann (née Galton), 230
Scotland, 85
  Chief Baron of, 193, 199
Scott, Walter, 5, 88, 176, 246, 389
  "The Wild Huntsman," 57
  Waverley, 5
Scully, William, 203, 204, 207, 210, 211, 212, 214, 220, 222, 227–228, 230, 233–234, 235, 239, 242, 252, 253, 259–260, 266, 282, 285, 286–287, 292, 297, 298, 302, 303, 359–360, 361, 363, 368
Sculpture, An Essay on, 5

"Sea-Mew, The," 34, 88, 378, 387
"Sea-Side Meditation, A," 395
Seraphim, The, 15, 18, 20, 21, 22, 23, 25, 27, 29n, 30, 31, 32–33, 34, 38, 41, 42, 45, 49, 52, 55, 59, 62–63, 71, 72, 81, 86n, 88, 120, 157, 178n, 181, 188, 193, 337, 338, 353, 369
  reviews of, 50n, 53, 59–60, 65, 69, 71, 72, 73, 74–75, 93, 96n, 99, 337, 340, 372–387, 397–400, 408–409, 413–416
Seraphina-Angelica, Sister, 75
Serpentine (lake), 294
Sette, *see* Barrett, Septimus Barrett Moulton-
Sévigné, Marquise de, 10
Seward, Anna, 5
  Letters of, 3–4
Shakespeare, William, 120, 124, 182, 207, 209, 237, 244, 284, 390, 392, 413
  autograph of, 33, 55
  Farther Particulars Regarding, 113
  King Lear, 273
  quotations from, 5, 28, 46, 49, 67, 71, 98, 101, 107, 139, 144, 147, 148, 149, 155, 157, 167, 169, 174, 179, 181, 184, 186, 189, 204, 207, 214, 218, 223, 227, 239, 248, 249, 282, 295, 296, 301, 304, 307, 310
Sheepshanks, J., 224
Sheil, Richard Lalor, 184
Shelley, Percy Bysshe, 76n, 251n, 330, 383, 400, 409
  Adonais, 330
  Essays, 233
  Poetical Works, 113, 328
  quotation from, 28
  RB's essay on, 330
Shepherd, Miss (Lady Mary's daughter), 193–194, 199–200
  letters from, 200
Shepherd, Miss (Mr. Townsend's bride), 83
  letter from, 102
Shepherd, Henry John, [vol. 3: 181n], 193, 199
  Pedro of Castile, 193, 194, 207, 222, 229
Shepherd, Lady Mary (*née* Primrose), [vol. 2: 156n], 56, 60–61, 193, 194, 199–200
Shepherd, Samuel, 193, 199
Shepherd, The Sad, 263
Shepherdess, The Faithful, 263
Sheridan, Richard Brinsley
  The Critic, 11
Sidmouth, 94, 122, 228
  Viscountess, 82

Sidney, Philip, 261
Siècle, Le, 138
Sinbad the Sailor, 17
Sinclair, Lord, 134
Skerrett, Marianne, 244, 266, 364
Sketches of a Sea Port Town, 185
"Sleep, The," 381
Smallfield & Son, Messrs., 13
Smith, Miss, 128
Smith, Edmund, 17
Smith, George Murray, 330
Smith, John Pye, [vol. 3: 149n], 72, 89, 345
  letter to, 129
Smith, Mary Ann (*née* Clarke), 7, 8, 29n
Smith, Robert Percy ("Bobus"), 55
Smith, Sydney, 55
Smith, William
  letter to, 267
Socrates, 114
Somers, Lord, [vol. 1: 43n], 162
"Song Against Singing, A," 86n
Sophocles, 383, 391, 392, 413
  Œdipus Tyrannos, 18
  Philoctetes, 18
Sordello, 24, 67, 253, 254, 256, 257, 261, 265, 267, 268, 269, 295, 296n, 316, 324, 326, 329
  reviews of, 263n, 416–417, 420–424
"Soul's Travelling, The," 384
"Sounds," 34, 73n
Southampton, 57, 171
Southey, Robert, 39, 48, 57, 75, 149, 246, 255, 368, 382, 388, 389
  quotation from, 73
Spallanzani, Lazaro, 43
Sparrow, Lady Olivia (*née* Acheson), [vol. 2: 105n], 26
Spectator, The, 416
Spenser, Edmund, 157, 162, 187n, 351, 383
  quotations from, 162, 294
Sphinx, The, 27
Spowers, G., 153n
Sprat, Thomas, 17
Spring-Rice, *see* Rice, Spring-
Squeers, Wackford, 174, 232
Staël, Anne Louise Germaine de (*née* Necker), 249
State Prisoner, The, 189
State Trials, 188, 191
Statesman, The, 284
Stepney, Catherine, Lady, 97
Sterne, Laurence
  quotation from, 254
Stokes, 261
Storey's Gate, 265
Storm/Stormie, *see* Barrett, Charles John Barrett Moulton-

Strafford, 417, 420, 421
Stratten, James, 93, 129
Stratten, Mrs. James (*née* Wilson), 93
Styles, The Misses, 270
Styx (river), 170, 240
Sullivan, Arabella Jane (*née* Wilmot), 119
Sunbeam, The, 93, 99, 102, 340, 387
Sun's Darling, The, 100
Swedenborg, Emanuel, 247, 328
Swift, Jonathan, 292
Sylvia; or The May Queen, 263, 284

Tagle, Mr., 234
Tait, William, 131
Tait's Edinburgh Magazine, 44, 143, 149, 213, 214, 406, 412
Tales of the Genii, The, 241, 249
Talfourd, Rachel (*née* Rutt), [vol. 3: 161n]
  letters to, 2, 218, 308
Talfourd, Thomas Noon, [vol. 3: 323–324], 82, 160, 166, 193, 207, 218, 247, 328, 330
  An Athenian Captive, 42, 47, 69
  Glencoe, 286
  Ion, 207, 264, 286, 324
  letters from, 41, 47, 208n
  letters to, 1, 47
Tasso, Torquato
  Aminta, 263
  "Song for," 113
Taygetus, Mt., 148
Taylor, Jeremy, 131
Temperance Society, The, 122
"Tempest, The," 394–395
Tennyson, Miss, 148
Tennyson, Alfred, 24, 28, 75, 79, 132, 148, 165, 172, 175, 315, 319, 320, 328, 329, 373, 400, 408, 414
  quotations from, 131, 186, 289, 292
"Teresa del Riego, The Death-Bed of," 396
Tertullian (Q. Septimus Florens Tertullianus), 376
  quotation from, 236
Thackeray, William Makepeace, 331
Thatcher, Mr., 97
Theatre Act (1737), 284, 289, 296n
Thebes, 158
Thomas à Becket, 263, 264, 274, 282, 284
Three Mile Cross, 57, 64, 167, 183, 243, 311, 319
Tieck, Johann Ludwig, 270
Tilsit, 67
Tilt, Charles, [vol. 3: 253n], 9, 38, 109, 119, 149, 186, 212, 214
Times, The, 150n, 197, 295
  quotations from, 33n, 59n, 69n, 202n, 255n, 288n
Titania, 66, 224
"To a Boy," 396–397

"To a Poet's Child," 396
Tolerance, Rhymed Plea for, 12
Torquay, 30, 37, 71, 74, 78, 89, 98, 118, 128, 139, 142, 155, 164, 171, 176, 195, 204, 210, 211, 219, 221, 224, 234, 252, 277, 299, 302
  EBB goes to, 70, 73–74, 75, 77, 78, 79, 80–81, 337, 338
  EBB's opinion of, 117, 277
Townsend, Richard Edwin Austin, 11, 53n, 61, 75, 83, 84, 102, 108, 225, 306
  letter from, 61
  letter to, 58
  marriage, 149
  poems, 52, 58, 61, 101, 403, 404, 406
Treherne, William, 80n
Trent, 68
Treppy, *see* Trepsack, Maria
Trepsack, Maria ("Treppy"/"Trippy"), [vol. 1: 301–302], 88, 95, 125, 129, 137, 142, 158, 159, 177, 203, 235, 271, 288, 337–338, 346, 349
Treviso, 68
Trieste, 68
Trippy, *see* Trepsack, Maria
Triumphs of Temper, The, 5
Trollope, Mr., 245
Trollope, Frances (*née* Milton), 245
  Michael Armstrong, 232
  One Fault, 230
Tulk, Charles Augustus, 2
Tunbridge Wells, 3
Turner, Joseph Mallord William, 36
Turpin, Dick, 232
"Two Harps," 12
Two Old Men's Tales, 189
Tyburn, 82
Tyrol, The, 68

United Service Gazette, The, 213, 403, 412
Upton, 202

Valentine's Eve, 61
Valpy, Abraham John, [vol. 2: 237n], 14, 15–16
Van Amburgh, Isaac A., 120, 150n, 284
Vanneck, Mr., 271, 366
Velino (river), 48
Venice, 138, 139, 174
  RB goes to, xii–xiii, 24, 68
Venice, 261, 315
Venus, 114
  "The Complaint of Mars and ___," 307
Verona, 68
Vestris, Mme., 296
Vicenza, 68

Index

Victoria, Queen, 58, 120, 149, 159, 171, 200, 213n, 233–234, 235, 244–245, 255, 264, 266, 302, 317, 364
  "The Crowned and Wedded Queen," 237, 244, 261n, 266n, 364
  "Victoria's Tears," 384–385
"Virgin, The Shrine of the," 104
"Virgin Mary to the Child Jesus, The," 53–54, 78n
Virginius, 295
"Vision of Life and Death, A," 396
"Vision of Poets, A," 135n
Visions of the Western Railways, 52, 58, 61

Wales, 57, 185
Walrond, Agnes, 155
Walters, Miss, 177
Wanderer, Notes of a, 158
"Waring," 316
"Waters, The Meeting of the," 104
Watson, David, 269
Waverley, 5
Weale, Mr., *155*, 156–157, 351, 352, 353
  letter to, 162
Weale, Mrs., 155, 157, 351
Webb, E., 305
Webster, Benjamin Nottingham, 296
Webster, Daniel, 168n, 184
"Wedding Slippers," 40, 44
Welcome and Farewell, 18
Wellington, Duke of, 238, 255n
West Indies, 17, 20, 274, 301
Westmacott, Mrs. Horatio, 119
Westminster, 2, 52
  —— Abbey, 93, 124
Wight, Isle of, 124
Wightman, William, 107

"Wild Huntsman, The," 57
Willyams, Sarah Brydges (*née* da Costa), 178
Wilson, Effingham, 329
Wilson, Elizabeth, 321, 324
Wilson, John (Christopher North), 69, 71, 72, 74, 88, 382
Wimpole Street, 10, 18, 28, 83, 98, 99, 104, 112, 115, 120, 122, 133, 140, 141, 145, 152, 163, 165, 166, 167, 170, 171, 176, 180, 195, 206, 221, 239, 247, 277, 307
Windsor, 235
  —— Park, 67
Wither, George, 398
Woodforde, Mr., 8
"Woods, A Story of the," 103n, 405
Woolsack, The, 114, 166, 288n
Worcester, 9
Wordsworth, William, 76n, 104, 109, 123, 130, 131, 137, 149, 249, 251n, 302n, 307, 309, 325, 328, 329, 331, 351, 365, 383, 389, 396, 398, 418
  quotations from, 27, 49, 228, 244, 247, 249, 289
Würzburg, 68
Wyatt, Matthew Cotes, 235
Wye (river), 61, 64, 131, 132

Xenophon, 77

York, 279
Young, Frederick, 316
Young, William Curling, 316

Zendavesta, 15, 16
Zenobia, 215
Zoological Gardens, 65, 88, 259

DATE DUE

DEMCO 38-297